Handbook of Communication in the Public Sphere
HAL 4

Handbooks of Applied Linguistics
Communication Competence
Language and Communication Problems
Practical Solutions

Editors
Karlfried Knapp and Gerd Antos

Volume 4

De Gruyter Mouton

Handbook of Communication in the Public Sphere

Edited by
Ruth Wodak and Veronika Koller

De Gruyter Mouton

ISBN 978-3-11-022605-8

Library of Congress Cataloging-in-Publication Data

> Handbook of communication in the public sphere / edited by Ruth Wodak, Veronika Koller.
>   p. cm. − (Handbooks of applied linguistics ; 4)
>   Includes bibliographical references and index.
>   ISBN 978-3-11-022605-8 (pbk. : alk. paper)
>   1. Communication.   2. Language and languages.   3. Critical discourse analysis.   I. Wodak, Ruth 1950−   II. Koller, Veronika, 1973−
>   P91.H363   2010
>   302.2−dc22
>   2010010873

Bibliographic information published by the Deutsche Nationalbibliothek

The Deutsche Nationalbibliothek lists this publication in the Deutsche Nationalbibliografie; detailed bibliographic data are available in the Internet at http://dnb.d-nb.de.

© 2010 Walter de Gruyter GmbH & Co. KG, Berlin/New York

Cover design: Martin Zech, Bremen
Typesetting: Dörlemann Satz GmbH & Co. KG, Lemförde
Printing: AZ Druck und Datentechnik GmbH, Kempten (Allgäu)
∞ Printed on acid-free paper

Printed in Germany

www.degruyter.com

Introduction to the handbook series
Linguistics for problem solving

Karlfried Knapp and Gerd Antos

1. **Science and application at the turn of the millennium**

The distinction between "pure" and "applied" sciences is an old one. According to Meinel (2000), it was introduced by the Swedish chemist Wallerius in 1751, as part of the dispute of that time between the scholastic disciplines and the then emerging epistemic sciences. However, although the concept of "Applied Science" gained currency rapidly since that time, it has remained problematic.

Until recently, the distinction between "pure" and "applied" mirrored the distinction between "theory and "practice". The latter ran all the way through Western history of science since its beginnings in antique times. At first, it was only philosophy that was regarded as a scholarly and, hence, theoretical discipline. Later it was followed by other leading disciplines, as e.g., the sciences. However, as academic disciplines, all of them remained theoretical. In fact, the process of achieving independence of theory was essential for the academic disciplines to become independent from political, religious or other contingencies and to establish themselves at universities and academies. This also implied a process of emancipation from practical concerns – an at times painful development which manifested (and occasionally still manifests) itself in the discrediting of and disdain for practice and practitioners. To some, already the very meaning of the notion "applied" carries a negative connotation, as is suggested by the contrast between the widely used synonym for "theoretical", i.e. "pure" (as used, e.g. in the distinction between "Pure" and "Applied Mathematics") and its natural antonym "impure". On a different level, a lower academic status sometimes is attributed to applied disciplines because of their alleged lack of originality – they are perceived as simply and one-directionally applying insights gained in basic research and watering them down by neglecting the limiting conditions under which these insights were achieved.

Today, however, the academic system is confronted with a new understanding of science. In politics, in society and, above all, in economy a new concept of science has gained acceptance which questions traditional views. In recent philosophy of science, this is labelled as "science under the pressure to succeed" – i.e. as science whose theoretical structure and criteria of evaluation are increasingly conditioned by the pressure of application (Carrier, Stöltzner, and Wette 2004):

> Whenever the public is interested in a particular subject, e.g. when a new disease develops that cannot be cured by conventional medication, the public requests science to provide new insights in this area as quickly as possible. In doing so, the public is less interested in whether these new insights fit seamlessly into an existing theoretical framework, but rather whether they make new methods of treatment and curing possible. (Institut für Wirtschafts- und Technikforschung 2004, our translation).

With most of the practical problems like these, sciences cannot rely on knowledge that is already available, simply because such knowledge does not yet exist. Very often, the problems at hand do not fit neatly into the theoretical framework of one particular "pure science", and there is competition among disciplines with respect to which one provides the best theoretical and methodological resources for potential solutions. And more often than not the problems can be tackled only by adopting an interdisciplinary approach.

As a result, the traditional "Cascade Model", where insights were applied top-down from basic research to practice, no longer works in many cases. Instead, a kind of "application oriented basic research" is needed, where disciplines – conditioned by the pressure of application – take up a certain still diffuse practical issue, define it as a problem against the background of their respective theoretical and methodological paradigms, study this problem and finally develop various application oriented suggestions for solutions. In this sense, applied science, on the one hand, has to be conceived of as a scientific strategy for problem solving – a strategy that starts from mundane practical problems and ultimately aims at solving them. On the other hand, despite the dominance of application that applied sciences are subjected to, as sciences they can do nothing but develop such solutions in a theoretically reflected and methodologically well founded manner. The latter, of course, may lead to the well-known fact that even applied sciences often tend to concentrate on "application oriented basic research" only and thus appear to lose sight of the original practical problem. But despite such shifts in focus: Both the boundaries between disciplines and between pure and applied research are getting more and more blurred.

Today, after the turn of the millennium, it is obvious that sciences are requested to provide more and something different than just theory, basic research or pure knowledge. Rather, sciences are increasingly being regarded as partners in a more comprehensive social and economic context of problem solving and are evaluated against expectations to be practically relevant. This also implies that sciences are expected to be critical, reflecting their impact on society. This new "applied" type of science is confronted with the question: Which role can the sciences play in solving individual, interpersonal, social, intercultural, political or technical problems? This question is typical of a conception of science that was especially developed and propagated by the influential philosopher Sir Karl Popper – a conception that also this handbook series is based on.

2. "Applied Linguistics": Concepts and controversies

The concept of "Applied Linguistics" is not as old as the notion of "Applied Science", but it has also been problematical in its relation to theoretical linguistics since its beginning. There seems to be a widespread consensus that the notion "Applied Linguistics" emerged in 1948 with the first issue of the journal *Language Learning* which used this compound in its subtitle *A Quarterly Journal of Applied Linguistics*. This history of its origin certainly explains why even today "Applied Linguistics" still tends to be predominantly associated with foreign language teaching and learning in the Anglophone literature in particular, as can bee seen e.g. from Johnson and Johnson (1998), whose *Encyclopedic Dictionary of Applied Linguistics* is explicitly subtitled *A Handbook for Language Teaching*. However, this theory of origin is historically wrong. As is pointed out by Back (1970), the concept of applying linguistics can be traced back to the early 19th century in Europe, and the very notion "Applied Linguistics" was used in the early 20th already.

2.1. Theoretically Applied vs. Practically Applied Linguistics

As with the relation between "Pure" and "Applied" sciences pointed out above, also with "Applied Linguistics" the first question to be asked is what makes it different from "Pure" or "Theoretical Linguistics". It is not surprising, then, that the terminologist Back takes this difference as the point of departure for his discussion of what constitutes "Applied Linguistics". In the light of recent controversies about this concept it is no doubt useful to remind us of his terminological distinctions.

Back (1970) distinguishes between "Theoretical Linguistics" – which aims at achieving knowledge for its own sake, without considering any other value –, "Practice" – i.e. any kind of activity that serves to achieve any purpose in life in the widest sense, apart from the striving for knowledge for its own sake – and "Applied Linguistics", as a being based on "Theoretical Linguistics" on the one hand and as aiming at usability in "Practice" on the other. In addition, he makes a difference between "Theoretical Applied Linguistics" and "Practical Applied Linguistics", which is of particular interest here. The former is defined as the use of insights and methods of "Theoretical Linguistics" for gaining knowledge in another, non-linguistic discipline, such as ethnology, sociology, law or literary studies, the latter as the application of insights from linguistics in a practical field related to language, such as language teaching, translation, and the like. For Back, the contribution of applied linguistics is to be seen in the planning of practical action. Language teaching, for example, is practical action done by practitioners, and what applied linguistics can contribute to this is, e.g., to provide contrastive descriptions of the languages involved as a foundation for teaching methods. These contrastive descriptions in turn have to be based on the descriptive methods developed in theoretical linguistics.

However, in the light of the recent epistemological developments outlined above, it may be useful to reinterpret Back's notion of "Theoretically Applied Linguistics". As he himself points out, dealing with practical problems can have repercussions on the development of the theoretical field. Often new approaches, new theoretical concepts and new methods are a prerequisite for dealing with a particular type of practical problems, which may lead to an – at least in the beginning – "application oriented basic research" in applied linguistics itself, which with some justification could also be labelled "theoretically applied", as many such problems require the transgression of disciplinary boundaries. It is not rare that a domain of "Theoretically Applied Linguistics" or "application oriented basic research" takes on a life of its own, and that also something which is labelled as "Applied Linguistics" might in fact be rather remote from the mundane practical problems that originally initiated the respective subject area. But as long as a relation to the original practical problem can be established, it may be justified to count a particular field or discussion as belonging to applied linguistics, even if only "theoretically applied".

2.2. Applied linguistics as a response to structuralism and generativism

As mentioned before, in the Anglophone world in particular the view still appears to be widespread that the primary concerns of the subject area of applied linguistics should be restricted to second language acquisition and language instruction in the first place (see, e.g., Davies 1999 or Schmitt and Celce-Murcia 2002). However, in other parts of the world, and above all in Europe, there has been a development away from aspects of language learning to a wider focus on more general issues of language and communication.

This broadening of scope was in part a reaction to the narrowing down the focus in linguistics that resulted from self-imposed methodological constraints which, as Ehlich (1999) points out, began with Saussurean structuralism and culminated in generative linguistics. For almost three decades since the late 1950s, these developments made "language" in a comprehensive sense, as related to the everyday experience of its users, vanish in favour of an idealised and basically artificial entity. This led in "Core" or theoretical linguistics to a neglect of almost all everyday problems with language and communication encountered by individuals and societies and made it necessary for those interested in socially accountable research into language and communication to draw on a wider range of disciplines, thus giving rise to a flourishing of interdisciplinary areas that have come to be referred to as hyphenated variants of linguistics, such as sociolinguistics, ethnolinguistics, psycholinguistics, conversation analysis, pragmatics, and so on (Davies and Elder 2004).

That these hyphenated variants of linguistics can be said to have originated from dealing with problems may lead to the impression that they fall completely into the scope of applied linguistics. This the more so as their original thematic focus is in line with a frequently quoted definition of applied linguistics as "the theoretical and empirical investigation of real world problems in which language is a central issue" (Brumfit 1997: 93). However, in the recent past much of the work done in these fields has itself been rather "theoretically applied" in the sense introduced above and ultimately even become mainstream in linguistics. Also, in view of the current epistemological developments that see all sciences under the pressure of application, one might even wonder if there is anything distinctive about applied linguistics at all.

Indeed it would be difficult if not impossible to delimit applied linguistics with respect to the practical problems studied and the disciplinary approaches used: Real-world problems with language (to which, for greater clarity, should be added: "with communication") are unlimited in principle. Also, many problems of this kind are unique and require quite different approaches. Some might be tackled successfully by applying already available linguistic theories and methods. Others might require for their solution the development of new methods and even new theories. Following a frequently used distinction first proposed by Widdowson (1980), one might label these approaches as "Linguistics Applied" or "Applied Linguistics". In addition, language is a trans-disciplinary subject par excellence, with the result that problems do not come labelled and may require for their solution the cooperation of various disciplines.

2.3.   Conceptualisations and communities

The questions of what should be its reference discipline and which themes, areas of research and sub-disciplines it should deal with, have been discussed constantly and were also the subject of an intensive debate (e.g. Seidlhofer 2003). In the recent past, a number of edited volumes on applied linguistics have appeared which in their respective introductory chapters attempt at giving a definition of "Applied Linguistics". As can be seen from the existence of the Association Internationale de Linguistique Appliquée (AILA) and its numerous national affiliates, from the number of congresses held or books and journals published with the label "Applied Linguistics", applied linguistics appears to be a well-established and flourishing enterprise. Therefore, the collective need felt by authors and editors to introduce their publication with a definition of the subject area it is supposed to be about is astonishing at first sight. Quite obviously, what Ehlich (2006) has termed "the struggle for the object of inquiry" appears to be characteristic of linguistics – both of linguistics at large and applied linguistics. Its seems then, that the meaning and scope of "Applied Linguistics" cannot be taken for granted, and this is why a wide variety of controversial conceptualisations exist.

For example, in addition to the dichotomy mentioned above with respect to whether approaches to applied linguistics should in their theoretical foundations and methods be autonomous from theoretical linguistics or not, and apart from other controversies, there are diverging views on whether applied linguistics is an independent academic discipline (e.g. Kaplan and Grabe 2000) or not (e.g. Davies and Elder 2004), whether its scope should be mainly restricted to language teaching related topics (e.g. Schmitt and Celce-Murcia 2002) or not (e.g. Knapp 2006), or whether applied linguistics is a field of interdisciplinary synthesis where theories with their own integrity develop in close interaction with language users and professionals (e.g. Rampton 1997/2003) or whether this view should be rejected, as a true interdisciplinary approach is ultimately impossible (e.g. Widdowson 2005).

In contrast to such controversies Candlin and Sarangi (2004) point out that applied linguistics should be defined in the first place by the actions of those who practically *do* applied linguistics:

> […] we see no especial purpose in reopening what has become a somewhat sterile debate on what applied linguistics is, or whether it is a distinctive and coherent discipline. […] we see applied linguistics as a many centered and interdisciplinary endeavour whose coherence is achieved in purposeful, mediated action by its practitioners. […]
> What we want to ask of applied linguistics is less what it is and more what it does, or rather what its practitioners do. (Candlin/Sarangi 2004:1–2)

Against this background, they see applied linguistics as less characterised by its thematic scope – which indeed is hard to delimit – but rather by the two aspects of "relevance" and "reflexivity". Relevance refers to the purpose applied linguistic activities have for the targeted audience and to the degree that these activities in their collaborative practices meet the background and needs of those addressed – which, as matter of comprehensibility, also includes taking their conceptual and language level into account. Reflexivity means the contextualisation of the intellectual principles and practices, which is at the core of what characterises a professional community, and which is achieved by asking leading questions like "What kinds of purposes underlie what is done?", "Who is involved in their determination?", "By whom, and in what ways, is their achievement appraised?", "Who owns the outcomes?".

We agree with these authors that applied linguistics in dealing with real world problems is determined by disciplinary givens – such as e.g. theories, methods or standards of linguistics or any other discipline – but that it is determined at least as much by the social and situational givens of the practices of life. These do not only include the concrete practical problems themselves but also the theoretical and methodological standards of cooperating experts from other disciplines, as well as the conceptual and practical standards of the practitioners who are confronted with the practical problems in the first place. Thus, as Sarangi and van Leeuwen (2003) point out, applied linguists have to become part of the respective "community of practice".

If, however, applied linguists have to regard themselves as part of a community of practice, it is obvious that it is the entire community which determines what the respective subject matter is that the applied linguist deals with and how. In particular, it is the respective community of practice which determines which problems of the practitioners have to be considered. The consequence of this is that applied linguistics can be understood from very comprehensive to very specific, depending on what kind of problems are considered relevant by the respective community. Of course, following this participative understanding of applied linguistics also has consequences for the Handbooks of Applied Linguistics both with respect to the subjects covered and the way they are theoretically and practically treated.

3. Applied linguistics for problem solving

Against this background, it seems reasonable not to define applied linguistics as an autonomous discipline or even only to delimit it by specifying a set of subjects it is supposed to study and typical disciplinary approaches it should use. Rather, in line with the collaborative and participatory perspective of the communities of practice applied linguists are involved in, this handbook series is based on the assumption that applied linguistics is a specific, problem-oriented way of "doing linguistics" related to the real-life world. In other words: applied linguistics is conceived of here as "linguistics for problem solving".

To outline what we think is distinctive about this area of inquiry: Entirely in line with Popper's conception of science, we take it that applied linguistics starts from the assumption of an imperfect world in the areas of language and communication. This means, firstly, that linguistic and communicative competence in individuals, like other forms of human knowledge, is fragmentary and defective – if it exists at all. To express it more pointedly: Human linguistic and communicative behaviour is not "perfect". And on a different level, this imperfection also applies to the use and status of language and communication in and among groups or societies.

Secondly, we take it that applied linguists are convinced that the imperfection both of individual linguistic and communicative behaviour and language based relations between groups and societies can be clarified, understood and to some extent resolved by their intervention, e.g. by means of education, training or consultancy.

Thirdly, we take it that applied linguistics proceeds by a specific mode of inquiry in that it mediates between the way language and communication is expertly studied in the linguistic disciplines and the way it is directly experienced in different domains of use. This implies that applied linguists are able to demonstrate that their findings – be they of a "Linguistics Applied" or "Applied Linguistics" nature – are not just "application oriented basic research" but can be made relevant to the real-life world.

Fourthly, we take it that applied linguistics is socially accountable. To the extent that the imperfections initiating applied linguistic activity involve both social actors and social structures, we take it that applied linguistics has to be critical and reflexive with respect to the results of its suggestions and solutions.

These assumptions yield the following questions which at the same time define objectives for applied linguistics:
1. Which linguistic problems are typical of which areas of language competence and language use?
2. How can linguistics define and describe these problems?
3. How can linguistics suggest, develop, or achieve solutions of these problems?
4. Which solutions result in which improvements in speakers' linguistic and communicative abilities or in the use and status of languages in and between groups?
5. What are additional effects of the linguistic intervention?

4. Objectives of this handbook series

These questions also determine the objectives of this book series. However, in view of the present boom in handbooks of linguistics and applied linguistics, one should ask what is specific about this series of nine thematically different volumes.

To begin with, it is important to emphasise what it is not aiming at:
– The handbook series does not want to take a snapshot view or even a "hit list" of fashionable topics, theories, debates or fields of study.
– Nor does it aim at a comprehensive coverage of linguistics because some selectivity with regard to the subject areas is both inevitable in a book series of this kind and part of its specific profile.
Instead, the book series will try
– to show that applied linguistics can offer a comprehensive, trustworthy and scientifically well-founded understanding of a wide range of problems,
– to show that applied linguistics can provide or develop instruments for solving new, still unpredictable problems,

Introduction to the handbook series   xiii

- to show that applied linguistics is not confined to a restricted number of topics such as, e.g. foreign language learning, but that it successfully deals with a wide range of both everyday problems and areas of linguistics,
- to provide a state-of-the-art description of applied linguistics against the background of the ability of this area of academic inquiry to provide descriptions, analyses, explanations and, if possible, solutions of everyday problems. On the one hand, this criterion is the link to trans-disciplinary cooperation. On the other, it is crucial in assessing to what extent linguistics can in fact be made relevant.

In short, it is by no means the intention of this series to duplicate the present state of knowledge about linguistics as represented in other publications with the supposed aim of providing a comprehensive survey. Rather, the intention is to present the knowledge available in applied linguistics today firstly from an explicitly problem solving perspective and secondly, in a non-technical, easily comprehensible way. Also it is intended with this publication to build bridges to neighbouring disciplines and to critically discuss which impact the solutions discussed do in fact have on practice. This is particularly necessary in areas like language teaching and learning – where for years there has been a tendency to fashionable solutions without sufficient consideration of their actual impact on the reality in schools.

5. Criteria for the selection of topics

Based on the arguments outlined above, the handbook series has the following structure: Findings and applications of linguistics will be presented in concentric circles, as it were, starting out from the communication competence of the individual, proceeding via aspects of interpersonal and inter-group communication to technical communication and, ultimately, to the more general level of society. Thus, the topics of the nine volumes are as follows:

1. Handbook of Individual Communication Competence
2. Handbook of Interpersonal Communication
3. Handbook of Communication in Organisations and Professions
4. Handbook of Communication in the Public Sphere
5. Handbook of Multilingualism and Multilingual Communication
6. Handbook of Foreign Language Communication and Learning
7. Handbook of Intercultural Communication
8. Handbook of Technical Communication
9. Handbook of Language and Communication: Diversity and Change

This thematic structure can be said to follow the sequence of experience with problems related to language and communication a human passes through in the course of his or her personal biographical development. This is why the topic areas of applied linguistics are structured here in ever-increasing concentric circles: in line with biographical development, the first circle starts with the communicative competence of the individual and also includes interpersonal communication as belonging to a person's private sphere. The second circle proceeds to the everyday environment and includes the professional and public sphere. The third circle extends to the experience of foreign languages and cultures, which at least in officially monolingual societies, is not made by everybody and if so, only later in life. Technical communication as the fourth circle is even more exclusive and restricted to a more special professional clientele. The final volume extends this process to focus on more general, supra-individual national and international issues.

For almost all of these topics, there already exist introductions, handbooks or other types of survey literature. However, what makes the present volumes unique is their explicit claim to focus on topics in language and communication as areas of everyday problems and their emphasis on pointing out the relevance of applied linguistics in dealing with them.

Bibliography

Back, Otto
    1970   Was bedeutet und was bezeichnet der Begriff 'angewandte Sprachwissenschaft'? *Die Sprache* 16: 21–53.
Brumfit, Christopher
    1997   How applied linguistics is the same as any other science. *International Journal of Applied Linguistics* 7(1): 86–94.
Candlin, Chris N. and Srikant Sarangi
    2004   Making applied linguistics matter. *Journal of Applied Linguistics* 1(1): 1–8.
Carrier, Michael, Martin Stöltzner, and Jeanette Wette
    2004   *Theorienstruktur und Beurteilungsmaßstäbe unter den Bedingungen der Anwendungsdominanz.* Universität Bielefeld: Institut für Wissenschafts- und Technikforschung [http://www.uni-bielefeld.de/iwt/projekte/wissen/anwendungsdominanz.html, accessed Jan 5, 2007].
Davies, Alan
    1999   *Introduction to Applied Linguistics. From Practice to Theory.* Edinburgh: Edinburgh University Press.
Davies, Alan and Catherine Elder
    2004   General introduction – Applied linguistics: Subject to discipline? In: Alan Davies and Catherine Elder (eds.), *The Handbook of Applied Linguistics*, 1–16. Malden etc.: Blackwell.
Ehlich, Konrad
    1999   Vom Nutzen der „Funktionalen Pragmatik" für die angewandte Linguistik. In: Michael Becker-Mrotzek und Christine Doppler (eds.), *Medium Sprache im Beruf. Eine Aufgabe für die Linguistik*, 23–36. Tübingen: Narr.

Ehlich, Konrad
  2006   Mehrsprachigkeit für Europa – öffentliches Schweigen, linguistische Distanzen. In: Sergio Cigada, Jean-Francois de Pietro, Daniel Elmiger, and Markus Nussbaumer (eds.), *Öffentliche Sprachdebatten – linguistische Positionen. Bulletin Suisse de Linguistique Appliquée/VALS-ASLA-Bulletin* 83/1: 11–28.
Grabe, William
  2002   Applied linguistics: An emerging discipline for the twenty-first century. In: Robert B. Kaplan (ed.), *The Oxford Handbook of Applied Linguistics*, 3–12. Oxford: Oxford University Press.
Johnson, Keith and Helen Johnson (eds.)
  1998   *Encyclopedic Dictionary of Applied Linguistics. A Handbook for Language Teaching*. Oxford: Blackwell.
Kaplan, Robert B. and William Grabe
  2000   Applied linguistics and the Annual Review of Applied Linguistics. In: W. Grabe (ed.), *Applied Linguistics as an Emerging Discipline. Annual Review of Applied Linguistics* 20: 3–17.
Knapp, Karlfried
  2006   Vorwort. In: Karlfried Knapp, Gerd Antos, Michael Becker-Mrotzek, Arnulf Deppermann, Susanne Göpferich, Joachim Gabowski, Michael Klemm und Claudia Villiger (eds.), *Angewandte Linguistik. Ein Lehrbuch*. 2nd ed., xix–xxiii. Tübingen: Francke – UTB.
Meinel, Christoph
  2000   Reine und angewandte Wissenschaft. In: *Das Magazin*. Ed. Wissenschaftszentrum Nordrhein-Westfalen 11(1): 10–11.
Rampton, Ben
  1997 [2003]   Retuning in applied linguistics. *International Journal of Applied Linguistics* 7 (1): 3–25, quoted from Seidlhofer (2003), 273–295.
Sarangi, Srikant and Theo van Leeuwen
  2003   Applied linguistics and communities of practice: Gaining communality or losing disciplinary autonomy? In: Srikant Sarangi and Theo van Leeuwen (eds.), *Applied Linguistics and Communities of Practice*, 1–8. London: Continuum.
Schmitt, Norbert and Marianne Celce-Murcia
  2002   An overview of applied linguistics. In: Norbert Schmitt (ed.), *An Introduction to Applied Linguistics*. London: Arnold.
Seidlhofer, Barbara (ed.)
  2003   *Controversies in Applied Linguistics*. Oxford: Oxford University Press.
Widdowson, Henry
  1984 [1980]   Model and fictions. In: Henry Widdowson (1984) *Explorations in Applied Linguistics 2*, 21–27. Oxford: Oxford University Press.
Widdowson, Henry
  2005   Applied linguistics, interdisciplinarity, and disparate realities. In: Paul Bruthiaux, Dwight Atkinson, William G. Egginton, William Grabe, and Vaidehi Ramanathan (eds.), *Directions in Applied Linguistics. Essays in Honor of Robert B. Kaplan*, 12–25. Clevedon: Multilingual Matters.

Acknowledgements

Comprehensive volumes take a long time to prepare, edit, and finish.

We would like to thank Gerd Antos and Karlfried Knapp for their help throughout this difficult process. Moreover, we are very grateful to Barbara Karlson and Wolfgang Konwitschny, de Gruyter Publishers, for their continuous support and feedback. Brian Walker edited and revised the manuscript very well indeed and helped us greatly with the index. Finally, we would like to thank all our contributors for their excellent cooperation and their patience.

February 2008																																	Ruth Wodak
Veronika Koller

Contents

Introduction to the handbook series
Karlfried Knapp and *Gerd Antos* v

Acknowledgements xvii

Introduction: Shifting boundaries and emergent public spheres
Veronika Koller and Ruth Wodak 1

I. Theoretical foundations

1. Language, communication and the public sphere: Definitions
   Scott Wright 21

2. Public space, common goods, and private interests: Emergent definitions in globally mediated humanity
   Phil Graham 45

3. Media discourse and the naturalisation of categories
   Nick Couldry 67

4. Language, communication and the public sphere: A perspective from feminist critical discourse analysis
   Michelle M. Lazar 89

II. Language and communication in business

5. Advertisements and Public Relations
   Guy Cook 113

6. Language and communication design in the marketplace
   Gerlinde Mautner 131

7. Identity, image, impression: Corporate self-promotion and public reactions
   Veronika Koller 155

8. Creating a "green" image in the public sphere: Corporate environmental reports in a genre perspective
   Aud Solbjørg Skulstad 181

9. Britain™ and "corporate" national identity
   Lidia De Michelis 203

III. Language and communication in politics

10. Political terminology
    Paul A. Chilton. 223

11. Rhetoric of political speeches
    Martin Reisigl 243

12. Dissemination and implementation of political concepts
    Florian Oberhuber. 271

13. The contribution of critical linguistics to the analysis of discriminatory prejudices and stereotypes in the language of politics
    Ruth Wodak 291

14. Tabloidisation of political communication in the public sphere
    Werner Holly. 317

IV. Language and communication in the media

15. News genres
    Theo van Leeuwen 343

16. Specific genre features of new mass media
    Helmut Gruber. 363

17. Specific debate formats of mass media
    Kay Richardson 383

18. The sounds of silence in the media: Censorship and self-censorship
    Christine Anthonissen 401

19. Technology, democracy and participation in space
    Rodney H. Jones. 429

Biographical notes 447
Index 453

Introduction: Shifting boundaries and emergent public spheres

Veronika Koller and Ruth Wodak

1. The emergent public sphere – defining the concept of 'public sphere'

Throughout the 1990s and early 2000s, we witnessed a growing academic interest in the issue of the *public sphere*. Significantly fostered by the first English translation of Jürgen Habermas' book *Structural Transformation of the Public Sphere* (Habermas 1989/1996), research on the public sphere has provided a variety of theoretical approaches which either postulated the imminent demise of the public sphere in (late) modern democracies (Calhoun 1992; Crossley and Roberts 2004) or related the evident crisis of the (national) public sphere(s) to the growth of global tendencies rooted in the emergent trans-nationalisation of media production and reception (Fraser 2003) (see Schulz-Forberg 2005 for an extensive discussion).

What is a public sphere? The *public sphere* is a concept in Continental philosophy and critical theory that contrasts with the private sphere, and is that part of life in which one interacts with others and with society at large. In *Civil Society and the Political Public Sphere*, Habermas (1992) defines the public sphere as "a network for communicating information and points of view" which eventually transforms them into a public opinion.

The contemporary debate about the public sphere is characterised by voices claiming authority on the definition of what might constitute a/the public sphere. For many, the public sphere is a political one, which enables citizens to participate in democratic dialogue. For others, the public sphere is found in the media.

In the field of theory, late modernists (Garnham 1986; Weintraub and Kumar 1997), postmodernists (Villa 1992; Fraser 1995), feminists (Siltanen and Stanworth 1984), and others have marked their terrain within the debate, which began – as mentioned above – with Jürgen Habermas in 1962. In *Strukturwandel der Öffentlichkeit* (Structural Transformation of the Public Sphere), he believed to have found a time and space in which a true public sphere – true to his definition of it – existed and thrived. The German term *Öffentlichkeit* (public sphere) encompasses a variety of meanings, implying as a spatial concept the social sites or arenas where meanings are articulated, distributed and negotiated. "Public sphere" also denotes the collective body constituted by this process, i.e. "the public" (Negt and Kluge 1993).

The public sphere denotes specific institutions, agencies, practices; however, it is also a general social horizon of experience integrating everything that is actually or seemingly relevant for all members of society. Understood in this sense, the public sphere is a matter for a handful of professionals (e.g., politicians, editors, union officials) on the one hand, but, on the other, it is something that concerns everyone and that realises itself only in people's minds, in a dimension of their consciousness (Negt and Kluge 1993).

Viewed historically, Habermas suggests that in the late eighteenth and nineteenth century in Germany, France, and Britain, for a short period of time only, an effective bourgeois public sphere had emerged. Large numbers of middle class men (!), i.e. private individuals, came together and engaged in reasoned argument over key issues of mutual interest and concern, creating a space in which both new ideas and the practices and discipline of rational public debate were cultivated (Habermas 1962). Habermas thus formulated an ideal-type Western approach, which reconfirmed the classic construction of European history in which the Enlightenment features as a key period for the constitution of social and moral values and practices in which many Europeans still believe and on which they build societies even today. This interpretation of history remains an ideal type, however. The values are surely partial to the discourse and self-understanding of Europe and its population and states, not to other parts of the world. Habermas was convinced that an independent reason almost forced the interlocutors in the public sphere to find a consensus based on the most acceptable and logical argument: "Public debate was supposed to transform *voluntas* into a *ratio* that in the public competition of private arguments came into being as the consensus about what was practically necessary in the interest of all" (Habermas 1989/1996: 83).

Forty years after Habermas' first contribution, the understanding of the public sphere has changed drastically as will become visible throughout this volume (see also Wright, this volume). Habermas developed an ideal type of a white and male middle-class community that has no reverberations in today's social structures and communicative behaviour. In general, "Habermas (…) seems too satisfied with a narrow perspective through which to explore the public sphere, namely that of the bourgeoisie" (Crossley and Roberts 2004: 11). Moreover, critics have accused Habermas of having bought into the "dumbing down" effect of the media that Theodor W. Adorno and Max Horkheimer had proclaimed in the 1950s. However, Habermas' explanations for the disappearance of the traditional public sphere are to a certain extent convincing when he claims that public opinion today is more and more thought of as the result of an opinion poll which politicians use and seek to manipulate for their own ends.

Before sketching very briefly three main developments in public sphere theory, it should be mentioned that Habermas was prominent among his critics himself (Habermas 1992). The highly idealised "rational dialogue" between citizens, and between citizens and the state, was later replaced by systemic and strategic exchanges of power in his model (Ingram 1994). Legitimacy is negotiated and citizens offer this legitimacy to the state in return for the benefits of the welfare state (Habermas 1988). However, Habermas is convinced that ever more areas of social life are bureaucratised and commodified while communicative engagement and reasoning within them is undermined, open dialogue replaced by bureaucratic procedures and economic transactions (see also Fairclough's concepts of marketisation and commodification which draw on Habermas; Fairclough 1992). Habermas did, however, continue to disentangle reason from discourse. That is to say that objective reasoning, i.e. critique and reflection on the status quo, remains a positive force for him that is not a form of rational domination by discourse as a negative force (Habermas 1988). In this scenario, even the representative ruler of a country, in the case of the Enlightenment the French king, could have theoretically joined the group of the "reasoning" would he have sat at the doorstep of a café and joined the world of objective argument.

2. Three theories of the public sphere

Criticism of Habermas led to three main trends in public sphere research (Schulz-Forberg 2005): a late-modern school, a postmodern school and a relational school (Crossley and Roberts 2004). The first one builds on Habermas by accepting Habermasian prerequisites such as general accessibility to information, eradication of privilege, the quest for truth and the quest for general norms, along with their rational legitimisation (Koopmans and Erbe 2004). While this public sphere rests on normative foundations, these norms do not apply to white middle-class men exclusively. A critical division of social concepts is introduced here: the "system" and the "lifeworld", which has become very important in sociolinguistics and critical discourse analysis (see Wodak 1996). The modern world falls into these two categories and the public sphere, i.e. communication between people through language and representation, belongs to the lifeworld and not to the system.

The postmodern school, on the other hand, opens up the public sphere to plurality. Instead of one consensus-driven public sphere, many so-called subaltern counter-publics exist: Parallel discursive arenas where members of subordinated social groups invent and circulate counter-discourses. Reason can thus be broken down into a myriad of practical and habitual modes of regulating public dialogue. Nancy Fraser (1995: 295) formulated three characteristics of a postmodern conception of the public sphere:

> 1) it must acknowledge that participatory parity [is] not merely the bracketing, but rather the elimination, of systematic social inequalities; 2) where such inequality persists, however, a postmodern multiplicity of mutually contesting publics is pre-

ferable to a single modern public sphere oriented solely to deliberation; 3) a postmodern conception of the public sphere must countenance not the exclusion, but the inclusion, of interests and issues that bourgeois masculinist ideology labels "private" and treats as inadmissible.

For the relational or institutional school, as it is sometimes called, the public sphere manifests itself in historical milieux and within wider social relations. Relational and institutional settings are defined as a "patterned matrix of institutional relationships among cultural, economic, social, and political practices" (Somers 1993). The public sphere is one of those relational or institutional arenas. The public sphere is furthermore "a contested participatory site in which actors with overlapping identities as legal subjects, citizens, economic actors, and family and community members, form a public body and emerge in negotiations and contestations over political and social life." From this point of view the theoretical development began to yield increasingly dialogical approaches, but not in the sense of the Habermasian rational dialogue, rather in the sense of Bakhtin's participatory dialogue, heteroglossia, and the semiotic understanding of meaning creation and perception (Bakhtin 1979).

Another definition of the public against this theoretical background claims that the public sphere represents

> open-ended flows of communication that enable socially distant interlocutors to bridge social-network positions, formulate collective orientations, and generate psychical "working alliances", in pursuit of influence over issues of common concern. Publics are not simply spaces or worlds where politics is discussed (...), but, rather, interstitial *networks* of individuals and groups acting as citizens. States, economies, and civil societies may all be relatively "bounded" and stable complexes of institutions, but publicity is emergent (Emirbayer and Sheller 1998: 738).

From this emergent, overlapping, never-ending communicative space, the notion of symbolic codes, i.e. a semiotic approach, developed. The public sphere is a special space for the articulation of symbolic codes, values and representations that help to formulate individual and political orientations (Crossley and Roberts 2004). Recently, terms such as "fluidity", "networks" and "dynamic" have entered this debate which relate, of course, to the development of new media and the change in time-space distantiation (Preston 2001; Mattelart 2003; see Couldry, Gruber, Jones, all this volume).

Recent research has also put forward the notion of a global public sphere in which money, people and ideas travel ever faster and in ever increasing numbers. Changes on a global level have altered the meaning of the public sphere, some argue, in four ways: First, new forms of leisure and consumption patterns can be detected, associated with global events and organisations like the World Cup or MTV. Second, global economic public spheres have emerged that revolve around organisations like the World Bank and IMF. Third, global political publics exist that act as "states", examples being the EU, UN and UNESCO, and global political publics exist in the form of NGOs such as Amnesty International, along with global social movements. Fourth, globalisation has reconstituted what is meant by the term "general public". People increasingly know about global events and global organisations and this knowledge helps them construct a fluid cosmopolitan identity in small but significant ways (Sheller and Urry 2003; see Koller and van Leeuwen, both this volume).

The four points sketched above can surely be agreed upon to some extent, but certainly not in all of their implications. The definition of the globally integrating public sphere still addresses a minority of globally interested citizens. MTV, for example, is not a channel watched by the majority of a population but only by a very small share (Chalaby 2002). However, a growing transnational quality of media coverage and a growing transnational interest in global events such as the Tsunami catastrophe point towards the further integration of public spheres not only on a European, but also on a global level.

Within Europe, a de-centralising trend in the national public spheres has gained momentum ever since the 1980s. Satellite TV, cable TV, and the Internet further fragmented the media while at the same time reaching a growing transnational audience. While transnational television existed already in the 1950s, the individual usage of the channels only became possible with the instalment of satellites that boosted the possibility for TV channels to utilise an ever-growing number of frequencies. National media regulations have been softened and are now increasingly penetrated by transnational, or non-national television production companies (Chalaby 2002; see Triandafyllidou, Wodak, and Krzyżanowski, forthcoming). This implies that communication has also become decisively multi-directional. On a transnational level, two forms of broadcasting spaces and configurations of culture have emerged: global broadcasting regions link populations of neighbouring countries on the basis of proximity, common cultural heritage and language, while on the other hand, diasporic transnational broadcasting spaces are established which gather different national communities scattered across the globe into a single audience. In addition to the growth in transnational communication, a focus on local communities, marginalised populations and civic activists can be found just as well (Busch 2004). Furthermore, media formats and genres have proliferated. Today, reading the quality newspapers only provides a partial view of the political debate, supplemented by infotainment, edutainment and reality soaps. Political discourse is not confined to the information genre anymore, but has left its mark on the entertainment sector as well (see Holly, this volume).

During the production process of the media, the media producer imagines an implicit reader (Iser 1972). In the context of the public sphere, this has an important implication: On the one hand the reader can still be understood as a member of civil society, as a citizen of the state, and the relationship to the audience as imagined by the media producer remains paternal and aims at transmitting values, habits and tastes. The transmission model of communication thus persists, in which the ordered transfer of meaning is the intended consequence of the communication process (Gardiner 2004; see also Bourdieu 2005 for a definition of the journalistic field). On the other hand, however, readers/receivers that constitute the audience are not citizens, but consumers. They consume media products and potentially also the products advertised for in the media. Unfortunately, in this configuration of media communication, the scoop, i.e. the extraordinary and the scandal, gains in importance since getting attention is regarded as being more important than the transmission of content. Media production is an economic enterprise and even the public service media is dependent on quotas. Thus, media production always walks the line between content orientation, factual representations, and the necessity to reach and entertain as many people as possible.

3. Main dimensions throughout this volume

In terms of structure, the book is divided into four sections, drawing on and related to the developments in Social Theory briefly summarised above, with the opening chapters laying the theoretical foundations for the study of communication in the public sphere (Part I). Subsequent contributions address the related public spheres of business (Part II), politics (Part III) and the media (Part IV). Cutting across these sections, the volume is organised around the three major themes of public vs private, inclusion vs exclusion, and globalisation. Of course, these themes also overlap and are separated here merely for analytical reasons.

The public sphere is impossible to think without demarcating it from the private sphere. As Lazar elaborates in chapter 4, this binary opposition has traditionally been gendered, in that the private sphere was feminised while the public sphere was co-constructed as masculine. However, the two are less of a dichotomy than the negative definition of "public" as "non-private" might suggest. Indeed, the boundaries between the two are increasingly blurred, not least under the impact of computer-mediated communication that, as Rodney Jones argues in the final chapter of the book, blends virtual public spaces with the user's private space. And it is not only practices that lead to a hybrid public-private sphere, but the ongoing informalisation, conversationalisation and "tabloidization" (as Holly calls the trend, see chapter 14) of public discourses equally contribute to an appropriation of the private by the public sphere.

Reversely, discourses originating in the private sphere cannot only influence discourses in the public sphere, but become part of such public discourses as well. A case in point is the grassroots activism that has impacted on corporate policies and genres promoting corporate social and environmental responsibility (see Skulstad, chapter 8). Now an established part of corporate communications, corporate environmental reports have been accused of being an example of "greenwashing", i.e. incorporating activist demands into new genres in order to manage a company's public image. Similarly cynical attitudes can be established for consumers' reactions to other forms of corporate impression management (Koller, chapter 7). As far as manipulation is an inherent element of all public discourse to secure consumer loyalty, political majorities or media reach, access to the public sphere is constrained by structures of inclusion and exclusion.

Inclusion/exclusion in fact cuts across all other dimensions. As Wodak points out in chapter 13, the public sphere consists of shifting groups, subject positions and social identities. As these are constantly being negotiated, the parameters of inclusion and exclusion change along with them. Throughout the following chapters, exclusion is discussed in its extreme form, as in Anthonissen's study on censorship in South African newspapers (chapter 18), where the political culture meant that silencing no longer required any legitimisation. However, exclusion from public discourse is also shown to work more covertly, relying on consensus-based hegemonic forms such as public debate formats (Richardson, chapter 17).

On the other hand, groups traditionally excluded from public discourse are striving to gain access to the public sphere through strategies referred to as discourse design or discourse engineering. A case in point is the "professionalisation" of the discourse of non-governmental organisations (see Mautner, chapter 6), which have gained media attention for their agendas. Rodney Jones' study of the impact of technology on access to (virtual) public spheres (chapter 19) further shows how newly included groups and individuals bring with them new genres and new subject positions. Here, emergent genres offer new constraints and options for participants to articulate themselves. Finally, in as far as features of communication in the private sphere impact on media discourse, e.g. in the case of tabloidisation (see Holly, chapter 14), we can see how particular discourses shape the media and thereby make them more accessible. Conversely, media also shape public discourses, making for new boundaries that define who is included and who is excluded. One example is the "digital divide" (see Gruber, chapter 16) that has broadened access for many while leaving behind others.

As mentioned above, Parts II, III and IV in turn address the public spheres of business, politics and the media. Despite the exclusion of many potential discourse participants in different localities, each of these three public spheres can be seen as global in its outreach. In fact, Graham (chapter 2) speaks of a "globally mediated humanity" to capture this phenomenon. This quest for holding the defining power in a potentially global discourse community is perhaps most obviously the case for multi-national corporations, who metaphorically style themselves as "global players" and seek to communicate a unified brand image (see Koller, chapter 7).

The sphere of politics is increasingly characterised by the decline of the nation state and the concomitant rise of supra-national and corporate organisations. Parallel to that trend, however, we are witnessing a rise in sub-national politics, as in the "Europe of regions". Such "glocalisation" retains historically grown constraints on discourse participants; for example, Richardson (chapter 17) discusses the participation by proxy that we can see in public debate formats as specific to British political culture. On a related note, Oberhuber (chapter 12) shows how political concepts, such as "sustainability", are disseminated and implemented differently in different political cultures.

Glocalisation is also seen at work in media communication, where a homogenising force of global media conglomerates communicating the brand values of their different publication channels is counterbalanced by media use and media features indebted to local histories and cultures. Examples of the latter are Jones' study of Hong Kong teenagers' use of internet chat forums (chapter 19), Lazar's discussion of the gendered public and private spheres in Singapore (chapter 4) and Anthonissen's account of exclusionary practices in South African media discourse (chapter 18). Given the tension between global and local forces shaping public discourses, it comes as no surprise that views on participation in the global sphere range from the pessimistic (see Graham, chapter 2) to the cautiously optimistic (see Mautner, chapter 6), with some contributions holding a balanced middle ground in their assessment (see Holly, chapter 14).

4. Structure of the volume

The nineteen chapters of this volume unfold as follows: The book opens with Scott Wright's overview of definitions of both the public sphere and the various concepts and terms which inform the debate on it. This first chapter shows how the very idea of the public sphere is contested, and particularly addresses how language and communication can themselves be used to construct "the" public. Wright links the political and sociological literature on the public sphere with discourse analytical, sociolinguistic and communication approaches and thus grounds the subsequent chapters. More specifically, he critically discusses the seminal approach by Jürgen Habermas on "deliberative public spheres", which has influenced many recent approaches. As Habermas integrates a linguistic/ pragmatic approach to communication with Critical Theory, we believe this debate to be salient for our volume.

Taking over from Wright, Phil Graham discusses how theorists of public space have emphasised the centrality of language to the production and maintenance of political, cultural, economic and social commonalities. He juxtaposes such notions of public space with ideas of private, proprietary or otherwise exclusive spaces and demonstrates how such spaces have usually been construed as existing "inside" public space. Recent trends toward globalisation, privatisation and commercialisation have led to a "privatised" global space emerging from the political and economic integration of nationalised public spaces. Importantly, Graham discusses how language itself becomes a central object of contention as evidenced, for example, by the intellectual property and trademark battles that continue over symbols of all kinds.

Laying the theoretical foundations for many of the chapters in Part IV (language and communication in the media), Nick Couldry turns towards media discourse to confront the problem of "media effects": While we know that media are consequential for social life, the question of how they achieve to have such an impact is a thorny one, given that specific effects of a particular media text are unlikely to be traceable. By way of a tentative answer to what might be the causal link between media discourse patterns and the patterning of social practice, the chapter reworks the notion of "category" as such a linking concept within mediated cultures. Couldry suggests that media discourse naturalises categories of social description in at least two ways: first, through general media-related categories (such as "liveness" or "reality") that are involved in media institutions' constant attempt to legitimate themselves as "central" social institutions; second, through specific categories of social description whose constant reinforcement through media is tied to the structural conditions of media production.

Closing the first part of the book is Michelle Lazar, whose contribution traces how the public sphere has been a central focus in debates on gender (in)equality: Women's access to, and participation in, the public sphere – the traditional stronghold of men in most societies – have been among the key indicators in measuring women's emancipation. The fact remains, however, that in many social, cultural and geographical contexts, communities of women have yet to achieve equality in these terms, so that entry and presence in the public sphere continue to be a struggle and an abiding goal. At the same time, Lazar outlines the growing public discourse of post-feminism that claims that once indicators of women's participation in public life are met, as is the case for sectors of women in modern industrialised societies, gender discrimination ceases to exist. According to the author, what such claims overlook is that subtle forms of sexism have emerged, which hinder (further) successes of women in public life; indeed in spite of all gender mainstreaming policies (for example in the European Union or at the level of the UN). Lazar proposes the dismantling of the deeply gendered public/private divide and a radical re-visioning of the gender order. To this end, critical feminist analysis of discourse is a form of analytical resistance that contributes to socially transformative goals.

The remaining three sections address, in turn, language and communication in the public spheres of business, politics and the media. Beginning with business, Guy Cook looks at public relations (PR) discourse, in which organisations seek to present themselves and their activities to outsiders in a favourable light. The chapter shows how PR has become particularly salient and powerful in the contemporary world of competitive corporate capitalism and global communication, addressing PR and advertising, as its most spectacular and ubiquitous form, from an applied linguistics perspective: Firstly, it establishes a theoretical basis for enquiry by defining PR and advertising, and showing how they relate to each other. It examines their functions, and the degree to which contemporary PR and advertising are (un)like other uses of language for display and persuasion. Particular attention is paid to the construction of "the public" in PR, and to the conflation of the public and private spheres in advertising. Secondly, the chapter considers possible methods for the study of PR and advertising, examining how linguistic and multimodal analyses can be integrated, what role automated corpus linguistic analysis can play, and how public reactions to PR and advertising can be studied through surveys, interviews and focus groups.

In another applied approach, Gerlinde Mautner outlines how organisational communication is increasingly the subject of interventionist policies, with management regulating who communicates what to whom and how. Pursuing "integrated" corporate and marketing communications, organisations attempt to acquire a uniform and unique "voice" which reinforces their core brand values and helps distinguish them from competitors. Internal homogenisation is meant to enhance external differentiation. This chapter demonstrates that impacts of these trends can be felt at both the macro-level of communications strategy as well as the meso-level of genre and the micro-level of lexical choice. Design initiatives are brought to bear on written and spoken communication, and on verbal and visual modalities. The author places particular emphasis on the discursive fallout of communications design in the public and nonprofit sectors, which have only fairly recently been exposed to market forces.

Corporations' textually mediated projections of themselves into the public sphere is also the subject of Koller's chapter, which looks at the corporate language used to this end and addresses the reaction of various publics to this communicated corporate identity (CI). It argues that CI represents a separate form of collective identity and therefore promises valuable new insights into the production, distribution and, most importantly, reception of self in discourse. In its empirical part, the contribution is based on the qualitative research into a sample mission statement. In terms of reception, systemic-functional analysis is employed to investigate texts by customers (e.g. chatroom data providing word-of-mouth testimonials). Results suggest that corporate impression management is at odds with customers' evaluation of the companies, thus pointing to a widening gap between narcissistic corporate self-promotion and grass-roots public sentiment about corporations and their role in society.

Still on the topic of corporate image creation, Skulstad discusses how the growing awareness of environmental issues among individuals, companies and governments has evoked a number of textual responses. One of these is corporate environmental reports, and the chapter looks at this genre at a relatively early stage of emergence: reports issued by British companies between 1991 and 1993. The chapter shows that genre analysis is not a unified approach, and that the analysis of new (emerging) genres represents specific problems. While examining specific linguistic strategies used to achieve the communicative aim of creating a positive corporate image in the public sphere, the chapter also shows that the use of visuals plays an important role in achieving specific communicative functions. Links are drawn to other genres in the public sphere, particularly corporate annual reports and corporate documents on animal testing issues.

Bridging the public spheres of business and politics, de Michelis' contribution aims to reveal the ideological dimension underpinning the language used by New Labour in its discourse on British national identity. De Michelis demonstrates how New Labour's agenda in projecting a more flexible, accommodating sense of "Britishness" is consistently expressed using forms of specialised communication. In particular, its discourse of nationhood focuses on the key metaphor of "the nation as corporation", given currency by an enthusiastic use of marketing techniques in politics. Empirically, the chapter draws on a variety of different communicative forms including think-tank reports, official surveys and British Council publications. The analysis shows that New Labour's rhetoric of "nationhood" and "change" is in reality a vehicle for a fundamentally ideological attempt to alter the very process of political culture by adapting it to managerial and corporate discourses. As a consequence, such alignment leads to a ritualisation of politics and political discourse along quasi-corporate lines, which translates into a loss of power on the part of political actors.

De Michelis' chapter shows how persuasion and discursive re-alignment operates at both a micro- and a macro-level. Historically, persuasive rhetoric gave rise to politics and was adopted wholeheartedly by companies in their public relations efforts (see Cook, chapter 5). The wheel has come full circle by political actors adapting marketing tactics, such as advertising (see Reisigl, chapter 11) and blogging to communicate with carefully targeted markets, formerly known as constituencies. Part II comprises contributions on what historically constituted, and is often still equated with, the public sphere: politics. The section starts out with Paul Chilton's treatment of political terminology. Seeing political behaviour as largely dependent on the human language faculty, and given that political structures and processes vary across space and time, linguistic practices are assumed to vary accordingly. Considering political terminology found in English, in the context of British and American polities, the chapter investigates the shared vocabulary that is required by political actors to conventionally refer to shared structures and processes. The contribution discusses the semantics of a number of key political terms, including the conceptualisations that cluster around them: Since politics involves difference and disagreement as well as coordination and cooperation, there will be semantic and conceptual variation within political communities. The chapter closes by raising the question if, despite variations in polity, there could be some universals in the vocabulary of politics.

In the subsequent chapter, Reisigl extends the treatment of language and communication in politics from the lexical level to that of genre. In his contribution, political speeches are seen as having potentially strong perlocutionary effects and sometimes even constituting important driving forces in political history. Seen as such, political speeches are socially integrative by contributing to the formation of group solidarity. On the other hand, they can fulfil disintegrative and destructive functions by mobilising addressees to social exclusion and, at worst, to martial attacks against those excluded by the orator. The chapter gives an overview of attempts to typify political speeches on the basis of thematic, functional, rhetorical and other criteria. Sub-genres such as presidential speeches, parliamentary speeches and commemorative speeches are included in this typological discussion. Reisigl's contribution further shows that orally performed political speeches, rather than being monologic, in fact realise conventionalised activity patterns that involve different groups of participants. The chapter closes by outlining the main constitutive conditions of political oratory, reconstructing its genesis and delineating the distribution of modern political speeches in the age of computer-assisted text production and multimodal mass media. With respect to the mass-mediated distribution of political speeches, the role of public relations and the influence of media coverage and reception will be examined. The chapter thus links back to Cook's contribution on PR, as well as anticipating Part IV on media as a public sphere.

Further extending the notion of language and communication in politics, Oberhuber's entry on the dissemination and implementation of political concept draws on case studies and theoretical approaches from a variety of disciplines. In particular, this chapter reviews the literature from Anglo-American, German and French academic traditions, discussing contributions from lexicology and language history, as well as presenting selected studies on dissemination of political concepts. With respect to implementation, the focus is on several approaches of theorising the mediation between the social and the linguistic, including critical discourse analysis, cognitive metaphor theory and Foucault's work on "discursive formations" and "governmentality". This part of the chapter also reviews selected contributions from neighbouring disciplines like history and political theory. The chapter closes by presenting recent exemplary case studies with a view to identifying basic processes and research issues within dissemination and implementation of political concepts, such as social power and discursive hegemony.

Focusing on exclusion through discrimination, prejudice and stereotype in political discourse, Wodak discusses some of the many rhetorical devices used by politicians in their attempts to persuade the electorate of a specific agenda. The author argues that one of the most important and indeed, constitutive discursive macro-strategies, positive self-presentation and negative other-presentation, is crucial for the discursive construction of in- and out-groups. This division into US and THEM furthermore serves as precondition for derogating, debasing and discriminating against "Others" in all possible genres in public and private spheres. Drawing on examples from recent political discourses in European countries, the chapter demonstrates that Critical Linguistics and Critical Discourse Analysis (CDA) as well as research on multimodality allow investigating the subtle means of conveying discrimination through typical and also newly created stereotypes, often realised through insinuations and prejudiced discursive practices. This chapter draws on examples from recent political discourses in European countries to illustrate the manifold ways of excluding "Others", specifically in the now Europe-wide rightwing populist rhetoric.

Werner Holly's contribution on the tabloidisation of political communication in the public sphere charts the common ground between politics and media. The author here makes a case that the public sphere has undergone fundamental structural changes, often referred to as a "colonisation" of the political by the media system, or as a "mediocracy" that has replaced even democratically legitimated power. Like the major mass media, which are increasingly pursuing commercial aims, politics has thus become subject to a process of tabloidisation, re-orienting itself towards mainstream tastes and their need for entertainment. However, as the chapter argues, "symbolic politics" does so for persuasive rather than commercial reasons, using strategies such as visualisation, staging, dramatisation and aestheticisation of political communication. Re-orientation towards aspects of entertainment and clarity does not necessarily translate into inferior quality and more trivial, banal politics. As long as political communication still adheres to the basic categories of information value, truth, relevance and comprehensibility, we may be witnessing a popularisation, even democratisation, rather than tabloidisation of political communication.

The final section of the book, language and communication in the media, opens with van Leeuwen's chapter on the role of genre in global media communication. Introducing first a specific approach to the analysis of media genres, it argues that, under globalisation, media genres are becoming increasingly homogeneous, while media content can remain local. Genre is therefore becoming the key ensuring cohesion in a discursively diverse world, not only in the media. A number of media genres is considered, including newspaper pages and magazine celebrity profiles.

Helmut Gruber complements the preceding chapter by looking specifically at genre features of new mass media, such as e-mail and newsgroup communication, internet relay chat, hypertext, and short text messages. He defines genres as specific combinations of communicative factors like the direction of communication (monologue vs. dialogue), communication channels (visual vs. verbal, synchronous vs. asynchronous) and modes of communication (spoken vs. written). The chapter starts by characterising the different genres on these dimensions, discussing commonalities and differences. Following that, the contribution discusses linguistic and communicative characteristics of each of the genres, giving special attention to interpersonal and textual characteristics. Gruber closes by addressing the impact of different access to, and use of communication in, the new media ("digital divide"), which again links to the overall theme of "inclusion/exclusion". Gruber argues that although the new media initiated a "democratisation" of communication among those who have access to them, the gap between new media users and non-users has severe social consequences.

In a different angle on mass media, Kay Richardson focuses on specific debate formats, principally in the broadcast media (radio and television) with some comparative reference to print media (the newspaper letters page) and electronic media (online chat). The chapter begins with a short discussion of how the varying broadcast "debate" formats; including one-to-one interviews, audience discussion programmes and phone-ins fulfil different functions in the broadcasting schedule, concentrating on different areas of social life from high politics to lifestyle issues, and being designed for different audiences. In the central section of the paper she analyses extracts from two programmes chosen for maximum contrast, namely material from *Any Questions*, the long-running British radio audience participation programme, and extracts from the kind of "lifestyle" programming represented by Jerry Springer's American talk show. In both cases attention is given to the different type of public which these programmes seek to establish and the discursive means they use to do this.

In her chapter on silencing and censorship, Christine Anthonissen extends the scope from uses to abuses of the mass media. She considers two kinds of censorship that are prevalent in media discourses, namely censorship of the powerful, who may violate the rights of lesser subjects, and censorship of weaker subjects, whose rights have been violated or are under threat of being violated. Her chapter investigates state censorship which relies on the legislative and retributive powers of government and which is introduced on various grounds such as concern for public morality, state security etc. Such state censorship may retrospectively remove already published texts, or may disallow future publication of potentially harmful matter. The contribution also investigates self-censorship of subjects who prefer to keep information from public scrutiny in the media on various grounds such as fear of self-incrimination, fear of state prosecution or fear of public humiliation. By way of illustration, the chapter draws on material from recent South African media.

The last chapter in this section, and in the book, revisits a question that is fundamental to this book, namely participation in emergent public spheres with their shifting boundaries. To this end, Rodney Jones outlines how computer mediated communication (CMC) has shifted flows of discourse and power in the "public sphere", opening up spaces for new discursive practices and identities and giving people access to a myriad of "imagined communities". He argues that an understanding of how CMC has changed participation on the social, cultural and political levels also means considering how it has changed patterns and possibilities of participation on the more basic level of situated social actions in everyday life. This is why Jones explores the way young people in Hong Kong use computers to strategically manage their social worlds and their relationships. Computers, for these young people and for many others, are not so much tools for communication as they are tools for managing and navigating social networks and resisting and redrawing social boundaries imposed by parents, teachers and other authorities. In closing, the author argues that understanding the mechanics of power and resistance in situated, everyday actions with technology is the first step to understanding technology's potential to affect power relations and ideologies in larger social, institutional and cultural contexts.

Apart from bringing together contributors from four continents, the volume also shows a wide interdisciplinarity range, combining various areas of linguistics such as critical discourse analysis (Reisigl, Wodak), genre analysis (Skulstad), multimodal analysis (van Leeuwen), pragmatics (Cook) and cognitive semantics (Chilton, Koller). These fields within linguistics act in concert with management studies (Mautner, Skulstad), political science (Oberhuber, Wright) and media studies (Couldry, Richardson). What these different approaches have in common is that they link social theories and social change (see section 1) back to concrete textual instances of a whole range of genres. As such, each contribution can be located in the framework of Applied Linguistics. Broadly conceived, the discipline seeks to harness the linguistic analysis of naturally occurring data in the solution of real-life, often social, problems. To the extent that communication in the public sphere is characterised by power asymmetries, marginalisation and exclusion along different dimensions, interdisciplinary applied linguistic research can help to uncover the mechanisms that disadvantage particular groups and thus – at least – raise awareness; or even, in a really applied way, propose new and different communicative patterns. The problem-based research underlying the contributions means that the instruments for linking macro-level theories back to their micro-level textual instantiations, such as rhetorical or semantic analysis, are handed flexibly yet consistently.

On the whole, then, we hope that this volume will contribute to an interdisciplinary treatment of how language and communication work to shift the boundaries of ever-emergent public spheres.

References

Bakhtin, Mikhail M.
    1979   *Die Ästhetik des Wortes*. Edited by R. Grübel. Frankfurt/Main: Suhrkamp.
Bourdieu, Pierre
    2005   The political field, the social science field, and the journalistic field. In: Rodney Benson and Erik Neveu (eds.), *Bourdieu and the Journalistic Field*, 29–47. Cambridge: Polity Press.
Busch, Brigitte
    2004   *Medien im Disput*. Klagenfurt: Drava.
Calhoun, Craig (ed.)
    1992   *Habermas and the Public Sphere*. Cambridge, MA: MIT Press.
Chalaby, Jean K.
    2002   Transnational television in Europe: the role of pan-European channels. *European Journal of Communication* 17(2): 183–203.
Crossley, Nick and John M. Roberts (eds.)
    2004   *After Habermas: New Perspectives on the Public Sphere*. Oxford: Blackwell.
Emirbayer, Mustafa and Mimi Sheller
    1998   Publics in history. *Theory and Society* 27(6): 727–79.
Fairclough, Norman
    1992   *Discourse and Social Change*. Cambridge: Polity.
Fraser, Nancy
    1995   Politics, culture, and the public sphere: toward a postmodern conception. In: Linda Nicholson and Steven Seidman (eds.), *Social Postmodernism: Beyond Identity Politics*, 287–314. Cambridge: Cambridge University Press.
Fraser, Nancy
    2003   *Transnationalizing the Public Sphere*. Paper presented at the Conference 'Identities, Affiliations, Allegiancies', Yale University, 3–4 October.
Gardiner, Michael E.
    2004   Wild publics and grotesque symposiums: Habermas and Bakhtin on dialogue, everyday life and the public sphere. In: Nick Crossley and John M. Roberts (eds.), *After Habermas: New Perspectives on the Public Sphere*, 28–48. Oxford: Blackwell.
Garnham, Nicholas
    1986   The media and the public sphere. In: Golding, Peter, Graham Murdock and Philip Schlesinger (eds.), *Communicating Politics: Mass Communications and the Political Process*, 37–54. Leicester: Leicester University Press.
Habermas, Jürgen
    1962   *Strukturwandel der Öffentlichkeit*. Frankfurt/Main: Suhrkamp.
Habermas, Jürgen
    1988   *Legitimation Crisis*. Cambridge: Polity.
Habermas, Jürgen
    1989/1996   *The Structural Transformation of the Public Sphere*. Cambridge: Polity Press.

Habermas, Jürgen
  1992   Civil society and the political public sphere. In: Craig Calhoun (ed.), *Habermas and the Public Sphere*, 421–461. Cambridge, MA: MIT Press.
Ingram, David
  1994   'Foucault and Habermas on the subject of reason. In: Gary Cutting (ed.), *The Cambridge Companion to Foucault*, 215–262. Cambridge: Cambridge University Press.
Iser, Wolfgang
  1972   *Der implizite Leser*. Munich: Fink.
Koopmans, Ruud and Jessica Erbe
  2004   Towards a European public sphere? Vertical and horizontal dimensions of Europeanised political communication. *Innovation* 17(2): 97–118.
Negt, Oskar and Alexander Kluge
  1993   *Öffentlichkeit und Erfahrung*. Frankfurt/Main: Suhrkamp.
Mattelart, Armand
  2003   *The Information Society: An Introduction*. London: Sage.
Preston, Pascal
  2001   *Re-Shaping Communications: Technology, Information and Social Change*. London/Thousand Oaks, CA: Sage.
Schulz-Forberg, Hagen
  2005   *The Meaning of Europe and the European Public Sphere after 1945: Crisis, Transformation and Change*. EMEDIATE Project Report, WP1 – State of the Art, EUI Florence and Humboldt University, Berlin. Available online at/http://www.eui.eu/RSCAS/Research/EMEDIATE. Accessed 4 February 2008.
Sheller, Mimi and John Urry
  2003   Mobile transformations of "public" and "private life". *Theory, Culture and Society* 20(3): 107–125.
Siltanen, Janet and Michelle Stanworth (eds.)
  1984   *Women and the Public Sphere: A Critique of Sociology and Politics*. London: Hutchinson.
Somers, Margaret R.
  1993   Citizenship and the place of the public sphere: law, community, and political culture in the transition to democracy. *American Sociological Review* 58: 587–620.
Triandafyllidou, Anna, Ruth Wodak and Michał Krzyżanowski (eds.)
  forthcoming   *Europe in/and Crisis*. Basingstoke: Palgrave.
Villa, Dana
  1992   Postmodernism and the public sphere. *American Political Science Review* 86: 712–721.
Weintraub, Jeff and Krishan Kumar (eds.)
  1997   *Public and Private in Thought and Practice: Perspectives on a Grand Dichotomy*. Chicago: University of Chicago Press.
Wodak, Ruth
  1996   *Disorders of Discourse*. London: Longman.

I. Theoretical foundations

1. Language, communication and the public sphere: Definitions

Scott Wright

> The art of talking, the thing that makes human beings what they are, has become a refuge for recusants. Our public discourse has become unworthy of the name and will remain so unless and until we decide to change it. Maybe it is time we talked about it. (Kettle 2005)

1. Introduction

Language and communication are two of the building blocks of any conceptualisation of a public sphere. If people do not communicate, or could not communicate because they were linguistically incomprehensible, a public sphere cannot be said to exist. The notion that people can and do communicate is essential, though often left as a given and not made explicit. Moreover, it is not just the fact that people communicate that is important, but which people are communicating, exactly how they do this, and to what effect. Put simply, who is this public, and how do they conduct themselves?

This chapter will firstly briefly define language. Secondly, two broad schools of thought about communication – the process school and the semiotic school – are outlined. I will argue that the two are not incompatible before providing an initial, layered, definition of communication. My analysis will begin with Jürgen Habermas's conceptualisation of the public sphere. I will then outline the various criticisms and alternative conceptualisations of this model. This will be developed into an account of why many assume that the contemporary public sphere is in crisis before outlining the debate between those who argue that the internet is a potential solution to these problems and those who argue that it will be its death knell. The chapter will conclude that there is no such thing as "the" public sphere. Rather, there are public spheres. Any definition must take account of this distinction, and this, combined with the growing number of alternative approaches to public sphere theorising, necessitates a multi-definitional, transdisciplinary approach.

2. Language and the public sphere

Language, at its most basic, is a set of symbols and sounds governed by rules of grammar for conveying information. Formal linguistics, for its part, studies the properties of natural language (as opposed to artificial, created languages). Early linguistics (that is, prior to Chomsky) tended to collect a corpus of data (text), which was then collated and categorised into its "constituent" parts (Searle 1972). This was achieved by using research methodologies derived from theories of language construction. In essence, linguistics provided the tools to deconstruct the text. In the behaviouralist vein, linguistics did not, however, concern itself with the meaning of sentences.

Noam Chomsky was prominent in revising such attitudes. Chomsky (1957, 1965) showed through an analysis of syntax that structural linguistic methods were not sufficient for analysing sentences; they struggled to cope with the notion that, in principle, the number of sentences was infinite. Moreover, Chomsky showed that structural linguistics struggled to determine (and, indeed, categorise) the internal relationships of certain "ambiguous" sentences.[1] The categorising approach employed in the analysis of phonemes and morphemes, although fine for analysing words, was often redundant when analysing whole sentences.

Chomsky's response was to adopt a Universalist approach to grammar "that accommodates the creative aspect of language use and expresses the deep-seated regularities which, being universal, are omitted from the grammar itself" (Chomsky 1965: 6). The Universalist approach, which places Chomsky in the rationalist philosophical tradition, argues that language is a toolset of specific universal principles, intrinsic in the human mind, derived from human beings' genetic structure.[2] This was developed into his theory of generative grammar, which provided a series of grammatical rules that could be used to account for the infinite number of possible sentences. This was subsequently developed as Chomsky (1965) attempted to explain all linguistic relations between sound and meaning system. Grammar, for Chomsky, had three parts. The syntactical element as previously outlined, plus two interpretative elements: a phonological component and a semantic component that describe the sound and meaning produced by the syntax.

Chomsky's theory has generated considerable debate. Of particular importance here are the generative semanticists who argue that Chomsky did not go far enough; for insisting that syntax should be studied independent from meaning when meaning is thought to shape syntax. Put more strongly, generative grammar is inadequate because it separates the study of language form from the study of its communicative function (Stringer 1973). As John Searle (1972) argues, Chomsky's approach is eccentric because viewing language as a formal system sidelines languages' importance for communicating meaning. Such arguments have been deeply influential in the debates about language and communication, and will be returned to later when I discuss the semiotic school. It would be useful now though to express some of the more general claims that have derived (at least implicitly) from this.

Neil Thompson (2003: 37), following Martin Montgomery (1995), argues that "language is not simply the ability to use words"; it "refers to the complex array of interlocking relationships which form the basis of communication and social interaction." They use this position to argue that language is central to society – and we know that societal identification is central to the public sphere. Montgomery (1995: 251) argues that: "Language informs the way we think, the way we experience, and the way we interact with each other." He goes further, to argue that language is "the basis of community (…) Systematic knowledge about language and practical awareness of how it works is fundamental to the process of building mature communities." Similarly, Thompson (2003: 36) states that language is "a primary factor in terms of the make-up of society in relation to both cultural and structural factors." We can see this most obviously in phatic communication, which can help to maintain the cohesiveness of a public sphere by reinforcing bonds through confirming that the communication is being received and understand (Jakobson 1960).[3]

These arguments suggest that language is central to the construction of the public sphere because it helps to determine who is "in" and who is "out". It also raises important questions about communication between different languages in the public sphere. This is most obviously problematic in transnational, multilingual forums. (Wodak and Wright 2007) The (admittedly controversial) Sapir-Whorf linguistic relativity hypothesis, for example, proposes that language determines (and not just influences) a person's thought. Thus, according to the hypothesis, people with different languages actually perceive the world differently rather than perceiving it the same but expressing their perceptions in different languages.

Less controversially, a distinction has been made between predominantly collectivistic cultures (for example, Japan) and individualistic cultures (Europe/North America), and how this can affect the nature of communication. Edward Hall (1976) argues that collectivist cultures tend to use high context communication, in which the context (relative status, for example) and visual signs are important in determining meaning. Individualistic cultures, on the other hand, tend to use context to a lesser degree, thus requiring more explicit use of language.[4]

One can clearly see the potential confusion that could occur when communicating inter-culturally. This has been highlighted in business communications by an HSBC bank advert expounding on how important their "local knowledge" is in ensuring effective communication/trading in the global economy (see also Koller 2007). Although these arguments are moving more into the field of communication as opposed to language, the two are obviously linked, with various factors such as culture helping to shape the relationship. It is, thus, necessary to move towards a definition of communication.

3. Defining communication

Numerous chapters, articles and books are devoted to defining communication. As John Fiske (1990: 1) notes, communication "is one of those human activities that everyone recognizes but few can define satisfactorily." Fiske (1990: 2) describes communication simply: "social interaction through messages". Arthur Asa Berger (2000: 271), adopting a media-based approach, defines communication as "a process that involved the transmission of messages from senders to receivers." John Corner and Jeremy Hawthorne (1993: 2), meanwhile, state that "communication studies is about how human meanings are made through the production and reception of various types of sign. It is about visual and verbal sign systems and the technologies used to articulate, record and convey them." The problem with any definition of communication is that, in trying to be broad enough to cover the subjects' diversity, the explanatory power of the definition can be lost. For example, we might say that communication is, in essence, about how human beings interconnect with each other. But what does this actually tell us? In an attempt to fully account for the complexities of communication, many studies have used diagrams to visualise communication. Broadly speaking, there are two schools of thought. I will take each in turn.

3.1. The process school

The Process School involves the transmission of messages (it is also known widely as the transmission model or sender-receiver model, as indicated by Berger's definition above) from a sender to the receiver (Fiske 1990). One of the founding contributions to the process school was published by Claude Shannon and Warren Weaver (1949). Although it has similarities to Harold Lasswell's preceding formula[5] (1948), the attempt to visually model communication was distinctive (and helped to create a tradition of using diagrams as explanatory tools). In the Process School, the sender initiates the communication by encoding some piece of information in the form of a message. A message is typically denoted by the intention to communicate, and thus often excludes "unintended" messages. Messages are transmitted through some method (such as face-to-face or by the media) to one or more persons. The message is then successfully decoded, dependent on distortions (noise) within the communicative process, by the receiver. Thus, this model emphasises the transporting of "the message" from A to B – and is particularly useful for mediated forms of communication; the sender/medium being particularly important as they shape the extent to which the receiver successfully decodes the message. It is in this stage of the model that language is important. However, particularly in earlier models, language is given an almost formulaic, neutral quality. If this school is correct, we can imagine that communication in the public sphere would be a relatively simple process.

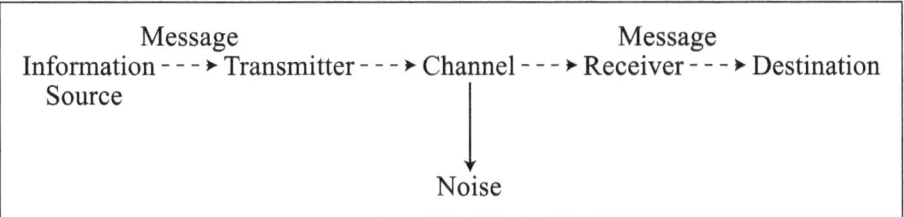

Figure 1. Shannon and Weaver's (1949) Transmission Model

Shannon and Weaver's basic "straight-line" model has been extensively developed to take account of the obstacles that, in real life situations, may block the "direct" path of "the message". There are a number of (often related) impediments. These can include the relative status of the sender and receiver (be it a gender, educational or class difference); the cognitive state of the receiver (who may not decode the message as intended and therefore receive a different message (Sless 1981; Streeck 1994); the fact that communication often involves a reply, and this may alter the message and suggests a loop rather than straight line (Dance 1967),[6] and technical impediments such as loss of communicative signal. Such impediments may make it more realistic to describe the process as the transmission of "the intended message". Two process models stand out for their attempts to account for communicative complexity.

George Gerbner (1956) was particularly interested in perceptions and context. Gerbner believed that events and messages were perceived differently by the communicator and receiver, and that this was influenced by the context – in a dynamic relationship. The model also includes factors such as the availability, access and control of (and to) the means of communication, which is particularly important for mediated environments.[7] In Gerbner's model we begin to see a cross-over between the Process School and the Semiotic School.

Gerbner's model begins with an external event (E), which is received (clearly or unclearly) and interpreted by a human or machine (M) and understood to a greater or lesser extent (E^1). It is in the complex relationship between the event and the receiver that meaning is developed. And this is itself influenced by education, culture and various other socio-political factors. The second stage of Gerbner's model relates to the medium (form) by which the mes-

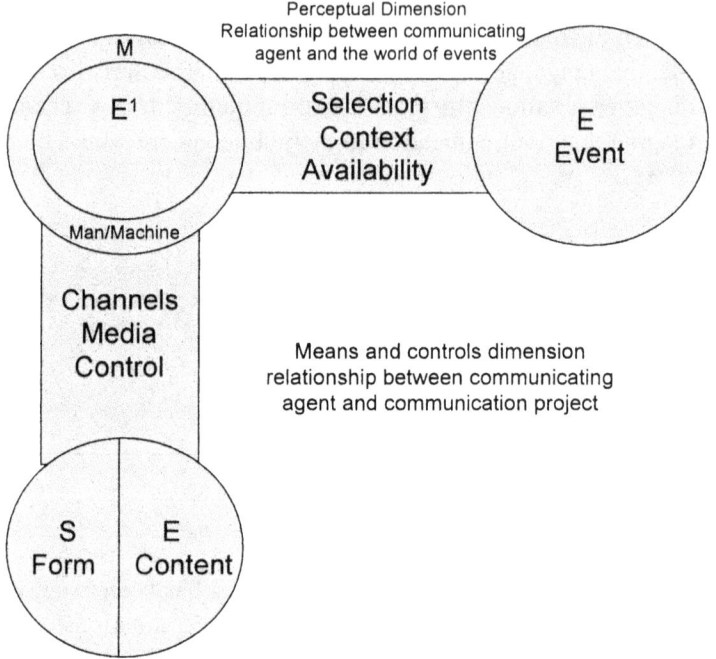

Figure 2. Gerbner's (1956) General Model of Communication

sage is communicated (S), and its content (E). These are directly related: the form of the message affects the content, and communicators make choices about what forms to use to best communicate each message they intend to send. The choices are limited by the available communication channels. For example, many people fall on the wrong side of a digital divide and do not have the access or skills to use the internet.

Gerbner's model was followed by one from Dean C. Barnlund (1970); it was designed (quite literally!) to take account of the complexities of communication between humans. For Barnlund, meaning was invented, assigned or given, rather than something which was received. The process was shaped by a variety of cues, both internal and external (and could be transferred between internal and external), with encoding and decoding represented by Barnlund as a continuous spiral. Moreover, Barnlund distinguished between intrapersonal communication (relatively simple) and interpersonal communication (multiplication of cues and the message is introduced).[8] The model is arguably sophisticated enough to withstand Ruth Finnegan's (2002: 17) criticism of process models; namely that they assume that there are essentially two main parties in the process without acknowledging the "multiple overlapping interchange" that takes place. It is in such interchanges that the Semiotic School has its roots.

3.2. The semiotic school

The Semiotic School is particularly interested in the production or exchange of meanings (as opposed to the transmission of messages from A to B) and has its roots in the works of C. S. Peirce and Ferdinand de Saussure. It is particularly associated with fields such as Semiology, Structural Linguistics and Cultural Studies. This grouping emphasises the signs, codes, rules and signifying systems by which meaning is constructed. According to the semiotic school we create meaning by sending signs. Signs include words, sounds, smells and images. For Peirce (1931–1958), an act can only be a sign if it is interpreted as such. In this sense, anything can actually be a sign; moreover, the emphasis is placed on the receiver as the interpreter. Peirce adopted a triadic model:

- The Representamen: the form which the sign takes (not necessarily material)
- An Interpretant: *not* an interpreter but rather the sense made of the sign;
- An Object: to which the sign refers.

This is distinguished from Saussure's dyadic model of signifier (our perception of the physical sign) and signified (the mental concept to which the signifier refers) by the object. Of particular interest is Saussure's (1959) argument that language is part of the science of signs, something which Roland Barthes (1967) believed needed to be inverted; semiology was one part of comprehensive linguistics.

From the cultural studies tradition Stuart Hall (1997: 36) argues that "since all cultural objects convey meaning, and all cultural practices depend on meaning, they must make use of signs; and in so far as they do, they must work like language works". Thus, for Hall, the music a person listens to, the clothes they wear, and the car they drive all communicate meaning. This arguably has elements of both the semiotic and process schools.

The semiotic school places the emphasis on the receiver, and how they interpret signs. The message is typically made up of a combination of signs. We make sense of the message; interpret it if you will, to the extent that we share the same signs or coding systems. This places a much greater emphasis on the structured relationships which enable a message to signify something. The marks on this page have a meaning beyond marks because the reader (and in the semiotic school messages are read rather than received) shares a similar signifying system. Firstly, the reader understands the letters and words – the signs – because they share the vocabulary. These words are given further meaning because they are organised by a code or signifying system – grammar. However, there are further factors which shape our interpretation.

Referring back to Stuart Hall (1997) again, there are a range of socio-political factors such as education, culture and economic conditions that shape how we understand and interpret messages. In the corporate world, Ronald Scollon and Suzanne Wong Scollon (1995) argue that corporate culture influences communication because of the differential power relationships that exist. They are particularly concerned with limiting the chances of miscommunication that can occur in inter-cultural contexts. To help limit such problems they put forward an analytical model to enable people to interpret the context which they are in.

When thinking about such factors, and the various signs which we put together to make up a message, we can see that communication is much more than language. Finnegan (2002) advises against narrow definitions of communication, and is particularly critical of the assumed equation between communication and language present in the works of Paul Cobley (1996) and Jürgen Habermas (1998). She takes a diverse approach, arguing that "communication through human-made artefacts and through their facial expressions, dress or bodily positioning form as relevant a part of their dynamic interacting as verbally-articulated sentences" (Finnegan 2002: 8). This relates to Pierre Bourdieu's argument about the importance of symbolic capital – and symbolic forms more generally – for understanding both the cognitive and social function of symbols (Bourdieu 1977: 183). Similarly, his famous account of habitus, as "a system of durable, transposable dispositions which functions as the generative basis of structured, objectively unified practices" (Bourdieu 1979: vii), suggests that a person's own knowledge and experience does not just reflect the "real" world but has a constitutive effect (Harker, Mahar, and Wilkes 1990: 11).

Communication is not just about spoken and written interaction, but also includes forms such as art, photography, dance and facial expressions (Finnegan 2002). Moreover, media such as television, the internet and radio, themselves the source of considerable debate, bring particular issues and possibilities in the ways they facilitate communication. From the political perspective, communicative formats such as pop and rock can be used to influence people's beliefs and voting behaviour (Street 1986: 2002). From the business perspective, we do not just have verbal and visual corporate communication (Skulstad, this volume; Koller, this volume), but logistical communications and the moving of goods and services that are necessary in making business work.

Defining language and communication, particularly in relation to the public sphere, depends on the theoretical and normative lenses through which you view the public sphere: This affects their relative weighting and precisely what the communication is intended to achieve. If you adopt a "folk" conceptualisation of the public sphere, that is, a public space outside of the house such as a market or other meeting point, a public sphere can be said to have existed since the early days of humanity. Agonistic conceptualisations of the public sphere, in the vein of Hannah Arendt, competition the emphasise for acclaim and immortality among the political elite (Benhabib 1992; Arendt 1998). Classical liberal theory argues that the public sphere is the space between government and the people in which private individuals influence the state – be it formally through elections or informally through the weight of public opinion. The liberal view of the public sphere has similarities to Habermas's model, but constrains free speech with the principle of neutrality (Ackerman 1980).[9] To begin this discussion I will start with Habermas's conceptualisation of the public sphere.

4. Habermas and the public sphere

In his classic (1989) work, *The Structural Transformation of the Public Sphere*, Habermas argued that an ideal(ised) public sphere rose during the late eighteenth century. The spark was the increasing separation of political from everyday life created by the centralisation of power he associated with the rise of the nation state, and the separation of church and state – a so-called decoupling (Habermas 1989). Combined with rising tax burdens to pay for military action, this led, Habermas argued, to a demand for accountability that constituted itself in agents forming into publics in an effort to control the state.

The publics were formed in the relief of a growing, privatised bourgeoisie. A private sphere was necessary for a public sphere to be possible, for Habermas, because the public sphere is the filter/space/mediator between private individuals and the state. There was, thus, a distinction between public and private individuals. Two further factors fed the rising public sphere: developments in printing technology increased the amount and (latterly, as censorship decreased) variety of information available; and the rise of the salon and coffee shop as forum for debate. These developments were important for Habermas because they fostered a critical rationality (in the bourgeois public), and because they were powerful enough to influence or steer the socio-political world.

As fast as the conditions that led to the evolution of a public sphere materialised, Habermas highlights a range factors that led to its eventual demise. For example, Habermas argues that the demarcation between state and society was blurred by interventionist welfare states, creating a dependent, supplier-consumer dynamic. Political debate was also gradually relegated to bartering over who gets what from the state, and not what the state should do. Such debates were increasingly transferred to parliaments and political parties – who pandered to the floating voter rather than trying to (re)educate the electorate. Finally, Habermas felt that the commercialisation of the public sphere was deeply worrying. Public debate was subjected to market forces, and this led to what we now know as "dumbing down" to increase (or at least maintain) market share (Franklin 1994, 1997; Holly, this volume).

This is combined with an historical account of the separation of economic and political systems from the communicatively rational sphere of everyday life. He uses this distinction as a basis to argue that the economic and political systems side-line, or at least distort, rational argument because they are steered by money and political power. This is compounded by their colonisation of the lifeworld (or everyday life), which is particularly problematic for Habermas. Communicative reasoning is increasingly squeezed out by bureaucracy and economics.

Habermas's subsequent work served to strengthen and, occasionally, revise his original argument. Of particular relevance here is Habermas's work on discourse, rationality and ethics. *The Theory of Communicative Action*, (1984, 1987) alongside *Legitimation Crisis* (1975) and *Communication and the Evolution of Society* (1979), strengthen Habermas's normative position by developing a communicative conception of rationality based around dialogue, argument and the exchange of reason. He distinguishes between communicative rationality and rational (or strategic) domination. This is grounded in Habermas's belief that argumentative speech is unifying and consensus-building when not coerced.

These are the building blocks for Habermas's discourse ethics. Discourse ethics are founded in a procedural conception of political theory. Unlike substantive theories which are grounded in accounts of reason and human nature, such discursive approaches develop rules (or at least procedures) that can legitimate social and institutional practices – when followed. In effect, a moral community can be produced because, for Habermas, publicly binding norms can claim to be rationally legitimate only if said norms are produced from a free and open discourse and argument between all parties affected by them. Claims to rationality (i.e. what any "reasonable" person would do) can only be justified if they are tested: no one person or group (such as politicians or political parties) can claim to speak or know what another person would, or should, do. In many instances, de facto acceptance of norms may suffice to ensure coordination amongst actors. Where there are different normative validity claims these may be overcome by discussants having compatible expectations: incomplete communicative action. (Moon 1995: 147) Nevertheless, the coordination is disturbed and must (generally) be overcome through further discussion – that is, a reflexive stance so that consensus can be restored (Moon 1995: 148).

5.   Critiquing Habermas

Habermas's work has been the subject of sustained, often critical, debate. The practical problems identified in the literature will be briefly outlined. Firstly, Habermas is criticised for implying that there was free and equal access to the bourgeois public: He tends to ignore its coerciveness and susceptibility to powerful groups. That rational communication was (at least for Habermas) the end result does not defend it from critiques of how it was produced: Structural arrangements and the distribution of power are crucial if the debate is to be truly democratic and rational (Fraser 1992: 115). For some, this may not be the case: The public sphere "is often dominated by the most powerful interests and tends to reflect their perspectives and exclude the most disadvantaged social groups, limiting their capacity to contribute with their issues and concerns to the political agenda" (Lombardo 2004: 3; see also Young 1990; Armstrong 2002) Such fears led Emilios Christodoulidis (2003) to argue that the public sphere must remain disorganised and anarchic if it is to resist co-optation.

Secondly, Habermas has been criticised for over-simplifying the effects of media colonization, if this can be said to exist at all. (Street 2001) Habermas has been accused of elitism and cultural snobbery (Dahlgren 1995; McGuigan 1996). Studies have argued that a "dumbed down" media has positive effects: better to give them cornflakes[10] than nothing at all (Street 1996). It follows from this that commercialisation of the media can have positive effects for public debate rather than being the death of it. Other studies argue that there was no media golden age as Habermas tends to assume in his account of the growth of the printing press (Winston 1998); and that people are not passive consumers of the media but engage critically with it (Norris 1999). Of particular importance, as highlighted by several of the subsequent chapters, the media can actually create new public spheres through debate programmes such as Question Time (see Richardson, this volume).

A related concern is whether the media are a public or a private sphere. On the one hand, Eric Hobsbawm (1983: 11–12) argues that the media (particularly television) constitutes a private sphere because the audience is atomised and because it is primarily consumed in the home. Similarly, Mark Poster (1995) argues that "the media, especially television but also other forms of electronic communication isolate citizens from one another and substitute themselves for older spaces of politics." On the other hand, Denis McQuail (1983: 33–34) argues that "the media operates almost exclusively in the public sphere." According to David Chaney (1986: 120), there is "no contradiction" between these perspectives as mass society has become so privatised that the media often provide the only means of publicly articulating societal concerns. James Curran has argued that beyond the public/private dichotomy, the conceptualisation of the media's role as mediator or "fourth estate" between government and citizens is restrictive; the media actually perform – or should perform – this role in all relations when power is exercised over others (Curran 1991: 32). Thus, the media can, for example, bring business discourses into the public sphere and highlight business corruption.

Thirdly, Habermas's conceptualisation of the public sphere has been criticised as unrealistic. It is thought to have rational biases (Dahlgren 2005: 155) and ignore more informal types of communication (Finnegan 2002). Put simply, Habermas has a rather dry, and perhaps elitist, conceptualisation of the kind of communication desirable for the public sphere. It promotes deliberation as *the* form of communication for the public sphere. The diversity of communication forms put forward by Finnegan (2002) is in contradiction to this. To develop a more holistic view of communication in the public sphere, Peter Dahlgren has put forward the notion of civic culture; it is "a way to conceptualize the factors that can enhance or impede political participation – the enactment of citizenship understood as forms of social agency" (Dahlgren 2005: 157). Of particular importance is the notion that the quality (and kind) of debate does not necessarily adhere to Habermas's model.

In a similar vein, the goal of reaching consensus put forward by Habermas (and by deliberative democracy theorists more generally) has been criticised by Chantal Mouffe. Mouffe (1999) develops her critique from the agonistic position, arguing that deliberative democracy cannot cope with deep differences of opinion; the passions raised cannot, and, indeed, should not, be denied by the force of consensus but be encouraged: agonistic pluralism. The point is not to reach consensus – which can be forced and have hidden power imbalances (see for example Wodak's [1996: 96] analysis, which raises serious questions about just how consensual apparently consensual decisions actually are) but to be open to other points of view in a process of continued contestation and deep respect for the adversary. The term "dissensus" is adopted (see also Ziarek's (2001) use of dissensus in her attempt to develop an ethical framework that avoids prescriptive norms).

A polar opposite "critique" comes from the consociational school put forward by Arend Lijphart (1977), which argues for grand coalitions to be built between the different political groups. In this model, issues are often only debated in private amongst the different leaders – particularly in deeply divided countries where there are fears of serious political instability and violence. The public sphere, in this model, is more or less neutered in the sense that the Habermasian sluice into political decision-making is missing. John Dryzek (2005) goes so far to as to draw a medicinal analogy, calling this an analgesic form of democracy because it suppresses deliberation.

Fourthly, Habermas is criticised for focusing on only the male, bourgeois, white public sphere at the expense of all others (Landes 1988; Benhabib 1992; Fraser 1992; Ryan 1994; Lazar, this volume), and for failing to develop a post-Bourgeois model (Fraser 1992: 111). Habermas's male-defined, liberal bourgeois account of the public sphere was historically revised by Geoff Eley (1992). Eley argued that it was a training ground for government amongst certain sections of the male bourgeois public leading to hegemonic rather than repressive rule. In fact, citing Ryan and Eley, Nancy Fraser (1992) argues that women were involved in the public sphere, just not the bourgeois public sphere: there were a host of competing counter-publics. Such counter-public spheres perform a dual role, both separate from, and linked to, the general public sphere. We can see the emergence of such spheres in the use of new technologies by protest groups to create "a temporary space of resistance, which has enabled (…) movements to move in a new direction typified by global grassroots solidarities, multi-issue campaigns and anti-hierarchical forms of organising" (Pickerill 2003: 170).

On an interpersonal level, Fraser (1992: 118–121) argues that it is not possible for people to bracket their different statuses and deliberate as if equal, as required by Habermas. Instead, Fraser suggests that bracketing should be dropped in favour of a requirement of social equality. This is to be achieved by their elimination and the development of some "rough equality" (1992: 121). However, Fraser does not extrapolate how this would be achieved in detail. James Fishkin (1992, 1995), and Fishkin and Ackerman (2004) have attended to many of these issues of representativeness in their deliberative polling experiments, by using representative sampling techniques. Fraser, for her part, does argue that a diverse range of (subaltern counter) public spheres are beneficial to democracy (and not negative as Habermas originally suggested). This, in turn, can help mitigate the problem of inequality by giving excluded groups an alternative locus for discussion. However, evidence from an innovative study of various institutionalised discourses (combining the theory of critical discourse analysis with the methods employed by socio-linguistics) suggested that there are many potential blocks to communication (Wodak 1996). Thus, it is questionable whether people can move vertically between these different spheres.

The idea that the contemporary public sphere operates on many levels, not just the local or national, has broader significance beyond Fraser's subaltern counter-publics. Erik Eriksen (2004: 1), for example, argues that the nation-state perspective "is rapidly becoming deficient, as the EU manifests more and more the characteristics of a supranational polity." Similarly, the transnationalisation of communication and capital flows, combined with localising concepts such as subsidiarity, is at odds with the nation-state perspective. Alvin Toffler (1970: 422) has characterised this as "Anticipatory Democracy", a series of locally based democratic constituent (or social future) assemblies where everyone would be wired. Toffler (1990: 251) has since argued that we are moving toward "mosaic democracy" – the fracturing of "mass" democracy into highly charged and fast-moving pieces. While obviously not taking it to this extreme, Habermas has (at least partially) recognised this diversity in the public sphere as *einen wilden Komplex*, "a wild complex", similar to a common room (Habermas 1996: 307, 373).

To summarise, however we describe the contemporary public sphere, of more importance are the alternative normative positions that underpin this. On the one hand, diverse, multi-sectoral public spheres can be considered positive (which would suggest a strong contemporary public sphere), while on the other hand, this can be viewed as a negative (and thus a weak contemporary public sphere). It is generally held that the public sphere is in crisis. For example, Poster (1995) argues that:

> Contemporary social relations seem to be devoid of a basic level of interactive practice which, in the past, was the matrix of democratizing politics: loci such as the agora, the New England town hall, the village Church, the coffee house, the tavern, the public square, a convenient barn, a union hall, a park, a factory lunchroom, and even a street corner. Many of these places remain but no longer serve as organizing centers for political discussion and action.

6. A virtual public sphere?

That the public sphere is widely thought to be in crisis because it is increasingly privatised, features an unrepresentative group of participants with mass society largely apathetic, and because the quality of the debate has been neutered or trivialised with a trenchant for the spectacular (McKee 2005). The internet and online discussion forums in particular have been posited as a solution to many of the ills that have, allegedly, infected the contemporary public sphere. As Kees Brants (2005: 144) puts it, "the Internet is often prescribed as the medicine for democracy in a midlife crisis." Such forums, it is thought, can help to create virtual Habermasian public spheres (Tsagarousianou, Tambini, and Bryar 1998; Keane 2000; Wilhelm 2000; Sassi 2001) or an electronic commons (Abramson, Arterton, and Orren 1988; Blumler and Coleman 2001), Such arguments are typically based on three assumptions: that the internet is free from domination, that it is interactive, and that it can facilitate consultation (Brants 2005: 144–145).

Perhaps unsurprisingly, there is a distinct divide between those who believe the internet will reinvigorate or revolutionalise the public sphere (and the political system more generally) and those who believe the internet will be normalised into existing practices. On the revolutionary side, Yoneji Masuda (1990: 83) argues that "the technical difficulties that until now have made it impossible for large numbers of citizens to participate in policy making have now been solved by the revolution in computer-communications technology". Similarly, Roza Tsagarousianou (1999: 195–196) argues that "new technologies clearly have the potential to sustain such spaces [public spheres] as they enable both deliberation (citizen to citizen communication) and hearing (citizen to authority communication)". Anthony Corrado and Charles M. Firestone (1996: 17), meanwhile, believe that online discussion will create a "conversational democracy".[11]

On the other side, Michael Margolis and David Resnick (2000: 2) argue that the internet has been normalised:

> Cyberspace has not become the locus of a new politics that spills out of the computer screen and revitalizes citizenship and democracy. If anything, ordinary politics and

commercial activity, in all their complexity and vitality, have invaded and captured cyberspace. Virtual reality has grown to resemble the real world.

Others suggest that the internet might have negative effects. Christine Bellamy and Charles Raab (1999: 169) argue that "there is a real danger that ICTs will not only reflect but amplify the fragmentation of the public sphere, balkanising politics into multifarious and shifting constituencies that are incapable of being aggregated by any means". Richard Davis and Diana Owen (1998: 124) follow up this concern: "Discussions via the internet are more likely to be as narrow or perhaps even narrower than those across the backyard fence. Those with differing views gravitate to their own discussion groups."

To test such claims, the nature and quality of debate being facilitated by online forums has been empirically measured. Analysis of Usenet discussion forums has suggested that the internet is not providing a Habermasian public sphere. Anthony Wilhelm (2000: 97) concludes that the debates are primarily "self-expression and monologue, without in large measure the listening, responsiveness, and dialogue that would promote communicative action" and that "[e]merging technologies (…) undermine severely the rhythm of democratic discourse" (2000: 101). Further research from Richard Davis (1999: 167) leads him to conclude that "even the internet's most democratic corner is not as democratic as it appears"; "it more closely resembles the Jerry Springer show rather than National Public Radio or CNN" (2005: 67). However, recent research now suggests that we should not automatically be so pessimistic; government-run online discussion forums can provide a deliberative public sphere (Wright 2007; Wright and Wodak 2007; Wodak 2007), and that the design and structuring of the forums (Wright 2005; Wright and Street 2005) and the use of moderation (Wright 2006) is crucial to their success. Put simply, it is too soon to discount the internet as an emergent public sphere because it is precisely that: emerging. We must be careful, however, to analyse existing practice and learn from these experiences.

7. Conclusion

As the contemporary public sphere has become increasingly complex, so have the debates that surround it. Language and communication are absolutely crucial to our understanding of the public sphere. But this cannot be disconnected from our normative position on what the public sphere should be like. The public sphere is undoubtedly growing – yet it is considered to be in crisis – and this is because theorists (as well as those using such ideas to empirically test it) have a certain understanding of what it should look like. To paraphrase Benjamin Barber (2004), we have a growing weak public sphere and (perhaps) a shrinking strong public sphere.

Notes

1 For example, "I like her cooking" contains no ambiguous words and has a simple grammatical structure but has numerous meanings (Searle 1972).
2 As opposed to the empiricist philosophical tradition which argues that all knowledge is derived from actual experience.
3 Phatic communication is associated with societal conventions (i.e. it is a socio-cultural factor). For example, it is expected that one person will greet another. In the West this might be by saying hello, while in Japan it might be by bowing.
4 Of course, this is not always the case: when communicating with one's "mates" or family the communication may be less explicit because of the greater communicative understanding that exists.
5 Lasswell's formula: Who says What, in which Channel, to Whom, with what Effect.
6 Dance (1967) developed a helical model of communication that is prefaced on the belief that, although looped models are preferable to linear ones, they assume a boomerang effect whereby the communication comes full-circle, which is "manifestly erroneous".
7 The shortcoming in Gerbner's model is that it takes a static view of the message; that is, it does not account for how people derive meaning from the message, which semiologists (see below) believe to be crucial. (Watson and Hill 2003: 117; see for example, Jakobson's [1960] model, which, although still broadly within the Process School, was particularly concerned with meaning and the internal structure of messages.)
8 Although many would argue that in intrapersonal communication we send out many messages and that it is, thus, not "simple".
9 Neutrality, here, means that reasons put forward within a discourse of legitimation can only be "good" reasons if citizens do not assert that their concept of the good is better than other citizens', or that they are intrinsically superior to other citizens (Ackerman 1980: 11). Thus, where people realise they disagree about aspects of the moral truth they should not talk about this in the public sphere (Ackerman 1980: 16–17).
10 Bob Franklin (1994) drew an analogy between dumbing down and the consumption of processed white bread, arguing that having a fibreless product was bad for people's health. Street (1996), in many ways following Dahlgren and McGuigan, argue that if people will only eat white bread then better they eat that than nothing at all.
11 Crucial to these debates is the role of government, and whether it suppresses the radical potential (Winston 1998) and inhibits freedom (De Sola Pool 1990) or whether it can help to promote deliberation by providing an institutional context.

References

Abramson, Jeffrey B., Christopher F. Arterton and Garry Orren
    1988   *The Electronic Commonwealth: The Impact of New Media Technologies on Democratic Politics.* New York: Basic Books.

Ackerman, Bruce
 1980 *Social Justice in the Liberal State.* New Haven: Yale University Press.
Arendt, Hannah
 1998 *The Human Condition.* Chicago: University of Chicago Press.
Armstrong, Kenneth
 2002 "Rediscovering Civil Society: the European Union and the White Paper on European Governance". *European Law Journal* 8(1): 102–132.
Barber, Benjamin
 2004 *Strong Democracy: Participatory Politics for a New Age.* Berkeley, CA: University California Press.
Barnlund, Dean C.
 1970 A transactional model of communication. In: Kenneth K. Sereno and C. David Mortensen (eds.), *Foundations of Communication Theory*, 83–102. New York: Harper & Row.
Barthes, Roland
 1967 *Elements of Semiology.* (Transl. A. Lavers and C. Smith). London: Jonathan Cape.
Bellamy, Christine and Charles D. Raab
 1999 Wiring up the deck-chairs? In: Coleman Stephen, John Taylor and Wim van de Donk (eds.), *Parliament in the Age of the Internet*, 156–172. Oxford: Oxford University Press.
Benhabib, Seyla
 1992 Models of public space: Hannah Arendt, the liberal tradition, and Jürgen Habermas. In: Craig Calhoun (ed.), *Habermas and the Public Sphere* 73–98. Cambrigde, MA: MIT Press.
Berger, Arthur A.
 2000 *Media and Communication Research Methods: An Introduction to Quantitative and Qualitative Approaches.* London: Sage.
Blumler, Jay G. and Stephen Coleman
 2001 *Realising Democracy Online: A Civic Commons in Cyberspace.* London: IPPR.
Bourdieu, Pierre
 1977 *Outline of a Theory of Practice.* (Transl. R. Nice). Cambridge: Cambridge University Press.
Bourdieu, Pierre
 1979 *Algeria 1960* (Transl. R. Nice). Cambridge. Cambridge University Press.
Brants, Kees
 2005 Guest editors' introduction: the Internet and the public sphere. *Political Communication* 22(2): 143–146.
Chaney, David
 1986 The symbolic form of ritual in mass communication. In: Golding Peter, Graham Murdock and Philip Schlesinger (eds.), *Communicating Politics: Mass Communications and the Political Process*, 115–132. Leicester: Leicester University Press.
Chomsky, Noam
 1957 *Syntactic Structures.* The Hague: Mouton de Gruyter.
Chomsky, Noam
 1965 *Aspects of the Theory of Syntax.* Cambridge, MA: MIT Press.

Christodoulidis, Emilios
 2003 Constitutional irresolution: law and the framing of civil society. *European Law Journal* 9(4): 401–432.
Cobley, Paul (ed.)
 1996 *The Communication Theory Reader*. London: Routledge.
Corner, John and Jeremy Hawthorne
 1993 *Communication Studies: An Introductory Reader.* London: Edward Arnold.
Corrado, Anthony and Charles M. Firestone (eds.)
 1996 *Elections in Cyberspace: Towards a New Era in American Politics*. Washington DC: The Aspen Institute.
Curran, James
 1991 Rethinking the media as a public sphere. In: Peter Dahlgren and Colin Sparks (eds.), *Communication and Citizenship: Journalism and the Public Sphere in the New Media Age*, 27–57. London: Routledge.
Dahlgren, Peter
 1995 *Television and the Public Sphere*. London: Sage.
Dahlgren, Peter
 2005 The Internet, public spheres, and political communication: dispersion and deliberation. *Political Communication* 22(2): 147–162.
Dance, Frank E. (ed.)
 1967 *Human Communication Theory:* London: Holt, Rinehart & Winston.
Davis, Richard
 1999 *The Web of Politics: the Internet's Impact on the American Political System*. Oxford: Oxford University Press.
Davis, Richard and Diana Owen
 1998 *New Media and American Politics*. Oxford: Oxford University Press.
De Sola Pool, Ithiel
 1990 *Technologies of Freedom: On Telecommunications in a Global Age*. Cambridge, MA: Harvard University Press.
Dryzek, John
 2005 Deliberative democracy in divided societies: alternatives to agonism and analgesia. *Political Theory* 33(2): 218–242.
Eley, Geoff
 1992 Nations, publics, and political culture: placing Habermas in the nineteenth century. In: Craig Calhoun (ed.), *Habermas and the Public Sphere,* 289–339. Boston: MIT Press.
Eriksen, Erik O.
 2004 Conceptualizing European public spheres general, segmented and strong publics. Arena Working Paper series 3(04). Available online at http://www.arena.uio.no/publications/working-papers2004/papers/wp04_3.pdf. Accessed 8 October 2007.
Finnegan, Ruth
 2002 *Communicating: The Multiple Modes of Human Interconnection*. London: Routledge.
Fishkin, James S.
 1992 *Democracy and Deliberation: New Directions for Democratic Reform*. New Haven: Yale University Press.

Fishkin, James S.
  1995   *The Voice of the People: Public Opinion and Democracy.* New Haven: Yale University Press.
Fishkin, James S. and Bruce Ackerman
  2004   *Deliberation Day.* New Haven: Yale University Press.
Fiske, John
  1990   *Introduction to Communication Studies.* 2nd ed. London: Routledge.
Franklin, Bob
  1994   *Packaging Politics: Political Communications in Britain's Media Democracy.* London: Edward Arnold.
Franklin, Bob
  1997   *Newszak and News Media.* London: Arnold.
Fraser, Nancy
  1992   Rethinking the public sphere: a contribution to the critique of actually existing democracy. In: Craig Calhoun (ed.), *Habermas and the Public Sphere*, 109–142. Cambridge, MA: MIT Press.
Gerbner, George
  1956   Toward a general model of communication. *AV Communication Review* 4(3): 171–199.
Habermas, Jürgen
  1975   *Legitimation Crisis* (Transl. T. McCarthy). Boston: Beacon Press.
Habermas, Jürgen
  1979   *Communication and the Evolution of Society* (Transl. T. McCarthy). Boston: Beacon Press.
Habermas, Jürgen
  1984   *The Theory of Communicative Action, Volume 1: Reason and the Rationalization of Society* (Transl. T. McCarthy). Boston: Beacon Press.
Habermas, Jürgen
  1987   *The Theory of Communicative Action. Volume 2: Lifeworld and System: A Critique of Functionalist Reason* (Transl. T. McCarthy). Boston: Beacon Press.
Habermas, Jürgen
  1989   *The Structural Transformation of the Public Sphere: Inquiry into a Category of Bourgeois Society* (Transl. T. Burger). Cambridge, MA: MIT Press.
Habermas, Jürgen
  1996   *Between Facts and Norms: Contributions to a Discourse Theory of Law and Democracy* (Transl. W. Rehg). Cambridge: MIT Press.
Habermas, Jürgen
  1998   *On the Pragmatics of Communication* (Transl. M. Cooke). Cambridge Polity Press.
Hall, Edward
  1976   *Beyond Culture.* Garden City, NY: Anchor Press.
Hall, Stuart
  1997   *Representation: Cultural Representations and Signifying Practices.* London: Sage.
Harker, Richard, Cheleen Mahar and Chris Wilkes
  1990   *An Introduction to the work of Pierre Bourdieu.* New York: St. Martin's Press.

Hobsbawm, Eric
    1983   Introduction: inventing traditions. In: Eric Hobsbawm and Terence Ranger (eds.), *The Invention of Tradition*, 1–14. Cambridge: Cambridge University Press.

Jakobson, Roman
    1960   Closing statement: linguistics and poetics. In: Thomas A. Seboek (ed.), *Style in Language,* 350–377. Cambridge, MA: MIT Press.

Keane, John
    2000   Structural transformations of the public sphere. In: Kenneth L. Hacker and Jan van Dijk (eds.), *Digital Democracy: Issues of Theory and Practice*, 70–89. London: Sage.

Kettle, Martin
    2005   It's good to talk, but we've lost the art of conversation, *The Guardian*, 16 August 2005. Available online at http://www.guardian.co.uk/Columnists/Column/0,5673,1549875,00.html. Accessed 27 February 2006

Koller, Veronika
    2007   "The world's local bank": glocalisation as a strategy in corporate branding discourse. *Social Semiotics* 17(1): 111–131.

Landes, Joan
    1988   *Women and the Public Sphere in the Age of the French Revolution*. Ithaca, NY: Cornell University Press.

Lasswell, Harold
    1948   The structure and function of communication in society. In: Lyman Bryson (ed.), *The Communication of Ideas*, 37–51. New York: Harper and Row.

Lijphart, Arend
    1977   *Democracy in Plural Societies: A Comparative Exploration*. New Haven: Yale University Press.

Lombardo, Emanuela
    2004   The participation of civil society in the European constitution-making process. Paper presented at CIDEL Workshop, London. Available online at: http://www.arena.uio.no/cidel/WorkshopLondon/Lombardo.pdf. Accessed 8 October 2007.

Margolis, Michael and David Resnick
    2000   *Politics as Usual: The Cyberspace Revolution*. London: Sage.

Masuda, Yoneji
    1990   *Managing in the Information Society*. Oxford: Blackwell.

McGuigan, Jim
    1996   *Culture and the Public Sphere*. London: Routledge.

McKee, Alan
    2005   *The Public Sphere: An Introduction*. Cambridge: Cambridge University Press.

McQuail, Denis
    1983   *Mass Communication Theory*. London: Sage.

Montgomery, Martin
    1995   *An Introduction to Language and Society*. New York: Routledge.

Moon, J. Donald
    1995   Practical discourse and communicative ethics. In: Stephen K. White (ed.), *The Cambridge Companion to Habermas*, 143–164. Cambridge: Cambridge University Press.

Mouffe, Chantal
  1999   Deliberative democracy or agonistic pluralism. *Social Research* 66(3): 745–758.
Norris, Pippa (ed.)
  1999   *Critical Citizens: Global Support for Democratic Government.* Oxford: Oxford University Press.
Peirce, Charles S.
  1931–1958   *Collected Writings* (8 Vols.). (Ed. Charles Hartshorne, Paul Weiss and Arthur W Burks). Cambridge, MA: Harvard University Press.
Pickerill, Jenny
  2003   *Cyberprotest: Environmental Activism On-line.* Manchester: Manchester University Press.
Poster, Mark
  1995   CyberDemocracy: Internet and the public sphere. Available online at http://www.hnet.uci.edu/mposter/writings/democ.html. Accessed 27 February 2006.
Ryan, Mary
  1994   Gender and public access: women's politics in nineteenth-century America. In: Craig Calhoun (ed.), *Habermas and the Public Sphere*, 259–288. Cambridge, MA: MIT Press.
Sassi, Sinikka
  2001   The transformation of the public sphere. In: Barrie Axford and Richard Huggins (eds.), *New Media and Politics*, 89–108. London: Sage.
de Saussure, Ferdinand
  1959   *Course in General Linguistics.* New York: McGraw-Hill.
Scollon, Ronald and Suzanne W. Scollon
  1995   *Intercultural Communication: A Discourse Approach.* Oxford: Blackwell.
Searle, John R.
  1972   Chomsky's revolution in linguistics. *The New York Review of Books*, June 29.
Shannon, Claude E. and Warren Weaver
  1949   *The Mathematical Theory of Communication.* Urbana, IL: University of Illinois Press.
Sless, David
  1981   *Learning and Visual Communication.* London: Croom Helm.
Streeck, Jürgen
  1994   Culture, meaning, and interpersonal communication. In: Mark L. Knapp and Gerald R. Miller (eds.), *Handbook of Interpersonal Communication*, 286–319. Thousand Oaks, CA: Sage.
Street, John
  1986   *Rebel Rock: The Politics of Popular Music.* Oxford: Blackwell.
Street, John
  1996   In praise of packaging? Political coverage as popular culture. *Harvard Journal of Press/Politics* 1(2): 126–133.
Street, John
  2001   *Mass Media, Politics and Democracy.* Basingstoke: Palgrave.

Street, John
    2002   Bob, Bono and Tony B: the popular artist as politician. *Media, Culture and Society* 24(3): 433–441.
Stringer, David
    1973   *Language Acquisition, Learning and Cognition.* Milton Keynes: Open University Press.
Thompson, Neil
    2003   *Communication and Language: A Handbook of Theory and Practice.* Basingstoke: Palgrave.
Toffler, Alvin
    1970   *Future Shock.* New York: Random House.
Toffler, Alvin
    1990   *Power Shift.* New York: Bantam.
Tsagarousianou, Roza
    1999   Electronic democracy: rhetoric and reality. *Communications* 24(2): 189–208.
Tsagarousianou, Roza, Damian Tambini and Cathy Bryar
    1998   *Cyberdemocracy: Technology, Cities and Civic Networks.* London: Routledge.
Watson, James and Anne Hill
    2003   *Dictionary of Media and Communication Studies.* 6th ed. London: Arnold.
Wilhelm, Anthony G.
    2000   *Democracy in the Digital Age: Challenges to Political Life in Cyberspace.* London: Routledge.
Winston, Brian
    1998   *Media, Technology and Society: a History from the Telegraph to the Internet.* London: Routledge.
Wodak, Ruth
    1996   *Disorders of Discourse.* London: Longman.
Wodak, Ruth and Scott Wright
    2007   The European Union online: language, policy and practice. In: Brenda Danet and Susan C. Herring (eds.), *The Multilingual Internet: Language, Culture and Communication in Instant Messaging, E-mail and Chat,* 385–407. Oxford: Oxford University Press.
Wright, Scott
    2005   Design matters: the political efficacy of government-run online discussion forums. In: Oates Sarah, Diana Owen and Rachel Gibson (eds.), *The Internet and Politics: Citizens, Voters, and Activists,* 80–99. London: Routledge.
Wright, Scott
    2006   Government-run online discussion for a: moderation, censorship and the shadow of control. *British Journal of Politics and International Relations* 8(4): 550–568.
Wright, Scott
    2007   A virtual European public sphere? The Futurum Discussion Forum. *European Journal of Public Policy,* 14(8): 1167–1185.
Wright, Scott and John Street
    2005   Democracy, deliberation and design: the case of online discussion forums.

Paper presented at the Political Studies Association Annual Conference, 5–7 April, Leeds UK.

Young, Iris M.
1990   *Justice and the Politics of Difference.* Princeton: Princeton University Press.

Ziarek, Ewa P.
2001   *An Ethics of Dissensus: Postmodernity, Feminism, and the Politics of Radical Democracy.* Stanford, CA: Stanford University Press.

2. Public space, common goods, and private interests: Emergent definitions in globally mediated humanity

Phil Graham

1. A history of public spaces

> In the dark ages, the public was squeezed out by the private (…) As the Roman Empire slid into the depth of the Dark Ages, the private gradually squeezed out the public until effectively the private sector swallowed everything and the public sector disappeared. The intense devotion of the Romans to the *Res Publica* was lost. Instead of being a citizen of Rome, every individual was attached to a feudal master who controlled all aspects of his or her life: work, housing, reproductive rights, and justice. Almost by definition, feudalism is public power in private hands – (Thurow 1996: 264–265)

Historical investigation into the nature of human association reveals waxings and wanings in the scale, scope, and character of what is construed as public space and, as a corollary, what elements of existence are considered to be common goods and private interests. Conceptions of public and private goods expand and contract along the lines of the political systems that enact them. Each different stage in the development of public spaces is marked by assumptions about what is required for its proper functioning. Those assumptions contain reference to dominant media forms, the correspondent perfection of appropriate political forms, and their relation to deep cultural values (Graham 2005: chapter 7). From the city-state of ancient Greece emerge the definitive statements of Aristotle on the essential characteristics of public space:

> Hence it is evident that the state is a creation of nature, and that man is by nature a political animal. And he who by nature and not by mere accident is without a state, is either a bad man or above humanity (…) Nature, as we often say, makes nothing in vain, and man is the only animal whom she has endowed with speech. And whereas mere voice is but an indication of pleasure or pain, and is therefore found in other animals (…) the power of speech is intended to set forth the expedient and inexpedient; and therefore likewise the just and the unjust. And it is characteristic of man that he alone has any sense of good and evil, of just and unjust, and the like, and the association of living beings who have this sense makes a family and a state. (Aristotle [1941] 2001: 1129)

Here we see a perennial tendency in political tracts written by the privileged (as political tracts typically are): the naturalisation of existing political orders. For Aristotle, the Greek state is a creation of *nature*.[1] Aristotle identifies *speech* as a definitive aspect of the state, linking speech and state with a theory of politics and ethics. To live well is to live together in a family and a state united by common speech. No explanation is necessary. Nature is aimed at the good. The state is the highest form of political association produced by nature. Therefore the state itself is the greatest of political goods.

> When several villages are united in a single complete community, large enough to be nearly or quite self-sufficing, the state comes into existence, originating in the bare needs of life, and continuing for the sake of a good life. And therefore, if the earlier forms of society are natural, so is the state, for it is the end of them, and the nature of a thing is its end. For what each thing is when fully developed, we call its nature, whether we are speaking of a man, a horse, or a family. Besides, the final cause and end of a thing is the best, and to be self-sufficing is the end and the best. (Aristotle 2001: 1129)

The final cause and end seems eternally linked to the very beginnings: when "men say that the Gods have a king (…) they imagine, not only the forms of the Gods, but their ways of life to be like their own" (Aristotle 2001: 1129).

It seems that no political development in recorded history has managed to go beyond these discoursal features: dominant political forms are construed as *natural, final, superordinate, ordained* by one or more deities, and are totally *mediated* products. They are achievements of discourse and are sustained by founding myths and hegemonic historical narratives (Wodak and de Cillia 1999). From Aristotle's final cause in the *Politics* to Fukuyama's (1992) *End of History and the Last Man*, these features of discourse about the public sphere prevail. As in antiquity, we find the principles of superordination, naturalism, and thorough mediation at work during the middle ages. The King is the "image of God on earth" because "[a]ll power is from the Lord God; the power which the prince has is therefore from God, for the power of God, for the power of God is never lost or severed from him, but he merely exercises it through a subordinate hand" (John of Salisbury 1121, as cited in Dickinson 1926: 313). The King's power is "instituted by God for the punishment of evil-doers and for the reward of good men" and sits "at the apex of the commonwealth by the divine governance" (Dickinson 1926: 13). Once again the moral dimension of public goods is definitive of political order. And in an era ruled by the word of God, the King "is subject only to God and the priesthood, who represent God upon earth" (Dickinson 1926: 13). In this view, "the public" is incapable of influencing the King's behaviour. But, as Dickinson notes, there arose at the same time, a corporatist "idea that seems to have its source among the Roman lawyers, and it consisted in identifying the corporate or organized community with the whole membership of the group – the *universitas* with the *populus*" (Dickinson 1926: 333). Herein lie the seeds of many revolutions and many incremental changes associated with the rise of the public sphere in the 17th and 18th centuries that Habermas ([1962] 1991) identifies. Rather than being an inert object of the King's "stewardship", the public sphere "becomes an active unity, bearing its own persona, and capable of speaking and acting for itself, against the prince if needs be" (Dickinson 1926: 33). For Habermas, this marks the beginning of "the public" as an active force in the shaping of political ends and the fundamental redefinition of public and private goods.

> By "the public sphere" we mean first of all a realm of our social life in which something approaching public opinion can be formed. Access is granted to all citizens. A portion of the public sphere comes into being in every conversation in which private individuals assemble to form a public body. They then behave neither like business or professional people transacting private affairs, nor like members of a constitutional order subject to the legal constraints of a state bureaucracy. Citizens behave as a public body when they confer in an unrestricted manner – that is, with the guarantee of freedom to express and publish their opinions – about matters of general interest. In a large public body this kind of communication requires specific means for transmitting information and influencing those who receive it. Today newspapers and magazines, radio and television are the media of the public sphere. We speak of the political public sphere in contrast, for instance, to the literary one, when public discussion deals with objects connected to the activity of the state. Although state authority is so to speak the executor of the political sphere, it is not part of it. (Habermas, Lennox, and Lennox 1974: 50)

The modern notion of a politically active public emerges with a public space occupied by an increasingly influential, post-mercantilist, propertied citizen-class that rose to dominance to the demise of the sacred order of Kings and Popes (Habermas 1991). This kind of public space emerges in history when "private people come together as a public" to freely form "public opinion" and claim "the public sphere regulated from above against the public authorities themselves" (Habermas 1991: 27). Habermas's "public sphere" is a space that firstly arose upon a flood of printed words pumped out by "the press", swelling the tide of bourgeois radicalism that began in the proliferation of coffee houses and *salons* of Western Europe during the early eighteenth century (Habermas 1991: 24–33). It was rare, says Habermas, to find any "great writer in the eighteenth century that would not have first submitted his essential ideas for discussion in lectures before the *academies* and especially in the *salons*"(Habermas 1991: 34). The moral basis of this communication revolution was enlightenment notions of *rationality*: informed discussion among equal persons about matters of common concern on a rational basis rather than automatic deterence to the ordained authority (*volantus*) of church and monarchy to which the new "public" stood opposed (Habermas 1991: 80–81). Thus "education was the one criteria [sic] for admission – property ownership the other. De facto both criteria demarcated largely the same circle of persons; for formal education at that time was more a consequence than a precondition of social status, which in turn was determined primarily by one's title to property" (Habermas 1991: 85). For Habermas, the emergence of a bourgeois public sphere, private property, public opinion, and the rise of enlightenment rationality are inextricably linked in a network of practices designed to promote common goods along a moral dimension. Consequently the public sphere developed in a "tension-charged field between state and society" (Habermas 1991: 141).

Later, as new media forms and their associated institutions emerged, and as societies massified and industrialised, the public sphere was to be eroded, firstly as a result of policies oriented towards "refeudalization" and "neomercantilism" (Habermas 1991: 142). These would later result in monopolies of industrial commodity markets on an international scale and, accordingly, in communication industries. While Habermas does not put it as such, he clearly describes the dynamics of what Harold Innis calls "knowledge monopolies" (Innis 1951), the rise of electronically fortified and massive "culture industries" (Horkheimer and Adorno [1947] 1998), and the recurrent historical effects of new media in respect of these (Graham 2000). In an ironic twist of history, the social impacts of a diffuse press, the rise in literacy, and the liberal erosion of "faith-based" power gave impetus to a system which, by the mid-twentieth century, had reverted to a top-down public space dominated by corporate interests, managed in a large part to shape public opinion – another symptom of "the dialectic of enlightenment" (Horkheimer and Adorno 1998). Hence Habermas's lament that the "communication network of a public made up of rationally debating private citizens has collapsed; the public opinion once emergent from it has partly decomposed into the informal opinions of private citizens without a public and partly become concentrated into formal opinions of publicistically effective institutions" (Habermas 1991: 247). For Habermas, whether or not a new public space can "assume its proper function" is a matter of "whether the exercise of domination and power persists as a negative constant (...) of history – or whether as a historical category itself, it is open to substantive change" (Habermas 1991: 250).

2. Public opinion and public goods in an age of global mediations

The proliferation of globally internetworked digital media may be a facilitating force for the "substantive change" that Habermas stipulates. Certainly many have argued that a new public sphere – in the sense of a politically influential field of discussion through which a global public opinion is emerging – is a desirable, if not inevitable, result of new media environments (cf. Kellner 1995; Poster 1995; Dutton 1999; Robins and Webster 1999). Throughout the developed world, "cyberdemocracy" initiatives have been developed to promote a form of direct democracy that was first imagined in the 1930s, just as "public opinion" was becoming a refined, scientifically objectified focus in the conduct of mass manipulation:

> With the development of the science of measuring public opinion, it can be stated with but few qualifications, that this stage in our democracy is rapidly being reached. It is now possible to ascertain, with a high degree of accuracy, the views of the people on all national issues. (Gallup 1938: 9)

Consequently, Gallup held that "with many of our leading psychologists and social scientists" interested in the problem of measuring public opinion, "it will not be long before the final stage in the development of our democracy (...) has been reached – that the will of the majority of citizens can be ascertained at all times" (Gallup 1938: 14). At about the same time Gallup was announcing that the pinnacle of democracy was soon to be reached, Harold Lasswell (1941) had come to the conclusion that the combined results of advanced technology, increased literacy, and the widespread "ventilation of opinions and the taking of votes" amounted to a "dictatorship of palaver" and that "the technique of dictating to the dictator is named propaganda" (Lasswell 1941: 631). Even at this relatively early moment in electronic mass media history, the techniques of manipulating opinion had reached quite sophisticated levels, their apotheosis being Goebbels's aggressive campaigns waged against the German people and, through them, the rest of the world. Goebbels displays a clear grasp of radio's implications as a new, instantaneous mass medium; its implications for shaping conceptions of public and private goods; and the internal relations between meaning making, international power, social values, and national politics:

> A government that has determined to bring a nation together so that it is once more a center of power in the scales of great world events has not only the right, but the duty, to subordinate all aspects of the nation to its goals, or at least ensure that they are supportive. That is also true for the radio. The more significant something is in influencing the will of the broad masses, the greater its responsibility to the future of the nation.
> That does not mean we want to turn the radio into a spineless servant of our partisan political interests. The new German politics rejects any partisan limitations. It seeks the totality of the people and nation, and the reconstructive work it plans or has already begun includes all who are of good will. Within the framework of these great tasks, the radio, if it is to remain living, must hold to and advance its own artistic and spiritual laws. Just as its technical methods are modern and distinct, so too are its artistic capacities. It is only distantly related to the stage and film. It is rarely possible to bring a powerful stage or film presentation to the radio with no changes. There is a style of speaking on the radio, a style of drama, of opera, of radio show. The radio is in no way a branch of the stage or film, but rather an independent entity with its own rules. (Goebbels 1938)

As with the rise of every new medium, new political, economic, and cultural disruptions emerge (Graham 2005: chapter 9).

Similar arguments about the possibility of "direct democracy" and the reinvigoration of the public sphere emerged with the proliferation of globally networked information and communication technologies (ICTs) (cf. Kellner 1995;

Poster 1995; Coleman 1999; Dutton 1999; Dahlberg 2001; Gruber this volume). Poster (1995) is instructive here. He notes the difficulty of defining a "public" cyberspace:

> This difficulty is amplified considerably once newer electronically mediated communications are taken into account, in particular the Internet. Now the question of "talk," of meeting face-to-face, of "public" discourse is confused and complicated by the electronic form of exchange of symbols. If "public" discourse exists as pixels on screens generated at remote locations by individuals one has never and probably will never meet, as it is in the case of the Internet with its "virtual communities," "electronic cafés," bulletin boards, e-mail, computer conferencing and even video conferencing, then how is it to be distinguished from "private" letters, printface and so forth? The age of the public sphere as face-to-face talk is clearly over: the question of democracy must henceforth take into account new forms of electronically mediated discourse. What are the conditions of democratic speech in the mode of information? What kind of "subject" speaks or writes or communicates in these conditions? What is its relation to machines? What complexes of subjects, bodies and machines are required for democratic exchange and emancipatory action? For Habermas, the public sphere is a homogeneous space of embodied subjects in symmetrical relations, pursuing consensus through the critique of arguments and the presentation of validity claims. This model, I contend, is systematically denied in the arenas of electronic politics. We are advised then to abandon Habermas' concept of the public sphere in assessing the Internet as a political domain. (Poster 1995).

The internet is populated by far-from-homogenous persons. Its current scope, scale, and cultural diversity exceed present possibilities for a global public space in which all persons can contribute equally to the definitions of common goods and private interests. Apart from issues of culture and language which can often result in a complete inability for people to communicate, strong nationalistic and cultural tendencies have re-emerged with the global permeation of all manner of discourses into all others. The inversions and disruptions that have marked historical transformations in the public sphere appear to be happening as a result. Understanding the historical implications of current circumstances means understanding what Walter Ong (1962) calls the "synchronic present":

> The purely linear sense of time, what we have called the purely diachronic sense, the sense that events are strung through time and no more, fails to do justice to the present situation because one of the characteristics of the present is the way in which it appears to have caught up into itself the entire past. Our mid-twentieth century sense of time is synchronic – and that at least in two ways: first, it feels the present as the front of a past which was vastly different from itself and yet which is in a multitude of ways continuous; secondly, it feels diverse fronts of the past as existing in the present in terms of the various cultures across the face of the earth which are variously related to the past and thus to the present, but which are now all part of us since, with our global awareness, all cultures are more and more present to one another. (Ong 1962: 250).

I believe Ong's conception of time here needs some modifications in light of recent developments: although the entirety of our histories are converging upon each other and are present all at once on many fronts, so to speak, it is clear that more recent historical formations have an immediacy that is more obvious and compelling, which is only to say that although older historical phenomena have deep and enduring effects upon those who grow up within them, new media environments have the effect of assaulting time and memory, if only by the sheer amount of information generated (Innis 1951; Postman 1985).

The character of an emergent global public space sprang for the most part from the mediation practices of large corporations whose "core business" is to shape and organise attitudes and understandings on mass scales in order to maximise profit and control public discourse (McChesney 2000; see also Koller, this volume). It has been widely documented how this has entailed the commodification, and therefore the expropriation, of public space throughout the 20th century (Habermas 1962/1991: chapter 7; Bourdieu 1988/1998; Chomsky 1992; Bagdikian 1997; Schiller 1999; Graham 2000; McChesney 2000). The introduction and diffusion of globally networked digital information and communication technologies (ICTs) appeared at first to herald a new global space, celebrated in policy, education, and reactivated social movements (Kellner 1995; Dahlberg 2001). In itself this space was to be a global commons free from corporate interests (Lessig 2004). The numerous policy initiatives launched worldwide, and which continue to be launched today, touting an unswerving faith in the democratic benefits of ICTs, has been central in the creation of opposite, balkanising movements (Poster 2005). The events of September 11, 2001 marked an abrupt halt to globalising discourses (Graham and Luke 2003). The global public space has been increasingly re-militarised and balkanised ever since (Graham and Luke 2003, 2005). This has had quite dramatic effects on the character of the emerging public sphere, moving it from the many and various technological enthusiasms that characterised the 1990s to the fear-ridden "us and them" paranoia of post-9/11 intercultural aggression reminiscent of the early crusades (Graham, Keenan, and Dowd 2004).

3. The re-emergence of private interests in public goods

The following exemplar of contemporary discourse on public opinion comes from the United States *Report of the Defense Science Board Task Force on Strategic Communication* (Office of the Undersecretary of Defense for Acquisition, Technology, and Logistics [OUD] 2004):

> Interests, not public opinion, should drive policies. But opinions must be taken into account when policy options are considered and implemented. At a minimum, we should not be surprised by public reactions to policy choices. Policies will not suc-

ceed unless they are communicated to global and domestic audiences in ways that are credible and allow them to make informed, independent judgments. Words in tone and substance should avoid offence where possible; messages should seek to reduce, not increase, perceptions of arrogance, opportunism, and double standards. These objectives mean officials must take full advantage of powerful tools to measure attitudes, understand cultures, and assess influence structures – not occasionally but as an iterative process. *Policies and strategic communication cannot be separated.* (OUD 2004: 3, original emphasis).

At the core of the OUD document are three assumptions identical to those of Habermas: first that the public sphere is a product of communication; second, that public attitudes and opinions motivate action; and third, that manipulative mass mediation practices are definitive of contemporary public spaces. Also, both assume that politics is in direct opposition to the public, although this is largely implicit in the OUD text. Habermas's view is that the public sphere is a modern, bourgeois creation that emerged in the eighteenth century as a space of interaction that mediated between the political and social aspects of existence, and which was directly linked to the development of private property and public opinion more generally:

> It is no coincidence that these concepts of the public sphere and public opinion arose for the first time only in the eighteenth century. They acquire their specific meaning from a concrete historical situation. It was at this time that the distinction of "opinion" from "opinion publique" and "public opinion" came about. Though mere opinions (cultural assumptions, normative attitudes, collective prejudices and values) seem to persist unchanged in their natural form as a kind of sediment of history, public opinion can by definition only come into existence when a reasoning public is presupposed. (Habermas 1991: 50)

For Habermas, the public sphere emerged as "a sphere which mediates between society and state, in which the public organizes itself as the bearer [of] public opinion" and is based on a mass mediated "principle of public information" (Habermas 1991: 150). Habermas sees the emergence of a public sphere as a triumph over feudal orders of information, or what Innis (1951) calls "knowledge monopolies".

The OUD document, while theoretically in agreement with Habermas on the character of the present public sphere, does not share Habermas's view of the public sphere's role in the development of democracy. Whereas Habermas claims the ideal public sphere shapes policy through the free development of reasoned public opinion, the OUD sees public opinion as an object to be shaped by means of "strategic communication", a marketing term. This implies that a politically derived public opinion must be "sold" to the public by every possible means of persuasion, including "information and analysis" of how "culture, values, and religion in shaping human behavior", "media trends and influences on audiences", and the role of "information technologies" in the development of favourable "global public opinion" towards the United States (OUD 2004: 69). In addition to analysis and governmental action, commercial multimedia producers and the academic sector are to be subcontracted

> for a range of products and programs that communicate strategic themes and messages to appropriate target audiences. Broad themes and messages would include respect for human dignity and individual rights; individual education and economic opportunity; and personal freedom, safety, and mobility. Examples of products would be a children's TV series (Arabic Sesame Street); video and interactive games; support for the distribution and production of selected foreign films; and web communications including BLOGs, chat rooms, and electronic journals. Programs might include training and exchanges of journalists, support for selected foreign television documentaries; maintenance of databases of third party validators and supporters for conferences; and the design and implementation of country and regional campaigns to support themes and messages and de-legitimize extremism and terrorism (OUD 2004: 67–68).

The OUD proposal extends strategies and practices that began with George Creel and the Committee for Public Information in 1916 and have continued ever since (Graham and Luke 2003, 2005). It relies on centralised occupation of a global public sphere. Its purpose is to inculcate the value system of the United States on a global basis, a national stragey since 1916. To put it in Woodrow Wilson's words, American business has a mission to "go out and sell goods that will make the world more comfortable and more happy, and convert them to the principles of America" (Wilson 1916).

To succeed in the broadest terms, such a strategy must be insinuated into education systems; media forums of all kinds, including games, blogs, databases, chat rooms, toys, newspapers; and every form of communal interaction. It must also be translated into every "target" language. Hence there has been a boom in requirements for trained linguists in the US (Edwards 2000):

> More than sixty-five federal departments and agencies have language requirements, ranging from the Department of Defense to the Central Intelligence Agency to the Peace Corps to the National Institute of Standards and Technology. (…) Including the intelligence sector, the department is the largest federal employer of language personnel. The end of the cold war has increased the need for more and different languages. Since 1991, United States defense personnel have been stationed in 110 nations, not counting the NATO countries and Japan. There are 140 different languages spoken in these nations. (Edwards 2000)

The computer mediated global public sphere was supposed to be a "global village" (McLuhan 1964). It was supposed to herald an age of peace, security, intercultural harmony led by unbridled markets which would bring with them a general move towards democratic participation (Friedman 1999). Instead, it has become a space in which language, linguistics, and communication have become the "core business" of warfare, marketing, and intellectual property battles. Censorship and surveillance are on an exponential increase (Miller 2004; Anthonissen, this volume). Intercultural aggression is at an historical high.

4. Commandeering discussion space in the global agora

The aims and means identified by the OUD respond to an emergent global public sphere that is a *potentially* free space of rational debate which is both a threat to established power relations and a legitimating force for the formation of new ones. Whether consciously or otherwise, governments and other powerful influences throughout the world are responding to the challenges posed by the emergence of a global, non-broadcast, instantaneous media environment that permits people to write, speak, and meet in ways that are theoretically uncontrollable (Markoff 2005). While it is true that the majority of human beings still do not have access to the means of participation in this sphere, more than one billion people do. The responses of vested interests to the new global communication environment are many and varied. Most common are the many banal "e-government" and "e-commerce" initiatives that allow people to fill in forms, buy things, and so on via the internet, to locate community services, to provide a point of contact, and to make legislation public. In China, censorship is a policy solution. For example, there was much uproar about the actions of Yahoo! after it turned over to the Chinese government the details of a journalist accused of spreading dissent and compromising national security via email (South China Morning Post 2005). The journalist was subsequently jailed for 10 years (United Press 2005). In contrast to China's strategy of censorship, we see the Arabic world responding quite differently. Aljazeera, often seen as notorious in the West for allegedly supporting terrorist activities, has expanded its services to include a worldwide news service in English.[2] The service includes news from all areas of the world, from multiple viewpoints, with the explicit values of "objectivity, accuracy, and a passion for truth" (Aljazeera 2005). Aljazeera explains the significance of its English language service as follows:

> Today, as we officially break the "language barrier" with Aljazeera.net English, our dream of bringing "people and continents together" is coming true. A new window of opportunity to see the world through is now opening.
> Aljazeera.net English goes behind the scenes to provide every visitor with "the news they don't see", daringly and boldly as Aljazeera always does.
> The website promises to raise traditionally sidelined questions and issues. It upholds the same philosophy of the mother organisation: "The right to speak up". This translates into allowing everyone to express their opinion freely, encouraging debates, viewpoints and counter viewpoints. (Aljazeera 2005)

Ironically, this summary of a new, alternative international news service looks more like the "freedom of speech" discourses associated with the United States.

As Aljazeera moves outwards toward a global public sphere, with the *Intelligence Reform Bill* (US Senate 2004) the US has made it a matter of national policy to move upon broadcast media space in the Muslim world to promote a single, centrally coordinated, clearly articulated *message* tailored to specific cultural contexts:

> If the United States does not act to vigorously define its message in the Islamic world, the image of the United States will be defined by Islamic extremists who seek to demonize the United States.
> Recognizing that many Arab and Muslim audiences rely on satellite television and radio, the United States Government has launched promising initiatives in television and radio broadcasting to the Arab world, Iran, and Afghanistan. (US Senate 2004: 331)

The same legislation specifies the centrality of language to national security, identifying "specific requirements for the range of linguistic skills necessary for the intelligence community, including proficiency in scientific and technical vocabularies of critical foreign languages" and "comprehensive plan" for the "the education, recruitment, and training of linguists" (US Senate 2004: 139–140). From electromagnetic spectrum, to broadcast media, to education systems, to language, the Bill targets media of communication at every level as a matter of national security.

At the same time, the global advertising industry continues to try and "tame" the unruly new mediascape, just as its leading members have done since the web emerged as viable advertising space in the mid-nineties (Graham 1999):

> Market research firm Compete today is expected to unveil a new private-label behavioral marketing platform. Called Voicebox, it uses desktop applications and Web toolbars to help marketers reach customers as they're on the verge of decision-making.
> "Today's consumers are more informed and more elusive than ever," said Don McLagan, chairman, president and CEO of Compete. "The battleground for consumer attention has moved to the desktop." (Newcomb 2005)

The aggressive tone of behavioural marketing discourse indicates its provenance in the techniques of warfare (Graham and Luke 2003). Marketing and advertising operate on a *battleground*. They target the *attention* of consumers who, to the detriment of mass marketers, are more *informed* and, by extension, more *elusive*. In other words, and in distinction to those who would use new media for the revitalisation of democracy, advertising aims to overcome public knowledge in order to persuade people to buy this or that commodity or service by breaking into the decision-making processes of consumers. Newcomb's text confirms that advertising and marketing aim at overcoming rationality, knowledge, questioning, and discussion by resorting to behavioural techniques that intervene automatically on behalf of the advertiser at the moment a decision is about to be made.

This is the same technique propounded as effective close quarters combat strategy by the marketing arm of the Blackhawk company:

> *you must strive to disorient your opponent.* Note I did not say, out shoot, out run, out shout, the prime directive is to disorient your opponent. Once in this state, he or she should be overcome by events as you move smoothly on to the next phases and around the clock again and again. The opponent's perception of time becomes distorted, incoming data is dismissed, decisions are irrational, and actions become erratic and ineffective. This is an immensely powerful and often overlooked tactical tool. (Good 2004, original emphasis)

The behavioural techniques of inciting disorientation in order to negatively affect a person's decision making capacity in order to control their reactions is focused on conquest by *disinformation*. It involves language and communication in an essentially negative sense: What is "said" or "meant" (by whichever means) is explicitly directed towards dominating others' behaviour by keeping them in a constant state of *irrational reaction* rather than one of deliberative action. Deliberative, rational action is essential for the development of a political commons at any scale of human organisation. The possibility of such action is threatened by the influence of militaristic strategies in the new media environment, whether those of advertisers, governments, or the many corporate interests at play.

It ought not to be surprising to see aggressive moves made by vested interests faced with new media threats. History is rife with such examples. But because every civilization "appears to have its own means of suicide", there is certainly no historical evidence to support the assumption that particular vested interests will prevail in the long run (Innis 1951). The historical evidence suggests that to understand current trends, we should understand three elements of context in the analysis of language and communication in the public sphere: *social function*, *entrenched cultural values*, and *mediation processes*.

5. Implications for analysis

5.1. Social function

In the context of mass mediated societies with broad access to the internet, a public sphere can be thought of in two very distinct ways: as a space of shared stories and rituals or as a space of shared discussions. That is an important (meta)functional distinction and the first, I think, that needs to be considered in any discussion of public commons. When viewed as a discussion space, the public sphere looks something like Habermas theorised: people gathering as equals to discuss and decide upon matters of common concern. As a space of shared stories and ritual, the public sphere appears as culture in the broadest sense (Carey 1989): that is, as a set of institutions performed in rituals, stories, or other entertainments. These two interact in interesting ways: Stories and ritual form the basis of culture, which in turn frames discussion and evaluations (Carey 1989: chapter 1). In mass industrialised culture, as we have seen, shared stories are also mass-industrialised, whether it is the latest news story or the oldest folk tale (cf. Horkheimer and Adorno 1947/1998; Adorno 1991; Carey 1989; Wasko 2001). But there is little or no space for discussion in this view, merely entertainmentised "performance" (Postman 1985). The billion or so people with access to internet communication are engaged in various degrees of discussion with varying amounts of enthusiasm and political influence, and this appears as a public sphere in so far as it is a large discussion space. But separated by language, culture, interest, profession, age, and so on, persons engaged in conversation with the internet do not form a singular sphere in any sense that might add up to a public. Also, it appears that ritual story space (culture) historically tends to overwhelm discussion space (public space); that culture, by definition, tends towards stasis; and, perhaps, that ritual reproductions of stories are simply less work and more efficient for cultural maintenance than discussion (Malinowski 1921; Carey 1989: chapter 7). This initial functional distinction between story and discussion is similar to the distinction between "ideational" and "interpersonal" (because discussion requires the presence of actively engaged persons, not spectator audiences) metafunctions but takes into account the social function of discourses in respect of their role in constituting a public space. The many "publics" that constitute the new mediascape can also be fruitfully considered in functional terms: whether as dominant vested interest, professionals, intellectuals, hobbyists, activists, political parties, advertisers, or in any functional (or dysfunctional) capacity whatsoever. The many "publics" of the internet are investing in new discussion spaces, with elements of new and emergent cultures evident. Just as democracy and capitalism emerged from the hybridity of science, theocracy, feudalism, and mercantilism, the emergence of new, hybrid cultures will entail the telling of new, hybrid stories. As far as analysis is concerned, the development in the emergence of a coherent global public sphere (if this is at all possible) will be indicated by the emergence of these kinds of stories from new discussion spaces. Their establishment as culture will be an indication that a "public sphere" is emerging as a social force.

5.2.   Entrenched cultural values

Entrenched cultural values are the most truculent of social forces. They are reproduced and conserved by stories that are essentially mythological (Campbell [1949] 2004). Two great theoretical themes that run through recorded history have entirely opposite conceptions of the relationship between persons and the public spheres they inhabit. The first of these is probably best recognised as

Adamic myth in which an "original" man and woman appear as the basis of human association. These "originals" give birth to all of humanity. It is a myth that pervades Norse, Judaic, Japanese and Samoan civilizations, among many others, and underlies cultural values that extol the virtues of heroic individualism. The opposite pole of creation mythology emphasises the originality of the family from which all else flows, giving each individual a socially situated meaning and identity. These last are evident in many African and Australian creation myths and underpin cultural values systems that privilege cooperation and sharing. What all creation mythologies have in common is that they describe how order is brought forth from chaos according to certain principles ordained by one or more deities. Because of the cultural hold they have on whole masses of people, they must be central to any discussion of public space, common goods, and private interests in a globally connected world. They provide the most ancient and enduring influences upon what it means to be human and to exist together as humans, as evidenced by the resurgence of deep cultural and religious conflicts in the current period when intercultural communication is at an all time high. Creation myths can be seen as simultaneously reflecting "the unique contexts of their inception" and as ongoing "political practice", with their interpretation being the object of power plays from both inside and outside the communities in which the myths originate (Blier 2004: 38). Contemporary explanations of creation have clear political implications in their origins and interpretation, as evidenced by the heated debate over whether theories of "intelligent design" (an allegedly scientific version of Old Testament creationism) should be taught alongside theories of evolution in classroom curricula (Mooney and Nisbet 2005). This debate has significant political implications, not the least of which is the legitimation of a Christian fundamentalist world view in curricula throughout the US, Canada, Australia, and elsewhere. Fuller (2001) investigates the political implications of competing perspectives on evolutionary theory, focusing on the "'handicap principle', which purports to explain altruism as a limited form of self-sacrifice that animals undergo to mark their status to members of their own species and sometimes of others" (Fuller 2001). What Fuller identifies is "contrasting genealogies of the selfishness- and altruism-based accounts of evolution" (Fuller 2001). He argues that once "the Iliad replaces Genesis as the creation myth" in Western societies "it becomes easy to see how the handicap principle may instill a spirit of 'competitive altruism' as you and I try to outdo each other in displays of superiority" (Fuller 2001). Fuller is describing the effects of a synthesis of religious and secular creationism and its impetus towards an individualist view of the world, as per the doctrine of neoliberalism – a doctrine with its roots set firmly in the soil of creation mythology; its theology overtly Christian; its modern pedigree stemming from a devoutly Christian Scottish moralist, Adam Smith (Noble 2005). The deleterious effects of ultra-competitive neoliberalism in the current context have been thoroughly documented and debated elsewhere and I need not rehearse the arguments here (Saul 1997; Schiller 1999; Fairclough 2000)

Almost as important as creation myths are "*re*-creation" myths, or myths of cultural, social, and political rebirth – present discourses of "reform" is its latest manifestation. The many "renaissances" and "enlightenments", with corresponding "dark ages" against which they are set, have been deployed to propagate the idea that some historical break with the past has happened. This has been so at least since mediaeval humanists used the term to identify the pre-Christian era; "to contrast the light, which Christ had brought into this world, with the darkness in which the heathen had languished before his time" (Mommsen 1942: 227). It has been a recurring device deployed to describe the Fourteenth Century rennaisance of "arts and letters" which attained "its greatest currency in the age of Enlightenment, and the very name of that period was a manifest declaration of war against the era of 'darkness' and its scale of values" (Mommsen 1942/227).

Re-creation myths promise new beginnings, new lives, new opportunities. They are also political strategies that shape conceptions of public space and public goods. Like creation mythologies, "rebirth" myths are achievements of language, communication, and mediations of all types – discourse in the broadest sense. One function of re-creation myths is to signal a break with the past, a denial of the pedagogical usefulness of history other than in a negative sense (Graham and Hearn 2000). Here is a current example of re-creation mythology in the formation of a new public space:

> As President al-Yawar said last week, "These people who are doing these things are the armies of the darkness." That's what the President said, of Iraq. These are the enemies of the Iraqi nation. They are trying to take Iraq back to the dark ages that we used to live in, until last year. The President and I share the same resolve – Iraq will never return to the dark ages of tyranny. Iraq will be a free nation. (Bush 2004)

References to *the armies of darkness*, the *dark ages of tyranny*, and the future in which *Iraq will be a free nation* reference typical elements of re creation myths since at least the 14th century (Mommsen 1926). They provide orators with an easy means to define enemies as enemies of progress, freedom, prosperity, or whatever values the host culture holds dear: enemies are conspirators against the public good: a menace to the private lives of persons (Lasswell 1941). In re-creation myths, the principal lesson of the past is that it was evil and must be erased once and for all. In this respect, re-creation myths may be seen to be at odds with creation myths, an integral part of the past. Typically, though, re-creation myths are intensely conservative because they are oriented towards the values embedded in the creation myths to which they ultimately refer (see Martin and Wodak 2003). In the above example, Bush prevails upon the appeal of an idealised natural Freedom which only the mythical Adam and Eve alone enjoyed. Let us leave aside here that the United States' (US) administration has assumed authority to define the future of foreign countries for almost a century, other than to note the necessity of including a "mediation" perspective for understanding our newly emerging global public sphere: that is to say, the point of emphasising myth in analysis of the public sphere is to emphasise that an incomprehensibly deep past dwells in the language of the most contemporary dreams of the future. The means of mediation for these myths are also their means of reproduction, transformation, and subversion. In this view, the current round of aggression can be seen as a necessary birth pain in the latest round of rebirth and renewal.

5.3. Mediation

Tensions between individual and group in notions of the public can, in some significant way, be understood through the lenses of creation myths that are part of every culture, including business cultures (Wasko 2001). Cultural differences, once brought into contact and underpinned by opposing myths, cannot be left to rest. In defense of culture, myths are mobilised; they are propagated and intensified throughout every department of a culture according to the principles of its (re-) creation myths: in politics, economics, education, entertainment, sport, technology, communication, and language (Graham and Luke 2003). Any public space can extend only as far as its technologies of mediation permit. The scale, pace, and complexity, along with the means by which it communicates, will largely determine the character of knowledge in a given culture (Innis 1951; Carey 1989). What that means, quite literally, is that what passes for "rational" or "good" for the public at any given time and place is greatly affected by the mediation processes through which public space is enacted. Just as the Greek city-state was principally achieved and limited by oral technologies, modern nation-states were established and held together principally through the organisation and standardisation of language practices inculcated through mass education systems, mass mediated print, and its corresponding literacies (Bourdieu 1991). The first production line was the printing press and it heralded a massive and dominant new political economic form (Ong 1969). Similarly, the emergent global public sphere is being achieved through meaningful practices mediated through communication networks that can potentially reach every human being almost instantaneously. The new media network's first function was as a weapons control system. Mediation is movement of meaning from context to context, culture to culture, institution to institution, and person to person (Silverstone 1999: 13). In each stage of movement, meanings change as they move through cultural frameworks: whether professional, religious, or nationalistic, every cultural frame changes and filters meanings that move through it. Media are not collections of mere things. They are technological forces that extend our capacities for discourse through time, space, and large groups of people. As Iedema (1999) has shown through ethnographic analysis of a major building project, linguistic analysis of mediation processes can reveal how cultural differences at micro-levels change meaning potentials at different levels of social organisation, and how those changed meanings are made manifest in more enduring and magnified forms, such as buildings. Changes in mediation processes are changes in the ways we make and move meanings. They change who can participate in stories and discussions. They change the scale and scope of our existence, and size and quality of the public spaces we make and live in. Mediation processes are also implicated in the political economic: the mixture of public and private, i.e., the point at which *polis* and *oikos* intersect in every person's life.

Any linguistic analysis of public space can benefit greatly by taking these elements into account when considering how common goods and private interests are achieved through the interplays and movements of discourse through time and space. Function, entrenched cultural values, and mediation are not language *per se*, but they shape language to a significant extent and are present in every form of human expression. Combined as categorical frameworks for linguistic analysis, they are the most significant parts of the contextual framing in any analysis of a network of emerging public spaces characterised by light speed, global communication; fragmented social structures; and ephemeral forms of association. Approaching analysis with these elements of context in mind provides essential perspectives on the character and form of existing and emergent public spaces.

The currently emerging global public space – the space of attitude formation and discussion – is clearly dominated by aggressive storytelling rather than discussion. It is militaristic, and its aggression is focused on meaning in general and language in particular. The current state of the emerging global public sphere is analogous to a world war of sorts. It is a war of raw meaning against understanding, reaction against action, vested interest against would-be usurpers, stories against discussions, entertainment against political engagement, discourse against discourse. The result of present conflicts, at least according to many Pentagon strategists, will in a large part be determined by warfare conducted between linguists, media strategists, and cultural experts. Given this state, it becomes imperative for linguists to study the contextual factors influencing "synchronically present" dynamics in discourse with both history and the future in view.

Notes

1 It would not be a shock to find that Greek slaves held opposing views. But like most subjugated people in history, their voices remain silent and we will never know.
2 See: http://english.aljazeera.net/HomePage

References

Adorno, Theodor W.
    1991   *The Culture Industry: Selected Essays on Mass Culture*. London: Routledge.
Aljazeera
    2005   *About Aljazeera*. Available online at http://english.aljazeera.net/NR/exeres/5D7F956E-6B52-46D9-8D17-448856D01CDB.htm. Accessed 1 October 2005.
Aristotle
    2001   The Politics. In R. McKeon (e.). *The Basic Works of Aristotle*, 1127–1324. New York: The Modern Library.
Bagdikian, Ben H.
    1997   *The Media Monopoly.* 5th ed. Boston, MA: Beacon Press.
Blier, Suzanne P.
    2004   African creation myths as political strategy. *African Arts* 37(1): 38–47.
Bourdieu, Pierre
    1998   *On Television and Journalism.* (Transl. P. Parkhurst Ferguson). London: Pluto Press.
Bourdieu, Pierre
    1991   *Language and Symbolic Power* (Transl. G. Raymond and M. Adamson). London: Polity.
Bush, George W.
    2004, June 18   *President Bush Salutes Soldiers in Fort Lewis, Washington.* Remarks by the President to the Military Personnel Fort Lewis, Washington. Available online at http://www.whitehouse.gov/news/releases/2004/06/20040618-1.html Accessed 7 March 2005.
Campbell, Joseph
    2004   *The Hero with a Thousand Faces*. Princeton, NJ Princeton University Press.
Carey, James
    1989   *Communication as Culture: Essays on Media and Society.* London: Routledge.
Chomsky, Noam
    1992   *Deterring Democracy*. New York: Hill and Wang.
Coleman, Stephen
    1999   The new media and democratic politics. *New Media & Society* 1(1): 67–74.
Dahlberg, Lincoln
    2001   The internet and democratic discourse: Exploring the prospects of online deliberative forums extending the public sphere. *Information, Communication & Society* 4(4): 615–633.

Dickinson, John
  1926 The mediaeval conception of kingship and some of its limitations, as developed in the Policratus of John of Salisbury. *Speculum* 1(3): 308–337.
Dutton, William
  1999 *Society on the Line: Information Politics in the Digital Age.* Oxford: Oxford University Press.
Edwards, J. David
  2000 Working beyond the Academy: The Federal Government. *ADFL Bulletin* 32(1). Available online at http://www.adfl.org/cgi-shl/docstudio/docs.pl?bulletin_321048. Accessed 9 September 2005.
Fairclough, Norman
  2000 Discourse, social theory, and social research: The discourse of welfare reform. *Journal of Sociolinguistics* 4(2): 163–195.
Friedman, Thomas L.
  1999 A manifesto for the fast world. *New York Times Magazine* (28 March): 40–44, 61, 70–71, 84, 96.
Fukuyama, Francis
  1992 *The End of History and the Last Man.* New York: Avon.
Fuller, Steve
  2001 The Darwinian Left: A rhetoric of realism or reaction? *Poroi* 1(1). Available online at http://inpress.lib.uiowa.edu/poroi/poroi/v1n1toc.html. Accessed 2 March 2005.
Gallup, George
  1938 Testing public opinion. *Public Opinion Quarterly* [Special Supplement: Public opinion in a democracy] 2(1): 8–14.
Goebbels, Josef
  1938 Der Rundfunk als achte Großmacht (Radio as the eighth great power). *Signale der neuen Zeit. 25 ausgewählte Reden von Dr. Joseph Goebbels.* 197–207. Munich: Zentralverlag der NSDAP. (Transl. Randall Bytwerk). Available online at http://www.calvin.edu/academic/cas/gpa/goeb56.htm. Accessed 17 September 2007.
Good, Kenneth J.
  2004 *Got a second? Boyd's OODA cycle in the close quarter battle environment.* Lee's Summit, MO: Strategos International.
Graham, Phil
  1999 Critical systems theory: A political economy of language, thought, and technology. *Communication Research* 26(4): 482–507.
Graham, Phil
  2000 Hypercapitalism: A political economy of informational idealism. *New Media & Society* 2(2): 131–156.
Graham, Phil
  2005 *Hypercapitalism: Language, New Media, and Social Perceptions of Value.* New York: Peter Lang.
Graham, Phil and Greg Hearn
  2000 The digital Dark Ages: A retro-speculative history of possible futures. *Internet Research 1.0: The State of the Interdiscipline.* Paper for the First Conference of the Association of Internet Researchers, 14–17 September: University of Kansas.

Graham, Phil and Allan Luke
  2003   Militarising the body politic: New media as weapons of mass instruction. *Body & Society* 9(4): 149–168.
Graham, Phil and Allan Luke
  2005   The language of neofeudal corporatism and the war on Iraq. *Journal of Language and Politics* 4(1): 11–39.
Graham, Phil, Thomas Keenan and Anne-Maree Dowd
  2004   A call to arms at the End of History: A discourse-historical analysis of George W. Bush's declaration of war on terror. *Discourse & Society* 15(2–3): 199–221.
Habermas, Jürgen
  1991   *The Structural Transformation of the Public Sphere: An Inquiry into a Category of Bourgeois Society.* (Transl. T. Burger). Cambridge, MA: MIT Press.
Habermas, Jürgen, Sara Lennox and Frank Lennox
  1974   The public sphere: An encyclopedia article. *New German Critique* 3: 49–55.
Horkheimer, Max and Theodor W. Adorno
  1998   *The Dialectic of Enlightenment* (Transl. J. Cumming). New York: Continuum.
Iedema, Rick
  1999   Institutional responsibility and hidden meanings. *Discourse & Society* 9(4): 481–500.
Innis, Harold A.
  1951   *The Bias of Communication.* Toronto: Toronto University Press.
Kellner, Doug
  1995   Intellectuals and new technology. *Media, Culture & Society* 22(1): 109–116.
Lasswell, Harold D.
  1941   World attention survey. *Public Opinion Quarterly* 5(3): 456–462.
Lessig, Lawrence
  2004   *Free Culture: How Big Media Uses Technology and the Law to Lock down Culture and Control Creativity.* New York: Penguin Press.
Malinowski, Bronislaw
  1921   The primitive economics of the Trobriand Islanders. *The Economic Journal* 31(121): 1–16.
Markoff, John
  2005   Control the Internet? A Futile Pursuit, Some Say. *New York Times* (14 November). Available online at http://www.nytimes.com/2005/11/14/business/14register.html?th&emc=th. Accessed 14 November 2005.
Martin, James R. and Ruth Wodak (eds.)
  2003   *Re/reading the Past: Critical and Functional Perspectives on Time and Value.* Amsterdam: Benjamins.
McChesney, Robert W.
  2000   The political economy of communication and the future of the field. *Media, Culture & Society* 22(1): 109–116.
McLuhan, Marshall
  1964   *Understanding Media: The Extensions of Man.* London: Routledge.

Miller, David
   2004   *Information Dominance: The Philosophy of Total Propaganda Control*. Georgetown, ON: Coldtype. Available online at http://www.coldtype.net/Assets.04/Essays.04/Miller.pdf. Accessed 12 July 2005.

Mommsen, Theodor F.
   1942   Petrarch's conception of the Dark Ages. *Speculum* 17(2): 226–242.

Mooney, Chris and Matthew C. Nisbet
   2005   Undoing Darwin. *Columbia Journalism Review*. September/October. Available online at http://www.cjr.org/issues/2005/5/mooney.asp. Accessed 22 September 2005.

Newcomb, Kevin
   2005   Behavioral marketing baked into new toolbar. *ClickZ News* (10 October). Available online at http://www.clickz.com/news/article.php/3554851. Accessed 10 October 2005.

Noble, David F.
   2005   *Beyond the Promised Land: The Movement and the Myth*. Toronto: Between the lines.

Ong, Walter J.
   1962   Synchronic present: The academic future of modern literature in America. *American Quarterly* 14(2): 239–259.

Ong, Walter J.
   1969   World as view and world as event. *American Anthropologist* 71(4): 634–637.

Office of the Undersecretary of Defense for Acquisition, Technology, and Logistics [OUD]
   2004   *United States Report of the Defense Science Board Task Force on Strategic Communication*. Washington DC: US Government.

Poster, Mark
   1995   *CyberDemocracy: Internet and the Public Sphere*. Available online at http://www.uoc.edu/in3/hermeneia/sala_de_lectura/mark_poster_cyberdemocracy.htm. Accessed 22 September 2005.

Postman, Neil
   1985   *Amusing Ourselves to Death*. London: Methuen.

Robins, Kevin and Frank Webster
   1999   *Times of the Technoculture: From the Information Society to the Virtual Life*. New York: Routledge.

Saul, John R.
   1997   *The Unconscious Civilization*. Maryborough, Australia: Penguin.

Schiller, Dan
   1999   *Digital Capitalism*. Cambridge, MA: MIT Press.

Silverstone, Roger
   1999   *Why Study the Media?* London: Sage.

South China Morning Post
   2005, 8 September   Yahoo office accused of betraying journalist. Available online at http://www.asiamedia.ucla.edu/article.asp?parentid=29547. Accessed 8 September 2005.

Thurow, Lester C.
   1996   *The Future of Capitalism: How Today's Economic Forces Will Shape Tomorrow's World*. St. Leonards, Australia: Allen & Unwin.

United Press
   2005, 9 September   The China Yahoo! welcome: You've got Jail!. Available online at http://www.physorg.com/news6368.html. Accessed 9 September 2005.
US Senate
   2004, 6 October   *An act to reform the intelligence community and the intelligence and intelligence-related activities of the United States Government, and for other purposes.* Washington DC: US Senate.
Wasko, Janet
   2001   Challenging Disney myths. *Journal of Communication Inquiry* 25(3): 237–257.
Wilson, Woodrow
   1916   Address to the 1st World Congress on Salesmanship, 10 July, Detroit, MI. Available online at htpp://wwl12.dataformat.com/Document.aspx?doc=30491. Accessed September 2004.
Wodak, Ruth, Rudolf de Cillia, Martin Reisigl, and Karin Liebhart
   1999   *The Discursive Construction of National Identity.* (Transl. Angelika Hirsch and Richard Mitten). Edinburgh: Edinburgh University Press.

3. Media discourse and the naturalisation of categories

Nick Couldry

What is the relationship between text and social action? This question must be asked not just of individual texts but also of the larger social practices that shape texts (discourses). At that most general level, there is undeniably a complex dialectic – as Fairclough and Wodak put it "discourse is social constitutive as well as socially shaped" (Fairclough and Wodak 1997: 258) – but it is a dialectic whose specific causal processes are difficult to disentangle. If however we are interested in a particular textual source – for example, media institutions – then such causal isolation is essential; otherwise whole areas of academic research (media sociology and media studies) and policy formulation (media regulation, media literacy) will lack definition.

This chapter reviews what progress has been made towards isolating the specific contribution of media institutions to the shaping of social action; it suggests that current important approaches – including versions of Critical Discourse Analysis (CDA) and the work within media studies identified with the Glasgow Media Group (GMG) – can usefully be supplemented by another approach that draws on the theoretical tradition within sociology of Durkheim and Bourdieu via the notion of social "categories". There is no space here to offer a comprehensive account of how within discourse analysis or media studies text and social action have so far been related. The point instead is to tell a more selective story that sharpens our understanding of the possible approaches to this question.

1. Background

At least the difficulty of understanding the causal relationship between text and social action for media discourse is clear. John Corner expressed it in terms of media power when he wrote that "the conception of 'power' within a notion of televisual process has now become a matter of the utmost importance and difficulty" (Corner 1997: 258). More crudely: We know media outputs have causal consequences (if they were inconsequential, why would we spend so much time studying them?), but how exactly?

At the outset it is worth distinguishing two very different approaches to this question. The first approach (which I do not pursue in detail here) is to take the media text as social action. This, broadly speaking, is the principle adopted by those who have applied conversation analysis to media texts, and looked specifically at the talk embodied in DJ-hosted radio and television talk shows (Scannell 1991; Tolson 2001; and for a related approach to the conversations on which "public opinion" reported in media are based, see Myers 2004). This approach draws on Garfinkel's famous proposal that:

> The activities whereby members produce and manage settings of ordinary everyday affairs are identical with members' procedures for making those settings "accountable". (Garfinkel 1967: 1, quoted in Heritage 1984: 179)

In a particular setting, according to Garfinkel, talk that gives an account of that setting is direct evidence of the activity that produces that setting, since it is part of that activity. If therefore we treat a media text as evidence of a setting (a talk show transcript as evidence of the studio setting where the talk show was produced), then the accounts of that setting recorded in that text are direct evidence of the principles by which the setting was itself produced.

This approach to the problematic link between media texts and social action (which resolves it by interpreting those texts as social action) is quite different from the approach given most attention in this chapter. This latter approach is concerned with what happens when media texts are circulated to countless settings beyond the talk setting presented by a television or radio programme itself, and so faces very different explanatory problems from the first. For, if we prioritise the causal implications of transmission then there is no reason to suppose that the principles which produced the setting in a talk show studio are the same principles which produced the setting of its interpretation, say, in the livingroom. Indeed there is every reason to suppose that settings of interpretation may differ significantly among themselves (I may be watching the talk show alone, with a group of friends, in a family situation of barely suppressed conflict, in an airport among people I've never seen before, and so on). It is the difficulties faced by this second approach, and how we might resolve them, on which I will concentrate in this chapter.

The question – what do transmission and reception contribute to the relationship between media texts and social action? – is complex. It emerges at specific points of explanations of media discourse itself. For example, Norman Fairclough interrupts his authoritative account of the structural patterning of "media discourse" as follows:

> We have then [in the TV text *Crimewatch*] a crossing of boundaries and a merging of voices and practices which powerfully domesticates and so legitimizes police work. *Or at least appears to do so: it would be fascinating to know what audiences make of this programme.* (Fairclough 1995: 168, emphasis added)

We will come to the tradition of audience research shortly, but before we do so it is important to note the explanatory challenge audience research faces. For it tries to answer the question that "pure" textual analysis offered by media analysis in the literary tradition avoids. Justin Lewis formulated the issue of text and social action in a particularly pointed way:

> The question that should be put to textual analysis that purports to tell us how a cultural product "works" in contemporary culture is almost embarrassingly simple: where's the evidence? Without evidence, everything is pure speculation. (Lewis 1991: 49)

It was precisely the search for "hard" evidence of the link between media texts and social action that generated the controversial US tradition of Cultivation Analysis headed by George Gerbner from the 1960s onwards (see a useful review in Morgan and Signorielli 1990). This approach moved away from the "effects" of individual texts and sought to show on the basis of statistical analysis how people's higher exposure to media was associated with a greater likelihood of possessing certain "conceptions of social reality" reflected in media outputs (Morgan and Signorielli 1990: 19–20). At a statistical level, however, the attempt to isolate heavy media consumption as a variable separate from its possible causes (lack of social status, education, and so on) proved inconclusive. While the explanatory intent of Cultivation Analysis should be admired, this disappointing outcome was perhaps inevitable given the causal complexity of how media (or indeed any major textual source) work in large societies with multiple flows of discourse.

A very different approach to this issue, using small-scale qualitative analysis, emerged from the British school of audience research started at the Birmingham Centre for Contemporary Cultural Research in the 1970s. But this tradition too encountered key difficulties. David Morley's early work (1980) on the audience for the BBC TV current affairs programme *Nationwide* was original not so much in studying audiences (already part of American mass communications research), but in connecting viewing as a complex cultural practice to issues of power and ideology. Morley, drawing on Stuart Hall's (1980) encoding-decoding model, insisted that the audience's "decoding" of the media text was connected with the wider "complex field of communications" (work, school, family, and so on) to which viewers belong (Morley 1992: 77). Morley aimed to relate the moment of audience interpretation to that more widely structured field.

Hall's model had famously simplified this relation through two key assumptions: first, that each media text is encoded in analysable ways, which determine a "preferred meaning" for that text, related to dominant ideology; second, that there are basically three interpretative positions for an audience to adopt – a decoding that uses the same codes with which the programme was encoded to produce the *dominant* reading, one which adjusts the programme's codes to produce a *negotiated* reading, and one which uses a quite different code, to produce an *oppositional* reading. An example would be the reading of a news bulletin:

We might (1) take it as direct evidence of the storyline it contains (reproducing the "dominant reading"), or (2) broadly accept its status as factual, but contest certain interpretations contained within it (a "negotiated" reading), or (3) contest its status as fact and offer a quite different interpretation of what we believe are the facts (an "oppositional reading"). Morley then, using focus groups where people were shown programme episodes and asked to interpret them, attempted to connect such decoding possibilities to sociological variables such as class and occupation, an ambitious move that promised to unlock in precise ways the connections between text-as-interpreted and social action.

Since then, the limitations of this model (even though it retains influence) have been extensively discussed, not least by Morley himself (1992). First, the term "decoding" – basically, a literary model of textual interpretation derived from semiotics – distorts what audiences actually do with media texts. People may have multiple levels of engagements which cannot be mapped onto forms of decoding (Corner and Richardson 1986; Buckingham 1987; Liebes and Katz 1990). What, for example, about irony, scepticism and willing suspension of disbelief, not to mention the ways in which media texts, like all texts, may invite various types of engagement (for example, ritual engagement: Dayan and Katz 1992)? These arguments derived from the specific complexity of the text/reader relationship can be supplemented by others with a wider focus. If we accept that we are simply saturated with media contents, then the impact of any particular media text is impossible to establish (see, for example, Ang 1996: 41, 67). As we have already seen, cultivation analysis had acknowledged this point, but Ang pushes it towards a more radical conclusion: "if television is an 'ideological apparatus' (...) then this is not so much because its texts transmit certain 'messages', but because it is a cultural form through which (...) constraints are negotiated" (Ang 1996: 51). Ang invites us to look away from the details of media texts and towards wider questions of media form.

There is also the argument from inattention: many television analysts, for example, claim that viewing is generally a "low involvement" activity (Barwise and Ehrenberg 1988) which fills non-work time at the lowest cost (Lodziak 1987), is often performed "parergically" in a state of distraction (Bausinger 1984), and amounts to little more than "routine reality maintenance" (Kubey and Csikszentmihalyi 1990). What if most media material (for example news stories) is simply forgotten (Graber 1988)? Certainly some media consumption continues to involve close attention (Caldwell 1996: 25–27), but that does not make a model of text/social action influence dependent on a presumed moment of active textual reading any easier to sustain.

At this point there has been a historical bifurcation. Whereas some of the leading members of the audience studies tradition (Morley 1980, 1986, 1992; Ang 1996) moved, in the early or mid 1990s, away from detailed empirical work into audiences, a new version of the audience research tradition has retained the momentum of the (predominantly textual) early work of the Glasgow Media Group (see Philo 1999a, for a useful overview). The next section will cover some of the detailed insights from this work, but for now it is worth noting the Glasgow Media Group's systematic attempt to do empirical analysis across a wide range of news types (from AIDS coverage to foreign political news), and their combination of well-targeted qualitative research (focus groups created to discuss particular news themes) with exhaustive analysis of relevant media coverage.

We must also note the quite independent tradition of research into the relationship between media discourse and social action that developed out of discourse analysis and linguistics in the 1990s (Fairclough 1995; van Dijk 1991; Meinhof and Richardson 1994; and for a review Wodak and Busch 2004). Again, we will defer detailed consideration, particularly of van Dijk's work, till later, but for now note two points: First, the Discourse Analysis tradition is bolder than the Glasgow Media Group in raising theoretical questions about how texts influence social practice, for example van Dijk's socio-cognitive model (van Dijk 1991); second, the versions of Discourse Analysis in which I am interested here, namely Critical Discourse Analysis, are quite open to working with complementary approaches from disciplines outside linguistics (Fairclough and Wodak 1997: 278). This is linked to a crucial similarity between Critical Discourse Analysis and the sociological approach that informs this chapter: Both are based on an explicit and unapologetic foregrounding of questions of power (compare Fairclough and Wodak 1997; Couldry 2000: 196). If the aim is to unmask operations of power (not merely to further academic debate) then it matters all the more to get the causal analysis right (by acknowledging, not hiding, causal complexity),[1] and it matters less what exact location in the disciplinary terrain we are working from.

2. Text and social action: Analysing interpretation

In this section I want to look in more detail at approaches which prioritise the analysis of how media texts are interpreted, as a route to understanding how the circulation of media texts influences social action. As just noted, there has since the early classic audience research been a considerable amount of work within media studies and discourse analysis that contributes to this question. My account will be necessarily brief, and aimed specifically at bringing out a point central to the argument of this chapter: namely, how the explanatory logic of these recent accounts has emphasised most the moment of individual interpretations of a media text (often recorded in a focus group setting), and so given less attention to the wider processes which might pre-structure contexts of interpretation. My point will be that, while the emphasis on the moment of interpretation (and how individual and group interpretations vary) is valid and important, it is in tension with a different emphasis at least implied in such writings, on the wider social context of interpretation and the possibility that media also influence that wider social context. It is this latter possibility that is developed in the alternative approach offered later in the chapter.

2.1. Explaining media influence through interpretation: Some tensions

One approach to understanding the complexity of how, and to what extent, media texts influence social action has been to offer ever more precise accounts of how particular audience members interpret particular texts in particular contexts, and of the different resources, skills, habits and preferences that they bring to the act of interpretation.

2.1.1. Studying the language of interpretation (Richardson; Meinhof)

A number of writers in the late 1980s and early 1990s aimed to take account of the uncertainties and complications noted in the last section, while still advancing David Morley's attempt to understand how the interpretation of media texts is socially embedded; for example Buckingham (1987); Corner, Richardson, and Fenton (1990); Livingstone (1990). Corner, Richardson and Fenton showed how particular groups (differentiated by political persuasion, class, age) "privilege[d] different frames of interpretation" (Corner, Richardson, and Fenton 1990: 92) when interpreting a TV programme about the nuclear industry, concluding that we must understand media influence not as a "top-down process" but instead grasp "the active and differentiated processes of interpretation" (Corner, Richardson, and Fenton 1990: 106). In a study of how people understood broadcasts on poverty, Kay Richardson (1994) explored both differences and convergences in interpretation between various groups, suggesting a complex overlap between the "discursive repertoires" which individuals brought to a programme (Meinhof and Richardson 1994: 23). Meinhof and van Leeuwen (2000) applied a similar approach to interpretations of media texts that were themselves particularly complex both in generic status and intertextual reference. Their comment at the end of a study of viewers of the TV series *The Rock'n'Roll Years* is striking:

> There is (…) a tension between the complex viewing habit presupposed in the viewers – an ability simultaneously and instantaneously to process information (…) – and at the same time a general resolution of these into myth, in Barthes' sense. Unsurprisingly viewers responded to the programme in highly divergent ways which were partly the result of differences in world knowledge, but more significantly a result of the divergent social attitudes, political beliefs and aesthetic preferences of each individual viewer. (Meinhof and van Leeuwen 2000: 74)

There is an explicit tension here between a supposed generalising effect ("myth") and the irreducibly individual process of interpretation; this tension is not, I suggest, resolvable because of the tendency towards a certain methodological individualism built into approaches that place most emphasis on the immediate process of interpretation. This tension is not resolved by Meinhof and Van Leeuwen in spite of their clear interest in addressing broader questions of social influence through the concept of discourse (Meinhof and Richardson 1994: 22). The way to resolve this tension, I suggest, is to develop a supplementary account of less direct forms of media influence that operates not just through the moment of interpretation.

2.1.2. Retelling the news: The Glasgow Media Group's research

Let us now turn to the work of the Glasgow Media Group which sought to avoid the risk of methodological individualism in an interesting way. While sharing some obvious starting-points with earlier audience research (viz. the use of demographically differentiated focus groups to comment on specific media outputs: compare Philo 1990 and Morley 1980), the Glasgow Media Group has in recent years sought to overcome the difficulty of isolating media outputs as a causal factor in what it readily acknowledges is a complex intertextual environment (Kitzinger 1999: 10–11). A bold Glasgow Media Group innovation has been to ask focus group participants to retell news stories, for example from a television news still or a press photo presented to them (Kitzinger 1999: 5). If conducted in tandem with detailed background analysis of news coverage of the same issues, this method provides insights into how ready-made formulas of story-telling (their regular inclusions and exclusions) may be shared between focus group participants and media texts.

While not proving, of course, that such formulas have been absorbed by audiences directly (and only) from media – sometimes, clearly, there may be common and pre-existing social and historical sources (cf. Kitzinger 1999: 5) – this technique can, in some cases, yield persuasive evidence of a significant causal connection. This approach works well, for example, when audiences, in their retelling of something far removed from their personal experience (a sexual abuse scandal), are found to reproduce the key features of the corresponding narrative in media coverage a few weeks before (Kitzinger 1999: 9). This account of how media texts influence social action becomes even more compelling when combined with an account of how alternatives to media narratives are excluded. There are certainly important cases where people's personal experience of events, or event-types, covered by media allows them to doubt those media narratives (Philo 1990). However, audiences may discount their personal experience, even if *prima facie* relevant, and the basis for a counter-narrative to dominant media stories (Kitzinger 1999: 16–17), where they lack a broader narrative which can make sense of personal experience being drawn upon in that way.

What emerges from the Glasgow Media Group's work in the 1990s, alongside a clear confirmation that media audiences are very capable interpreters of media, is a strong scepticism about some cultural studies' belief in the positive consequences of audiences' interpretative freedoms. We have to recognise, Jenny Kitzinger notes, that how people read media (even when they are active readers and decoders) may "reinforce, rather than undermine, broad media influence over public understandings" (Kitzinger 1999: 19).

The Glasgow Media Group also suggest other forms of influence. Media narratives may resonate because they play into and help reproduce particular ways of thinking or arguing, or because they help reproduce particular cultural affinities and value systems (Philo 1999b: 284–285). Media influence, here, is clearly seen to span cognitive and evaluative dimensions. In addition, Philo suggests that media may influence key categories that organise cognition and emotion:

> It seems likely that media portrayals can shape audience understandings of what is legitimate or desirable, and of which characters are likely to be seen as 'cool', 'amazing' or the sort of person who 'everyone' would wish to be like. (Philo 1999b: 285)

This, I suggest, is exactly right, but it cannot be accounted for simply through an account of how people read and understand news stories. We need a wider explanatory focus and it is therefore important to separate out here distinct and complementary models of how text/ social action relationship might work. The Glasgow Media Group however has been less concerned with developing abstract theoretical models: its aim has been more to intervene across the policy terrain of news production.

2.1.3. *Van Dijk and Critical Discourse Analysis*

At this point it is useful to turn to van Dijk's more formal approach to how texts might influence social action, as perhaps the most detailed account within Critical Discourse Analysis of how media texts have consequences for social action. Van Dijk (2001: 353) is careful to distinguish various levels on which texts might have causal consequences, for example at an organizational level (motivating or summoning groups to act in certain ways or requiring social actors to follow instructions) or, quite differently, by influencing processes of personal and social cognition. The latter involves a mixture of positive and negative factors (van Dijk 2001: 357–358): not just a readiness to accept particular beliefs but also the lack of knowledge with which to challenge them or the discourse with which to articulate alternatives. Van Dijk's account of personal and social cognition in relation to news reports is particularly rich. Drawing on a detailed model of how textual comprehension involves various levels of long-term, personal and short-term memory (van Dijk and Kintsch 1983), van Dijk (1991:

chapter 9) shows how, given their limited recall of the details of news items, news audiences need, in retelling stories about the world, to draw on a variety of schemas acquired over a longer period; in doing so, they tend to be confined, whatever their detailed differences of opinion, within an overall ideological framework that matches the framework of media's own coverage, unless of course they have been exposed consistently to alternative ideological frameworks. If van Dijk's model of how exactly this works is more detailed than the Glasgow Media Group's, the main outcome is similar, that when people use the news, they "are engaged in the active construction of their 'own' interpretations of news reports" (van Dijk 1991: 228) – not just incidentally but, as van Dijk suggests, necessarily. The schemas and patterns through which they do so are therefore of vital importance in deepening our understanding of how media influence works.[2] Indeed, if there were more space it would be important to sketch in other approaches within communications research to how media texts influence social action that overlap with this analysis (for example, research on agenda-setting and news "framing").[3]

2.2.   Towards a resolution

So far in this section, I have tried to show that, for all their virtues, there has been a tension in earlier accounts of how circulated media texts influence social action between (1) emphasising the moment of individual interpretation and (2) the desire to explain more broadly how interpretation is socially shaped. To clarify how to resolve this tension, it is helpful to look at work by the Viennese School of Critical Discourse Analysis.

Wodak et al.'s (1999) account of the discursive construction of Austrian national identity is not primarily concerned with the influence of media texts on groups or individuals, but rather with how to explain a wider set of relations between different forms of elite discourse (of which media are only one) and lifeworld discourse (Wodak et al. 1999: 3). Very useful, however, is their characterisation of the explanatory gap they aim to fill: "the aim of the present study is to throw light on the largely contingent and imaginary character of nation and to sharpen awareness of dogmatic, essentialist and *naturalising conceptions* of nation and national identity" (Wodak et al. 1999: 9, emphasis added). In understanding more precisely how "naturalising conceptions" might be effective, Wodak and her collaborators draw broadly on Bourdieu's concept of habitus, as a way of understanding how the identities of those who in everyday life reinterpret and reuse elite discourses of the nation are themselves shaped. They are interested in how the state "shapes those forms of perception, of categorisation, of interpretation, and of memory which serve as the basis for more or less immediate orchestration of the habitus which forms the basis for a kind of 'national common sense', through the school and the educational system" (Wodak et al.

76   Nick Couldry

1999: 29). Clearly there is no reason to limit our account of the mechanisms through which this orchestration of habitus works to the educational system: what about media themselves?

The formulation of Wodak and her collaborators opens up a much wider range of causal influences on how we might come to interpret a media text in a particular context. Common sense forms of categorisation are, after all, involved in (1) how we make sense of the types of things we do or do not do every day (our general practice), (2) how we make sense of choosing to watch, let alone pay attention to, a particular programme (our viewing practice), (3) how we interpret particular contexts of interpretation (interpretation contexts), and (4) how we interpret and generate uses to which we can put what we learn from a programme in the future (practices of reuse or adaptation). The difference between this formulation of how media texts might influence social action and the approaches discussed earlier in the section can be summarised diagrammatically.

Approaches discussed earlier were concerned with the largely closed causal circuit that explains the individual act of interpretation or story retelling; they therefore understand media's social influence through media's direct influence on that circuit (see Figure 1a).

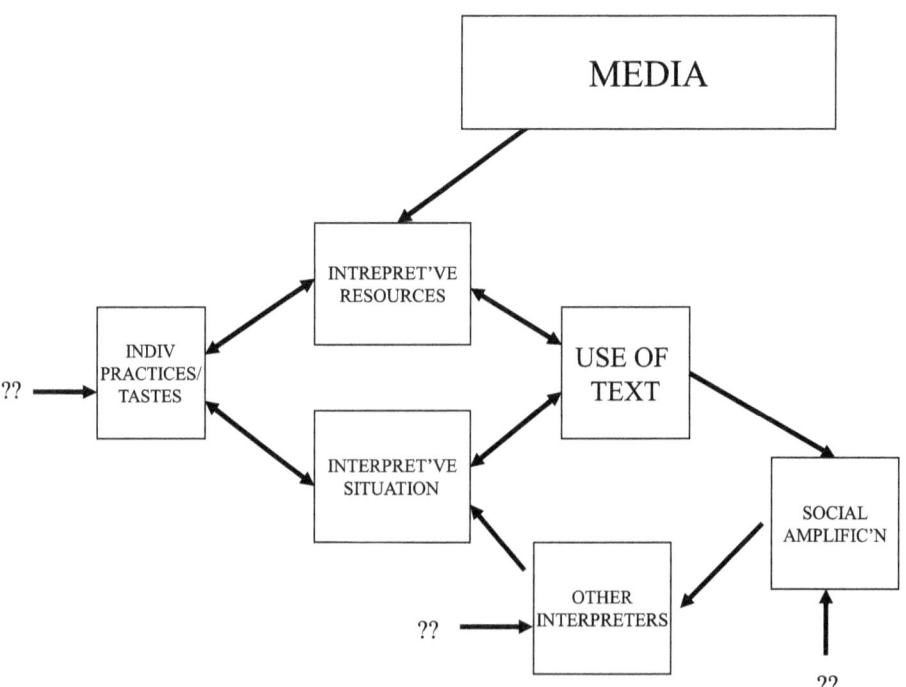

Figure 1a. Explaining media influence through individual interpretation

As a result, various other causal influences (structuring the practices of the interpreter, and those around them, and processes of social amplification) are not explicitly considered (these are indicated by the question-marks in Figure 1a): what of media's influence on these processes? In so far as, for example, the Glasgow Media Group's analysis does point to such wider explanations, they cannot be fitted into the causal circuit around the act of interpretation.

By contrast Wodak et al. suggest a broader explanatory canvas in which media influences on the overall practice of viewers/audiences can be understood: see Figure 1b.

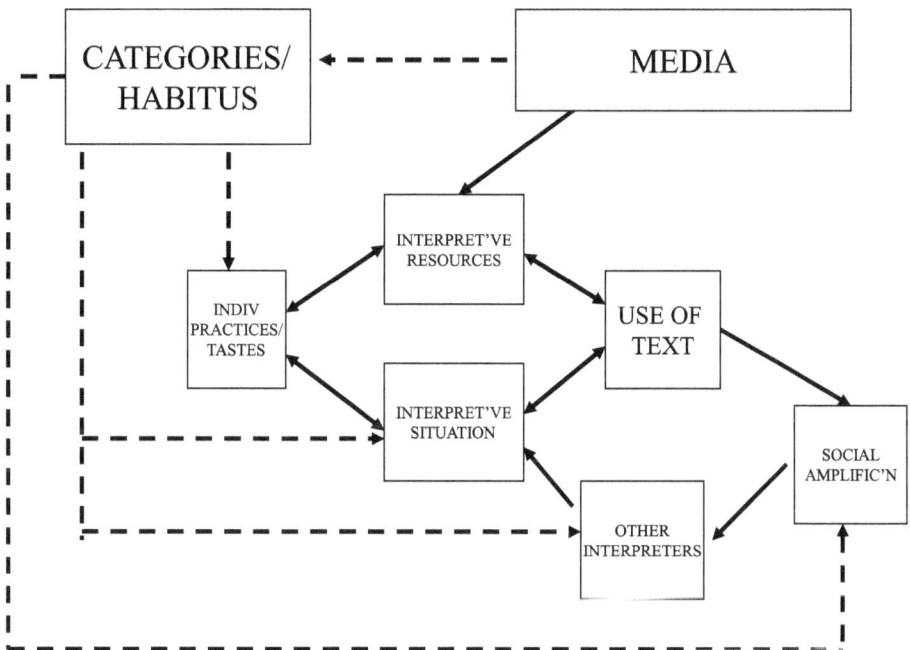

Figure 1b. Expanded explanatory field

Note in particular the additional dotted lines indicating how media influence might explain why individuals interpret a programme a particular way, beyond the brute fact of individual variability.

In the next section, I want to explore how an approach analogous to Wodak et al.'s might be developed in more detail, as a supplement to approaches more closely focussed on the moment of interpretation. In doing so, I will attempt to fill in the explanatory space suggested by the dotted lines in Figure 1b, drawing on my previous work (Couldry 2000, 2003a and 2003b).

3. An alternative approach: media and social categories

This alternative approach aims to supplement the approaches to the text/ social action link considered so far by considering certain feedback loops (in media discourse and in the use of media outputs in everyday practice) that are not considered, explicitly at least, by those other approaches. One such feedback loop is internal to media discourse (Couldry 2000: 42–52), the other ranges far beyond media discourse (or even its interpretations) and encompasses the whole range of practices oriented to media (Couldry 2000: 52–57, 2003a).

An example of the first type of feedback loop is media's habit of continually referring back to themselves as the assumed privileged reference-point for accessing social "reality" (cf. Zelizer 1993). While this feedback loop is not crucial to an individual's interpretative resources, it is a context for these resources to develop. It is also crucial in the construction of types of media consumption as socially legitimate (or even necessary), and in the construction of audiences as just audiences (i.e. people that are in the process of making sense of social reality) rather than valid social interpreters (Couldry 2000: 44–50; cf. Hall 1973; Fairclough 1995: 40; van Dijk 2001: 355–356). This feedback loop therefore begins to explain influences (1) on individual practice, (2) on the practices of other interpreters as well as (3) the wider interpretative situation (see points where question-marks are located in Figure 1a).

An example of the second feedback loop would be the huge range of everyday practices that reproduce media-oriented values in contemporary societies. For example, the values of celebrity reproduced through various acts, from the banal act of flicking through a celebrity magazine while we wait to have our hair cut, or (at the other extreme of organisation) the ritually orchestrated final minutes of a reality TV game-show, such as *Big Brother*, when the crowd cheer the exit of the winner (and new-found celebrity) from the *Big Brother* house marking, in spectacular fashion, her or his return to the "everyday world". In this latter type of the feedback loop, we see an influence on the process of social amplification (see Figure 1a, bottom right).

To foreground such feedback processes is to think in a distinctive way about how regular patterns of media discourse structure social action, emphasising not the factual content of media (as remembered by audiences or registered in their persistent patterns of story-telling, important though that is), but rather a longer process of naturalisation whereby elements and categories of media discourse, and its overall forms, become embedded in everyday practice and so become self-reproducing simply by being taken-for-granted as "natural". In a sense this approach extends van Dijk's insight that we need to understand better the consequences of media representations for "action and interaction" (van Dijk 1991: 225), but emphasises action well beyond the immediate context of reception or even the retelling of news. Action – for example, how people behave when they go on TV or when they meet a celebrity – can condense patterns of thinking or evaluation and so reproduce them as "natural" even without (in fact precisely when not) articulating them: a reproduction "below" the level of consciousness as Bourdieu puts it (1990). This is one reason why ritualised action (cf. Rappoport 1999; for discussion see Couldry 2003a: 22–24) matters in this approach.

This approach towards understanding the "effects" of media discourse is concerned with "habitus" in the broadest sense of Bourdieu's term (that is, "history turned into nature": Bourdieu 1977: 78), and so with "effects" that work over a long time and only by saturating whole territories with their patterns: such "effects" therefore far exceed in temporal duration or spatial extension those generally foregrounded by Critical Discourse Analysis and the Glasgow Media Group, while at the same time illuminating some of the broader effects implied by those approaches. I am not claiming this alternative approach is better, merely different in emphasis from those other approaches. It is interested in consequences of media institutions (both of their very existence – cf. Lazarsfeld and Merton 1969 – and of the structuring of their outputs). This might seem inordinately ambitious if it were not that we can see on a regular basis both the outcomes and the everyday traces of such influences. We see the outcomes in, for example, taken-for-granted beliefs (acted out in daily routines) in the privileged position of media institutions as our access-point to what is "going on" in our world; we see traces of the mechanisms that reproduce such wider outcomes when we notice fragments of ritualised practice, as when everyone turns around if a major media celebrity enters the room.

Most importantly – the last point to be made in introducing this alternative approach – an important mechanism that links language and action on this large scale is the category, that is, a reproducible principle for organising thought and action on the basis of which both can be organised in self-replicating ways. The concept of "category", while it can be adapted in any theoretical framework, was introduced into sociology and anthropology in the early 20th century by Emile Durkheim (1995; cf. Durkheim and Mauss 1963), and drawn upon in the late 20th century by Pierre Bourdieu (1990). A "category" (in Durkheim's sense) is not just any distinction in language thought or action; it is an organising distinction which serves as a principle for organising thought and action more widely. Durkheim and Mauss were concerned with fundamental logical categories and certain other very pervasive categories such as left and right, man and woman, sacred and profane. There is, however, no limit to what type of distinction can be a social category in Durkheim's sense and, as we see in the next section, one key feature of the approach to media discourse offered here is to suggest that media institutions are associated with the gradual emergence of new categories which help organise everyday action and thought: for example, the categories of "celebrity" and "liveness".

If the general principle of (organising) social categories is accepted, it is important to realise that we do not need to import with it Durkheim and Mauss's (1963) curious theory about the origins of categories of thought in so-called "primitive" societies. This is just as well; for that theory – of how all thought-categories in "primitive" societies derive from the actual spatial organisation of social life (for example, the division of people into tribes) – is not only implausible (Needham 1963) but also inapplicable to complex societies as Durkheim and Mauss (1963: 86) themselves realised. However, the broader principle of social categories is not at all strange; in fact it addresses the recent call of one cultural sociologist (Swidler 2001) for ways of understanding how in practice the maelstrom of cultural practices is hierarchized and so how their implicit order can be grasped (Swidler draws here on ritual, a term which, for Durkheim at least, is closely linked to the concept of categories). What I am proposing is that media discourse and practices oriented to media are organised through specific media-related categories whose pervasive work helps explain some of the consequences that media discourse has well beyond contexts of textual interpretation or textual consumption.

4. The long-term consequences of media discourse

In this section I want to explain in more detail why this alternative approach to the social consequences of media texts usefully supplements other approaches. Clearly, any hypothesis on the scale just indicated requires a large number of studies to become convincing. In the space of this chapter, I can at best provide it with some initial plausibility, as well as sketch how the different elements of this approach fit together.

This application of Durkheim's notion of social category to media discourse makes, as just explained, no claims about the current relevance of the specific categories that Durkheim and Mauss discussed a century ago, and for so-called "primitive" societies. The question instead is whether in contemporary mediated societies we can see the emergence of one or more new category distinctions in terms of which language and practice oriented to media are organised, deserving the description of "category" in Durkheim and Mauss's sense. My claim is that there are such category distinctions based on an underlying distinction between what is in/on/related to "media" and what is not (that is, what is "non-media" or "ordinary"). This underlying distinction implies a hierarchy, marking off anything (whether object, person, world) that is "in" or "on" media from anything that is not.[4] Let's take some examples of the media/ ordinary distinction being used in everyday language and media discourse.

First an example of the cliché (but as Michael Billig has argued it is precisely banal language that works with least explicit resistance: Billig 1995,

1997) that "ordinary" people can only get into media if they do something "extraordinary" (cf. Langer 1998: 41). Take this excerpt from a television company's bid to run a major new current affairs programme, leaked to the Guardian's media section:

> Profiles could involve a celebrity (...) alternatively it could be a politician (...) Or, we could even focus on an ordinary person in an extraordinary situation, e.g. a day in the life of a Lottery jackpot winner, or the parents caring for a teenage daughter with CJD (...) (*Guardian* 19 January 1999, Media Section)

This quote is interesting because it reproduces exactly, even while appearing to invert it, the media/ordinary boundary; ordinary people must be non-ordinary (extraordinary) if they are to be "in" the media, whereas media people – those usually in media – need just be themselves; which implies that it is extraordinary, and therefore also worthy of media comment, when media people such as celebrities are caught doing something "ordinary". The latter, after all, is one appeal of celebrity magazines and many recent television shows about celebrities in their "ordinary" "real life".

Or take this description from a fan's description of what distinguishes pop stars from others: "you think of them as being wonderful people (...) everybody that everybody ordinary isn't" (cited in Vermorel and Vermorel 1985: 175). The contentlessness of the distinction confirms it as a more fundamental category distinction that, like the "sacred/profane" distinction in Durkheim's account of the social bases of religion, is absolute and so can mark literally anything off from anything else (Durkheim 1995: 35). Yet this contentless distinction can still be glossed so that it appears less arbitrary, as in this TV producer's "explanation" of what he does when he selects people for TV: "I wouldn't pick someone to be a [game-show] contestant who wanted to be a star. I want nice ordinary people who just come along for a bit of fun: some of them are so ordinary that they are surprised to be chosen" (cited in Root 1986: 98). Notice how the term "ordinary" only appears to explain here; its content is never unpacked as such.

What of the "world" that the media/ ordinary distinction marks off from the (apparently separate) world outside media? It is a world that appears to be automatically different: "to be transposed into television *is* to be elevated out of the banal realm of the off-screen and repositioned in the privileged on-screen world" (Tichi 1991: 40, emphasis added). Sometimes the transition is more seamless as when cameras come into your life, but no less dramatic: "you feel everything you do is imbued with significance because there is a camera crew there pointing a lens in your face" (as one early participant in MTV's programme *The Real World* put it).[5]

Examples could be multiplied, but note that none of the examples quoted come from media texts themselves and all are from wider discourse around the process of making media. The point is that texts are not the only place where we can, or should, look for the more general patterns of naturalisation at work in and around media discourse. Yet this wider discourse is surely relevant both to the contexts of interpreting media and to people's practices oriented to media.

The media/ordinary distinction is however only one part of an interlocking structure of naturalised distinctions and discursive patterns relating to media. The centralisation of media resources underlies, I suggest, a whole series of naturalised patterns of thinking that are pervasively reproduced in and around media. Let me set these out abstractly first:

1. The assumption that media provide a privileged access-point to what is constructed as a social "centre".
2. A set of categorical distinctions and hierarchies between worlds, agents, and things, based on the assumption (linked to 1) that everything associated with media is "higher" than everything which isn't (for example the privilege given to "liveness", that is in current and "direct" connection to a mediated social "centre": cf. Feuer 1983).
3. A set of practices which encode those hierarchies and categories (for example, "magic" of mediated locations embodied in tourist "pilgrimages").
4. Formalisations of action that further reinforce the naturalness of 1, 2 and 3 through ritual (Couldry 2003a) (including here more or less formalised media genres such as talk shows and "reality TV": Here we might come closer to approaches drawing on Garfinkel in analysing the talk of those shows).

What I am attempting, through this list, is to capture how an increasingly complex set of practices can be linked by, and serve to naturalise further, the concentration of symbolic resources in media institutions that characterise contemporary societies. Crucially, the media/non-media distinction works not just on its own, but by being mappable onto other category distinctions, just as in Bourdieu's well-known account of the Kabyle house (1990) a key category distinction (male/female) is reproduced by being transposed onto other distinctions (right/left, high/low). The assumption (point 1) that media are not just a powerful but a privileged (that is, legitimately powerful) source of representations of the social world would be weak, if it were only a single assumption, unconnected to daily practice. But it is condensed in category distinctions which naturalise the difference between things "in" media and those not, including distinctions that on the face of it are not about the quality of media, but about the quality of events themselves (the quality of "live" events to which media give us "direct" access: point 2). These categories are more effectively naturalised if they come to organise whole practices, whether organising your routine around the watching of live news or organising leisure time around visits to places in the media (as in the "pilgrimages" to media locations: point 3). The naturalness of such organisation is further enhanced when media practices linked to them are incorporated in formalised activities with a ritualised quality (point 4), whether at media locations (as explored in my work on visits to Granada Studios Tour: Couldry 2000, Part Two; cf. Couldry 2003a: chapter 5) or in new forms of media output such as reality TV (once again, recall the staged return to "ordinary reality" of the winning contestant on the final night of *Big Brother*). "Reality television" presents perhaps the most interesting reproduction of all, since it purports on one level to undermine media's privileged status and present "ordinary reality". The naturalisation of media's representative power works here not through people's credulity in these programme's claims to "reality" (people may well be quite sceptical: cf. Hill 2004), but through the embedding of the paradoxical category "reality *television*" in practices of television production, and everyday talk and consumption.

In addition, of course, there are feedback loops that work within media discourse itself. Media institutions occupy a position quite distinct, say, from other major concentrations of symbolic power (such as religious institutions) since they do not so much provide the authoritative source for particular beliefs (a credo about media, as it were), but instead a constant source of often banal facts about the world. The result is a self-reinforcing process of legitimation across at least three "dimensions" which elsewhere (Couldry 2000: chapter 3) I have expressed formally as "naming" (the identification of what counts as significant in the world), "framing" (acting as the taken-for-granted access-point or "window" to whatever, whether general or specific, is significant in the world) and "ordering" (the hierarchy of "media" versions of the world over others). Let me quote from my earlier account of this point:

> The media's status as reporter of "the facts" about social reality (Naming) helps naturalise their status more generally as the "frame" through which we obtain access to social reality (Framing). This helps reinforce the symbolic hierarchy between "media" and "ordinary" "worlds" (Ordering), which in turn helps reinforce the status of media material (whether fact or fiction) as social "reality" or "actuality" (Naming again). A largely closed cycle of reproduction whose overall result constitutes what I call the "symbolic hierarchy of the media frame". (Couldry 2000: 52)

At this point, you might have some questions. First, I have referred throughout to "media" or "the media" without differentiation between specific media: why? This is not because there are no distinctions between media (on the contrary, there are many important distinctions); the point instead is that the pattern of naturalisation we are trying to capture precisely overrides those differences in favour of a broader and wholly constructed sense that the specific, and historically contingent, media institutions installed in particular societies are themselves a "natural" and privileged access-point to our social "reality".

Second, does the naturalised structure that I have argued is somehow embedded within media discourse appear in the same way in every society? The answer is that we don't know without further research; indeed we may be able to use the general account of this chapter as the basis for investigating how "media cultures" differ from territory to territory; there is a palpable difference in "media culture" between, say, Britain and the USA and maybe this has some basis in differences in how the structure of naturalisation sketched above is worked out across those societies and in relation to their different institutional structures. No claim however is made here that the structure just sketched is universal. What I do claim however is that, because the notion of social category spans talk, text and action, it can link the organising patterns in both media text and the huge range of practices oriented towards media; this breadth of application gives the term "category" its advantage in helping grasp the pervasiveness of media influences on the social world, whatever the term's odd historical provenance.

5. Conclusion

This chapter has reviewed a range of approaches to a fundamental question: how do media texts shape social action? At the outset, we put to one side approaches influenced by Conversation Analysis that treat media texts as social action, and concentrated on a range of approaches that address media influence through an analysis of the factors that shape people's variable interpretations of media texts. While those approaches (including the work of the Glasgow Media Group and approaches linked to Critical Discourse Analysis, such as van Dijk's and Meinhof's) offer valuable insights, I have argued that there remains a tension between (1) the tendency of accounts of textual interpretation to reduce to the variability of individual interpretation and (2) the desire in all such accounts to find broader social explanations of media influence, which however are not easily contained within an account of the dynamics of textual interpretation itself.

As a way of resolving that tension, I have in the second half of the chapter sketched a different approach to explaining media influence that connects with an insight from Wodak et al.'s (1999) study of Austrian nationalism into the classificatory and naturalising power of certain discourses. This alternative approach thinks about media influences not just directly on the resources with which individuals are able to interpret media texts, but more broadly on the whole social context and pattern of social organisation in which media-oriented practices are situated, agents are formed, and particular contexts of interpretation come to seem natural. Inevitably, to suggest this broader canvas is to start on a very long explanatory journey which cannot be completed here. The chapter's aim however has been to show how this broader canvas provides a useful context for evaluating and supplementing more familiar approaches to the relation between media texts and social action.

Notes

1. Here there is also a clear similarity with the Glasgow Media Group's explicit concern with questions of power (Philo 1999).
2. Cf. van Dijk's criticisms of what he sees as the superficiality of earlier approaches to media influence (1991: 225–227).
3. See on agenda-setting Iyengar and Kinder (1987); McCombs and Shaw (1972); and on framing Pan and Kosicki (2001).
4. There is of course a larger question about how this distinction acquired such force. I have argued elsewhere (2000: 14–16, 2003a: 5–9) that it is the long-term historical result of the gradual organization of everyday practice on the basis that media representations are central to them (cf. Couldry 2003b which relates this analysis to Bourdieu's field theory). I cannot expand on such broader explanations here, nor is this necessary to understand the account offered here of how media-oriented language and social action are related.
5. Quoted in *Independent on Sunday*, 16 July 1995.

References

Ang, Ien
    1996   *Living Room Wars*. London: Routledge.
Barwise, Patrick and Andrew Ehrenberg
    1988   *Television and its Audience*. London: Sage.
Bausinger, Herman
    1984   Media, technology and daily life. *Media Culture & Society* 6(4): 343–352.
Billig, Michael
    1995   *Banal Nationalism*. London: Sage.
Billig, Michael
    1997   From codes to utterances: cultural studies, discourse and psychology. In: Marjorie Ferguson and Peter Golding (eds.) *Cultural Studies in Question*, 205–226. London: Sage.
Bourdieu, Pierre
    1977   *Outline of a Theory of Practice*. Cambridge: Cambridge University Press.
Bourdieu, Pierre
    1990   *The Logic of Practice*. Cambridge: Polity.
Buckingham, David
    1987   *Public Secrets: Eastenders and its Audience*. London: BFI.
Caldwell, John
    1996   *Televisuality: Style, Crisis and Authority in American Television*. New Brunswick: Rutgers University Press.
Corner, John
    1997   Television in theory. *Media Culture & Society* 19(2): 247–62
Corner, John and Kay Richardson
    1986   Documentary meanings and the discourse of interpretation. In: John Corner (ed.) *Documentary and the Mass Media*, 141–160. London: Edward Arnold.

Corner, John, Kay Richardson and Nathalie Fenton
　1990　　*Nuclear Reactions.* Luton: John Libbey.
Couldry, Nick
　2000　　*The Place of Media Power: Pilgrims and Witnesses of the Media Age.* London: Routledge.
Couldry, Nick
　2003a　*Media Rituals: A Critical Approach.* London: Routledge.
Couldry, Nick
　2003b　Media meta-capital: extending the range of Bourdieu's field theory. *Theory and Society* 32(5–6): 653–77.
Dayan, Daniel and Elihu Katz
　1992　　*Media Events: The Live Broadcasting of History.* Cambridge, MA: Harvard University Press.
Durkheim, Emile
　1995　　*The Elementary Forms of Religious Life.* (Transl. K. Fields). Glencoe: Free Press.
Durkheim, Emile and Marcel Mauss
　1963　　[1903] *Primitive Classification.* London: Cohen and West.
Fairclough, Norman
　1995　　*Media Discourse.* London: Edward Arnold.
Fairclough, Norman and Ruth Wodak
　1997　　Critical Discourse Analysis. In: Teun van Dijk (ed.), *Discourse as Social Interaction*, 258–271. London: Sage.
Feuer, Jane
　1983　　The concept of live television: ontology as ideology. In: E. Ann Kaplan (ed.), *Regarding Television*, 12–22. Los Angeles: The American Film Institute.
Garfinkel, Harold
　1967　　*Studies in Ethnomethodology.* Englewood Cliffs: Prentice Hall.
Graber, Doris
　1988　　*Processing the News.* 2nd ed. London: Longman.
Hall, Stuart
　1973　　The "Structured Communication" of Events. Stencilled Occasional Paper no. 5. Birmingham: Centre for Contemporary Cultural Studies.
Hall, Stuart
　1980　　Encoding/decoding. In: Hall, Stuart, Dorothy Hobson, Andrew Lowe and Paul Willis (eds.), *Culture, Media, Language*, 128–138. London: Unwin Hyman.
Heritage, John
　1984　　*Garfinkel and Ethnomethodology.* Cambridge: Polity.
Hill, Annette
　2004　　*Reality TV.* London: Routledge.
Iyengar, Shanto and Donald Kinder
　1987　　*News That Matters.* Chicago: Chicago University Press.
Kitzinger, Jenny
　1999　　A sociology of media power: key issues in audience reception research. In: Greg Philo (ed.), *Message Received*, 3–20. Harlow: Longman.
Kubey, Richard and Mihai Csikszentmihalyi
　1990　　*Television and the Quality of Life.* Mahwak, NJ: Lawrence Erlbaum.

Langer, John
    1998   *Tabloid Television*. London: Routledge.
Lazarsfeld, Karl and Robert Merton
    1969   Mass communication, popular taste and organised social action. In: Wilbur Schramm (ed.), *Mass Communications.* 2nd ed., 492–512. Urbana: University of Illinois Press.
Lewis, Justin
    1991   *The Ideological Octopus*. New York: Routledge.
Liebes, Tamar and Elihu Katz
    1990   *The Export of Meaning*. Oxford: Oxford University Press.
Livingstone, Sonia
    1990   *Making Sense of Television*. Oxford: Pergamon.
Lodziak, Konrad
    1987   *The Power of Television*. London: Frances Pinter.
McCombs, Maxwell and Donald Shaw
    1972   The agenda-setting function of the mass media. *Public Opinion Quarterly* 36: 176–187.
Meinhof, Ulrike and Kay Richardson
    1994   Introduction. In: Ulrike Meinhof and Kay Richardson (eds.), *Text, Discourse and Context: Representations of Poverty in Britain*, 1–24. London: Longman.
Meinhof, Ulrike and Theo van Leeuwen
    2000   Viewers' worlds: image, music, text and *The Rock 'n' Roll Years*. In: Ulrike Meinhof and Jonathan Smith (eds.), *Intertextuality and the Media: From Genre to Everyday Life*, 61–75. Manchester: Manchester University Press.
Morgan, David and Nancy Signorielli
    1990   Introduction. In: Nancy Signorielli and David Morgan (eds.), *Cultivation Analysis*, 13–34. Newbury Park: Sage.
Morley, David
    1980   *The "Nationwide" Audience*. London: BFI.
Morley, David
    1986   *Family Television*. London: BFI.
Morley, David
    1992   *Television, Audiences and Cultural Studies*. London: Routledge.
Myers, Greg
    2004   *Matters of Opinion: Talking About Public Issues*. Cambridge: Cambridge University Press.
Needham, Rodney
    1963   Introduction. In: Emile Durkheim and Marcel Mauss, *Primitive Classification*. London: Cohen and West.
Pan, Zhongdan and Gerald Kosicki
    2001   Framing as a strategic action in public deliberation. In: Reese, Stephen, Oscar Gandy and August Grant (eds.), *Framing in the New Media Landscape*, 35–66. Mahwah, NJ: Lawrence Erlbaum.
Philo, Greg
    1990   *Seeing and Believing*. London: Routledge.
Philo, Greg (ed.)
    1999a   *Message Received*. Harlow: Longman.

Philo, Greg
   1999b   Conclusion on media audiences and message reception. In: Greg Philo (ed.), *Message Received*, 282–288. Harlow: Longman.

Rappaport, Roy
   1999   *Ritual and Religion in the Making of Humanity*. Cambridge: Cambridge University Press.

Richardson, Kay
   1994   Interpreting *Breadline Britain*. In: Ulrike Meinhof and Kay Richardson (eds.), *Text, Discourse and Context: Representations of Poverty in Britain*, 93–121. London: Longman.

Root, Jane
   1986   *Open the Box*. London: Comedia.

Scannell, Paddy (ed.)
   1991   *Broadcast Talk*. London: Sage.

Swidler, Ann
   2001   What anchors cultural practices. In: Schatzki, Theodore, Karin K. Cetina and Eike von Sariguy (eds.), *The Practice Turn in Contemporary Theory*. Chicago: Chicago University Press.

Tichi, Cecilia
   1991   *Electronic Hearth: Creating an American Television Culture*. New York: Oxford University Press.

Tolson, Andrew (ed.)
   2001   *Television Talk Shows*. Mahwah, NJ: Lawrence Erlbaum.

van Dijk, Teun
   1991   *Racism and the Press*. London: Routledge.

van Dijk, Teun
   2001   Critical Discourse Analysis. In: Schiffrin, Deborah, Deborah Tannen and Heidi Hamilton (eds.), *The Handbook of Discourse Analysis*, 352–371. Oxford: Blackwell.

van Dijk, Teun and Walter Kintsch
   1983   *Strategies of Discourse Comprehension*. New York: Academic Press.

Vermorel, Fred and Julie Vermorel
   1985   *Starlust*. London: WH Allen.

Wodak, Ruth and Brigitte Busch
   2004   Approaches to media texts. In: John Downing (ed.), *The Sage Handbook of Media Studies*, 105–123. Newbury Park: Sage.

Wodak, Ruth, Rudolf de Cillia, Martin Reisigl and Karin Liebhart
   1999   *The Discursive Construction of National Identity*. Edinburgh: Edinburgh University Press.

Zelizer, Barbie
   1993   *Covering the Body: The Kennedy Assassination, Media and the Collective Memory*. Berkeley: University of California Press.

4. Language, communication and the public sphere: A perspective from feminist critical discourse analysis

Michelle M. Lazar

1. Introduction

The public sphere has occupied a central focus in debates on gender (in)equality. The insistence by feminists in the 1960s and 70s that "the personal is political" highlighted the importance of public dialogue and consciousness of oppressive social conditions experienced routinely by many women as merely personal in the private and intimate spheres. This remains a pertinent issue today in the light of resistive, regressive government policies and social practices in some societies, as well as an abiding concern especially for gay and lesbian people within hetero-patriarchal structures.

Further, women's access and participation in the public sphere – the traditional stronghold of men in most societies – have come to be accepted as key indicators in "measuring" women's emancipation. Undeniably, this has been historically important for women and other politically disadvantaged groups for whom access to sectors of employment, literacy and education, and legal and citizenship rights have been systematically denied. Yet, equality and freedom, defined in liberal terms, have proven to be limited. For in spite of growing visibility of women in the public sphere, including some occupying senior positions in companies and governments, gender discrimination in the public sphere continues. In modern industrialised societies, general awareness of feminism and women's growing presence in the public sphere may have displaced, to some extent, overt forms of sexism. However, it continues to persist covertly through naturalised, deep-seated androcentric assumptions (Lazar 2000, 2005a).

In liberal states, discussions about the "public" have tended to be premised upon a dichotomous division and separation from the "private", instead of viewing them as interconnected. As a result, misguided public policies and perceptions that women's ability to succeed in the public sphere largely depends upon women's personal resources have prevailed, without taking into account the double (sometimes triple) shift work shouldered by many women across the public and private spheres.

This chapter focuses on how language and communication, which are imbricated in the social (Kress 1985; Fairclough and Wodak 1997), constitute, reflect, and challenge gendered power asymmetries which underscore participation in the public and private spheres. The perspective adopted here is from "feminist critical discourse analysis" (FCDA),[1] which critiques from a feminist perspective hierarchically ordered gender structures sustained in/through language and other forms of communication, as part of a radical emancipatory project (Lazar 2005a). In what follows, the key principles of FCDA are outlined, which then are collectively used as the critical feminist lens in discussing the three sets of issues: (i) the private in need of public expression, (ii) the gendered public sphere, and (iii) the public/private dualism. The issues will be discussed in relation to selected examples and case studies on language, communication and gender. The FCDA lens is used both to critique the persistent and prevailing patriarchal social order at the heart of the public and private debate, as well as the liberal reformist perspective (even though embraced by some feminists), as inadequate for a radical emancipatory politics of gender.

2. Principles of Feminist Critical Discourse Analysis

Below is an outline of five interrelated principles of FCDA, which will form the basis for the following discussion on issues of language and communication in terms of the public and private spheres:

2.1. Analytical activism

FCDA is a radical discursive critique of prevailing unequal social arrangements. Because the imbrication of power and ideology in discourse is sometimes not apparent to participants involved in particular social practices, discursive critique from the point of view of critical feminist theorisation and analysis of their interrelation is necessary. The goal of critique is to contest the social status quo in favour of radical emancipation and change, based upon a feminist vision of social justice that opens up possibilities for both women and men as human beings, instead of having gender predetermine and constrain our relationships with others, and our sense of who we are or might become. As a radical emancipatory discourse politics, FCDA is a form of analytical activism.

2.2. Gender as an ideological structure

In patriarchal societies, gender is an ideological structure that divides people into two classes. Based upon sexual difference, the gender structure imposes a social dichotomy of labour and human traits for women and men. Although variable for particular communities and individuals across time and place, the ideological structure of gender systematically privileges men as a social group – accruing to them a "patriarchal dividend" (Connell 1995) – and disadvantaging, excluding and disempowering women as a social group. The prevailing social arrangement is hegemonic in that it appears natural and complementary, and innocuous and consensual, mystifying the hierarchical relations of power at work. Gender permeates social practices and institutions in the public and private spheres both as an interpretive category that enables participants in a community to make sense of and structure their social activities, and as a social relation that enters into and partially constitutes all other social relations and activities (Connell 1987; Flax 1990). Based on the specific asymmetrical meanings of "man" and "woman", and the consequences being assigned to one or the other within actual social practices, such an allocation becomes a constraint on further practices.

2.3. Complexity of gender and power relations

Feminist Critical Discourse Analysis aims to provide contextualised analyses of gender and sexism in contemporary societies in their complex and multiple forms. Complexity refers to current feminist appreciation that the gender structure does not function in isolation, but intersects with other structures of power such as those based on sexuality, ethnicity, age, (dis)ability, social class and position, and geography (notably, the global north, or the "west", in relation to the rest of the world). This means that gender asymmetry is neither materially experienced nor discursively enacted in the same way by (and for) women everywhere. Patriarchy as an ideological system also interrelates with, for example, corporatist and consumerist ideologies.

Multiplicity refers to the variety of modalities, extents, and degrees of explicitness through which power relations are exercised, reflected, maintained and resisted. Along with overt forms of sexism (such as blatant exclusionary gate-keeping practices, physical violence, and verbal harassment/denigration) are subtle and seemingly innocuous forms of power pervasive in modern societies, which are substantively discursive in nature. This form of power is embedded and dispersed throughout networks of relations, is self-regulating, and produces subjects in both senses of the word (Foucault 1977) – although differentially affecting gendered subjects, as well as crystallizing in hegemonic relations of dominance. The effectiveness of modern power (as with hegemony) is that it is mostly cognitive (van Dijk 1998), based on an internalisation of gendered norms and acted out routinely and "naturally" in the texts and talk of everyday life. Relations of power and dominance, however, can be discursively resisted as well as co-opted in a dynamic struggle over securing and challenging the interests at stake.

2.4. Discursive de/construction of gender

Feminist Critical Discourse Analysis takes the view of discourse as one element of the social (Chouliaraki and Fairclough 1999). It takes as the object of analysis those aspects of social practices that are discursive in character: talking and writing, for instance, are part of (and constitutive of) many social practices and events; also, social practices are discursively represented (through texts and talk) in particular ideological ways. The relationship between discourse and the social is dialectical, in which discourse constitutes as well as is constituted by social situations, institutions and structures (Fairclough 1992, passim). The notion of constitution both applies in the sense that every act of meaning-making through (spoken and written) language and other forms of semiosis contributes to the reproduction and maintenance of the social order, and also in the sense of resisting and transforming that order. Relatedly, the concepts of "accomplishment" and "performance", although from different theoretical traditions (from ethnomethodology and poststructuralism, respectively), can be used fruitfully in Feminist Critical Discourse Analysis (see Lazar 2005b; West and Zimmerman 1987), where the active production of social identities and relationships in/ through discourse is emphasised, cognizant though of the particular material conditions and constraints of these discursive actions. Underlying a critical feminist analysis of discourse is also the principle of "gender relationality", which is cued explicitly or implicitly in studies. It refers to the discursive co-constructions of ways of doing and being a "woman" and a "man", vis-à-vis each other, in particular communities of practice, as well as interrelations between forms of masculinity and between forms of femininity within existing gender orders.

2.5. Critical feminist reflexivity

Just as Feminist Critical Discourse Analysis is concerned to raise awareness on how taken-for-granted gender norms and asymmetrical power relations are discursively produced (and can therefore be challenged), critical reflexivity on the take-up of emancipatory knowledge and practice is important. There are two aspects to this. The first concerns institutional reflexivity, both in regard to progressive practices such as the implementation of gender-parity programmes in organisations and schools, as well as in regard to recuperative practices that use feminist values strategically for non- or anti-feminist ends. The second aspect switches the focus to feminist analysts and the need for feminists to be critically reflexive of our own theoretical positions and practices lest these inadvertently contribute to the perpetuation, rather than the eradication, of hierarchically differential treatment of groups of women. At its core is the issue of what we mean by "emancipation". This is because from a critical feminist perspective, where a radical transformation of existing dualistic gender structures is the goal (Grant

1993), a liberal reformist position, even when embraced by some feminists, is inadequate. Indeed, it may be quite easily co-opted by the dominant structures. Also, required is critical distance from our own feminist academic practices in terms of whom we include and exclude through a range of gate-keeping activities.

3. Issues and analyses of the public and private from the perspective of Feminist Critical Discourse Analysis

3.1. The personal is political

"The personal is political" encapsulated second-wave feminist critique of the social dichotomisation between the private and the public, which has resulted in asymmetrical power relations between women and men in the private sphere to be naturalised and obscured from public, political scrutiny. The critique does not intend to jettison a distinction between the private and the public, for self-determination of privacy is an abiding feminist concern, but seeks a balance between the dangers of loss of privacy and the political uses of publicity, which are viewed as necessary for the emancipation and empowerment of subordinate groups (Fraser 1998; Young 1998). Politicising the personal means that any and all matters should be brought into the open for critical, democratic dialogue, instead of predefining the nature of the issues as public versus private, and thence excluding those considered private from public discussion and expression (Benhabib 1998). Among the many private practices that feminists have made into public issues, which will be dealt with in this section in terms of their relatedness to language and communication practices, include naming, and representations of sexual assault against women as well as the sexual division of labour in the intimate sphere. The politicisation of sexist and androcentric assumptions in private practices needs to be considered alongside the appropriation and/or subversion by mainstream patriarchal discourses in the public domain as well.

In the 1970s and 1980s, feminists highlighted linguistic sexism, for instance, in the meaning of pronouns, naming practices and lexical gaps in language. In the case of English, for example, the masculine pronoun that was instituted ever since the eighteenth century to be the "correct" form for gender-indefinite referents is not at all generic as it is purported to be, but refers quite specifically to men. Such a usage, it is found, encodes the "male as norm", as universal, and renders women invisible (Martyna 1983; Bodine 1990). Gender inclusive alternatives (such as "they" or "he or she") have been suggested instead by feminists for contemporary usage. Awareness of the gender bias and the take-up of alternative usages, however, have been greatly variable across communities and individuals using English – from dogged insistence on "conventional" usage that maintains the status quo, to reflection and change in pronoun (and other language) choices, and to the adoption of half measures. The latter is indicated in the following example from West, Lazar and Kramarae (1997), which was taken from the preface of a compendium of protocol for diplomats among the British white upper classes.

> We have been conscious that in the twentieth century for the first time in known history, diplomacy has become in many countries a profession open to both sexes. The English language has not yet provided a grammatically elegant way of dealing with this change. We have, therefore, used the compromise of occasionally employing the "he or (she)" formula to show our absence of prejudice; but its constant repetition would be intolerably tedious, and for this edition, the male pronoun has had, once again, to serve both sexes.

By using the rhetorical strategy of disclaimer ("our absence of prejudice, but …") (cf. van Dijk 1998), the authors of the compendium here demonstrate what may be called "strategic reflexivity". On the one hand, through representations of positive agency attributed to themselves ("we have been conscious"; "we have used the compromise … to show"), the authors portray themselves as socially aware and progressive. Yet, on the other hand, through negative agency attributed to "the English language", the latter is blamed for not keeping up with changed social realities ("has not provided a grammatically elegant way"). Represented thus, it is not the language users' fault for reverting to the "generic" male pronoun for the sake of convenience – as if language users and the language they use do not mutually influence each other. By opting for the disclaimer strategy, therefore, the authors of the compendium remain complicit with the sexist conventions, although manifestly distancing themselves from sexism.

Address terms also reflect sexism at work. Unlike men, women in many cultures are denied an autonomous existence through titles that distinguish them on the basis of marital status – for example Mrs/Miss (English), Madame/Mademoiselle (French), Puan/Cik (Malay), Senora/Senorita (Spanish), and Thirumathi/Kumari (Tamil). In the case of the English language, American feminists coined "Ms" as a neutral equivalent to "Mr" so that in both cases one's sexual (un)availability is not by default public knowledge. As mentioned, the take-up of this has been variable. In mainstream public discourse in Singapore, for instance, although "Ms" is in circulation in some contexts, it is devoid of its intended feminist signification. Either it signifies divorced status for women or is used as a contracted form for "Miss" in the written mode. Out of twelve application and feedback forms I randomly collected in 2005 at banks, hospitals, universities, theatres and public transportation booths, ten had the options printed thus: "Mr/Mrs/Ms", where "Ms" evidently stands for "Miss". (The remaining two forms had this in full: "Mr/Mrs/Miss").[2] Therefore, although the intended neutral title is in use, there is no concomitant change in meaning or mindsets –

a point that has been raised by feminist linguists on the issue of reforming sexism in languages – instead, the title has been co-opted into mainstream discourse and maintains the status quo.

Giving a name to experiences regularly encountered by women as a social group has been one of feminists' achievements in going 'public' on matters considered 'private'. In her study of white, middle class women living in the American suburbia in the 1960s, Friedan (1962) had noted the pervasiveness of a "problem without a name" experienced by many of these women. The notion of the "problem without a name", however, can be extended to describe a range of other practices routinely experienced by women in other social and historical contexts as well. Because of their namelessness, the experiences are either dismissed as imaginary by men (and some women), or endured by women as part of life. Terms such as "chauvinism", "sexism", "sexual harassment", "domestic violence", "date/acquaintance rape" and "marital rape" were coined by feminists over the years to give expression to some of these experiences, and render them open to public scrutiny and redress. Across cultural and national contexts, social and legal penalties for such acts have become, in varying extents, possible as a consequence.

Naming an oppressive practice and highlighting issues of linguistic sexism constitute an important first step. However, unless accompanied by a radical dismantling of dominant institutionalised gender ideologies, social justice for women will continue to be elusive. Studies on representations of sexual assault of women in judiciary settings as well as in the media have shown that although women are the victims (or survivors), the attacks get recontextualised in these institutions by prevailing androcentric assumptions that mitigate the perpetrator's blame and/or question the victim's credibility. Ehrlich's (2001) study of adjudication processes involving a case of acquaintance rape in a university tribunal and a criminal court in Canada, on the one hand, attests to the success in seeking legal/disciplinary action on a 'private', and until quite recently unnamed, problem. Yet, on the other hand, as her analysis shows, the adjudication proceedings deny women justice by diminishing the severity of the action committed by their male perpetrators. Consider the following excerpt (emphasis as in original):

SC: And how did that all take place?
MA: Well, my shirt came off (...)
Q: And when you say your shirt came off, how did your shirt come off?
MA: I mean, I gather that I took it off (...)

Ehrlich argues that the non-personal agency in the unaccussative construction of the perpetrator's (MA) initial response distances him from his actions. It is compounded by his later response ("I gather ..."), which represents him as not having directly experienced the event, thereby reducing his responsibility for it.

The diminished culpability resonates culturally with deep-seated androcentric assumptions of men's naturally uncontrollable sex drive. At the same time, directed at the complainant are such questions as "Did it occur to you that you could lock the door so that they may not return to your room?" and "Why didn't you ask him to leave? ... Why did you let ah what you say happened happen?", which presuppose a legal definition of "active resistance". Ehrlich explains that based upon a theory of "the universal, rational individual", active resistance discounts other forms of resistance exercised by women as passive, and as amounting to consensual activity.

In a separate earlier study on the representation of rape in a British tabloid press, Clark (1992) suggests an implicit patriarchal framework that underlies the newspaper's reports of sexual assault. The conceptual framework distinguishes between "fiend" and "non-fiend" attackers, and between "genuine" and "non-genuine" victims. A fiend is one who attacks a sexually unavailable, "respectable" woman, named by the newspaper as "wife", "mother", "young woman", and "daughter", and a stranger to the attacker. However, a perpetrator is not labelled a fiend when the act is committed against a "sexually available" woman, who is named "blonde", "blonde divorcee" or "unmarried woman". Moreover, when husbands are attackers they are never fully culpable. For example, in a headline such as "hubby kicked no-sex wife out of bed", the attacker is sympathetically represented through affectionate naming, and the blame mitigated. The representations shown in the study not only present women stereotypically in terms of their sexual availability to men, and thus appallingly imply that some women ask to be raped, but also perpetuate the dangerous myth that violent attacks against women are quite rare and only committed by lurking strangers.

The politicisation of the personal has included also the sexual division of labour in the intimate private sphere. Power relations in this realm is often treated as non-existent (Benhabib 1998), which makes natural and unexamined the unremunerated work that women do in the private sphere such as caring for the family, maintaining relationships and running the household. In a set of pro-natalist government advertisements in Singapore, I undertook to show how naturalisation of women's emotional labour in personal relationships was accomplished multimodally through systematic cultivation of intense devotedness to men (boyfriends and husbands) and children, which I termed "other-centredness" (Lazar 2002). This was developed in various ways across a heterosexually-staged narrative life course, so that central in courtship, marriage and motherhood was a normative, other-focused subject position offered to educated Singaporean women as an authentically feminine identity. In courtship, other-centredness was cultivated by getting women invested in romantic love. The following example from an ad addressed to women, for instance, shows how through a series of elaborating clauses, the focus on the romantic other is gradually built up:

"Falling in love.
Having someone to love and care for us.
Someone who shares our hopes and dreams (…)
Someone special who'll make our life more complete."

According to the copy, a romantic relationship is in women's interest, and this entails an emotional reliance upon "someone special" (men, in this context), needed to complete women's lives. (Note that the comparative in "more complete" implies that a woman is actually less complete without a partner). In marriage, an accommodating, enduring love that overlooks the husband's shortcomings is emphasised, as seen in the contrastive sentence pairs such as "Maybe he's no Romeo. But he's my loving one-man show". Finally, on becoming a parent, other-centredness is honed into a self-effacing and sacrificial maternal love. Through narrative sequences in the ads, the 'good' wife and mother is represented as someone who prioritises her husband's or child's desire for a baby. Consider the text in an ad titled "Lonely Child":

"You may give your child the best things that money can buy.
But the most precious gift of all is a brother or a sister."

The presence of the adversative conjunction indicates that the mother's care for her child's welfare is wanting until she provides a sibling. Working along with the copy are visual sequences of a boy looking sad and positioned out of frame in a pose that Goffman (1979: 57) would call "licensed withdrawal", but who visibly cheers up when his mother – fulfilling her ex-centric maternal obligations – returns home with a new-born baby in her arms, whom she gives over to the delighted boy. Ideologically, the cultivation of other-centredness in these representations stands to benefit the state, men and children, but seemingly at the expense of women's own needs and life choices. Furthermore, it is suggested that the ideological potency of this kind of heterosexual feminine identity is that women's discontent (experienced in the domestic sphere, and in their negotiations between the private and the public) becomes difficult to articulate and challenge when at the same time they are bound to others in a labour of love.

3.2. The myth of the neutral public sphere

The ideals of liberalism have long promised women formal equality and emancipation through provision of civil and political rights, and their participation in public and political life. In many industrialised societies today, these rights and access to public and political life have been achieved, to a large extent, and even taken as a given. Yet after many decades, the *full* emancipation of women remains elusive, and the reason for this is that equality and liberty extended to women have been granted on the same terms as men. That is, the yardstick used for women is one that is already set by men, thereby requiring women to play by the rules set by a group with the power to define the norms of practice. Hence, the critical feminist aphorism: 'women who want to be equal to men have no ambition'.

Androcentrism in the public sphere, however, frequently assumes the status of universality, rationality and impartiality, all of which generally contribute to the ethos of professionalism in the public sphere. Yet, as feminists have noted, such claims often belie a totalising perspective that is intolerant of divergent points of view of different groups. The proverbial playing field in the public, in other words, is still not a level one.

Recent studies on language and communication in professional organisations have indicated that with growing numbers of women entering the public sphere of work, some organisations have responded by implementing gender equity programs that would not unfairly discriminate against women. Wodak (2005) reports on a "gender mainstreaming" program adopted in the European Union, which aims to promote comprehensive changes in gender roles and organisational practices. This has enabled women politicians in the European Parliament to negotiate their multiple identities in a range of ways, not usually possible in more rigidly structured institutions. In fact, one of the Members of the European Parliament (MEP) interviewed in Wodak's study reveals how very different she is from a typical MEP:

> "I'm (…) a very special bird in this (…) you don't feel like you fit into sort of a typical MEP (…) I'm not. I'm left I'm a woman I'm Swedish and I'm also everything – everything's wrong (laughs)".

Through self-irony, self-reflection and assertiveness, as Wodak notes, this woman has been able to discursively re-define as positive traditionally negative and marginalising social attributes.

Other instances of gender related initiatives in response to the growing presence of women in the public workforce include changing management models and affirmative action policies in institutions. Martín-Rojo and Esteban (2005) report on an emerging relational management model in Spanish companies, which is different from traditional hierarchical models associated with masculine management styles. The implication of the shift is that it will potentially benefit women, as the relational styles of interaction are culturally associated with female sociality. McElhinny's (1998) study indicates that as a result of affirmative action measures implemented in an American city (Pittsburgh) there has been a steady increase in numbers of women police officers in an otherwise male-dominated profession.

However, in spite of these various overtly progressive institutional measures to equitably integrate women into public organisations, androcentrism tacitly (and manifestly) prevails in the cultural norms and social interactions within these workplaces. Wodak's quantitative findings reveal that in the EU, representation of women "at the top" is uneven across member states and that women are grossly underrepresented at the highest levels of decision-making. In the Spanish context, regardless of a changing trend in corporate management models, Martín Rojo and Gómez-Esteban find that the accepted communicative style of power and authority is still definitively masculine in terms of tone of voice, intonation in giving orders and a preference for direct speech acts. Accordingly women managers are criticised for not getting their communicative styles "right". Either they are caricatured as too "soft" or "hard" as revealed in the following assessment by a group of male employees of female bosses:

> "Well there is, for example, the typical conservative and *shit-scared* one, who's just not up to it, poor thing. And then there's the *super-aggressive* one, who steps on your foot as she walks by you, and *screams at you*, to boot" [emphasis as in original]

As a result, it is a challenge for women managers in Spanish companies, whose authority is undermined by peers and subordinates alike, who do not respect or take them seriously.

In the case of the Pittsburgh police force, McElhinny (1998) shows that female police officers learn to integrate into their workplace by adopting interactional styles that are culturally masculine, although not viewed as such but rather as part of professional police conduct. The approved interactional conduct includes "objective" non-involvement and emotional reserve. As one female police officer puts it:

> "*When I'm at work I I always feel like I have to be so* (.) *so like gruff you know.* (umhm) *And normally I'm not like that* (...). *Sometimes I try to be like such a hard ass. I I don't smile as much*" [emphasis as in original, ellipsis added].

Women officers' adoption of interactional behaviour of this nature, augmented by the rejection of traditional practices of femininity at work (e.g. attention to one's physical appearance), according to McElhinny, redefine and resist hegemonic interpretations of gender. One could argue, however, that instead of constituting a radical reinterpretation of gender, women officers in this hegemonic social order seem obliged to adapt to normatively masculine styles, albeit misrecognised as "doing professionalism" in this context, or else risk disapproval by their male (and female) peers ("as being unable to work the job", as McElhinny puts it).

The public sphere, of course, refers not only to actual, but also virtual spaces of general access. In recent decades, the internet has ushered in a new medium for public expression and exchange (see also Jones, this volume). In the absence of non-verbal status cues and the preclusion of verbal markers of dominance such as interruptions, the internet represents a potentially democratic public sphere, as envisaged by Habermas, for unfettered public dialogue and debate on issues of common interest. The reality at present, however, is that cyberspace, too, appears to have become generally a male stronghold, with boys and men overwhelmingly using, controlling and administering its rules of conduct (West, Lazar, and Kramarae 1997). Even in contexts where women are the purported authorities, for example, in electronic discussion groups focused on issues of concern to women, men appear to be in control. West, Lazar and Kramarae (1997) found that in one such discussion list, 63 per cent of the participants comprised of men, their messages received more responses than women's, and their interests dominated discussions. Similarly, another study by Herring, Johnson, and DiBenedetto (1998) reported that in a women-friendly academic list, women's overall contributions came up to only 30 per cent of the total postings. Yet on one occasion when, for two days, women's contributions on a feminist topic exceeded men's, this became perceived as a threat. The discussion got disrupted by complaints from some of the men, who threatened to unsubscribe from the list, claiming that they were being "silenced", and that the women's tones were "vituperative" and "unreasonable". Herring, Johnson, and DiBenedetto (1998: 202) found this to be unsubstantiated. If anything, they found that the only message indisputably negative in tone was posted by one of the men, who

> accused women on the list of "posting without thinking [their contributions] through carefully first", of levelling "charges" [rather than questions] at the men, and in general, of "bashing", "guilt-tripping", and "bullying" men who didn't toe the strict feminist line.

The study supports Spender's (1979, 1980) earlier observations based on face-to-face interactions that, in general, even 30 per cent of talk by women is considered as speaking "too much", and that, in particular, when women express feminist views in public, no matter how rationally and calmly, they tend to be perceived by some men as hostile and emotional.

While critique of androcentric bias in the public sphere is rightfully a major feminist concern, feminist self-reflexivity of our own public practices ought to also merit critical attention, if our goal is radical emancipation for all women. I shall refer here to a discussion thread on a gender and language list, which offers a good example, both of feminists' critique of the male dominated public sphere – in this case, in the academic linguistic sub-field of sociolinguistics – as well as feminists' self-critique of exclusionary practices among women in the academic public sphere. The discussion, titled "female sociolinguists", ran from 24 May 2005 until 2 June 2005, and comprised a total of 27 posts (twenty-four by women, two by men, and one an anonymous forward). The thread began as a critique on the substantial bias towards "white, Anglophone (or European) male academics" noticed in the entries of a newly released sociolinguistics dictionary. The initiator of the thread commented that "[i]t's not like there aren't excellent female and/or non-white researchers out there" and ended by asking fellow List members "How do you feel about this? If you support my view, who would you like to see included?" Except for the first respondent, who overtly agreed with the dearth of female representation in sociolinguistics references before she proceeded to offer a list of women's names for inclusion, others simply supplied a name or a list of names without commenting further on the male bias. Clearly for this group of feminist-conscious subscribers, the issue was undisputed.

Although the fact of androcentrism in sociolinguistics references was not in contest, the subsequent exercise of nominating female sociolinguists for inclusion in the coveted reference list was critiqued by four of the women on the discussion forum, who pointed out that neither the criteria for the nominations nor the definition(s) of sociolinguistics were made evident in the contributions. Their use of metaphorical and analogical expressions in their posts highlighted the profoundly exclusionary practice at work in the feminist naming [italics mine]:

> "some kind of weird *popularity contest*, the rules of which never seem to be clearly articulated by anyone involved"
>
> "now we know who happens to be in some people's *radar* today, and the more names that pile up the more glaring the omissions"
>
> "the naming (…) has been hilarious, as if it was some *party invitation list*"

Indeed, what had emerged from most of the initial posts were names of female sociolinguists from the English-speaking North. Consequently, a few posts asked for the inclusion of scholars working on languages other than English and one appealed that female sociolinguists from the South not be forgotten. Signalling a discourse of critical awareness, therefore, the critics called the exercise of feminist naming itself "a nice object lesson in academic politics", and as indicative of the "operative disciplinary hegemony". In fact, one of the four women pointed out the ironically masculinist and elitist practice that underlay this particular exercise. She wrote

> The name request is at the heart of the old boys system – Harvard uses it to initiate searches, CASBS uses it to develop a list of potential fellows – and we know how badly (or how well, depending on your perspective) it works in those kinds of cases.

The critical reflexivity demonstrated in these posts point to the deeply exclusionary practices in the academic public sphere, misrecognised and perpetuated as normal and self-evident professional activities. There are no easy solutions to this dilemma, but the first step, as shown by this case, lies in recognising that professional practices are not neutral and objective and that their biases need to be called into question. As feminists struggle to break hierarchical relations of power between men and women, critical self-reflexivity of this kind must be a safeguard against inadvertently re-producing hierarchical relations among groups of women in the public sphere.

3.3. The imbrication of the public and the private

Any theory of the public sphere and public dialogue must presuppose some distinction between the public and the private (Benhabib 1998). The patriarchal ideological structure based upon the gendered opposition between men and women has been mapped onto the public and private spheres, such that these too have been historically conceptualised as binary opposites. Whereas the public sphere, traditionally associated with men, has been characterised as rational, impartial and universal, the private sphere, conventionally associated with "female activities" like housework, childbearing and care for the young and the elderly, has been characterised as emotional, personal and particular. Consequently, as Benhabib (1998) has noted, matters of the private sphere have been cut off and kept from the public agenda in the liberal state (see my discussion above).

The gendered division of public and private life has carried into gender-typed occupational sectors in the public domain. In Singapore, construction work, operating public transportation, and working as engineers and doctors are largely considered "men's jobs" either because of the physical strength required, or the outdoor nature of the job, or the long, irregular hours spent at work outside the home. The latter got cited as the main reason in the government's discourse and practice of maintaining a reduced quota (that was only recently rescinded) on the numbers of female students admitted into the medical faculty in Singapore's national university. According to the discourse, women, especially after marriage and motherhood, could not possibly be as dedicated to the requirements of the profession as men and, therefore, it would be wasteful of the state's resources to invest in the education and training of female doctors. Instead of working towards eradicating the distinction between public and private responsibilities along gender lines, the government opted to react to the conflict between women's domestic duties and medical practice by reinforcing traditional gender roles.

Production line factory work, domestic help, teaching and nursing, however, are all 'women's jobs', for repetitive tasks and jobs that require care-giving and nurturance are considered natural extensions of work that women do at home. The commercially successful 'Singapore Girl' (the global marketing icon for Singapore Airlines SIA) is a case in point, where women's domesticity is made saleable for public consumption. As the lyrics for one of SIA's television commercials sung in a male voice (and from a mate perspective) goes:

> "Let me share your gentle smile. Give me all your caring. Singapore Girl. You're a great way to fly".

Clad in a batik print sarong kebaya uniform, created by French designer Pierre Balmain, the "Singapore Girl" also indexes an orientalist fantasy of a stereotypical "Asian femininity". Female flight attendants selected, among other things, for their appearance (height, complexion, youth and slenderness) have been expected, since the 1970s, to uniformly perform the represented stereotype of the petite and demure, warm and attentive Asian woman, who is always willing to serve with a smile.

A significant implication of the division between public and private life is that the domains have been kept separate and unrelated, whereas critical feminists would argue for the need to view the two as mutually imbricated. Liberal theorists have steadfastly believed that social provision of equal opportunities to gain literacy and education is key for women's liberty and empowerment in societies. However, without attending to the relationship between the provision of opportunities in the public and the lived, material realities of women's lives in the private, the emancipatory goal is seriously misguided. Rockhill's (1994) study, based on life history interviews with working class Hispanic adults learning English in Los Angeles, illustrates this point well. The mainstream official American discourse equates communicative literacy in English with liberty, and holds the view that because literacy programs are provided, it is up to "rational" individuals to avail themselves of these opportunities and rights. Conversely, non-participation or absence from sustained participation is a reflection of individuals' lack of motivation and unwillingness to learn, and represent a threat to the American tradition of liberty and development. Such a universalistic liberal view fails to recognise its own ethnocentrism, and overlooks the situated differences of gender, ethnicity and culture. Rockhill's (1994) findings reveal that contrary to the official discourse, the Hispanic adults are willing to learn English; women especially yearn to do so: "God willing, I will learn one day" is a common refrain she found in her interviews with them. At play, though, is a gendered politics of literacy, whereby the extent of women's literacy practices, including participation in schools, is hampered by family relationships. Whereas the Hispanic men are said to "own the public", Hispanic women's access to the public is constrained by the men in their lives, who control their movements and prevent them from attending classes for fear that an (English) educated woman would challenge their authority or leave them. A vicious cycle for women thus is set in motion. Because women have limited access to mainstream public life, they have fewer opportunities to acquire English, which limits the types of jobs available to them; jobs which, in turn, do not provide opportunities to learn and use the language confidently. For these women, the liberal concept of "right", which underlies the public official discourse, is alien. Instead, they experience the learning of English as a desire which offers the promise of a way out of their working-class lives. However, often the desire must be put aside because the family's needs come first. In the following excerpt, the woman reframes the experience of success in terms of the achievements and desires of others, and not her own:

> "I consider myself to be a successful woman because I went to the school and they told me that my son was the best and he likes to study. That is a triumph for me. And then, my husband says to me, 'My work is going better and better.' This is also a success for me."

The treatment of the public sphere as divorced from the private also has differential entailments for the way women may negotiate those dual spaces compared to men. The differences were documented in another study related to the Singaporean government advertising campaign that I earlier discussed (Lazar 2002). Although the public and private spheres are separate, the representations show that the negotiation between them is fairly smooth and unproblematic for men. They could concentrate their energies full-time on their careers, without at the same time having to assume responsibilities full-time at home as well. As shown in the advertisements, fathers can decide on the type and the extent of their involvement at home, which characteristically are fun and leisurely type activities with children.[3] Because the cultural assumption is that Singapore men are the primary breadwinners, their absenteeism from home on account of their professional careers is represented as normal and expected. Note, for instance, how this is presupposed by the concessive adjunct and the abstract agency in "even though my work takes me away, my children are my hope and joy supreme". The representations indicate the positive effect children have on fathers, but not the effect of fathers' absence on children. In fact, the central message is that men stand to personally and professionally benefit from having a family, as portrayed in the clauses where through the selection of active material processes and causative constructions, "family life" is the helping, enabling agent and men are the recipients:

> "Family life has made my life really good."
> "It also provides stability, encouragement and support (…) Isn't that what you need for a successful career?"
> "It's broadened my horizon."
> "It gives you a direction, a purpose. And most of all it gives you a future."

The negotiation between domains, however, is remarkably different for women. Whereas for men the relationship is relatively harmonious, the analysis shows that for women it is fraught with tension. Consider the following clauses:

> "I'm really excited about parenthood, but I also love my job."
> "How will you divide your time between the kids, housework and the office?"

In the first example, the presence of the adversative conjunction cues the presupposition that the two interests are mutually conflicting. In the second case, such a question may be asked of women (but not men) because of the gendered cultural presupposition that women are primarily responsible for the home. As these examples show, women who work full-time outside the home also have full-time domestic commitments, and must learn to "balance" the two (something never broached in the ads for men):

"One of my major concerns right now is balancing family and career".
"(...) I'm sure you'll do very well, Lin. But do balance your career with a family."

The representations further show that mothering (unlike fathering) requires care work that is intensive and mundane, and neglect of the home on account of their professional careers carries the sanction of being labelled a 'bad' mother. The analysis, therefore, shows not only that the public and private spheres are gendered, but that their dichotomisation is not as challenging for men (for they can maintain and experience the public and private separately), as it is for women (for whom the separation, and thus the balance, of the two is complex).

It is no wonder that the double-shift undertaken by women in many parts of the world, therefore, often results in conflicts of interest and exhaustion for them. In October 2003, the *New York Magazine* ran an article titled "The Opt-Out Revolution", in which the writer, Belkin, reported on how some professional career women in the USA were leaving the public sphere of work as a consequence. The introduction to the article read:

> Many high-powered women today don't ever hit the glass ceiling, choosing to leave the workplace for motherhood. Is this the failure of one movement or the beginning of another?

The question points to the shortcomings of liberal feminism, as I have discussed, reflected in the article of women's dissatisfaction with public work life once they have got there. The latter part of the question entertains the possibility that professionally accomplished women's rejection of the workplace, by "opting out" of it, is the start of a new "revolution". However, by presenting the public sphere per se as problematic, Belkin overlooks the rigid dichotomisation between public and private life; a separation that does not fit the lived experiences of many women, especially mothers. In other words, that women are leaving the public workplace is symptomatic of a structural failure, and is not simply a 'failure' of (liberal) feminism that had enabled women's entry into a domain previously denied to them. Therefore, women's exit from the public workforce does nothing to challenge the gendered, dualistic structures of social life; indeed, it perpetuates the normativeness of those structures. This then can hardly be considered a revolution. By way of substantiating this viewpoint, I shall offer a short critique of the "opt-out" discourse in the article. First, an analysis of the narratives of the women whom Belkin interviewed shows that the women's career pursuits hit a snag in their life trajectories when they became mothers. The "resolution" in their life stories (following Labov and Waletsky's [1967] narrative categories) is represented by them leaving their full-time professional careers. For example,

> One night she and her husband sat down, and he asked, "What is the ultimate goal?"
> "In theory", she answered, "the goal is to become a partner" [in her law firm]
> "Does your life get better or worse if you become a partner?"
> "Well, financially it gets better, but in terms of my actual life, it gets worse."

And that is when Brokaw quit. She now cares full time for that eldest daughter, as well the other two children who followed. "I wish it had been possible to be the kind of parent I want to be and continue with my legal career", she says, "but I wore myself out trying to do both jobs well."

Second, the decision to leave the workforce is emphasised throughout the article as a personal "choice":

"'This play group is the reason I feel so happy with my choice."
"Talk to any professional woman who has made this choice"
"This is not a trap. This is a choice."

Although having options and being able to make self-determined choices are unarguably positive (indeed, a goal of feminism), there needs to be recognition that structural constraints make this a limited choice, and the decision to quit unsurprising. More importantly, from these statements as well as in the women's narratives, what is not questioned is that this is a choice that primarily women make. Also unchallenged is the underlying assumption that the family is primarily women's concern. Third, the phrase "opt-out revolution" masks the fact that not all women can choose to leave as a result of work and life conflict. All the women interviewed were of privileged backgrounds: highly educated and professionally successful middle-class women, with husbands earning substantial incomes. Clearly the same cannot be said about women from low income households, and who are the main or sole providers. Finally, although the women interviewed recognised that the relationship between work and home life is different for women than for men (cf. Lazar 2000), their explanations were based on essentialist arguments of biology and evolution, and a simple transference from biological to sociological imperatives. Belkin reports on one woman's viewpoint:

"'It's all in the M.R.I.' – of studies that show the brains of men and women 'light up' differently when they think and feel. And those different brains, [Sarah Amsbary] argues, inevitably make different choices".

This goes to show the powerful hold of dominant gender ideology, which through people's internalisation (women and men alike), keeps entrenched the normalcy of the gendered public/private split. Further, through such media reports, the gender assumptions and stereotypes are unwittingly kept in constant circulation, and thus are perpetuated.

4. Conclusion

Pertinent to this chapter were two interrelated social dichotomies that have been central to issues of language and communication: the oppositional division between the public and private, and the dualistic gender organisation and entailments of that divide. Underlining the dichotomisation of the social structures and practices, as we have seen, are asymmetrical relations of power between women and men that are often obscured discursively as natural, commonsensical and innocuous. Yet the lived, material implications, as discussed, are very real and profound for different groups of women. For example, in terms of possibilities for access to and participation in literacy and educational opportunities (which could enable women to achieve some measure of self-determination); having to fit into androcentrically-defined professional work-styles that require women to accommodate their interactional behaviour accordingly; shouldering a largely unacknowledged double-shift in the workplace and in the home; having their experiences and unremunerated work at home made invisible; and being denied an autonomous existence as a result of keeping private issues off the public agenda.

As discussed, the dominant gender ideologies are enshrined institutionally in that they are systematically regulated, but not in the sense that they are imposed from "out there". Rather, the potency is in their internalisation and acceptance by both women and men in their everyday communities of practice. An emancipatory discourse politics, therefore, is important for mobilising theory to create critical awareness for resistance and change of existing social structures and practices within different communities and contexts. This must be an emancipatory politics that is not only alert to co-optations by dominant structures, but also exercises critical self-reflexivity on its practices.

Notes

1 The focus of this chapter is on Feminist Critical Discourse Analysis, a perspective at the nexus of feminist studies and Critical Discourse Analysis, which is used here to discuss and interrogate issues of language, communication and the public/private. It is neither the aim nor within the scope of this chapter to provide an overview or development of the gender and language field. The reader is referred to other sources for this, for example, West, Lazar, and Kramsrae 1997; Wodak 1997, and Holmes and Meyerhoff 2003.
2 Additionally, "Dr" was sometimes included in the list. So, too, "Mdm", short for "Madam", a title conventionally used in Singapore for and by married women who do no adopt their husbands' surname.
3 The association of fathering with fun and leisure has been similarly observed by Lupton and Barclay (1997) and Sunderland (2002) in the British context.

References

Belkin, Lisa
    2003   The Opt-Out Revolution, *The New York Times Magazine*.
Benhabib, Seyla
    1998   Models of public space: Hannah Arendt, the liberal tradition, and Jürgen Habermas. In: Joan B. Landes (ed.), *Feminism, the Public and the Private*, 65–99. Oxford: Oxford University Press.
Bodine, Ann
    1990   Androcentrism in prescriptive grammar: singular "they", self-indefinite "he", and "he or she". In: Deborah Cameron (ed.), *The Feminist Critique of Language: A Reader*, 124–138. London: Routledge.
Chouliaraki, Lilie and Norman Fairclough
    1999   *Discourse in Late Modernity: Rethinking Critical Discourse Analysis*. Edinburgh: Edinburgh University Press.
Clark, Kate
    1992   The linguistics of blame: representations of women in the *The Sun's* reporting of crimes of sexual violence. In: Michael Toolan (ed.), *Language, Text and Context*, 206–224. London: Routledge.
Connell, Robert W.
    1995   *Masculinities*. Berkeley: University of California Press.
Connell, Robert W.
    1987   *Gender and Power: Society, the Person and Sexual Politics*. Stanford, CA: Stanford University Press.
Ehrlich, Susan
    2001   *Representing Rape: Language and Sexual Consent*. London: Routledge.
Fairclough, Norman
    1992   *Discourse and Social Change*. Cambridge: Polity Press.
Fairclough, Norman and Ruth Wodak
    1997   Critical discourse analysis. In: Teun A. van Dijk (ed.), *Discourse as Social Interaction*, 258–284. London: Sage.
Flax, Jane
    1990   Postmodernism and gender relations in feminist theory. In: Linda J. Nicholson (ed.), *Feminism/Postmodernism*, 39–62. New York: Routledge.
Foucault, Michel
    1977   *Discipline and Punish*. London: Allen Lane.
Fraser, Nancy
    1998   Sex, lies, and the public sphere: reflections on the confirmation of Clarence Thomas. In: Joan B. Landes (ed.), *Feminism, the Public and the Private*, 314–337. Oxford: Oxford University Press.
Friedan, Betty
    1962   *The Feminine Mystique*. New York: Norton.
Goffman, Erving
    1979   *Gender Advertisements*. London: Macmillan.
Grant, Judith
    1993   *Fundamental Feminism: Contesting the Core Concepts of Feminist Theory*. New York: Routledge.

Herring, Susan C., Deborah A. Johnson and Tamra DiBenedetto
  1998   Participation in electronic discourse in a "feminist" field. In: Jennifer Coates (ed.), *Language and Gender: A Reader*, 197–210. Oxford: Blackwell.
Holmes, Janet and Miriam Meyerhoff
  2003   *The Handbook of Language and Gender.* Malden, MA: Blackwell.
Kress, Gunther
  1985   *Linguistic Processes in Sociocultural Practice.* Victoria: Deakin University Press.
Labov, William and Joshua Waletzky
  1967   Narrative analysis: oral versions of personal experiences. In: June Helm (ed.), *Essays on the Verbal and Visual Art*, 12–44. Seattle, WA: University of Washington Press.
Lazar, Michelle M.
  2000   Gender, discourse and semiotics: The politics of parenthood representations. *Discourse & Society* 11(3): 373–400.
Lazar, Michelle M.
  2002   Consuming personal relationships: The achievement of feminine self-identity through other-centredness. In: Lia Litosseliti and Jane Sunderland (eds.), *Gender Identity and Discourse Analysis*, 111–128. Amsterdam: Benjamins.
Lazar, Michelle M.
  2005a   Politicizing gender in discourse: Feminist Critical Discourse Analysis as political perspective and praxis. In: Michelle M. Lazar (ed.), *Feminist Critical Discourse Analysis: Gender, Power and Ideology in Discourse*, 1–28. Basingstoke: Palgrave.
Lazar, Michelle M.
  2005b   Performing state fatherhood: The remaking of hegemony. In: Michelle M. Lazar (ed.), *Feminist Critical Discourse Analysis: Gender, Power and Ideology in Discourse*, 139–163. London: Palgrave.
Lupton, Deborah and Lesley Barclay
  1997   *Constructing Fatherhood: Discourses and Experiences.* London: Sage.
Martín Rojo, Luisa and Concepción Gómez Esteban
  2005   The gender of power: The female style in labour organizations. In: Michelle M. Lazar (ed.), *Feminist Critical Discourse Analysis: Gender, Power and Ideology in Discourse*, 61–89. London: Palgrave.
Martyna, Wendy
  1983   Beyond the he/man approach: The case for nonsexist language. In: Thorne Barrie, Cheris Kramarae and Nancy Henley (eds.), *Language, Gender and Society*, 25–37. Rowley, MA: Newbury House.
McElhinny, Bonnie
  1998   "I don't smile much anymore": affect, gender and the discourse of Pittsburgh police officers. In: Jennifer Coates (ed.), *Language and Gender: A Reader*, 309–327. Oxford: Blackwell.
Rockhill, Kathleen
  1994   Gender, language and the politics of literacy. In: Janet Maybin (ed.), *Language and Literacy in Social Practice: A Reader*, 233–251. Clevedon: Multilingual Matters.

Spender, Dale
    1979   Language and sex differences. In: *Osnabrücker Beiträge zur Sprachtheorie: Sprache and Geschlecht* II: 38–59.
Spender, Dale
    1980   *Man Made Language*. London: Pandora Press.
Sunderland, Jane
    2002   Baby entertainer, bumbling assistant and line manager: discourses of paternal identity in parentcraft texts. In: Lia Litosseliti and Jane Sunderland (eds.), *Gender Identity and Discourse Analysis*, 293–324. Amsterdam: Benjamins.
van Dijk, Teun A.
    1998   *Ideology: A Multidisciplinary Approach*. London: Sage.
West, Candace and Don Zimmerman
    1987   Doing gender. *Gender & Society* 1(2): 125–51.
West, Candace, Michelle M. Lazar and Cheris Kramarae
    1997   Gender in discourse. In: Teun A. van Dijk (ed.), *Discourse as Social Interaction*, 119–143. London: Sage.
Wodak, Ruth
    1997   Introduction: some important issues in the research of gender and discourse. In: Ruth Wodak (ed.), *Gender and Discourse*, 1–23. London: Sage.
Wodak, Ruth
    2005   Gender mainstreaming and the European Union: interdisciplinarity, gender studies and CDA. In: Michelle M. Lazar (ed.), *Feminist Critical Discourse Analysis: Gender, Power and Ideology in Discourse*, 90–113. London: Palgrave.
Young, Iris M.
    1998   Impartiality and the civic public: some implications of feminist critiques of moral and political theory. In: Joan B. Landes (ed.), *Feminism, the Public and the Private*, 421–447. Oxford: Oxford University Press.

II. Language and communication in business

5. Advertisements and Public Relations

Guy Cook

1. Definitions

Advertisements (ads) and public relations communications (PR) are difficult to define, and the relation between them is complex and changing.

1.1. Ads

As a starting point, we might say that a prototypical ad has the following features. It is a brief high-budget, carefully-designed, multi-modal act of communication and widely-distributed through TV, posters or print. It is initiated by a big business, and attempts to sell a product or service by associating it with desirable outcomes for the purchaser, through the presentation of some positive image, person, or fictional vignette.

Such prototypical ads are characterised by maximum exploitation of the linguistic code and its interaction with other modes. The form of the linguistic message – distinctive letter shapes, rhythm, innovative lexis and grammar, puns and memorable phrases – is integral to the effect of the whole. A recent British television chocolate-bar ad displayed some of these typical characteristics. A young couple are shown sitting side by side on a beach. The woman is unwrapping a Mars Bar. The man edges tentatively closer as though shy about a first kiss. Then he suddenly leans forward and bites off the end of the Mars Bar. Up come the punning words (written in the product's distinctive calligraphy)

Love Bite

and then the product's latest slogan:

Mars. Pleasure you can't measure

Such uses of rhythm and rhyme are almost as old as advertising itself. An earlier product slogan was

A Mars a day
Helps you work, rest and play.

And the very name "Mars Bar" has internal rhyme. This earlier slogan illustrates another common advertising technique, allusion to another text: in this case the proverb

An apple a day
keeps the doctor away

The echo is achieved both through the repeated structure (*An x a day*) of the first line, and the identical rhythm of the whole.

It is ads of this kind which most readily come to mind, on which the greatest amount of money is spent (AA 2005), and which are the subject of the majority of academic studies of advertising language (to be discussed in detail below).

Such ads are of particular interest to applied linguistics, as we shall see. Yet the term "advertisement" embraces acts of communication which depart from this initial description in a variety of ways. Firstly, there is a distinction to be made between "big ads" and "small ads"[1] – numerically the largest category. In the latter it is typically individuals rather than businesses who are selling something. Small ads are not so widely distributed, nor so often repeated as big ads, and usually their focus is upon factual information, couched in prosaic and formulaic terms, without artistic embellishment (Bruthiaux 1996) – though a notable sub-category is the "lonely hearts ad", seeking a relationship, and prone to more creative uses of language (Thorne and Coupland 1998). Secondly, among big ads, there is a distinction to be made between those selling products or services, and those which exhort their recipients to do something other than spend money, such as: vote Republican, drive safely, use condoms, stop smoking, join the army and so forth. A further departure from our initial characterisation is that not all ads use positive images. Several high-profile campaigns, notably by Benetton (Falk 1997), have contained very negative images: a teenage mercenary soldier holding a human bone, an AIDS death, the electric chair. Then, not all big ads occur in print or TV. They are found in all the major media, notably including the internet and in the mail, but also, in "ambient advertising", in unpredictable places too. There have been ads on the side of cows, in vapour trails in the sky, on scraps of paper looking like banknotes dropped in the back of taxis. Lastly, it is hard to draw a line between ads and other promotional genres: information leaflets, packaging, labels, instructions, shop signs, logos on clothing etc. There is even a sense in which any object (such as a can of Coca Cola) or activity (playing a song) is an ad for itself.

Such broad definitions of ads raise the problematic distinction between advertising, branding and marketing, which varies depending on how these three terms are defined. In a narrow sense, a brand is

> a name, sign or symbol used to identify items or services of the seller(s) and to differentiate them from goods of competitors.[2]

and famous examples would be the McDonalds golden arches or the loopy lettered Coca Cola.[3] These logos (if that is all a brand is taken to be) appear within adverts. But in a broader sense the brand is the whole identity of the product or company:

> A set of assets (or liabilities) linked to a brand's name and symbol that adds to (or subtracts from) the value provided by a product or service (Aaker 1996: 7–8)

In this larger sense, advertising is only a constituent of the much larger activity of branding. The relationship of advertising to marketing on the other hand is more straightforward.

> Marketing is the process of planning and executing the conception, pricing, promotion, and distribution of ideas, goods, services, organizations, and events to create and maintain relationships that will satisfy individual and organizational objectives. (Boone and Kurtz 1998)

If we accept this definition, then advertising is a constituent of it, albeit the most glamorous and high-profile one.

Thus ads are a particularly diverse and various genre with complicated relations to other promotional activities. Any attempt to define ads precisely is likely to be easily refuted. The principle of surprise and unpredictability which guides their design, together with their tendency to imitate or attach themselves to other genres, creates many problematic cases. For these reasons it is preferable to talk of prototype definitions (Rosch 1977) of the kind with which I began, rather than any checklist of defining features.[4]

1.2. Public Relations

PR presents similar problems for definition, and has a similar tendency to merge with other genres. We might say for example that PR is "mostly a category of persuasive communications done by interests in the political economy to advance themselves materially and ideologically through markets and public policy making" (Moloney 2000: 60). Yet, as Moloney also points out, any such characterisation is inevitably fuzzy at the edges as almost any organisational communication might come under such a heading. In addition, there is some overlap between PR and propaganda, though the connection is either vigorously denied or simply ignored by PR practitioners (Moloney 2000: 85–86).

Yet despite this inherent fuzziness, PR is readily recognisable, and perceived as a genre. There are PR departments within organisations. It has a growing workforce, its own institutions,[5] rapidly expanding university degrees, its own journals,[6] and a growing literature – both laudatory (e.g. Grunig et al. 1992) and condemnatory (e.g. Stauber and Rampton 1995).

Given its scope and variety, it may be best to begin with a prototype as we did with ads, and to specify certain typical – but not necessary – features. Prototypical PR emanates from a large business and is primarily intended to present that organisation in a favourable light. It may do this either by talking directly (*"About Us"* or *"Our Mission"* etc.)[7] or by using some event or development described in a press release (*"McDonald's launches new low fat Salad dressings"*) as a hook on which to hang positive comments (*"These new choices reflect a wider culture of change at McDonald's"*).[8] There is emphasis on the culture of the organisation, its trustworthiness and moral responsibility, on social, health, and environmental issues, and on responsiveness to shareholders, customers and society in general (*"the community"*, *"communities"*) with emphasis on listening and dialogue. The tone is conversational and familiar, though treading very carefully where there are legal implications. These emphases lead to certain lexical and linguistic characteristics. The organisation is "we", though it is unclear who is included in this term (owners, managers, employees) or who is the actual author of the PR (presumably the corporation's PR department though there may be quotations from the Chief Executive Officer or other company officials); the addressee is either vaguely "you" or indeterminate (see Koller, this volume). There is frequent use of evaluative terms with positive connotations but imprecise denotation ('high-quality products (…) beneficial to our customers and to the environment (…) sound and innovative science (…) thoughtful and effective stewardship');[9] intensifiers ('we place strong emphasis on personal accountability');[10] measures, comparatives and superlatives without reference points (lower fat dressings, fewer calorie dressings); mitigators of numerals ('Some 10 million people shop with us each week in over 375 stores'),[11] a penchant for innovation ('we aim to deliver best-in-class financial results') and catchy metaphors (contemporary university PR talks of 'enterprise hubs, incubators for ideas, pump-priming funding, drilling down assessments', and 'seed-corn research').[12] Many of these favoured "PR words and constructions" can be omitted without altering propositional content. Consider the adverb "simply" in simply+imperative as in, for example 'Simply tell us where you want to go. We'll search for the lowest fares offered (…)'.[13] (Emphases added throughout.)

2. Ads and Public Relations compared

While in ads, expensive limited space and time motivate both an economical use of language and maximum exploitation of multimodal communication, PR is in contrast typically more verbose while less witty and creative. Its purpose is also more general than ads, to the point of vagueness. Though the overall perlocution is clear (to persuade the receiver to view the organisation favourably) there is often no clear illocution in PR as there is in ads ("Buy this", "Do that").

Nevertheless, the boundary between the two genres is by no means always clear, nor their relation to other related activities and genres such as sponsoring, marketing, branding, and – more controversially – propaganda. Big ads, as they imply a favourable view of the manufacturer, might seem in a sense to be simply a sub-category of PR. Such a simple relation, however, belies the reality. Prototypical advertising is markedly different from prototypical PR: more precise, concise, and more creative. This makes it the higher profile and probably the more respected of the two discourses (Moloney 2000: 28) with PR following and learning from advertising rather than *vice versa*. Recently however, as many commentators have observed, the distinction between ads and PR is shifting, with the latter increasingly seen as a more effective part of marketing than ads, especially when it successfully disguises its partisan nature (Moloney 2000: 100).

3. Ads and Public Relations in Applied Linguistics

Yet however we define them, two aspects of ads and PR make them of particular interest to Applied Linguistics. First is their increasing social influence and ubiquity in a world where corporations are becoming ever more powerful, and communications technology ever more sophisticated. Ads permeate all of the mass media. PR is used extensively, not only by governments, governmental organisations and political parties (Franklin 2003) and non-governmental organisations including pressure groups (Deacon 2003), but also by a vast range of organisations and individuals including monarchies, churches, universities, schools, trade unions, celebrities and people accused of crimes (Moloney 2000: 17–18). While ads, with the exception of the "advertorial",[14] remain generally distinct from the genres they inhabit, PR exploits the blurring of its boundary with news and politics. News is increasingly derived from PR press releases (Cottle 2003), and political policy increasingly dictated by PR advisers (Goldman 1992). Second is the fact that both advertising and PR rely heavily, though not exclusively, upon language in order to persuade. Analysis of them is likely to shed light on the relationship of language use and social power.

Yet an AL analysis needs to do more than describe the language of ads and PR, and the social relations they embody. In a problem-oriented AL (Brumfit 1995: 27) of the kind adopted in this handbook, we need to specify both what the problems are, and how solutions to them might be framed. With ads and PR, there are in theory two possible and conflicting directions, one seeking to influence the producers, the other the receivers. A first direction would be for AL analysis to form the basis of advice to producers on how to achieve their ends more effectively. Two factors however mitigate strongly against this. One is the anti-capitalist political commitment of many applied linguists which would lead them to reject such a course of action. The other is that producers of advertising and PR have their own research base – largely in psychology and survey techniques rather than linguistic analysis (Myers 1999: 151–169) and are resistant to outsider academic influence which they regard with some reason as generally antagonistic. The second and more likely possible direction for AL analysis would be to establish if and how ads and PR are persuading their audiences to perceive organisations and products more favourably than they deserve, to reveal their ideological content and their effects on social and economic relations. Having established this, AL might then contribute both to public awareness of this manipulation and resistance to it. In either case, AL analysis needs to be assessed for its capacity to contribute to changes, either in the production of ads and PR or their reception.

4. Ads and Public Relations research

There are broadly speaking two types of publications on ads and PR, which we might characterise as insider and outsider. The former category, written by present or former practitioners, comprises work aimed both at students and practitioners (often of the "How to become a successful" variety) (e.g. on PR: Grunig et al. 1992; Gregory 2000; Heath and Vasquez 2001; Oliver 2001; e.g. on ads: Butterfield 1999; White 2000). This insider literature is marked by an implicit approval of ads and PR, and an absence of any criticism of their manipulative and deceptive characteristics, or of the market economy of which they are an integral part. Though there is some limited reference by this insider literature to social and political theory (see for example Botan and Hazleton 1989), there is, extraordinarily, very little reference to language. The outsider literature, on the other hand, questions, to a greater or lesser degree, the ethics and politics of ads and PR. With some exceptions,[15] neither literature makes much reference to the other. This mutual mirror-image cold-shouldering is regrettable: firstly because, irrespective of their opposed ideological positions, both contain valuable insights and descriptions; and secondly because the arguments of both might be sharpened by an encounter with opposition (see Mautner, this volume). Both are open to the charge of preaching only to the converted.

4.1. Research on the language of advertising

The outsider academic literature on the language of advertising may be characterised as focusing to differing degrees upon one or more of the following, and the interaction between them:

- the language of ads in itself, e.g. prosody, grammatical innovation, word-coinage, puns and other word play, literariness, metaphor.
- the use of other semiotic systems: the paralanguage of speech (such as uses of voice, face and body); the paralanguage of writing (such as letter and/or character shapes, colour, size, animation and layout (see Walker 2001); non-linguistic modes such as pictures and music; the use of different media, substances and locations (see Scollon and Scollon 2003)
- the micro social (i.e. the pragmatics of ads as acts of communication between individuals)
- the macro social (i.e. the political and ideological significance of ads).

Research on the language of ads was initiated by Leech (1966). Drawing upon techniques from literary stylistics and descriptive linguistics, he concentrated upon linguistic innovation, patterning and deviation in advertising language. His analysis, though seminal, implicitly adopts the mainstream-linguistics tenet of the time that language, whether studied as a system or in use, can be separated from other communicative resources. While such analysis undoubtedly provides insights into language, it is of limited value to the analysis of most adverts *as adverts* (as opposed to as instances of language) as it ignores the interaction of language choices with other semiotic systems. Arguably essential to the analysis of any language use (Finnegan 2002; Norris 2004 Kress and van Leeuwen 2001, 2006) the integration of text with other modes is particularly important in the analysis of ads, given that the specific semiotic choices and their combinations are so particular to their identity, and that the visual is particularly powerful in enticing receivers into the illusion of belonging to a credible "consumption community" (Fairclough 1989: 208).

Realisation of this limitation has been a prime motive in the development of a second approach, analysing the language in ads[16] in interaction with other modes, considered in a social and communicative context. From the 1980s onwards, there has been a growing tendency for work on advertising language to draw to a greater or lesser extent upon analyses from traditions outside linguistics: notably general semiotic analyses of ads (e.g. Williamson 1978; Umiker-Sebeok 1987) and pragmatics. But there is also recognition that these techniques for elucidating how ads signify on a micro-social level need to be complemented by a more macro-sociological analysis which sees ads as players in a larger political arena. Analyses of the language of ads have thus increasingly drawn upon a further tradition of a political and social critique of ads which goes back to the work of Marshall McLuhan (1964), Erving Goffman (1979), Raymond Williams (1980) and continues more recently in such works as Goldman (1992), Nava et al. (1997), and Cronin (2000). Nevertheless, while the major books on advertising language which followed Leech's lead may be said to draw to some extent on all of these traditions, each one is also all distinguished by a particular emphasis of its own. Geis (1982) examines the pragmatics and propositional truth of television advertising; Vestergaard and Shrøder (1985) are concerned particularly with the targeting of specific consumer groups in print ads; Cook (2001) considers the creativity, poetics and literariness of ads; Myers (1994) deals with word choices in ads; Tanaka (1994) uses a relevance-theoretical pragmatics approach to Japanese and British print ads; Forceville (1996) examines how pictures and words interact to create "visual metaphors"; Goddard (1998) presents techniques of language analysis in print ads for school students, and Myers (1999) considers the meanings of ads in the context of their production, distribution and reception.

Political analyses of advertising language can be found in works of Critical Discourse Analysis (CDA) taking their cue from comments on advertising and consumerism in Fairclough's seminal book *Language and Power* (1989: 199–211). Fairclough regards the influence of advertising as primarily ideological, reflecting and advancing the values of late capitalism (e.g. efficiency as an aspiration transferred from industrial to personal life), flourishing in a consumerist culture with increased mass communication, and "colonising" society with "consumption communities" in which identity is defined more by what one consumes than by other more traditional allegiances. He notes how ads are characterised, like many other instances of contemporary institutional discourse, by "synthetic personalisation", a tendency "to give the impression of handling each of the people handled *en masse* as an individual" (Fairclough 1989: 62). These themes are taken up and amplified in later CDA analyses of ads such as Goodman (1996: 150–16), Chouliaraki and Fairclough (1999: 10–15), and Goatly (2000: 183–213).

Though most of the work listed here (with some exceptions such as Tanaka 1994) draws its examples almost exclusively from advertising in English aimed at English speaking countries, there is also a growing body of literature looking at ads across languages and cultures, both in the outsider literature (e.g. Bhatia 1992; Wang 2000) and in the insider literature (e.g. Usunier 1999).

4.1.1. Public and private

The merger of public and private is taken up from a different angle in Cook (2001) and Cook (2000), who observes how ads, like several other powerful genres, not only mix the language of intimacy and power, but also make private subject matter public, and are delivered in both the most public and private places. Through selling such commodities as medicines, condoms, toilet cleaners, sanitary towels, deodorants, diet aids and underwear, ads are able to talk openly about otherwise potentially taboo topics: health, contraception, sanitation, menstruation, food, sexual relationships, and personal self-image. Typically, in tackling such topics, they adopt the linguistic and paralinguistic features of casual conversation. In sanpro ads, for example, almost without exception, another woman addresses the receiver as though she were a close friend and confidante in close physical proximity, using eye-contact, smiles, personal pronouns (Freitas 2003: chapter 7). Yet while ads are encountered in private situations, such as watching TV at home or flicking through the pages of a magazine, they are also very public, both in the sense that they occur on other people's TV screens at the same time, and that they are also shown in public places (poster ads etc.). This combination of public and private is one which ads have in common with some of the most valued discourses. Thus prayer and religious worship also deal with intimate subjects (birth, marriage, ill health and death), and occur also in the most private and public places (at the bedside or in the cathedral). Literature and song depict intimate events and emotions and are encountered either in the most intimate circumstances (the private reading of a book, the singing of a song in solitude) or public places (the theatre, the concert stadium). The prerogative of ads to enter this élite class of discourses,[17] in which, through ritual, society enables the public discussion of the most private matters, imbued with strong evaluation and explicit or implicit behavioural guidance by the sender, signals the degree to which ads have achieved a very high status in contemporary society. Yet on the other hand, unlike religious and literary discourse, ads' solutions to personal problems are material. While a religious discourse might tell us for example that our personal relationships would be enriched by faith and prayer, or a literary discourse make us reflect more deeply upon them, so an ad might imply that they will be enhanced by the purchase of a particular product.

Ironically this brings us full circle back to Leech's emphasis on the linguistically creative features of advertising language, for the high status of such ritual discourses is marked by poetic uses of language (rhythm, sound patterning, repetition, linguistic innovation, marked register, specialised vocabulary), obscurity of meaning, discussion of vital subject matter, and the presentation of alternative realities. These formal characteristics are ones which advertising shares with much literary and religious language (Cook 2000: 86–91).

4.2.   Research on Public Relations language

Despite a prolific and growing insider literature on PR, reflecting its clear identity as an area of enquiry for practitioners, there are relatively few outsider analyses making specific use of the term "PR" – in marked contrast to the many specifically about "advertising". The absence reflects not only difficulties of definition, which exist also for advertising, but also some contestation over whether PR is a genuinely distinct and discrete area at all. The term "public relations" may itself be viewed by critics as a PR euphemism, reifying the concept of "public" and treating largely one-way communication as "relations". This imbalance between studies of ads and PR is particularly marked in the area of language analysis, reflecting perhaps the fact that PR, being verbose, less multimodal, and tamer in its subject matter, is understandably less attractive to linguists as an object of analysis.

There are however linguistic analyses of areas of language use which are relevant to PR: for example Nash (1993) on *Jargon*, Shuy (1998) on *Bureaucratic Language in Government and Business*, Koller (2004) on *Metaphor and Gender in Business Media English*, and a chapter by Goodman (1996) entitled "Market Forces Speak English". In addition there are more specific analyses of aspects of PR, such as Swales and Rogers (1995) on the mission statement as a genre, Lemke (1999) on institutional web pages, Cook (2004: 62–74) on the presentations of genetically modified food by supermarkets and biotech companies, and Mautner (2005) on "buzz-words" in higher education. Yet while current analyses are often only implicitly about PR, outsider research may be increasing, reflecting the growing power and profile of PR itself. Even *within* business studies we can find reference to "critical public relations research" (Motion and Weaver 2005) and the theme of creativity in PR (Green 2002). Similar themes are developed in other fields concerned with the interaction of institutions and the public, such as health studies (Traynor 1996). Perhaps in the future we shall see a growth of studies which do make explicit use of the term.

A key work of language analysis is Deborah Cameron's (2000) *Good to Talk? Living and Working in a Communication Culture* which examines "styling": the training of workers in service industries, especially retail outlets and call centres, to speak and act in designated ways, no matter how badly the customer treats them, and no matter what their own personalities or feelings at the time. Thus, for example, employees at Wal-Mart supermarkets swear an "oath" that "every time a customer comes within ten feet of me, I will smile, look him in the eye and greet him", and McDonald's trainees were told to answer the question "how are you feeling today?" by saying "outstanding", raising the pitch of their voices and punching the air with their hands (Cameron 2000: 53–54). Cameron uses her analysis to make points of much broad relevance to language use in contemporary society. She criticises the widespread belief, frequently implied in PR, that "good communication" and more dialogue will somehow heal disagreements; she shows how the growth of "language work" and "emotional labour" has affected the roles of males and females; she argues that communication is debased if language becomes a controlled commodity rather than a medium for the speakers themselves.

A key work from the public relations literature is Kevin Moloney's (2000) *Rethinking Public Relations*, an informative and well argued critique arguing for reform of PR, and highlighting a number of problems. One is the unclear boundary between PR, news and political policy

> The concerns about PR come alive when it reduces, or is perceived to reduce, through manipulative communications popular access to three institutions which are nearly universally viewed as important public goods. Those three institutions are free markets which claim to give public choice and value, a political system which claims to be democratic and representative, and a media which calls itself independent. (Moloney 2000: 88)

A second is the lack of transparency in the sources and motives of PR statements

> modern PR lends itself to debased forms because its sources are often undeclared, making it difficult to establish the motives and intent which produce it. (Moloney 2000: 87)

and a third is the nature of the persuasion itself

> The data in its messages is asserted rather than argued; reasoned persuasion is downplayed and emotional appeal is strong. (Moloney 2000: 87)

5. Ads and Public Relations as persuasion

Both ads and PR favour an emotional over a rational approach to persuasion, placing – in functional linguistic terms – a greater emphasis upon the interpersonal than the ideational (Halliday 1973: 22–46, 1976: 19–27). Linguistically, this is evident in a predilection for emotive and evaluative language, and, particularly in advertising, in the foregrounding of poetic effects which deflect attention from the propositional content of the message. It is also evident in the strong reliance on paralanguage (the friendly eye contact, reliable voice) and non-linguistic modes such as music and pictures. A critical view of these emphases might remark that they derive from the poverty of the propositional content. There is often no particular factual case to be made for the benefits of one product over another[18] and business PR often seeks to distract from, rather than explore, factual details about the company.

Within the PR insider literature, not surprisingly, a rather different view pertains, either denying the primacy of persuasion as the main function of ads and PR, or seeing its nature in contemporary society as distinctive from earlier eras. Yet while there are aspects of ads and PR which are specific to a consumerist, pluralist, capitalist society with high-tech mass communication, it is debatable whether there is anything profoundly new in the techniques (as opposed to the content) of either as persuasive discourse. Effective persuasion has always deployed similar techniques, however different the causes they espouse. Evangelists and political rhetoricians have used the paralanguage of voice and body, and rhythmic, emotional language. Ceremonies of power – such as coronations, military parades – are thoroughly multimodal, integrating linguistic, musical, visual, spatial, and tactile communication. Mottos (*Per Ardua Ad Astra*, *Who Dares Wins*)[19] and political slogans (*Power to the People*) achieve support by their vagueness, and uncannily echo the modern slogan or strapline (*Pursuing Excellence in Education*, *Putting the Community First*, *Britain Forward Not Back* etc.).[20] In all these cases, the function of the communicative event is less to convey new information, or move social relationships forward, as to indulge in what Goffman (drawing on Darwin) characterises as equivalent to "display" in the animal kingdom:

> the capacity and inclination of individuals to portray a version of themselves and their relationships at strategic moments – a working agreement to present each other with, and facilitate the other's presentation of, gestural pictures of the claimed reality of their relationship and the claimed character of human nature. (Goffman 1979: 7)

This raises the issue of the whether ads and PR are a substantially new phenomenon or merely a recent manifestation of propaganda – a term which since the mid-20th century has had very negative connotations, largely through its association with fascism, National Socialism and Stalinism. The insider post-war literature on PR has inevitably argued energetically that they are not. Both have been presented instead as an important constituent of liberal pluralist democracy, and as a form of dialogue rather than one-way acts of manipulative persuasion: as "the planned and sustained effort to establish goodwill and *mutual understanding between* and organisation and its publics" (Institute of Public Relations, quoted in Moloney 2000: 59, emphasis added). To many this may seem to be simply PR for PR. While ads may merit some credit for artistic merit (Cook 2001) PR in many ways reflects the worst aspects of propaganda with its

> bias, intent to influence, high-pressure advocacy, simplification and exaggeration, avoidance of argumentative exchange, and reluctance to give and take views. (Moloney 2000: 84)

6. Conclusion

Ads and PR are both promotional activities, most prominently so for corporations and their products and services. Yet, despite many overlaps between them, they are also different in character, and the relationship between them is changing. Whereas in the past it was advertising which was the higher profile of the two, and arguably the more powerful, that situation has now to a degree reversed. One reason for this may be that ads, being now (in most parts of the world) a long-established genre, can be easily identified. They have lost some of their persuasive edge, and are treated with a degree of scepticism by an increasingly sophisticated and advert-literate audience.

PR on the other hand is both more recent and less distinct. Like ads it permeates all media, and has taken full advantage of new modes of electronic communication. But being produced by its originators rather than bought out of other outlets, it is less regulated than advertising, and less constrained by cost and space limitations. Taking advantage of this freedom, it has become deeply implicated in news reporting, political persuasion, to such an extent that the degree of power which it exercises in the social sphere should give cause for concern in supposedly democratic societies.

AL needs to respond to this situation. As noted above, while there is a wealth of literature on advertising, there is relatively little on contemporary PR as such. Let us hope that in the near future, applied linguists will meet this challenge by subjecting PR to an ongoing detailed and critical analysis.

Notes

1. This distinction relates to, but does not equate with, numerous other dichotomous classifications such as those between "hard" and "soft sell" (Bernstein 1974: 18), "sudden burst" and "slow drip", "reason" and "tickle" (Brierley 1995: 116).
2. Quoted on http://www.articlehub.com/Marketing/What-Is-A-Brand.html. Accessed 19 December 2005.
3. For an outstanding critique of the power and influence of brands and logos, see Klein 2001.
4. Though see Cook (2001: 219–221) for a list and discussion of 26 features typifying contemporary advertisements (see Appendix).
5. Such as the Institute of Public Relations in Britain and the Public Relations Society of America in the USA.
6. Such as Public Relations Quarterly and Public Relations Review and Journal of Public Relations Research.
7. Both very common tabs on corporate websites.
8. Both quotations in this sentence from http://www.mcdonalds.co.uk/pages/global/dressing.html. Accessed 20 September 2007.
9. Monsanto Pledge http://www.monsanto.com/monsanto/layout/our_pledge/living_the_pledge/creating/default.asp. Accessed 21 April 2005.
10. http://www.imperial-tobacco.com/index.asp?pageid=65. Accessed 26 April 2005.
11. http://www2.marksandspencer.com/thecompany/whoweare/index.shtml. Accessed 26 April 2005.
12. The unifying metaphor here seems to be UNIVERSITY IS FARMYARD.
13. http://svc.travelocity.com/info/info_main/0,,BUSINESSTRAVEL:EN%7CSITE_GUIDE,00.html?source=BT&BIZTRACK=bizbottom_guide. Accessed 28 April 2005.
14. An advert which poses as a news report or article.
15. e.g. among insiders, White (2000) and, among outsiders, Cook (2001) and Myers (1999).
16. Conversely this analysis of ads has contributed to a general trend in discourse analysis away from monomodal analysis, just as ads themselves have contributed to a general trend towards more multimodal communication in general.
17. Another candidate for this group of discourses is legal proceedings where for example intimate sexual details are discussed in public forum.
18. In the case of formula milk powder for babies in the EU for example, the contents of different brands is identical due to very tight regulation (Cook and O'Halloran 1999).
19. The mottos of respectively The British Royal Air Force (Latin for Through Adversity to the Stars) and Special Air Service.
20. The slogans of respectively: The London University Institute of Education, Barnet Council in London, the British Labour Party.

References

AA (Advertising Association)
    2005   *Advertising Statistics Yearbook 2005*. Henley on Thames: World Advertising Research Center.
Aaker, David A.
    1996   *Building Strong Brands*. New York: The Free Press.
Bernstein, David
    1974   *Creative Advertising*. London: Longman.
Bhatia, Tej K.
    1992   Discourse functions and pragmatics of mixing: Advertising across cultures. *World Englishes* 11(2–3): 195–215.
Boone, Louise E. and David L. Kurtz
    1998   *Contemporary Marketing Wired*. 9th ed. Fortworth: Dryden Press.
Botan, Carl and Vincent Hazleton
    1989   *Public Relations Theory*. Hillside, NJ: Lawrence Erlbaum.
Brierley, Sean
    1995   *The Advertising Handbook*. London: Routledge.
Brumfit, Christopher J.
    1995   Teacher professionalism and research. In: Guy Cook and Barbara Seidlhofer (eds.), *Principle and Practice in Applied Linguistics*, 27–41. Oxford: Oxford University Press.
Bruthiaux, Paul
    1996   *The Discourse of Classified Advertising: Exploring the Nature of Linguistic Simplicity*. New York: Oxford University Press.
Butterfield, Leslie (ed.)
    1999   *Excellence in Advertising: The IPA Guide to Best Practice*. Oxford: Butterworth Heinemann.
Cameron, Deborah
    2000   *Good to Talk? Living and Working in a Communication Culture*. London: Sage.
Chouliaraki, Lilie and Norman Fairclough
    1999   *Discourse in Late Modernity*. Edinburgh: Edinburgh University Press.
Cook, Guy
    2000   *Language Play, Language Learning*. Oxford: Oxford University Press.
Cook, Guy
    2001   *The Discourse of Advertising*. 2nd ed. London: Routledge.
Cook, Guy
    2004   *Genetically Modified Language*. London: Routledge.
Cook, Guy and Kieran O'Halloran
    1999   Label literacy: factors affecting the understanding and assessment of baby food labels. In: Theresa O'Brien (ed.), *Language and Literacies, BAAL Studies in Applied Linguistics* 14: 145–157. Clevedon: British Association for Applied Linguistics in association with Multilingual Matters.
Cottle, Simon (ed.)
    2003   *News, Public Relations and Power. Media in Focus*. London: Sage.

Cronin, Anne
    2000   *Advertising and Consumer Citizenship*. London: Routledge.
Deacon, David
    2003   Non-governmental organisations and the media. In: Simon Cottle (ed.), *News, Public Relations and Power*, 99–115. London: Sage.
Fairclough, Norman
    1989   *Language and Power*. London: Longman.
Falk, Pasi
    1997   The Benetton-Toscani effect: testing the limits of conventional advertising. In: Nava, Mica, Andrew Blake, Ian MacRury and Barry Richards (eds.), *Buy this Book: Studies in Advertising and Consumption*, 64–83. London: Routledge.
Finnegan, Ruth
    2002   *Communicating: The Multiple Modes of Human Interconnection*. London/ New York: Routledge.
Forceville, Charles
    1996   *Pictorial Metaphor in Advertising*. London: Routledge.
Franklin, Bob
    2003   "A good day to bury bad news?": Journalists' sources and the packaging of politics. In: Simon Cottle (ed.), *News, Public Relations and Power*, 45–62. London: Sage.
Freitas, Elsa S. L.
    2003   *Taboo in Advertising: a textual study of Portuguese and UK magazine and television advertisements*. Unpublished PhD thesis, Department of Linguistics and English Language, University of Lancaster.
Geis, Michael L.
    1982   *The Language of Television Advertising*. New York: Academic.
Goatly, Andrew
    2000   *Critical Reading and Writing*. London: Routledge.
Goddard, Angela
    1998   *The Language of Advertising*. London: Routledge.
Goffman, Erving
    1979   *Gender Advertisements*. London: Macmillan.
Goldman, Robert L.
    1992   *Reading Ads Socially*. London: Routledge.
Goodman, Sharon
    1996   Market forces speak English. In: Sharon Goodman and David Graddol (eds.), *Redesigning English: New texts, New Identities*, 141–164. London: Routledge and the Open University.
Green, Andy
    2002   *Creativity in Public Relations*. London: Kogan Page.
Gregory, Anne
    2000   *Planning and Managing a PR Campaign: A Step-by-step Guide*. London: Kogan Page.
Grunig, James E., David M. Dorier, William P. Ehling, Larissa A. Gronig, Fred C. Repper and Jon White
    1992   *Excellence in Public Relations and Communication Management*. Hillsdale, NJ: Lawrence Erlbaum Associates.

Halliday, Michael A. K.
  1973   *Explorations in the Function of Language.* London: Arnold.
Halliday, Michael A. K.
  1976   *System and Function in Language.* Oxford: Oxford University Press.
Heath, Robert L. and Gabriel Vasquez (eds.)
  2001   *Handbook of Public Relations.* Thousand Oaks, CA: Sage.
Klein, Naomi
  2001   *No Logo: No Space, No Choice, No Jobs: Taking Aim at the Brand Bullies.* London: Flamingo.
Koller, Veronika
  2004   *Metaphor and Gender in Business Media Discourse: A Critical Cognitive Study.* Basingstoke: Palgrave.
Kress, Gunther and Theo van Leeuwen
  2001   *Multimodal Discourse.* London: Arnold.
Kress, Gunther and Theo van Leeuwen
  2006   *Reading Images: The Grammar of Visual Design.* 2nd ed. London: Routledge.
Leech, Geoffrey N.
  1966   *English in Advertising.* London: Longman.
Lemke, Jay L.
  1999   Discourse and organizational dynamics: website communication and institutional change. *Discourse & Society* 10(1): 21–48.
Mautner, Gerlinde
  2005   The entrepreneurial university: a discursive profile of a higher education buzzword. *Critical Discourse Studies* 2(2): 95–120.
McLuhan, Marshall
  1964   *Understanding Media.* London: Routledge & Kegan Paul.
Moloney, Kevin
  2000   *Rethinking Public Relations: The Spin and the Substance.* London: Routledge.
Motion, Judy and C. Kay Weaver
  2005   A discourse perspective for critical public relations research: life sciences network and the battle for "truth". *Journal of Public Relations Research* 17(1): 49–67.
Myers, Greg
  1994   *Words in Ads.* London: Arnold.
Myers, Greg
  1999   *Ad Worlds: Brands, Media, Audience.* London: Arnold.
Nash, Walter
  1993   *Jargon: Its Uses and Abuses.* Blackwell: Oxford.
Nava, Mica, Andrew Blake, Ian MacRury and Barry Richards (eds.)
  1997   *Buy this Book: Studies in Advertising and Consumption.* London: Routledge.
Norris, Sigrid
  2004   *Analyzing Multimodal Interaction: A Methodological Framework.* New York and London: Routledge.
Oliver, Sandra
  2001   *Public Relations Strategy.* London: Kogan Page.

Rosch, Eleanor
    1977   Human categorization. In: Neil Warren (ed.), *Advances in Cross Cultural Psychology.* Volume 1, 1–49. New York: Academic Press.

Scollon, Ron and Suzie Scollon
    2003   *Discourse in Place: Language in the Material World.* London: Routledge.

Shuy, Roger
    1998   *Bureaucratic Language in Government and Business.* Washington DC: Georgetown University Press.

Stauber, John and Sheldon Rampton
    1995   *Toxic Sludge is Good for You: Lies, Damn Lies and the Public Relations Industry.* Monroe, ME: Common Courage Press.

Swales, John and Rogers, Priscilla
    1995   Discourse and the projection of corporate culture: the mission statement. *Discourse and Society* 6(2): 233–242.

Tanaka, Keiko
    1994   *Advertising Language: A Pragmatic Approach to Advertisements in Britain and Japan.* London: Routledge.

Thorne, Adrian and Justine Coupland
    1998   Articulation of same-sex desire: lesbian and gay-male dating advertisements. *Journal of Sociolinguistics* 2(2): 233–257.

Traynor, Michael
    1996   A literary approach to managerial discourse after the NHS reforms. *Sociology of Health and Illness* 18(3): 315–40.

Umiker-Sebeok, Jean (ed.)
    1987   *Marketing and Semiotics.* Amsterdam: Mouton de Gruyter.

Usunier, Jean-Claude
    1999   *Marketing Across Cultures.* New York: Prentice Hall.

Vestergaard, Torben and Kim Schrøder
    1985   *The Language of Advertising.* Oxford: Blackwell.

Walker, Susan
    2001   *Typography and Language in Everyday Life: Prescriptions and Practices.* Harlow: Longman Pearson Education.

Wang, Jian
    2000   *Foreign Advertising in China: Becoming Global, Becoming Local.* Iowa City: Iowa State Press.

White, Roderich
    2000   *Advertising.* 4th ed. London: McGraw Hill.

Williams, Raymond
    1980   *Advertising: the Magic System: Problems in Materialism and Culture.* London: Verso.

Williamson, Judith
    1978   *Decoding Advertisements.* London and Boston, MA: Marion Boyars.

Appendix

From Cook (2001: 219–221)
features which are characteristic of the materials, language and participants of ads (…)

1. ads use a variety of substances, including some which are not used in communication elsewhere (e.g. soap, vapour)
2. ads are embedded in an accompanying discourse
3. ads are presented in short bursts
4. ads are multi-modal, and can use pictures, music and language, either singly or in combination, as the medium permits
5. ads, in their use of language, are multi-submodal, and can use writing, speech and song, either singly or in combination, as the medium permits
6. ads contain and foreground extensive and innovative use of paralanguage
7. ads foreground connotational, indeterminate and metaphorical meaning, thus effecting fusion between disparate spheres
8. ads make dense use of parallelisms, both between modes (e.g. the pictures and music have elements in common), and within modes (e.g. the words rhyme)
9. ads involve many voices, though they tend to be dominated by one
10. ads are parasitic: appropriating the voices of other genres, and having no independent existence
11. ads are often heard in many contradictory ways simultaneously
12. ads merge the features of public and private discourse, and the voices of authority and intimacy, exploiting the features which are common to these poles
13. ads make extensive use of intertextual allusion, both to other ads and to other genres
14. ads provoke social, moral and aesthetic judgements ranging from the most positive to the most negative (they are "harmful" or "beneficial", "bad" or "good", "not artistic" or "artistic"). (…)
15. ads provoke controversy. (…)
16. ads have the typical restless instability of a new genre
17. ads are a discourse on the periphery of attention
18. ads constantly change
19. ads follow a principle of reversal, causing them to change many features, as soon as they become established, to their opposite
20. ads seek to alter addressees' behaviour but this is understood by default, and need not occupy space or time
21. ads are identified by their position in an accompanying discourse, and need not use space or time to establish their identity as an ad
22. ads use their space and time in an attempt to give pleasure
23. ads use code-play
24. ads answer a need for display and repetitive language
25. ads are unsolicited by their receivers
26. ads, as verbal art, are detrimentally constrained by the need to obey the orders of their clients

6. Language and communication design in the marketplace

Gerlinde Mautner

1. Introduction

In industrialised economies, "designed" communication is ubiquitous. The letterhead on your Air Miles account statement has the same colour as the flight attendants' shirts; phone the airline to book a seat and the operator will steer the conversation along the prescribed path laid down in the Call Centre's interactional guidelines – including, you may be disillusioned to hear, a seemingly spontaneous, rapport-building comment on what a "lovely place" you have chosen to fly to (Thompson, Callaghan, and van den Broek 2004: 139); signage you see in the airline's airport lounge will be in the same font as the letterhead of your account statement, making the cycle of "integrated corporate communication" [*integrierte Unternehmenskommunikation*] (Bruhn 2003) complete. Many other organisational discourses that surround us are similarly streamlined. Everyday consumer goods, for example, are almost invariably "branded", and it is marketing *communications* that are "the means by which products become brands" (Fill 2002: 353). Nonetheless it would be misleading to associate language and communication design *exclusively* with profit generation in the commercial sector. These days, sophisticated design is equally at home in public and voluntary sector organisations (such as the police force, local councils, higher education institutions, hospital trusts, and charities). Also, there are types of language and communication design that offer very real benefits not just to producers, but also to consumers, as is the case with, for example, design initiatives aimed at making the World Wide Web more accessible to people with disabilities.

The type of design process discussed in this chapter is related to, but distinct from, advertising and public relations (see Cook, this volume). In a nutshell, advertising promotes individual products, and PR establishes goodwill among an organisation's stakeholders. Although language and communication design, as conceived here, has a role in both advertising and PR, it is not co-extensive with either of them. It aims to standardise a wide variety of texts and interactions, reaching beyond the narrower remit of advertising, and harnessing linguistic intervention to corporate goals that are broader than the promotion of individual products or services. Also, whereas advertising is aimed at external audiences (though internal ones are of course exposed to it as well), language and communication design is instrumental in shaping a distinctive corporate identity and as such impacts in equal measure on both internal and external constituencies. Public relations, on the other hand, include many activities which are not exclusively constituted by communication, such as sponsorship, events management, and crisis management (Pickton and Broderick 2002: 493–495). The present contribution differs from Koller (this volume) by the specific focus applied. While I shall be concentrating on the impact of design on texts and discourses, Veronika Koller adopts a cognitive approach to discourse reception, investigating the impact on an organisation's publics.

The chapter is structured as follows. Section 2 clarifies what each of the concepts mentioned in the title is taken to mean in the context of this particular contribution. Section 3 traces key socio-political trends that have encouraged language and communication design to develop and expand from its commercial roots to the public and nonprofit sectors. Section 4 outlines several dimensions along which different forms of language and communication design may be distinguished. In Section 5, the account shifts back to issues surrounding the implementation of design schemes on an organisational and managerial level, before turning to two case studies in Section 6, and concluding in Section 7 with a discussion of linguists' role as critics and potential practitioners.

2. The chapter title unpacked: Key concepts

2.1. Language and Communication

In the context of this chapter, the case for coupling *language* with *communication*, rather than using only one or the other, rests on the following arguments. First, if we do applied research situated in social and organisational contexts, there is clearly a need to include a purview wider than what is covered by the purely verbal systems of meaning making which the term *language* commonly refers to. Second, in the domains of application that this chapter talks about it is *communication* that strikes all the right chords, not *language*. In the "marketplace" – the worlds of business, management consulting, and public relations – *language* is associated primarily either with "foreign language" or has overtones of "grammar" and "correctness". Third, the case for not using *communication* on its own is tied to a wish (on the part of this author and, I assume, a majority of the applied linguistics readership of this Handbook) to bolster a linguistic agenda, with the specific theoretical and methodological competencies this entails, rather than remain in the ill-defined and crowded multi-disciplinary space inhabited by "communication".

2.2. Design

I understand language and communication design to be utilitarian intervention in texts and communicative processes, aimed at shaping discourse in the long term. Let me examine each element of this definition in turn.

Language and communication design is "utilitarian" in the sense that it is meant to serve a purpose that reaches beyond the actual discursive process and textual product, and beyond any personal expressive needs the author may have. In this, it contrasts with other consciously manipulated forms of symbolic expression, such as poetry or painting. Language and communication design is not an end in itself. In the marketplace, where it is situated and which is the domain this chapter talks about, that purpose is to attract more customers, make a profit, enhance the image of the organisation concerned, or, put more generally, to gain an advantage over competitors (which of these purposes is predominant depends on the kind of organisation and on environmental factors, both of which I shall return to in Section 5). It follows that language and communication design is generally an activity undertaken by and for organisations rather than individuals, and is directed at public not private spheres. An individual carefully crafting personal letters, for example, would not, under this definition, be said to be engaging in language and communication design. It is tempting, and in most cases perfectly accurate, to see language and communication design as an "organisational discursive practice" (Iedema and Wodak 1999: 10). Yet some caution needs to be exercised with regard to hitching the concept of design to an explicitly organisational framework, and thus to the theoretical and interdisciplinarily complex baggage that *organization* carries with it. Although the size of the organisation is one of the factors determining how language and communication design will be implemented, *large* size is not a prerequisite for language and communication design to play a role. Thus, if we wish to call language and communication design *organisational*, we will have to waive those parts of definitions of *organisation* which specify size – cf. Giddens' (2001: 346) definition, "an organisation is a *large* grouping of people, structured on impersonal lines and set up to achieve specific objectives [emphasis mine]". Indeed, even the smallest of economically active units, such as one-person businesses, can and often do design their corporate communications in systematic, goal-oriented ways. In such cases the label *organisational* is not strictly speaking appropriate, even if one takes recourse to definitions of *organisation* which make more modest demands in terms of size than Giddens'.[1] However, when language and communication design *is* carried out within the framework of a large organisation, which it often is, it is heavily intertwined with organisational structures and relationships of power, and impinges on the identities of the organisation's members. Furthermore, design, as an institutional practice, spawns its own culture of professionalisation and "experthood" – elements of what Fairclough (1996) refers to as the "technologisation of discourse".

The final part of my definition above – "aimed at shaping discourse in the long term" – is intended to differentiate language and communication design from ad hoc interventions in individual texts. Language and communication design lays down the law in specified areas of organisational communication. Guidelines are written, templates published, sanctions for non-compliance devised (and executed). Within the confines of an organisation's discourse, language and communication design is essentially an exercise in semiotic standardisation.

2.3. The marketplace

In this chapter, *marketplace* is shorthand for any public setting in which competitive exchange takes place. *Marketplace* is a general and pre-theoretical expression which, unlike *market*, has no scholarly or "textbook" definition.[2] From popular Web dictionaries, *marketplace* emerges as vaguely synonymous with *business* or *trade*.[3]

However, it would be misleading to tie the concept of the marketplace exclusively to the commercial arena. Agents may be pursuing the profit motive, but this need not be the case. In fact, one of the key socio-economic developments recently shaping the nonprofit and public sectors has been the adoption of market-based approaches and the discourses that come with them (Mautner 2005a). As a result, the social space governed by the market, or market-like structures, has expanded, and the rest of the public sphere – notably areas traditionally inhabited by the state and civil society – has shrunk accordingly. This is not just a question of symbolic expansion. Pertinent though accounts of the market as a metaphor are (Bourdieu 1991; Rigney 2001), they should not blind us to the fact that marketisation can, mundanely, also refer to the perfectly non-metaphorical process of buying and selling goods at prices set by supply and demand, in areas where other mechanisms, such as provision by state monopolies and financing through taxation, used to be the norm. Effectively, the boundaries between the various spaces that make up the public sphere are being redrawn, with growing territorial claims falling to the market. As literal markets expand, so does the appeal (and the conventionality) of the market as a metaphor, so that marketised discourses can be seen to invade even those niches of the public sphere that have not yet been marketised in a literal sense. As a result, discursive practices originating in the commercial sector have been spreading throughout the public sphere. Language and communication design is one of these practices.

3. The socio-political environment

Language and communication design is not an isolated phenomenon. It is embedded in, and nourished by, a cluster of environmental factors. None of these factors can be said to "result in" language and communication design in a superficially causal sense, but taken together they create the social climate in which language and communication design has gained momentum, spreading from the for-profit to the non-profit and public sectors. The "environmental forces" listed by Balmer and Gray ([1999] 2003: 127) include (1) *acceleration of product life cycles,* increasing the importance of strong brands which reduce customers' uncertainty in choosing between competing products; (2) *mergers and acquisitions*, in which language and communication design is instrumental in forging a brand image for the entity created by the merger; and (3) *increased competition through deregulation, privatisation, and globalisation,* which makes organisations rely increasingly on communication to differentiate themselves from a growing number of competitors. Key branding strategies and tools include precise brand positioning, the development of clear brand values, and a distinctive "Brand Tone of Voice" (Delin 2005).

In service industries, these trends are compounded by the fact that many services consist primarily in communication. Cameron (2000) reports that in one of the call centre training materials she looked at, operators were in fact told, "you *are* the brand [emphasis mine]" (Cameron 2000: 100). In knowledge-intensive industries, there is stiff competition not only for customers, but also for highly qualified staff, for whom the reputation of the organisation they work for, or intend to work for, provides "a certain psychic income" (Balmer and Gray 2003: 130). Also, reputations are increasingly formed by companies' willingness to engage in corporate responsibility initiatives (Fombrun and Shanley 1990: 239; Fombrun 1995), and this is a strong incentive to commit to – and persuasively flaunt – schemes that promote, for example, minority rights or environmental sustainability.[4]

In the public and voluntary sectors, deregulation and competition have led not only to "marketlike behaviours" (Slaughter and Leslie 1997: 11) on the part of organisations, but also to a wholesale "discursive shift" (Gewirtz and Ball 2000: 253), which both reflects and further encourages the modelling of organisations along business lines in an environment frequently referred to as the "enterprise culture" (Keat and Abercrombie 1991; Mautner 2005b). In this environment, a positive image is a competitive asset, and the importance of branding increases accordingly (Tapp, Lindsay, and Sorrell 1999). As Gewirtz, Ball and Bowe (1995: 126) note in relation to schools facing market conditions, "the production of signs assumes an enhanced significance" and "new semiologies" are being created. Another environmental factor which can impact on language and communication design is the legal framework, which, in turn, is conditioned both by social and technological developments (see Section 6.2 on Web accessibility).

4. Dimensions of analysis

There is now a wide variety of "designed" texts and discourses, including standardised stationery, Powerpoint presentations and Web pages, forms, bills, memos, annual reports, and signage, as well as receptionists' and call centre operators' interactional routines. Obviously, these differ considerably in terms of (a) which mode (spoken/written) is involved, (b) which modality (verbal/visual), and (c) which medium (e.g. face-to-face, telephone, E-mail, WWW, paper, 3D/outdoor [in the case of signage]). I shall raise issues related to each of these dimensions below.

(a) Mode
As the list of examples above suggests, the majority of design initiatives are directed at written communication. Among the most notable exceptions are schemes to standardise the communication of staff in "call centres", that is, centralised operations that provide customer service over the phone in industries such as direct banking and mail-order businesses. An in-depth study of these outfits is provided by Cameron (2000: 91–124), who calls them "communication factories", pointing out that

> the call centre regime is of particular interest because it represents an unusually thoroughgoing attempt to regulate many aspects of talk – indeed, to "Taylorize" it, as if it were a kind of automated production process. (Cameron 2000: 123)

As far as cases of language and communication design in the written mode are concerned, it is worth spelling out specifically that this not only includes genres that the popular imagination would see as texts, but also genres almost entirely devoid of continuous prose, such as forms, bills and bank statements, whose textual properties are recognised by linguists, but hardly by lay language users. Increasingly, these genres, too, are subjected to language and communication design. The idea is to reduce ambiguity and improve comprehensibility as well as to exploit their potential for projecting a positive and consistent company image. Expending design effort on even the most mundane, formalised, and apparently factual texts recognises that, as a communications consultancy puts it poignantly on its website, "of all the communications your customers are exposed to, they spend most time looking at bills and statements" (http://www.enterpriseidu.com/bill.htm).[5]

(b) Modality
Design activities may be brought to bear on elements of verbal and visual expression. Along the verbal dimension, design may be directed at (i) lexical choice (e.g. adjusting job titles so as to reflect corporate-level marketing strategies, or adapting the lexis used to the linguistic competence of particular publics), (ii) syntax (e.g. simplifying sentence structure to facilitate comprehension), (iii) text (e.g. standardising textual structure, increasing cohesion to

improve coherence, or laying down rules for question-and-answer sequences in telephone conversations).

Visual language and communication design, on the other hand, which is generally referred to as "corporate design", is concerned with the consistent use of trademarks, logos, corporate colour, layout, the use of graphic design and distinctive proprietary typography. The area of application that comes to mind most readily are genres such as letters, memos, annual reports and the like. However, conveying a consistent visual identity is also central to packaging design, product design and environmental design, that is, the appearance of points of sale and other physical spaces associated with the organisation (Brun 2002: 137).

(c) Medium

Which types of semiosis are available for design intervention obviously depends on the specific "affordances" (Lemke 2002), or semiotic potential, of the medium involved in each case, and need not be elaborated here. There are four points though that do merit attention. First, there are cases where the challenge for language and communication design is to overcome the limitations inherent in a particular medium. Much of the design effort that goes into telephone conversations, for example, is geared towards making up for the limited affordance of the auditory channel, which means that operators' oral communication is the only way in which the desired brand image can be conveyed (Cameron 2000: 100). Second, where many different media are employed simultaneously, we find both overlapping and complementary affordances. Accordingly, some design features will be shared (such as the use of a company slogan as a running head in an annual report), and others unique (such as the animation of that slogan on the company website). Third, the Internet not only offers corporate text producers unique opportunities for communication design, but also empowers users by giving them equally unique opportunities to substitute their own design. So-called "cascading style sheets" (Vassallo 2003) enable disabled users to override Web sites' original style and customise them to suit their specific needs (e.g. with clearer layout or larger fonts).

Finally, advantages in word processing, computer graphics, presentations software and web design have made the tools for language and communication design not only more sophisticated, but also more accessible to individuals, small businesses and charities. On the upside, these groups too can now professionalise their communications in ways that used to be the reserve of large and powerful organisations. On the downside, the availability of these resources *de facto* increases the pressure to use them, and organisations with outdated hardware, a shortage of funds and/or an insufficient skills base among their staff are likely to lose out. This mirrors, on an organisational level, the general patterns of disadvantage referred to as the "digital divide".[6]

Separating out individual modes, modalities and media helps coming to terms analytically with the diversity of the field, but it should not obscure the fact that in reality the language and communication design practiced by any one organisation is generally a highly complex and multi-dimensional undertaking. Many things will be going on at the same time – from interactional training for switchboard operators to the development of a design manual for annual reports, to name just two examples. Organisations intent on conveying a unified brand image will make sure that different design activities do not remain compartmentalised and diverse, but are brought together, streamlined, and diffused throughout the organisation. Also, language and communication design should be in sync with other aspects of corporate strategy and contribute to what is known as integrated (corporate or marketing) communication (Kotler 1991: 781; Schultz, Tannenbaum, and Lauterborn 1996; Kitchen 1999: 89–110; Pickton and Broderick 2002; Balmer and Gray 2003; Bruhn 2003; van Riel 2003: 165).[7] For multinational companies (MNCs) a key strategic question is how much to integrate their communications across different national subsidiaries, and in the face of conflicting evidence about the convergence versus divergence of organizational structures, cultures, and communicative practices (Stohl 2001). In terms of responses, the two opposing ends of the spectrum are global standardisation, yielding to "company-level centripetal forces", and local adaptation, reacting to "centrifugal country-level forces" (Pickton and Broderick 2002: 130). In between, there is a gamut of strategies responding in varying degrees to global similarities and local specifics of the cultural and competitive environment, the oganisation, the brand, and the product.[8] The dovetailing of global and local approaches is neatly captured in the notion of "glocalisation" (Robertson 1995; Melewar and Saunders 1999; Koller 2007).

5. Broader organisational and human resource issues

In Section 2, I referred to language and communication design as "utilitarian intervention", hinting only briefly at what the utility was, and what it implied within a larger organisational framework. Having surveyed, in Section 4, key dimensions along which manifestations of language and communication design may be analysed, I would now like return to these broader organisational issues.

The imputed relevance of language and communication design rests on the assumption that "consistency in communication is one of the crucial factors in increasing success with corporate communication" (van Riel 2003: 169). If consistency contributes to success, and language and communication design improves consistency, then language and communication design contributes to success. Cogent though it is, the syllogism should not tempt one to skirt underlying questions which a critical appraisal of language and communication design ought to address. From an applied linguistics perspective it is crucial to ask, for example, who is in charge of planning and implementing this consistency? In the corporate communications literature, this question is often backgrounded, with agency being obscured through the familiar techniques of nominalisation, passivisation and the use of collective and non-human agents – witness statements such as "Organisations are aware of the dangers of fragmented communication", and "the clear trend now to strive towards an increase in the mutual cohesion of all forms of communication" (van Riel 2003: 164).

In practice, the "orchestration of communication at a holistic company level" (van Riel 2003: 169) is planned, executed and monitored by communications professionals who are either affiliated to a specialised communications division or else part of individual functional divisions, such as marketing, public relations, or investor relations. These, in turn, are likely to outsource some elements of the design process to consultancies and agencies (Daymon 1999: 76). In so far as corporate communication, and language and communication design as part of it, is more than a purely operational matter but also has strategic implications (Balmer and Gray 2003: 131) for the creation of brand image, the involvement of top-level management is crucial and increasingly the norm. As one executive said of public relations management, it "has rocketed up the corporate agenda" and now "sits ever more close to centre stage on the boardroom agenda" (Sandler 2003). This is equally true of public sector organisations, such as universities (see Section 6.1 and Mautner 2002) and even schools, about which Gewirtz, Ball and Bowe (1995: 126) report that "headteachers appear to be taking more control over the processes of semiotic production".

A related question of key interest to the applied linguist is how the language and communication design that is instigated and approved by top management, and developed by a central planning division, is then made to cascade down, through various reporting lines, to the communications "coal face", that is, those people who are routinely engaged in customer contacts. The main vehicles for the dissemination of language and communication design are memos, manuals, electronic templates, and staff training (both at induction level and in-service).[9] Implementation is secured by surveillance, assessment, and, in the case of non-compliance, sanctions. The precise nature of all of these directive mechanisms will obviously vary according to the organisation's structure and corporate culture, and according to which aspect of language and communication is subjected to design efforts. In a call centre, staff training materials are likely to include detailed instructions for interactional routines (Cameron 2000: 103–104) as well as techniques to control emotion and build rapport with the customer (Thompson, Callaghan, and van den Broek 2004: 139). In a university environment, on the other hand, staff training in oral communication skills is still the exception rather than the rule. Characteristically, one of the communications guidelines examined in Section 6.1.2, from the University of Bristol, says in relation to the communicative side of customer care, "it would be unrealistic to advocate a programme of formal training" – a comment that would sound very odd indeed in a commercial environment.

Finally, focussing on the point of "delivery", where a member of the organisation interacts through designed language with a person from outside, we need to ask what this involves for those whose language is being modelled according to top-down demands. Again, it is call centre work that throws these issues into particularly sharp relief. Korczynski et al. (2000: 670) argue that such forms of work "are informed by dual and potentially contradictory logics – of customer-orientation, on the one hand, and of efficiency and rationalisation, on the other". As organisations in the public and non-profit sectors adopt the practices and discourses of service industries, they, too, will increasingly face the tensions inherent in a "customer-oriented bureaucracy" (Korczynski et al. 2000: 670).

Quite generally, and even where the discourse involved is less immediate and intimate than one-to-one oral communication, it has to be borne in mind that language and communication design subjects what is a hugely personal aspect of human behaviour to managerial command and control, supplanting what is individual and diverse with something that is collective and uniform. When such control is exercised in organisations whose members are not used to being "managed" at all, the effect is compounded. In Section 6.1, the close-up on language and communication design in universities will elaborate this point.

6. Close-up: Two examples of language and communication design

In this section, I am looking at two examples of language and communication design: one where the overarching function of language and communication design is to project a consistent brand image; and one where language and communication design is to ensure equality of access to information. They have more in common than may appear at first sight. For one thing, although their goals differ, they draw essentially on the same repertoire of interventionist moves (though which items are actually selected from the repertoire is likely to differ). Also, their functions – ostensibly "competitive" in one case, and "altruistic" in the other – should not be pigeonholed so easily. As I shall demonstrate below, language and communication design for improved web accessibility also has commercial relevance. Finally, they are related in that they are both examples of language and communication design at a formative stage, and are thus better suited than fully routinised and institutionalised forms of language and communication design to bring to the fore the socio-political and discursive processes involved.

6.1. University branding

6.1.1. The socio-political context

In higher education, the emergence of centralised language and communication design reflects the growing importance of marketing in this sector (Kotler and Fox 1995), a development which has arguably gone furthest in the United States (Kirp 2003). As governments have reduced funding and introduced deregulation, universities, like other public and nonprofit institutions, have been exposed to competition in the marketplace. They compete for public and private-sector funds, sponsorship deals, first-rate faculty, and the best and/or wealthiest students. Many universities have also established so-called "spin-off" companies in order to market research-based, knowledge-intensive products and services, and have thus entered into direct competition with commercial rivals. It is against this background that "corporate branding", which "is about creating differentiation and preference" (Melewar 2003: 206), is considered to be as important for universities as for commercial organisations.

Nevertheless, marketing and the streamlining of external communications that goes with it still do not sit easily with traditional academic cultures and values. Although the days are long gone when a university could be described, facetiously though aptly, as "a series of separate schools and departments held together by a central heating system" (Kerr 1964: 20),[10] vestiges of a strong sense of individual, departmental, and disciplinary independence remain. Used to the de-centralised, collegial styles of governance typical of "loosely coupled organisations" (Weick 1976), faculty still tend to bristle at the idea that their vice-chancellor, rector or dean is now a powerful chief executive officer rather than what he (or, much less likely, she) used to be, a rather remote ceremonial figure-head – or "old fogey academic", as Prichard and Willmott (1997: 289) irreverently label the type. The "dull but worthy administrator who supported the professional", Parker and Jary (1995: 324) point out, "becomes the dynamic leader-manager who directs and inspires other professionals". Joined by others in a senior executive team, these new "manager-academics" (Deem 2003) can and do exercise strategic leadership for the whole organisation. The impact on organisational communication is profound and keenly felt by all those affected. As a complex, centrally controlled branding machinery falls into gear, individual organisational units need to brace themselves for persistent intrusions from top-down language and communication design initiatives.

On the level of organisational structure, the drive towards homogenised external communications has led to the creation of dedicated administrative units whose sole purpose it is to devise and implement communication strategies, develop marketing campaigns, liaise with the media, and monitor the execution of language and communication design schemes. These units – headed by communications professionals with job titles such as *corporate communications officer* – generally report directly to the highest echelons of university management.

Although such streamlined brand management and concomitant language and communication design is fast becoming the norm, implementation across the sector as a whole is still patchy. It is not unusual for the homepage of the university and its central management units to sport slickly professional, uniform design, while individual departments hang on to idiosyncratic forms of presentation, with only minimal deference to university-wide design templates.[11] However, given the sector-wide push for consistent branding, it is highly probable that the homogenising forces will eventually prevail.

6.1.2. Areas of intervention

At present, language and communication design in universities is confined to the written mode and visual modality. Typically, the media and genres involved are websites, newsletters, prospectuses, posters, invitation to events, stationery, and public signage. The main thrust is to harmonise the use of fonts, layout, colours, and logos. Management may still decide to allow departments some leeway in preserving their individual visual identity, but whatever freedom is granted is likely to be tightly regulated, with guidelines specifying exactly where a department logo is allowed to go, how big it can be, and so on.

There are not, as yet, similar trends towards streamlining oral communication, and interactions between staff and students, face-to-face and by telephone, are still a design-free zone, just as lexical choice (and with it, tone of voice) remains unregulated in 1:1 written communication. However, in certain domains at least, even that may change. While it would clearly be dysfunctional to attempt to homogenise oral interactions between faculty and students in tutorial or pastoral contexts, a good case can and probably will be made for deliberate interventions in the text and talk at the centre of service encounters. With students increasingly expecting to be treated as "customers" (inappropriate though the metaphor may be),[12] university management will feel increasingly compelled to make staff project a customer service ethos through consistently adhering to discursive choices decreed from above. In staff-student interactions, tight call-centre routines may be a long way off, and mindlessly routinised exchanges of the *have a nice day* variety would certainly be considered quite inappropriate. At the same time, there is some evidence, albeit scarce and anecdotal at this stage, that universities are beginning to nudge language and communication design into hitherto unregulated areas. Bristol University's *Communications & Marketing Strategy,* for example, includes a section headed "Precinct enhancement and customer care" which notes that "there is at least anecdotal evidence that standards of customer care are not uniformly high across the University" (University of Bristol 2002/03: 45). Moving on to suggestions for improvement, the paper argues (University of Bristol 2002/03: 46) that

> it would be unrealistic to advocate a programme of formal training. However, it would be helpful to the image of the University if it were taken as read that people should be treated with courtesy and consideration at all times. One practical step that some departments might wish to take would be to review any standard letters they send – for example, to applicants who are refused a place.

Between the carefully crafted lines, with their distancing, low-affinity modals[13] ("it *would be* helpful *if it were taken as read* [...]; one practical step departments *might* wish to take *would* be to") we can sense that the university's communications professionals have identified a very real problem. What is more, they obviously recognise the role that "frontline" communications play for the creation of a positive image. Tightening the screws on visual identity guidelines is not the end of the story; if anything, it is only the beginning.

6.1.3   Compliance and enforcement

The strategies, principles and practices that universities have adopted for language and communication design are enshrined in official guidelines, administrative memos, manuals and other such documents,[14] which acquire normative force because they are endorsed by management. Compliance by faculty can be reluctant – witness the off-the-record comments by a British colleague of mine who, jokingly but with acerbic irony, referred to his university's Communications and Marketing Services as "the brand police".

Indeed, protracted arguments between vice-chancellors and professors over what a department's headed notepaper should look like are not unknown. In spite of the aura of quaint pettiness that hangs over such bickering, it is a surface symptom of a deeper problem – formerly independent agents having to adjust to centralised managerial control, in matters as closely linked to professional identity as presentation to external audiences. However, with reluctance or indifference (though rarely enthusiasm), most academics have now accepted that language and communication design is here to stay and, if anything, will be made more streamlined and more pervasive as universities become ever more thoroughly enmeshed in both the practices and communicative conventions that rule the marketplace. Academics are also likely to be aware that, no matter how participative and conciliatory their vice-chancellor's or rector's style of leadership may be, non-compliance with the university's marketing policy, of which language and communication design is a core element, will not be tolerated for long. If nothing else, they will, eventually, succumb to the supremely persuasive force of resource allocation – further proof, if proof was needed, that the enforcement of homogenised discourse is fundamentally an issue of power.

6.2. Web accessibility

6.2.1. *The socio-political context*

Web accessibility improvement is a case of language and communication design being driven mainly by legislation and codes of practice. The relevant pieces of legislation in the US and the UK are, respectively, Section 508 of the Rehabilitation Act of 1998 (applying to Federal Government websites)[15] and the Disability Discrimination Act (DDA) of 1995.[16] As is the nature of such acts, they contain only very general provisions about information access for people with disabilities, and it is up to government departments, pressure groups and organisations such as the World Wide Web Consortium (http://www.w3.org) and Euroaccessibility (http://www.euroaccessibility.org) to flesh out the general legal provisions with detailed guidelines for design practices.[17]

At present, implementation of language and communication design for Web accessibility is still in its infancy. In a study carried out in 2003, the UK Disability Rights Commission found that 81 per cent of websites did not in fact fulfil even the most basic accessibility requirements (Disability Rights Commission 2004b: 9).[18] This means lost opportunities on all sides. From a disabled person's point of view, being empowered to engage in the full range of economic transactions is as important as exercising citizen's rights. From a producer's point of view, aside from any social responsibility issues and legal pressures, widening access to web pages means more potential and actual customers (Sloan et al. 2000: 213).[19] As both the importance of the Web as a communications channel and public awareness of disability rights continue to grow, it will make more and more sense for organisations, with a view to boosting both image and sales, to design their websites with accessibility in mind.

6.2.2. *Areas of intervention*

According to the *Web Accessibility Guidelines* developed by the World Wide Web Consortium (W3C), the goal of their design principles is to make Web content (1) "perceivable", (2) "operable", (3) "understandable" and (4) "robust" (World Wide Web Consortium 2004). Of these four, it is the first three that are relevant from a semiotic rather than purely information technology point of view.[20] Satisfying the criterion of perceptibility is essentially about assessing, adjusting and changing the nature of multimodality to suit the needs of users unable to process certain types of information. For example, "text alternatives" need to be provided which can then be converted into whichever format the disabled user *can* access (such as audio or Braille) with the help of "assistive technologies". The complex multimodality of hypertext is disentangled, its layers of meaning-making separated out, and then reassembled in ways that suit specific disabilities. If colour, for example, is functional but cannot be processed by a user, then whatever meaning it conveys has to be separated from colour as its carrier, and made available without colour. The second criterion, operability, includes some technical issues (such as the use of variable input devices), but also some that are related to information processing, such as a guideline against time-outs, so that users with reading, learning or motor-control disabilities can control the speed at which they read and interact. Finally, the third criterion, "understandability", informs several guidelines intended to clarify and disambiguate discourse through intervention at various levels of linguistic organisation – including lexis (e.g. "avoid jargon"), cohesion (e.g. "making clear pronoun references", "indicating logical relationships between phrases"), syntax (e.g. "using the simplest sentence forms consistent with the purpose of the content") and macro-structural issues (e.g. "developing a single topic or subtopic per paragraph", "providing summaries to aid understanding", "organize content consistently from 'page to page'") (World Wide Web Consortium 2004).

6.2.3. Compliance and enforcement

At present, compliance with the W3C *Web Accessibility Guidelines* is voluntary. However, legal enforcement will no doubt gain momentum soon. In the UK, there is no reported case law yet on the provisions of the Disability Discrimination Act (1995) being applied to websites, but there is "a very strong anticipation that any future case law will support this interpretation of the Act" (Disability Rights Commission 2004b: 4). Sloan (2001), too, argues that "a disabled person could bring an action under the Act" (Sloan 2001: 19), while also acknowledging that:

> it is only through the power of the media and potential damage to a high profile service provider's goodwill that a culture change will actually be initiated and an accessible Web site will become the expected standard (Sloan 2001: 20).

This is where language and communication design for web accessibility and for branding, described in Section 6.1, can be seen to have more in common than might initially have been supposed. What they share, over and above certain technicalities of the design process, is the potential they have for impacting on organisations' publicly projected image and reputation.

7. Summary and conclusion

This chapter has explored the role which language and communication design plays in organisations operating in a market or under market-like conditions. Developments that have contributed to the rise of language and communication design include accelerated product life cycles, increased merger activity, deregulation, privatisation and globalisation.

When examining individual instances of language and communication design, key dimensions of analysis are mode, modality and medium. Also, one needs to address the implications for organisational structure and culture. These are particularly salient when organisations are in transition, with the distribution of power shaken up and members' roles and identities left in a state of flux. Universities adapting to a competitive environment, and adopting language and communication design schemes as part of top-down branding initiatives, are a case in point. That certain types of language and communication design can benefit the customer as well as enhance the organisation's image is illustrated by interventions aimed at making Web sites more accessible, particularly to people with disabilities.

In society generally, a paradigm shift has been occurring. Sections of the public sphere that used to be under the influence of the state or civil society are increasingly being governed both by forces characteristic of markets (the law of supply and demand, as well as competition) and by cognitive, social and discursive practices following in their wake: adherence to the economic principle, a preoccupation with quantifiable outputs, and the large-scale adoption of managerial discourse. That language is subjected to design interventions – and, in the process, functionalised, homogenised, and commodified – is a symptom of this paradigm shift. Through a process of "dialectical internalization" (Fairclough 2003: 22), it is also one of its causes, contributing its share to marketisation by reinforcing market-oriented perspectives on practices, roles and identities.

In this context, issues of power loom large. The ability to impose design on language and communication is a function of agents' symbolic capital (Bourdieu 1991: 72). Typically, in organisations, such capital is conferred on individuals by management positions. Conversely, less powerful agents who conform to design rules imposed by managerial fiat are likely to accumulate more social capital than those that do not. Towing the line pays off handsomely all round. Vis-à-vis management, complying with language and communication design schemes marks you off as obliging and supportive of organisational goals. In the organisational environment, language and communication design contributes to an image of professionalism and, ideally, promotes a consistent corporate brand distinguished clearly from competitors. Both inside and outside the organisation, social capital is often converted into monetary capital (e.g. in the form of increased budgets or profits) so that symbolic and financial power in fact converge. However, some doubts are in order as to whether all language and communication design schemes do, in fact, make a sustainable contribution to organisational success. Call centre talk, for example, with its heavily prescribed, impersonal interactional routines, operates according to the logic of short-term cost-effectiveness, when it may in fact make sounder business sense to prioritise factors that pay off in the long term, such as customer satisfaction and loyalty.

An account of language and communication design would be incomplete if it did not address the ethical dimension. Is it "good" or "bad" to design language and communication? Can language and communication design be accommodated within the framework of a broader "organizational communication ethics" (Seeger 2004)? How (un)comfortably does language and communication design sit with a critical research agenda, how well does it resonate with people brought up on a diet of anti-capitalist critique, and is it something that linguists should be actively involved in?

In principle, applied linguists are well positioned to put their expertise to both emancipatory and conformist uses. We can study design mechanisms in order to bolster resistance against them, or to help maximise the efficiency of their application. Which role any one linguist might prefer in a given situation will depend as much on his or her *Weltanschauung* ("worldview") as it does on the merits of each case, which could be determined by the answers to questions such as: what does a particular instance of *Weltanschauung* aim to achieve? Which agenda does it promote, and whose position does it help strengthen? There are echoes here of the debate on political correctness. In both cases, we find that one and the same type of "linguistic engineering" can be put to different uses which can be judged quite differently, depending on the ideological stance of whoever makes the judgement (cf. Johnson, Culpeper, and Suhr 2003: 30–31).

Clearly, not all design interventions are a capitalist ruse intended to foist a corporate persona on dependent individuals. There are scenarios in which language and communication design protects the vulnerable; where, for example, the creativity of people writing for the Web is curbed in order to make sure that users with cognitive disabilities find Web documents easier to understand; where strict interactional guidelines are given to shopping mall security guards about how to address ethnic minority shoppers; and where university staff are trained how to be courteous when talking or writing to students. If guidelines protect people against verbal abuse and racism, we are unlikely to say about a security guard what Cameron says about the call centre worker, that he or she "is not the 'stylistic agent' and does not 'own' the style s/he adopts" (Cameron 2000: 101) even though this is, technically, as true of the security guard exposed to language and communication design as of the call centre operator. It is not the design processes as such that are laudable or reprehensible, but the social goals they help achieve.

There is no doubt that a certain amount of tension is inevitable between the linguist-as-critic and the linguist-as-consultant. Apart from having to ask themselves, on a case-by-case basis, whether they are willing to put their expertise actively to the service of particular social goals, linguists will have to adjust, among other things, to the shorter time frames and reduced level of detail that distinguishes corporate from academic work. Yet, as several authors have argued (Sarangi and Roberts 1999: 40; Grant and Iedema 2005: 56), it is possible to straddle the divide between critical and pragmatic approaches, opening up opportunities for integrated projects which address organisations' practical tasks and problems, while also leaving researchers' scholarly integrity intact.

Notes

1 Cf. Gibson, Ivancevich, and Donnelly (1994: 5), "An organization is a coordinated unit consisting of *at least two* people who function to achieve a common goal or set of goals [emphasis mine]".
2 *Market*, on the other hand, does. In economics, *market* is defined as "a mechanism through which buyers and sellers interact to determine prices and exchange goods and services" (Samuelson and Nordhaus 2005: 26). In marketing it stands for "the set of actual and potential buyers of a product" (Kotler et al. 2002: 10). Both definitions include elements relevant to the issues under discussion here, but would have been too specific. Hence the preference in this chapter for the less technical term *marketplace*.
3 One source defines it as "the world of commercial activity where goods and services are bought and sold" (http://www.wordwebonline.com/en/MARKETPLACE), another as "a set of trading conditions or the business environment" (http://www.freesearch.co.uk/dictionary/marketplace; both accessed 1 September 2005).
4 See Skulstad (this volume).
5 Accessed 11 February 2005.
6 The "digital divide" refers to inequality of access to information technology. The lines along which the world is digitally divided include geographic location, gender, ethnic origin and other sources of social exclusion (Kendall 1999: 63 and http://www.digitaldividenetwork.org/). For a discussion of the digital divide in relation to people with disabilities, see Waddell (1999).
7 According to Kotler (1991: 781), integrated marketing communications is "[t]he concept under which a company carefully integrates and co-ordinates its many communications channels to deliver a clear, consistent and compelling message about the organisation and its products". It seems fairly typical of marketing textbook discourse for Kotler to name the channels as the object of managerial intervention rather than the people using them, or the language they use. While the concept of integrated marketing communications has recently gained wide currency, doubts have also been voiced, on the basis of empirical research, about its actual application in practice (Hartley and Pickton 1999: 98–100; Stuart and Kerr 1999: 177).
8 Pickton and Broderick (2002) identify four key strategies: a global strategy, assuming a high degree of homogeneity between the cultures involved; a global niche strategy, which is based on cross-cultural similarities between sub-groups (e.g. students); a multinational strategy, which adapts communications to each foreign market; and a customisation strategy, which follows the assumption that both inter- and intra-cultural differences are high (Pickton and Broderick 2002: 130–131).
9 On dissemination see Oberhuber (this volume).
10 Kerr (1964: 20) attributes this remark to "Hutchins" (presumably, the educator Robert Maynard Hutchins, 1899–1977) without giving a source. As a google search shows, the quote is now frequently (and it would seem, wrongly) attributed to Kerr.

11 At the time of writing (February 2005), the website of the University of Bristol is a good example of how the implementation of "corporate" design can vary between the centrally managed organisational core and the departmental periphery. Some of its schools and departments, such as the School of Chemistry (http://www.chm.bris.ac.uk/) use the same template as the university homepage (http://www.bris.ac.uk/); others, such as the Department of Philosophy (http://www.bris.ac.uk/Depts/Philosophy/index.html) and the Department of Physics (http://www.phy.bris.ac.uk/) do not; and a third group, such as the Department of Italian (http://www.bris.ac.uk/Depts/Italian/) display the university logo, but have nothing else in common with the main university homepage. In a strategy paper (University of Bristol 2002/03), the university's Communications & Marketing Services recognise that their Web presentation is "a mish-mash of different styles" (p. 21), and go on to outline a project for web development aimed at the "separation of design and content". That is, design is supposed to be standardised, "safeguarding the overall look and feel of the site" and "creating consistency" (p. 22), but content "should be generated, updated and 'owned' by those closest to the subject matter" (p. 23).
12 Cf. McMillan and Cheney 1996.
13 On the affinity of modal verbs, see Fairclough (1993: 148).
14 For an example from the US, see Stanford's *Design Guidelines* (http://www.stanford.edu/group/identity, accessed 25 January 2005), from the UK, the afore-mentioned *Visual Identity Guidelines* from the University of Bristol (http://www.bris.ac.uk/cms/pro/visualidentity/, accessed 24 January 2005), from Canada, the *Logo Usage Standards* of the University of Calgary (http://www.ucalgary.ca/mp2003/logo, accessed 31 January 2005) as well as the guidelines related specifically to the University of Calgary's Haskayne School of Business, published, appropriately, under the heading *Managing the Haskayne Brand* (http://www.haskayne.ucalgary.ca/about/brand, accessed 31 January 2005).
15 Even so, Section 508 "is expected to act as a significant driver in raising the importance of accessibility in the commercial IT sector, particularly for companies wishing to secure federal contracts" (Sloan et al. 2000: 213).
16 The latter has also been followed by a code of practice published by the Disability Rights Commission (2002). Furthermore, educational institutions, whether public or private, are covered by a 2001 amendment to the DDA, the Special Educational Needs and Disability Act (SENDA). For an audit of UK academic websites with regard to compliance with SENDA, see Witt and McDermott (2004).
17 The current version (2.0) of the *Web Content Accessibility Guidelines* published by the World Wide Web Consortium is available at http://www.w3org/TR/WCAG20 (accessed 1 February 2005).
18 Davis (2002: 361) reports a similar percentage for Internet-based health information. Only 19 per cent of the home pages investigated satisfied the accessibility criteria of the World Wide Web Consortium.
19 The spending power of the disabled community is currently put at £50 billion for the UK (according to Catherine Casserley, a Senior Legislative Advisor for the UK Disability Rights Commission, quoted in Disability Rights Commission 2004a), and $220 billion for the US (according to a marketing study conducted in 2003 by the National Organization on Disability and reported on their website at http://www.nod.org/marketing/index.cfm, accessed 2 February 2005).

20 The fourth, "robustness", refers to compatibility with "current and future technology" (World Wide Web Consortium 2004), and need not concern us here.

References

Balmer, John M. T. and Edmund R. Gray
    2003   Corporate identity and corporate communications: Creating a competitive advantage. In: John M. T. Balmer and Stephen A. Greyser (eds.), *Revealing the Corporation. Perspectives on Identity, Image, Reputation, Corporate Branding, and Corporate-Level Marketing,* 124–135. London/New York: Routledge. First published in *Corporate Communications: An International Journal* 4(4): 171–176 [1999].

Bourdieu, Pierre
    1991   *Language and Symbolic Power.* Cambridge: Polity Press.

Bruhn, Manfred
    2003   *Integrierte Unternehmens- und Marketingkommunikation* [Integrated Corporate and Marketing Communication]. Stuttgart: Schäffer-Poeschel.

Brun, Monique
    2002   Creating a new identity for France Télécom. Beyond a visual exercise? In: Bertrand Moingeon and Guillaume Soenen (eds.), *Corporate and Organizational Identities. Integrating Strategy, Marketing, Communication and Organizational Perspectives,* 133–155. London/New York: Routledge.

Cameron, Deborah
    2000   *Good to Talk? Living and Working in a Communication Culture.* London etc.: Sage.

Davis, Joel J.
    2002   Disenfranchising the disabled: The inaccessibility of Internet-based health information. *Journal of Health Communication* 7: 355–367.

Daymon, Christine
    1999   The organizational context of marketing communications. In: Philip J. Kitchen (ed.), *Marketing Communications: Principles and Practice,* 73–88. London etc.: International Thomson Business Press.

Deem, Rosemary
    2003   Gender, organizational cultures and the practices of manager-academics in UK universities. *Gender, Work and Organization* 10(2): 239–259.

Delin, Judy
    2005   Brand tone of voice: a linguistic analysis of brand position. *Journal of Applied Linguistics* 2(1): 1–44.

Disability Rights Commission
    2002   *Code of Practice. Rights of Access. Goods, Facilities, Services and Premises.* London: The Stationery Office.

Disability Rights Commission
    2004a   UK businesses "cannot run and cannot hide" from equal access laws after October 1st. http://www.drc-gb.org/newsroom/newsdetails.asp?id=715&section=1, accessed 4 February 2005.

Disability Rights Commission
    2004b   *The Web. Access and Inclusion for Disabled People.* London: The Stationery Office. Available online at http://www.drc-gb.org/publicationsandreports/2.pdf. Accessed 2 February 2005.

Fairclough, Norman
    1993   Critical discourse analysis and the marketization of public discourse: the universities. *Discourse & Society* 4(2): 133–168.

Fairclough, Norman
    1996   Technologisation of discourse. In: Carmen Caldas-Coulthard and Malcolm Coulthard (eds.), *Texts and Practices*, 71–83. London: Routledge.

Fairclough, Norman
    2003   "Political correctness": the politics of culture and language. *Discourse & Society* 14(1): 17–28.

Fill, Chris
    2002   *Marketing Communications: Contexts, Strategies, and Applications.* 3rd ed. London: Prentice Hall.

Fombrun, Charles J.
    1995   *Reputation. Realizing Value from the Corporate Image.* Boston: Harvard Business School Press.

Fombrun, Charles and Mark Shanley
    1990   What's in a name? Reputation building and corporate strategy. *Academy of Management Journal* 33(2): 233–258.

Gewirtz, Sharon and Stephen Ball
    2000   From "Welfarism" to "New Managerialism": Shifting discourses of school headship in the education marketplace. *Discourse: Studies in the Cultural Politics of Education* 21(3): 253–268.

Gewirtz, Sharon, Stephen Ball and Richard Bowe
    1995   *Markets, Choice and Equity in Education.* Buckingham: Open University Press.

Gibson, James L., John M. Ivancevich and James H. Donnelly
    1994   *Organizations. Behavior, Structure, Processes.* Burr Ridge etc.: Irwin.

Giddens, Anthony
    2001   *Sociology.* 4th ed. Cambridge: Polity Press.

Grant, David and Rick Iedema
    2005   Discourse analysis and the study of organizations. *Text* 25(1): 37–66.

Hartley, Bob and Dave Pickton
    1999   Integrated marketing communications requires a new way of thinking. *Journal of Marketing Communications* 5: 97–106.

Iedema, Rick and Ruth Wodak
    1999   Introduction: organizational discourses and practices. *Discourse & Society* 10(1): 5–19.

Johnson, Sally, Jonathan Culpeper and Stephanie Suhr
    2003   From "politically correct councillors" to "Blairite nonsense": discourses of "political correctness" in British newspapers. *Discourse & Society* 14(1): 29–47.

Keat, Russell and Nicholas Abercrombie (eds.)
    1991   *Enterprise Culture.* London/New York: Routledge.

Kendall, Lori
   1999   Recontextualizing "cyberspace". Methodological considerations for on-line research. In: Steve Jones (ed.), *Doing Internet Research: Critical Issues and Methods for Examining the Net*, 57–74. Thousand Oaks, CA: Sage.

Kerr, Clark
   1964   *The Uses of the University.* Cambridge, MA: Harvard University Press.

Kirp, David L.
   2003   *Shakespeare, Einstein, and the Bottom Line. The Marketing of Higher Education.* Cambridge, MA/London: Harvard University Press.

Kitchen, Philip J.
   1999   *Marketing Communications: Principles and Practice.* London etc.: International Thomson Business Press.

Korczynski, Marek, Karen Shire, Stephen Frenkel and May Tam
   2000   Service work in consumer capitalism: customers, control and contradictions. *Work, Employment and Society* 14(4): 669–688.

Koller, Veronika
   2007   "The world's local bank": Glocalisation as a strategy in corporate branding discourse. *Social Semiotics* 17(1): 111–130.

Kotler, Philip
   1991   *Marketing Management – Analysis, Planning, Implementation and Control.* 7th ed. Harlow etc.: Prentice Hall.

Kotler, Philip and Karen F. A. Fox
   1995   *Strategic Marketing for Educational Institutions.* 2nd ed. Englewood Cliffs: Prentice Hall.

Kotler, Philip, Gary Armstrong, John Saunders and Veronika Wong
   2002   *Principles of Marketing. Third European Edition.* Harlow etc.: Prentice Hall.

Lemke, Jay
   2002   Travels in Hypermodality. *Visual Communication* 1(3): 299–325.

Mautner, Gerlinde
   2002   Universitäten online – Die Kommerzialisierung des Diskurses in der tertiären Bildung am Beispiel von "Business Schools" [Universities online. The commercialisation of higher education discourse, with special reference to business schools]. In: Caja Thimm (ed.), *Unternehmenskommunikation On- und Offline. Wandelprozesse interner und externer Kommunikation durch neue Medien,* 209–229. Vienna/New York: Peter Lang.

Mautner, Gerlinde
   2005a   For-profit discourse in the nonprofit and public sectors. In: Guido Erreygers and Geert Jacobs (eds.), *Language, Communication and the Economy,* 24–46. Amsterdam: John Benjamins.

Mautner, Gerlinde
   2005b   The entrepreneurial university: A discursive profile of a higher education buzzword. *Critical Discourse Studies* 2(2): 95–120.

McMillan, Jill J. and George Cheney
   1996   The student as consumer: The implications and limitations of a metaphor. *Communication Education* 45: 1–15.

Melewar, T. C.
  2003   Determinants of the corporate identity construct: a review of the literature. *Journal of Marketing Communications* 9: 195–200.
Melewar, T. C. and John Saunders
  1999   International corporate visual identity: standardization or localization? *Journal of International Business Studies* 30(3): 83–98.
Parker, Martin and David Jary
  1995   The McUniversity: Organization, management and academic subjectivity. *Organization* 2(2): 319–338.
Pickton, David and Amanda Broderick
  2002   *Integrated Marketing Communications.* Harlow: Financial Times Prentice Hall.
Prichard, Craig and Hugh Willmott
  1997   Just how managed is the McUniversity? *Organization Studies* 18(2): 287–316.
Rigney, Daniel
  2001   *The Metaphorical Society. An Invitation to Social Theory.* Lanham/Oxford: Rowman and Littlefield.
Robertson, Roland
  1995   Glocalization: time-space and homogeneity-heterogeneity. In: Meike Featherstone, Scott Lash and Roland Robertson (eds.), *Global Modernities*, 25–44. London: Sage.
Samuelson, Paul and William D. Nordhaus
  2005   *Economics.* 18th ed. Boston etc.: McGraw-Hill.
Sandler, Ron
  2003   A review of the PR industry today. Speech delivered at the Guild of Public Relations Practitioners' Fourth Installation Dinner. Available online at http://www.ipr.org.uk/News/speeches/sandler.htm. Accessed 15 January 2005.
Sarangi, Srikant and Celia Roberts
  1999   The dynamics of interactional and institutional orders in work-related settings. In: Srikant Sarangi and Celia Roberts (eds.), *Talk, Work and Institutional Order. Discourse in Medical, Mediation and Management Settings*, 1–57. Berlin/New York: Mouton de Gruyter.
Schultz, Don E., Stanley Tannenbaum and Robert F. Lauterborn
  1996   *The New Marketing Paradigm: Integrated Marketing Communications.* Boston: McGraw Hill.
Seeger, Matthew W.
  2004   Organizational communication ethics. Directions for critical inquiry and application. In: Dennis Tourish and Owen Hargie (eds.), *Key Issues in Organizational Communication*, 220–233. London/New York: Routledge.
Slaughter, Sheila and Larry L. Leslie
  1997   *Academic Capitalism: Politics, Policies, and the Entrepreneurial University.* Baltimore: Johns Hopkins University Press.
Sloan, Martin
  2001   Web Accessibility and the DDA [Disability Discrimination Act]. *The Journal of Information, Law and Technology (JILT)* 2001(2). Available

online at http://elj.warwick.ac.uk/jilt/01-2/sloan.html. Accessed 1 February 2005.

Sloan, David, Rowan Murray, Paul Booth and Peter Gregor
2000 Ensuring the provision of accessible digital resources. *Journal of Educational Media* 25(3): 203–216.

Stohl, Cynthia
2001 Globalizing organizational communication. In: Fredric M. Jablin and Linda L. Putnam (eds.), *The New Handbook of Organizational Communication. Advances in Theory, Research, and Methods*, 323–375. Thousand Oaks/London/New Delhi: Sage.

Stuart, Helen and Gayle Kerr
1999 Marketing communication and corporate identity: are they integrated? *Journal of Marketing Communications* 5: 169–179.

Tapp, Alan, Graeme Lindsay and Rosemary Sorrell
1999 Towards a branding framework for cause-, funding- and need-oriented charities. *Journal of Marketing Communications* 5: 39–50.

Thompson, Paul, George Callaghan and Diane van den Broek
2004 Keeping up appearances: Recruitment, skills and normative control in call centres. In: Stephen Deery and Nicholas Kinnie (eds.), *Call Centres and Human Resource Management. A Cross-National Perspective,* 129–152. Basingstoke: Palgrave.

University of Bristol
2002/03 *Communications & Marketing Strategy.* Available online at http://www.bris.ac.uk/cms/cmsstrategy2.pdf. Accessed 10 January 2005.

van Riel, Cees B. M.
2003 The management of corporate communication. In: John M. T. Balmer and Stephen A. Greyser (eds.), *Revealing the Corporation. Perspectives on Identity, Image, Reputation, Corporate Branding, and Corporate-Level Marketing,* 161–170. London/New York: Routledge.

Vassallo, Sandra
2003 Enabling the Internet for people with dyslexia. Available online at http://e-bility.com/article/dyslexia.shtml. Accessed 1 February 2005.

Waddell, Cynthia D.
1999 *The Growing Digital Divide in Access for People with Disabilities. Overcoming Barriers to Participation in the Digital Economy.* Available online at http://www.icdri.org/CynthiaW/the_digital_divide.htm. Accessed 10 February 2005.

Weick, Karl E.
1976 Educational organizations as loosely coupled systems. *Administrative Science Quarterly* 21: 1–19.

Witt, Neil and Anne McDermott
2004 Web site accessibility: what logo will we use today? *British Journal of Educational Technology* 35(1): 45–56.

World Wide Web Consortium
2004 *Web Content Accessibility Guidelines* 2.0. Working Draft 19 November 2004. Available online at http://www.w3org/TR/WCAG20. Accessed 1 February 2005.

7. Identity, image, impression: Corporate self-promotion and public reactions*

Veronika Koller

1. Corporate communication in the public sphere

Despite its stated aim to identify and denaturalise the ways in which discourse constructs and maintains power asymmetries in society (van Dijk 1993; Fairclough and Wodak 1997), Critical Discourse Analysis has a curious tendency of largely overlooking that sector of the public sphere where the most, and the most unequally distributed, power is amassed today, i.e. the corporate sector and its discourses.[1] By leaving corporate discourse largely unchallenged, critical researchers leave corporate voices in a position to shape the public sphere to an ever greater extent and thus contribute to the power asymmetries they set out to remedy. In this chapter, I will adapt the three-fold model of text, interaction and social context developed within Critical Discourse Analysis to account for how corporate authors project images of their company into the public sphere, and for how far texts by employees and customers show these stakeholders to accept that image. To this end, I will analyse a mission statement and look at the practices of production, distribution and reception surrounding it. The analysis will also extend to employees' and customers' blogs to ascertain possible explicit recontextualisations of the mission statement and implicit reliance on its concepts. In this way, I attempt to give an account of the perceived power status of corporate elites and their stakeholders, and of the textually mediated relations between them.

2. Literature review: Work on corporate discourse

The area of corporate discourse that has received most attention from linguists, often in tandem with management and organisational theorists,[2] is companies' and other institutions' internal spoken and written communication, also referred to as organisational discourse (Mumby and Clair 1997; Iedema and Wodak 1999, 2005; Jablin and Putnam 2001; Grant et al. 2004). While the study of organisational discourse in general is characterised by combining concepts from sociology, philosophy, psychology and semiotics at a high level of theoretical abstraction, increasing specificity in the area usually goes hand in hand with an increased focus on empirical data and/or practical application (see Koester 2004 for a practically oriented analysis of a wide variety of business discourses and genres). Thus, work with a specific research interest such as intercultural business communication (Candlin and Gotti 2004) or gendered discourse in an organisational context (Kendall and Tannen 1997, Holmes 2006, Mullany 2007), while still covering a broad range of genres and media, typically applies theory to empirical data analysis rather than engaging in theory development. This trend continues when one looks at the possible sub-division of spoken and written genres in corporate discourse (see Iedema 2003 for a multi-modal analysis). Research into spoken genres in organisational discourse continues to be influenced by Boden and Zimmerman's (1991) as well as Drew and Heritage's (1992) seminal works. In harnessing conversation analysis and the ethnography of communication as methods to investigate talk in professional settings, these early anthologies provided an influential toolkit for researchers interested in spoken organisational genres (Boden 1994; Sarangi and Roberts 1999) and its various aspects such as intercultural communication (Bargiela-Chiappini and Harris 1997a; Yuling, Scollon, and Scollon 2002), politeness (Holmes and Stubbe 2003) or gendered talk (Tannen 1995). Some recent studies of spoken discourse in organisations have adopted a critical stance that takes into account the broader socio-economic context and the historical development of late capitalism (Iedema and Scheeres 2003).

Research into written genres in corporate discourse has likewise drawn on discourse analysis, often combining it with genre analysis (Bargiela-Chiappini and Nickerson 1999; Dieltjens and Heynderickx 2001). Again, crucial foci are gender (Kessapidou and Makri-Tsilipakou 2001), intercultural written communication (Gimenez 2002; Zhu 2005), as well as the impact of new technologies on communicative practices and genres within organisations (Yates, Orlikowski, and Okamura 1999; Ducheneaut 2002). A sub-field of corporate discourse analysis that spans both spoken and written communication is the growing body of research looking at narratives and their function in institutional contexts (Czarniawska-Joerges 1997; Czarniawska and Gagliardi 2003). Discourse and genre analysis are once more the central methods employed in the study of both spoken (Hopkinson 2003) and written narratives (Rhodes 2001), with researchers in management and organisational theory also using content analysis (see Boje 2001 on methods to analyse narratives).

Another genre that has been studied extensively is that of business meetings (Putnam and Roloff 1992; Bargiela-Chiappini and Harris 1997b; Menz 1999), especially those involving participants from different cultures (Bargiela and Turra forthcoming; Poncini 2004) and of different genders (Baxter 2003: 128–180; Martín Rojo and Gómez Esteban 2003). While this persistent focus on culture and gender bears witness to the growing importance of diversity management in contemporary organisations, studies on gender in particular have gone beyond discourse and genre analysis to include a critical discussion of the discursive construction of gendered social roles in institutional settings.

Although the focus of this chapter, and indeed this volume, is communication in the public sphere, it is worth noting that internally and externally oriented corporate discourse cannot always be clearly demarcated. Van de Mieroop's (2005) study on corporate identity construction in speeches given at business seminars is a case in point. The speech situations investigated were seminars involving academic and corporate experts, but not the general public, making for interorganisational but not public discourse. Genres such as mission statements have multiple internal and external audiences (employees, shareholders, suppliers), leading to shifts in address and reference. In the following, categorisation as external will hinge upon specimens of the genre being available in the public sphere, e.g. the company website.

When thinking of corporate discourse in the public sphere, it is advertising that comes first to mind. Given the ubiquitous, pervasive and even intrusive nature of advertising, this is little wonder; advertising is the one facet of corporate communication that affects each and every member of the general public to a greater or lesser extent. As an object of research, advertising is first and foremost the concern of studies in marketing, of which it is a part, and advertising research in this framework has been going strong for almost a century (see Taylor 2005 for a review of recent work in the field). However, given the fact that management, including marketing, studies necessarily rely on feeder disciplines,[3] studies in advertising, its design, proliferation and effectiveness in terms of recall, raised brand awareness and buying behaviour, have relied mostly on (cognitive) psychology, but also on semiotics and linguistics (McQuarrie and Mick 1996, 1999, 2003; Phillips and McQuarrie 2004). Just as research on advertising has drawn on linguistics, the growing importance of advertising in the saturated markets of post-industrial societies has also rendered it interesting for linguists. An early study to look at how (the English) language is used for promotional purposes is Leech's (1966) seminal account. Naturally, the changing nature of advertising in the past forty years has given rise to further linguistic investigations (Myers 1994, 1998; Cook 2001).

Apart from the admittedly significant research on advertising, however, other forms of corporate discourse in the public sphere remain under-researched to date. This is despite the growing importance of public relations (PR) vis-à-vis advertising (see Cook, this volume):[4] At a time when even the "irony and reflexivity [used] to distance the brand from the overly hyped and homogenizing conceits of conventional advertising" has itself degenerated into a cliché (Holt 2002: 84, 86), companies are adopting ethically questionable techniques such as "viral" (Grauel 2004), "subliminal" (Bakan 2004: 132–134) or "stealth" marketing (Holt 2002: 85). Alternatively, they seek to build goodwill through increased transparency, good citizenship and social responsibility. Obviously, the latter strategy requires the use of text genres from the field of PR.

Research into some of these text types directed at various stakeholder groups includes studies of spoken genres such as call centre interaction (see Cameron 2000, for a critical analysis of its gendered features) and other service encounters (Bowles and Pallotti 2004; Ventola 2005) as well as face-to-face interviews and phone calls dealing with customer complaints (Morales-López, Prego-Vásquez, and Domínguez-Seco 2005; Schnieders 2005). The methods used in these studies, i.e. conversation analysis and ethnography of communication as well as genre analysis, have – with or without a critical edge – also been employed to account for the multimodal nature of genres like environmental reports (Skulstad, this volume) or company brochures and websites (Koller 2007). Probably because they are more easily obtainable, written genres have received most attention to date. Thus, Delin (2005) has looked at the layout and tone of voice used in, for instance, bills issued by telephone and utilities companies. Going beyond description and interpretation alone, she has complemented her systemic-functional analysis by suggesting ways to extend branding to less obvious instances of corporate communication.

In fact, the ongoing marketisation of the public sphere (Fairclough 1993) means that especially promotional discourses colonise, and are appropriated by, other discourses. Thus, public discourse has become increasingly managerial and promotional, including all the typical features of advertising, such as persuasive rhetoric, explicit positive evaluation and direct address, making for a "synthetic personalisation" which reconstructs citizens as consumers and consumers as the close friends of product and service providers. This trend has seen many genres that used to be mostly informative being recast as hybrid genres combining information and self-promotion. Evidence of this trend can be found in job advertisements, which increasingly adopt the up-beat tone prevalent in the sunshine world of advertising. Another case in point is annual reports and letters from the chief executive officer to shareholders, the producers of which react to the increased pressure that comes with shareholder value by including promotional features such as persuasive narratives (Jameson 2000) or positive description and evaluation (Bhatia 2004: 81–84). A focal point of interest is again intercultural communication (Garzone 2004). Other externally oriented specimens of corporate discourse are press releases (Jacobs 1999: chapter 7) as well as company profiles and mission statements. The latter genre has been investigated from a rhetorical point of view, looking at how it appeals to credibility and emotion (Isaksson 2005). The multiple audiences of a mission statement and its concomitant multiple orientations, or lack thereof, have also attracted attention (Gurau and McLaren 2003). Other accounts stress the function of the mission statement as a carrier of ideology, analysing parameters such as tense and aspect, modality or pronoun use (Swales and Rogers 1995). Interestingly, the latter study briefly mentions the

Identity, image, impression: corporate self-promotion and public reactions 159

need of taking into account the socio-cognitive factors impacting on the production and interpretation of mission statements (Swales and Rogers 1995: 237). Cognitive theories of communication and message interpretation are also discussed by Hackley (1998), who, however, contrasts them with social constructionist views on meaning making.[5] Swales and Rogers' call for an analysis of mission statements that takes socio-cognitive aspects into consideration finds a partial answer in Koller's (forthcoming) study of mission statements, which discusses the textual construction of corporate brands as socio-cognitive representations.

The various areas of research in corporate discourse, as well as methods and special foci, are summarised in Figure 1 below. This brief overview of the literature on corporate discourse shows that – except for advertising – research into externally oriented discourse, while gaining ground, remains relatively scattered. In the following, I will propose a comprehensive approach to researching corporate public discourse that relates texts to their conditions of production, distribution and reception and these in turn to the wider socio-economic context as it maps out at the situational, institutional and societal level. The same framework also takes cognitive aspects of text production and interpretation into account. Given the object of study, this approach relies on linguistic tools that can potentially also be employed in marketing research.

3. Researching corporate discourse in the public sphere

Faced with growing pressure from consumers and critics who demand that they behave according to ethical standards, companies

> have come to realise that organisational practices which traditionally have been thought of as strictly internal (...) are now becoming central themes in the public discourse and thus part of the communication that the organisation (...) carries on with its surroundings. (Christensen and Askegaard 2001: para. 22)

This relative strengthening of corporate public discourse calls for a comprehensive research paradigm that incorporates the analysis of texts with their production by corporate authors, their distribution in the public sphere and the reception of such texts, and the concepts expressed therein, by various stakeholder groups. These interactions around a text are in turn seen as embedded in a wider socio-economic context that operates at various levels. Importantly, a full-fledged analysis should also account for the cognitive aspects of discourse production and reception, since "marketing, and marketing communication, has become the 'business of meanings'" (Hackley 1998: 97) and organisations in general "need to be seen as specialized sites for the construction, maintenance, as

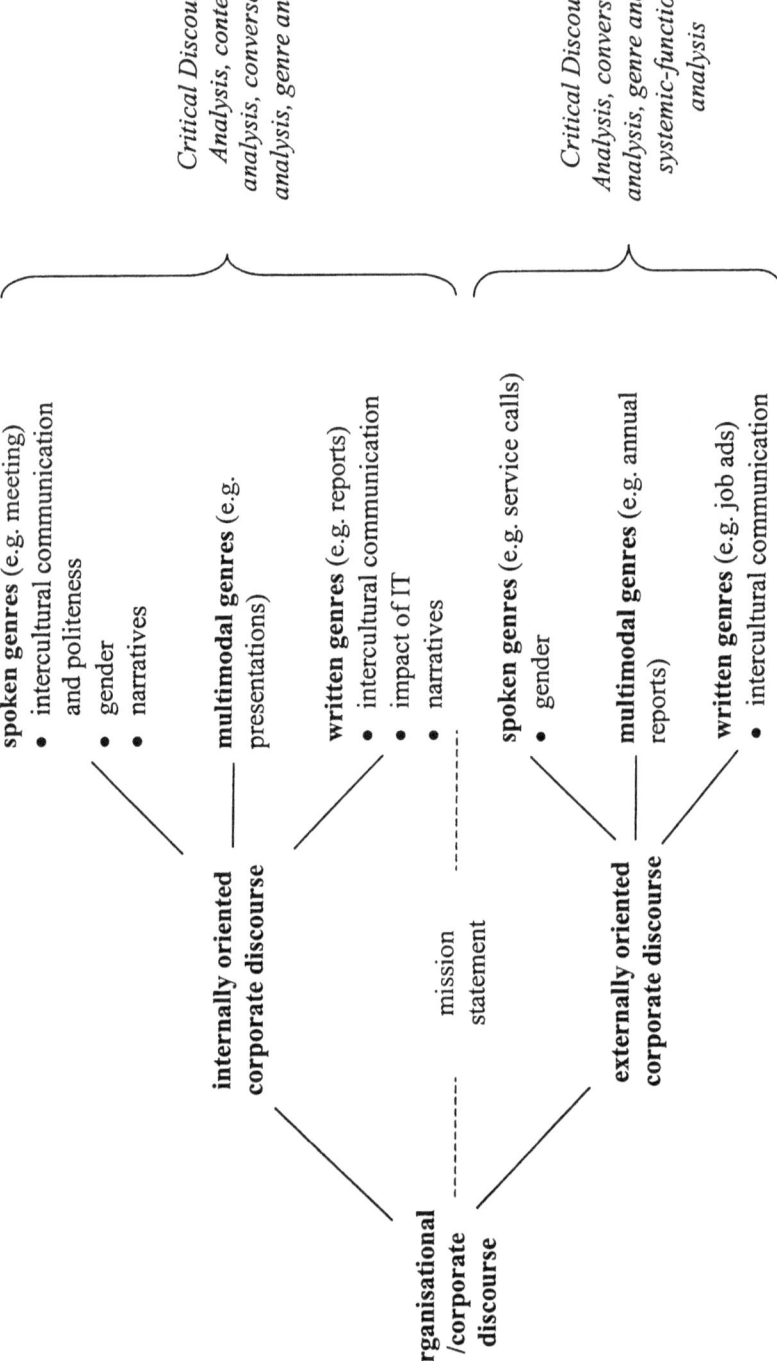

Figure 1. Areas and methods in researching corporate discourse

well as the contestation of meanings" (Iedema and Wodak 2005: 1605; see Graham, this volume).

Texts that instantiate corporate discourse in the public sphere can be located in a tripartite framework like the one graphically represented and explained in Figure 2 (see also Koller 2004: 21–23):

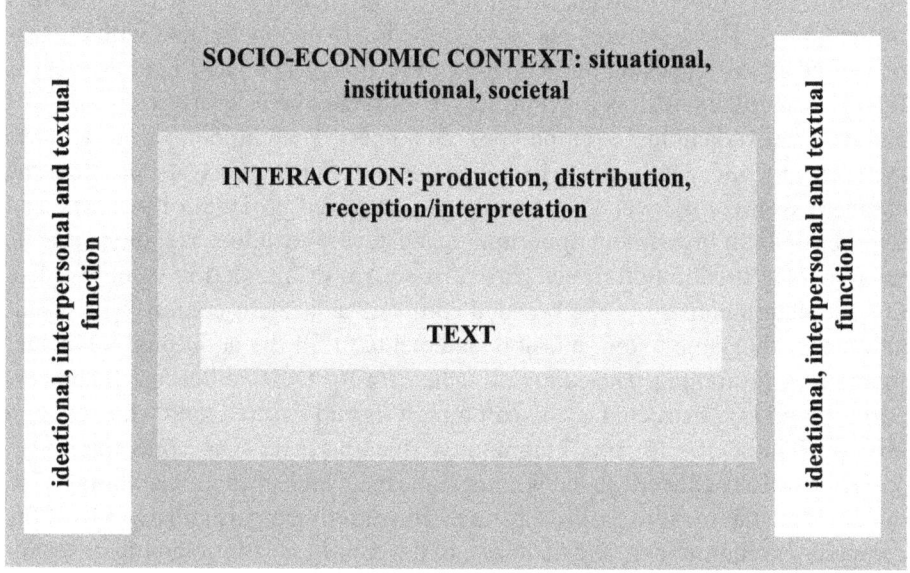

Figure 2. Three-level framework for researching discourse (adapted from Fairclough 1995: 98)

Research based on the above model incorporates a notion of discourse as "texts in contexts" (van Dijk 2005), including the specific processes of text production, distribution and reception/interpretation.[6] Together, these processes represent the textually mediated interaction between discourse participants in their respective roles and relations. Interaction is in turn embedded in a wider socio-economic context that plays out at the situational, institutional and societal level. All three levels are mutually constitutive so that texts mediate and reflect discursive interaction as well as instantiate and reproduce socio-economic contexts. As all three levels in the above model are embedded in and (re)produce each other, each level includes all three Hallidayan meta-functions of the textual, interpersonal and ideational (Halliday and Matthiessen 2004: 29–30). In addition, personal and social cognition are intertwined with discourse as particular cognitive models are usually over-represented in discourse. Such discursive prominence may in turn lead to these models being even more firmly anchored in recipients' cognition.

Text is here defined as an instance of written or spoken language use (often combined with other semiotic systems, see van Leeuwen 2005) that is of indeterminate length. To illustrate, take the genre of the mission statement as one instance of corporate discourse in the public sphere. The text itself will combine various semiotic modes (written language and still images, sometimes complemented by video clips) and be characterised by particular linguistic features such as high-affinity modals, direct address or mental process types (Koller forthcoming). These features obviously function to endow the text with the textual standards of cohesion and coherence (de Beaugrande and Dressler 1981). Interpersonally, the text as a whole serves to define the role of various internal and external stakeholders (employees, customers, shareholders) in relation to the company and vice versa. Mission statements further serve to promote the company as the employer of choice, as the preferred provider of products and services or as an investment opportunity. Whatever the objectives, the text in its interpersonal function promotes particular scripts of interaction while its ideational function constructs the branded company as a socio-cognitive representation.[7] By the same token, mission statements fulfill the additional ideational function of promoting particular self-schemata for their audiences: If the corporate brand is constructed as my community/friend/partner, then who am I and how do I interact with this community/friend/partner? The concomitant research questions concern a) the linguistic means which corporate authors use in the mission statement to make it a site of constructing a particular image of the company in relation to its stakeholders, b) the conditions of producing, distributing and receiving the text as they are indicative of the wider socio-economic context discourse participants operate in, and c) if and how the text itself and the main concepts and values expressed therein are taken up by stakeholders' texts. The analysis needed to answer these questions can, at the textual level, employ a range of methods, including quantitative corpus analysis and qualitative genre analysis. However, quantitative methods in discourse analysis can only ever be a first step and will have to be complemented by a more qualitative approach looking at genre features, genre-mixing and interdiscursivity.

As for the conditions of their production, distribution and reception/interpretation, mission statements are addressed at, and received by, various audiences, which at the textual level is reflected in features such as the presence of multiple actors with different actions and attributions ascribed to them. Further, mission statements are typically commissioned by board-level executives, who thus act as principals, and authored by staff of the communications department, sometimes with the help of external consultants. Although input from across the company is occasionally sought, "creating mission statements is viewed as a senior manager privilege/prerogative" and external stakeholders are hardly ever involved (Baetz and Bart 1996: 530). Status comes into play when considering that the executives with more responsibility and power are likely to produce and dis-

Identity, image, impression: corporate self-promotion and public reactions 163

tribute the texts while lower-level employees are mostly at the receiving end of texts. Mission statements are mostly distributed on the company's intranet as well as on its public website. Using these media for distribution to internal and external audiences means that the text in question is widely accessible. Still, it requires proactive audiences, i.e. readers need to search for the text of their own accord. Given the diverse internal and external audiences, reception conditions will differ vastly, ranging from office to domestic environments, from deliberate viewing to merely coming across the text while surfing the company's website. At the textual level, the distribution channel imposes particular constraints on the text, for instance a certain brevity and emphasis on the visual that may be considered appropriate for the medium and the literacy practices of its users.

Interpersonally, the usually top-down process of production and distribution again defines roles of the interactants and rules for their interaction around the text. For instance, in an old-economy, hierarchical organisation, top-down production and distribution that confine employees and other audiences to passive reception will reinforce these audiences' self-schema of being relatively powerless and discourage them from challenging the rules of text production in the company. For a text whose propositions are to be owned by all employees, excluding a significant layer of staff from drawing up the text is clearly problematic. In the corporate culture of a more lateral organisation, the same top-down process may be inappropriate and thus cause cognitive and other psychological unease. Ideationally, textually mediated interaction not only constructs, reinforces or challenges the scripts for organisational interaction but also impacts on the socio-cognitive representation that is the corporate brand.

Production and distribution processes can be ascertained relatively easily by interviews and questionnaires with the people involved; sometimes the information is even offered on the corporate website itself. Reception and interpretation, however, are more elusive. In a first step, one will have to decide what addressees to focus on and then decide on the method accordingly. In the case study below, for instance, consumer reaction was gauged by analysing blogs on the company's products and image for intertextual reference and traces of the central notions expressed in one company's mission statement.[8] To this end, I used the Google blog search engine to find occurrences of the key word "IBM" in blogs no older than three months. From the results, I singled out a few entries that started threads, as replies tend to be too short to warrant analysis. Blogs as an emergent genre have met with both approval for enabling "participatory democracy" (Blood 2004) and with criticism for filtering opinions and thus obstructing democratic processes and variety of opinion (Sunstein 2004; Massing 2005: 24–26). Also, the "blogosphere" is heavily skewed towards the US and Canada, with little or no participation from regions that are bogged down by censorship and/or less advanced technology (Kumar et al. 2004). It seems uncontroversial, however, that blogging creates communities of practice centering on special interests that enable their members to spread and thereby reinforce or challenge opinions, beliefs and attitudes. Business is increasingly trying to harness this power of blogging by drawing up guidelines for employees who engage in blogs relating to the company, or by issuing their own blogs (Baker and Green 2005; see Cass, Munroe, and Turcotte 2005[9] for the effectiveness of corporate blogging). For the researcher, independent blogs offer an opportunity to tap into the reception of a company, its products and image, by consumers.

Textually mediated interaction is in turn positioned in a mutually constitutive relation with a broader socio-economic context that impacts on the levels of situation, institution and society as such. The context of a more or less deregulated market economy determines, via the phenomenon of the limited company, particular situations of production, distribution and reception/interpretation, which have an impact on the interpersonal interaction between various groups that are more or less loosely affiliated with the company. The company as found in late capitalism also has a structure that is traditionally hierarchical, although the New Economy starting around the mid-1990s has seen a flattening of hierarchies and the advent of lean management. This changing situation again impacts on interpersonal relationships in quite distinct ways, not least by bringing about simultaneous and often conflicting scripts for interaction and, ideationally, schemata of the organisation and the self in relation to it. Interpersonally and ideationally, the framework of late capitalism again redefines corporate structures and ideas about the role and nature of the company and its various stakeholders. This last stage of the analysis will invariably draw on work done in organisational theory, political economy and the sociology of work.

In the remainder of this chapter, I shall illustrate the above research paradigm by briefly looking at some empirical data.

4. Case study: IBM's mission statement and stakeholder reactions

The following brief case study centres on an aspect of IBM's construction of itself as a corporate brand in the public sphere, looking at how IBM constructs its corporate brand by promoting its ideal self in its mission statement. This will be followed by an investigation into how the company and its values as expressed in the mission statement feature in blogs run by employees and customers, in particular if there are any intertextual traces to the IBM text. The analysis will account for the textual, interactional and socio-economic dimension in both cases.

4.1. IBM mission statement

IBM's mission statement, reproduced in Appendix A, is at its macro-level structured by exemplifying, echoing, extending and elaborating chains. These are formed by the expressions from the word fields of emotion and partnership and tend to cluster in the middle part, especially lines 10–40, forming two sets of interrelated chains (lines 10–25 and 29–40). Looking at those chains, we can see that the first chain begins in line 11 ("uncertain, conflicted or hesitant"), with the negatively evaluated emotional state being extended to "painful to read" in line 25. All other instances refer to positively connoted emotional states and processes, the first of which ("we needed to find a way to engage everyone" in lines 16–17) being elaborated by "we invited all 319,000 IBMers (...) to engage" in lines 21–22. The next set of chains starts in line 29, with "enthusiastic consensus" being extended to "dedication to every client's success" and "every CEO craves" in lines 33 and 38–39, respectively. All three instances are linked by the intensity they convey. The widest-spanning chain starts with the sub-heading in line 35 ("trust and personal responsibility in all relationships"). Its three element all trigger chains across the remainder of the text: They are each echoed in line 45 ("our values of trust and personal responsibility") and 48 ("our relationships with investors"), respectively. From there, the three concepts, while retaining their sequence, are spread still further apart, with "trust" being exemplified as "we are trusting [our people]" (lines 61–62) and "responsibility" and "relationships" being echoed in lines 68–69. As these three are the only items to be repeated in a three-link chain, they can be identified as central concepts.

The text further employs a number of persuasive devices. Certainty is conveyed by the pronounced use of deontic modality (including "we needed to affirm" in lines 14–15, "I must tell you", line 36, and "we have to innovate" in line 67). Direct address and use of first person singular are another particularity of the IBM text (e.g. "I must tell you, this process has been very meaningful to me", line 36). As the linguistic equivalent of significant eye contact, these phrases are meant to engage the reader and lend further credibility to the text.

The most frequent personal actor is we/our, which occurs 38 times (as contrasted with 12 times for they/them/their and 9 times for I/me), suggesting its dominant status. Further, the first person plural actor is always found as acting, while second and third person also feature as affected entities. The two audiences addressed by the mission statement are employees and investors. In the first case, the top-down communication is potentially at odds with the intention to make employees identify with the corporate brand conveyed, a tension that is eased by positive politeness strategies such as compliments ("smart [...] independent-minded workforce", lines 18–19), showing interest ("we needed to [...]

engage everyone", lines 16–17), claiming common ground ("grass-roots consensus", line 29) and claiming reciprocity ("keeping the dialog free-flowing", line 28). Investor communication in the latter half of the text is equally characterised by positive politeness, notably claims to reciprocity ("we work for each other's success", lines 65–66) and self-deprecation ("investors first receive meaningful returns [...] before [...] executives can realize a penny of profit", lines 50–52). Again, the lack of negative politeness ties in with the overall direct and unhedged nature of the text.

The tense used is the present, making the ideal self converge with the actual self. The narrative in lines 48–58 also reflects perceived expectations of investors after the early 2000s flurry of corporate scandals, and thus incorporates the company's "ought self" (Kunda 1999: 472). All in all, the corporate brand is presented as a reliable, fair and responsible partner who shows an engaging and trustworthy behaviour while putting themselves last. Nevertheless, actor roles are ambiguous in that the predominant *we* refers to the categorised actor "IBMers" (lines 9–12) but is backgrounded everywhere else. Strikingly, IBMers are later allocated third-person status (lines 23–25), leaving the reader to infer that *we* refers to the board or executives. Still, these are referred to as "they" in lines 49–52 and set apart from investors. It seems that the principal of the text, i.e. senior management, avoids fully identifying with either employees or executives, making "we" a paradoxical actor that is simultaneously inclusive and exclusive because backgrounded (Dieltjens and Heynderickx 2001). In line with its "political role", the text is therefore "vague, inclusive and persuasive" (Iedema and Wodak 2005: 1607). It is also contradictory in its purpose, with the other-centered persuasive devices being at odds with a narcissistic focus on the corporate self and a detached managerial class unwilling to identify themselves. This tension, created by the multiple internal and external audiences, is indeed characteristic of the genre.

4.2. IBM blogs and bloggers on IBM

Moving on to blogs to which users of IBM's products contribute, it has to be kept in mind that customers are not the primary target group of the company's mission statement. Rather, we could see above that the text is first and foremost addressed at employees and shareholders. Nevertheless, distributing it via IBM's webpage acknowledges secondary audiences by rendering the mission statement a publicly available document that is open to reactions by various stakeholders, including customers. In an attempt to regain control of the "anarchic" Internet, companies now publish their own blogs on products and services. IBM pioneered this movement by launching developerWorks (http://www.ibm.com/developer-works), a site aimed at IT professionals that includes downloads, tutorials and blogs on various topics and is hosted by IBM employees. These obviously not only happen to be members of the company; by acting as hosts, they also repre-

Identity, image, impression: corporate self-promotion and public reactions 167

sent the corporate voice. It is therefore little wonder that some of the conceptualisations featured in the mission statement are recontextualised in the blogs and taken up by discussants from outside IBM. For instance, the following example features the metaphoric notion of "a company's DNA", which is visually represented on the mission statement webpage as well:

> Should SOA [service-oriented architecture] start to be embedded in the DNA of the Enterprise or is it something that should be left as best addressed piecemeal, project by project, on an "as need" basis? What do you think? (...)
> Let it evolve like DNA. The more we put in the DNA, the more restrictive the future generation of SOA will be, the less we put in the DNA the more fragile our SOA generation will be.
> (http://www.128.ibm.com/developerworks/blogs/dw_blog_comments.jspa?blog=490&entry=96867&roll=0#comments, 7 October and 7 November 2005)

However, the impact of IBM's in-house blogs in the public sphere may be limited: Cass, Munroe and Turcotte (2005: 52–53) observe that developerWorks bloggers do not discuss products in enough detail to garner much user feedback and that their attempt to build a brand community has therefore not been entirely successful.

Halfway between in-house commercial blogs and targeted customer blogs (Lankshear and Knobel 2003), we find IBM employees contributing to external blogs. Again, IBM was among the first companies to issue blogging guidelines for its employees (http://www.snellspace.com/IBM_Blogging_Policy_and_Guidelines.pdf). Employees adhere to the guidelines whenever they include disclaimers in their blogs and provide balanced accounts of IBM products compared to competitors':

> It's now been a few months since the Toshiba M200 Tablet PC I bought last year unceremoniously fell apart just out of warranty, and I've finally gotten over my annoyance with that experience sufficiently to begin thinking about buying a replacement. The leading contender has been the IBM X41 Tablet, partly because I love ThinkPads (full disclosure, I work for IBM), and have been looking forward to a Thinkpad tablet since before I bought the M200, and because the reviews have been good, and it seems like a nice solid little machine. (...)
> (http://davidgaw.typepad.com/cuzwesaidso/2005/11/index.html, 4 and 7 November 2005)

Beyond such rather vague brand loyalty, however, none of the central goals and values expressed in the mission statement are drawn upon by employees.

Identification with the company does not seem to extend to external customers. In customers' blogs, IBM and its corporate brand as laid out in their mission statement features in three different ways: Firstly, the mission statement, or parts of it, can be quoted verbatim. Strikingly, such direct quotes like other promotional communication such as press releases attract no comments whatsoever. In general, bloggers are rather cynical about corporate branding in the blogosphere:

the only solution (of course) is to buy overpriced IBM software products (...) that require extensive IBM training and IBM consulting service and enormous (...) investments in (I suppose why not) IBM hardware. I get it, and (...) the fact that [tech news blog] ZDnet earns a good buck from IBM advertising [is just a coincidence]. Thank you ZDnet once again for such an unbiased and even handed news story.
(http://www.zdnet.com.au/forums/0,39029293,39193420-20117729o,00.htm, 2 June 2005)

Secondly, and rather predictably, we find members of the nerdier tech communities rejecting the grand values expressed in the mission statement. Instead, the above cynicism is intensified by endowing IBM and its executives with a range of colourful invectives.

Finally, more mainstream users of IBM products also show little appreciation of IBM's "dedication to every client's success". Brand affiliation is questionable, and users' experiences with IBM's flagship products[10] ThinkCentre (desktop), ThinkPad (laptop) and PalmOne (palmtop) tend towards the factual and slightly disgruntled:

I have an IBM ThinkCentre that serves (no pun intended) as our "home server". (...) Every once in a while I back the drive up to a DVD. And that's where my current problem begins. (...) This machine is only about 2 years old. It should NOT be as decrepit as it is!
(http://b-n.blogspot.com/2005/10/i-hate-computers.html, 25 October 2005)

After recounting a negative customer service experience, another blogger asks: "If you can't trust brands like IBM (...) who can you trust?" (http://www.280group.com/2004/11/customer-service-brands.html, 9 November 2004). While this still acknowledges the "blue-chip" nature of IBM, the overall discursive and mental representation is again tilted towards the negative. Brand endorsements like the following are extremely rare:

Earlier this morning I met my new best friend that will be my companion for at least the next two years. He will help me with all my homework, projects, and assignments and I will trust him with all my deepest and darkest secrets. It's my new IBM Thinkpad T43.
(http://journals.aol.com/buckyhoo/UNC/entries/326, 7 July 2005)

However, even this marketer's dream of bonding with a personalised and gendered brand goes on to reiterate the criticism found in most blogs that IBM products are overpriced.

To sum up then, we can see that IBM's mission statement may reach its aim of building brand loyalty with employees and in this respect, "the act of communicating this mission message to certain parties" could indeed "further the ends expressed in it" (Hackley 1998: 95). However, customers, although they have access to the mission statement, are probably less interested in reading it. More importantly still, their IBM-related blogging shows that the company's expressed value of dedication to client success does not, in the absence of satisfactory products and services, generate brand loyalty. Clearly, disseminating a company's values in the public sphere alone does not suffice to implement them in the discourse and cognition of external stakeholders. The above testimonials show that lofty goals and laudable values need to translate into reliable and competitively priced products and services if customers are to accept the image expressed in corporate statements. Otherwise, the consequences are as betrayed in the above quotes from customer blogs, which are largely devoid of any appreciation for IBM's values. On the contrary, attitudes reflected in the above sample tend to range from the factual at best to the spiteful and cynical at worst.

Customers can be assumed to care more about good products and services than about whether they are addressed by corporate statements. Nevertheless, the authors' focus on employees and the all-powerful shareholders, and their failure to include customers in the textually mediated interaction, is further proof of the often narcissistic and exclusive nature of corporations. This disregard for anyone outside the company is bound to be reflected in other forms of externally oriented communication as well (and will ultimately show in inferior products). Such self-centred pseudo-communication will inevitably lead to a widening gap between companies' self-image and their image in parts of the public sphere.

5. Conclusion

We are witnessing the ongoing colonisation of various areas of the public sphere by discourses originating in the context of corporations. This interdiscursive alignment necessitates critical research into corporate discourse itself. While intra-organisational discourse continues to attract broad, if not always critical, scholarly interest, investigations into corporate discourse in the public sphere are only just increasing in number and scope. However, if we are to understand how companies' discourse can continue to impact on various public spheres despite the elitist detachment and narcissism of corporate leaders, and despite cynical public attitudes towards it, it is necessary to look at the points where companies discursively intersect with the wider public. This includes analysing not only the respective texts and genres themselves. Given that "a useful understanding of the roles of genres in institutional and community affairs requires more sociocognitive input than the texts themselves provide" (Swales and Rogers 1995: 237), it is also paramount to consider the production, distribution and reception of texts and the socio-economic context in which such textually mediated interaction takes place. By accounting for at least part of the network of texts that surround a nodal text such as a mission statement, it is possible to ascertain how corporate authors succeed, or fail, in disseminating and implementing corporate images and corporate discourse in the public sphere. In this way, linguistic and discourse analysis can complement research in marketing and its feeder disciplines, psychology and sociology. Crucially, textual analysis will take a differentiated view of the public sphere by discussing the power status of its different members. In the present case, the decision to exclude any but the most formulaic reference to customers from the text suggests that the corporate authors regard this particular stakeholder group as less powerful and therefore more negligible than employees, let alone shareholders. This exclusion may well be just one facet of a lack of regard for customer needs and wants, which will ultimately bring about products and services of inferior quality and/or user-friendliness. Companies thus risk alienating this most important stakeholder group.

Lemke (2003) has argued that in postmodernism, texts, text types and specific ways of relating texts lend cohesion to social systems such as multinational corporations, which are often only held together by "empty or hyperreal signifiers" (Lemke 2003: 134) such as brands. If companies become brands, promotional genres are crucial in sustaining corporate systems through garnering public support. Yet, if the data sample analysed above is anything to go by, blogs are another central outlet for both positive and negative PR and may thus bring about a level of consumer empowerment that could make it impossible for companies to continue prioritising other stakeholder groups over them. Critical analysis of corporate discourse in the public sphere is ideally positioned to monitor, analyse and discuss this shift in social relations.

Appendix A (IBM n.d.)

asterisks: partnership and emotion lexis

At IBM, we strive to lead in the invention, development and manufacture of the industry's most advanced information technologies, including computer systems, software, storage systems and microelectronics. We translate these advanced technologies into value for our customers through our professional solutions, services and consulting businesses worldwide.
Business value, and a company's values
We've been spending a great deal of time thinking, debating and determining the fundamentals of this company. It has been important to do so. When IBMers have been crystal clear and united about our strategies and purpose, it's amazing what we've been able to create and accomplish. When we've been *uncertain, conflicted or hesitant*, we've squandered opportunities and even made blunders that would have sunk smaller companies.
It may not surprise you, then, that last year we examined IBM's core values for the first time since the company's founding. In this time of great change, we needed to affirm IBM's reason for being, what sets the company apart and what should drive our actions as individual IBMers. Importantly, we needed to find a

way to *engage* everyone in the company and get them to speak up on these important issues. Given the realities of a smart, global, independent-minded, 21st-century workforce like ours, I don't believe something as vital and personal as values could be dictated from the top.

So, for 72 hours last summer, we invited all 319,000 IBMers around the world to *engage* in an open "values jam" on our global intranet.

IBMers by the tens of thousands weighed in. They were *thoughtful and passionate* about the company they want to be a part of. They were also brutally honest. Some of what they wrote was *painful* to read, because they pointed out all the bureaucratic and dysfunctional things that get in the way of serving clients, working as a team or implementing new ideas.

But we were resolute in keeping the dialog free-flowing and candid. And I don't think what resulted broad, *enthusiastic*, grass-roots consensus could have been obtained in any other way.

In the end, IBMers determined that our actions will be driven by these values:

Dedication to every client's success

Innovation that matters, for our company and for the world

Trust and personal responsibility in all *relationships*

I must tell you, this process has been very meaningful to me. We are getting back in touch with what IBM has always been about and always will be about in a very concrete way. And I feel that I've been handed something every CEO *craves*: a mandate, for exactly the right kinds of transformation, from an entire workforce.

Where will this lead? It is a work in progress, and many of the implications remain to be discovered. What I can tell you is that we are rolling up our sleeves to BRING IBM's values to life in our policies, procedures and daily operations.

I've already touched on a number of things relating to clients and innovation, but our values of *trust and personal responsibility* are being managed just as seriously from changes in how we measure and reward performance, to how we equip and support IBMers' community volunteerism.

Our values underpin our *relationships* with investors as well. In late February, the board of directors approved sweeping changes in executive compensation. They include innovative programs that ensure investors first receive meaningful returns a 10 percent increase in the stock price before IBM's top 300 executives can realize a penny of profit from their stock option grants. Putting that into perspective, IBM's market value would have to increase by $17 billion before executives saw any benefit from this year's option awards. In addition, these executives will be able to acquire market-priced stock options only if they first invest their own money in IBM stock. We believe these programs are unprecedented, certainly in our industry and perhaps in business.

Clearly, leading by values is very different from some kinds of leadership demonstrated in the past by business. It is empowering, and I think that's much healthier. Rather than burden our people with excessive controls, we are *trusting* them to make decisions and to act based on values – values they themselves shaped.

To me, it's also just common sense. In today's world, where everyone is so interconnected and interdependent, it is simply essential that we work for each other's success. If we're going to solve the biggest, thorniest and most widespread problems in business and society, we have to innovate in ways that truly matter. And we have to do all this by taking *personal responsibility* for all of our *relationships* with clients, colleagues, partners, investors and the public at large. This is IBM's mission as an enterprise, and a goal toward which we hope to work with many others, in our industry and beyond.

Samuel J. Palmisano
Chairman, President and Chief Executive Officer

Notes

*   I would like to thank Greg Myers for his helpful comments on an earlier version of this chapter.

1. "Corporate" here denotes the nature of any institution that exists for the purpose of profit generation, i.e. a business, partnership or limited company. However, non-profit organisations increasingly adopt the linguistic and semiotic features, genres and discourses of for-profit entities (Fairclough 1993; Mautner, this volume).

2. Grant and Iedema (2005) distinguish between organisational discourse studies, the origins of which they locate in management and organisational theory, on the one hand, and organisational discourse analysis, which emerges from the sphere of linguistics, on the other.

3. Although management schools are undoubtedly an integral part of any contemporary university, not least with regard to the funds they generate, the claim of business administration to be viewed as a science in its own right has to be refuted. Rather, it draws on and combines "soft" disciplines such as psychology or sociology on the one hand and "hard" ones like statistics and IT on the other to provide the theoretical framework to what is ultimately high-level vocational training. This view of management studies fully acknowledges the importance of a practically oriented university education provided that it takes place against a sound academic background but does not accept the notion of a management "science". Others are even less benevolent in their judgement: "Originating from book keeping and cost calculating and having little in common with what is commonly referred to as science, [business administration] does not hold the slightest appeal for anyone interested in theory and culture" (Koch 2001: 59–60, transl. VK).

4. The idea that advertising has become an add-on to PR rather than a tool to increase sales in its own right has also been propounded in popular management literature

(Ries and Ries 2002). While self-appointed consulting "gurus" have a habit of maximising their income by presenting their personal approach as a new panacea to a company's every worry, the above-mentioned book still includes some noteworthy studies on consumer reception of advertising as opposed to PR.
5 This opposition ignores work in social cognition that had by the late 1990s already been recognised by, and indeed been integrated into, linguistic discourse studies (van Dijk 1993; see also 2003, 2005 for more recent accounts). Hackley's disregard thus illustrates the negative consequences of non-interdisciplinary research.
6 In the social constructionist view, recipients actively construct a text's meaning, making reception coincide with interpretation.
7 Scripts are culturally determined mental models that involve a temporal sequence, e.g. a meeting script. Social representations are defined as the cognitive structures jointly held by members of a particular group and as such are the subject of "continual renegotiation (…) during the course of social interaction and communication" (Augoustinos and Walker 1995: 178).
8 The reactions of sub-sections of the public can moreover be tested in focus groups (Kitzinger and Barbour 1999; Myers 2004; Markova and Linell 2006).
9 As a white paper published by a consulting agency specialising in online marketing communication, the latter study is hardly an unbiased account. Clearly, more non-commercial research into blogging is very much needed (for research to date, see Bruns and Jacobs 2006; Lankshear and Knobel 2003 as well as the papers presented at the 2005 Blogtalk conference, available from http://incsub.org/blogtalk/; see also Gruber, this volume).
10 After selling its personal computing division to Chinese company Lenovo in December 2004, IBM in fact now generates the bulk of its revenues with consulting services. However, it is safe to say that despite an awareness-raising ad campaign ("The Other IBM") the company is still overwhelmingly associated with PCs, especially notebooks.

References

Augoustinos, Martha and Iain Walker
   1995   *Social Cognition: An Integrated Introduction*. London: Sage.
Baetz, Mark C. and Christopher K. Bart
   1996   Developing mission statements that work. *Long Range Planning* 29(4): 526–533.
Bakan, Joel
   2004   *The Corporation: The Pathological Pursuit of Profit and Power*. London: Constable & Robinson.
Baker, Stephen and Heather Green
   2005   Blogs will change your business. *Business Week*, 2 May. Available online at http://www.businesweek.com/print/magazine/content/05_18/b3931001_mz001.htm. Accessed 22 April 2005.
Bargiela, Francesca and Elisa Turra
   forthcoming   Organizational change from Old to New Economy: exploring consen-

sus and conflict in business meetings. In: Giuliana Garzone and Srikant Sarangi (eds.), *Discourse, Ideology and Ethics in Specialized Discourse.* Bern: Peter Lang.

Bargiela-Chiappini, Francesca and Sandra Harris
1997a *The Language of Business: An International Perspective.* Edinburgh: Edinburgh University Press.

Bargiela-Chiappini, Francesca and Sandra Harris
1997b *Managing Language: The Discourse of Corporate Meetings.* Amsterdam: Benjamins.

Bargiela-Chiappini, Francesca and Catherine Nickerson (eds.),
1999 *Writing Business: Genres, Media and Discourses.* New York: Longman.

Baxter, Judith
2003 *Positioning Gender in Discourse: a Feminist Methodology.* Basingstoke: Palgrave.

Bhatia, Vijay K.
2004 *Worlds of Written Discourse: A Genre-Based View.* London: Continuum.

Blood, Rebecca
2004 How blogging software reshapes the online community. *Communications of the ACM* 47(12): 53–55.

Boden, Deirdre
1994 *The Business of Talk.* Cambridge: Polity Press.

Boden, Deirdre and Don H. Zimmerman (eds.),
1991 *Talk and Social Structure: Studies in Ethnomethodology and Conversation Analysis.* Berkeley: University of California Press.

Boje, David M.
2001 *Narrative Methods for Organizational and Communication Research.* Thousand Oaks, CA: Sage.

Bowles, Hugo and Gabriele Pallotti
2004 Conversation analysis of opening sequences of telephone calls to bookstores in English and Italian. In: Christopher N. Candlin and Maurizio Gotti (eds.), *Intercultural Discourse in Domain-Specific English.* Special issue of *Textus* 17(1): 63–88.

Bruns, Axel and Joanne Jacobs (eds.)
2006 *Uses of Blogs.* New York: Peter Lang.

Cameron, Deborah
2000 *Good to Talk? Living and Working in a Communication Culture.* London: Sage.

Candlin, Christopher N. and Maurizio Gotti (eds.)
2004 *Intercultural Aspects of Specialized Communication* [Linguistic Insights, 14]. Bern etc.: Peter Lang.

Cass, John, Kristine Munroe and Stephen Turcotte
2005 Corporate blogging: is it worth the hype? White paper available online at http://www.backbonemedia.com/blogsurvey/blogsurvey2005.pdf. Accessed 4 November 2005.

Christensen, Lars T. and Søren Askegaard
2001 Corporate identity and corporate image revisited: a semiotic perspective. *European Journal of Marketing* 35(3/4): 292–315.

Cook, Guy
 2001 *The Discourse of Advertising.* 2nd ed. New York: Routledge.
Czarniawska, Barbara and Pasquale Gagliardi (eds.)
 2003 *Narratives We Organize By* [Advances in Organization Studies 11]. Amsterdam: Benjamins.
Czarniawska-Joerges, Barbara
 1997 *Narrating the Organization: Dramas of Institutional Identity.* Chicago: University of Chicago Press.
de Beaugrande, Robert and Wolfgang Dressler
 1981 *Introduction to Text Linguistics.* London: Longman.
Delin, Judy
 2005 Brand tone of voice: a linguistic analysis of brand position. *Applied Linguistics* 2(1): 1–44.
Dieltjens, Sylvain and Priscilla Heynderickx
 2001 Evasive actions in top-down communication: strategies for avoidingdirect sender and receiver references. *Document Design* 2(2): 210–219.
Drew, Paul and John Heritage (eds.)
 1992 *Talk at Work: Interaction in Institutional Settings.* Cambridge: Cambridge University Press.
Ducheneaut, Nicolas
 2002 The social impacts of electronic mail in organisations: a case study of electronic power games using communication genres. *Information, Communication & Society* 5(2): 153–188.
Fairclough, Norman
 1993 Critical Discourse Analysis and the marketization of public discourse: the universities. *Discourse & Society* 4(2): 133–168.
Fairclough, Norman
 1995 *Critical Discourse Analysis.* London: Longman.
Fairclough, Norman and Ruth Wodak
 1997 Critical discourse analysis. In: Teun A. van Dijk (ed.), *Discourse Studies: A Multidisciplinary Introduction. Vol. 2. Discourse as Social Interaction*, 258–284. London: Sage.
Garzone, Guilian
 2004 Annual company reports and CEOs' letters: Discoursal features and cultural markedness. In: Christopher N. Candlin and Maurizio Gotti (eds.), *Intercultural Aspects of Specialized Communication* [Linguistic Insights 14], 311–341. Bern etc.: Peter Lang.
Gimenez, Julio C.
 2002 New media and conflicting realities in multinational corporate communication: a case study. *International Review of Applied Linguistics in Language Teaching* 40: 323–343.
Grant, David and Rick Iedema
 2005 Discourse analysis and the study of organizations. *Text* 25(1): 37–66.
Grant, David, Cynthia Hardy, Cliff Oswick and Linda Putnam (eds.)
 2004 *The Handbook of Organizational Discourse.* London etc.: Sage.
Grauel, Ralf
 2004 Mitarbeiter des Monats: der Kunde [Employee of the month: the customer]. *Brand eins*, November: 18–20.

Gurau, Calin and Yvonne McLaren
    2003   Corporate reputations in UK biotechnology: an analysis of on-line "company profile" texts. *Journal of Marketing Communication* 9(4): 241–256.
Hackley, Christopher
    1998   Mission statements as corporate communications: the consequences of social constructionism. *Corporate Communication* 3(3): 92–98.
Halliday, Michael A. K. and Christian M.I.M. Matthiessen
    2004   *Introduction to Functional Grammar*. 3rd ed. London: Arnold.
Holmes, Janet
    2006   *Gendered Talk at Work*. Oxford: Blackwell.
Holmes, Janet and Maria Stubbe
    2003   *Power and Politeness in the Workplace: A Sociolinguistic Analysis of Talk at Work*. London: Pearson Education.
Holt, Douglas B.
    2002   Why do brands cause trouble? A dialectal theory of consumer culture and branding. *Journal of Consumer Research* 29(1): 70–90.
Hopkinson, Gillian
    2003   Stories from the front-line: how they construct the organisation. *Journal of Management Studies* 40(8): 1943–1969.
IBM
    (n.d.)   Our values at work. Available from http://www–03.ibm.com/ibm/history/exhibits/valveone/valveone_valveone_intro.html. Acessed 20 August 2007.
Iedema, Rick
    2003   *Discourses of Post-Bureaucratic Organization* [Document Design Series 5]. Amsterdam: Benjamins.
Iedema, Rick and Hermine Scheeres
    2003   From doing work to talking work: renegotiating knowing, doing, and identity. *Applied Linguistics* 24(3): 316–337.
Iedema, Rick and Ruth Wodak
    1999   Analysing organizational discourses and practices. *Discourse & Society* 10(1): 5–19.
Iedema, Rick and Ruth Wodak
    2005   Communication in institutions. In: Ammon, Ulrich, Norbert Dittmar, Klaus J. Mattheier and Peter Trudgill (eds.), *Sociolinguistics: An International Handbook of the Science of Language and Society*. Volume 2. 2nd ed., 1602–1615. Berlin: Walter de Gruyter.
Isaksson, Maria
    2005   Ethos and pathos representations in mission statements: identifying virtues and emotions in an emerging business genre. In: Anna Trosborg and Poul Erik Flyvholm Jørgersen (eds.), *Business Discourse: Texts and Contexts*, 111–138. Bern: Peter Lang.
Jablin, Fredric M. and Linda L. Putnam
    2001   *The New Handbook of Organizational Communication: Advances in Theory, Research, and Methods*. Thousand Oaks, CA: Sage.
Jacobs, Geert
    1999   *Preformulating the News: An Analysis of the Metapragmatics of Press Releases*. Amsterdam: Benjamins.

Jameson, Daphne A.
2000 Telling the investment story: a narrative analysis of shareholder reports. *Journal of Business Communication* 37(1): 7–38.
Kendall, Shari and Deborah Tannen
1997 Gender and language in the workplace. In: Ruth Wodak (ed.), *Gender and Discourse*, 81–105. London: Longman.
Kessapidou, Sevasti and Marianthu Makri-Tsilipakou
2001 Gender and corporate discourse. In: Eliza Kitis (ed.), *The Other Within. Volume II: Aspects of Language and Culture*, 63–86. Thessaloniki/Greece: Athanassios A. Altintzis.
Kitzinger, Jenny and Rosaline S. Barbour
1999 Introduction: the challenge and promise of focus groups. In: Rosaline S. Barbour and Jenny Kitzinger (eds.), *Developing Focus Group Research: Politics, Theory and Practice*, 1–20. London: Sage.
Koch, Joachim
2001 *Megaphilosophie: Das Freiheitsversprechen der Ökonomie* [Megaphilosophy: the Economy's Promise of Freedom]. Göttingen: Steidl.
Koester, Almut
2004 *The Language of Work*. London: Routledge.
Koller, Veronika
2004 *Metaphor and Gender in Business Media Discourse: A Critical Cognitive Study*. Basingstoke: Palgrave.
Koller, Veronika
2007 "The world's local bank": Glocalisation as a strategy in corporate branding discourse. *Social Semiotics* 17(1): 111–130.
Koller, Veronika
forthcoming "Our customers embrace us as an essential partner": corporate brands as socio-cognitive representations. In: Gitte Kristiansen and René Dirven (eds.), *Cognitive Sociolinguistics: Language Variation, Cultural Models, Social Systems*. Berlin: de Gruyter.
Kumar, Ravi, Jasmine Novak, Prabhakar Raghavan and Andrew Tomkins
2004 Structure and evolution of blogspace. *Communications of the ACM* 47(12): 35–39.
Kunda, Ziva
1999 *Social Cognition. Making Sense of People*. Cambridge, MA: MIT Press.
Lankshear, Colin and Michele Knobel
2003 Do-it-yourself broadcasting: writing weblogs in a knowledge society. Paper presented at the American Educational Research Association Annual Conference, 21 April. Chicago/USA, Available online at http:// www.geocities.com/c.lankshear/blog2003.html. Accessed 4 November 2005.
Leech, Geoffrey N.
1966 *English in Advertising: A Linguistic Study of Advertising in Great Britain*. London: Longman.
Lemke, Jay
2003 Texts and discourses in the technologies of social organization. In: Gilbert Weiss and Ruth Wodak (eds.), *Critical Discourse Analysis: Theory and Interdisciplinarity*, 130–149. Basingstoke: Palgrave.

Markova, Ivana and Per Linell
2006   *Dialogue in Focus Groups: Exploring Socially Shared Knowledge*. London: Equinox.
Martín Rojo, Luisa and Concepción Gómez Esteban
2003   Discourse at work: when women take on the role of managers. In: Gilbert Weiss and Ruth Wodak (eds.), *Critical Discourse Analysis: Theory and Interdisciplinarity*, 241–271. Basingstoke: Palgrave.
Massing, Michael
2005   The end of news? *The New York Review of Books* 52(19): 23–27.
McQuarrie, Edward F. and David Glen Mick
1996   Figures of rhetoric in advertising: language. *Journal of Consumer Research* 22(4): 424–438.
McQuarrie, Edward F. and David Glen Mick
1999   Visual rhetoric in advertising: text-interpretive, experimental, and reader-response analyses. *Journal of Consumer Research* 26(1): 37–54.
McQuarrie, Edward F. and David Glen Mick
2003   Visual and verbal rhetorical figures under directed processing versus incidental exposure to advertising. *Journal of Consumer Research* 29(4): 579–587.
Menz, Florian
1999   Self-organisation, equivocality, and decision-making in organisations. *Discourse & Society* 10(1): 101–129.
Morales-López, Esperanza, Gabriela Prego-Vásquez and Luzia Domínguez-Seco
2005   Interviews between employees and customers during a company restructuring process. *Discourse & Society* 16(2): 225–268.
Mullany, Louise
2007   *Gendered Discourse in Professional Communication*. Basingstoke: Palgrave.
Mumby, Dennis K. and D. Clair
1997   Organizational discourse. In: Teun A. van Dijk (ed.), *Discourse Studies: A Multidisciplinary Introduction. Vol. 2; Discourse as Social Interaction*, 181–205. London: Sage.
Myers, Greg
1994   *Words in Ads*. London: Edward Arnold.
Myers, Greg
1998   *Ad Worlds: Brands, Media, Audiences*. New York: Arnold.
Myers, Greg
2004   *Matters of Opinion: Talking about Public Issues*. Cambridge: Cambridge University Press.
Phillips, Barbara J. and Edward F. McQuarrie
2004   Beyond visual metaphor: a new typology of visual rhetoric in advertising. *Marketing Theory* 4(1/2): 113–136.
Poncini, Gina
2004   *Discursive Strategies in Multicultural Business Meetings* [Linguistic Insights 14]. Bern etc.: Peter Lang.
Putnam, Linda L. and Michael E. Roloff
1992   *Communication and Negotiation*. Thousand Oaks, CA: Sage.

Rhodes, Carl
    2001   *Writing Organization: (Re)presentation and Control in Narratives at Work* [Advances in Organization Studies 7]. Amsterdam: Benjamins.
Ries, Al and Laura Ries
    2002   *The Fall of Advertising and the Rise of PR*. New York: Harper Collins.
Sarangi, Srikant and Celia Roberts (eds.)
    1999   *Talk, Work and Institutional Order: Discourse in Medical, Mediation and Management Settings*. [Language, Power and Social Process 1] Berlin: de Gruyter.
Schnieders, Guido
    2005   *Reklamationsgespräche: Eine diskursanalytische Studie*. [Complaints: a discourse-analytical study]. Tübingen: Gunter Narr Verlag.
Sunstein, Cass R.
    2004   Democracy and filtering. *Communications of the ACM* 47(12): 57–59.
Swales, John and Priscilla S. Rogers
    1995   Discourse and the projection of corporate culture: the mission statement. *Discourse & Society* 6(2): 223–242.
Tannen, Deborah
    1995   *Talking from 9 to 5*. London: Virago.
Taylor, Charles
    2005   Moving international advertising research forward. *Journal of Advertising Research* 34(1): 7–16.
van Dijk, Teun A.
    1993   Principles of critical discourse analysis. *Discourse and Society* 4(2): 249–283.
van Dijk, Teun A.
    2003   The discourse-knowledge interface. In: Gilbert Weiss and Ruth Wodak (eds.), *Critical Discourse Analysis: Theory and Interdisciplinarity*, 85–109. Basingstoke: Palgrave.
van Dijk, Teun A.
    2005   Contextual knowledge management in discourse production: a CDA perspective. In: Ruth Wodak and Paul A. Chilton (eds.), *A New Agenda in (Critical) Discourse Analysis*, 71–100. Amsterdam: Benjamins.
van Leeuwen, Theo
    2005   *Introduction to Social Semiotics*. London: Routledge.
van de Mieroop, Dorien
    2005   An integrated approach of quantitative and qualitative analysis in the study of identity in speeches. *Discourse & Society* 16(1): 107–130.
Ventola, Eija
    2005   Revisiting service encounter genre: some reflections. *Folia Linguistica* 39(1–2): 19–44.
Yates, Joanne, Wanda J. Orlikowski and Kazuo Okamura
    1999   Explicit and implicit structuring of genres in electronic communication: reinforcement and change of social interaction. *Organization Science* 10(1): 83–103.
Yuling, Pan, Suzanne Wong Scollon and Ron Scollon
    2002   *Professional Communication in International Settings*. Malden, MA: Blackwell.

Zhu, Yunxia
   2005   *Written Communication across Cultures: A Sociocognitive Perspective on Business Genres*. Amsterdam: Benjamins.

8. Creating a "green" image in the public sphere: Corporate environmental reports in a genre perspective

Aud Solbjørg Skulstad

1. Introduction

Corporate environmental reports form part of a large number of documents on sensitive social issues. Companies aim to create an image where being environmentally friendly is good business practice: "In RTZ, responsibility towards the environment is considered good business practice and an integral part of daily operations as well as long term strategy" (RTZ plc 1991: 3). Some companies project the image that being environmentally friendly is also good business: "For us, long-term profitable performance goes hand-in-hand with the understanding that being environmentally friendly and socially responsible is good business" (Hydro 2005). Similarly, some companies such as The Body Shop have made their concern for environmental issues a key element in their marketing strategy and their corporate image:

> (1) Anita [the founder of the company] has always been driven by her vision of a better world. From the very beginning she wanted to encourage positive change and establish a new work ethic that would enable her business to thrive while being environmentally responsible on both local and global levels. This vision is still as true today and emerges in every aspect of our operations (The Body Shop International plc 2005: 2, Environmental Performance Report).

The genre of corporate environmental reports has emerged as a response to the strategic aim of creating a "green" image in the public sphere. Gunnarsson (1997) specifies three different aspects of corporate image:

– Internal images
Such images appear in documents and presentations addressed to staff.
– Externally addressed images
These images appear in communication aimed at customers, owners, governments and the general public.
– Externally constructed images
These images are constructed outside the company by the media, pressure groups etc. Such images are not always favourable.

Compared to established genres, emerging genres are heterogeneous in form and content, and the conventions are less stabilized. As *The Economist* (1993: 75) observes, "Outside the United States, rules are rare. So what companies call an 'environmental report' can be almost anything printed on recycled paper with a few nice pictures of birds and flowers." This variation is also characteristic of the documents in my corpus.

Requests for corporate environmental documents were sent to 88 companies in Britain in 1993. I received 22 such documents from 21 different companies. Two of these documents were not included in my corpus. These were booklets addressed to shoppers, and these documents contained a mixture of advertising and environmental discourses (J. Sainsbury plc, *Packaging*; and Reckitt & Colman plc, *Making a Clean Home a "Green Home" with Down to Earth*). In addition to the 21 companies mentioned above, a few companies sent a copy of their environmental policy statement. These policy statements consisted of single sheets of paper and were not included in my corpus.

Corporate environmental reports are multisemiotic documents. That means that they combine various semiotic resources such as words, pictures, colour, bar charts, tables, etc. Thus, in my analysis of image creation both visual and verbal strategies are important. In this chapter, however, verbal strategies are given the most space.

The section following the introduction of this chapter briefly presents three research traditions of genre analysis to show that there are alternatives to the method frequently associated with the analysis of discourse within the professions (the English for Specific Purposes (ESP) or Languages for Specific Purposes (LSP) traditions). As emerging genres are characterized by variation and heterogeneity, there may be specific problems of assigning genre and subgenre membership, and this is discussed in the next section. The next two sections look at examples of written and visual strategies chosen to create and contest corporate images in the public sphere in two subgenres of corporate environmental reports.

2. Research traditions

In literary studies, the concept of genre can be traced as far back as the work of Aristotle. Within linguistics and discourse analysis, however, *genre* is a relatively recent concept. Genre analysis is not a unified set of approaches within linguistics and discourse analysis. Within the Anglo-American and Australian research traditions three approaches are conventionally identified: English for Specific Purposes studies, (North American) New Rhetoric studies and the Sydney School (Hyon 1996; Yunick 1997; Johns 2002). (For an introduction to German research traditions see Muntigl and Gruber 2005.) However, as Swales (2007: 147) points out, "the divisions among the traditions have become much less sharp – although by no means disappeared".

Creating a "green" image in the public sphere   183

As the name indicates, the first tradition is rooted in English for Specific Purposes studies (e.g. Swales 1981, 1990; Dudley-Evans and Henderson 1990; Bhatia 1993; Skulstad 1996, 2002). Within an English for Specific Purposes context, the term *genre* was used for the first time by Tarone, Dwyer, Gillette and Icke in 1981 in an article on the use of passive voice in two journal articles of astrophysics (Dudley-Evans 1994). The English for Specific Purposes tradition takes an eclectic approach to theories of linguistics, but Hallidayan ideas of the relationship between language and its social functions are evident. The most quoted definition of genre within the English for Specific Purposes tradition is the one proposed by Swales (1990: 58):

> A genre comprises a class of communicative events, the members of which share some set of communicative purposes. These purposes are recognised by the expert member of the parent discourse community, and thereby constitute the rationale for the genre. This rationale shapes the schematic structure of the discourse and influences and constrains the choice of content and style.

The role of a genre within a discourse community is central in this definition. Discourse communities are occupational or recreational groups where the members perform specific activities typical of a profession or connected to a hobby such as making widgets in a factory, playing in an orchestra or being active members of a local bicycle club, and in doing these things the members acquire, use and modify the language that goes along with these activities (Swales 1998: 20). Swales goes on to say that "these discourse communities evolve their own conventions and traditions for such diverse verbal activities as running meetings, producing reports, and publicizing their activities. These recurrent classes of communicative events are the *genres* that orchestrate verbal life" (Swales 1998: 20; original emphasis). As will be demonstrated later on in this chapter, genres are increasingly multisemiotic today (cf. Kress and van Leeuwen 2001; Kress 2003; Lemke 2005), and to separate the verbal aspect of a "text" does not give a true picture of the genre, but the important point about the conventionality of these activities remains. The importance of conventionality is echoed in Bhatia's (2004: 10) definition of genre analysis:

> [a] framework for the investigation of conventionalized or institutionalized genres in the context of specific institutional and disciplinary practices, procedures and cultures in order to understand how members of specific discourse communities construct, interpret and use these genres to achieve their communicative goals and why they write them the way they do.

The ideas and theories of Bourdieu (1977, 1991), Vygotsky (1978, 1986), Foucault (e.g. 1980, 2001), and Bakhtin (1981, 1986), have been influential in the development of the second tradition, (North American) New Rhetoric studies. Examples of studies within this tradition are Miller (1984), Bazerman (1988), Yates and Orlikowski (1992), Berkenkotter and Huckin (1995), and Adam and

Artemeva (2002). Important for the development of the North American tradition was Hymes's concept of communicative competence and his point that "[t]here are rules of use without which the rules of grammar would be useless" (Hymes 1979 [1971]: 8). Levinson's (1979) notion of *activity type* has also been influential in the development of the concept of genre as used in New Rhetoric studies (Muntigl and Gruber 2005). Levinson (1979: 368; original emphasis) defines activity type as:

> a fuzzy category whose focal members are goal-defined, socially constituted, bounded, events with *constraints* on participants, setting, and so on, but above all on the kinds of allowable contributions. Paradigm examples would be teaching, a job interview, a jural interrogation, a football game, a task in a workshop, a dinner party, and so on.

Here Levinson states that an activity type is "goal-defined". In all three traditions genre membership is assigned according to a set of shared communicative goals or purposes. However, Levinson's notion of activity type differs from genre in that it is a broader category that includes events that do not entirely consist of language and visual images (e.g. a football game). Levinson's concept of activity type is reflected in Miller's (1984: 159) definition of genres, which includes the notion of "typified rhetorical actions based in recurrent situations". As Bazerman (1988: 62) puts it, in his rephrasing of Miller's concept of genre, "[a] genre is a socially recognized, repeated strategy for achieving similar goals in situations socially perceived as being similar".

Yet another frequently quoted definition is Berkenkotter and Huckin's (1995: 4) sociocognitive theory of genre:

> *Dynamism.* Genres are dynamic rhetorical forms that are developed from actors' responses to recurrent situations and that serve to stabilize experience and give it coherence and meaning. Genres change over time in response to their users' sociocognitive needs.
> *Situatedness.* Our knowledge of genres is derived from and embedded in our participation in the communicative activities of daily and professional life. As such, genre knowledge is a form of "situated cognition" that continues to develop as we participate in the activities of the ambient culture.
> *Form and Content.* Genre knowledge embraces both form and content, including a sense of what content is appropriate to a particular purpose in a particular situation at a particular point in time.
> *Duality of Structure.* As we draw on genre rules to engage in professional activities, we *constitute* social structures (in professional, institutional, and organizational contexts) and simultaneously *reproduce* these structures.
> *Community Ownership.* Genre conventions signal a discourse community's norms, epistemology, ideology, and social ontology.

The idea of community ownership echoes the English for Specific Purposes tradition's emphasis on the relationship between genre and discourse community, and the idea of situatedness echoes the Sydney School's emphasis on the relationship between language and context (see below). Thus this characterization of genre may serve to illustrate the fact that there are many similarities between the three research traditions.

The Sydney School is influenced by functional views of language as presented by the anthropologist Bronislaw Malinowski in the 1920s and 1930s and which were further developed by the linguist John Rupert Firth in the 1950s, particularly their emphasis on the relationship between language and the situational and cultural context (Ventola 2005). Another source of influence is M.A.K. Halliday's work in systemic functional linguistics. Muntigl and Gruber (2005: 3–5) list six characteristics of genre identified by systemic functional linguistics:

- Genres are goal oriented
- Genres unfold in terms of stages or phases
- The set of genres, taken together, realize a cultural potential or all possible contexts of culture
- Genres consist of families that contain fuzzy borders
- Genres often pattern together to form what are termed *macro-genres*
- Genres may be realized by various semiotic modes such as spoken/written language, gesture, image, body position and others.

Examples of research studies within the Sydney School are Martin, Christie, and Rothery (1987); Ventola (1987); Halliday and Martin (1993), and Macken-Horarik (2002).

Alternatively, the theoretical camps associated with genre analysis could be divided according to the criterion of whether they are linguistically or non-linguistically grounded. Flowerdew (2002: 91) groups the English for Specific Purposes tradition and the Sydney School together on the ground that they both "take a linguistic approach, applying theories of functional grammar and discourse and concentrating on lexico-grammatical and rhetorical realization of the communicative purposes embodied in a genre". The New Rhetoric group, on the other hand, "is less interested in lexico-grammar and rhetorical structure and more focused on situational context – the purposes and functions of genres and the attitudes, beliefs, values, and behaviours of the members of the discourse communities within which genres are situated" (Flowerdew 2002: 91).

There is a corresponding contrast in methodology in that the New Rhetoric group often uses ethnographic methods whereas the English for Specific Purposes and Sydney schools apply methods of discourse analysis, mainly systemic functional linguistics, "but with more concern for social context than is usual in that tradition" (Flowerdew 2002: 91). The inclusion of the contextual dimension is evident in Swales's (1998: 1) term *textography*, by which he refers to "something more than a disembodied textual or discourse analysis, but something less than a full ethnographic account". Flowerdew (2002) sums up the differences in the following way: The English for Specific Purposes tradition and the Sydney School both look to the situational context to interpret discursive manifestations whereas the New Rhetoric tradition may look to textual strategies to interpret the situational context.

The Sydney School is rooted in educational linguistics in an L1 context. The type of educational context associated with New Rhetoric is primarily L1 teaching in disciplines such as rhetoric, composition studies and professional writing, whereas the English for Specific Purposes tradition is mainly associated with English for Specific Purposes (Language for Specific Purposes) teaching of L2 students.

3. Assigning genre and subgenre membership

As we have seen, there are a number of different genre definitions. Even when one sticks to the English for Specific Purposes school, assigning genre membership may pose problems in the case of new genres. Like Swales, Bhatia (1993) claims that the main defining characteristic of texts belonging to the same genre is a set of shared communicative purposes. This leads Bhatia to regard sales promotion letters and job application letters as belonging to one genre, a genre he calls promotional genres. The main reason behind this conclusion is that he sees these two types of letters as sharing a set of communicative purposes. They are both persuasive in nature and their communicative purposes are reflected in a similar rhetorical organization:

Establishing credentials
Introducing the offer/introducing candidature
Offering incentives
Enclosing documents
Soliciting response
Using pressure tactics
Ending politely (see Bhatia 1993: 46–68).

By regarding these two letter types as belonging to the same genre, Bhatia ignores one of Swales's defining characteristics of genre: "A discourse community's nomenclature for genres is an important source of insight" (Swales 1990: 54). *Sales promotion letters* and *job application letters* are well established names of two different types of letters in the discourse communities where they are used.

There is a parallel situation in the case of corporate environmental reports: Companies issue a number of different types of documents, all of which in different ways aim to create or reinforce a favourable corporate image (annual reports, company brochures, public relations booklets, animal testing booklets, etc.). Consequently, it could be argued that these documents are members of the same genre. However, this would mean to ignore the discourse community's nomenclature for these different types of documents.

In the case of new genres, the metadiscourse used to characterize the documents in the texts themselves may give valuable information about how the authors see these texts. Some of the introductions to the corporate environmental reports in my corpus give a *global preview* of the report (Skulstad 2005b). This type of metadiscursive element signals that the global function and aim of the document are being anticipated. Here the documents are referred to by various lexical choices: *report, review, brochure, booklet, leaflet* and *environmental report*:

(2) This first environmental report (...) describes what we are doing to harmonise our activities with the natural environment, to limit environmental impacts and to make efficient use of natural resources and gives targets that we have set ourselves which we will report back on in future annual environmental reports (Nuclear Electric plc 1993: 1, Environmental Performance Report).

This range of lexical choices may be taken as an indication of the fact that *environmental report* was not an established genre name within the discourse community at this point in time. The word *leaflet* is used in the smallest of these documents. It consists of only four pages, and there is no proper front cover (Wellcome plc). This contrasts sharply with the longest of the corporate environmental reports in my corpus which consists of 48 pages (The Body Shop International plc 1992). As pointed out above, being environmentally friendly is a central aspect of the corporate image of this company.

Move-Step analysis, an identification of the rhetorical movement writers or speakers conventionally make when operating in a specific genre (Skulstad 2005a), is the most quoted type of analysis within the English for Specific Purposes tradition. Examples include Swales's (1990) analysis of the rhetorical movement writers conventionally make in introductions of research articles, the Create a Research Space (CARS) model and Skulstad's Relationships and Confidence (RECON) model of chairmen's statements in corporate annual reports (Skulstad 2002, 2005a). A Move-Step approach is not possible in the case of emerging genres due to the variation and heterogeneity that characterize such a genre. However, emerging genres may demonstrate systematic variation as to rhetorical strategies chosen. This was the case in my data, and as a consequence of this fact two subgenres were identified. In the majority (14) of these documents, reporting on the company's environmental performance is given the most space. These documents will be referred to as *Environmental Performance Reports* (EPRs). The term itself appears on the front page of one of the documents in my corpus (PowerGen plc 1993) and another document uses the label *environmental performance review* (National Power plc 1992). The Environmental Performance Reports signal their commitment to improve the company's environmental performance by announcing the company's environmental policy and objectives. They give examples of the company's environmental performance, which serve as evidence of the company's commitment:

- signalling commitment towards environmental issues
  - announcing environmental policy and objectives
    - making "promises"
- signalling good business practices (business ethics)
  - reporting on the company's environmental performance
    - giving "evidence".

Environmental Performance Reports often indicate that this type of document is issued annually, which may not always be the case with the other subgenre.

The minority (six) of the documents on environmental issues draw on an alternative set of rhetorical strategies:

- signalling environmental awareness (and commitment)
  - putting the issue(s) into perspective
- signalling good business practices (business ethics)
  - challenging/shaping public opinion.

This group of documents will be referred to as *Environmental Awareness Booklets* (EABs). However, Environmental Awareness Booklets have a less well-defined form than do Environmental Performance Reports. The nomenclature *Environmental Awareness Booklet* is entirely my own in that this label is not used by members of the discourse community. It is applied merely for pragmatic reasons as a convenient way of referring to these documents for descriptive purposes.

The nomenclature of the two subgenres reflects some important characteristics of the two types of documents. Environmental Performance Reports present reviews of the performance of the company regarding environmental issues, whereas in Environmental Awareness Booklets reports or reviews of company performance are given very little space.

To signal environmental awareness is a central aim in the Environmental Awareness Booklets. Typically, these documents in my corpus concentrate on one sensitive issue which is central to the company such as the greenhouse effect (British Coal Corporation plc), nuclear waste (BNFL plc) and deforestation (Donald Murray Paper Ltd). The remaining three Environmental Awareness Booklets show greater variation. In the two booklets on chemical activities, the focus is on the environmental advantage of the products themselves (Allied Colloids Group plc and W. Canning plc). One of these companies stresses that it creates "products which improve the environment and quality of life – such as our pollution control and water treatment processes that are used worldwide" (Allied Colloids Group plc 1993: 1). Similarly, another of the Environmental

Awareness Booklets outlines the environmental advantages of the company's basic product, a 210 litre steel container called "the green drum", which is designed for storage and transportation of hazardous and highly toxic products (Blagden plc). The communicative purpose "signalling good business practices (business ethics)" is often realized by various rhetorical strategies which are aimed at challenging public opinion (see below).

Todorov (1976: 161) suggests that "[a] new genre is always the transformation of one or several old genres: by inversion, by displacement, by combination". The Environmental Performance Reports in my corpus draw heavily on corporate annual reports, whereas the Environmental Awareness Booklets bear closer resemblance to public relations booklets and sales brochures. As will be evident from the discussion above, these two groups of documents are seen as textual responses to similar strategic needs. This view is supported by the subtitle of one of the Environmental Awareness Booklets, *A British Coal Environmental Review*, which could just as well have been the subtitle of an Environmental Performance Report.

4. Externally addressed images

The specification of internal, externally addressed and externally constructed images implies that the identification of corporate image has to be seen in relation to the intended audience of the documents in question. Two of the Environmental Performance Reports in my corpus list the intended audience. They both mention staff, suppliers and shareholders. One of the companies also mentions franchisees, and the other one includes the public, regulators and customers. As the Environmental Performance Reports are addressed to both the staff and people outside the company it is not easy to separate internal images from those that are externally addressed. This section will concentrate on the latter, the public sphere. If we look at Environmental Awareness Booklets, the intended audience is even more heterogeneous when compared to the Environmental Performance Reports. Three of the Environmental Awareness Booklets (the three most homogenous of these documents) are addressed both to the public and the business community (one of the Environmental Awareness Booklets specifies this specifically) (British Coal Corporation plc, BNFL plc and Donald Murray Paper Ltd). The other three Environmental Awareness Booklets are addressed to customers and will not be discussed in any detail here (Allied Colloids Group plc, Blagden Industries plc and W. Canning plc) (see Skulstad 2002).

As for choice of rhetorical strategies, eleven of the 14 Environmental Performance Reports have a separate environmental policy section. Central here are various strategies of "promise-making". A characteristic feature of the aims and objectives set out in this section is that they are not easily testable.

Above all, they show the company's commitment to further environmental improvement.

It is important to notice that the Environmental Performance Reports typically give examples to illustrate the company's commitment to and their high levels of performance on environmental issues instead of giving a comprehensive survey. In one of the reports, for instance, there is a section headed "Emissions and effluents" (The Shell International Petroleum Company Ltd 1992: 5, Environmental Performance Report). This section opens by stating that the strategy of continuous improvement in environmental performance "requires a detailed, quantitative inventory of the present emissions, effluents and discharges from each Shell operation" (Shell 1992: 5). However, data on these aspects of operation are not given in this report. Instead, the writer gives examples of improved environmental performance: "One advance has been a state-of-the-art biological effluent treatment plant (...) Another contribution towards reducing emissions and effluents has been (...)" (Shell 1992: 5). Thus, the reports on environmental performance have a clear image-creating function, emphasizing the improvement and environmental advantages of the business. Only five of the 14 Environmental Performance Reports provide data on emissions to the atmosphere, solid residues and wastes, water quality, and other aspects related to the environmental performance of the company (ICI plc, National Power plc, Nuclear Electric plc, PowerGen plc and Thames Water plc). With a few exceptions, the data presented show improved environmental performance, but only a minority of the examples given specify the exact investments made to reduce pollution. A typical example of the type of "evidence" provided is related to recycling. This is a type of environmental action which everybody in the public sphere understands as every household is expected to recycle parts of its domestic waste. The Environmental Performance Reports give concrete examples of recycling, ranging from the recycling of office paper and plastic cups to the recovering of waste energy from process plants. Other examples of externally addressed images in the Environmental Performance Reports are sections of the documents which emphasize the company's active role in establishing a "good neighbour" policy such as community relations programmes involving facilities for school visits or regular visitor centres. Such examples are to be found in seven of the Environmental Performance Reports in my corpus. The companies demonstrate their active involvement in raising the environmental awareness of school children and other members of the public.

A company's appraisal of its own excellence would not be particularly convincing in terms of the creation of externally addressed images. Quotations from people outside the company, in which the company is praised have much greater force, because such quotations represent objective assessment (cf. Koller's idea of narcissistic corporate self-promotion, this volume):

(3) Thanks to new technology, ICI was able to launch the first solvent-free emulsions in the USA and UK in March 1992. Following the launch, the US Environmental Protection Agency wrote to Glidden, the US arm of ICI Paints, to say: "Your company's work to reduce air emissions sends a positive message to other businesses and sets an example of innovation that we would like to see adopted throughout corporate America" (ICI plc 1992: 17, Environmental Performance Report).

Direct discourse presentation is not used extensively in the Environmental Performance Reports, except in one of these reports. The instances of direct discourse presentation that are included generally aim to persuade a sceptical audience of the company's role in environmental improvement.

As mentioned above, the Environmental Awareness Booklets in my corpus do not announce the company's environmental policy and objectives explicitly in the same way as do the Environmental Performance Reports. The Environmental Awareness Booklets make an argument on a specific issue such as the use of coal or the activities of the chemical division of the company. The discussion typically goes beyond the company's immediate business and products to the company's awareness of environmental problems. The Environmental Awareness Booklet on nuclear waste, for instance, opens by discussing how a high standard of living leads to enormous amounts of domestic waste, and the Environmental Awareness Booklet on coal discusses the greenhouse effect as a natural phenomenon. In this way, the commitment to environmental improvement is implicit, in contrast to the "promises" made and the "evidence" given in the Environmental Performance Reports. In the Environmental Awareness Booklets the companies conventionally present themselves as being above the controversy of central environmental issues and as making a reasoned response to the problems:

(4) If the predictions of some global climate analysts are to be believed, the world could be facing a great disaster. But the economic upheaval of a hasty reaction to the possibility of the Greenhouse Effect could reduce living standards throughout the developed world. (…) But (…) it would be prudent for the world to take out an "insurance policy" by adopting sensible measures which reduce the possibility of climate change while causing minimal economic disruption (British Coal Corporation plc n.d.: 1, Environmental Awareness Booklet).

This particular company also presents itself as an advisory body on global environmental action in Eastern Europe and developing countries.

A recent trend in documents of the Environmental Performance Report-type is to include other issues beside environmental impact and local community relations. Let us take The Body Shop as an example. In 1993 they published their first environmental report called *The Green Book*. In 1995 the company published a document entitled *The Values Report*. They characterize this document as their first "social audit" where they presented the results of consultation with 5000 stakeholders. The document dealt with environmental and animal protection performance. In 2005 they published their first independently verified values report, and the range of issues was widened:

> (5) For this report, we have invited five stakeholders to comment on the role of The Body Shop on business in general and on some of the global community's greatest challenges, such as HIV/AIDS, tropical deforestation, domestic violence, animal testing and economic development of the poorest communities (The Body Shop International plc 2005: 3).

The focus on the global threat of HIV/AIDS is also seen in Rio Tinto's *Sustainable Development Review* (2004: 17): "Rio Tinto's southern African operations are nearing full implementation of the Group HIV/AIDS strategy, which provides access to antiretroviral therapy which is affordable for employees and a partner". Thus, environmental protection has increasingly become one issue among several of corporate social responsibility.

5. Responses to externally constructed images

As mentioned above, externally constructed images are not always favourable. Thus, corporate environmental reports sometimes have to contest this type of image in order to realize their communicative aims. Example 6 characterizes opposition and challenges public opinion:

> (6) These chemicals [chlorine and dioxins], in themselves dangerous substances, are widely associated with the papermaking industry. As this section explains, however, there is no real risk to the end user of paper products, or to the environment in any substantial way. This "dangerous" image has been largely exaggerated by poorly informed environmental campaigners and the marketing industry looking for selling points like "unbleached", to encourage consumers to favour their brands. They are confusing the product with the production process – the important factor in environmental terms is the reduction of chlorine emissions during production, as opposed to the far less damaging chlorine content in paper (Donald Murray Paper Ltd n.d.: 7, Environmental Awareness Booklet).

Example 6 identifies the source of the assertion this text maker is contesting, "poorly informed environmental campaigners and the marketing industry". Hence, this writer draws attention to the intertextual perspective of the text (see below).

Negation is a frequent strategy in these Environmental Awareness Booklets (see e.g. Tottie 1982, 1987; Pagano 1994 on the use of negatives in written language). One of the booklets is entitled *Papermaking Is Not Killing the Forests*. Fairclough (1992) treats negation intertextually, and interpreted this way, the title of this Environmental Awareness Booklet presupposes the existence of the proposition found in antecedent texts (spoken or written) that papermaking *is* killing the forests. In relation to the aim of challenging public opinion, negative sentences become particularly powerful precisely in their intertextual force, as they contest propositions in some other text, produced by environmental campaigners or environmentalists, which is (assumed to be) within the reader's experience. I have found Pagano's (1994) category of denials of background information particularly useful in my analysis of negatives in Environmental Awareness Booklets. She defines this category as "denials used when the writer assumes that the reader entertains certain mistaken ideas from his previous background knowledge" (1994: 258). In other words, the writer denies misconceptions which he or she assumes the imagined reader to have prior to reading the present text. Such implicit denials (Pagano 1994) may be seen as a way of contesting unfavourable images in antecedent texts:

(7) *Contrary to popular belief*, radiation is *not* something solely produced by the nuclear industry or nuclear weapons. In fact, about 87% of the radiation dose we receive comes from natural sources. [emphasis added] (BNFL plc 1992b: 6, Environmental Awareness Booklet).

Example 7 may be seen to attribute misconceptions about radiation to the imagined reader. The category denials of background information is also found in some of the Environmental Performance Reports in my corpus, but is not a dominant strategy. Another way of contesting propositions in antecedent texts is simply to label them "wrong" or to identify certain propositions as "myth". Such propositions are not grammatically negative, but semantically negative (see Fairclough 1992: 122).

One way of contesting externally constructed images is to provide contrasts with "competing" industries to minimize the problem. In the example below the environmental advantages of nuclear power are contrasted with the environmental disadvantages of the use of coal:

(8) All industries produce waste. (...) burning coal produces large quantities of waste – a large coal-fired power station emits yearly some 11 million tonnes of carbon dioxide and about 200,000 tonnes of sulphur dioxide and nitrous oxide. In addition, a million tonnes of coal ash is produced, of which some 4,000 to 7,000 tonnes is emitted up the chimney, (...) Compared with other energy producers, nuclear power results in significantly smaller amounts of waste (BNFL plc 1992b: 4, Environmental Awareness Booklet).

The Environmental Awareness Booklet on coal, in turn, argues that nuclear power is not the solution to the problems of the greenhouse effect:

(9) It is true that nuclear power plants release negligible amounts of greenhouse gases during operation, although some are released indirectly during fuel preparation and reprocessing. However, nuclear plants are only suited to electricity production, and even if it were possible to replace all coal-fired power stations, the Greenhouse Effect could only be reduced by about 10% (British Coal Corporation plc n.d.: 18, Environmental Awareness Booklet).

Figure 1. Persuasive function of a visual in an Environmental Awareness Booklet (British Coal Corporation plc n.d.: 7).

Note that example 9 opens by confirming readers' preconceptions about the release of greenhouse gases from nuclear power plants and then dismisses nuclear power as a viable option.

It may be fruitful to extend a Swalesian approach to the analysis of visual communication. Put simply, this means that the choices of visuals and visual strategies are directly related to the communicative purpose(s) of the genre as perceived by the text maker. In the Environmental Awareness Booklet issued by British Coal there is a photograph of an oil rig from which thick, black smoke is released into the atmosphere (see Figure 1). The caption reads: "Leaks from natural gas distribution networks and from oil and gas producing plants are a significant source of atmospheric methane". The document goes on to argue that "Releases of methane from the production and use of coal around the world account for less than 7% of global emissions, and are estimated to contribute less than 0.8% to the Greenhouse Effect" (British Coal Corporation plc n.d.: 7, Environmental Awareness Booklet).

An environmental report issued by an oil company, on the other hand, is not likely to choose a visual that shows the emission of methane. One of the oil companies in my corpus chose a photograph of some seals basking on a buoy in the foreground and a drilling platform in the background (see Figure 2). The photograph could be seen to argue that if offshore drilling did produce high levels of pollution, the seals would not choose to bask so close to an oil rig. Thus, visual and verbal strategies interact in building the reputation of the company. However, visuals may be seen to be more effective compared to verbal argu-

Creating a "green" image in the public sphere 195

Figure 2. Persuasive function of a visual in an Environmental Performance Report (Esso UK plc 1992: 13).

ments. The reason for this is that most people know how to respond in words to a verbal argument by having been socialized into a number of written and spoken genres in "lifeworld" and institutional discourse. Visual arguments, on the other hand, are harder to identify and respond to (cf. Myers 1994). The visual argument in Figure 2, for instance, is more subtle compared to the verbal claim that offshore drilling is in complete harmony with maritime life.

Conclusion

During the past two decades companies have generally come to realize their role in environmental harm and protection. They have seen the need to make discursive moves to respond to externally constructed images which may harm the business and to construct externally addressed images that demonstrate their environmental awareness and willingness to act. Environmental reports have also become an important factor in the creation and projection of what Mautner (this volume) calls a uniform and unique voice. Today, this "voice" increasingly includes the projection of a social responsibility beyond environmental protection.

This chapter has argued that studies of genres should not ignore the information provided by the names given to the texts in question by competent users of those texts. However, in the case of new genres, a problem arises as such information may be minimal or even misleading. Because image creation and the contesting of externally constructed images are overall aims, the generic label *environmental report* is somewhat misleading as few of the documents are true reports of the company's environmental action and data concerning emissions, waste, etc.

Another problem when faced with genres at an early stage of emergence is that the texts are typically heterogeneous in terms of content, length and rhetorical strategies chosen to realize the shared set of communicative purposes. If there is systematic variation, the analyst may respond to this by the identification of subgenres.

Corporate environmental reports generally assume a sceptical audience. As we have seen, this means that the documents often use a number of persuasive strategies to convince the sceptical reader. They tend to use easily understood examples, such as recycling of office paper, rather than quantifying the environmental impact of the company's operations.

We have seen that visual and verbal strategies interact in corporate image creation in the public sphere. By using a Swalesian approach, this chapter has tried to demonstrate that the use of visuals may have a parallel function to written arguments, only more effective.

This chapter started with an overview of three research traditions within genre analysis. In the mid and late 1980s and early 1990s, analysts of genres in institutional and professional discourse tended to focus on single genres. Increasingly genres are not viewed as discrete phenomena, but as part of larger chains of oral and written discourse (Berkenkotter [with Thein] 2005). A consequence of this recognition would be to look at a network of genres in the public sphere instead of examining environmental reports in isolation. The choice made in the present chapter is purely practical, and there is a need for analyses of how this particular genre is networked into larger chains of discourse. There is also a need for further research which explores the relationship between visual and verbal strategies in the creation of externally addressed images and the contesting of externally constructed images. Yet another area for further study is to document the current move from corporate environmental reports to values reports.

References

Adam, Christine and Natasha Artemeva
    2002   Writing instruction in English for academic purposes (EAP) classes: introducing second language learners to the academic community. In: Ann M. Johns (ed.), *Genre in the Classroom: Multiple Perspectives*, 179–196. Mahwah, NJ: Lawrence Erlbaum Associates.

Bakhtin, Mikhail M.
    1981   *The Dialogic Imagination: Four Essays by M. M. Bakhtin.* Edited by Michael Holquist. (Transl. Caryl Emerson and Michael Holquist). Austin: University of Texas Press.

Bakhtin, Mikhail M.
    1986   The problem of speech genres. In: Caryl Emerson and Michael Holquist (eds.), *Speech Genres and Other Late Essays*, 60–102. (Transl. Vern W. McGee). Austin: University of Texas Press.

Bazerman, Charles
    1988   *Shaping Written Knowledge: The Genre and Activity of the Experimental Article in Science.* Madison, Wisconsin: The University of Wisconsin Press.

Berkenkotter, Carol and Thomas N. Huckin
    1995   *Genre Knowledge in Disciplinary Communication: Cognition/Culture/Power.* Hillsdale, NJ: Lawrence Erlbaum Associates.

Berkenkotter, Carol (with Amanda Haertling Thein)
    2005   Settings, speech genres, and the institutional organization of practices. *Folia Linguistica: Acta Sociatatis Linguisticae Europaeae* 39: 115–141.

Bhatia, Vijay K.
    1993   *Analysing Genre: Language Use in Professional Settings.* London: Longman.

Bhatia, Vijay K.
    2004   *Worlds of Written Discourse: A Genre-based View.* London/New York: Continuum.

Bourdieu, Pierre
    1977   *Outline of a Theory of Practice.* (Transl. Richard Nice). Cambridge: Cambridge University Press.

Bourdieu, Pierre
    1991   *Language and Symbolic Power.* Edited by John B. Thompson. (Transl. Gino Raymond and Matthew Adamson). Cambridge: Polity Press.

Dudley-Evans, Tony
    1994   Genre analysis: an approach to text analysis for ESP. In: Malcolm Coulthard (ed.), *Advances in Written Text Analysis*, 219–228. London: Routledge.

Dudley-Evans, Tony and Willie Henderson (eds.)
    1990   *The Language of Economics: The Analysis of Economics Discourse*. ELT Document 134. London: Modern English Publications/British Council.

The Economist
    1993   A Green Account 4 September: 17.

Fairclough, Norman
    1992   *Discourse and Social Change*. Cambridge: Polity Press.

Flowerdew, John
    2002   Genre in the classroom: a linguistic approach. In: Ann M. Johns (ed.), *Genre in the Classroom: Multiple Perspectives*, 91–102. Mahwah, NJ: Lawrence Erlbaum Associates.

Foucault, Michel
    1980 [1970]   *The Order of Things: An Archeology of the Human Sciences*. London: Tavistock Publications.

Foucault, Michel
    2001   *Power: The Essential Works of Michel Foucault, 1954–1984*. Volume 3. Edited by James D. Faubion. (Transl. R. Hurley et al.) London: The Penguin Press.

Gunnarsson, Britt-Louise
    1997   The writing process from a sociolinguistic viewpoint. *Written Communication* 14: 139–188.

Halliday, Michael A. K. and James R. Martin
    1993   *Writing Science: Literacy and Discursive Power*. London: The Falmer Press.

Hymes, Dell H.
    1979 [1971]   On communicative competence [extensive extracts]. In: Christopher J. Brumfit and Keith Johnson (eds.), *The Communicative Approach to Language Teaching*, 5–26. Oxford: Oxford University Press. First published University of Pennsylvania Press, Philadelphia 1971.

Hyon, Sunny
    1996   Genre in three traditions: implications for ESL. *TESOL Quarterly* 30: 693–722.

Johns, Ann M. (ed.)
    2002   *Genre in the Classroom: Multiple Perspectives*. Mahwah, NJ/London: Lawrence Erlbaum Associates.

Kress, Gunther
    2003   Genres and the multimodal production of "scientificness". In: Carey Jewitt and Gunther Kress (eds.), *Multimodal Literacy*, 173–186. New York: Peter Lang.

Kress, Gunther and Theo van Leeuwen
    2001   *Multimodal Discourse: The Modes and Media of Contemporary Communication*. London: Arnold.

Lemke, Jay L.
    2005   Multimedia genres and traversals. *Folia Linguistica: Acta Sociatatis Linguisticae Europaeae* 39: 45–56.

Levinson, Stephen
    1979   Activity types and language. *Linguistics* 17: 356–399.

Macken-Horarik, Mary
    2002   "Something to shoot for": a systemic functional approach to teaching genre in secondary school science. In: Ann M. Johns (ed.), *Genre in the Classroom: Multiple Perspectives*, 17–42. Mahwah, NJ: Lawrence Erlbaum Associates.
Martin, James R., Frances Christie and Joan Rothery
    1987   Social processes in education: a reply to Sawyer and Watson (and others). In: Ian Reid (ed.), *The Place of Genre in Learning: Current Debates*, 58–82. Deakin University: Centre for Studies in Literary Education.
Miller, Carolyn R.
    1984   Genre as social action. *Quarterly Journal of Speech* 70: 151–167.
Muntigl, Peter and Helmut Gruber
    2005   Introduction: approaches to genre. *Folia Linguistica: Acta Sociatatis Linguisticae Europaeae* 39: 1–18.
Myers, Greg
    1994   *Words in Ads*. London: Edward Arnold.
Pagano, Adriana
    1994   Negatives in written text. In: Malcolm Coulthard (ed.), *Advances in Written Text Analysis*, 250–265. London: Routledge.
Skulstad, Aud Solbjørg
    1996   Rhetorical organization in chairmen's statements. *International Journal of Applied Linguistics* 6: 43–63.
Skulstad, Aud Solbjørg
    2002   *Established and Emerging Business Genres*. Kristiansand: Høyskoleforlaget (Norwegian Academic Press).
Skulstad, Aud Solbjørg
    2005a   Move-step models: their rationale and application. In: Bäcklund, Ingegerd, Ulla Börestam, Ulla Melander Merttala and Harry Näslund (eds.), *Text at Work. Essays in Honour of Britt-Louise Gunnarsson*, 349–357. Uppsala: Association Suédoise de Linguistique Appliquée and Department of Scandinavian Languages at Uppsala University.
Skulstad, Aud Solbjørg
    2005b   The use of metadiscourse in introductory sections of a new genre. *International Journal of Applied Linguistics* 15: 71–86.
Swales, John M.
    1981   *Aspects of Article Introductions*. Birmingham: The University of Aston, Language Studies Unit.
Swales, John M.
    1990   *Genre Analysis: English in Academic and Research Settings*. Cambridge: Cambridge University Press.
Swales, John M.
    1998   *Other Floors, Other Voices: A Textography of a Small University Building*. Mahwah, NJ: Lawrence Erlbaum Associates.
Swales, John M.
    2007   Worlds of genre metaphors of genre. In: Bonini, Adair, Débora de Carvalho Figueiredo and Fábio José Raren (eds.), *Proceedings of the 4th International Symposium on Genre Studies*, 147–157. Tubarão, Brazil: University

of Southern Santa Catarina. Available online at http://www3.unisul.br./paginas/ensino/pos/linguagem/cd/English/15i.pdf. Accessed 21 September 2007.

Tarone, Elaine, Sharon Dwyer, Susan Gillette and Vincent Icke
1988 [1981]   On the use of passive in two astrophysics journal papers. In: John M. Swales (ed.), *Episodes in ESP: A Source and Reference Book on the Development of English for Science and Technology*. Hertfordshire: Prentice Hall International. First published *The ESP Journal* 1: 2 [1981].

Todorov, Tzvetan
1976   The origin of genres. *New Literary History* 8: 159–170.

Tottie, Gunnel
1982   Where do negative sentences come from? *Studia Linguistica* 36: 88–105.

Tottie, Gunnel
1987   Rejections, denials and explanatory statements – a reply to Fretheim. *Studia Linguistica* 41: 154–163.

Ventola, Eija M.
1987   *The Structure of Social Interaction: Systemic Approach to the Semiotics of Service Encounter Interaction*. London: Frances Pinter.

Ventola, Eija
2005   Revisiting service encounter genre – some reflections. *Folia Linguistica: Acta Sociatatis Linguisticae Europaeae* 39: 19–43.

Vygotsky, Lev S.
1978   *Mind in Society: The Development of Higher Psychological Processes*. Edited by Cole Michael, Vera John-Steiner, Sylvia Scribner and Ellen Souberman. Cambridge, MA: Harvard University Press.

Vygotsky, Lev S.
1986   *Thought and Language*. Edited by Alex Kozulin. Cambridge, MA: The MIT Press.

Yates, Joanne and Wanda J. Orlikowski
1992   Genres of organizational communication: a structurational approach to studying communication and media. *Academy of Management Review* 17: 299–326.

Yunick, Stanley
1997   Genres, registers and sociolinguistics. *World Englishes* 16: 321–336.

Corpus of corporate environmental reports

Allied Colloids Group plc (1993). *Caring Chemistry.* (EAB).
Blagden Industries plc (Packaging) (n.d.). *Environmental Protection.* (EAB).
BP (The British Petroleum Company) plc. (1991) *New Horizons 1991.* (EPR).
The Body Shop International plc (1992). *The Green Book.* (EPR).
The Body Shop International plc (2005) *The Body Shop Values Report 2005.* Available online at http://valuesreport.thebodyshop.net/. Accessed 26 January 2006.
British Coal Corporation plc. (n.d.) *Coal and the Climate: A British Coal Environmental Review.* (EAB).
BNFL (British Nuclear Fuels) plc (1992a). *BNFL and Environmental Care.* (EPR).
BNFL (British Nuclear Fuels) plc (1992b). *Nuclear Waste: What's to Be Done About It?.* (EAB).
W. Canning plc. (n.d.) *Making Chemistry Work.* (EAB).
Donald Murray Paper Ltd. (n.d.) *Papermaking Is Not Killing the Forests.* (EAB).
Esso UK plc (1992). *Esso and the Environment: Policy and Practice.* (EPR).
Hydro (2005) Sustainability rating. Available online at http://www.hydro.com/en/global_commitment/sustainability_rating/index.html. Accessed 25 May 2005.
ICI (Imperial Chemical Industries) plc. (1992) *Environmental Report 1992: Improvement By Design.* (EPR).
National Power plc. (1992) *Environmental Performance Review 1992.* (EPR).
Nuclear Electric plc. (1993) *Nuclear Electric and the Environment 1990–1993: A Progress
Report.* (EPR).
Pilkington plc (1992). *Environmental Policy.* (EPR).
PowerGen plc (1993). *Environmental Performance Report: Analysis of PowerGen's Achievements.* (EPR).
Rio Tinto plc (2004) *Sustainable Development Review: Meeting Global Needs for Minerals and Metals.*
The RTZ Corporation plc (1991). *RTZ and the Environment.* (EPR).
The Shell International Petroleum Company Ltd (1992). *Shell and the Environment.* (EPR).
SmithKline Beecham plc. (n.d.) *The Environment.* (EPR).
Thames Water plc (1993). *Environmental Review.* (EPR).
Wellcome plc (1993). *Wellcome and the Environment.* (EPR).

9. Britain™ and "corporate" national identity[1]

Lidia De Michelis

1. Introduction

The main focus of this article is the so-called "rebranding of Britain", which elicited such outraged press coverage throughout New Labour's first term (1997–2001). This paradigmatic attempt to implement a consistent, pervasive project of national self-refashioning is in fact an impressive tool of domestic and foreign policy. New Labour's agenda of engaging with the vexed question of British national identity and amplifying its discussion through the naturalising channels of today's media-saturated public sphere, involves projecting a more flexible, accommodating sense of "Britishness" alongside the party's revision and representation of Britain's role in the world. In line with the pervasive, difference-erasing technologization and commodification of public discourse typical of neo-liberal agendas (Fairclough 1999), this vision is consistently expressed via forms of specialised communication. In particular, New Labour's discourse of national rebranding is developed around clusters focusing on the key NATION AS CORPORATION metaphor, and the ensuing view of governance as a type of entrepreneurial expertise. These issues are at the heart of *Britain*™. The apparently objective marketing communication approach adopted in this pamphlet, sponsored by the progressive think-tank Demos, in fact displays a strong ideological undercurrent which goes well beyond endorsing the view of the public sphere as merely an "increasingly deregulated 'market' for ideas" (McLennan 2004). By placing the rhetoric of "reasonableness" at the core of its discursive strategies, *Britain*™ upholds that process of "corporatisation of the public sphere" (Marden 2003: XV) which necessarily bears on conceptions of governance and citizenship. I shall argue that Leonard's (1997) attempt to repackage "concept U.K." as a more attractive brand label helps channel public debate along lines consistent with New Labour's discourse, which Fairclough (2000) deconstructed from a Critical Discourse Analysis standpoint, of a "New Britain" or a "Young Country" and its obsession with "novelty", "rejuvenation" and "renewal".

2. Literature review

Before proceeding to the core of this analysis, a brief overview of recent insights into the increasingly interconnected domains of destination marketing and national identity may be helpful, with particular emphasis on their discursive and strategic recontextualisation.

2.1. From "destination marketing" to "nation branding"

Specialist literature on product and destination marketing has for some time now concurred on the importance of what is generally referred to as the "place-of-origin" factor, that is, the psychological and emotional impact of a product's source on consumer behaviour. Development of this factor's enormous potential for engaging customers' imagination and loyalty has been coterminous with the growth of brand theory, and has taken on increasing prominence as more sophisticated insights into the performative and discursive dynamics of branding have been yielded. The idea of "place", here very broadly understood as an experienced and "culturally" meaningful reconfiguration of the more neutral concept of "space", carries emotional connotations also inherent in the concept of "brand". The latter, which Lindsay (2000: 2) describes as "the executive summary (…) of all the expectations, thoughts, feelings, associations that we carry in our minds" regarding a product, is actually described in specialised literature as being comprised of such humanising characteristics as identity, image, personality, essence, character and even culture. The ensuing triangulation between such core constituents of individual self-definition as "place", "identity" and "brand" has proved especially important in the process of marking out the fields of tourism and destination marketing as uniquely suited for appropriation by the discourse of public diplomacy.

The flurry of academic studies being published over the past two decades shows that serious research into tourism, marketing and culture has been steadily gaining momentum, with the most recent theoretical contributions coming from, amongst others, Gallarza, Saura, and Garcia (2002); Kotler and Gertner (2002); and Morgan, Pritchard, and Pride (2002). At the same time, the study of destination branding similarly began to broaden its analytical scope, cross-breeding productively, for example, with sociological texts, which emphasised the status of tourism as a cultural practice (Lash and Urry 1994; Urry 1995). It has also been influenced by the increasing appeal of the emerging specialist discipline known as "place branding", where the choice of the term "place" signals the pervasive, overall culturalization of "space" within the discourses and practices of globalisation (Rojek and Urry 1997).

The ascendancy of place branding over "mere" destination marketing equally owes much to the parallel shift from product brands to "corporate" branding, which took place towards the end of the 1980s. Heralded in the 1960s and 1970s, the conceptual cluster underlying the idea of "corporate brand" (which Balmer and Gray [2003: 982] describe as "an explicit covenant" between the organization behind the brand and its "key stakeholder groups, including customers") was given a more thorough theoretical grounding in the decade that followed.[2]

In those same years, the practical insight, culture and "lore" of corporate branding were popularised most effectively by Wally Olins (1978, 1989). His innovative thinking about branding had been honed and given a communicative cutting edge by his frontline experience as a renowned practitioner and advisor of choice with public administrations and agencies worldwide. This helped him become one of the first to investigate the ways in which countries and companies are becoming increasingly similar to the point of exchanging roles (Olins 1999; see also Elwes 1994). His 1996 case study and corporate branding report "Made in U.K." had a conspicuous influence on the British Tourist Authority's ongoing project of strategic refashioning which led to the launch of the "Branding Britain Campaign" early in 1997. Revived and updated, Olins' findings were broadcast by the BBC2 *Money* programme on 18 May 1997, just a fortnight after New Labour's election victory, and three months ahead of the launch of Mark Leonard's *Britain*™. Olins' (1999) *Trading Identities*, which was published by the pro-Labour, pro-European think tank, The Foreign Policy Centre (directed at the time by Mark Leonard himself), marks the shift of nation branding from the domain of marketing to that of governance, as its two sections address the following questions respectively: "Countries: From nation-state to national brand?" and "Companies: The global rise of the corporate state?". Olins' book helped to popularise the idea that a nation's brand-building project should be a collective enterprise, involving and affecting both public and private concerns and discourses. While maintaining that such a project could only be furthered by adhering to "corporate brand management" patterns which emphasise the holistic involvement of all stakeholders in communicating the corporation's/nation's mission, identity, image and "culture", Olins was also pointing to the unequivocally political nature of such cross-breeding between statecraft and marketing.

Indeed, since the mid-1990s a new discourse representing the need and desirability for "country", "state" or "nation branding" had begun to emerge, gaining unprecedented momentum from the economic, social, cultural and political *humus* of late modernity.

The economic and political rationale for national branding (and *re*-branding) clearly draws on the discourse and logic of new capitalism, with its emphasis on the globalisation, competitiveness and/or partnership, homogenisation and culturalisation of consumer behaviour (Fairclough 2000, 2003; Bourdieu and Wacquant 2001). At the same time, the concept of "nation branding" owes much of its cultural, imaginative and discursive grounding to "modernist" insights such as Hobsbawm's "invention of tradition" (Hobsbawm and Ranger 1983), and, even more so, to post-modernist views of national identity which emphasise the largely imaginary (Anderson 1991: 6), narrative (Bhabha 1990:

291–322), symbolic and discursive nature (Hall 1996a: 612) of national communities (Wodak et al. 1999). From a quite different angle, Anthony Giddens' (1994: 23) description of "a post-traditional social order" in which traditions, far from disappearing, have to "become open to interrogation and discourse", even to the point of implying their own "selective preservation, or perhaps reinvention" (Giddens 1994: 29), similarly offers an attractive theoretical standpoint for "rebranding" projects.

Drawing on the scientific insight of product and corporate marketing, national "brand-building" projects were implemented at first on a public economy-oriented basis: their primary aim was to bend the emotional and cultural potential of marketing towards attracting inward investment, and promoting exports and tourism against an increasingly undifferentiated global product offering. The end of the Cold War and the demise of communism paved the way for the expansion of this scenario, which has increasingly been defined by the largely unchallenged tenets of new capitalism and the consolidation of a so-called "new world order" in which, according to the British diplomat Robert Cooper (1997, 2002), prosperous and well-governed "post-modern" states are invited to expand their powers of attraction through a new kind of benign imperialism. In this world, as Joseph S. Nye argues, "soft" power should supplant military might, and a country might be able to "obtain the outcomes it wants in world politics because other countries want to follow it, admiring its values, emulating its examples, aspiring to its levels of prosperity and openness" (Nye 2002: 5).

This ideological environment, whose discourses have been extensively mediated and circulated in the public sphere, has helped bring about another area of recent specialism within the domain of "nation branding": one which, while still largely concerned with the "national interest" in terms of revenues and tourism (Olins 2003: 148–169), is now openly being conceptualised as a tool of public diplomacy. In a special issue of *The Journal of Brand Management* (2002), Simon Anholt, himself editor of the journal *Place Branding* and one of the most authoritative practitioners in this field, listed a number of ideologically and politically sensitive issues contributing to the overall definition of "nation branding". These included questions of domestic public communication, global competitiveness and "the relationship between nation branding and the (rumoured) demise of the nation-state" (Anholt 2002: 231).

Tourism, which constitutes a highly sophisticated branch of public administrations' managerial and cultural expertise, has long been a privileged contact zone where a nation's brand-building efforts may be put to the test, and its cultural "brand equity" (the whole set of assets and liabilities determining the worth of a brand) may be tracked and evaluated. Within the wider framework of neo-liberalism and the post-nationalist world order, however, this sector now tends to be seen as just one frontline asset in a nation's "corporate" bid for global visibility. Indeed, its emotionally and culturally charged discursivity and largely visual appeal tend to be increasingly subsumed and recontextualised within the more comprehensive and far-reaching political strategies of "national brand management".

Anholt (2005: 118) has recently lamented that "destination branding" (a term pertaining to the language of tourism in the first instance) is all too often confused with "nation branding", which is one of the practices of public diplomacy. Choosing "place branding" as a softer and more comprehensive label for this specialised domain, he maintains that a "convergence of advanced brand theory and statecraft is potentially epoch-making". Place branding as an act of public diplomacy, he adds, differs from propaganda insofar as it is not deliberately manipulative, but stems from "a realization that public opinion is an essential component of achieving a political end" (Anholt 2005: 120). This opinion is similarly reflected in Leonard, Stead, and Smewing's (2002: 9) statement that public diplomacy in fact "is based on the premise that the image and reputation of a country are public goods which can create either an enabling or disabling environment for individual transactions". Unlike traditional diplomacy, it involves multiple (i.e. governmental and non-governmental) stakeholders, and relies on a three-dimensional communicative process ("news management", "strategic communication" and "relationship building"), cutting across the three "spheres on which it is played out: political/military, economic and societal/cultural" (Leonard, Stead, and Smewing 2002: 10).

In Anholt's view, the equation of a country as a corporate brand, which aims to bring all the messages of its "related sub-brands" under an "umbrella of trust" (Anholt 2003: 130), is especially valuable as a working "metaphor". Indeed, the whole strategy of managing and tracking the brand consistency of a nation through the full range of its semiotic practices is described metaphorically as the invisible magnet which in school experiments is often shown to pull iron filings scattered randomly on a sheet of paper into a predictable shape (Anholt 2003: 122–123). Implicit in this metaphor is, of course, an attempt to portray "nation branding" as a dual democratic process, i. e. bottom-up and top-down, harmonising the popular component of local attachment and pride which is undoubtedly important in destination branding, with the unemotional top-down approach of public diplomacy. However, the neat, compelling beauty of Anholt's oddly hybrid discursive strategy scarcely manages to conceal the frighteningly *dirigiste* nature of the unchallenged power of "attraction" wielded by the magnet/corporate brand/public diplomacy. This is all the more disquieting when one considers Anholt's recent definition of branding as a "paradigm" for managing places in the future (Anholt 2005: 119): "The driver of the new paradigm", he concludes, "is *simply* globalisation" and branding "is not something that you add on top: it is something that goes *underneath*" (Anholt 2005: 121, emphasis added). But globalisation, in fact, is neither simple nor transparent.

2.2. "Nation branding" and the discourse of national identity

The third major constituent of the discursive domain of 'nation branding', along with place and marketing, is the discourse of nationhood, with the notion of identity as the common conceptual and emotional denominator between them.

It is beyond the remit of this study to engage in in-depth analysis of the academic literature on the question of national identity, and the way its conceptual boundaries are incessantly renegotiated against a backdrop of post-nationalism and globalisation, from the perspectives of anthropology, history, politics, social science, cultural studies and, increasingly, critical discourse analysis and applied linguistics. However, a brief overview is at least required of some of the recent hypotheses and strategies which bear most directly on the specialist discourse of "nation branding" and its ramifications in the public sphere.

The "discourse-historical" approach described by Wodak et al. (1999) is especially rewarding in tackling concepts such as national identity (and, in this case, national "brand") which involve complex relational dynamics between persistence and change that imply a temporal dimension. Its comprehensive overview and discussion of conceptualisations of identity (Wodak et al. 1999: 10–18) and the nation (Wodak et al. 1999: 18–30) are taken here as prerequisites not only for engaging with the discursive construction of national identity, but also for deconstructing the public diplomacy discourse of "rebranding".

Starting from Ricoeur's (1992) dual description of identity as "sameness" and "selfhood", Wodak et al. (1999: 14–15) review his concept of "narrative identity" (the basis for all reinterpretation and harmonisation of the past) in the light of its elaboration by Martin (1995: 8) as "an open-ended" identity capable of affecting the future. Distinctions between individual and social identities are then introduced (Wodak et al. 1999: 15–16), followed by an analysis of the conventional understandings of a nation as *Kulturnation* (an entity defined by culture, with a strong ethnical and linguistic component) or as *Staatsnation* (defined on a political and territorial basis) (Wodak et al. 1999: 18–21).

The paragraphs that follow (Wodak et al. 1999: 21–27) are especially relevant to an interdiscursive approach to "nation branding". They discuss Anderson's thesis that nations are imagined communities to be distinguished primarily "by the *style* in which they are imagined" (Anderson 1991: 6), and Hall's position that they are "systems of cultural representations" through which an imagined community is transformed into a "symbolic" one by the interpretive act of its citizens partaking in the national culture (Hall 1996a: 612). This is explained as a national "discourse", "a way of constructing meanings about the nation with which we can identify" (Hall 1996a: 613) through shared "stories". Such stories make up what Hall (1996a: 613–14) also describes as the "narrative of the nation": one that, in the words of Wodak et al. (1999: 24) "is presented in national narratives, in literature, in the media and in everyday culture", and which "creates a connection between stories, landscapes, scenarios, historical events, national symbols and national rituals which represent shared experiences and concerns". This same emphasis on social narrativity is an overriding characteristic of the discourse of "nation branding", which often seems to conflate that "discursive constitution and regularization of both the capitalist economy and the national state as *imagined entities*" which Jessop (1999: 2, original emphasis) has noted. Equally influential are Hall's definitions of "hybrid", "fragmented" and "multiply-constructed" identities (Hall 1996b: 4), which are extensively subsumed and recontextualised in the jargon of marketing.

While agreeing with Wodak et al. (1999: 24–30) that concepts such as "habitus", "collective memory", "historical memory", and their various articulations and critiques are central to the discursive construction of national identity, I shall not be discussing them in this paper on the grounds that they are largely absent from the top-down, future-oriented discursivity of nation branding. Rather, in considering the role of memory in shaping narratives of national identity, I shall draw on Duncan Bell's (2003) definition of "mythscape" as a notion which seeks to overcome the theoretical tensions that arise from conflating memory and myth under the "monolithic" category of collective memory. A mythscape, in Bell's words, is "the temporally and spatially extended discursive realm wherein the struggle for control of peoples' memories and the formation of nationalist myths is debated, contested and subverted incessantly. (…) it is the perpetually mutating repository for the representation of the past for the purposes of the present" (Bell 2003: 66).

While the in-depth analyses of a "national character" and the linguistic construction of a *homo nationalis* carried out suggestively in Wodak et al. (1999: 193–199) are, of course, relevant in the case of destination marketing, they are largely absent from the public diplomacy discourse of "nation branding". In fact, far from projecting any preferred stereotype of an "ideal" national subject, this discipline explicitly articulates and promotes "flexible" definitions of nationhood, loosely echoing Bauman's view that today "the snag is no longer how to discover, invent, construct, assemble (even buy) an identity, but how to *prevent it from sticking*. Well-constructed and durable identity turns from an asset into a liability. The *hub* of post-modern life strategy is not identity building, but *avoidance of fixation*" [emphasis mine] (Bauman 1996: 24).

However, such notions of flexibility and "avoidance of fixation" are themselves discursively constructed according to tested formulas and updated stereotypes, a practice which, in Billig's words, "means that the imagination is not unfettered, for stereotyping involves repetition" (Billig 1995: 102). Bond, McCrone, and Brown (2003: 371) put forward a rewarding theoretical model for mapping out exactly how distinct conventional features of national identity are deconstructed and refashioned in order to serve contemporary agendas, most notably when they are recontextualised within the discursive domain of economic development.

This reconciliation of the past with the present in order to affect the future is attained via four processes: "reiteration, recapture, reinterpretation or repudiation, which derive from economic agents' *perceptions* of their nation's economic attributes, and their *normative beliefs* regarding the qualities necessary for economic success" [emphasis mine] (Bond, McCrone, and Brown 2003: 377). Reiteration denotes the mobilisation of a positive historic feature of national identity to serve contemporary economic ends, whereas recapture refers to the same process when this feature is seen as fading out or problematic. On the negative side, reinterpretation signals the presentation of negative historic characteristics as potential contemporary assets, and repudiation refers to the omission or erasure of negative historic features from contemporary discourses on identity (Bond, McCrone, and Brown 2003: 377–385).

These processes, moreover, entail a strong discursive focus, which renders Bond, McCrone and Brown's model especially suitable to laying bare the underlying rhetorical power of *Britain*™ as a multi-genre, multi-source message, drawing on the specialist languages of economics, marketing, social science and national culture in order to disseminate a fundamentally political view of national identity for its own flexible, public diplomacy agenda.

3. Case study: Britain™

3.1. Background

Britain™ was launched on 3 September 1997, hot on the heels of the BTA's "Branding Britain Campaign" and Olins' BBC2 *Money programme* of 18 May 1997 (De Michelis 2005: 92–94; De Michelis forthcoming).[3] "Cool Britannia"[4] was still at its peak, and the pamphlet received great attention from the press. Opinions ranged from overall endorsements of New Labour's modernising project to Stephen Bailey's flaying of Leonard's portrait of "New Britain" as a place governed by a newly-established "Department of Corporate Identity" (*New Statesman*, 12 September 1997). Other voices claimed that a country could not be branded and resold as a consumer good. Some, more neutrally, inscribed *Britain*™ within the broader mid-1990s craving for "modernisation", or simply dismissed it as a mere recasting of popular management clichés in the shape of political advice (Frank 2000).

However, Leonard's nation-branding exercise commanded appreciative comments and extensive quotations in specialised literature on tourism, branding and marketing (Lindsay 2000), as well as being echoed, of course, in contemporary speeches by politicians and public officials. Irrespective of their differing standpoints, most of these approaches locate *Britain*™ among the disciplines of business marketing. To some extent this is still the case, although, in the run-up to the 2001 general election, several columnists have highlighted the shift in the political affiliations of various high-ranking figures in the Demos[5] think-tank, who moved from posts held on the editorial board of *Marxism Today* in their youth, to realigning their philosophies with the defining positions assumed by New Labour during its first term in office.

In the light of these issues, and building on an indepth reading of several other pamphlets published by Demos between 1995 and 1999, I shall endeavour to deconstruct the dual ideological function of *Britain*™. On one hand, Leonard tells an optimistic, compelling story about what Britain will become under New Labour, which entails a selective view of national identity which is projected as factual and universally shared, presented in the seemingly disinterested format of the executive report. On the other, in a manner which closely resembles Fairclough's "genre chains" (Fairclough 2003: 31–32, 65–66), *Britain*™ and the other contemporary publications by Demos, discussed below, form part of an attempt to saturate the public sphere with converging variations on the themes of "New Britain" and the "Third Way".

For instance, Philip Dodd (1995: 14) laments that his impending vision of Britain as "an outward-looking nation in love with change" goes against the grain of the contemporary orthodox "tale of backward-looking insularity, melancholy, decline and loss". What Britain will really need "in an increasingly globalised world (…) is politicians who are willing to enter this turbulence and find ways of telling national stories that are inclusive and open-ended" (Dodd 1995: 38). Anticipating, as it were, Tony Blair's idea of the "Big Conversation",[6] Dodd rounds off his argument by underlining the likely role of the internet in this act of collective re-imagining. Likewise, Geoff Mulgan and Perri 6 (1996: 5) proclaim their vision of "active popular capitalism" where companies and countries will have "to create the future", and planning will be seen as "exploration and creation" (Mulgan and Perri 6 1996: 18). Mulgan and Perri 6 reiterate their standpoint in another Demos pamphlet published in March 1997, in which Britain is heralded as being "brimful of energy" and "now ready for Spring" (Mulgan and Perri 6 1997: 3–4). But for such "signs of Britain's potential for rejuvenation" to deliver their promises, the authors warn, "there are legacies – psychological as well as institutional – that need to be shed" (Mulgan and Perri 6 1997: 4). Underneath this statement lies the hidden agenda driving much of the public discourse on modernisation and rebranding, where concerns over what "to leave behind" have proved far more divisive than "imagining" the shape of the new.

After this brief overview of *Britain*™'s interdiscursive environment, the next section will focus on its linguistic and discursive parameters. Special attention will be given to structure, intertextuality and lexis: metaphorical references, modality and deixis shall also be investigated.

3.2. Textual analysis

Britain™ is an interesting example of that "proliferation of promotional genres" that Fairclough (2003: 33) identifies as an outstanding feature of new capitalism. Accordingly, it may be ascribed to the broader category of "genres of governance", which is characterised by high levels of recontextualization, genre-mixing, intertextuality and interdiscursivity (Fairclough 2003: 32–39). From a functional viewpoint, it may be defined, again in Fairclough's words, as a "hortatory report" (see also van Leeuwen, this volume), encompassing cross-disciplinary domains such as "policy formation" and "management literature" (Fairclough 2003: 96). At the same time, Leonard's pamphlet features the same mobilization of the vocabulary of national identity "for economic ends" by public agencies not motivated by "the pursuit of nationalism as a political project *per se*" which constitutes the focus of Bond, McCrone, and Brown (2003: 371).

In line with the precepts of communications design (Mautner, this volume), *Britain*™ is structured and interspersed with elements such as figures, statistics, graphs and text boxes reporting decontextualized quotations, which, while typical of business communication, help keep readers' attention focused on a narrowly predetermined track. A wealth of specialized vocabulary and catchphrases also draw attention to the fields of management and marketing. Occasionally, however, this comes across as an almost cosmetic device, for identity and the whole symbolic domain of nation-building (with globalisation looming large as its discursive "other") are set firmly at the heart of *Britain*™ and inform a number of its ideological subtexts.

Its summary, which begins with the realis statement that "Britain's identity is in flux" (Leonard 1997: 1), is followed by a kind of executive report, which peremptorily declares itself to be about "The facts". However, chapter headlines soon open up to the language of "identity", first by asking "What is identity for", and second "What are the tools for constructing an identity?".

These questions reveal the underlying notion that identity is a "construct", which may be "shaped", "projected" and "renewed". The same view is deeply embedded in the metaphoric topography of the pamphlet, which, due to its hybrid positioning astride the discursive domains of marketing, public diplomacy and nationalism, mobilises conceptual metaphors conducive to all these fields. However, 'identity' (133 occurrences, plus 48 in chapter headings) is most frequently figured as AN OBJECT, made of diverse "components" and "parts", and displaying "shapes" or "forms" ("a national identity" is presented, even, as being a "useful thing" [Leonard 1997: 32]). Consequently, it may be "constructed", "built", "shaped", "re-shaped", "forged" and "regalvanized" by resorting to appropriate "tools" (Leonard 1997: 36–42). One further example of this is the conceptual metaphor AN IDENTITY IS A SET / A CHANGE OF CLOTHES, which may be "fashioned" and "re-fashioned", "redesigned", "shed" and, of course, once updated, "worn", as in Leonard's confident remark that "today identities are worn more lightly than in the past" (Leonard 1997: 70).

Other conceptual metaphors reiterating the identity nexus include EVOLUTIONARY STRUGGLE (Koller, forthcoming) and, somewhat jarringly, both ORGANIC GROWTH and INORGANIC DEVELOPMENT, the latter to be achieved via ASSEMBLING, ARCHITECTURAL and CONSTRUCTIVE practices. Occasionally identity is conceptualized as A LIVING ORGANISM, which may be "cultivated" and "strengthened", and may appear "confused", "robust" or "outward-looking". Finally, traditional understanding of "Britishness" is discussed in terms of a temple standing on six timeworn pillars: "Institutions", "Empire", "Industry", "Language", "Culture and religion" and "Sport" (Leonard 1997: 21–26; cf. the architectural metaphors above).

On the strength of this pervasive metaphoric network, and building on Olins, Leonard's summary proceeds to argue emphatically that the British should proactively engage in "re-imagining" their national identity and improve Britain's national brand management so as to be able to leverage on what he enticingly refers to as "the identity premium" (Leonard 1997: 3).

> The renewal of identity does not imply casting off what has gone before. Our challenge is to find a better fit between our heritage and what we are becoming. The time is now ripe for Britain to do that. Britain has a spring in its step and a new mood of confidence. Two hundred years ago our ancestors invented a new identity that proved enormously successful. They pioneered new institutions, new images and new ways of thinking, free from any sentimental attachment to the traditions they had inherited. Today we need to do the same again (Leonard 1997: 5).

Due to the unparalleled reach and self-reflexivity of expert knowledge nowadays, the task of renewing British identity for the twenty-first century goes far beyond "our ancestors'" seemingly effortless *invention* of Britishness, as *identity*, especially *national* identity, tends to be seen as elusive and tricky, and badly in need of being "tracked" and, of course, "managed". Accordingly, the stem "manag-" occurs a total of 27 times, generally in association with the "techniques", "mechanisms", "centralized machinery", "central body" and "institutions" related to the manipulation of national identity. This is consistent not only with brand communication practice, but, more relevantly, with Leonard's own public diplomacy call for establishing "a small 'vision group' chaired by the Prime Minister to agree strategic objectives and a working party with representatives from all the agencies – government and business – involved in promoting Britain abroad" (Leonard 1997: 4).

While echoing the same seasonal metaphor and categorical epistemic mode adopted in Mulgan and Perri 6 (1997: 3), the excerpt quoted above is a good example of the way the present tense is used pervasively as a structural device throughout this pamphlet. Traditional constructions of Britishness are left undetermined and dismissed lightly as "what has gone before". Conversely "Britain" (meaning "New Britain") is portrayed as an energetic actor, capable of moods and feelings, and seen in the very act of coming back to life. Hence its representation is firmly grounded in the semantic fields of becoming, renewal, and ripeness. More generally, the stem "Brit-" may be regarded as something of a "logo", and is overwhelmingly present throughout the pamphlet with 522 total occurrences (314 of which are for "Britain", 160 for "British", and 33 for "Britishness"). Often it is used deictically, and is therefore clearly neutral, whereas it bears positive connotations when associated with creativity, novelty and innovation, as in the case of the excerpt quoted above, or with ideals of youthfulness, inclusiveness, imagination and the future. When it is associated, instead, with representations of a traditional past, British identity is described as something "confused and outdated", even "archaic" (Leonard 1997: 24), valuable at best as a "reassuring certainty" (Leonard 1997: 70), but most often an obstacle and a liability.

The ambivalent status of *new* in this passage is also worth noting: univocally positive in connection with the "now", it acquires a somewhat diminished resonance when referred to "our ancestors" and "two hundred years ago". This oscillation is a result of Leonard's attempt to embed a re-interpretive (and possibly recuperative) script within his future-oriented agenda (see above), in order to overcome resistance to his argument that "renewal" is not tantamount to casting off the past. Such reconciliation of the past to a desirable future reality via selective approaches to memory and history entailing processes of narrative recasting is also central to the discursive construction of national identity. Postmodern emphasis on the performativity of national narratives is a striking feature of *Britain*™. This pamphlet's endorsement of the narratedness of experience is apparent in its different use of "story" and "history". While "history", which occurs only 12 times in the pamphlet, sounds at best neutral, "story" and "stories", of course, carry the day. Sometimes they have negative connotations, as in "traditional stories of Britishness" (Leonard 1997: 2) now appealing "if at all, only to an *ageing* minority" [emphasis mine] (Leonard 1997: 2). Most often, however, they are "new stories" with a primarily "bridging" (or reconciling) function, which concur to make up a "new story of Britain at the forefront of creativity and invention" (Leonard 1997: 47).

Six "brand-new" national "stories" are described as "a toolkit for a new sense of identity" (Leonard 1997: 58) and represent *Britain*™'s contact zone between the discourses of identity and branding. Their titles, "Hub UK", "Creative Island", "United Colours of Britain", "Open for Business", "Silent revolutionary" and "Nation of fair play" are apparently indebted to the short, pithy expressions of marketing, and their strategic conception is reinforced by a graph showing six interlinking circles. Put forward uninhibitedly as "our trademarks – at the heart of all promotional activity as we start the new century" (Leonard 1997: 58), these narratives basically represent a subtle recasting of those six "traditional stories of Britishness" previously dismissed as semi-neglected "pillars" of a monolithic, outdated identity.

Each "story" is actually made up of an attractive "tale" developing its brand promise in narrative form between inverted commas, and a list of data, figures and quotes as its supporting evidence and impressive "scientific" rationale. No "once upon a time", however, is to be found in *Britain*™. As a brief analysis of the "Hub UK" story will show, Leonard's re-energizing mix of "Cool Britannia" and advertising styles endorses a conceptual and political scenario which is defined by global cosmopolitanism and reflexive modernity, and often mobilized for the purpose of legitimizing change.

> Britain is an *island*, but it is never insular. It is more *connected* to the *world* than any land-bound nation. It is a *hub*: a place where goods, messages and ideas are *exchanged*; a *bridge* between Europe and America, north and south, east and west. This aspect of Britain helped to define the empire as much as a splash of pink on the map. Britain's empire was also a *web of connections*, from the transoceanic *cables* and radio *links* to the *trading routes*, and the *financial exchanges* of the City of London.
> (...)
> Today, Britain is more than ever a *hub*: the old *links* still exist and have been re-energised through membership of the European Union, the strength of industries like finance and telecommunications, *our favourable position in the world's time zones* and the success of the English language. That *place* prepares Britain well for a *new century*. We are strong not just in the creative industries but also in the knowledge market – creating ideas, researching and importing and exporting students and materials. We are strong in the *industries of speed and connections* – with the world's third largest aerospace industry and dominance in Formula One racing and in telecommunications. Far from being unchanging or closed off, Britain is a country *at ease with change*, a place of *coming and going*, of *import and export*, of *quickness and lightness*. [emphasis mine] (Leonard 1997: 44).

The beginning of this "story" is structured along two main axes. Drawing on the familiar stereotype of the "island race", the first one sets out to construct Britain in the light of psycho-spatial paradigms such as "island" and "world". Three statements of fact, forming a pattern of description, modification and elaboration, define this relationship primarily in terms of "connectedness". The second axis consists of a series of functional equivalences, or at best slight variations on a theme, between "island", "hub" and "bridge", a rhetorical strategy which conflates stereotypes pertaining to the discursive fields of Britain's identity, economy and foreign policy. At the same time, "connectedness" is recontextualized in terms of "exchanges", acquiring an "economic national interest" focus reflected in the hierarchy implicit in the list "goods, messages and ideas". While the use of the present tense is again dominant in an attempt to naturalize a desired future socioscape as an accomplished fact, it is followed by a tentative sally back into the past where empire is selectively reinterpreted as a "web of connections" in an apparently ambivalent assessment. These connections are again defined by "cables", "links", "routes" and "exchanges", terms ultimately conducive to the "City of London" and the fundamentally "metropolitan" vein of Leonard's recipe for rebranding.

The second part of the "story" is meant to cohere the different threads under the brand concept "hub": while the "*old* links" are viable only insofar as they have been "*re*-energized", the passage hinges on the almost oxymoronic spatial and temporal nexus implied in "our favourable *position* in the world's *time zones*" [emphasis mine]. This and the link between "place" and "new century" which follows help to create a discursive and political "space-time" (Fairclough 2003: 224), consistent with New Labour's rhetoric of connectedness. While this is also made clear in the sudden, repeated shift to inclusive first-person deixis, terms such as "creative industries" and "knowledge market", and hints to international economic ratings marry the world of business with the odd lyricism of the last sentence, marked by a crescendo of nominalizations and most appropriately concluded with a reference to "lightness".

While thoughts also inevitably drift to what many editorialists and foreign policy experts have dubbed the "Blair bridge project" (Garton Ash 2004: 41–52), the end of the story is equally consistent with New Labour's projection of itself as the party of change. A paradigm of post-modern porousness and liquidity, new Britain is also "a peculiarly creative nation" (Leonard 1997: 47), where devolution is presented as self-reformation, membership of the European Union is sold as "inventing new forms of supranational governance", and constitutional reform is a matter of the parliamentary system "being reinvented" (Leonard 1997: 57).

Leonard's discursive construction of "Hub UK" helps disseminate a story of "New Britain", which is in line with the redefinition of Britishness put forward in New Labour's 1997 manifesto, characterizing, to quote but one famous example, the late Robin Cook's so-called "Chicken tikka masala speech" (19 April 2001).[7] This is consistent with Leonard's choice of branding Britain as a "global island". The reconciliation of opposites implied in this brand name not only reiterates the difference-erasing agenda underlying the discourse of New Labour, but it also helps project an "imagined community" whose "distinctiveness" consists largely in erasing both spatial and temporal differences from the "imagining".

As is unanimously agreed, the mobilization of memories (whether "authentic" or "invented") lies at the heart of discursive constructions of national identity. However, "memory", "memories" and "remember" feature barely at all in *Britain*™. Leonard, rather, seems to promote a timeless imagining. He goes even further, advocating the creation of "a 'brand space' where people can go to absorb values, vocabulary, imagery and re-energise their conception of the national brand" (Leonard 1997: 62). Identity, thus, increasingly comes to overlap with "image", against the backcloth of a global brandscape where the new "brand states", to borrow van Ham's (2001) expression, compete fiercely for political brand recognition and brand loyalty. The imagining, too, risks being debased to a mere production of "images" to be brokered across an increasingly mediatised public sphere, even though these images, like other "on message" national stories, speeches and reports, are constructed narratively for the purpose of "re-galvanising excitement around Britain's core values" (Leonard 1997: 70).

Leonard's rationale is consistent also with Anholt's celebration of place branding as "fascinating, far-reaching and potentially world-changing" (Anholt 2005: 118; 2006). This notion of *managing* change by resorting to imagination seems, again, to lie at the heart of both public diplomacy and marketing, the aim of which has been described as making people "want to change their minds – to offer to replace what they think with something so much more interesting and captivating, and yet equally portable, that they will happily oblige" (Anholt 2003: 110).

4. Conclusion

Anholt's opinion fits well with Leonard's strategic prescription contained in chapter five of *Britain*™ ("Projecting a new identity"): "The first priority is *to cultivate a national consensus*. Just as the new identity that was forged in the late eighteenth and early nineteenth centuries was born *out of public debate and argument*, today *we need the widest possible participation* in rethinking our identity" [emphasis mine] (Leonard 1997: 60). While this is reminiscent of Demos' metaphorization of its own role as "a greenhouse for ideas" (see Demos website http://www.demos.co.uk), this statement contains useful clues for understanding the link between works such as *Britain*™ and current reconfigurations of the public sphere. In line again with his own reiterative agenda, Leonard appropriates the Habermasian view of the public sphere as a product of the Enlightenment, born out of the rational, dialogical activities of arguing and debating, only to legitimize the emotional, often unaccountable style of democratic participation which increasingly is a defining feature of the current marriage between mood politics and expert knowledge.

Leonard's "pedagogical" agenda (Fairclough 2003) of popularising the insights of public diplomacy, and more generally influencing political debate, inevitably leads to the wider issue of the place occupied by think-tanks in contemporary British politics, and the way they interact with the public sphere as "carriers and interpreters of new ideas and new ways of thinking" (Worpole 1998: 154). This is, of course, beyond the remit of this study, but an allusion at least must be made to the "special relationship" between works such as *Britain*™ and the media. These have been largely instrumental, not only in establishing Leonard's reputation for agenda-setting, but also in commodifying and lending currency to increasingly unchallenged reconfigurations of both the political and economic public spheres as porous discursive environments, where "ideas are 'floated' and 'promoted'" by means of "sustained 'branding' exercises" (McLennan 2004) against a busy backcloth of global networking and connections.

Analysis of the intricate discursive network, whereby the languages of market and national identity are blurred under the terms of Leonard's public diplomacy agenda in *Britain*™, serves, I trust, to raise consciousness of the extent to which corporate discourse exploits the inherent interdiscursivity of supposedly distinct public spheres, in order to acquire public consensus for this agenda over privileged ideological meanings.

Notes

1 A paper centred on the ideological dimension of Mark Leonard's promotion of British national identity was presented at the conference "Discourse, Ideology and Ethics in Specialised Communication", Milan, 11–13 November 2004, and is being published in Garzone and Sarangi (forthcoming). De Michelis (2005: 92–109) also includes a differently tailored Italian version of this study, focusing on political aspects in particular. I would like to thank the editors of the present volume for helpful and constructive comments on the first draft. My thanks also go to Dr. David Gibbons for his stimulating insights.
2 On the ever more complicated topography of corporate brand management studies, see Olins (1978, 1989, 1999); Ind (1997); Balmer and Gray (2003).
3 See "Britain Case Study" (http://www.wollf-olins.com/britain1.htm).
4 First used in a 1967 song by the Bonzo Dog Dooh Dah Band, the phrase "Cool Britannia" was revived in the late 1990s after a *Newsweek* article in October 1996 described London as the "coolest" city in the world. The phrase was immediately taken up by fashion designers, advertisers and popular music critics, and was briefly associated with the modernizing agenda characterizing the onset of New Labour.
5 Geoff Mulgan, Demos co-founder and its first director, has long been a member of 10 Downing Street's Policy Unit, and is currently director of the Young Foundation, London. Mark Leonard, co-founder and former director of the Foreign Policy Centre, and later Director of Foreign Policy at the Centre for European Reform, London, is currently Executive Director of the European Council on Foreign Relations. On Demos, its mission and its history, see Bale (1996) and Frank (2000).
6 On 27 November 2003 Tony Blair launched his "Big Conversation" initiative, which aimed to sound voters' opinions ahead of the 2005 election manifesto by opening "a conversation with the British people about the challenges Britain faces and how together we can meet them" (http://newswww.bbc.net.uk/1/hi/wales/3247994.stm). This initiative was based largely on an interactive website (http://www.bigconversation.org.uk) where citizens could express their suggestions and priorities after registering, or by email.

7 Speech by the then Foreign Secretary to the Social Market Foundation in London in which he asserts that the Indian dish "is now a true British national dish" on which "the Masala sauce was added to satisfy the desire of British people to have their meat served in gravy". This is presented as a "perfect illustration of the way Britain absorbs and adapts external influences" (http://www.guardian.co.uk/racism/Story/0,2763, 477023,00.html).

References

Anderson, Benedict
   1991 [1983] *Imagined Communities: Reflections on the Origin and Spread of Nationalism.* London: 2nd ed. Verso.
Anholt, Simon
   2002 Foreword. *Journal of Brand Management* 9(4–5): 229–239.
Anholt, Simon
   2003 *Brand New Justice. The Upside of Global Branding.* Oxford/Amsterdam/ Boston: Butterworth Heinemann.
Anholt, Simon
   2005 Editorial: some important distinctions in place branding. *Place Branding* 1(2): 116–121.
Anholt, Simon
   2006 *Competitive Identity: The New Brand Management for Nations Cities and Regions.* Basingstoke: Palgrave.
Bailey, Stephen
   1997 Don't phone the identity man yet: as Heisenberg's uncertainty principle reminds us, there's far more to creating a new brand image for Britain than marketing soap powder. *The New Statesman*, 12 September.
Bale, Tim
   1996 Demos: populism, eclecticism and equidistance in the post-modern world. In Michael D. Kandiah and Anthony Seldon (eds.), *Ideas and Think Tanks in Contemporary Britain*, vol. 2, 22–34. London: Frank Cass.
Balmer, John and Edmund Gray
   2003 Corporate brands: What are they? What of them? *European Journal of Marketing* 37(7–8): 972–997.
Bauman, Zygmunt
   1996 From pilgrim to tourist – or a short history of identity. In Stuart Hall and Paul DuGay (eds.), *Questions of Cultural Identity*, 18–36. London: Sage.
Bell, Duncan
   2003 Mythscapes: memory, mythology, and national identity. *British Journal of Sociology* 54(1): 63–81.
Bhabha, Homi K. (ed.)
   1990 *Nation and Narration.* London/New York: Routledge.
Billig, Michael
   1995 *Banal Nationalism.* London: Sage.

Bond, Ross, David McCrone and Andrew Brown
  2003   National identity and economic development: reiteration, recapture, reinterpretation and repudiation. *Nations and Nationalisms* 9(3): 371–391.
Bourdieu, Pierre and Loïc Wacquant
  2001   New-liberal speak: notes on the new planetary vulgate. *Radical Philosophy* 105: 2–5.
Cooper, Robert
  1997   *The Post-Modern State and the World Order.* London: Demos.
Cooper, Robert
  2002   The post-modern state. In Mark Leonard (ed.), *Re-ordering the World*. London: Demos.
De Michelis, Lidia
  2005   *L'Isola e il Mondo. Intersezioni culturali nella Gran Bretagna d'oggi.* Milano: FrancoAngeli.
De Michelis, Lidia
  forthcoming   "A forward-looking country": *Britain*™ and the unbearable lightness of "corporate" national identity. In Giuliana Garzone and Srikant Sarangi (eds.), *Discourse, Ideology and Ethics in Specialised Communication*. Frankfurt/Main: Peter Lang.
Dodd, Philip
  1995   *The Battle over Britain.* London: Demos.
Elwes, Anneke
  1994   *Nations for Sale*. London: BMP DDB Needham.
Fairclough, Norman
  1999   Global capitalism and critical awareness of language. *Language Awareness* 8(2): 71–83.
Fairclough, Norman
  2000   *New Labour, New Language?* London/New York: Routledge.
Fairclough, Norman
  2003   *Analysing Discourse: Textual Analysis for Social Research.* London: Routledge.
Frank, Thomas
  2000   Review of *Britain*™. *Harper's Magazine*. May.
Gallarza, Martina G., Irene Gil Saura and Haydée Calderon Garcia
  2002   Destination image: towards a conceptual framework. *Annals of Tourism Research* 29(1): 56–78.
Garton Ash, Timothy
  2004   *Free World: Why a Crisis of the West Reveals the Opportunity of Our Time.* London: Allen Lane.
Giddens, Anthony
  1994   Brave New World: the new context of politics. In: David Miliband (ed.), *Reinventing the Left*, 21–38. Cambridge: Polity Press.
Hall, Stuart
  1996a   The question of cultural identity. In: Hall, Stuart, David Held, Don Hubert and Kenneth Thompson (eds.), *Modernity: An Introduction to Modern Societies*, 595–634. Oxford: Blackwell.

Hall, Stuart
　1996b　　Introduction: who needs "identity"? In: Stuart Hall and Paul DuGay (eds.), *Questions of Cultural Identity*, 1–17. London: Sage.
Hobsbawm, Eric and Terence Ranger (eds.)
　1983　　*The Invention of Tradition*. Cambridge: Cambridge University Press.
Ind, Nicholas
　1997　　*The Corporate Brand*. London: Macmillan.
Jessop, Bob
　1999　　Narrating the future of the national economy and the national state? Remarks on remapping regulation and reinventing governance. Department of Sociology, Lancaster University. Available online at http://www.lancs.ac.vk/fass/sociology/papers/jessopnarrating-the-future.pdf. Accessed 24 September 2007.
Koller, Veronika
　forthcoming　　"Our customers embrace us as an essential partner": corporate brands as socio-cognitive representations. In: Gitte Kristiansen and René Dirven (eds.), *Cognitive Sociolinguistics: Language Variation, Cultural Models, Social Systems*. Berlin/New York: Mouton de Gruyter.
Kotler, Philip and David Gertner
　2002　　Country as brand, product and beyond: a place marketing and brand management perspective. *Journal of Brand Management* 9(4/5): 249–262.
Lash Scott and John Urry
　1994　　*Economies of Signs and Space*. London: Sage.
Leonard, Mark
　1997　　*Britain™: Renewing Our Identity*. London: Demos.
Leonard, Mark, Catherine Stead and Konrad Smewing
　2002　　*Public Diplomacy*. London: Foreign Policy Centre.
Lindsay, Marsha
　2000　　The brand called Wisconsin™: can we make it relevant and different for competitive advantage. (Economic Summit White Paper). Available online at http://www.wisconsin/edu/summit/archive/2000/papers/pdf/lindsay.pdf). Accessed 20 April 2005.
McLennan, Gregor
　2004　　Big ideas. *re:search*, 19 July. Available online at http://www.bris.ac.uk/researchreview/2004/1113908911. Accessed 12 January 2006.
Marden, Peter
　2003　　*The Decline of Politics: Governance, Globalization and the Public Sphere*. Aldershot: Ashgate.
Martin, Denis-Constant
　1995　　The choices of identity. *Social Identities* 1(1): 5–20.
Morgan, Nigel, Annette Pritchard and Roger Pride (eds.)
　2002　　*Destination Branding: Creating the Unique Destination Proposition*. Oxford/Auckland/Boston: Butterworth Heinemann.
Mulgan, Geoff and Perri 6
　1996　　*The New Enterprise Culture*. London: Demos.
Mulgan, Geoff and Perri 6
　1997　　*The British Spring: A Manifesto for the Election after the Next*. London: Demos.

Nye, Joseph S.
> 2002 Hard and soft power in global Information Age. In: Mark Leonard (ed.), *Re-Ordering the World*, 2–10. London: Demos.

Olins, Wally
> 1978 *The Corporate Personality: An Inquiry into the Nature of Corporate Identity*. New York: Mayflower Books.

Olins, Wally
> 1989 *Corporate Identity: Making Business Strategy visible through Design*. London: Thames & Hudson.

Olins, Wally
> 1999 *Trading Identities: Why Countries and Companies Are Becoming More Alike*. London: The Foreign Policy Centre.

Olins, Wally
> 2003 *On Brand*. London: Thames and Hudson.

Ricoeur, Paul
> 1992 *Oneself as Another*. Chicago: The University of Chicago Press.

Rojek, Chris and John Urry (eds.)
> 1997 *Touring Cultures: Transformations of Travel and Theory*. London: Routledge.

Urry, John
> 1995 *Consuming Places*. London: Routledge.

van Ham, Peter
> 2001 The rise of the brand state: The postmodern politics of image and reputation. *Foreign Affairs*, September–October. Available online at http://www.foreignaffairs.org. Accessed 10 June 2005.

Wodak, Ruth, Rudolf de Cillia, Martin Reisigl and Karin Liebhart
> 1999 *The Discursive Construction of National Identity*. Edinburgh: Edinburgh University Press.

Worpole, Ken
> 1998 Think-tanks, consultancies and urban policy in the UK. *International Journal of Urban and Regional Research* 22(1): 147–155.

III. Language and communication in politics

10. Political terminology

Paul A. Chilton

1. Introduction

In book three of his *Politics* Aristotle asks: "How should we define 'citizen'?" He goes on to give a definition for "practical purposes". The latter phrase is significant because it suggests that Aristotle acknowledges the contingency of the term. Aristotle goes on to give a detailed classification of types of kingship and democracy. Though the *Politics* is a detailed discussion and questioning of historical cases, it is also the most influential example in the western tradition of an attempt to classify a set of political terms in terms of the social facts that they refer to. However, Aristotle does not discuss the *semantics* of political terms, although at the beginning of the *Politics* there is a passage that strongly suggests a link between language and political behaviour (cf. Chilton 2004).

When, then, do we begin to find a literature concerned with political terms as bearers of particular kinds of meaning? I shall consider briefly only twentieth-century and contemporary scholarship. A landmark is the rise of totalitarian societies in the mid-twentieth century. In the second half of the century German scholars in particular produced a large literature investigating the language of the national-socialist era, as well as that of the German Democratic Republic and its aftermath: the reader is referred to the overview of this literature provided by Oberhuber (this volume). In the English-speaking world, the first public voice addressing political terminology is perhaps George Orwell (1946, 1949), but Orwell's approach to meaning was scarcely scientific and was highly prescriptive. However, his critical stance was taken up in academia and was reflected in the "critical linguistics" of Fowler, Kress, Hodge (and associates) and the subsequent Critical Discourse Analysis (CDA) movement (Fairclough, van Dijk, Wodak and others). This body of scholarship has had much more to say about the linguistic processes that are involved in the production of political meaning: for an overview of this literature, again see Oberhuber (this volume). Meanwhile, the academic disciplines of philosophy and political science were giving attention to political terms and their associated concepts. In political science, there was a tendency to take for granted the processes whereby terminology is historically produced and to concentrate on the history and definition of salient terms in the western political tradition such as "state" and "citizen" (e.g. Ball et al. 1989). A new current emerged in the so-called "linguistic turn" of post-modernist scholars in political science (e.g. Shapiro 1984), who took up the ideas of Foucault and Derrida, without adopting or developing a theory of meaning recognisable within a linguistics perspective, however. In a parallel current, some thinkers in the tradition of analytic language philosophy, ordinary language philosophy and pragmatism have in fact addressed the problem of political semantics. It is with these currents of thought that the present essay initially engages, but only in order to move towards contemporary theories of meaning that have developed with the cognitive revolution in linguistics and discourse analysis.

2. How can the meanings of political terms be analysed?

What I understand by "political terms" is lexical items that would be recognised by native speakers as typically used to refer to entities and processes in that domain of social life concerned with politics, where politics is understood to be primarily activities associated with the public institutions of the state. Political terminology in this sense is therefore to be distinguished from political discourse, which is the use of language to do the business of politics and includes persuasive rhetoric, the use of implied meanings, the use of euphemisms, the exclusion of references to undesirable realities, the use of language to rouse political emotions, and the like. Political discourse thus includes political terminology but is not coterminous with it. However, as will be seen, this means that there is an interaction between political terms that appear to be stable over time and certain discourse processes.

There is no existing theory of political terminology. What follows is an outline of the possible elements of such a theory. It draws on pragmatic and cognitive theories, but also considers how such theories can be informed by observations about political concepts and the social nature of language that have been put forward by philosophers.

The question that we are seeking to address is very broad: What are the meanings expressed by political terms? To answer this question, we need a short excursus into semantic theory. The most formalised semantic theory is truth-conditional semantics. Essentially, the principle is as follows. We know the meanings of sentences because we know what it means to say that such-and-such an expression is true in some model of the world. So, for example, to say that we know the meaning of the word "democracy" would mean that we know when a sentence using this word is true in some model of the world. This approach does in fact go to the heart of the concern that political semantics has, namely the concern with truth. But the begged question is, which model of the world, whose model of the world? This question then obliges us to enquire into the different models of the world – presumably in this case the political world – in which such a sentence is or is not true.

Another aspect of truth-conditional semantics, one which goes back to the foundational work of the mathematician and logician Gottlob Frege, stresses that words have a relationship, called "reference", to things in the world, not directly but by way of a further notion called "sense" (Frege 1960 [1892]). Frege wanted to distinguish sense from subjective individual meanings and associations. Consequently, he claimed that sense is a public and shared meaning. However, the line is difficult to draw, because of the difficulty of formulating criteria to define "public". After all, a shared meaning might be public and shared in the sense that it is a conventional meaning among only members of some group, e.g. the local branch of a "ban the bypass" lobby group, as opposed to being public and shared by members of a much larger community such as a state. This must mean that the truth conditions of a term vary from one group of users to another.

In order to establish the meaning of an expression we have to turn to what is in people's minds, that is, to what is in the mind of certain people in some group. This brings us back to a specific aspect of discourse, one that has to do with contention between groups concerning the meaning of some term, the truth conditions of some term. I now look at a theory of meaning that has an implicit relevance for political terminology, one that starts in philosophy as a theory of concepts, but which, as I will suggest below, is best understood in terms of discourse.

3. "Essentially contested concepts"

It is often maintained that political terms are associated with concepts that are "essentially contested". That is, it is maintained that political terms are members of a subset of the lexicon of a language whose members are associated with such concepts.

The notion of "essentially contested concepts" was expounded by the philosopher and political scientist W. B. Gallie. Gallie sought to establish a set of concepts that are logically distinct from other types of concepts, in that they are always necessarily open to contest. He contrasts such concepts with other kinds of concepts for which, he assumes, rational argument or evidence can establish definite criteria for proper use. Essentially contested concepts can never be defined in this way, he claims. Such concepts can endlessly be both supported and contested by rational arguments of different kinds, all of which are valid (Gallie 1956: 169). It is clear that Gallie is operating with a certain understanding of the term concept, one which assumes that concepts are rationally constructed categories amenable to empirical or logical testing.

Gallie claims that the special category of essentially contested concepts relates in particular to "a number of organised or semi-organised human activities" (Gallie 1956: 169), including the concept "democracy". He provides a list of criteria that define the category (Gallie 1956: 171–180). In brief, the necessary conditions of an essentially contested concept are the following: (1) it is "appraisive", i.e. it implies a valued achievement, (2) it shows internal complexity, (3) its internal components can be ranked in different ways by competing speakers, (4) the attributed achievement is "open", i.e. it can be modified over time and (5) users of some concept recognise that others use it differently, i.e. that the concept is contested, which means that it is used both aggressively and defensively.

In addition, Gallie claims that two further criteria are required in order to distinguish "essentially contested concepts" from another class of concepts that he believes to exist, namely, those concepts that can be demonstrated to be inherently confused or erroneous. These criteria are: (6) that the true essentially contested concept is derived from an "exemplar", some kind of schematic concept perhaps, that all contestants accept as validly underlying the concept they are contesting, (7) that the continuous contestation regarding the exemplar implies its maintenance and development over time "in optimum fashion".

There are several objections that could be brought against Gallie's notion. One relates to (5). While (5) may be an ideal criterion, it is surely not the case in practice that users of a term such as "democracy" recognise that it is contestable: most users would assert that their use is the only correct one. A second objection is more general and relates to the Gallie's concept of "concept" itself. Linguistic semantics, especially cognitive semantics, has long accepted that to some degree all concepts associated with linguistic expressions are fuzzy categories whose precise denotation (not to mention the looser notion of connotation) varies over time. It is therefore highly questionable whether any particular *subset* of the lexicon is *essentially* contested. However, it is intuitively plausible to think that, as a matter of *degree*, political concepts are especially prone to change, variable interpretation, re-interpretations and deliberate attempts by political actors to bring about re-interpretation in the minds of hearers. A third objection could be raised against (7) on the grounds that "in optimum fashion" is not definable.

Nonetheless, Gallie's discussion of "democracy" as an essentially contested concept draws attention to important characteristics. By criterion (1), the term "democracy" is clearly appraisive: it has developed as a term that can be used to express approval of a certain polity or procedure. With reference to (2) and (3), the term democracy can be said to denote a variety of states of affairs that can be ordered in different ways. Gallie notes that the term covers at least the following aspects: (a) It can mean the power of citizens to choose and remove their government; (b) it means that all citizens, irrespective of their backgrounds, can attain political positions; and (c) it can mean self-government or the continuous active participation of citizens in government. Gallie then points out that (a) is not necessarily more fundamental, in practice, than the other two aspects, which enables him to say that the three aspects (a), (b) and (c) can be varied in number and ranking by different contesting groups of utterers. With reference to (4) and (5), the meaning of the term "democracy" is modified over time and is used aggressively and defensively by different groups. Finally, invoking condition (6), Gallie (1956: 186) argues that users of the term "democracy" lay claim in general to "the authority of an exemplar, i.e. of a long tradition of (…) demands, aspirations, revolts and reforms of a common anti-*in*egalitarian character".

What is interesting about Gallie's discussion is that his notion of "essentially contested concepts" points toward an alternative methodology. As noted earlier, Gallie's fundamental theoretical frame appears to assume that concepts are conscious rational categories with clear boundaries. However, this is not self-evident. Internal complexity, recognition of contesting conceptual variation, conceptual change over time – these ideas all stand in need of detailed explanation. For instance, one can reasonably ask, in what medium or by what vehicle complexity, variation, contestation and change are manifested. The only reasonable answer is human linguistic communication. Once this is admitted, to say that democracy is an "essentially contested concept" amounts to using compressed shorthand for multiple communicative acts (i.e. discourse) in which different individuals and groups of individuals seek to get their own conceptualisation of, let us say, the term "democracy" recognised and accepted by other individuals and groups of individuals. The study of "political terms" can therefore only be approached by way of the study of political discourse, in the sense of the dynamic process of language use in the domain that constitutes "politics". Equally, Gallie's observations in terms of criteria (2) and (3), namely, the contestable ranking of the aspects (a), (b) and (c), can be understood in terms of "discourse", where "discourse" is understood as an ordered set of stable and communicable beliefs. The latter can also be characterised as "ideologies".

4. The division of labour theory of meaning

As Gallie's framework suggests, the degree of variation in conceptualisation of political terms allows for consensual communication at a minimum level in a polity, but can also lead to a lack of conceptual consensus at the level of fuller conceptualisation. This means that political terminology is always to some extent liable to be in the process of negotiation among individuals and groups. There will doubtless be a stable "core" ultimately linked to constitutional and historical knowledge, but historical change and contingencies will produce complex renegotiations of meanings.

However, Gallie's framework is not enough to deal with other observations that can be made concerning political terminology, for example those that are not contested but which are, on close scrutiny, variable. For example, what does the term "prime minister" mean? On a referential theory of meaning, most people in the UK, asked the question "who is the prime minister?", would probably correctly identify the person whom the term denotes. But in this particular case, identifying the extension of the category provides a very limited notion of the meaning of the term. We might go further, still within a referential truth-conditional framework, and say that the sense of the term "prime minister" is the set of properties that it is true to predicate of the term in English in the UK. At this point, if we now ask who knows this set, the answer has to be: probably very few people in the UK, possibly just a handful of constitutional lawyers. Most people are likely to use the term in communicating with other members of the polity quite happily with knowledge of only one or two, possibly vague, properties (e.g. "the head of the government") that serve for all practical purposes to correctly identify the holder of the office in question.

Where does this leave us if we are asking what the term means? It could imply that the "true" or "full" meaning is not instantiated in the minds of the relevant population at all, but exists in some metaphysical realm of concepts or sense. I assume that this is wrong. It could mean that only the denotational meaning is the meaning of the term "prime minister", but this seems to yield a depleted notion of meaning. Another possibility, however, is the one outlined by Putnam (1975: 227–229) and summarised in his "hypothesis of the division of linguistic labour", which runs as follows:

HYPOTHESIS OF THE UNIVERSALITY OF THE DIVISION OF LINGUISTIC LABOR:
Every linguistic community exemplifies [division of linguistic labor]: that is, possesses at least some terms whose associated "criteria" are known only to a subset of the speakers who acquire the terms, and whose use by the other speakers depends upon a structured cooperation between them and the speakers in the relevant subsets. (Putnam 1975: 228)

To substantiate this hypothesis, Putnam points out that the meaning of a word such as "gold" does not depend on everyone in the relevant speech community having acquired the expert's method for recognising gold. It is perfectly possible for someone to use the term meaningfully, without knowing how to perform an appropriate metallurgical test, relying on a special community of speakers who do know such a test. Certain political terms can be considered in the same fashion. Such terms cannot be defined as members of a conceptual category on the basis of necessary and sufficient conditions ("criteria"), as one would expect to do within a truth-conditional semantic theory. That is to say, for some members of the relevant speech community, there will be some people who do not have all the criteria to unequivocally define a referent as a member of the extension "prime minister" under, for example, the British constitution. However, as Putnam argues (1975: 228), one can consider the entire political community, with varying criteria across the population, as the domain over which the necessary and sufficient conditions are found in the minds of expert and non-experts *considered as a collective body*.

It is important to note, however, that even if we consider the case of an expert with the fullest conceptual representation of "prime minister", we need to enquire into the nature of this representation. This will lead us to a consideration of the frame-semantic theory of meaning. A comparison of political concepts across languages demonstrates what is at issue. Consider the French translation equivalent of "prime minister", namely *premier ministre*. The meanings of these terms, used in actual utterances, would depend on the location and situation of the utterance. For example, *le premier ministre* could still refer to Tony Blair in the relevant context. However, if we take these two terms to be used one in a British context the other in a French context, then not only will they each denote separate individuals at any one historical moment, but also they will be potentially linked to different conceptual frames (perhaps only in the minds of the appropriate Putnamian experts). What I mean by this is that the meaning of the terms "prime minister" and *premier ministre* is related to two different sets of concepts, each of which is differently structured. The British constitution is different from the French constitution in regard to prime ministers (e.g. with respect to how they are appointed). It is in this sense that the terms have different meanings.

5. Structural and frame semantics

In the sections above, we have begun with denotational theories of meaning, which focus on a relationship between words or sentences and entities or states of affairs in the world. We have, however, argued that it is necessary to consider both what is in the minds of speakers and how speakers use these words in particular situations. In this section I broach the subject of how linguistic expressions relate to one another in people's minds.

The Swiss linguist, Ferdinand de Saussure (1857–1913), developed a theory of meaning (or "signification") that crucially depended on the network of relationships between linguistic expressions in the minds of speakers in a speech community (Saussure 1964/1916, 1983). Saussure had in mind an abstract system of all the terms in a language (*langue*) viewed as a supra-individual social fact, rather than language in use (*parole*). But of course the two perspectives, *langue* and *parole*, are related to one another, and perhaps in two directions. On the one hand, a speaker has knowledge of the expressions in a language and of which ones typically go together in certain semantic patterns. On the other hand, which particular terms get into the stored set of terms and what they mean, is a function of a historical process of language use. Thus, "democracy" and "party" in their modern senses (whatever they are) have not always existed in English, but start to enter the knowledge base of speakers at a certain period (perhaps the eighteenth and nineteenth centuries).

In actual utterances, we have two dimensions at least – the words that are in the utterance and that typically do or do not go together in a string. For example, "democratic" might co-occur in a *syntagmatic relation* with "country", "elections", "freedom", "America" in some particular sentence. We also have words that are associated with one another but are not actually present. So for example, "democratic" is contrasted with "undemocratic", and also (depending on the speaker) with "tyranny", "communist", etc. This approach to the meaning of terms leads us to a view of meaning in which political terms (like any other terms) are linked to background conceptualisation. This linking can be viewed in a narrow or a wide fashion. A term like *vote* takes its sense (is "profiled" as cognitive linguists would say) in relation to a conceptual "base". Just as the term "hypotenuse" can only have a meaning in relation to a concept of a right-angled triangle, so *vote* can only be understood in terms of a set of interrelated concepts.

That is to say, *vote* only makes sense if we have stored in our long term memory (or "semantic" or "encyclopaedic" memory, as it is sometimes called) a relatively complex set of connected concepts. Such a set is variously referred to as a "mental model" (Lakoff 1987), a "frame" (Fillmore 1982) or a "base" (Langacker 1987: 183–9; Taylor 2002: 192–202). In the case of the concept associated with *vote*, we would expect the base to contain concepts relating to the entire procedure of elections in a particular political culture. In the cognitive linguistic approach to meaning, it would be said that the meaning of *vote* is a conceptual element of the base that is "profiled". This approach helps to explain how an isolated term like *vote* has the meaning it does. It also prompts a question – how much encyclopaedic knowledge is in the base? This is an important question, but in the domain of political terminology at least, it can be understood in relation to some of the ideas introduced in sections 3 and 4, specifically the ideas of contested concepts and expert meanings. For it can be admitted that the amount of detail, and indeed any variability in the detail, depends on the social role of the language user – for instance, whether he or she is a political scientist by training, a constitutional lawyer, professional politician, a journalist, a lay person who encounters politicians only in TV programmes, or a member of a political organisation with a particular political ideology.

The upshot of all this is that there are degrees of conceptualisation alongside referential meanings. Somehow a population coordinates itself sufficiently to be able to meaningfully talk about prime ministers. What is of interest is that it emerges that meaning is not fixed but unevenly distributed in the minds of people in a population. Moreover, it is possible that quite minimal conceptual content is sufficient for an adequate level of communication across the political community.

The linguistic concept of "frame" has been popularised by George Lakoff (2002, 2004). Lakoff uses the term "frame" roughly in the sense already outlined above. For example, he considers the expression "tax relief" (Lakoff 2004: 3–4, 24–26). Lakoff's argument is, in effect, that the meaning of the word *relief* depends on a conceptual frame in which there is an affliction, an afflicted party and an heroic reliever of the affliction. Consequently, in public discourse, an expression such as "tax relief" evokes the notion that taxation is an affliction. This might seem to be naturally the case. However, as Lakoff points out, taxation could be framed differently, for example one could speak of taxation as investment in the future or as paying one's dues. Lakoff also argues that frames govern the ideologies of the two major political parties in the United States: the public discourse of the Democrats is framed by a "nurturant parent" model and that of the Republicans by a "strict father" model. Lakoff also claims that the concept of the "nation" and "America" is framed by a metaphor, namely "the nation is a family" (on metaphor, see below). It follows that the Democrats will conceptualise America in one way and the Republicans in a different way, and that this difference will be expressed in their public discourse. For example, the strict father model will include the requirement that fathers discipline children in order to make them tough and self-reliant, while "nurturant" parents will be sensitive to their needs and feelings. Such values and attitudes are, it is claimed, metaphorically transferred to political ideologies and into policies. There are several assumptions here that may be questioned, at least in so far as they appear to be generalised claims about a highly complex and differentiated population.

6. Deep and shallow processing of political terms

The considerations above have led to the conclusion that political terminology is variable in its content and that it may also be quantitatively different in different individuals or groups of individuals, with expert communities, for example, having a greater amount of conceptual information linked to a particular lexical item. There is, however, a further possibility. It is plausible to think that even an individual who links a particular lexical item – say, the term "democracy" – with a large amount of conceptual structure may not always, in all circumstances of communication, draw on all of this encyclopaedic background knowledge. One might say that it is not indeed relevant to draw on all the linked background conceptual structure on all the occasions when the term is uttered or understood.

This approach to the question of political terminology carries interesting implications, not merely for an understanding of the nature of political terms (the points we have just made apply equally to many non-political expressions), but also for an understanding of how political terms can be exploited or manipulated during the course of political communication. Allott (2005), for example, outlines a theory to explain how the term *democracy* – and other similar terms such as "communist", "extremist", "terrorist" – are, as Allott would put it, misused. The notion of "misuse" of a term is not our prime concern here. Suffice it to say that the word "misuse" seems to presuppose the existence of a proper or correct use of a term, and if this is the case, then a question is begged and it may be that all we can say is that one person's correct use is another person's misuse. Be that as it may, what is clear is that terms such as "democracy" and "terrorism" have variable meanings for different individuals of a speech community, and conceivably at different times for the same individual. It is even possible that in some sense a speaker can use such terms in different senses on the same occasion.

The question that we need to address as linguists is what sort of theory of meaning we need to account for the sort of linguistic behaviours just alluded to. As Allott (2005) suggests, we can refocus this question. Since we are talking about subtle kinds of meaning construction via language in use, we should address the issue through cognitive pragmatics. Allott's claim is that we should expect the manipulative uses of political terms to be implicit in human pragmatic capacities, and to be potentially universal, although perhaps particularly well developed in western democracies from the beginning perhaps of the twentieth century (Allott 2005: 150).

An appropriate cognitive pragmatic theory is Relevance Theory (Sperber and Wilson 1995 [1986], Wilson and Sperber 2004). Relevance Theory, which takes its inspiration from Grice (1989) but disagrees with significant elements of Grice's theory, is, at the most general level, a theory about human cognition, More particularly it is a theory about the use and understanding of utterances. According to Relevance Theory, in deriving mental representations on the basis of utterance input the human brain seeks to maximise relevance. What is relevance? In this theory relevance is a ratio between positive cognitive effects and processing effects. Positive cognitive effects are those that matter to an individual, because they make a "worthwhile difference to the individual's representation of the world", e.g. by improving that person's information on a certain topic (Wilson and Sperber 2004: 608). There are two further crucial ingredients. One is the assumption that lexical expressions are associated with "mental addresses" that consist of (a) phonetic and syntactic information, (b) logical inferences based on meaning postulates or "core meaning", and (c) a variable amount of encyclopaedic information. The other is the claim that processing utterances for relevant representations involves "ad hoc concepts". Such concepts arise in the process of getting relevant meaning from the literal or "encoded" meaning of linguistic expressions in relation to their context, and can involve "narrowing" or "loosening" of the conventional core meaning. People processing utterances in certain contexts for certain purposes might find they achieve relevance by "narrowing" or "loosening" the core meaning of a certain linguistic expression. Such processing has been termed "shallow" processing.

Now Allott's (2005) argument in relation to democracy is precisely that in many contexts this and other political terms undergo "shallow processing", which Allott thinks might be typical of public discourse because of the low expectations hearers have for the relevance of such discourse. Assuming that there is an agreed common core meaning of democracy (and this is a big assumption), then what would happen in shallow processing might be that individuals only access part of the core meaning if they reach relevance in the context. For example, suppose the core meaning includes something like "political system with popular influence over decisions" (as Allott 2005: 152). This core might be known to the hearer, but not accessed; merely elements such as "good political system" might be accessed. While this account provides an interesting hypothesis as to the mechanisms of "shallow processing" and an interesting explanation of the "slippage" in the use of political terms, it remains problematic that one "correct" core meaning appears to be assumed by the theory. Core meanings vary between groups of individuals (as Putnam's hypothesis proposes) and over time through contestation (as Gallie's ideas lead us to think).

7. New political terms: Metaphor and policy change

It is important to be aware that political terms come into being as a result of historical processes. These processes do of course consist of discourse, viewed over relatively long periods of time – innumerable acts of linguistic communication in various sectors of societies that are involved in the enactment and control of political processes. There is no linguistic or sociolinguistic theory of innovation in political terminology, but it does seem to be an important area for potential research, since there appears always to be a semantic penumbra around political terms that is constantly changing, while new terms are also added to the lexicon utilised in political discourse.

A suggestive, though very informal and linguistically under-informed current of thought, is to be found in the ruminations of the American philosopher Richard Rorty. An important idea in Rorty's thinking is that what he calls "metaphor" provides new concepts in the culture of a community, including the political culture. A further idea is that liberal democratic societies provide the most conducive environment for innovative metaphor in political "language", and that such an environment, together with the kind of "language" that it fosters, is likely to reflect the best conditions for human freedom and amelioration of suffering. The point here is not to discuss this second thought-provoking claim, but to examine further the notion that "metaphor" is an essential element in the innovation and renovation of political discourse.

Rorty's view of metaphor, which is never defined and fails to take account of work in linguistics and cognitive science, reflects his espousal of the Romantic strand in European philosophy and his critique of the formal truth-conditional theory of meaning found in analytic philosophy. Thus Rorty speaks of metaphor as if it were an almost mystical act of creation, typically generated by "an idiosyncratic genius"; metaphor in his view is opposed to a "representational" or denotational notion of language. Furthermore, metaphor is "a call to change one's language and one's life, rather than a proposal about how to systematize either" (Rorty 1991: 13). Following Heidegger and more specifically Davidson (1984), Rorty refuses to see metaphor as already a part of a language – a view that is at odds with the findings of cognitive linguistics (e.g. Lakoff and Johnson 1980).

However, an interesting point made by Davidson and Rorty is that certain expressions (and the ideas that go with them), which they term metaphors, are unfamiliar on their first appearance in a culture but subsequently become absorbed and eventually understood as literal. One of their examples is "the earth moves round the sun", which, they claim, would initially have been regarded as (merely) metaphorical. In this, they are actually in accordance with the cognitive linguistic approach, which treats metaphor as more than mere ornamentation, and in fact as "on a par with perception and inference" (Rorty 1991: 14). But Rorty (1991, 1995) appears also, in essence, to be going beyond cognitive linguistics in claiming a much grander role for metaphor, one that leads to "conceptual revolutions" and that has major importance for scientific thought, ethical norms, political culture and political actions. His examples relate to major cultural and scientific shifts, such as the Galilean paradigm shift, in line with his assumption that metaphor is the product of creative genius. While he does introduce the idea that liberal democracies have a close reciprocal relationship with the possibility of absorbing (and literalising) metaphorical expression, he appears to overlook the contestation that can occur over alternative metaphors, as well as the potential that metaphors have for being wielded by political forces that are not liberal or democratic.

In this section I will briefly address some of the issues that Rorty's ideas raise – the nature of metaphor, the pervasiveness of metaphor and the relationship between metaphor and political power or influence. The notion of metaphor I adopt is that developed by cognitive linguists on the foundation of ideas in Lakoff and Johnson (1980). According to this view, metaphor is a cognitive not a linguistic process. Metaphorical expressions are possible because of cognitive operations that map concepts from a known source domain to another conceptual domain. The source domains include image schemas, which are non-linguistic and arise in the human mind-brain as, for instance, spatial, kinaesthetic, visual, etc., perception and cognition. The target domains vary and the mappings are to some degree constrained by the pre-metaphorical contents of the target concepts. But there is an element of selection arising in discourse in specific circumstances.

An example of the selection of a metaphor that led to policy change with some significant historical effects is examined in Chilton (1996), where it is argued that the cold war policy of "containment" arose in a particular policy-making milieu and crystallised around a few key texts and one key metaphor. As in Davidson's and Rorty's perspective, "containment", at first metaphorical, became literal containment. One influential text was George Kennan's "Long Telegram", which had a great impact on the way officials thought and talked in the State Department and National Security Council in the late 1940s. Now, it could be argued, and generally is, that containment was the policy that was simply required because of the real facts of the situation. However, there could have been alternative policies (e.g. negotiation, trade, aid), so it is worth considering the functioning of the term in providing a mode of thought, a conceptual framework that caught on and appeared to work for a community of experts.

How do such metaphorical political terms work? First, it may be noted that "containment" requires, for at least part of its meaning, that speakers access the image schema of spatial containment – a naturally meaningful concept that is part of human mental equipment, including language. Second, like all metaphorical mappings, this mapping provides an inferential system, a means of simplifying, reasoning about and talking about a complex situation. For example, with the "containment" metaphor the Soviet Union could now be thought about as an expanding substance that had to be physically kept in a delimited geopolitical space. There are also linkages with other conceptual systems, since diseases are also conceptualised as in need of containment, as are the insane and criminals (cf. Musolff 2007). Third, there are two aspects to the acceptance and to what Rorty would think of as the literalisation of the containment metaphor. On the one hand, the metaphor is taken up and passed on because of its seeming naturalness; on the other hand, it was first promulgated by an authoritative individual (Kennan, a diplomat based in Moscow) to other supposed expert and influential individuals. This may not be a case of "an idiosyncratic genius" (though it may be a case of a talented writer) but the key point is that it was the product of somebody in a position of influence purveyed to people who were anxious to find a solution to an international crisis. The case of "containment" is important for world politics, but it was not of the order imagined in some of Rorty's reflections; moreover, it is not self-evident that its consequences were part of a process of liberalisation.

Another case in which an innovative expression went along with the definition of policy is the use of the expression "war on terrorism" by the administration of George W. Bush in response to the atrocities of 11 September 2001. One long-standing issue is the meaning of the term "terrorism". As is well known, the meanings of the term depend on who you are and what your political ideology is, and include the meaning that makes it possible to use "terrorist" to refer to states as well as to sub-state actors. Accordingly, the meaning of this type of term can only be theorised in terms of a semantic theory that includes the elements of variation, contestation and shallow processing outlined above.

Here, however, I want to address the whole phrase, which, in some respects like *containment*, had the function of offering a conceptualisation of a policy in unprecedented political circumstances. The question is what are the semantic workings of a phrase of this type?

Expressions such as "war on poverty", "war on drugs", seem to be unequivocally metaphorical, in the sense that poverty and drugs are not entities against which war can be waged, in the conventional senses of the term *war*. However, war on terrorism is a different matter, because "terrorism" is a metonymy for human actors who use violence, and who thus can fill slots in the conceptual frame for agents or victims of war. Even so, "war on terrorism" is not a literal expression for some speakers, or not completely literal. One reason for this might be that war (for some speakers) belongs to a conceptual frame in which war is, amongst other things, waged between sovereign states after a declaration of war that has status in international law, and specifically between the organised armed forces of those states.

None of these elements correspond to the facts about the hostility and violence between terrorists and their victims. There should therefore be some sort of conceptual problem with "war on terrorism". This may be resolved in several ways. One way is to redefine the conceptual frame of war so that it includes substate agents and units other than institutionalised armed forces. Such a reconceptualisation of the frame can accompany or lead to change in the practice of war and in the attitude toward international law relating to war. A different way in which the potential conceptual clash can be resolved is by shallow processing. It is possible that in using or hearing the expression "war on terrorism" individuals access only part of whatever core meaning and encyclopaedic mental structure they have for "war". Thus some people may, for example in the post-attack crisis, maximise relevance by limited processing effort that yields positive cognitive effects by accessing a minimal meaning such as "action against our enemy" or "action using physical force against our enemy". Such meanings would constitute positive cognitive effects since they would, one might assume, connect with security needs and emotional needs such as those of vengeance. In fact, the different types of conceptualisation are likely to vary, but within a range that does not include the more institutionalised or legalised concepts – these being perhaps in any case reserved to expert groups of speakers.

Another important way of looking at the functioning of expressions of the "war on terrorism" type is to apply Rorty's perspective, at least in part, as outlined earlier. Since war cannot literally, in its old sense, be waged against terrorists, the expression "war on terrorism" may be experienced, by some people at least, as metaphorical or as slightly odd semantically, as we have noted. The expression becomes banalised or literalised, through shallow processing. Or substantively it can be literalised by adjusting the concepts of the source domain. But there is a further substantive possibility for resolving the conceptual anomaly, if there is one. The old structure of the source domain may be retained but the target domain can be readjusted, so that the term *terrorism* is used to refer not to sub-state actors but to sovereign states. This is indirectly what the Bush administration did: terrorism was so closely associated, by means of discourse techniques not discussed in this article, with the sovereign state of Iraq that it made literal sense (by the old conceptual frame for war) to wage war against Iraq and to call it "war against terrorism". Since it has been widely claimed that there was no evidence that Iraq was supporting the perpetrators of the atrocities of 11 September 2001, the meaning of the expression "war on terrorism", in this particular context, did in fact rely on establishing an initial conceptual association between an entire sovereign state and a certain type of non-state violence.

8. Conclusion

We have noted some key intuitions about the nature of political terminology – that individuals contest concepts in the public arena, that such concepts vary across society and across time, that such concepts may be more or less detailed and that they may be part of or have an influence on political action. These observations are commonplace but have been developed to some extent by thinkers like Gallie, Putnam and Rorty. What we have emphasised here is that whatever meanings are, they are in the minds of individual humans. There is perhaps nothing linguistically special about political terminology. What we have seen is that, in order to explain what we intuitively know about political terms, we have to draw on theories of meaning, particularly cognitive and pragmatic theories of meaning. What the study of political terminology makes clear is that an adequate cognitive-pragmatic theory must take account of the fact that the phenomenon of lexical meaning occurs both in the mind and in the mind-in-society.

References

Allott, Nicholas
    2005   The role of misused concepts in manufacturing consent: a cognitive account. In: Louis de Saussure (ed.), *Manipulation and Ideologies in the Twentieth Century*, 147–168. Amsterdam: Benjamins.
Aristotle
    1992   *The Politics*. Transl. T. A. Sinclair. Revised and re-presented by Trevor J. Saunders. Harmondsworth: Penguin.

Ball, Terence, James Farr and Russell L. Hanson (eds.)
    1989   *Political Innovation and Conceptual Change*. Cambridge: Cambridge University Press.
Chilton, Paul A.
    1996   *Security Metaphors: Cold War Discourse from Containment to Common House*. New York: Peter Lang.
Chilton, Paul A.
    2004   *Analysing Political Discourse: Theory and Practice*. London: Routledge.
Derrida, Jacques
    1967   *De la grammatologie*. Paris: Editions de Minuit.
Davidson, Donald
    1984   *Inquiries into Truth and Interpretation*. Oxford: Clarendon.
Fairclough, Norman
    1989   *Language and Power*. London/New York: Longman.
Fairclough, Norman (ed.)
    1992a   *Critical Language Awareness*. London: Longman.
Fairclough, Norman
    1992b   *Discourse and Social Change*. Cambridge: Polity.
Fairclough, Norman
    1995a   *Critical Discourse Analysis: The Critical Study of Language*. London: Longman.
Fairclough, Norman
    1995b   *Media Discourse*. London: Edward Arnold.
Fairclough, Norman
    2000   *New Labour, New Language?* London: Routledge.
Fillmore, Charles
    1982   Frame semantics. In: Linguistic Society of Korea (ed.), *Linguistics in the Morning Calm*, 111–138. Seoul: Hanshin Publishing.
Foucault, Michel
    1971   *L'ordre du discourse*. Paris: Gallimard.
Fowler, Roger
    1991   *Language in the News: Discourse and Ideology in the Press*. London: Routledge.
Fowler, Roger
    1996   *Linguistic Criticism*. Oxford: Oxford University Press.
Fowler, Roger, Robert Hodge, Gunther Kress and Tony Trew
    1979   *Language and Control*. London: Routledge and Kegan Paul.
Frege, Gottlob
    1892   Über Sinn und Bedeutung. *Zeitschrift für Philosophie und philosophische Kritik* 100: 25–30.
Frege, Gottlob
    1960   On sense and reference. In: P. Geach and M. Black, *Translations from the Philosophical Writings of Gottlob Frege*, 56–78. Oxford: Blackwell.
Gallie, Walter B.
    1956   Essentially contested concepts. *Proceedings of the Aristotelian Society* 56: 167–198.
Grice, Herbert P.
    1989   *Studies in the Way of Words*. Cambridge MA: Harvard University Press.

Lakoff, George
    1987   *Women, Fire and Dangerous Things: What Categories Reveal about the Mind*. Chicago: University of Chicago Press.
Lakoff, George
    2002 [1996]   *Moral Politics: How Liberals and Conservatives Think*. Chicago: University of Chicago Press.
Lakoff, George
    2004   *Don't Think of an Elephant! Know your Values and Frame the Debate*. White River Junction, VT: Chelsea Green Publishing.
Lakoff, George and Mark Johnson
    1980   *Metaphors We Live By*. Chicago University Press: Chicago.
Langacker, Ronald W.
    1987   *Foundations of Cognitive Grammar*, Volume 1. Stanford, CA: Stanford University Press.
Musolff, Andreas
    2007   What role do metaphors play in racial prejudice? The function of anti-Semitic imagery in Hitler's Mein Kampf. *Patterns of Prejudice*, 41(1): 21–43.
Orwell, George
    1946   Politics and the English Language. *Horizon*, April: 252 – 265.
Orwell, George
    1949   *Nineteen Eighty-Four*. London: Secker and Warburg.
Putnam
    1975   *Mind, Language and Reality*. Cambridge: Cambridge University Press.
Rorty, Richard
    1991   *Essays on Heidegger and Others*. Cambridge: Cambridge University Press.
Rorty, Richard
    1995   *Contingency, Irony, and Solidarity*. Cambridge: Cambridge University Press.
Saussure, Ferdinand de
    1964   *Cours de linguistique générale*. Edited by C. Bally and A. Sechehaye. Paris: Payot. First published [1916].
Saussure, Ferdinand de
    1983   *Course in General Linguistics*. Transl. Roy Harris. London: Duckworth.
Shapiro, Michael (ed.)
    1984   *Language and Politics*. Oxford: Blackwell.
Sperber, Dan and Deirdre Wilson
    1995 [1986]   *Relevance: Communication and Cognition*. 2nd ed. Oxford: Blackwell.
Taylor, John R.
    2002   *Cognitive Grammar*. Oxford: Oxford University Press.
van Dijk, Teun A.
    1984   *Prejudice in Discourse: An Analysis of Ethnic Prejudice in Cognition and Conversation*. Amsterdam: John Benjamins.
van Dijk, Teun A. (ed.)
    1985   *Handbook of Discourse Analysis*. Volume 3. London: Academic Press.
van Dijk, Teun A.
    1987   *Communicating Racism. Ethnic Prejudice in Thought and Talk*. London: Sage.

van Dijk, Teun A.
   1990   Social sognition and discourse. In: Howard Giles and W. Peter Robinson (eds.), *Handbook of Language and Social Psychology*, 163–183. New York: John Wiley.
van Dijk, Teun A.
   1993   Discourse and cognition in society. In: David Crowley and David Mitchell (eds.), *Communication Theory Today*, 107–126. Oxford: Pergamon.
van Dijk, Teun A.
   1993   *Elite Discourse and Racism*. London: Sage.
van Dijk, Teun A.
   1997   What is political discourse analysis? In: Jan Blommaert and Chris Bulcaen (eds.), *Political Linguistics,* 11–52. Amsterdam: Benjamins.
van Dijk, Teun A. (ed.)
   1997   *Discourse as Social Interaction*. London: Sage.
van Dijk, Teun A.
   1998   *Ideology: An Interdisciplinary Approach*. London: Sage.
van Dijk, Teun A.
   2002   Ideology: political discourse and cognition. In: Paul A. Chilton and Christine Schäffner (eds.), *Politics as Talk and Text: Analytic Approaches to Political Discourse*, 203–237. Amsterdam: Benjamins.
van Dijk, Teun A. and Walter Kintsch
   1983   *Strategies of Discourse Comprehension*. New York: Academic Press.
Wilson, Deirdre and Dan Sperber
   2004   Relevance Theory. In: Gregory Ward and Laurence Horn (eds.), *Handbook of Pragmatics*, 607–632. Oxford: Blackwell.
Wodak, Ruth (ed.)
   1989   *Language, Power and Ideology*. Amsterdam: Benjamins.
Wodak, Ruth
   1996   *Disorders of Discourse*. London: Longman.
Wodak, Ruth
   2002   Fragmented identities: redefining and recontextualizing national identity. In: Paul Chilton and Christine Schäffner (eds.), *Politics as Text and Talk*, 143–169. Amsterdam: Benjamins.
Wodak, Ruth and Anton Pelinka
   2002   *The Haider Phenomenon*. London: Transaction Publishers.

11. Rhetoric of political speeches

Martin Reisigl

The present chapter starts with a general characterisation of political speeches from a rhetorical and a politolinguistic point of view (section 1). It then elaborates on various characterisations and types of political speeches on the basis of selected criteria (section 2). The rhetorical macro-structure and functional main sections of (political) speeches are discussed in section 3. Fourth, it will be shown that orally performed political speeches are not to be seen as monological "discursive events", but as semiotic realisations of conventionalised, multi-addressed activity patterns (section 4). Fifth, I will consider the main constitutive conditions of political oratory then and now, reconstructing the genesis and delineating the distribution of modern political speeches in the age of computer and internet supported text production and multimodal mass media (section 5). The article will conclude with an outline of possible tasks for applied linguists who engage in speech criticism and political language consulting (section 6).[1]

1. What are political speeches? – A rhetorical and politolinguistic approach

A speech is a structured verbal chain of coherent speech acts uttered on a special social occasion for a specific purpose by a single person, and addressed to a more or less specific audience (see Schmitz 2005: 698). Amongst other things, speeches differ from each other in length, with respect to their occasion (including time and place), their topic, their function, the speaker, their addressees, their form of presentation and degree of preparedness and with respect to their style and structure.

Speeches are normally "texts" – in the sense of materially durable products of linguistic actions (Ehlich 1983; Graefen 1997: 26; Reisigl 2000: 231). Usually, they are prepared in writing, although the wording of their verbal presentation may sometimes differ considerably from the written version. They are rarely produced *ad hoc* or spontaneously, and even the sporadic *ex tempore* speeches are never improvisations out of nothing, but compositions based on speech patterns and set pieces that have entered the linguistic and episodic memory of the speaker. The infrequency of spontaneous speeches is due to the fact that speeches are, for the most part, given in formal situations, and on occasions speakers have been familiar with for a long time.

In view of classical rhetoric,[2] speeches are analysed within the theoretical framework of rhetorical genre theory. Central criteria for the first rhetorical typology of speeches are the social function, the occasion and – related to that – the place of delivery. Classical rhetoric distinguishes three forms of oratory: the judicial (*genus iudiciale*), the deliberative (*genus deliberativum*) (Schild 1992) and the epideictic (*genus demonstrativum*) (Plett 2001: 17–18). This general rhetorical typology is summarised in Figure 1.[3]

The division – still reproduced in many rhetorical textbooks today – is abstract and ideal typical. Already the speech practitioners of antiquity knew that this theoretical distinction, in practice, is not as strict as suggested (Engels 1996: 702), and empirical speech analyses also demonstrate that the theoretical separation has first and foremost to be taken as a simplification produced for giving a didactic overview.

A first attempt to locate political speeches within this genre-theoretical framework of classical rhetoric leads to the finding that they are – primarily – associated with the deliberative genre and – in second place – with the epideictic genre. The first group of political speeches is especially related to differing opinions about political decisions in the ancient public sphere of the deliberative assembly or people's assembly. The latter group is concerned with the verbalisation of political values and – at least apparently – of political (inter-party, national or supra-national) consent in the public sphere of the assembled company that celebrates a victory, a jubilee, an anniversary, a birthday, a public personality etc. (Klein 2000: 748).

Since the first rhetorical genre theory was outlined by Aristotle, political situations, systems, conditions and circumstances have changed and become increasingly complex, and, with these transformations, the forms, types and functions of political speeches have also altered remarkably. Rhetorical theory has not always followed these developments closely. Thus, the ancient rhetorical view of speeches alone cannot do analytical justice to the many complex political changes. Consequently, the rhetorical view of political language and political speeches gains a lot if complemented by a transdisciplinary politolinguistic approach that tries to connect and synthesise rhetoric, political science, and linguistic discourse analysis (see Burkhardt 1996; Reisigl 2006).

Politolinguistics theoretically relies on actual concepts in political science, as well as on rhetorical and discourse analytical categories (see Reisigl 2003b: chapter 3; Reisigl and Wodak 2001: chapter 2). With respect to the topic in question, politolinguistics builds on a differentiated concept of "the political" that, amongst others, distinguishes amongst the three dimensions of polity, policy and politics, and tries to grasp the specific political functions of speeches with respect to these dimensions more accurately than the traditional rhetorical approach did. According to this theoretical distinction, political speeches can be "political" in a threefold sense.

The dimension of polity concerns the political frame for political actors, i.e. the formal or structural prerequisites and basic political principles of political

| | practical eloquence | | "artificial eloquence" |
	judicial genre	deliberative genre	epideictic genre
thematic focus or guiding norm	justice or injustice / right or wrong	expediency or harmfulness	honour and disgrace / worthiness or reprehensibility
main function	accusation or defence	exhorting or dissuading	praise or blame
aim / purpose	decision (court decision)	decision	contemplation
place of delivery	court	deliberative / people's / citizens' assembly, parliament	assembled company / public gathering
time reference	past	future	mostly present
appropriate "argumentation" form	enthymene ("abbreviated argumentation")	example (*exemplum*)	incrementation (amplification)
prototypical speakers	speakers in court (prosecutor, defender, defendant, witness)	speakers in deliberative / citizens' assembly (kings, consulates, senators, citizens) or in advisory / parliamentary committees (politicians, advisors)	speakers in assembled companies / public gatherings and in celebrations on various social occasions
role of addressees	those who pass judgement on the defendants' past (judges, jurors)	those who pass judgement on the future (deliberators and decision-makers)	spectators and observers who pass judgement on the rhetorical ability and ethos of the speakers
model cases	judicial / forensic oration (speech of accusation / speech of defence, apology / address to the jury), social-critical drama, lampoon, satire, polemic	political speech (debate, discussion), promotional speech, didactic poem, utopia, sermon	laudatory speech / eulogy, ode, admonitory speech, blaming speech / vituperation speech / invective / diatribe, occasion-specific speeches like welcoming speech, farewell speech / valedictory speech, pleading speech, speech of thanks, inaugural address, (official) opening speech, closing address / speech, birthday speech, wedding speech, jubilee or anniversary speech, commemorative speech, victory speech, funeral oration / epitaph / necrology, speech of consolation, ceremonial address / panegyric

Figure 1. The three classical forms of rhetorical speech oratory

action. This dimension relates to normative, legal procedural and institutional manifestations, which help to establish the political order. The constitution, the political system, the political culture, political norms and values as well as legal and institutional rules are associated with this dimension. Amongst the political speeches which primarily focus on polity are commemorative speeches, memorial speeches, jubilee speeches and anniversary speeches, speeches of principle, ceremonial addresses (Eigenwald 1996), funeral oration, necrology and speeches of consolation, laudatory speeches (Hambsch 1996; Matuschek 2001), speeches in honour of prize-winners, and birthday speeches. All these speeches aim to express common values of a political "in-group". They are mostly formulated according to the rules of epideictic genre (Matuschek 1994) and fulfil a laudatory or vituperative purpose. Many presidential speeches, including state of the union addresses, but also various speeches given by chancellors, ministers and mayors, are of this kind.

The dimensions of policy and politics both relate to political action, albeit in a different way. Policy concerns the content-related dimension of political action. It regards the formulation of political tasks, aims and programmes in the different fields of policy, such as foreign policy, domestic affairs, social policy, cultural and educational policy, economic policy, family policy etc. This political dimension answers the questions of what policy is aimed at whom and for what purpose. Its central purpose is shaping the social by political means. Political speeches strongly relating to policy are, amongst many others, chancellor's speeches like inaugural speeches, ministerial speeches, opening speeches on the occasion of commercial fairs, speeches of resignation and (presidential) speeches of appointment. Such speeches represent an important contribution to the "government by speaking" (Peters 2005: 754). Many speeches in parliamentary debates can, in particular, centre on this political dimension, especially those given by representatives of the government who attempt to justify their policies – despite the fact that parliamentary speeches are held within the field of the law-making procedure and thus necessarily relate to polity.

The dimension of politics, finally, concerns political processes, i.e. the question of how and with whose help politics are performed. Politics revolves around the formulation of political interests, the dissensual positioning against others, the conflict between political actors (be they single politicians or "collective actors" like parties, nations etc.), political advertising and fighting for followers and the acquisition of power. Its main purpose is to assert oneself against political opponents, in order to make a specific policy possible. The prototypical speech serving this political dimension is the election speech, but, in a wider sense, all speeches with the aim to advertise one's own political position and to gain influence and power strongly relate to this dimension.

Even though the differentiation between political dimensions is an ideal typical one, it helps speech analysts to orient themselves in the wide realm of political speeches. An additional politolinguistic differentiation of political speeches becomes possible if we introduce the "field of political action" as a functional concept. "Fields of action" (cf. Girnth 1996, 2002) can be conceived of as "places of social forms of practice" (Bourdieu 1991: 74) or as frameworks of social interaction (Reisigl 2003b: 148). They relate to at least eight different functions or socially institutionalised purposes of discursive practices. Further developing the initial division of Heiko Girnth (1996), who made distinctions between four different fields, I propose to distinguish, according to these functions, at least eight different political fields, viz.:

- the lawmaking procedure;
- the formation of public attitudes, opinions and will;
- the party-internal formation of attitudes, opinions and will;
- the interparty formation of attitudes, opinions and will;
- the organisation of international and (especially) interstate relations;
- political advertising;
- the political executive and administration; and
- the various forms of political control (for more details, see Reisigl 2003b: 128–142).

Moreover, bringing in the concept of "discourse"[4] and connecting it with the "fields of political action", it can be stated that a "political discourse" about a specific topic may have its starting point within one of the eight fields of action and proceed onward through another one, not least via recontextualisation and intertextual linking. So, discourses and discourse topics can "spread" to the different fields and cross between them, realised as thematically connected and problem-related semiotic (e.g. oral or written) tokens that can be assigned to specific semiotic types (i.e. textual types or genres), which serve particular political purposes (see Reisigl and Wodak 2001: 36–37 for more details).

The relationships between fields of political action, subgenres of political speech and discourse topics are illustrated in Figure 2 with the example of commemorative speeches and their functional roles in the discourse about the Austrian nation and identity (see also Reisigl 2003b: 140).

2. Types and functions of political speeches

Although Figure 2 focuses on the role of commemorative speeches in a specific discourse that has been studied extensively (see Reisigl 2003b; Wodak et al. 1994: 163–190, 1999: 70–105; for other studies on commemorative speeches see Ensink 1997, 1999; Sauer 1997; Ensink and Sauer 2003), the figure also shows the relationships amongst other subgenres of political speeches

248 Martin Reisigl

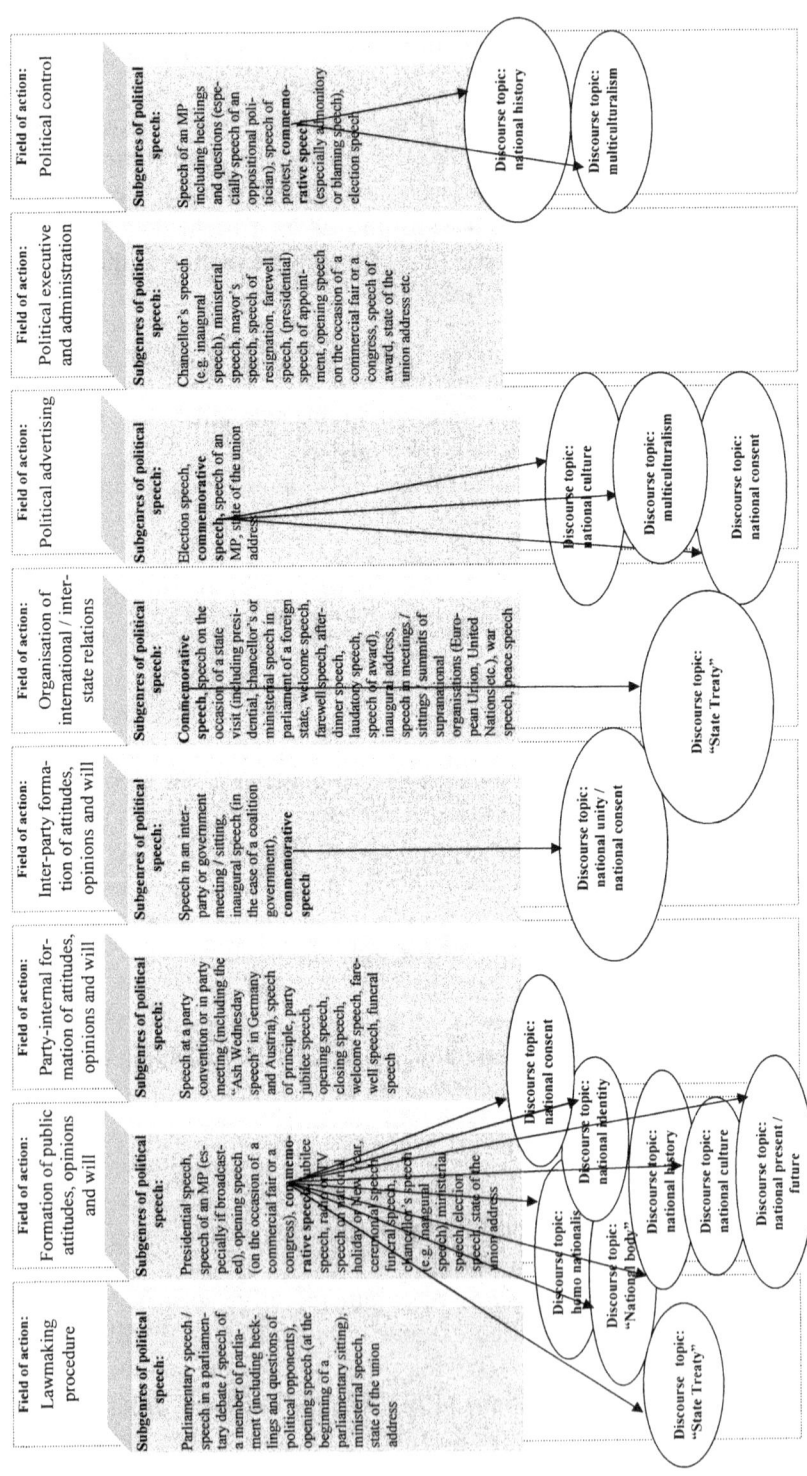

Figure 2. A systematisation of fields of political action, subgenres of political speeches and discourse topics (illustrated with the example of the commemorative speech and its functional roles in the discourse about the Austrian nation and identity; see Reisigl 2003b):

Rhetoric of political speeches 249

and the eight fields of political action. Similar to the commemorative speech, these other subgenres of the political speech can accomplish more than one of the eight political functions in a specific political discourse. The assignment of the subgenres to the action fields can therefore never be exclusive.

Other attempts to typify political speeches are not based on strictly disjunctive categorisations either, for the criteria of distinction partly overlap. Taking the most common criteria employed in speech typologies and in labelling speeches, political speeches can be characterised according to the following ten heuristic criteria (the criteria are not absolute, but selected for their main emphasis; this sometimes allows for cross-typifying):

	Question	Criterion for speech name		Examples of speech names
1	who?	the speaker or the political function of the speaker as political representative		*presidential speech, chancellor's speech, ministerial speech, speech of MPs, mayor's speech; King's/Queen's speech at the opening of parliament*
2	on what occasion?	the occasion		*"occasional speech"*
			performative/illocutionary quality	*inaugural address, speech of resignation, speech of appointment, speech of award, welcoming speech, farewell address*
			cyclical recurrence of the occasion	*anniversary speech, jubilee speech, commemorative speech, birthday speech, speech on national holiday or New Year, ceremonial address, memorial speech, Aschermittwochsrede[5] ("Ash Wednesday speech")*
			relative time of speech	*after-dinner speech, postprandial speech, opening speech, closing speech/address*
			intertextual or interdiscursive embedding in a greater communicative event	*speech at a party convention, speech in an election campaign, debate speech, counterspeech, funeral oration/eulogy, King's/Queen's speech at the opening of parliament*
			organisation of inter-state relations / relations to political opponents/enemies	*speech on the occasion of a state visit, victory speech, war speech, peace speech*
			one-off occasions	*funeral eulogy, speech of consolation, speech of award, victory speech*

	Question	Criterion for speech name	Examples of speech names
3	where?	the place (or place name)	speech in parliament, King's/Queen's speech at the opening of parliament (German: "Thronrede", i.e. speech from the throne), "soap-box speech", "Humboldt speech" (referring to the speech given by the former German foreign minister Joschka Fischer at the Humboldt University on May 12, 2000; see Weiss 2002)
4	when?	the time	
		relative time of speech	after-dinner speech, inaugural address
		cyclical recurrence of the occasion	anniversary speech, jubilee speech, commemorative speech, birthday speech, speech on national holiday or New Year, "Aschermittwochsrede" ("Ash Wednesday speech")
5	to whom?	the addressees/ hearers	
		explicit	"address to the nation"
		implicit	laudatory speech, admonitory speech, blaming speech/ vituperation speech, counterspeech
6	via what media?	(mass) media of transmission	TV speech, radio speech, orally delivered speech, written speech, live speech, recorded speech
7	for what purpose?	communicative main function, often naming the performative / illocutionary quality of the speech (closely related to the first group of 2)	speech of thanks, pleading speech, welcoming speech, farewell speech or address, valediction, laudatory speech/eulogy, admonitory speech, blaming speech/vituperation speech, speech of consolation, speech of appointment, speech of award, speech of protest
8	in what form?	form of speech, form of preparation, form of presentation	free speech, read out speech, long speech, short speech, abridged speech, unabridged speech, fighting speech (i.e. an aggressive, loud and often offensive speech), polemical speech
9	about what?	content, topic	speeches of principle, victory speech, war speech, state of the union address, "Europarede" ("speech on Europe")

Question	Criterion for speech name	Examples of speech names
10 belonging to which rhetorical genre?	rhetorical genre membership	*deliberative speech, epideictic speech*

Figure 3. Types of political speeches

Types of speeches like those in Figure 3 are language-dependent. Please note also that the two metalinguistic English words "speech" and "address", which widely correspond to German "Rede" and "Ansprache", are not always synonymous. Sometimes "address" and "Ansprache" denote a higher degree of formality and/or consensuality than "speech" and "Rede" (see also Klein 2000: 751).

In particular, speeches whose illocutionary quality is explicitly mentioned in the category name (see points 2 and 7) can easily be recognised as "deeds done in words" (Campbell and Jamieson 1990; see also Sternberger 1991). Political speeches are, however, not just actions in this speech act theoretical sense. They are, most generally speaking, interactional contributions to identity politics and accomplish the two political purposes of inclusion and exclusion. On the one hand, they are socially integrative by contributing to the formation of transindividual identity and to the foundation of group solidarity. On the other hand, they can fulfil disintegrative and destructive functions by mobilising addressees to social exclusion and, at worst, to violent attacks against those excluded and denigrated by the orator. The dual functionality manifests itself in all eight fields of political action, but this cannot be exemplified in the short overview of the present article.

To focus on just one extreme example: In his nationalistic speech on the occasion of the 600th anniversary of the "Battle at the Kosovo field in 1389", held at Gazimestan on June 28, 1989, the former Serbian leader Slobodan Milošević practiced a rhetorically cunning commemoration with both an integrative and a disintegrative political function. Under the veil of euphemistic high-value words like "harmony", "cooperation", "solidarity", "unity", "community" and "equality", which suggest a high degree of consent on the state unity of Yugoslavia, Milosevich announced a military conflict in passing.

Amongst the many subgenres of political speeches, five deserve special attention, viz. (1) the debate speech, (2) the inaugural speech, (3) the election speech, (4) the TV address and (5) the commemorative speech (for the fifth subgenre see section 4). The first three speeches are primarily dissent-oriented, whereas the last two are mainly consent-oriented (for details on these subgenres see Klein 2000: 748–752).

The debate speech can – according to Klein (2000: 749) – be subdivided into the "parliamentary debate speech" and into the "debate speech at a party convention or in a party meeting". Klein observes that the majority of parliamentary debate speeches are speeches aiming to (de)legitimise a specific policy, to positively present one's own political position, party or coalition, and to negatively present political opponents (as far as these speeches are concerned, the voting has mostly been fixed before the debate already), whereas debate speeches at a party convention or in a party meeting are much more designated to influence the vote on a bill, amendment etc. after the debate.[6] Parliamentary debate speeches are – apparently – mainly located in the field of law-making, but they are also associated with the fields of formation of public attitudes, opinions and will, of political advertising and of political control. By contrast, debate speeches at a party convention or in a party meeting are primarily performed in the field of party-internal formation of attitudes, opinions and will. They show a prevalence for high-value words that are related to one's own party and its programme, but also a tendency to denigrate political adversaries by stigma words and insults (Klein 2000: 750).

Inaugural addresses are mostly held by the head of the government (chancellor, prime minister) and sometimes by a minister or secretary. Their primary audience is composed of members of parliament. Their secondary audience is the extra-parliamentarian public of the respective nation state, as well as, in part, "foreign" public spheres (Volmert 2005: 210). Their main topic is the policy programme of the government in the most important policy fields for the next parliamentary or congressional term. One of their main functions is to show and promote a strong corporate identity of the government (see de Michelis, this volume; see also Campbell and Jamieson 1990: 17). In Germany, they are normally produced by teams of about five to ten speech writers and political advisors (Schwarze and Walther 2002: 39), who engage in the elaboration of the final speech manuscript for several weeks at least, if not months, whereas the speakers themselves rarely contribute to the formulation of the text (Volmert 2005: 213). Inaugural addresses are first and foremost located in the field of political administration, but they additionally play a role in the fields of formation of public attitudes, opinions and will, and – in the case of a coalition government – of interparty formation of attitudes, opinions and will (see Klein 2000: 750). In the United States, where political speeches play a more important role than in most European democracies, the inaugural address of the president is one of the central "speech events" in the national political culture. The highly ritualised event is characterised by an elaborated and conventionally scripted orality rich in metaphors. Spontaneous deviations from the written script, which has been carefully prepared by ghost writers and political advisers including spin doctors (Meinhart and Schmid 2000), are very rare. Under the influence of audiovisual mass media like radio, TV and internet, these speeches have become syntactically less complex and more colloquial in the past few decades (Herget 2005: 762–763; see Holly, this volume). Inaugural addresses are normally far less dissent-oriented than debate speeches and election speeches.

The election speech (Panagl and Kriechbaumer 2002; Efing 2005) is one of the central subgenres employed in the field of political advertising. The dimension of politics comes to the fore in this speech, since it aims to mobilise potential voters and party supporters for the speaker and his or her party. Of all political speeches, it is the most dissent-oriented, and, thus, the most crude and emotionalising in tone. It attacks the political "enemy" more fiercely than other speeches, as the assertion against the opponent and the acquisition of power are its main purpose. The election speech can also gain relevance in the field of political control, if the orator criticises the opponents' abuse of political power, as well as in the field connected with the formation of public attitudes, opinions and will.

Like the commemorative speech, the TV address belongs to the consent-oriented subgenres. It is primarily uttered in the field of the formation of public attitudes, opinions and will. Top-level political representatives such as presidents and heads of government are usually the orators. The TV address is designated to express consensual political values and political norms, frequently related to the imagined community of the nation (Anderson 1983) and to national identity. Thus, the dimension of polity is central. Elevated in language, it is often full of tropes, high-value words and flag words. Although it is mostly read from a teleprompter which projects the well-prepared manuscript of the speech, the orator often tries to suggest that she or he is speaking freely (Klein 2000: 752), hence hoping to produce good publicity as an eloquent politician in the TV-constituted public sphere.

3. Rhetorical macro-structure and functional sections of (political) speeches

The different functional sections of speeches are composed by sequences of speech acts that are combined with each other in a specific way. Following the rhetorical rules of disposition, the different speech acts are grouped together in the three macro-structural units of introduction, main part and conclusion, as well as in their respective subsections. The ideal typical rhetorical macro-structure of speeches is formed by the succession of the speech parts of (1) introduction (*exordium*), (2) narration (*narratio*) and argumentation (*argumentatio*), and (3) conclusion (*peroratio*) (see, amongst others, Plett 2001: 18–20; Ueding and Steinbrink 2005: 259–277).

In their composition, political speeches are often more freely organised than other speeches (Schmitz 2005: 699). They seldom contain clearly separate sections of argumentation and narration. This deviation from the antique rhetorical ideal is due to the fact that political orators – especially nowadays – are concerned with many new demands in addition to deliberative advising and epideictic demonstration. The conditions of political oratory have changed remarkably since antiquity, not least because of the transformation of political systems and the development of new means of mass communication that have led to new forms of public spheres. The influence of the political system and political culture (i.e. the polity) on the disposition of political speeches can best be illustrated with the example of argumentation (for the general relationship between political speeches and persuasive argumentation see Dedaić 2006). In history, whenever freedom of political decision had been restricted by the political form of rule (e.g. by despotism, dictatorship or strict absolutism), the consequence was that speeches for the most part lacked longer sequences of explicit plausible argumentation and contained – as in the case of many of Hitler's, Goebbels' and Mussolini's speeches – much more dramatisation, hyperbolic exaggeration and fallacious suggestion instead. On the other hand, in times of a strong democracy and parliament, that is to say, of the political participation of many, argumentation played and plays a much more important role in political speeches.

4. The "interaction structure" of political speeches as linguistic action patterns

Speeches are often misunderstood as monological linguistic events. This shortsighted, non-pragmatic view is even adopted by many of those who stress the appellative functions of speeches in principle and specific linguistic speech elements in particular. A functional pragmatic view immediately reveals that spoken political speeches are complex realisations of conventionalised linguistic action patterns with a clear interaction structure (Beck 2001), even though they have no transition relevance places and are, thus, not endowed with turn taking.

Following the functional pragmatic concept of "linguistic action pattern" (*sprachliches Handlungsmuster*; see Ehlich and Rehbein 1979), a political speech is an institutionally determined and institutionally embedded multipart pattern that fulfils specific social-psychological and political purposes. Commemorative speeches, for example, accomplish the purposes of establishing consent, solidarity, identification and the disposition to act as the speaker proposes to do. These purposes are achieved by the commemoration of a past event considered to be relevant for the political present and future of an in-group. As a complex action pattern, commemorative speeches show a variety of different specimens. These diverge with respect to the composition of the single parts that are related with different purposes. Amongst these are epideictic purposes such as the laudatory function, the vituperative function, the recalling function, the admonitory function, the consolatory function, the thanking function, the congratulatory function, the optative function, the promising function and the teaching function. Amongst the deliberative purposes of commemorative speeches are the conciliatory function, the admonitory function, the promising function and the teaching function (some of the deliberative and epideictic functions of commemorative speeches overlap). Finally, the three characteristic judicial purposes of commemorative speeches are the accusing function, the exculpatory function and the justifying function.

Normally, the only listener positions scheduled in the interaction pattern of many political speeches are those which articulate the listeners' accord or agreement with something the speaker just said and/or with the speaker her or himself. These speaker-supportive places are prototypically associated with non-verbal ratifications in the form of applause, if the speech occasion and situation is rather formal and solemn, as for example in commemorative speeches and ceremonial addresses. In less formal situations, as in the case of debate speeches given in parliament, listeners' approval can also be expressed through cheers or – as in the English parliament – through conventionalised directive attention getters like "Hear, hear!". Less formal speeches, as for example political speeches held during election campaigns, additionally allow for whistling as a "collective" reaction.

Whistling, however, is not just employed as a sign of approval. It can also signify the contrary. In most interaction patterns of political speeches (except for debate and election speeches), the articulation of disapproval on the part of the listeners is not desirable. It is considered to be a dispreferred response, a breach of the interaction pattern. In order to prevent the articulation of disapproval, the participation in a speech event and the concrete joining in the interaction structure is often regulated by the selective invitation of a group of listeners who are believed to behave themselves as prescribed by the rules.

If disagreement is expressed despite the cautious selection of listeners and the speaker is, for instance, disturbed by unwelcome hecklings and protest cries, those who have booed or interrupted are sometimes removed from the auditorium by security guards through physical force. A moderate form of protest can also be expressed by ostentatiously leaving the place or room of the speech. All these different articulations of disagreement break the regulated interaction patterns of many types of political speeches and – as a consequence – can provoke political scandals. A case in point is Philipp Jenninger, then president of the German parliament, who gave a commemorative address on November 9, 1988, on the occasion of the 50th anniversary of the so-called *Reichskristallnacht* ("night of broken glass", a euphemistic name for the antisemitic National Socialist pogrom in Germany and Austria in the night from November 8 to November 9, 1938; the name refers to the numerous broken windows of Jewish shops). He was accused of having demonstrated too much understanding for Nazi perpetrators, which is why about 49 members of the parliamentary audience ostentatiously left the room, and Jenninger subsequently resigned (Wodak et al. 1994: 180; for more details see, amongst others, Hoffmann and Schwitalla 1989; Ensink 1992; Krebs 1993).

Speeches during parliamentary debates, however, belong to linguistic action patterns in which interruptions and hecklings (Burkhardt 2004) are generally conventionalised and accepted as facultative reactions, as long as they do not consist of serious insults, which chairpersons of debates usually sanction by a call to order. This type of action pattern allows the speaker to spontaneously respond to the hecklings. The same holds for election speeches.

The pattern positions that permit applause – I call them "acclamation relevance places" in analogy to the conversation analytical concept of "transition relevance place" – are partly obligatory, especially before the beginning of the speech or address, when the speaker enters the room or place to speak, or when the speaker is introduced by the previous speaker, and after the end of the speech or address. The pattern positions that allow for intermediary acclamatory reactions of the audience during the speech or address are facultative. They can be initiated by appointed claques or be rhetorically triggered by prosodic and syntactic elicitation cues, as, for instance, in many histrionic speeches of dictators like Hitler (Reisigl 2003a; Beck 2001). By means of his marked intonation, which was very often technically augmented and transmitted by loudspeakers (Epping-Jäger 2003), in combination with syntactic parallelisms and the rhetorical figure of the three/four, the German dictator systematically elicited acclamations and other reactions from his listeners.

The reactions of the primary audience can – though do not necessarily – influence the media coverage addressed to the secondary or tertiary audience, be these expressions of dissent or acclamations. It is sometimes the case that press reports on speeches especially focus on those speech segments that have been met with acclamations by the primary audience (see Reisigl 2003b: 518). But it can also happen that the listeners' expression of disagreement is not covered in cases of consent-oriented speeches, if a journalist wants to paint a picture of consent.

Before the audio-visual media of news distribution was developed, the written version of a political speech had been the one that substantially decided on the speech reception, especially for the non-primary audiences. It was and is sometimes still today this version which journalists usually quote and report on in the press, although the speech manuscripts distributed to the press before the speech performance always stress that it is the spoken word which is valid.

Perhaps the one-sided focus on the written versions of political speeches will be overcome by the use of the new electronic media that facilitate the registration, dissemination and transcription of orally presented speeches. Electronic mass media and particularly new media like the internet increase the importance of oral speeches, since the co-present primary audience is no longer the only audience that enjoys the oral performance.

5. Constitutive conditions of political oratory in past and contemporary public spheres

The following typology gives an overview of constitutive conditions of political oratory then and now (more detailed explications can be found in Reisigl 2003b: 305–327). It is a revised and extended version of a schematic outline offered by Josef Klein (1995: 71) and taken up by Christoph Sauer (1997: 36–50) and Titus Ensink (1999: 80–83). The synopsis opposes, in an ideal typical manner, important basic factors and production conditions of classical and modern political rhetoric:

dimension	classical rhetorical type	modern political communication
time	momentariness /singularity: • primarily future (deliberative genre) or • primarily present (epideictic genre)	processuality / sequentiality: • reference to past, present and future
linguistic context	simple linguistic context: • monotextuality (speech without intertextual relations) • duotextuality (reference to the counterspeech of the opponent) • intertextual relation of imitation (celebration speech)	complex linguistic context: • multi- and intertextuality • multi- and interdiscursivity
speaker / author	individuality: • speaker = author	representation: • team of authors consisting of ghost writers, political advisers and the speaker
addressee	general homogeneity of addressees	plurality of audiences / multiple addressing: • primary audience (face to face) • secondary audience (audience listening to a live transmission via mass media) • tertiary audience (audience listening to a later transmission via mass media, or recipients reading the press)
medium	direct acoustic and visual contact (co-presence: sequential spatio-temporal unity of speech, reception and reaction)	direct acoustic and visual contact (co-presence) as well as acoustic and visual mass mediated / media echo (spatio-temporal dissociation: diatopia and diachrony)

dimension	classical rhetorical type	modern political communication
type of speech	two genres: • deliberative genre and • epideitic genre (laudatory speech or vituperation speech)	variety of genres and subgenres (see section 2)
aims / functions	two basic aims/functions: • preparation of a decision (including law making) on the basis of a persuasive exhortation or dissuasion (deliberative genre) • laudatory or blaming contemplation and creation of a distinctive positive image as a speaker (epideictic genre)	variety of aims/functions: • positive self and other-presentation (recognition, emphasis on the exemplariness) and negative self- and other-presentation (including admonition, warning) • political advertising aiming to acquire or maintain power • influence on the formation of public attitudes, opinions and will (identity construction, manufacturing of consent and solidarity, ratification / justification of political norms) • law-making procedure • party-internal formation of attitude, opinions and will • inter-party formation of attitudes, opinions and will • organisation of international / interstate relations • political administration • political control

Figure 4. Constitutive conditions of political oratory in past and present public spheres

Ideally and theoretically, the speech genres distinguished by classical rhetoric are realised as singular, momentary and point-blank speech events characterised by temporal, spatial, thematic and functional unity, by immediate sequential adjacency of the speech and its reception (including the audience reactions), by a relative uniformity of the audience and by monotextuality or textual duality (the latter is the case if a speech is followed by a counterspeech). In contrast to the classical rhetorical genres (in their idealised and in part counterfactual description), modern political communication is characterised by a great typological variety with multiple temporal relations to past, present and future, by a thematical ephemerality and by a procedural embedding into a complex network of discursive, interdiscursive and intertextual relations and sequences, which is constituted by an often selective, fragmentary or paraphrastic distribution of the speech via mass media to heterogeneous groups of audiences. Individuality of the political speech is a less important value today than it was in earlier times, since the principle of representation has gained significance (particularly in representative democracies). On the other hand, however, there is a strong tendency in politics towards personalisation, which is considered to be an antidote to the voters' political reluctance and political disinterest (see Holly, this volume).

5.1. How mass media influence the reception and success of a speech

Undeniably, the occasion of a speech and the audience which is being addressed – both the immediate audience and the one reached by the mass media – considerably influence the content, structure and form of a political speech. Many politicians nowadays are faced with the problem of multiple addressing (Kühn 1992, 1995), that is to say, with the problem that, due to new means of technical mediation, they often have to address various publics – different political groups with different problems, interests and political affiliations – at the same time. If these audiences are to be addressed as potential voters in their speeches, the speakers often apply the principle of calculated ambivalence (Klein 1996). The respective speeches are characterised by the deliberate use of conflicting theses, of contradictions often disguised by euphemisms and paraphrases, and of allusions and ambivalent expressions as well as unintentional slips.

In times of technical reproducibility and mass mediated dispersion, political communication is neither singular nor momentary, neither with respect to its uttering nor to its effect. Mass media reduce the importance of the original situation in which a speech is given, for the speech is to be multiplied and the speech situation dilated via technical mediation. Most of the addressees receive just small pieces of the speech in the form of later transmissions of selected speech fragments on the radio, TV or the internet, often in news formats. Even journalists who report on the speeches do not always participate in the original speech event. They are saved being present at the original scene, because industrious public relations workers cooperating with the political orators supply the press with copies of written versions of the speech in advance, or at least with press releases that selectively summarise the content of the speech. Concepts such as "textual chain", "(multi)modal transposition" and "recontextualisation" can help in the understanding of some of these complex semiotic interrelations and transformations.

It is a remarkable characteristic of modern political rhetoric that the reception history of a speech need not depend on the eloquence of the political orator (Jochum 1999: 143), and that even the applause of the primary audience need not indicate the overall impact of a speech on the public (Sauer 1997: 37).[7] Clever and targeted public relations work can actually compensate for the lack of rhetorical eloquence (Jochum 1999: 144–145). Political speeches are increasingly becoming parts of interrelated "textual chains" and of dialogically connected discursive practices. The reception of a political speech is decisively influenced by the journalists' intentional selection and quotation of single speech passages, and – even more – by exaggerating and reformulating interpretations of speech fragments. Above and beyond that, the impact of a speech sometimes depends on the media's hunt for wider circulation and – in relation to this – on accidental factors that can by no means be manipulated by the politicians. It is Jochum (1999: 145–146) who supplies us with a striking example of this. On 2 December 1993, the former German president Richard von Weizsäcker – who is well-known for his commemorative speech on the occasion of the 40th anniversary of the national socialist capitulation on 8 May 1945 – gave an address in Hamburg's council chamber on "Our common future: 1943 – 1993 – 2043". The address promised to become an important speech of principle for German foreign policy and was enthusiastically acclaimed by the 400 listeners in the room. About an hour after the address Weizsäcker was attacked by a thug and punched on the head. The media immediately decided that the content of the address was less newsworthy than the physical attack. As a consequence, the address was lost in the scandalising flurry of the media reports on the assault.

5.2.   The speeches' authorship and the division of labour during speech production

The genesis of political speeches under constitutive conditions of modern political rhetoric (Kammerer 1995; Klein 1995; Sauer 1997; Ensink 1999) is, amongst others things, characterised by team work, the importance of a "corporate political identity", and a strongly increased intertextuality and interdiscursivity, including multiple addressing via mass media. In view of these conditions, political speeches are often produced according to a clear division of labour. In classical rhetoric, the production of a speech is subdivided into five stages: finding of topics (*inventio*), arrangement of topics (*dispositio*), linguistic development of the arranged topics (*elocutio*), memory (*memoria*) and delivery (*actio*). Today, ghost writers and political advertisers including spin doctors (who gain importance especially in periods of election campaigns; see, amongst others, Hofer 2005) are engaged in conceiving and writing during the first three production stages (Kammerer 1995: 27). The political orator her or himself is then primarily concerned with making some proposals and giving some rough instructions with respect to the global content, the structure and linguistic peculiarities of the speech. After a first version of the speech has been drafted, this version is corrected and commented on by the speakers and in part also by the advisers. The ghost writers will then take the corrections and comments into account and rewrite the text. Sometimes, the final version is not finished until after several revisions that may occasionally lead to a complete rewriting. Memory and delivery of the final version are the sole responsibility of the politicians as "principals", who deliver their speeches as "animators" (Goffman 1981).

The increasing influence of the media on leading politicians results in something like rhetorical omnipresence. Politicians sometimes deliver more than 150 speeches a year (Kammerer 1995: 20; Schwarze and Walther 2002: 34). They obviously do not have the time to write all these speeches themselves. However, the increasing personalisation of politics forces them to conceal the origin of their speeches from the public and to obscure the fact that top political offices, such as those of the president, the chancellor, or the cabinet ministers[8] necessitate large teams with corporate identity status, of which speech writers and political advisors including spin doctors are important members (this has been shown by Campell and Jamieson [1990: 11] for the office of the President of the United States). On the other hand, former professional speech writers have increasingly started to put an end to the mystification of the production of political speeches and to publicly correct the idolising image of the eloquent politicians who purportedly write their speeches on their own (Volmert 2005: 213).

6. Speech criticism and political language advising – An issue for applied politolinguistics

Speech criticism is as old as the production of speeches itself. Speech criticism intends to evaluate and judge speeches with respect to their persuasive rhetorical structure, aesthetic criteria, the actual performance and the political, social and ethical dimension (Meyer 2005: 801). Speech criticism can relate to (1) the object of critique, (2) the norms and values followed or infringed by the speech, and (3) the functions and aims of the speech (Meyer 2005: 802).

As far as the object of critique is concerned, Meyer (2005: 802) distinguishes between (1a) the critique of speech theories (the present contribution may be considered to belong to this area of critique); and (1b) the critique of speech practices, that is to say, of single speeches and orators with respect to questions of eloquence.

As for the second area of speech criticism, Meyer (2005: 802–803) differentiates between: (2a) criticism relating to language internal norms and values such as clarity and understandability versus obscurity (*perspicuitas* versus *obscuritas*), dispositional order versus disorder, simplicity versus preciousness (*simplicitas* versus *ornatus*), literal speech versus tropic speech (*verbum proprium* versus *verbum improprium*, i.e. tropes), matter-of-factness versus poverty of content, shortness versus long-windedness (*brevitas* versus *taedium*) or choice of speech (sub)genre; and (2b) criticism relating to language external norms and values such as practice, ethics, religion or knowledge, but also pragmatic criteria such as free speech (improvisation) versus recitation or situational adequacy (e.g. of non-verbal means like gestures, facial expression and intonation).

The third criticism strives for an evaluation of the functions and aims of speeches and is either linked to (3a) positive criteria like dialogicality, sincerity, public, informativity, plausibility and convincingness, or to (3b) negative criteria like manipulation, demagogy, agitation, propaganda, defamation and fallaciousness. The latter have been most important in the 20th century, when analysing speeches of political leaders like Hitler, Goebbels, Mussolini and Stalin, and are still highly relevant when analysing current "war speeches" (see, for example, Fairclough 2005; van Dijk 2005).

All these areas of speech criticism and the respective criteria are significant for an applied linguistics that aims to combine rhetorical theory (including argumentation theory), political science and (critical) discourse analysis when approaching the topic of political speeches. The inclusion of concepts and theories of political sciences is advisable, since it enables speech analysts to take into consideration the influence of political systems and cultures of specific countries on the development of speech genres and subgenres.

There are three tasks that are amongst the main issues for applied linguistics concerned with the analysis of political speeches and their functions and impact in public spheres.

(1) Although there are several characterisations of different subgenres of political speeches, many of them are rather abstract and theoretical and, thus, do not do justice to empirical reality. Therefore, more empirical, transdisciplinary politolinguistic work is desirable, in order to get adequate analyses and descriptions of political speeches and their communicative, social, historical and political context. In trying to accomplish this task, applied politolinguistics has to research the conditions of production, distribution and reception of political speeches (see, for a case study, Reisigl 2003a).

(2) The second important task for an applied politolinguistics identifying with the programme of critical discourse analysis consists in the analysis of political speeches with the purpose to detect and expose the persuasive, propagandist, populist, "manipulative" character of political speeches, and to criticise orators' rhetoric if it infringes upon basic ethical and democratic principles. In keeping a watch on political speech practices related to political activities under democratic legitimation-obligation, this speech criticism locates itself in the action field of political control. It can sometimes take the form of linguistic expert reports produced for the juridical procedure (see, for instance, Wodak and Reisigl 2002).

(3) The third task of applied politolinguistics is to become even more practical and to try to change and improve the culture of political speech – which is regularly said to be terribly neglected (see, for example, Kopperschmidt 1999) – by means of consulting (see, for example, Rentrop 1992–2005; Duden 2000; Roth 2004: 173–201). Competent advisory critique presupposes the satisfying

fulfilment of the first task. Speech advisers who recognise ethical claims should not be tempted by payment to help politicians to rhetorically "manipulate" their audiences as effectively as possible. Rather, they will see their job as a possible contribution to the further development of a democratic political culture, since the quality of political speeches can be an important gauge of the state of a democracy.

Notes

1 I would like to thank Veronika Koller and Ruth Wodak for constructive comments on an earlier version of the article and Maura Bayer for correcting my English.
2 "Rhetoric" is here intended to denote both the practical art of speaking and writing well in public, and the theory of eloquence (*ars bene dicendi et scribendi*).
3 The schematic synopsis is primarily based on Aristotle (1994: 1358b–1359a), Plett (2001: 17–18), Kopperschmidt (1995: 91) and Zinsmaier (1999: 384), who quotes Pernot (1993: 38). Extending the epideictic oratory, the figure also takes into account the works of Matuschek (1994: 1258–1567), Sermain (1994: 1083–1086), Vallozza (1994: 1160) and Hambsch (1996: 1377–1392).
4 I see a "discourse" as a complex bundle of semiotic social practices that are topic-related, involve argumentation about validity claims such as truth and normative validity, and involve various social actors who participate in the discourse and set up different points of view (Reisigl 2003b: 92). I adopt Foucault's (2004: 106) general characterisation of "discourse" as socially constitutive and socially constituted practice, although I do not take up his enigmatic and linguistically inscrutable concept of *énoncé* ("statement"), which most of his theoretical characterisations of "discourse" are based on.
5 In Christian Germany and Austria, such speeches are given after the end of carnival. They are held in front of party members and party followers. Despite the fact that they are given at the beginning of the fasting period, they are often designated to attack political opponents polemically (Wodak and Reisigl 2002).
6 For parliamentary speeches see also Klein 2003; Van Dijk 2002; Illie 2006. For interactions during parliamentary question time see Chilton (2004: 92–109).
7 However, outstanding orators lived not only in the past (for example, Woodrow Wilson, Vladimir Ilich Lenin, Lev Trotsky, Winston Churchill or Martin Luther King, to mention just a few gifted orators of the 20th century), but act also in the present, where examples of political speeches can be still found which owe their public political impact for the most part to the eloquence of the speakers. The "Humboldt speech" given by the former German foreign minister Joschka Fischer at the Humboldt University on May 12, 2000 is just one good example of great public influence that is strongly based on the elevated quality of a speech. This speech did much to stimulate the discussion about European integration, constitution and identity and thus contributed to the constitution of an "European public sphere" (see, among others, Weiss 2002).
8 For the influence of the speaker's political position on the content of a speech see, among others, Wodak et al. (1999: 72–74).

References

Anderson, Benedict R. O'Gorman
    1983   *Imagined Communities: Reflections on the Origin and Spread of Nationalism.* London: Verso.
Aristotle
    1994   *The Art of Rhetoric. With an English translation by John Henry Freese. Reprint.* London: Heinemann.
Beck, Hans-Rainer
    2001   *Politische Rede als Interaktionsgefüge: Der Fall Hitler.* Tübingen: Niemeyer.
Bourdieu, Pierre
    1991   *Sozialer Raum und "Klassen": Leçon sur la leçon. Zwei Vorlesungen.* Frankfurt/Main: Suhrkamp.
Burkhardt, Armin
    1996   Politolinguistik: Versuch einer Ortsbestimmung. In: Josef Klein and Hajo Diekmannshenke (eds.), *Sprachstrategien und Dialogblockaden: Linguistische und politikwissenschaftliche Studien zur politischen Kommunikation,* 75–100. Berlin/New York: de Gruyter.
Burkhardt, Armin
    2004   *Zwischen Monolog und Dialog: Zur Theorie, Typologie und Geschichte des Zwischenrufs im deutschen Parlamentarismus.* Tübingen: Niemeyer.
Campbell, Karlyn Kohrs and Kathleen Hall Jamieson
    1990   *Deeds Done in Words: Presidential Rhetoric and the Genres of Governance.* Chicago/London: University of Chicago Press.
Chilton, Paul
    2004   *Analysing Political Discourse.* London/New York: Routledge.
Dedaić, Mirjana Nelson
    2006   Political speeches and persuasive argumentation. In: Keith Brown (ed.), *The Encyclopedia of Language and Linguistics.* Volume 9. 2nd ed., 700–707. Oxford: Elsevier.
Duden
    2000   *Reden gut und richtig halten: Ratgeber für wirkungsvolles und modernes Reden.* Mannheim etc.: Dudenverlag.
Efing, Christian
    2005   Rhetorik in der Demokratie: Argumentation und Persuasion in politischer (Wahl-)Werbung. In: Jörg Kilian (ed.), *Sprache und Politik: Deutsch im demokratischen Staat,* 222–240. Mannheim etc.: Dudenverlag.
Ehlich, Konrad
    1983   Text und sprachliches Handeln: Die Entstehung von Texten aus dem Bedürfnis nach Überlieferung. In: Assmann Aleida, Jan Assmann and Christof Hardmeier (eds.), *Schrift und Gedächtnis: Beiträge zur Archäologie der literarischen Kommunikation,* 24–43. Munich: Fink.
Ehlich, Konrad and Jochen Rehbein
    1979   Sprachliche Handlungsmuster. In: Hans-Georg Soeffner (ed.), *Interpretative Verfahren in den Sozial- und Textwissenschaften,* 243–274. Stuttgart: Metzler.

Eigenwald, Rolf
1996   Festrede. In: Gert Ueding (ed.), *Historisches Wörterbuch der Rhetorik.* Volume 3, 257–259. Tübingen: Niemeyer.
Engels, Johannes
1996   Genera causarum. In: Gert Ueding (ed.), *Historisches Wörterbuch der Rhetorik.* Volume 3, 701–721. Tübingen: Niemeyer.
Ensink, Titus
1992   *Jenninger. De ontvangst van een Duitse rede in Nederland: Een tekstwetenschappelijke en communicatiewetenschappelijke analyse (Jenninger. The reception of a German speech in the Netherlands: A textlinguistic and communicative analysis).* Amsterdam: Thesis Publishers.
Ensink, Titus
1997   The footing of a royal address: an analysis of representativeness in political speech, exemplified in Queen Beatrix' address to the Knesset on March 28, 1995. In: Christina Schäffner (ed.), *Analysing Political Speeches,* 5–32. Clevedon etc.: Multilingual Matters.
Ensink, Titus
1999   Epideiktik mit fehlendem Konsens: Die Tischrede der niederländischen Königin Beatrix beim Staatsbesuch in Indonesien im August 1995. In: Josef Kopperschmidt and Helmut Schanze (eds.), *Fest und Festrhetorik: Zu Theorie, Geschichte und Praxis der Epideiktik,* 75–101. Munich: Fink.
Ensink, Titus and Christoph Sauer (eds.)
2003   *The Art of Commemoration: Fifty Years after the Warsaw Uprising.* Amsterdam/Philadelphia: Benjamins.
Epping-Jäger, Cornelia
2003   Laut/Sprecher Hitler: Über das Dispositiv der Massenkommunikation in der Zeit des Nationalsozialismus. In: Josef Kopperschmidt (ed.), *Hitler der Redner,* 144–157. Munich: Fink.
Fairclough, Norman L.
2005   Blair's contribution to elaborating a new "doctrine of international community". In: Lilie Chouliaraki (ed.), *The Soft Power of War: Legitimacy and Community in Iraq war Discourses,* 41–63. (Journal of Language and Politics 4/1).
Foucault, Michel
2004 [1969]   *L'archéologie du savoir* Paris: Éditions Gallimard.
Girnth, Heiko
1996   Texte im politischen Diskurs: Ein Vorschlag zur diskursorientierten Beschreibung von Textsorten. *Muttersprache* 1: 66–80.
Girnth, Heiko
2002   *Sprache und Sprachverwendung in der Politik: Eine Einführung in die linguistische Analyse öffentlich-politischer Kommunikation.* Tübingen: Niemeyer.
Goffman, Erving
1981   *Forms of Talk.* Oxford/Philadelphia: University of Pennsylvania Press.
Graefen, Gabriele
1997   *Der wissenschaftliche Artikel: Textart und Textorganisation.* Frankfurt/Main: Lang.

Hambsch, Björn
  1996   Herrscherlob. In: Gert Ueding (ed.), *Historisches Wörterbuch der Rhetorik.* Volume 3, 1377–1392. Tübingen: Niemeyer.
Herget, Winfried
  2005   Rede: USA. In: Gert Ueding (ed.), *Historisches Wörterbuch der Rhetorik.* Volume 7, 758–765. Tübingen: Niemeyer.
Hofer, Thomas M.
  2005   *Spin Doktoren in Österreich: Die Praxis amerikanischer Wahlkampfberater. Was sie können, wen sie beraten, wie sie arbeiten.* Vienna etc.: LIT.
Hoffmann, Ludger and Johannes Schwitalla
  1989   Äußerungskritik oder Warum Philipp Jenninger zurücktreten mußte. *Sprachreport* 1: 5–9.
Illie, Cornelia
  2006   Parliamentary discourses. In: Keith Brown (ed.), *The Encyclopedia of Language and Linguistics.* Volume 9. 2nd ed., 188–196. Oxford: Elsevier.
Jochum, Michael
  1999   Der Bundespräsident als öffentlicher Redner: Zur Entstehung und Verbreitung der Reden Roman Herzogs. In: Josef Kopperschmidt and Helmut Schanze (eds.), *Fest und Festrhetorik: Zu Theorie, Geschichte und Praxis der Epideiktik*, 141–147. Munich: Fink.
Kammerer, Patrick
  1995   Die veränderten Konstitutionsbedingungen politischer Rhetorik. Zur Rolle der Redenschreiber, der Medien und zum vermeintlichen Ende öffentlicher Rede. In: Dyck, Joachim, Walter Jens and Gert Ueding (eds.), *Rhetorik. Ein internationales Jahrbuch*, Volume 14, 14–29.
Klein, Josef
  1995   Politische Rhetorik: Eine Theorieskizze in Rhetorik-kritischer Absicht mit Analysen zu Reden von Goebbels, Herzog und Kohl. *Sprache und Literatur in Wissenschaft und Unterricht (SuL)* 26 (75/76): 62–99.
Klein, Josef
  1996   Insider-Lesarten: Einige Regeln zur latenten Fachkommunikation in Parteiprogrammen. In: Josef Klein and Hajo Diekmannshenke (eds.), *Sprachstrategien und Dialogblockaden: Linguistische und politikwissenschaftliche Studien zur politischen Kommunikation*, 201–209. Berlin/New York: de Gruyter.
Klein, Josef
  2000   Textsorten im Bereich politischer Institutionen In: Brinker, Klaus, Gerd Antos, Wolfgang Heinemann and Sven F. Sager (eds.), *Text- und Gesprächslinguistik / Linguistics of Text and Conversation: Ein internationales Handbuch zeitgenössischer Forschung / An international Handbook of Contemporary Research.* 1. Halbband / Volume 1, 732–755. Berlin/New York: de Gruyter.
Klein, Josef
  2003   Parlamentsrede & Moderne Parlamentsrede. In: Gert Ueding (ed.), *Historisches Wörterbuch der Rhetorik.* Volume 6, 582–586 and 634–637. Tübingen: Niemeyer.

Kopperschmidt, Josef
   1995   Rhetorik als Medium der politischen Deliberation: z.B. Augustin. In: Josef Kopperschmidt (ed.), *Politik und Rhetorik: Funktionsmodelle politischer Rede*, 74–101. Opladen: Westdeutscher Verlag.

Kopperschmidt, Josef
   1999   Über die Unfähigkeit zu feiern: Allgemeine und spezifische deutsche Schwierigkeiten mit der Gedenkrhetorik. In: Josef Kopperschmidt and Helmut Schanze (eds.), *Fest und Festrhetorik: Zu Theorie, Geschichte und Praxis der Epideiktik*, 149–172. Munich: Fink.

Krebs, Birgit-Nicole
   1993   *Sprachhandlung und Sprachwirkung: Untersuchungen zur Rhetorik, Sprachkritik und zum Fall Jenninger*. Berlin: Erich Schmidt Verlag.

Kühn, Peter
   1992   Adressaten und Adressatenkarussell in der öffentlich-politischen Auseinandersetzung. In: Dyck, Joachim, Walter Jens and Gert Ueding (eds.), *Rhetorik: Ein internationales Jahrbuch*, Volume 11, 51–66.

Kühn, Peter
   1995   *Mehrfachadressierung: Untersuchungen zur adressatenspezifischen Polyvalenz sprachlichen Handelns*. Tübingen. Niemeyer.

Matuschek, Stefan
   1994   Epideiktische Beredsamkeit. In: Gert Ueding (ed.), *Historisches Wörterbuch der Rhetorik*. Volume 2, 1258–1267. Tübingen: Niemeyer.

Matuschek, Stefan
   2001   Lobrede. In: Gert Ueding (ed.), *Historisches Wörterbuch der Rhetorik*. Volume 5, 390–398. Tübingen: Niemeyer.

Meinhart, Edith and Ulla Schmid
   2000   *Spin Doktoren: Die hohe Schule der politischen Manipulation*. Vienna: Czernin.

Meyer, Urs
   2005   Redekritik. In: Gert Ueding (ed.), *Historisches Wörterbuch der Rhetorik*. Volume 7, 801–815. Tübingen: Niemeyer.

Panagl, Oswald and Robert Kriechbaumer (eds.)
   2002   *Wahlkämpfe: Sprache und Politik*. Vienna etc.: Böhlau.

Peters, Heiner
   2005   Rede: England. In: Gert Ueding (ed.), *Historisches Wörterbuch der Rhetorik*. Volume 7, 751–758. Tübingen Niemeyer.

Plett, Helmut
   2001   *Einführung in die rhetorische Textanalyse*. Hamburg: Buske.

Pernot, Laurent
   1993   *La rhétorique de l'éloge dans le monde gréco-romain*. Paris: Inst. des Ètudes Augustiniennes.

Reisigl, Martin
   2000   Literarische Texte als heuristische Quellen und kunstfertige Herausforderung für die Analyse gesprochener Sprache: Eine Fallstudie am Beispiel von Friedrich Glauser. In: Oswald Panagl and Walter Weiss (eds.), *Noch einmal: Dichtung und Politik. Vom Text zum politisch-sozialen Kontext, und zurück*, 237–319. Vienna: Böhlau.

Reisigl, Martin
  2003a   Rede als Vollzugsmeldung an die (deutsche) Geschichte: Hitler auf dem Wiener Heldenplatz. In: Josef Kopperschmidt (ed.), *Hitler der Redner*, 383–412. Munich: Fink.
Reisigl, Martin
  2003b   *Wie man eine Nation herbeiredet: Eine diskursanalytische Untersuchung zur sprachlichen Konstruktion der österreichischen Nation und österreichischen Identität in politischen Fest- und Gedenkreden*. Ph.D. Dissertation, Department of Linguistics, University of Vienna.
Reisigl, Martin
  2006   Rhetorical tropes in political discourses. In: Keith Brown (ed.), *The Encyclopedia of Language and Linguistics*. Volume 10. 2nd ed., 596–605. Oxford: Elsevier.
Reisigl, Martin and Ruth Wodak
  2001   *Discourse and Discrimination: Rhetorics of Racism and Antisemitism*. London/New York: Routledge.
Rentrop, Norman (ed.)
  1992–2005 *Der Redenberater: Handbuch für erfolgreiche Reden im Betrieb, in der Öffentlichkeit und im Privatleben*. Bonn: Verlag Norman Rentrop.
Roth, Kersten Sven
  2004   *Politische Sprachberatung als Symbiose von Linguistik und Sprachkritik: Zu Theorie und Praxis einer kooperativ-kritischen Sprachwissenschaft*. Tübingen: Niemeyer.
Sauer, Christof
  1997   Echoes from abroad – speeches for the domestic audience: queen Beatrix' address to the Israeli parliament. In: Christina Schäffner (ed.), *Analysing Political Speeches*, 33–67. Clevedon: Multilingual Matters.
Schild, Hans-Jochen
  1992   Beratungsrede. In: Gert Ueding (ed.), *Historisches Wörterbuch der Rhetorik*. Volume 1, 1441–1455. Tübingen: Niemeyer.
Schmitz, Thomas
  2005   Rede. In: Gert Ueding (ed.), *Historisches Wörterbuch der Rhetorik*. Volume 7, 698–709. Darmstadt: Wissenschaftliche Buchgesellschaft.
Schwarze, Antje and Antje Walther
  2002   Redenschreiben für den Bundeskanzler: Formulieren, Koordinieren und Beraten. In: Karl-Rudolf Korte (ed.), *"Das Wort hat der Bundeskanzler": Eine Analyse der Großen Regierungserklärungen von Adenauer bis Schröder*, 33–55. Wiesbaden: Westdeutscher Verlag.
Sermain, Jean-Paul
  1994   Eloge. In: Gert Ueding (ed.), *Historisches Wörterbuch der Rhetorik*. Volume 2, 1083–1086. Tübingen: Niemeyer.
Sternberger, Dolf
  1991   Auch Reden sind Taten [1979]. In: Dolf Sternberger, *Sprache und Politik*, 52–68. Frankfurt/Main: Insel.
Ueding, Gert and Bernd Steinbrink
  2005   *Grundriß der Rhetorik: Geschichte, Technik, Methode*. Stuttgart: Metzler.

Vallozza, Maddalena
    1994   Enkomion. In: Gert Ueding (ed.), *Historisches Wörterbuch der Rhetorik*. Volume 2, 1152–1160. Tübingen: Niemeyer.
Van Dijk, Teun A.
    2002   Knowledge in parliamentary debates. *Journal of Language and Politics* 2(1): 93–129.
Van Dijk, Teun A.
    2005   War rhetoric of a little ally: Political implicatures and Aznar's legitimatization of the war in Iraq. In: Lilie Chouliaraki (ed.), *The Soft Power of War: Legitimacy and community in Iraq war discourses* 65–91. (Journal of Language and Politics 4/1).
Volmert, Johannes
    2005   Kanzlerrede: Regierungserklärungen als Inszenierung von repäsentativ-parlamentarischer Herrschaft. In: Jörg Kilian (ed.), *Sprache und Politik: Deutsch im demokratischen Staat*. 210–221. Mannheim etc.: Dudenverlag.
Weiss, Gilbert
    2002   Searching for Europe: The problem of legitimisation and representation in recent political speeches on Europe. *Journal of Language and Politics* 1 (1): 59–84.
Wodak, Ruth, Florian Menz, Richard Mitten and Frank Stern
    1994   *Die Sprachen der Vergangenheiten: Öffentliches Gedenken in österreichischen und deutschen Medien*. Frankfurt/Main: Suhrkamp.
Wodak, Ruth, Rudolf De Cillia, Martin Reisigl and Karin Liebhart
    1999   *The Discursive Construction of National Identity*. Edinburgh: Edinburgh University Press.
Wodak, Ruth and Martin Reisigl
    2002   "Wenn einer Ariel heißt" – Ein linguistisches Gutachten zur politischen Funktionalisierung antisemitischer Ressentiments in Österreich. In: Ruth Wodak and Anton Pelinka (eds.), *"Dreck am Stecken": Politik der Ausgrenzung*, 134–172. Vienna: Czernin Verlag.
Zinsmaier, Thomas
    1999   Epideiktik zwischen Affirmation und Artistik: Die antike Theorie der feiernden Rede im historischen Aufriß. In: Josef Kopperschmidt and Helmut Schanze (eds.), *Fest und Festrhetorik: Zu Theorie, Geschichte und Praxis der Epideiktik*, 375–398. Munich: Fink

12. Dissemination and implementation of political concepts[1]

Florian Oberhuber

1. Introduction

"Dissemination and implementation of political concepts" does not constitute a systematic field of scientific enquiry, neither within research on political language nor within political science or sociology. There are no established approaches or schools of thought in this area, no classic texts, no repertoire of basic concepts or methods of data gathering and analysis. At the same time, one would find it hard to argue that "dissemination and implementation" do not refer to important processes in today's social reality, or that such processes could not be scientifically studied. And indeed, a second glance shows that a variety of disciplines have contributed to the investigation of such processes with case studies as well as with theoretical work. This chapter will draw some strands of this literature together, and in a concluding section will propose a heuristic framework for research.

A few words of caution are necessary at this point. The following literature review will not start from definitions of dissemination and implementation, but will work with a rather broad understanding of those concepts. It will draw on a variety of approaches which were not originally intended for the study of dissemination and implementation of political concepts, but, as will be shown, can in fact be used for such study. As a general rule, the character of the present subject lends itself to an interdisciplinary approach. Both dissemination and implementation refer to phenomena which are not to be found "in language", but to extra-linguistic processes. They cannot be fully apprehended by linguistic concepts only, and scholars have often found it useful to draw on methodological and conceptual resources from neighbouring disciplines such as sociology or political science.

The selection of the literature reviewed here does not claim completeness. Apart from my own subjective focus, I attempted to include recent contributions from various theoretical, geographical and disciplinary backgrounds. Special emphasis is put on research in linguistics and political science. Furthermore, dissemination and implementation are understood in this chapter from an actor-centred perspective, i.e. implying conscious, intentional activities: who disseminates what, where, why and by what means? Who implements what, why, in what context and by what means? Reception studies and agenda-setting will be not dealt with since they are separate and well-established fields of enquiry. Political terminology and contested concepts are discussed in Paul Chilton's chapter in this volume.

2. Dissemination and implementation in linguistics

2.1. Language history, lexicology and discourse semantics

In the German-speaking academic tradition, research on language and politics has a strong historical focus which can be traced back to the 19th century, when "historism" became the dominant intellectual paradigm in the humanities (cf. Oexle 1996). In the second half of the century, not only students of history, but also legal scholars, economists and linguists[2] turned to historical sources and tried to reconstruct the meaning of specific constellations of institutions and cultural production. They tried to understand (*verstehen*) the individuality of historical phenomena rather than explain social life by establishing the causal laws governing it, and consequently they put special emphasis on the historical roots of their objects of study.

Over the past ten years, three excellent overviews of the vast literature on the history of public communication in Germany were published by Armin Burkhardt (1996), Peter von Polenz (1999) and Hajo Diekmannshenke (2001).[3] As Burkhardt (1996: 85–86) observes, this body of literature failed to work out a unified and systematic terminology, and the theoretical concepts as well as methods applied are not specific, but reflect the general discussion in the historical disciplines. Moreover, neither "dissemination" nor "implementation" figure among the basic concepts (cf. Polenz 1991) or topics of mainstream research (cf. Burkhardt 1996: 85–89; Girnth 2002: 2–12). Nevertheless, many publications present historical case studies which are excellent resources for understanding the dissemination of political vocabulary such as the language of nationalism, antisemitism, women's rights or social reform.

2.1.1. Recent developments in research on language and politics in Germany

Since the mid 1970s, a growing interest in political communication can be noted among German linguists. Diekmannshenke (2001: 1) even speaks of an independent discipline of political linguistics or "politolinguistics" (Burkhardt 1996). Girnth (2002: 8–9) identifies the following main areas of research: language in the National-Socialist era, language in the German Democratic Republic, and the language of and after the 1989 *Wende* and German re-unification. Moreover, many of the public debates in post-war Germany have been intensively studied, for instance those on military politics, asylum and migration, ecology, nuclear power, womens' rights or the rise of the European Union (Polenz 1999: 561–562; Diekmannshenke 2001: 20–26). Among the main research foci were: political terminology, language use by politicians, genres of political language, language use in institutions, "semantic wars" (i.e. struggles over the meanings of concepts) and many more. In terms of methodology, scholars have drawn for instance on rhetoric, speech act theory, conversation analysis, various methods of text analysis, theory of argumentation and critical linguistics (Burkhardt 1996: 89). Dissemination and implementation, though, have not figured among the central concerns. As Klein and Diekmannshenke (1996: v) put it:

> Linguistische Analysen thematisieren politische Texte traditionell vor allem unter dem Gesichtspunkt der Absichten und Strategien der Politiker. Wie es mit dem Erfolg der Strategien aussieht, bleibt dabei unbeachtet. [Linguistic analyses traditionally look at political texts above all from the point of view of politicians' intentions and strategies. Yet the question of the success of such strategies remains untackled.]

On the other hand, a theoretical development in the field can be noted which tends to transcend the purely linguistic realm to include the extralinguistic context, and thus extends to the problem of dissemination and implementation. While earlier studies were often limited to the description and (critical) analysis of single words,[4] the seminal eight-volume conceptual history by Brunner, Conze, and Koselleck (1972–1997) marks an important turning point. Focussing on the communicative function of language and language use, the aforementioned authors developed a new approach to historical semantics which would integrate social and conceptual history.[5] In subsequent years, text and discourse oriented research came to complement lexicological studies, and emphasis was put on the relationship between language and its larger context. Authors like Dietrich Busse (1987) criticised traditional approaches in historical semantics and advocated the investigation of the communicative practices constituting social knowledge ("discourse semantics"), while Fritz Herrmanns (1995) coined the phrase of "language history as the history of mentalities" (*Sprachgeschichte als Mentalitätsgeschichte*).

Drawing on such theoretical developments, a research group at the University of Düsseldorf published a series of monographs on the "history of public communication in the Federal Republic of Germany" (e.g. Stötzel and Wengeler 1995; Böke, Liedtke, and Wengeler 1996). Aiming at reconstructing changes of perspectives on reality in language, they focussed on *Leitvokabeln*, 'the study of thematic complexes and key terms', i.e. concepts which are linked to the political programmes of contesting groups. In this context, the Düsseldorf school also looked at the persuasive interests of speakers and how they reach a broader public via the mass media (Böke 1996: 20). Wengeler (1995), for instance, reconstructed how conservative political parties succeeded after 1945 in disseminating their ideas of a "social market economy", and Böke (1995) looked at the changing terminology in political discussions on gender relations. Both studies used a broad range of sources including print media, political advertising, encyclopaedias, legal texts and texts produced by various political actors. They focussed on contested meanings, competing concepts and their changing roles in the political context. However, the conceptual and methodological elements of such a research programme were not spelled out in detail, and general inferences on how processes of dissemination of political concepts work were not drawn. Rather, faithful to the tradition of historism in German academia, the main focus remained on idiographic research, i.e. on the individual cases.

2.2. Theorising the mediation between the linguistic and the social: Critical Discourse Analysis

Critical Discourse Analysis (CDA) as a network of scholars emerged in the early 1990s, marked by the launch of van Dijk's journal *Discourse and Society* (1990) as well as books like *Language and Power* by Norman Fairclough (1989) or *Language, Power and Ideology* by Ruth Wodak (1989). Critical Discourse Analysis as such cannot be viewed as a strictly defined paradigm, but rather as a 'school', or a programme which many researchers find useful and to which they can relate. As Michael Meyer (2001: 18) notes: "there is no guiding theoretical viewpoint that is used consistently within CDA, nor do the CDA protagonists proceed consistently from the area of theory to the field of discourse and then back to theory".

As a basic premise, Critical Discourse Analysis shares the notion of "language as social practice" (Fairclough and Wodak 1997) contributing to the reproduction of society. As a consequence, Critical Discourse Analysis does not consider discursive and non-discursive practices as separated but, conversely, places particular emphasis on the context of language use as well as the problem of conceptualising the "mediation between the social and the linguistic" (Chouliaraki and Fairclough 1999).

Owing to this research focus, scholars have emphasised the need for interdisciplinary work in order to gain a proper understanding of how language functions in constituting and transmitting knowledge, in organising social institutions or in exercising power. Some of the ensuing theoretical issues are referred to in the following quote from Fairclough and Wodak (1997: 258):

> Describing discourse as social practice implies a dialectical relationship between a particular discursive event and the situation(s), institution(s) and social structure(s) which frame it: the discursive event is shaped by them, but it also shapes them. That is, discourse is socially constitutive as well as socially conditioned – it constitutes situations, objects of knowledge, and the social identities of and relationships between people and groups of people. It is constitutive both in the sense that it helps to sustain and reproduce the social status quo, and in the sense that it contributes to transforming it. Since discourse is so socially consequential, it gives rise to important issues of power.

The various research areas, protagonists and approaches of Critical Discourse Analysis cannot be dealt with here, nor its theoretical background reconstructed in detail (cf. Chouliaraki and Fairclough 1999; Wodak and Meyer 2001). Instead, let us consider an author who placed the linguistic/social interface at the centre of his work and who provided a theoretical framework which addresses some of the key problems concerning the dissemination and implementation of political concepts.

2.2.1. Dissemination and implementation in Critical Discourse Analysis

In the early 1990s, Norman Fairclough began looking for ways of combining his research on language with "social and political thought relevant to discourse and language, in the form of a framework which will be suitable for use in social scientific research and specifically in the study of social change" (Fairclough 1992: 62). With respect to the dissemination and implementation of political concepts, the main features of his account can be summarised in the following cyclical model (adapted from Fairclough 2005: 57):

1. Establishment and articulation: An emergent discourse (e.g. the "knowledge-based economy") brings elements of existing discourses (e.g. those of "lifelong learning", "social exclusion", "flexibility") into a particular, new articulation. Through processes of contestation ("semantic wars") and political struggle, it may become hegemonic in particular social fields.

2. Dissemination: Processes of dissemination may take place across structures (e.g. between governments, public and social services such as education and health) and scales (between global or international, national and local scales of social life). Those processes entail the recontextualisation (cf. below) of discourses in new social fields, institutions, organisations, countries, localities.

3. Implementation: Discourses change and reproduce discursive and non-discursive elements of social realities. They may be enacted as new ways of (inter)acting (like regulatory regimes), inculcated in new ways of being (identities), materialised in new institutional arrangements or ways of organising social relations (like monitoring agencies).

For each step of this model, different data and methodological tools are required. Fairclough proposes genealogy and interdiscursive analysis for studying the specific articulations of different discourses. This entails the collection and analysis of a historical series of texts, the identification of key terms, discursive strategies, and of interdiscursive relationships.[6] Moreover, texts are subject to or reflect discursive practices and are co-articulated with social practices: Discourse internalises and is internalised in other, non-linguistic elements (cf. Fairclough 2003).

The investigation of processes of dissemination requires focusing on the distributive aspects of discursive practice, which involves the comparative analysis of a large number of texts from various social fields and institutions. With respect to the factors determining successful dissemination, Fairclough (2005: 55–56) identified a number of *conditions*:

> First, "structural selectivities": structures are more open to some strategies than to others. Second, the scope and 'reach' of the discourse (narrative) – for instance, the discourses of 'globalization' or 'knowledge-based economy' might be seen as "nodal discourses" which articulate many other discourses (…). Third, the differential capacities and power of the social agents whose strategy it is "to get their messages across", e.g. their access to and their control over mass media and other channels and networks for diffusion. Fourth, the "resonance" of discourses, their capacity to mobilize people, not only in the institutions but also in the lifeworld.

As a key term for studying processes of dissemination, Fairclough draws on the concept of recontextualisation which has become widely used in discourse analysis (cf. Iedema 1997; Iedema and Wodak 1999; Kovács and Wodak 2003).[7] Recontextualisation can briefly be defined as the integration of elements borrowed from different contexts in a new context. Such processes can be studied by comparing texts in different social fields and at different scales. In a recent study, Fairclough (2007) has, for instance, looked at how Romanian policy texts integrate elements from discourses of the "knowledge-based economy" and "information society" formulated at the level of the European Union. At the textual level, this involved taking a close look at the "texturing" and "rhetorical structures" of the respective documents. Recontextualisation practices are never fully governed by external discourses, but they involve a dialectic of colonisation and appropriation (Chouliaraki and Fairclough 1999). Moreover, authors can never fully control the meaning of texts, but meaning is co-constituted by the interpretations of the readers. Thus, Kovács and Wodak (2003), for instance, studied different corpora from public, semi-public and quasi-private domains (focus groups) in order to investigate the various understandings of a discourse/topic/argument/topos by various publics.

Finally, the third step of the cyclical model takes us to implementation, i.e. the ways in which discourse may be inculcated, enacted, institutionalised and materialised. Arguably, implementation is the most difficult process to grasp both with respect to empirical research and theoretical conceptualisation. Fairclough proposes the use of ethnographic methods of data collection to study such processes in social organisations from the "inside". As a key analytical category, he draws on the concept of "genres", i.e. the practices of "(inter)acting semiotically" (Fairclough 2005: 58) such as meetings, reports, policy papers and so on. Genres can be seen as institutionalised ways of framing and regulating interaction (Chouliaraki 1995). Being organised in "chains" or "networks", they are "articulated together in intra-organisational or cross-organisational procedures, routines and practices" (e.g. practices of "evaluations" or of "benchmarking") (Fairclough 2005: 64–65). Thus, implementation can be conceptualised as the operationalisation and institutional enactment of a discourse by "a complex set of network relationships between genres" (Fairclough 2005: 59). Genres function as "filtering devices (...) selectively including or excluding discourses in the shift from one genre to another" (Fairclough 2005: 65). Moreover, certain genres (such as white papers of the European Commission or codes of conduct in companies) can govern other genres and also practices.

3. Discourse, power and the Foucauldian tradition

Studying processes of the implementation of political concepts requires a problem-oriented approach which permits the integration of a variety of theoretical, conceptual and methodological resources which are adequate for an understanding and explanation of the object under investigation. With respect to conceptualising the relationship between discursive and non-discursive practices, the writings of Michel Foucault have proved to be particularly influential. For many scholars in the humanities, Foucault's studies of the 1970s on bio-politics and the disciplinary society signalled a turn to a new kind of endeavour, namely analysing the constitutive function of discourse for the "construction of reality". To this end, Foucault provided a range of powerful conceptual notions such as "dispositive", "diagram", "discipline", the "microphysics of power", and "governmentality".

Foucault started out by analysing the internal structures and formative principles of discourse, and only later turned to social practices and institutions. From the very beginning, however, he vigorously defended a view of discourse as not being representative (i.e. mirroring reality), but as productive, i.e. constituting reality and, above all, human subjects (cf. Foucault 1982). Foucault achieved an important expansion of this perspective when he began investigating the "practical" dimension of the discursive processes of the production of subjects, namely power. With his perhaps most famous concept, power/knowledge, he coined an influential term for this new focus. Foucault (1977: 27) writes: "power and knowledge directly imply one another (...) there is no power relation without the correlative constitution of a field of knowledge, nor any knowledge that does not presuppose and constitute at the same time power relations."

The potential of such an approach for an examination of the implementation of political concepts cannot pass unnoticed: by emphasising the dialectical relations between regimes of power on the one hand, and orders of discourse on the other, Foucault pointed to the many pathways that language can take in influencing social reality. For Foucault, power, understood as the structuring of a possible field of action, can be literally everywhere. It circulates throughout the entire social field down even to the tiniest and apparently most trivial extremities. Thus, it is important to focus at the concrete, local techniques and micropractices of power. Furthermore, such local "dispositives" of power are always conceived as connected with a set of discursive practices. Knowledge is indispensable for the reproduction of institutionalised power. It can be translated into technologies of power, and it participates in the (self-)objectivisation of humans as subjects of power.

4. Exemplary applications: Policy and discourse

Recent years have brought an increased interest in social construction in political science research. Scholars of European Studies, for instance, have attempted to open up the "black box" of institutions and negotiations and to focus on the micro-level dynamics of social interaction and their institutional environments (for a literature review cf. Jupille, Caporaso, and Checkel 2003; Checkel 2004). Such efforts include research by linguists on problems traditionally treated by political scientists. Eugène Loos (2004), for instance, studied the text production of advisers in the European Parliament by drawing on sociolinguistic concepts such as "discursive interculture" and applying methods from discourse analysis. On the other hand, political scientists used concepts such as "speech community" or "shared language" in order to explain how language permits the reduction of contingency and thus successful co-operation in complex political organisations.[8] Furthermore, cognitive metaphor theory first formulated by Lakoff and Johnson (1980) has been applied in political science research for looking at the ways in which language shapes the ways of thinking and acting of political elites and civil servants (cf. Schön 1979; Schäffner and Wenden 1995; Lakoff 2004).

4.1. The rise of "sustainability" in public policy

As a reaction to the (re-)introduction of the concept of sustainability in the aftermath of the United Nations' Brundtlandt report *Our Common Future* (1987) and the Earth Summit held in Rio de Janeiro in June 1992, a vast literature emerged in the 1990s tracing the historical genealogy of the concept of "sustainability" (cf. Torgerson 1995), its ambiguous and contested meanings (cf. Williams and Millington 2004), as well as its dissemination and implementation in policy contexts. Summarising this literature on "sustainability", two basic foci can be highlighted, namely language on the one hand, and social practices on the other (see Skulstad, this volume). Pointing to the first of these two aspects, Yvonne Rydin (1999) asked "can we talk ourselves into sustainability?". The author took an actor-centred perspective and highlighted the central aspect of language and communication in policy processes, i.e. the constructive nature of "the ways in which we define issues, understand problems and delimit possible solutions" (Rydin 1999: 473). Applying such an approach, Rydin (2003) provided a comprehensive account of the role of talk within environmental planning and presented case studies on, for instance, air pollution control and housing land policy. Fischer and Black (1995) took a closer look at "sustainable development" as a policy discourse with a special focus on its cultural-political underpinnings (cf. also Dryzek 1997). At a more general level, Peet and Watts (1996) introduced the concept of "environmental imaginaries" understood as a set of "modes of thought, logics, themes, styles of expression and typical metaphors" through which social groups construct and communicate nature. Applying this concept in an empirical case study, McGregor (2004) developed a typology of environmental discourse with respect to "key narratives", "key terms" and "nature metaphors", and he used focus group discussions to study the relevance of those discursive frameworks in interpersonal communication.

At the level of material practices, the institutionalised forms of communication in policy processes as well as organisational practices such as scientific management, monitoring or risk assessment were investigated. In 1997, an edited volume on *The politics of sustainable development* would clearly place such research focus at the centre of interest, claiming that "sustainable development needs to be understood as a social and political construct and, as such, the study of the operationalization of sustainable development through the implementation of specific policies provides the critical focus for research" (Baker et al. 1997: 1). The concept of power/knowledge has been widely used in this respect (cf. Luke 1995), and the normative and cultural assumptions underlying institutional arrangements have been scrutinised (Hajer and Fischer 1999).

Maarten Hajer's book on *The Politics of Environmental Discourse* (1995) set a milestone for the discursive turn in policy analysis. Focussing on the case of the regulation of the problem of acid rain in Britain and the Netherlands, Hajer highlighted the constitutive function of discourse in defining and framing public policy: "ecological problems do not pose institutional problems by themselves, but only to the extent that they are constructed as such" (Hajer 1995: 40). Consequently, the two issues of dissemination and implementation of environmental discourse are closely linked. The ways in which the problem of acid rain is framed by certain actors often implies certain policy-relevant recommendations. A focus on the critical limits of emissions that nature can endure, for instance, clearly favours an end-of-pipe oriented regulatory regime. Thus, Hajer (1995: 30) conceives of discourse as an "organizing principle for the innovation of institutional procedures". "Discursive hegemony" and "discourse institutionalisation" are seen as mutually implying one another:

> We will speak of discourse institutionalization if a given discourse is translated into institutional arrangements, i.e. if the theoretical concepts of ecological modernization are translated into concrete policies (…) and institutional arrangements (…). If these two conditions are satisfied, a discourse can be said to be hegemonic in a given domain. (Hajer 1995: 61)

At the methodological level, Hajer implemented this theoretical programme by studying the construction of the problem of acid rain both at the level of programmatic statements (such as memoranda) and of concrete practices (such as regulatory regimes). The author analysed a wide variety of genres, including conference proceedings, scientific reports, mass media coverage of crucial events, parliamentary debates and many others. His main focus was on the various ways of defining an issue and on the main "story-lines" used by various actors. "Story lines" were conceptualised as "narratives on social reality through which elements from many different domains are combined and that provide actors with a set of symbolic references that suggest a common understanding" (Hajer 1995: 62). The "acid rain story-line", for example, relates "certain industrial emissions to the dying of fish, lakes, and trees" and thus gives meaning to "previously singular and unrelated events". Moreover, story-lines "are devices through which actors are positioned, and through which specific ideas of 'blame' and 'responsibility' (…) are attributed" (Hajer 1995: 64–65). When actors routinely utter these story-lines and actively relate their practices to one another, Hajer speaks of the formation of "discourse-coalitions". In the Dutch case, for instance, scientists, government officials and actors from the environmental movement built a coalition that challenged the mainstream regime of moderate ecological modernization, that is, they publicly made a much more wide-ranging statement on the "ecological crisis".

Another innovative characteristic of Hajer's approach is the broad attention he pays to all kinds of practices involved in the construction of the acid rain problem. The restructuring of ministerial departments, for instance, is used as an indicator for changing conceptions of environmental regulation. The practices and main concepts organising the negotiations between the government and representatives of industry are looked at (drawing on interviews with officials). The contribution of "sub-political" practices like tree health surveys, excursions and public awareness campaigns for the "public construction of damage" are analysed. Hajer even goes to great lengths to reconstruct the story-lines informing the set-up and model assumptions of the Dutch Priority Programme on Acidification, and he also dissects the practices of translating scientific knowledge into policy-relevant information.

With respect to methodology, Hajer often fails to provide a systematic account of how to approach textual material or how to operationalise the key concepts of "story-lines" and "discourse-coalitions". On the other hand, the creative use of a wealth of sources for reconstructing the relationships between discursive and non-discursive practices makes this study an invaluable resource for any student of processes of dissemination and implementation.

5. Conclusions: A heuristic framework for research

For the time being, there is neither an overarching theoretical framework for the study of dissemination and implementation of political concepts nor a specific set of concepts and methods. Consequently, conclusions have to be limited to a set of heuristic principles derived from the literature discussed. While those principles might be useful for designing individual research projects, any particular research design will mainly depend on the characteristics of the specific case that one wants to study.

Secondly, the above literature review implies that a focus on political concepts is too narrow. Generally speaking, concepts are always embedded in discourses, and discourses are always situated in social, political, economic etc. contexts (cf. Panagl and Wodak 2004). As pointed out above, recent years have seen a general shift of research from lexicology to discourse semantics.

A heuristic framework for studying dissemination/implementation:

Note: In practice, dissemination and implementation cannot be neatly separated since dissemination is a prerequisite for implementation, and implementation fosters dissemination.

1. Dissemination:
a) Possible foci of research at the discursive level:
   – How is a given discourse established (genealogy) and co-articulated with other discourses (cf. step 1 in Fairclough's [2005] model)
   – How is meaning transferred between various social fields and discourses (recontextualisation, interdiscursivity)?
   – What metaphors, story-lines, key terms, arguments etc., are widely accepted and routinely used?
   – How is a particular discourse interpreted and communicated in various social contexts and by various social groups?
b) At the level of situational context:
   – How are discourses situated and embedded in social fields, institutions, practices, etc.?[9] Depending on the case studied, this might include context at the macro and/or micro-level.
   – The actors' perspective: Who propagates a discourse, who adopts it, what are its strategic values and functions for particular actors? What are the practices in which this discursive activity is embedded?

- What are the media of dissemination, and how do they imprint on the semantics of a particular discourse?
- What are the communicative practices of dissemination, ranging from the everyday (like jokes) to the discourse of formal institutions (like education or administration)?

2. Implementation
a) Discourse as organising ways of thinking and talking:
   - How are social problems constructed and communicated through language? What are the normative and cultural assumptions underlying a given discourse?
   - How are issues defined and framed in such a way that they pose challenges for collective action or institutional change?
   - How does discourse (metaphors, story-lines, etc.) contribute to providing a cognitive and communicative framework for social practice (orienting actors, reducing contingency etc.)?
b) Discourse as organising ways of doing:
   - How are elements of a discourse translated into concrete policies and institutional arrangements?
   - What are the institutionalised practices that provide standardised ways for organising communication and implementing knowledge in administrative contexts (e.g. the use of scientific indicators, monitoring networks, expert committees, etc., cf. Muntigl, Weiss, and Wodak 2000; Wodak 2000)?
   - How are genres organised as ways of regulating interaction in institutional settings?
   - How are sub-political practices (such as scientific studies, information campaigns etc.) influenced by discourse and vice versa?

Again, it should be noted that it is the objectives and research questions of any particular study which should determine which concepts and methods are applied. Such a problem-oriented approach implies an eclectic use of theories and methods. A variety of data from multiple public spaces can be used, while the interpretation of particular texts should be linked to an examination of the practices and contexts they are embedded in.[10] Interdisciplinarity, in terms of theory, fieldwork and research teams, is thus called for.

Notes

1 A previous version of this research paper was presented at a meeting of the Language, Ideology and Power Group, Department of Linguistics and English Language, Lancaster University. Insights gathered from the discussion greatly benefited this article. I also would like to thank the colleagues who advised me on the literature in their respective disciplines, Teun van Dijk, Karin Liebhart, Oswald Panagl, and Martin Reisigl, as well as Ruth Wodak and Veronika Koller for their critical comments. The responsibility for what follows lies entirely with the author.

2 A historically oriented linguistics had developed in Germany since the beginning of the 19th century (See 1984: 242; cf. also Gardt 1999).

3 For English language publications see section 2.2 below as well as the literature review by van Dijk (1997). Reviews of publications in political communication (Johnston 1990; Kaid 2004) reveal that dissemination and implementation have not figured among the central topics of research in this field. – For French discourse analysis, I want to draw particular attention to the rich research on the "semiotics" of the French Revolution published since the late 1970s (cf. Guilhaumou 1989).

4 Already in the 19th century, various dictionaries of political communication were published. After 1945, dictionaries of language use in the National-Socialist era were among the first books in language and politics (e.g. Sternberger, Storz, and Süßkind 1957; Berning 1964).

5 "Hiermit wird deutlich, daß Begriffe zwar politische und soziale Inhalte erfassen, daß aber ihre semantische Funktion, ihre Leistungsfähigkeit nicht allein aus den sozialen und politischen Gegebenheiten ableitbar ist, auf die sie sich beziehen. Ein Begriff ist nicht nur Indikator der von ihm erfaßten Zusammenhänge, er ist auch deren Faktor. Mit jedem Begriff werden bestimmte Horizonte, aber auch Grenzen möglicher Erfahrung und denkbarer Theorie gesetzt." [This shows that concepts do grasp political and social phenomena, but that their semantic function and potential cannot be inferred only from the social and political realities they refer to. A concept is not only an indicator of the phenomena that it grasps, but it is also a factor. Every concept sets certain horizons and limits of possible experience and of conceivable theory.] (Koselleck 1989: 120)

6 Studying interdiscursive relationships entails reconstructing how meaning is transferred between various domains, how cognitive models from one domain (e.g. science) are used in another domain (e.g. politics), and how metaphors play a fundamental role for structuring discourse. The well-documented history of the dissemination of racist discourses since the 18th century provides an excellent example of this (cf. Weingart, Kroll, and Bayertz 1992; Hannaford 1996; Weikart 2004).

7 Recently, Ludwig Jäger (2004: 69–74) proposed the concept of "transcriptivity" for conceptualising processes of translation, transformation and "remediatisation" which are immanent to the generation of meaning. Such a research programme implies shifting the focus from content to operations and media, i.e.: What are the characteristics and preconditions of language use in politics, and how are political concepts integrated, employed and applied? Which concepts and which elements of, say, scientific discourses lend themselves to be transcribed in political contexts, and which do not? What functions does the implementation of concepts

from external sources play in various political contexts (e.g., reducing contingency, legitimising decisions)?
8   Gumperz (1968: 219) characterised a speech community as "any human aggregate characterized by regular and frequent interactions by means of a shared body of verbal signs and set off from similar aggregates by significant difference in language usage." Administrative codes or trade languages are used as examples of "shared language".
9   Reisigl and Wodak (2001) distinguished the following political "fields of action": legislation, self-presentation, the manufacturing of public opinion, developing party-internal consent, advertising and vote-getting, governing as well as executing, and controlling as well as expressing (oppositional) dissent. Particularly extensive literature is available on parliamentary debates (e.g. Bayley 2004; Ilie 2005).
10 Victor Klemperer ([1946] 2000), in his famous *Lingua Tertii Imperii*, already demonstrated such a broad use of quantitative as well as qualitative data. For recent examples of how to integrate fieldwork and ethnography with methods of text analysis, the discourse-historical research done by Ruth Wodak and co-workers can be referred to (cf. Wodak et al. 1999; Muntigl, Weiss, and Wodak 2000; Krzyżanowski and Oberhuber 2007; for an introduction to methodology, Wodak and Meyer 2001).

References

Baker, Susan, Maria Kousis, Dick Richardson and Stephen Yound (eds.)
    1997   *The Politics of Sustainable Development: Theory, Policy and Practice within the European Union*. London/New York: Routledge.
Bayley, Paul
    2004   *Cross-Cultural Perspectives on Parliamentary Discourse*. Amsterdam: Benjamins.
Berning, Cornelia
    1964   *Vom "Abstammungsnachweis" zum "Zuchtwart": Vokabular des Nationalsozialismus*. Berlin/New York: de Gruyter.
Böke, Karin
    1995   "Männer und Frauen sind gleichberechtigt": Schlüsselwörter in der frauenpolitischen Diskussion seit der Nachkriegszeit. In: Georg Stötzel and Martin Wengeler (eds.), *Kontroverse Begriffe: Geschichte des öffentlichen Sprachgebrauchs in der Bundesrepublik Deutschland*, 447–516. Berlin/New York: de Gruyter.
Böke, Karin
    1996   Politische Leitvokabeln in der Adenauer-Ära: Zu Theorie und Methodik. In: Böke, Karin, Frank Liedtke and Martin Wengeler (eds.), *Politische Leitvokabeln in der Adenauer-Ära. Mit einem Beitrag von Dorothee Dengel*, 19–50. Berlin/New York: de Gruyter.
Böke, Karin, Frank Liedtke and Martin Wengeler
    1996   *Politische Leitvokabeln in der Adenauer-Ära: Mit einem Beitrag von Dorothee Dengel*. Berlin/New York: de Gruyter.

Brunner, Otto, Werner Conze and Reinhart Koselleck
  1972–1997   *Geschichtliche Grundbegriffe: Historisches Lexikon zur politisch-sozialen Sprache in Deutschland*, 8 Volumes. Stuttgart: Klett-Cotta.
Burkhardt, Armin
  1996   Politolinguistik: Versuch einer Ortsbestimmung. In: Josef Klein and Hajo Diekmannshenke (eds.), *Sprachstrategien und Dialogblockaden: Linguistische und politikwissenschaftliche Studien zur politischen Kommunikation*, 76–100. (Sprache, Politik, Öffentlichkeit 7.) Berlin/New York: de Gruyter.
Busse, Dietrich
  1987   *Historische Semantik: Analyse eines Programms*. Stuttgart: Klett-Cotta.
Checkel, Jeffrey T.
  2004   Social constructivisms in global and European politics (a review essay). *Review of International Studies* 30(2): 229–244.
Chouliaraki, Lilie
  1995   Regulation in "progressivist" pedagogic discourse: individualized teacher-pupil talk. *Discourse & Society* 9(1): 5–32.
Chouliaraki, Lilie and Norman Fairclough
  1999   *Discourse in Late Modernity: Rethinking Critical Discourse Analysis*. Edinburgh: Edinburgh University Press.
Diekmannshenke, Hajo
  2001   Politische Kommunikation im historischen Wandel: Ein Forschungsüberblick. In: Hajo Diekmannshenke (ed.), *Politische Kommunikation im historischen Wandel*, 1–27. Tübingen: Stauffenberg Verlag.
Dryzek, John S.
  1997   *The Politics of the Earth: Environmental Discourses*. Oxford: Oxford University Press.
Fairclough, Norman
  1989   *Language and Power*. London: Longman.
Fairclough, Norman
  1992   *Discourse and Social Change*. Cambridge: Polity Press.
Fairclough, Norman
  2003   *Analyzing Discourse: Textual Analysis for Social Research*. London: Routledge.
Fairclough, Norman
  2005   Critical Discourse Analysis in transdisciplinary research. In: Ruth Wodak and Paul Chilton (eds.), *A New Agenda in (Critical) Discourse Analysis: Theory, Methodology and Interdisciplinarity*, 53–70. Amsterdam: Benjamins.
Fairclough, Norman
  2007   Discourse Transition in Central and Eastern Europe. In: Shi-xu (ed.), *Discourse as Cultural Struggle*, 49–72. Hong Kong: Hong Kong University Press.
Fairclough, Norman and Ruth Wodak
  1997   Critical Discourse Analysis. In: Teun A. van Dijk (ed.), *Discourse as Social Interaction*. Volume 2. *Discourse Studies*, 258–283. London: Sage.
Fischer, Frank and Michael Black (eds.)
  1995   *Greening Environmental Policy – The Politics of a Sustainable Future*. London: Paul Champman.

Foucault, Michel
[1977]   *Discipline and Punish: The Birth of the Prison.* Transl. A. Sheridan New York: Random House.
Foucault, Michel
1982   The subject and power. In: Hubert L. Dreyfus and Paul Rabinow (eds.), *Michel Foucault: Beyond Structuralism and Hermeneutics*, 208–226. Chicago: University of Chicago Press.
Gardt, Andreas
1999   *Geschichte der Sprachwissenschaft in Deutschland: Vom Mittelalter bis ins 20. Jahrhundert.* Berlin/New York: de Gruyter.
Girnth, Heiko
2002   *Sprache und Sprachverwendung in der Politik: Eine Einführung in die linguistische Analyse öffentlich-politischer Kommunikation.* Tübingen: Niemeyer.
Guilhaumou, Jacques
1989   *La langue politique et la Révolution Française. De l'événement à la raison linguistique.* Paris: Méridiens/Klincksieck.
Gumperz, John
1968   The speech community. In: Pier Paolo Giglioli (ed.), *Language and Social Context*, 219–231. London: Penguin Books.
Hajer, Maarten A.
1995   *The Politics of Environmental Discourse: Ecological Modernization and the Policy Process.* Oxford: Clarendon Press.
Hajer, Maarten A. and Frank Fischer
1999   Beyond global discourse: the rediscovery of culture in environmental politics. In: Frank Fischer and Maarten A. Hajer (eds.), *Living with Nature: Environmental Politics as Cultural Discourse*, 1–20. Oxford: Oxford University Press.
Hannaford, Ivan
1996   *Race: The History of an Idea in the West.* Baltimore: Johns Hopkins University Press.
Herrmanns, Fritz
1995   Sprachgeschichte als Mentalitätsgeschichte: Überlegungen zu Sinn und Form und Gegenstand historischer Semantik. In: Gardt, Andreas, Klaus J. Mattheier and Oskar Reichmann (eds.), *Sprachgeschichte des Neuhochdeutschen: Gegenstände, Methoden, Theorien*, 69–101. Tübingen: Niemeyer.
Iedema, Rick
1997   The language of administration: organizing human activity in formal institutions. In: Frances Christie and James R. Martin (eds.), *Genre and Institutions: Social Processes in the Workplace and School*, 73–100. London: Cassell.
Iedema, Rick and Ruth Wodak
1999   Introduction: organizational discourses and practices. *Discourse & Society* 10(1): 5–19.
Ilie, Cornelia
2005   Parliamentary discourses. In: Keith Brown (ed.), *Encyclopedia of Language and Linguistics*, 2nd ed. Oxford: Elsevier.

Jäger, Ludwig
    2004   Die Verfahren der Medien: Transkribieren – Adressieren – Lokalisieren. In: Jürgen Fohrmann and Erhard Schüttpelz (eds.), *Die Kommunikation der Medien*, 69–79. Tübingen: Niemeyer.

Johnston, Anne
    1990   Selective bibliography of political communication, 1982–1988. In: David L. Swanson and Dan Nimmo (eds.), *New Directions in Political Communication: A Resource Book*, 363–389. Newbury Park: Sage.

Jupille, Joseph, James A. Caporaso and Jeffrey T. Checkel
    2003   Integrating institutions: rationalism, constructivism, and the study of the European Union. *Comparative Political Studies* 36 (1–2) (special issue): 7–40.

Kaid, Lynda Lee (ed.)
    2004   *Handbook of Political Communication Research*. Mahwah, NJ: Erlbaum.

Klein, Josef and Hajo Diekmannshenke (eds.)
    1996   *Sprachstrategien und Dialogblockaden: Linguistische und politikwissenschaftliche Studien zur politischen Kommunikation.* (Sprache, Politik, Öffentlichkeit, Vol. 7) Berlin/New York: Walter de Gruyter.

Klemperer, Victor
    2000   *The Language of the Third Reich: LTI, Lingua Tertii Imperii: a Philologist's Notebook.* London: Athlone Press. First published [1946].

Koselleck, Reinhart
    1989   Begriffsgeschichte und Sozialgeschichte. In: Reinhart Koselleck, *Vergangene Zukunft: Zur Semantik geschichtlicher Zeiten*, 107–129. Frankfurt/Main: Suhrkamp.

Kovács, Andras and Ruth Wodak (eds.)
    2003   *NATO, Neutrality and National Identity: The Case of Austria and Hungary.* Vienna et al.: Böhlau.

Krzyżanowski, Michał and Florian Oberhuber
    2007   *(Un) Doing Europe: Discourse and Practices in Negotiating the EU Constitution.* Brüssels, etc.: P.I.E.-Peter Lang.

Lakoff, George and Mark Johnson
    1980   *Metaphors We Live By.* Chicago: University of Chicago Press.

Lakoff, George
    2004   *Don't Think of an Elephant! Know Your Values and Frame the Debate: The Essential Guide for Progressives.* White River Junction: Chelsea Green.

Loos, Eugène
    2004   Composing "panacea texts" at the European Parliament: an intertextual perspective on text production in a multilingual community. *Journal of Language and Politics* 3/(1): 3–24.

Luke, Timothy W.
    1995   Sustainable development as a power/knowledge system: the problem of "governmentality". In: Frank Fischer and Michael Black (eds.), *Greening Environmental Policy: The Politics of a Sustainable Future*, 21–32. London: Paul Chapman.

McGregor, Andrew
    2004   Sustainable development and "warm fuzzy feelings": discourse and nature within Australian environmental imaginaries. *Geoforum* 35: 593–606.

Meyer, Michael
  2001 Between theory, method, and politics: positioning of the approaches to CDA. In: Ruth Wodak and Michael Meyer (eds.), *Methods of Critical Discourse Analysis*, 14–31. London: Sage.
Muntigl, Peter, Gilbert Weiss and Ruth Wodak
  2000 *European Union Discourses on Un/employment: An Interdisciplinary Approach to Employment Policy-Making and Organizational Change.* Amsterdam: Benjamins.
Oexle, Otto Gerhard
  1996 *Geschichtswissenschaft im Zeichen des Historismus: Studien zu Problemgeschichten der Moderne.* Göttingen: Vandenhoeck & Ruprecht.
Panagl, Oswald and Ruth Wodak (eds.)
  2004 *Text und Kontext: Theoriemodelle und methodische Verfahren im transdisziplinären Vergleich.* Würzburg: Königshausen & Neumann.
Peet, Richard and Michael Watts
  1996 Liberation ecology: development, sustainability, and environment in an age of market triumphalism. In: Richard Peet and Michael Watts (eds.), *Liberation Ecologies: Environment, Development, Social Movements*, 1–45. London/New York: Routledge.
Polenz, Peter von
  1991 *Deutsche Sprachgeschichte: Vom Spätmittelalter bis zur Gegenwart*, Volume 1. Berlin/New York: de Gruyter.
Polenz, Peter von
  1999 *Deutsche Sprachgeschichte: Vom Spätmittelalter bis zur Gegenwart*, Volume 3, 19. und 20. Jahrhundert. Berlin/New York: de Gruyter.
Reisigl, Martin and Ruth Wodak
  2001 *Discourse and Discrimination: Rhetorics of Racism and Antisemitism.* London: Routledge.
Rydin, Yvonne
  1999 Can we talk ourselves into sustainability?: The role of discourse in the environmental policy process. *Environmental Values* 8: 467–484.
Rydin, Yvonne
  2003 *Conflict, Consensus, and Rationality in Environmental Planning: An Institutional Discourse Approach.* Oxford: Oxford University Press.
Schäffner, Christina and Anita L. Wenden (eds.)
  1995 *Language and Peace.* Dartmouth: Aldershot.
Schön, Donald A.
  1979 Generative metaphor: a perspective on problem-setting in social policy. In: Andrew Ortony (ed.), *Metaphor and Thought*, 254–283. Cambridge: Cambridge University Press.
See, Klaus von
  1984 Politisch-soziale Interessen in der Sprachgeschichtsforschung des 19. und 20. Jahrhunderts. In: Besch, Werner, Anne Betten, Oskar Reichmann and Stefan Sonderegger (eds.), *Sprachgeschichte: Ein Handbuch zur Geschichte der deutschen Sprache und ihrer Erforschung*, Volume 1, 242–257. Berlin/New York: de Gruyter.
Sternberger, Dolf, Gerhard Storz and Wilhelm E. Süßkind
  1957 *Aus dem Wörterbuch des Unmenschen.* Hamburg/Düsseldorf: Claassen.

Stötzel, Georg and Martin Wengeler (eds.)
  1995   *Kontroverse Begriffe: Geschichte des öffentlichen Sprachgebrauchs in der Bundesrepublik Deutschland*. Berlin/New York: de Gruyter.
Torgerson, Douglas
  1995   The uncertain quest for sustainability: public discourse and the politics of environmentalism. In: Frank Fischer and Michael Black (eds.), *Greening Environmental Policy: The Politics of a Sustainable Future*, 3–20. London: Paul Chapman.
van Dijk, Teun A.
  1997   What is political discourse analysis? In: Jan Blommaert and Chris Bulcaen (eds.), *Political Linguistics*, 11–52. [Belgian Journal of Linguistics 11.] Amsterdam: Benjamins.
Weikart, Richard
  2004   *From Darwin to Hitler: Evolutionary Ethics, Eugenics, and Racism in Germany*. New York: Palgrave.
Weingart, Peter, Jürgen Kroll and Kurt Bayertz
  1992   *Rasse, Blut und Gene: Geschichte der Eugenik und Rassenhygiene in Deutschland*. Frankfurt/Main: Suhrkamp.
Wengeler, Martin
  1995   "Der alte Streit 'hier Marktwirtschaft, dort Planwirtschaft' ist vorbei": Ein Rückblick auf die sprachlichen Aspekte wirtschaftspolitischer Diskussionen. In: Georg Stötzel and Martin Wengeler (eds.), *Kontroverse Begriffe: Geschichte des öffentlichen Sprachgebrauchs in der Bundesrepublik Deutschland*, 35–91. Berlin/New York: de Gruyter.
Williams, Colin C. and Andrew C. Millington
  2004   The diverse and contested meanings of sustainable development. *The Geographical Journal* 170(2): 99–104.
Wodak, Ruth. (ed.)
  1989   *Language, Power and Ideology: Studies in Political Discourse*. Amsterdam: Benjamins.
Wodak, Ruth
  2000   Recontextualization and the transformation of meanings: A critical discourse analysis of decision making in EU-meetings about employment policies. In: Srikant Sarangi and Malcolm Coulthard (eds.), *Discourse and Social Life*, 185–206. London: Pearson.
Wodak, Ruth, Rudolf de Cillia, Martin Reisigl and Karin Liebhart
  1999   *The Discursive Construction of National Identity*. Edinburgh: Edinburgh University Press.
Wodak, Ruth and Michael Meyer (eds.)
  2001   *Methods of Critical Discourse Analysis*. London: Sage.

13. The contribution of critical linguistics to the analysis of discriminatory prejudices and stereotypes in the language of politics

Ruth Wodak

1. Introduction

What form of "discrimination" are we talking about? Racism, ethnicism, difference, discrimination, multiculturalism.

The spectre of a new cultural racism is often invoked as a feature of present-day patterns of social exclusion and is, moreover, related to the existence of a more deeply rooted structural racism pervading some of the key institutions of contemporary society, in particular those pertaining to politics, the media, work, education, housing and state services. Racism, it would appear, despite the absence of clearly defined "races", is alive and well. But how pervasive is it and what kind of claims can be made about the relation between the obvious reality of racial inequality and social exclusion, on the one side, and the extent of racial discrimination within politics, social institutions and in everyday life on the other?

This chapter, of course, is not able to cover all these challenging dimensions. I will focus primarily on investigating discriminatory practices in various domains of politics from a critical perspective. Thus patterns of everyday racism will have to be neglected (see Essed 1991, Delanty and Wodak 2005); moreover, I am restricting myself to research on xenophobic, racist and anti-Semitic discriminatory practices (see Lazar, this volume, for other dimensions of discrimination).

In the following, after defining the notions of "difference/discrimination/racism", I will first summarize salient issues of Critical Linguistics[1] related to the field of politics (and related to it, media). Then important theoretical approaches in Critical Discourse Analysis on politics and discrimination will be briefly discussed. One example of an interview with a politician on TV will serve to illustrate the impact of such research. Due to space restrictions, I will have to refer readers to an extensive bibliography for more details.

At this point, I would like to emphasize a *caveat:* One way of looking at discourses of difference/discrimination is to examine the ways in which minorities or migrants actually experience racial discrimination in European societies today. Such an analysis will not and can not lead us to a casual explanation of racial inequality, but it will provide relevant knowledge about the many facets of racial discrimination from the perspective of the marginalized and vulnerable – i.e. "insider" perspective (see Delanty, Jones, and Wodak 2007; Krzyżanowski and Wodak 2007).[2]

The other way to proceed is from "outside", investigating the arenas where politics are performed, such as parliamentary discourses, election campaigns, public speeches, media reporting, and so forth. In these cases, we study discourses *about* minorities, as well as the frequently to be observed positive self-presentation of politicians which manifests itself, *inter alia*, in disclaimers and in the denial of racism.[3] This necessarily implies that we are confronted with a gap between self-assessment and other-assessment which can only be bridged in small ways, but never in its entirety (for example, by data triangulation, trans- and interdisciplinarity, and so forth; Weiss and Wodak 2003).

In this chapter I rely on a working definition of racism which considers at least two levels: the level of ideology and beliefs (about groups, minorities, "others") and the level of social practices (Who is included? Who is excluded?) (see also van Dijk 2005a). Moreover, it is important to stress that the term "racism" means different things in different languages: in English there is a tendency to label any discrimination as "racist" whereas in German, due to the semantic history of the terms (i.e. in National-Socialism), only biologically constructed inferiority is accounted for by the terms *rassistisch* or *Rasse*. Clearly not all discrimination experienced by migrants, for example, is racist in a sense that is universally acceptable. I have to neglect a more detailed discussion of the terminology here; however, this historical semantic tradition also accounts for major methodological difficulties in cross-cultural or cross-national comparison (see Reisigl and Wodak 2001 for an extensive discussion).

2. What is the New Racism? Difference and discrimination

Much discussed in recent times is the emergence of new kinds of racism in European societies, often referred to as "Euro-racism", "symbolic racism", "cultural racism", or, in France, a *racisme differentiel* (Holmes 2000; Macmaster 2001). While these approaches differ, there is widespread agreement that racism in Europe is on the increase and that its main feature is hostility to immigrants, refugees and asylum-seekers, who are often the new "Others". In this respect the new European racism is characterized by a focus of hostility that is not exclusively defined by the traditional terms of colour and race that were typical of "biological" racism in the industrial and colonial period. In many European countries the extreme right has refined their electoral programs under the rubric of nationalist-populist slogans and has adopted more subtle (i.e. coded) forms of racism (Wodak and Pelinka 2002; Rydgren 2003, 2005).

The move away from overt neo-fascist discourse has in fact allowed these parties to expand their electoral support as populist-nationalist parties (Delanty and O'Mahony 2002). This has paradoxically led to an increase in racist discourse, not to its decline, since racism often takes more pervasive, diffuse forms, frequently to the point of being expressed in the denial of racism (van Dijk 1989). There is considerable evidence of a normalization of racism in political discourse, and there is much to indicate that this is also occurring on all levels of discourse, ranging from the media to political parties and institutions (*Race and Class* 2001) to everyday life.

The distinctive feature of this is a confluence of racism and xenophobia. The "new" racism differs from the older kinds in that it is not expressed in overtly racist terms or in the terms of neo-fascist discourse, for instance by some notion of biological or racial superiority, white supremacy or skin colour. Instead, the repertoires of justification that are typically employed use social characteristics (e.g. protecting jobs, concern about welfare benefits) or cultural incompatibilities (immigrants lack "cultural competence", they are not "tolerant"). The new racism exploits xenophobic frames (fear of the "other"), ethnocentrism, masculinities, and "ordinary" prejudice in subtle ways and often, too, in ways that are subconscious or routinized (Wodak and van Dijk 2000; Geden 2005). For these reasons the new racism can be termed "xeno-racism", a mixture of racism and xenophobia. While being racist in substance, it is xenophobic in form: its outward defensive mode of expression disguises a stronger opposition to migrants and the continuation of racism in a new guise (Fekete 2001; Sivanandan 2001).

The new racism has also incorporated a *quasi* anti-racism into it, thus diffusing criticism. In ways that have been documented on the level of political discourse, but are not yet fully understood in wider socio-cognitive processes, liberal values are inverted. In this way, multiculturalism seems to become a defense of the "national" culture and of "tolerance" and thus becomes an argument to keep communities separate (this is why minorities reject the term "tolerance" and propose "acceptance, recognition and respect" instead).[4] This confluence of "nation and race" is occurring at a time when the nation-state is undergoing major transformations, and there are, as yet, unclear implications of EU enlargement. Where nationalism was once defined by reference to other nations, in the current post-industrial/information societies, nationalism is becoming more defensive and defined by reference to immigrants and other marginalized groups.[5]

Moreover, the border between xeno-racism and the more overt and explicit neo-fascist racism is frequently blurred in political discourse. In everyday discourse ordinary people tend to be more susceptible to xeno-racism than to the more explicit messages of neo-fascist racism (Essed 1991).

In order to capture the multidimensional nature of racism the concept of *syncretic racism* lends itself, which encompasses everyday racism, xeno-racism and other concepts of racism (such as racialisation, otherism etc). By *syncretic racism* I mean the construction of differences which serve ideological, political and/or practical discrimination on all levels of society. Old and new stereotypes form a mixed bag of exclusionary practices, they are used whenever seen to be politically expedient – such as in gaining votes.[6] It is a "racism without races" in which the discourse of racism has become removed from any direct relation with a specific constructed racial subject (Jews, Blacks, Roma), and is similar to an "empty discourse" (analogous to an "empty signifier" in the view of Ernesto Laclau and Chantal Mouffe) in which xenophobic attitudes are combined with racist stereotypes.

3. The discursive construction of US and THEM: The racialized subject

Who is the subject of the racist discourse constructed and disseminated by different agents and actors in the public sphere? There are at least three important points to be made here (see Delanty and Wodak 2005):

– First, the racialized subject today is different from the past in that skin colour and physical signs of racial difference are less important. Perhaps it is for this reason that "the veil and the scarf" have become key symbols of racially constructed "others" today and the debate about them has become integral to liberal values rather than to any direct assertions about inferiority. A significant number are poor whites and come from within Europe and are not identifiable in "race" terms (which is not to suggest that they are not racialized) (Richardson 2004).
– Second, non-European migrants generally fall into two categories, asylum-seekers or refugees on the one hand, and migrants from (East) Asia on the other. The first group are more likely to come from Africa, Afghanistan, Iran, and Russia and are smaller in number than other racialized groups. The second group is more likely to come from Asia and is more likely to be educated and, unlike refugees, have a quasi permanent right to work in areas of the economy that require professionally qualified workers. The new semantic process used here in public discourses is to conflate two notions, *refugees* with *migrants*, and to push both groups discursively into "criminality" and "illegality". How would one otherwise, for example, explain the term "illegal refugees"?[7]
– The third category presents the greatest difficulty for any comparative study since it calls into question the adequacy of the notion of "migrant". Migrants do not constitute a coherent group that is homogeneous, in which all "others" who are not national citizens can be subsumed. Indeed, it could be argued that if "migrant" refers to non-national citizens, it fails to address some of the most pervasive forms of racial discrimination, namely that associated with ethnic and/or religious groups and "others" who have already obtained citizenship in an EU country (Camus 2005).

We are thus presented with the paradox that the racialized subject is not easily connected with a simple and clear-cut person or group. The extreme example of this is the existence of strong anti-Semitism in Poland, where Jews do not exist in any numerical sense and yet anti-Semitism is rife. Bernd Marin has labelled this phenomenon, also true for Austria, as "anti-Semitism without Jews and without anti-Semites" (because of the contrast between the constant denial of being anti-Semitic in public discourses and the results of opinion polls which prove that anti-Semitism is strongest when no Jews live in the respective area and, moreover, when the interviewees have never met any in person) (Marin 2000).

What this finally draws attention to is the discursive nature of racism. Racism exists without concrete or observable "races"; it is bound up in language and proliferates in our societies on all levels in many subtle ways.

Differences between various social groups take on a negative character. It is not the existence of differences that produces discrimination or racism, but the generalization of such differences into negative categories and their attribution to whole groups, which constitutes stereotyping. Each individual experience with a foreigner, Jew, gay person etc. is viewed as explanatory for the whole group (while, interestingly, positive experiences with migrants, Jews, Others, are classified as exceptions).

Within the system of racism, discourse may be used to problematize, marginalize, exclude or otherwise limit the human rights of ethnic/religious/minority out-groups. Such may be the case either by direct discriminatory discourse in interaction with "Others", or indirectly by writing or speaking negatively *about* the Other.[8]

The discursive construction of US and THEM is thus the foundation of prejudiced and racist perceptions and discourses. This discursive construction starts with the labelling of social actors, proceeds to the generalization of negative attributions and then elaborates arguments to justify the exclusion of many and inclusion of some. The discursive realizations can be more or less intensified or mitigated, more or less implicit or explicit, due to historical conventions, public levels of tolerance, political correctness, the specific context, and public sphere.

4. Discourse/text/politics

Critical research in the field of language, politics and discrimination has expanded enormously in recent years.[9] According to the underlying theoretical approach the notion of discourse is often defined in many different ways. Since the 70s and 80s this notion has been subject to manifold semantic interpretations (see Reisigl 2004 for a recent discussion of the concepts of discourse). In the analysis of discourse and politics, the meaning of the notion of discourse is therefore closely linked to the respective research context and theoretical approach. Possible definitions range from a "promiscuous use of 'text' and 'discourse'" (Ehlich 2000), as it may be found predominantly in Anglo-Saxon approaches, to a strict definition from the perspective of linguistic pragmatics (see Lemke 1995; Titscher et al. 2000).

The notion of politics is also defined in many different ways depending on the theoretical framework. It ranges from a wide extension of the concept according to which every social utterance or practice of the human as a *zoon politikon* is "political", to a notion of politics referring only to the use of language by politicians in various settings and in political institutions:

> On the one hand, politics is viewed as a struggle for power, between those who seek to assert their power and those who seek to resist it. On the other hand, politics is viewed as cooperation, as the practices and institutions that a society has for resolving clashes of interest over money, influence, liberty, and the like. (Chilton 2004: 3)

Chilton (2004) embraces an interactive view of politics, which cuts through both of the above-mentioned dimensions. This is also the perspective endorsed in this chapter.

Furthermore, it is important to define the political domains and the genres which are relevant in this field (in the sense of Bourdieu's theory of fields, habitus and capitals). The most important domains can thus be summarized in Figure 1.

Reviewing the relevant theoretical concepts and studies, the following issues will be discussed in this chapter:

> a) How wide or narrow should political action (or political language behaviour) be defined? Should one restrict oneself to the study of the traditional political genres (like speeches, slogans, debates) or are all everyday actions in some way "political" and can all of them be functionalized for discriminatory means?
> b) What is the role of the political elites? Who determines political issues? Who produces and reproduces discrimination? These questions lead to the debate about possible causalities: "top down" or "bottom up"? Do people believe what politicians (or the media) tell them? Do citizens influence the slogans in an election campaign, etc.? What about grass root movements that exist increasingly outside party politics?
> c) Politics is tied to ideologies, party programs, opinion leaders, and political interests. How do ideologies and belief systems manifest themselves in various genres of political discourse? How are *topoi* and arguments recontextualized through various genres and public spaces? Which arguments and discursive strategies are frequently used for discriminatory purposes?

There are certainly many more related questions, such as the influence of globalizing processes, language change or the change of political rhetoric and its functions over time (Kovács and Wodak 2003; Mokre, Weiss, and Bauböck 2003; Beck 2004). In this chapter, I have to restrict myself to the functions of producing and reproducing stereotypes and racism in the public field of politics.

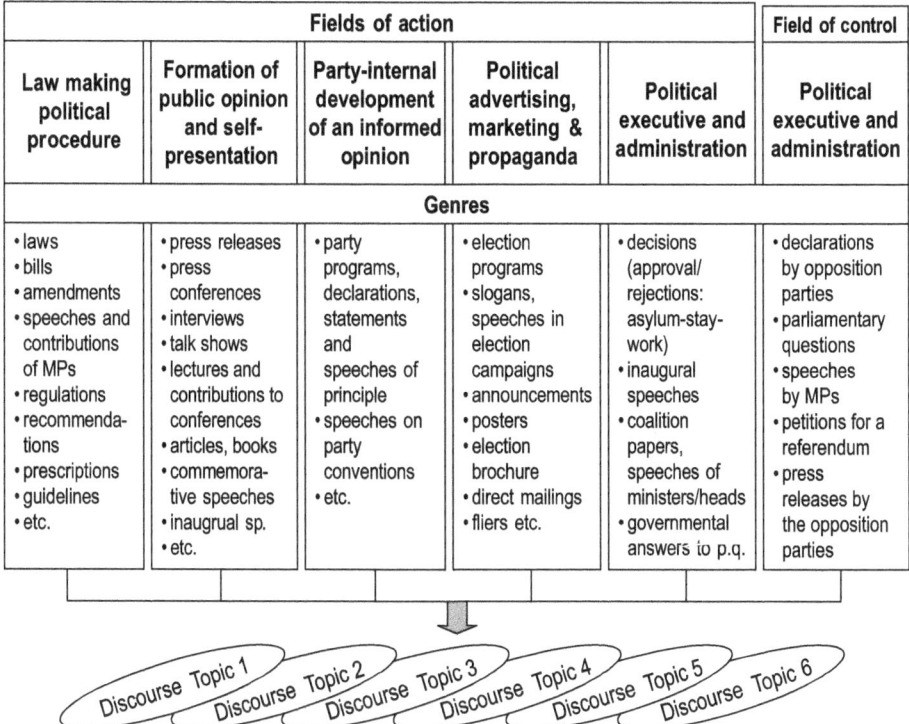

Figure 1. Selected dimensions of Discourse as Social Practice (see Wodak 2001).

5. Critical Linguistics and Critical Discourse Analysis

The terms Critical Linguistics (CL) and Critical Discourse Analysis (CDA) are often used interchangeably. In fact, it seems that the term Critical Discourse Analysis is preferred and is used to denote the approaches formerly identified as Critical Linguistics. Critical Discourse Analysis sees "language as social practice" (Fairclough and Wodak 1997), and considers the context of language use to be crucial (Anthonissen 2001; Weiss and Wodak 2003; Wodak and Weiss 2004a,b). Critical Linguistics and Critical Discourse Analysis may be defined as fundamentally interested in analyzing opaque as well as transparent structural relationships of dominance, discrimination, power and control, as they are manifested in language. Four concepts figure indispensably in all Critical Discourse Analysis: the concepts of critique, of power, of history, and of ideology. Let me elaborate these in turn:

"Critique" carries many different meanings. Some adhere to the Frankfurt School, others to a notion of literary criticism, some to Marx's notions (Reisigl and Wodak 2001; Sayer 2006 for overviews). Basically, "critical" could be understood as having distance to the data, embedding the data in the social, making the respective political stance explicit, and having a focus on self-reflection as scholars undertaking research. For all those concerned with Critical Discourse Analysis, application of the results is important, be it in practical seminars for teachers, doctors and bureaucrats or in the writing of expert opinions or devising schoolbooks.

Thompson (1990) discusses the concepts of ideology and culture and the relations between these concepts and certain aspects of mass communication. He points out that the concept of ideology first appeared in late 18th century France and has thus been in use for about two centuries. The term has been given a range of functions and meanings at different times. For Thompson, ideology refers to social forms and processes within which, and by means of which, symbolic forms circulate in the social world. Ideology, for Critical Discourse Analysis, is seen as an important means of establishing and maintaining unequal power relations. Critical Discourse Analysis takes a particular interest in the ways in which language mediates ideology in a variety of social institutions (see also Eagleton 1994).

Critical theories, thus also Critical Discourse Analysis, are afforded special standing as guides for human action. They are aimed at producing enlightenment. Such theories seek not only to describe and explain, but also to root out a particular kind of delusion. Even with differing concepts of ideology, critical theory seeks to create awareness in agents of how they might be deceived about their own needs and interests. This was, of course, taken up by Pierre Bourdieu's concepts of *violence symbolique* and *méconnaissance* (Bourdieu 1989). One of the aims of Critical Discourse Analysis is thus to "demystify" discourses by deciphering ideologies.

For Critical Discourse Analysis, language is not powerful on its own – it gains power by the use powerful people make of it. This explains why Critical Discourse Analysis often chooses the perspective of the vulnerable, and critically analyzes the language use of those in power, who are responsible for the existence of inequalities and who also have the means and the opportunity to improve conditions. In agreement with its Critical Theory predecessors, Critical Discourse Analysis emphasizes the need for interdisciplinary work in order to gain a proper understanding of how language functions in constituting and transmitting knowledge, in organizing social institutions or in exercising power.

An important perspective in Critical Discourse Analysis related to the notion of power is that it is very rare that a text is the work of any one person. In texts discursive differences are negotiated; they are governed by differences in power which is in part encoded in and determined by discourse and by genre. Therefore texts are often sites of struggle in that they show traces of differing ideologies contending and struggling for dominance (see also Jäger 2001).

Language provides a finely articulated vehicle for differences in power in hierarchical social structures. Very few linguistic forms have not at some stage been pressed into the service of the expression of power. Power is signalled not only by grammatical forms within a text, but also by a person's control of a social occasion by means of the genre of a text, or by access to certain public spheres. It is often exactly within the genres associated with given social occasions that power is exercised or challenged.

6. Different theoretical approaches to discourse, politics and discrimination

Chouliaraki and Fairclough (1999) illustrate extensively how Critical Discourse Analysis is useful in disclosing the discursive nature of much of contemporary social and cultural change. Particularly the language of the mass media is scrutinized as a site of struggle and social exclusion, and also as a site where language is apparently transparent. Media institutions often purport to be neutral in that they provide space for public discourse, that they reflect states of affairs disinterestedly, and that they give the perceptions and arguments of the newsmakers. Fairclough (1995) shows the fallacy of such assumptions, and illustrates the mediating and constructing role of the media with a variety of examples.

In critically analyzing various kinds of discourses that encode prejudice, van Dijk's interest lies in developing a theoretical model that explains cognitive processing mechanisms related to the production and reproduction of racism (van Dijk 1984). In his view, one of the main roles of discourse is the reproduction of social representations, such as knowledge, attitudes, ideologies, norms and values. This means that discourse constitutes the main interface between the social, emotional and cognitive dimensions of racism. On the one hand it may itself be a discriminatory social practice, and on the other, it expresses and helps reproduce the negative social representations (prejudices, etc.) that are socially shared. However, not all types of discourse are equally influential in the reproduction of society and of systems of domination such as racism. Obviously, public discourses are more influential throughout societies than private discourses, such as everyday conversations in the family, among neighbours or friends.

Those groups who are in control of most influential public discourses, that is symbolic elites such as politicians, journalists, scholars, teachers and writers, thus play a special role in the reproduction of dominant knowledge and ideologies in society (van Dijk 2003, 2004, 2005a). Since prejudices are not innate, but socially acquired, and since such acquisition is predominantly discursive, the public discourses of the symbolic elites are the primary source of shared ethnic prejudices and ideologies (van Dijk 1993). Popular racism, and its practices and discourse, are often based on, exacerbated or legitimated by such elite discourse and racism (van Leeuwen and Wodak 1999). It is unlikely for everyday discourses to have the widespread influence of public discourses such as parliamentary debates, news, TV programs, novels, movies or textbooks. Even when the media or politicians may "give voice" to popular racism, it is still the media and political elites who are responsible for this publication and reproduction in the public sphere. That is, the elites at least pre-formulate, legitimate or condone popular racism.

Obviously, the same arguments hold for the reproduction of antiracist practices and ideologies in society (van Dijk 1998). However, the antiracist elites in all domains of society – politics, media, education, research, etc. – have much less influence, and are themselves often problematized and marginalized (Pelinka and Wodak 2002).

A growing awareness in media studies of the importance of non-verbal aspects of texts has turned attention to semiotic devices in discourse other than linguistic ones. Particularly the theory put forward by Kress and van Leeuwen (2006) should be mentioned here, as this provides a useful framework for considering the communicative and also discriminatory potential of visual devices in the media and in politics. This type of work leads to a particular relation between discourse analysis, ethnography, history and theory in which these disciplines are no longer contributing to the whole through some kind of indefinable synergy or triangulation, but are complementary in quite specific ways. Van Leeuwen also focused on visual traits of carica tures in the media which manifest generalizing and racist traits/features (van Leeuwen and Jaworski 2003) and on specific sexist stereotypes as transmitted globally by the magazine *Cosmopolitan* (Machin and van Leeuwen 2003). Particularly, the latter research detects the power of white, upper middle-class feminine traits as symbolically prestigious and therefore selected as global role-models.

The discourse-historical approach created by Ruth Wodak and her collaborators at the University of Vienna combines theoretical discourse studies with ethnographic fieldwork and interdisciplinarity. The study for which the discourse-historical approach was actually developed tried to trace in detail the constitution of an anti-Semitic stereotyped image, or *Feindbild*, as it emerged in public discourse in the 1986 Austrian presidential campaign of Kurt Waldheim (Wodak et al. 1990; Wodak 2004, 2005).

To illustrate this context-dependent approach, I would like merely to mention some of the many layers of discourse investigated in the study of the Waldheim Affair. The context was that during the presidential election 1986, Waldheim had at first denied active involvement with Nazism and Nazi military operations in the Balkans. The data were collected from day to day during the whole election campaign and comprise a total set of the three months involved from March 3rd 1986 to June 6th 1986.

- There were documents of the *Wehrmacht* about the war in the Balkans in general, as well as documents relating specifically to Waldheim's activities there.
- There were also several statements and interviews with other *Wehrmacht* veterans who had served with Waldheim.
- One step removed from these was the research by historians on the Balkan war in general, and on Waldheim's wartime role specifically.
- At still another level there were the reports in Austrian newspapers on the Balkan war, on Waldheim's past, and on the historical research into war and Waldheim's role.
- There were reports in newspapers on Waldheim's own explanation of his past; on the other hand there was the reporting of all these previously mentioned aspects in foreign newspapers, especially in *The New York Times*.
- Simultaneously, the press releases and documents of the World Jewish Congress provided an autonomous informational and discursive source.
- Finally, apart from these, there were statements of and interviews with politicians, as well as the *vox populi* on all these topics.

Though sometimes tedious and very time consuming, such an approach allowed the recording of the varying perceptions, selections and distortions of information, i.e. the recontextualization of anti-Semitic *topoi*. As a result, we were able to trace in detail the constitution of an anti-Semitic stereotyped image, or *Feindbild*, of the "Others" as it emerged in public discourse in Austria in 1986 (see also Wodak and de Cillia 1988).

The discourse-historical approach has been further elaborated in a number of more recent studies, for example, on the genesis of discrimination and discourses of difference after 1989 (Wodak and Matouschek 1993; Matouschek, Wodak, and Januschek 1995), on right wing populist rhetoric as developed by Jörg Haider and the Freedom Party in Austria, on discourses about coming to terms with traumatic pasts as well as on the discursive construction of European identities.[10] Particularly, the complex mediation between context and text was further elaborated.

Five research questions have proven to be relevant for theoretical and methodological approaches to inclusion/exclusion from a discourse-historical perspective (Reisigl and Wodak 2001):

(1) How are persons named and referred to linguistically?
(2) What traits, characteristics, qualities and features are attributed to them?
(3) By what arguments and argumentation schemes do specific persons or social groups try to justify and legitimize the inclusion/exclusion of others?
(4) From what perspective or point of view are these labels, attributions and arguments expressed?
(5) Are the respective utterances articulated overtly, are they intensified or are they mitigated?

According to these questions, we are especially interested in five types of discursive strategies, which are all involved in positive self-presentation and negative other-presentation. By "strategy" we generally mean a more or less accurate and more or less intentional plan of practices (including discursive practices), adopted to achieve a particular social, political, psychological or linguistic aim. As far as the discursive strategies are concerned – that is to say, systematic ways of using language – we locate them at different levels of linguistic organization and complexity:

Strategy	Objective	Devices
reference/nomination	construction of in-groups and out-groups	membership categorization: biological, naturalizing and depersonalizing metaphors, metonymies and synecdoches (*pars pro toto, totum pro parte*)
predication	labeling social actors more or less positively or negatively, deprecatorily or appreciatively	stereotypical, evaluative attributions of negative or positive traits, implicit and explicit predicates
argumentation	justification of positive or negative attributions	*topoi* used to justify political inclusion or exclusion, discrimination or preferential treatment
perspectivization, framing or discourse representation	expressing involvement positioning speaker's point of view	reporting, description, narration or quotation of (discriminatory) events and utterances
intensification, mitigation	modifying the epistemic status of a proposition	intensifying or mitigating the illocutionary force or (discriminatory) utterances

Figure 2. Discursive strategies for positive self-presentation and negative other representation[11]

6. Example: Interviews with politicians on TV[12]

The Freedom Party in Austria (FPÖ), a rightwing populist party similar to Le Pen's Front National in France, launched a new party program in October 1997 which was discussed widely in the media. In contrast to the former positions of the Freedom Party, this new program contains two issues, which lead the party in a new direction and which – as they hoped – would attract new voters. Firstly, after having always been secular the Freedom Party adopts Christian values explicitly and underlines how important such values are for family life and everyday behaviour. Secondly, while originally rejecting patriotism and even labelling the Austrian nation *eine Mißgeburt* ("a freak birth"), they now champion the concept of an Austrian nation and Austrian patriotism. Jörg Haider, the then leader of the Freedom Party, was interviewed to comment on his party's new program.

The interviewer, Robert Hochner, was the most widely known moderator of the late evening news and known as an opponent to the ideas of the Freedom Party. The interview tradition in the Austrian Broadcast Company is very "soft" and avoids conflicts because politicians have been known to sue, claiming that they had been unfairly treated. Because of this, interviewers hold back with their opinions and allow the politicians much space to voice their positions and generally allow the interviewees a considerable margin of freedom in their answers. Austrian interview culture is thus very different from what we find in the United States or in Britain, both known for interviewers who are not afraid to challenge politicians openly.

> RH: "Doctor Haider, in this party-program, Christian values and the obligation to defend these Christian values are relatively strongly emphasized – uh, but there is no Christian xenophobia, Christianity does not distinguish between Austrians and foreigners and Christianity in fact obliges people – who don't have a lot, even to share what one has – how does – – does this in fact fit into the politics of your party?"
> JH: "First of all in that we are Christian when cutting back privileges because we are the only ones who are voluntarily making an income sacrifice – whereas, in times of the austerity package, from the Federal Chancellor right to all of the ministers, regional leaders, regional government members, everyone has given him- and herself the gift of salaryincreases. That's the first thing that's Christian about us. The second is – ah, that we take the words of the Pope seriously and – ah there – the cur- / current Pope made it very clear that neighbourly love really means to care for your immediate neighbour and not to embrace the whole world but also to think of the Austrians."
> RH: "So, your neigh- / the neighbour has to have an Austrian passport for you to love him."
> JH: "Not necessarily but he has to have a legal residency permit for th / this country because otherwise for us it'll be that one – ah – lets in illegals – and then in the end it creates a problem for the Austrians and the foreigners residing here legally. So, in that respect we are very much – on the basis of the rule of law – and because: / the

reactions of the government just show how we are completely on the right track, also with the – ah – "Austria First" principle that we are thinking about this country: and that we want to stop the sell-out, or rather an unrestrained immigration in any case." (see Appendix for the German text)

The first step of deconstructing this text applies the analysis by *topoi:* which argumentative strategies are employed and how pseudo-causalities and a certain logical argumentative structure are constructed:[13] On the one hand, Haider employs decontextualization and recontextualization (of the attribute Christian), on the other hand, he applies certain typical *topoi* which emphasize his arguments and give them authority. Moreover, through further references to other *topoi*, he discursively constructs salient discriminatory arguments. In a second step, I will consider some aspects of the microstructure of clauses on a syntactic level, to illustrate how the discourses of exclusion function on all levels of text and grammar.

Haider mainly exploits the *topos* of definition: He redefines a concept prominent in common knowledge and thus launches a new meaning into the public sphere. He subsequently presents a systematic three-step argument as to why the Freedom Party can be seen as being Christian. First of all, the Freedom Party has agreed to lower members' own salaries in an acknowledgment that "we are going through bad economic times. This is something none of the other parties have proposed or done; on the contrary, they have increased their salaries."

And then, employing the *topos of authority*, the pope is called on. "The pope has emphasized that we should be concerned about our neighbours." In an interesting twist, Haider proposes to take the meaning of neighbour literally: "our neighbours are those people close to us; that is, the Austrian people, and not the rest of the world." The pope's word can thus be interpreted, Haider suggests, as emphasizing that "we should consider Austrians and exclude foreigners", employing a pragmatic device, an implicature, as well as presupposing that the words of the pope would be acknowledged by all Austrians. In this way, the group of Austrians is constructed as being Catholic, thus excluding all people with other religious beliefs and labelling them as non-Austrians and non-neighbours.

This strategy is thus likely to have serious impact in a primarily Catholic country where the pope is highly respected. It was already put to good use during the petition "Austria First" in 1992/93 where the Freedom Party attempted to align their racist slogans with the statements of some Catholic bishops (see Reisigl and Wodak 2001).

The neighbours who could have been constructed as "the Other", which the interviewer tried to point to, are thus taken into the in–group and become insiders. Others (neighbours) in this sense are only Austrians and legal immigrants. Then there are positively evaluated others, the pope for example and other authorities. The "bad Others" are therefore construed as "foreigners" who are illegal and a threat. This *topos* is elaborated later. The *topos of being respon-*

sible for one's country and for the Austrians is central here. The FPÖ thus wants to present an image of being a state party, a party which could also be in government and not only in opposition (*positive self-presentation*).

Moreover, Haider emphasizes closeness and equality, not difference. Thus, he creates a possibility to identify with his argumentation because nobody would contradict the statement that politicians should think of their voters and be concerned for them (*argumentum ad populum*). This strategy of claiming positions which nobody would or could reject, is used to cover latent racist opinions and ideas. This argumentation device, of course, is an old rhetorical strategy which Haider combines with the *strawman principle*. Haider does this throughout the interview; he never comes close to uttering an explicit racist opinion. In alluding, however, to the "Austria First" petition of 1992/93 in his next turn, he presupposes previous and implicit knowledge of the contents of the petition, which were in some respects openly racist. But the petition is never really talked about in the interview and the interviewer does not challenge Haider on the issue of racism. But, because of the implicit accusation and insinuations of the moderator, Haider is enabled to push through his argumentation and employ all the above mentioned rhetorical devices, decontextualize and redefine central concepts and apply typical discriminating and populist *topoi*.

As always, interviews are interactions: other questions might have entailed other responses. But, an explicit accusation of being racist would have been easy to reject, as Haider himself stays with implicit presuppositions, insinuations, redefinitions and *topoi*. His attempt in presenting his party as responsible, considerate and "taking care of the real Austrians" is therefore successful. The cynical and ironic overtone of the moderator can not threaten such a discourse.

Moreover, clause analysis demonstrates how Haider delegates boundary drawing to the grammar, thereby rendering it "unseen" for most except discourse analysts (see Wodak and Iedema 2004). First, and more specifically, Haider reserves verbs to do with thinking, feeling and knowing (i.e. mental-affective processes) for those associated with the Freedom Party. And he allocates doing verbs (material and behavioural processes) to the "Other" ("An additional 150 000 people from Eastern Europe will enter Austria"). This strategy implies that people "on our side" are thinking and feeling human beings. The "Other" engages in material and behavioural acts only, with little or no ability to give their actions intellectual or moral depth.

Second, discriminatory statements are attributed to others, like the pope, the notion of the German language, as the official vague research and studies, and the like. We do not know which studies by whom came to which conclusions or when the pope stated the quoted utterance. This rhetorical-grammatical strategy places the responsibility for the views expressed with authorities other than Haider, thereby naturalizing his views as deriving from and as aligned with those of important sources of knowledge and morality, a common strategy of legitimization. Third, Haider buries the crux of his views very deeply in the rheme (the last part) of his sentences. Thematic (i.e. at the front of the sentence) are the authorities on whom Haider relies to authorize his points. The effect of leaving the crux of his divisive message until last in the sentence is that it is both most prominent (because most recent), and most difficult to retrieve for negotiation (due to the levels of embedding).

Finally, when Haider refers to himself or his party he does so in very short and pithy statements, using relational processes of being, which project stasis, positive evaluations, and no negatives: "We have clear principles; we are clear, and we are a party for all those who care about Austria". In these ways, Haider exploits different sources to edify his own views. He allocates negativity, causality and action to immigrants, while reserving for himself the appearance of a considerate and non-aggressive thinker. His evaluations of the people he discriminates against are not realized overtly, but as tokens of judgment whose mitigating effect rounds off the quasi rationality he manages to project.

7. Conclusions: The institutional and political logic of racial discrimination

Institutional and political discrimination is a striking feature of some of the key social institutions in European societies. Undoubtedly, it is true that in almost every society, the nation-state itself tended to exclude those at the periphery. However, in recent times there has been a major undermining of the dominant hegemonic designs as a result of a gradual move towards post-national membership, especially in European countries. More and more claims can be made by reference to the rights of individuals (Soysal 1994).

The Europeanization of the public sphere has given minorities and migrants more opportunities to mobilize and to bring counter-claims to challenge exclusionary and discriminatory practices. The result of this is that political and institutional discrimination has become a major site of public discourse and contestation.

Discrimination is both a discourse and a practice. It is obviously enough of a practice in that it is easy to prove that there is endemic, although variable, discrimination against minorities. It is a discourse in the sense that institutional discrimination does not take place in a pre-political context.

The evidence gathered in the research summarized in this chapter does not confirm the existence of a hegemonic apparatus of institutional-political and public racism, but does provide evidence of widespread institutional discrimination and even of institutional racism along with some of the traditional expressions of racist bigotry. The important finding is that such practices are resisted and contested. Such resistance takes place in a legal and public context.

Appendix

Interview with Jörg Haider about the new party program, in
"Zeit im Bild 2", 29th October 1997 (Interviewer: Robert Hochner)

RH: Herr Doktor Haider! In diesem Parteiprogramm sind christliche Werte und die Verpflichtung, diese christlichen Werte zu verteidigen, relativ stark unterstrichen. – Äh, es gibt keine christliche Ausländerfeindlichkeit. Das Christentum unterscheidet nicht zwischen Österreichern und Ausländern, und das Christentum verpflichtet eigentlich Menschen, – die wenig haben, das, was man hat, noch zu geben. Wie ver / paßt das eigentlich zur Politik ihrer Partei? –

JH: Zum ersten einmal, daß wir christlich sind bei Privilegienabbau, weil wir sind die einzigen, die freiwilligen Einkommensverzicht leisten, – während in Zeiten des Sparpaketes vom Bundeskanzler angefangen bis zu allen Ministern, Landeshauptleuten, Landesregierungsmitgliedern, jeder sich Gehaltserhöhungen verpaßt hat. So, einmal das erste Christliche an uns. Das Zweite ist, – ah daß wir das Papstwort ernst nehmen, und äh der – äh je / jetzige Papst hat ja ganz deutlich gemacht, daß Nächstenliebe bedeutet, wirklich sich um den Nächsten zu kümmern und nicht die ganze Welt zu umarmen, sondern auch an die Österreicher zu denken.

RH: Also, der Näch / der Nächste muß einen österreichischen Paß haben, daß Sie ihn lieben.

JH: Nicht unbedingt, aber er muß eine legale Aufenthaltsberechtigung hier in d / im Lande haben, denn sonst geht's uns so, daß man – äh Illegale hereinläßt – und dann letztlich den Österreichern und den hier legal lebenden Ausländern ein Problem schafft. Wir sind also da sehr – auf der rechtsstaatlichen Grundlage – und der / die Reaktionen der Regierung zeigen ja nur, daß wir völlig richtig liegen auch mit der Linie – äh "Österreich zuerst", daß wir an dieses Land denken und den Ausverkauf beziehungsweise eine ungehemmte Zuwanderung jedenfalls stoppen wollen.

Notes

1 I use this term as synonymous with CDA; see Wodak and Meyer 2001; Gee 2004; Wodak 2004; Blommaert 2005; Wodak and Chilton 2005.
2 Many results and insights reported in this chapter stem from an EU project (5th framework) in which I was involved as PI of the Austrian team: XENOPHOB, coordinated by Masoud Kamali in Uppsala. This research studied social exclusion and discrimination in eight EU countries from 2002 until 2005. A short summary of the theoretical considerations in sections 2, 3 of this paper were presented at a project meeting at Brussels, January 2005, together with Gerard Delanty. Other relevant results were obtained in another interdisciplinary and comparative project, together

with Teun van Dijk, funded by the Austrian Ministry of Science 1996. There, we investigated parliamentary debates on immigration in six EU countries (Wodak and van Dijk 2000). I am grateful to Gerard Delanty, Teun van Dijk, and Martin Reisigl for their important contributions to the research reported in this chapter.

3   See van Dijk 1984, 1989, 2005a; Wodak et al. 1990; Matouschek, Wodak, and Januschek 1995; Reisigl and Wodak 2000a, 2000b, 2001; Wodak and van Dijk 2000; Ensink and Sauer 2003; Heer et al. 2003; Martin and Wodak 2003; Chilton 2004; Richardson 2004; Camus 2005; Wodak and de Cillia 2005.

4   Most recently, the term "celebration" has also been used instead of tolerance, implying a proactive meaning of embracing and welcoming diversity (i.e. "celebrating diversity").

5   Among the many studies on racism, see Lauren 1988; Balibar and Wallerstein 1991; Essed 1991; Wrench and Solomos 1993; Wieviorka 1994; Solomos and Back 1996; Goldberg 1997, 2002; Bulmer and Solomos 1999, 2004; Back and Solomos 2000; Feagin 2000; Sears, Sidanius, and Bobo 2000; Boxill 2001; Feagin, Vera, and Batur, 2001; Essed and Goldberg 2002; Goldberg and Solomos 2002; Marable 2002; Cashmore 2003; Doane and Bonilla-Silva 2003.

6   I have created this term in analogy to the term "syncretic anti-Semitism", which grasps forms of anti-Semitic discourses and actions after WWII more adequately then the traditional concepts of Christian, racial or economic anti-Semitism; see Mitten 1992.

7   This is even more salient if one considers migrants in prestigious professions or from rich countries, such as "mobile academics" who are considered to be "flexible". The ranking of migrants from different countries and differing economic backgrounds is obvious; Boltanski and Thévenot (1991), see Brubaker (2002).

8   See, e.g. van Dijk 1984, 1987, 1989, 1991, 1993, 2005a,b; Jäger 1991, 1999; Wetherell and Potter 1992; Blommaert and Verschueren 1998; Reisigl and Wodak 2000, 2001.

9   See Wilson 1990; Jarren, Sarcinelli, and Saxer 1998; Wodak and van Dijk 2000; Chilton and Schäffner 1997, 2002; Girnth 2002; Gruber, Menz, and Panagl 2003; Chilton 2004; Wodak and Chilton 2005; Billig 2006.

10 Wodak et al. 1999; Wodak and Pelinka 2002; Heer et al. 2003; Martin and Wodak 2003, Wodak and Weiss 2004a, b.

11 For specific examples for all these categories see Reisigl and Wodak (2001: 40–52). Due to space restrictions, examples will be given while analyzing the TV interview in the last section of this chapter whenever they occur.

12 See Wodak and Iedema (2004) for an extensive analysis of this interview.

13 Within argumentation theory, *topoi* or *loci* can be described as parts of argumentation which belong to the obligatory, either explicit or inferable, premises. They are the content-related warrants or "conclusion rules" which connect the argument or arguments with the conclusion, the claim. As such, they justify the transition from the argument or arguments to the conclusion (Kienpointner 1992: 194).

References

Anthonissen, Christine
    2001   On the effectivity of media censorship: an analysis of linguistic, paralinguistic and other communicative devices used to defy media restrictions. Unpublished Ph.D. thesis, University of Vienna.
Back, Les and John Solomos (eds.)
    2000   *Theories of Race and Racism: A Reader.* London: Routledge.
Balibar, Etienne and Immanuel Wallerstein
    1991   *Race, Nation, Class.* London: Verso.
Beck, Ulrich
    2004   *Risikogesellschaft.* Frankfurt/Main: Suhrkamp.
Billig, Michael
    2006   Discrimination in discourse. In: *Elsevier Encyclopedia for Language and Linguistics*, 597–599. Oxford: Elsevier.
Blommaert, Jan
    2005   *Discourse.* Cambridge: Cambridge University Press
Blommaert, Jan and Jef Verschueren
    1998   *The Diversity Debate.* London: Routledge.
Boltanski, Luc and Laurent Thévenot
    1991   *De la Justification.* Paris: Gallimard.
Bourdieu, Pierre
    1989   *The Logic of Practice.* Cambridge: Polity Press.
Boxill, Bernard R. (ed.)
    2001   *Race and Racism.* Oxford: Oxford University Press.
Brubaker, Rogers
    2002   Ethnicity without groups. *Archives Européennes de Sociologie* XL111(2): 163–89.
Bulmer, Martin and John Solomos (eds.)
    1999   *Racism.* Oxford: Oxford University Press.
Bulmer, Martin and John Solomos
    2004   *Researching Race and Racism.* London: Routledge.
Camus, Jean-Yves
    2005   The use of racist, anti-Semitic and xenophobic arguments in political discourse. In: *ECRI: European Commission against Racism and Tolenrance*, March 2005.
Cashmore, Ernest
    2003   *Encyclopedia of Race and Ethnic Studies.* London: Routledge.
Chilton, Paul
    2004   *Analysing Political Discourse: Theory and Practice.* London: Routledge.
Chilton, Paul and Christine Schäffner
    1997   Discourse and politics. In: Teun van Dijk A. (ed.), *Discourse as Social Interaction.* 206–230. London: Sage.
Chilton, Paul and Christine Schäffner (eds.)
    2002   *The Politics of Text and Talk.* Amsterdam: Benjamins.
Chouliaraki, Lilie and Norman Fairclough
    1999   *Discourse in Late Modernity: Rethinking Critical Discourse Analysis.* Edinburgh: Edinburgh University Press.

Delanty, Gerard and Patrick O'Mahony
    2002   *Nationalism and Social Theory.* London: Sage.
Delanty, Gerard, and Ruth Wodak
    2005   Everyday and Institutional Racism. Interim Report, *EU Commission*, Brüssels.
Delanty, Gerard, Paul R. Jones and Ruth Wodak
    2007   *The Voices of Migrants.* Liverpool: Liverpool University Press.
Doane, Ashley W. and Edoardo Bonilla-Silva (eds.)
    2003   *White out: The Continuing Significance of Racism.* New York: Routledge.
Eagleton, Terry (ed.)
    1994   *Ideology.* London: Longman.
Ehlich, Konrad
    2000   Diskurs. In: Helmut Glück (ed.), *Metzler Lexikon Sprache*, 162–163. Stuttgart: Metzler.
Ensink, Titus and Christoph Sauer (eds.),
    2003   *The Art of Commemoration.* Amsterdam: Benjamins.
Essed, Philomena
    1991   *Understanding Everyday Racism.* Newbury Park: Sage.
Essed, Philomena and David T. Goldberg (eds.)
    2002   *Race Critical Theories.* Malden, MA: Blackwells.
Fairclough, Norman
    1995   *Media Discourse.* London: Edward Arnold.
Fairclough, Norman and Ruth Wodak
    1997   Critical Discourse Analysis. In: Teun A. van Dijk (ed.), *Discourse as Social Interaction*, 256–284. London: Sage.
Feagin, Joe R.
    2000   *Racist America: Roots, Current Realities, and Future Reparations.* New York: Routledge.
Feagin, Joe R., Hernan Vera and Paul Batur
    2001   *White Racism: The Basics.* New York: Routledge.
Fekete, Liz
    2001   The emergence of xeno-racism. *Race and Class* 43(2): 23–40.
Geden, Oliver
    2005   The discursive construction of masculinity in the Austrian Freedom Party. *Journal of Language and Politics* 4(3): 397–420.
Gee, James P.
    2004   *Discourse Analysis: Theory and Method.* London: Routledge.
Girnth, Heiko
    2002   *Sprache und Sprachverwendung in der Politik.* Tübingen: Niemeyer.
Goldberg, David T.
    1997   *Racial Subjects: Writing on Race in America.* New York: Routledge.
Goldberg, David T.
    2002   *The Racial State.* Oxford: Blackwell.
Goldberg, David T. and John Solomos (eds.)
    2002   *A Companion to Racial and Ethnic Studies.* Malden, MA: Blackwell.
Gruber, Helmut, Florian Menz and Oswald Panagl (eds.)
    2003   *Sprache und politischer Wandel.* Bern: Peter Lang.

Heer, Hannes, Walter Manoschek, Alexander Pollak and Ruth Wodak (eds.)
    2003   *"Wie Geschichte gemacht wird": Erinnerungen an Wehrmacht und Zweiten Weltkrieg*. Vienna: Czernin.
Holmes, David
    2000   *Integral Europe: Fast-Capitalism, Multiculturalism, Neofascism*. Princeton: Princeton University Press.
Jäger, Siegfried
    1991   *Text- und Diskursanalyse: Eine Anleitung zur Analyse politischer Texte*. Duisburg: DISS Verlag – Unrast.
Jäger, Siegfried
    1999   *Kritische Diskursanalyse: Eine Einführung*. Duisburg: DISS Verlag – Unrast.
Jäger, Siegfried
    2001   Discourse and knowledge: theoretical and methodological aspects of Critical Discourse Analysis. In: Ruth Wodak and Michael Meyer (eds.), *Methods of Critical Discourse Analysis*, 32–62. London: Sage.
Jarren, Otfried, Ulrich Sarcinelli and Ulrich Saxer (eds.)
    1998   *Politische Kommunikation in der demokratischen Gesellschaft: Ein Handbuch*. Opladen: Westdeutscher Verlag.
Kienpointner, Manfred
    1992   How to classify arguments. In: van Eemeren, Frans H., Robert Grootenhorst, John A. Blair and Charles A. Willard (eds.), *Argumentation Illuminated. Selected Proceedings of the Second International Conference on Argumentation in Amsterdam 1990*, 178–188. Amsterdam: Sicsat.
Kovács, Andras and Ruth Wodak (eds.)
    2003   *Nato, Neutrality and National Identity: The Case of Austria and Hungary*. Vienna: Böhlau Verlag.
Kress, Gunter and Theo van Leeuwen
    2006   *Reading Images: The Grammar of Visual Design*. 2nd ed. London: Routledge.
Krzyżanowski, Michał and Ruth Wodak
    2007   "Identities in-between": analyzing focus groups with migrants. In: Rick Iedema and Carmen Caldas-Coulthard (eds.), *Identity Politics*. Basingstoke: Palgrave (forthcoming).
Lauren, Paul G.
    1988   *Power and Prejudice: The Politics and Diplomacy of Racial Discrimination*. Boulder: Westview.
Lemke, Jay L.
    1995   *Textual Politics*. New York: Arnold.
Macmaster, Neil
    2001   *Racism in Europe*. London: Palgrave.
Machin, David and Theo van Leeuwen
    2003   Global schemas and local discourses in Cosmopolitan. *Journal of Sociolinguistics* 7(4): 493–512.
Marable, Manning
    2002   *The Great Wells of Democracy: The Meaning of Race in American Life*. New York: Basic Books.
Marin, Bernd
    2000   *Antisemitismus*. Munich: Campus.

Martin, James R. and Ruth Wodak (eds.)
   2003   Re/reading the Past. Critical and Functional Perspectives on Time and Value. Amsterdam: Benjamins.
Matouschek, Bernd, Ruth Wodak and Franz Januschek
   1995   Notwendige Maßnahmen gegen Fremde? Genese und Formen von rassistischen Diskursen der Differenz. Vienna: Passagen Verlag.
Mitten, Richard
   1992   The Politics of Antisemitic Prejudice. Boulder: Westview Press.
Mokre, Monika, Gilbert Weiss and Rainer Bauböck (eds.)
   2003   Europas Identitäten, Mythen, Konstruktionen, Konflikte. Frankfurt/Main: Campus.
Pelinka, Anton and Ruth Wodak (eds.)
   2002   "Dreck am Stecken". Politik der Ausgrenzung. Vienna: Czernin Verlag.
Race and Class
   2001   Special Issue: The Three Faces of British Racism, vol. 43(2).
Reisigl, Martin
   2004   "Wie man eine Nation herbeiredet": Eine diskursanalytische Untersuchung zur sprachlichen Konstruktion der österreichichen Nation und Identität in politischen Fest- und Gedenkreden. Unpublished Ph.D. thesis, University of Vienna.
Reisigl, Martin and Ruth Wodak
   2000b   "Austria first": a discourse-historical analysis of the Austrian "Anti-Foreigner-Petition" in 1992 and 1993. In: Reisigl, Martin and Ruth Wodak (eds.), The Semiotics of Racism, 269–303. Vienna: Passagen Verlag.
Reisigl, Martin and Ruth Wodak (eds.)
   2000a   The Semiotics of Racism. Vienna: Passagen Verlag.
Reisigl, Martin and Ruth Wodak
   2001   Discourse and Discrimination: Rhetorics of Racism and Antisemitism. London: Routledge.
Richardson, John E.
   2004   (Mis)Representing Islam. Amsterdam: Benjamins.
Rydgren, Jens
   2003   Mesolevel causes of racism and xenophobia. European Journal of Social Theory 6(1): 45–68.
Rydgren, Jens (ed.)
   2005   Moments of Exclusion. New York: Nova.
Sayer, Andrew
   2006   Language and significance – or the importance of import: implications for Critical Discourse Analysis. Journal of Language and Politics 5(3): 449–471.
Sears, David O., Jim Sidanius and Louis Bobo (eds.)
   2000   Racialized Politics. Chicago: University of Chicago Press.
Sivanandan, Ambalavaner
   2001   Poverty is the new Black. Race and Class 43(2): 1–5.
Solomos, John and Les Back
   1996   Racism and Society. New York: St. Martins Press.

Soysal, Yasmin
   1994   *The Limits of Citizenship.* Chicago: University of Chicago Press.
Thompson, John B.
   1990   *Ideology and Modern Culture.* Cambridge: Polity Press.
Titscher, Stephan, Ruth Wodak, Michael Meyer and Eva Vetter
   2000   *Methods of Text and Discourse Analysis.* London: Sage.
van Dijk, Teun A.
   1984   *Prejudice in Discourse.* Amsterdam: Benjamins.
van Dijk, Teun A.
   1987   Elite discourse and racism. In: Zavala, Iris, Teun A. van Dijk and Maria Diaz-Diocaretz (eds.), *Approaches to Discourse, Poetics and Psychiatry,* 81–122. Amsterdam: Benjamins
van Dijk, Teun A.
   1989   The denial of racism. In: Ruth Wodak (ed.), *Language, Power and Ideology,* 199–226. Amsterdam: Benjamins.
van Dijk, Teun A.
   1991   *Racism and the Press.* London: Routledge.
van Dijk, Teun A.
   1993   Principles of Critical Discourse Analysis. *Discourse & Society,* 4(2): 249–283.
van Dijk, Teun A.
   1998   *Ideology: A Multidisciplinary Approach.* London: Sage.
van Dijk, Teun A.
   2003   The discourse-knowledge interface. In: Gilbert Weiss and Ruth Wodak (eds.), *Critical Discourse Analysis: Theory and Interdisciplinarity,* 85–109. Basingstoke: Palgrave Macmillan.
van Dijk, Teun A.
   2004   Discourse, knowledge and ideology. In: Pütz, Martin, JoAnne Neff and Teun A. van Dijk (eds.), *Communicating Ideologies,* 5–38. Bern: Lang.
van Dijk, Teun A.
   2005a   Contextual knowledge management in discourse production: a CDA perspective. In Ruth Wodak and Paul A. Chilton (eds.), *A New Agenda in (Critical) Discourse Analysis,* 71–100. Amsterdam: Benjamins.
van Dijk, Teun A.
   2005b   Reproducing racism: the role of the press. Unpublished Paper, Congress on Immigration, Almeria, 21/22 April, 2005.
van Leeuwen, Theo and Adam Jaworski
   2003   The discourses of war photography: Photojournalistic representation of the Palestinan–Israeli war. *Journal of Language and Politics,* 1(2): 255–275.
van Leeuwen, Theo and Ruth Wodak
   1999   Legitimizing immigration control: a discourse-historical analysis. *Discourse Studies* 1(1): 83–118.
Weiss, Gilbert and Ruth Wodak (eds.)
   2003   *Critical Discourse Analysis: Theory and Interdisciplinarity.* Basingstoke: Palgrave.
Wetherell, Margaret and Jonathan Potter
   1992   *Mapping the Language of Racism: Discourse and the Legitimation of Exploitation.* New York, etc.: Harvester Wheatsheaf.

Wieviorka, Michel (ed.)
  1994   *Racisme et xenophobie en Europe: une comparison internationale.* Paris: la Decouverte.
Wilson, John
  1990   *Politically Speaking: The Pragmatic Analysis of Political Language.* Oxford: Basil Blackwell.
Wodak, Ruth
  2001   The discourse-historical approach. In: Ruth Wodak and Michael Meyer (eds.), *Methods in Critical Discourse Analysis,* 63 – 94. London: Sage.
Wodak, Ruth
  2004   Discourses of silence: anti-Semitic discourse in postwar Austria. In: Lynn Thiesmeyer (ed.), *Discourse and Silencing,* 179–209. Amsterdam: Benjamins.
Wodak, Ruth
  2005   Sprache und Politik: Einige Grenzen diskursanalytischer Vorgangsweisen. In Krisch, Thomas, Thomas Lindner and Ulrich Müller (eds.), *Analecta homini universali dicata: Festschrift für Oswald Panagl zum 65. Geburtstag.* vol. 2, 648–61. Stuttgart: Verlag Hans-Dieter Heinz.
Wodak, Ruth and Paul Chilton (eds.)
  2005   *A New Agenda in (Critical) Discourse Analysis.* Amsterdam: Benjamins.
Wodak, Ruth and Rudolf de Cillia
  1988   *Sprache und Antisemitismus.* Vienna: Institut für Wissenschaft und Kunst, *Mitteilungen 4.*
Wodak, Ruth and Rudolf de Cillia
  2005   Discourse and politics. In: Ammar, Ulrich, Herbert Mattheier and Norbert Dittmar (eds.) *Handbuch Soziolinguistik,* 1638–1653, Berlin: de Gruyter.
Wodak, Ruth and Rick Iedema
  2004   Constructing boundaries without being seen: the case of Jörg Haider, Politician. *Revista Canaria de Estudos Ingleses* 49: 157–178.
Wodak, Ruth and Bernd Matouschek
  1993   We are dealing with people whose origins one can clearly tell just by looking: Critical Discourse Analysis and the study of Neo-Racism in contemporary Austria. *Discourse & Society* 4(2): 225–248.
Wodak, Ruth and Michael Meyer (eds.)
  2001   *Methods of Critical Discourse Analysis.* London: Sage.
Wodak, Ruth and Anton Pelinka
  2002   From Waldheim to Haider: an introduction. In: Wodak, Ruth and Anton Pelinka (eds.) *The Haider Phenomenon,* vii–xxvii. London/New Jersey: Transaction Press.
Wodak, Ruth and Anton Pelinka (eds.)
  2002   *The Haider Phenomenon in Austria.* London/New Jersey: Transaction Press.
Wodak, Ruth and Teun A. van Dijk (eds.)
  2000   *Racism at the Top: Parliamentary Discourses on Ethnic Issues in Six European States.* Klagenfurt: Drava.

Wodak, Ruth and Gilbert Weiss
   2004a   Möglichkeiten und Grenzen der Diskursanalyse: Konstruktionen europäischer Identitäten. In: Oswald Panagl and Ruth Wodak (eds.) *Text und Kontext: Theoriemodelle und methodische Verfahren im transdisziplinären Vergleich,* 67–86. Würzburg: Verlag Königshausen & Neumann.
Wodak, Ruth and Gilbert Weiss
   2004b   Visions, ideologies and utopias in the discursive construction of European identities: organizing, representing and legitimizing Europe. In: Pütz, Martin, JoAnne Neff van Aertselaer and Teun A. van Dijk (eds.), *Communicating Ideologies: Multidisciplinary Perspectives on Language, Discourse and Social Practice,* 225–252. Frankfurt/Main: Peter Lang.
Wodak, Ruth, Rudolf de Cillia, Martin Reisigl and Karin Liebhart
   1999   *The Discursive Construction of National Identity.* Edinburgh: Edinburgh University Press.
Wodak, Ruth, Jürgen Pelikan, Peter Nowak, Helmuth Gruber, Rudolf de Cillia and Richard Mitten
   1990   *"Wir sind alle unschuldige Täter!": Diskurshistorische Studien zum Nachkriegsantisemitismus.* Frankfurt/Main: Suhrkamp.
Wrench, John and John Solomos (eds.)
   1993   *Racism and Migration in Western Europe.* Oxford: Berg.

14. Tabloidisation of political communication in the public sphere[1]

Werner Holly

1. Politics, democracy, media and communication

Media development has changed the structure of the public sphere fundamentally. Some speak of a "colonisation" of the political system by the media system, of a "mediocracy" (Meyer 2001) that has allegedly replaced even democratically legitimated power. Just as the major mass media themselves increasingly follow commercial interests, politics too has become subject to a process of tabloidisation, in that it caters to the taste of the masses and their entertainment needs, albeit for persuasive rather than commercial reasons. It is nowadays seen as sufficient for public communication to be "successful", irrespective of the quality of actual political decisions; "symbolic politics" functions as a replacement (Sarcinelli 1987). This process is accompanied by political communication becoming more visual, more performative, more theatrical and more aestheticised.

Admittedly, an orientation towards more entertainment and clarity does not necessarily lead to a loss in quality and in turn to more trivial, banal and, ultimately, seemingly "depoliticised" politics (which nevertheless have strong political implications). As long as political communication remains true to the basic categories of all good communication, i.e. stays informative, true, relevant and comprehensible, politics with a broad impact could signal a modernisation, popularisation or even democratisation of political communication rather than its tabloidisation. Thus, the development of public communication, up to the recent impact of electronic media, continues to be ambivalent.

First of all, however, we can state that communicative conditions are more than the merely external aspects of politics; rather, they are central and constitutive factors without which political processes would not be conceivable in the first place. Many definitions of politics therefore include a reference to (verbal) communication (e.g. Sternberger 1966: 98; Dieckmann 1975: 29; Strauß, Haß, and Harras 1989: 29; Heringer 1990: 9). After all, politics is about a "constrained use of social power" (Goodin and Klingemann 1996: 7), not about violence, which – to quote Proudhon (1843: 82) – is only "the last word in politics". Furthermore, what holds true for politics in general (see Frevert and Braungart 2004 for a historical perspective) is all the more relevant for democracy as the only truly legitimate form of power in present-day societies. Any democracy worth its salt will be measured against the quality of its public communication. Contemporary mass democracy, however, is by nature about media communication, or "mediated politics" (Bennett and Entman 2001).

In the beginnings of Attic democracy, it was still conceivable that the few free men who had civil rights would reach agreement through direct interaction and "noble dispute" (Meier 1983; Assmann and Assmann 1990: 91). Concerning the second attempt at democracy, which followed the model of "government by discussion", a well-known phrase for the notion of power legitimated by parliament (e.g. Mill 1864; Bagehot 1872), only the early parliaments consisting of notabilities from the aristocracy and bourgeoisie enabled small-scale deliberation without the media. As more groups gained suffrage, the "fourth power" in the form of the press became ever more important, bringing about a change in the structure of the public sphere (Habermas 1962). Under the new system, what counted was not only rhetorical prowess in more or less small assemblies, but also leaving a good impression with the "masses" of the electorate, who, however, mostly relied on debates being published in newspapers, then later broadcast on the radio and finally shown on television. Due to the triumph of television over other media, political communication underwent a number of fundamental changes (Meyrowitz 1985).

Parliamentary debates as the original centres of political processes have seen a substantial loss in persuasive force in many parliamentary systems, where they are now merely seen as an institutionalised and staged event that is kept on life support but has to all intents and purposes been replaced by television talk shows (Tenscher 2002). Thus, direct verbal agreement in the form of individual talk between citizens and their representatives is no longer seen as the basis for decision making in all democratic nations. Rather, such direct interaction has been replaced by the complex discursive process of the media interacting with the political system. As part of this process, political language has become the subject of professionally developed strategies and – despite or perhaps because of this – seems less effective now (Klein 1998b: 393).

Ever since the truly democratic form of verbal agreement (the unmediated interaction of authentic and lively debate) became backgrounded, the subsequent return to monologic forms of verbal interaction in the media and the mere staging of dialogue in parliament have led to problems with credibility. Where truth claims can no longer be challenged in interaction, the fact that linguistic signs can be used strategically becomes crucial, and verbal utterances are always regarded with suspicion. By the same token, the visual component of communication is rendered more important. Since the visual can be transmitted directly, body language regains importance, and the visual impressions afforded by the artificial closeness of the camera and its specific rules become a factor of public communication that is hard to gauge. As Meyrowitz (1985) has shown, electronic media not only re-introduce orality into public communication – albeit a "secondary orality" based on written language and technology (Ong 1982; Holly 1995) –, but also a new and equally secondary intimacy. As a multi-coded and multimodal one-way programming medium, television seems to meet the needs of modern societies perfectly. In this respect, it can still be regarded as the leading public medium (Holly 2004a), even if new electronic media – like all previous new media in history – further change and complement the overall mediascape.

When television started to blend the public and private spheres, it went against the traditional "sense of place" (Meyrowitz 1985): Politicians seem to enter the living rooms of the audience while the audience invades the privacy of politicians, making them their media friends or foes. Television transforms everything, including the political sphere, into a familiar and everyday object that is perceived and evaluated according to everyday criteria and everyday knowledge. However, this also means that politics are integrated more and more seamlessly into the stream of everyday communication. As a consequence, what is communicated via the media has no effect on its own; rather, the process of media communication is only made complete by the subsequent communications among the many and heterogeneous primary audiences (Livingstone and Lunt 1994; Holly, Püschel, and Bergmann 2001; Holly 2002; Couldry, this volume). Thus, communication in the public sphere becomes both more complex and more difficult to control for its protagonists. This is in contrast to the illusion of total manipulation by an effective machinery of political propaganda, which both the producers and the critics of grand ideologies still subscribed to, believing in significant effects of a centrally controlled one-way communication in the image of Orwell's Big Brother.

Today, the attempts of political players to achieve effects through communication seem much more subtle and sophisticated; they are both less conspicuous and less clandestine, but certainly no less elaborate, even if their success is by no means guaranteed. Power elites more than ever regard the media as key in their struggle for dominance. This is why even under the "pluralistic" conditions of modern democracies and their non-governmental mass media, be they regulated by public law or commercial political and media systems, are as inextricably linked as ever. Even if some already see such close links to be waning again, suspecting the media to be symbiotically linked to business (Jarren 1998: 77), it is safe to say that the framework for the media is still set by politics. The work of journalists and thus the media reporting on politics still depends on their access to government, parliament and other political arenas (Schneider 1998: 422), just as vast chunks of political media content are pre-structured through the ready-made information and publications issued, i.e. the public relations efforts made by the actors themselves. The "embedded journalism" of Iraq war reporting was an extreme case in point (see Anthonissen, this volume). On the other hand, there is no doubt that politicians not only need the media but increasingly also have to accommodate to the media's specific forms of communication and their anticipated conditions; this is most obvious in the growing importance of media consultants or "spin doctors", as well as in the proliferation of political "initiatives" and campaigns (Baringhorst 1998; Holly 2007), and public relations measures of various kinds. While researchers have long tried to answer the question of who was leading and controlling who in this context (e.g. Graber 1997; Iyengar and Reeves 1997; Norris 1997; Cook 1998), academic accounts now seem to subscribe to a model of "interpenetration" (e.g. Münch 1991; Choi 1995) which includes more than just occasional "structural relations" between the two systems (Luhmann 1996: 124). Weischenberg (1995: 239) characterises the model as follows:

> One of the features of such a model of interpenetration is the fact that while both systems show increasing interdependence, they nevertheless operate in a self-referential manner and can therefore not be steered from outside. In this context, the media – on the basis of their legal, economic and technological structures – make public political topics according to their own rules of editing and processing. In doing so, they are highly dependent on the information supplied by the political system. The political system, which has an ever more urgent need for the media in order to stage politics, in turn accommodates to the media-specific modes of operation insofar as it simulates the media's strategies of topic presentation.
> In the end, one system thereby subjects itself to the rules of the other: Media communication follows the logic of political decision-making and leadership, and political processes follow the media institutions' logic of selection and construction.

In his characterisation, Weischenberg distinguishes between a "system level", on which politics are mediatised and media are instrumentalised, and an "actor level", on which the "relationship games" (Donsbach et al. 1993) played by the various actors in political communication – the party spokespersons, the journalists and the audience – can be observed. To describe these relations, Weischenberg draws on a concept of roles developed by Michael Gurevitch and Jay G. Blumler in the 1970s (1977). By structuring hypotheses for the different constellations that can be deducted from the normatively organised relations between media and political institutions, their concept distinguishes "autonomous", "socially responsible", "commercial" and "government regulated" media systems. One constellation of roles which the authors ascribe to commercial media institutions seems prototypical of tabloidisation tendencies: Here, the audience remains in the role of "spectator", while journalists function as "entertainers" and politicians as "actors".

Thus, the focus is again on the actual sovereign in democratic systems, but only as a spectator. Other constellations conceivably cast him or her in other roles as well: as "party follower" (in authoritarian or totalitarian regimes with government control of the media), as "member of the electorate" (while politicians "argue" and journalists "mediate") or as "observer" (while the media play the role of "comptroller" and politicians are mere "informants"). Thus, even democratic systems allow for different relationships between the participants in political communication.

The range gets even broader when one distinguishes between different forms of democracy, according to the degree to which they involve the people (Schmidt 2000: 307–389). Following Meyer (2001: 17–21), these have vastly different requirements for political communication: the most common and, according to its advocates, "realistic" form is the "market model", in which voters only need to be provided with sufficient access to information to be able to take legitimate decisions. Other, more democratically ambitious models, however, need to account for very different forms of communication, in particular deliberation between present actors, which traditional mass media characteristically fail to afford. Their structures seem to promote a development that can be captured by the terms commercialisation and "tabloidization" (Sparks 2000: 35–36) and seems to square best with the "market model".

In the following, we will address the following questions: What constitutes such tabloidisation tendencies; which of the above-mentioned rules of editing and processing do they give rise to; how does the political system simulate the strategies of topic presentation; and finally, what notion of democracy do they imply.

2. The term "tabloidisation" and its common characteristics

"Tabloidisation" cannot be regarded as a scientific term (see also Esser 1999; Sparks 2000: 9). Even though its existence is uncontested and indeed considered important, it is best seen as a term used by media critics. As such, it needs to be elaborated further, because its negative connotations evaluate the phenomenon in a premature and biased way, and also because it lumps together different phenomena that require different evaluations. The German equivalent, *Boulevardisierung*, can be traced back to the term "boulevard papers" (papers sold on the street). The term has been used in Germany ever since the first wave of commercialisation and the advent of the mass press at the turn of the 20th century afforded cheap and sensationalist press products that could be marketed and sold without subscription. Both German and English associate the same characteristics with boulevard papers/tabloids: news presented in a brief and sensationalist form, large letters in the headlines, many pictures and cartoons. The specific features of tabloids pertain to their thematic and semiotic structure, as well as their layout and verbal style, as illustrated by the following two, more or less explicitly evaluative, quotes concerning the most successful German tabloid, the *Bildzeitung* published by Springer. These quotes are equally valid for British or Austrian papers like *The Sun* or the *Kronenzeitung* (see Esser 1999 for a comparison of the Anglo-American press with its German counterpart):

> The clever mixture of sensationalist cover stories, a predominance of sports reporting, human interest stories, conservative edification and pictures of attractive page-three girls, all of which adapt to the "modern illiterate" (to quote Hans Zehrer, whose brainchild this product is), proved to be extremely successful. (Schildt 1999: 638)
>
> The transition from a pure picture publication to an illustrated paper entailed the use of headlines as "eye catchers" and a more dynamic make-up aiming at maximum stimulation of the superficial reader. He had sensations and exclusive news announced to him in screaming headlines, but was fobbed off with trivia and banalities on one of the next pages. The increased amount of text led to a more pronounced politicisation, to more explicit opinions and to the conscious attempt to influence politics. (...) Since the reader was not supposed to think about but merely to scan the news, he was offered bite-sized chunks of the interesting, the incredible and the never-read-before, so that he could whet his appetite for the next bite while still chewing on the first one. This consumption of small bites was best achieved by a telegraphic language broken up into its components. (...)
> The *Bildzeitung* shows all elements of a repressive language, as the texts merely suggest informativity while their unusual and insufficient design makes them hard to understand and evaluate, providing no prompts for interpretation. They are mostly vague while at the same time notably stereotypical. Although stereotypical components facilitate text processing by activating models stored in the reader's mind, the fact that the text in itself is inconsistent and that the entertaining, baffling and jokey components always outshine the informative ones means that such language torsos can neither survive nor be remembered; they are mere disposable products. (Straßner 1997: 50–51)

More recently, media critique of "tabloidisation" has occasionally also addressed the changing layout of quality papers and magazines (e.g. the German news magazine *Focus*). Mostly, however, such critique concerns itself with commercial broadcasting (radio, television) and consequently also with broadcasting governed by public law, to which it ascribes a tendency for self-commercialisation (see some chapters in Holly and Biere 1998). The occasionally scathing evaluations are plausible and form part of a long-standing complaint that has already triggered an international debate on journalistic standards (Turner 1999; Sparks and Tulloch 2000): Although a tabloid-like style can be considered harmless in the area of pure entertainment, transferring it to the context of political communication is regarded as a danger to essential elements of political culture. Apart from institutional structures and professional standards, two aspects of this development in particular give rise to continuing discussion: On the one hand, media with visual affinities are said to render political communication increasingly visual, performative, theatrical and aestheticised. On the other hand, critics identify a predominant orientation towards the entertaining, which, in the form of different varieties of "infotainment", is said to already define the central domain of political communication, i.e. news reporting and debate. This latter phenomenon, although related to the former, is worth a specific mention as it clashes with the informativity and discursivity required by political communication. The following sections will therefore address these two areas: visualisation or aestheticisation, and entertainment.

2.1. Visualisation, performance, theatricality, aestheticisation

Media development has reinforced the mediation of politics through forms of communication that process mostly visual signs (Meyrowitz 1985). In contrast to a culture of books and newspapers that is imagined as, but in fact never was, non-visual, the contemporary public sphere of the media seems dominated by the visual medium television and a visually increasingly opulent (tabloid) press; it seems to be heavy on, if not dominated by, visuals (Meyer 2001: 104–110). In this context, we can also observe the revaluation of design and the emergence of globally distributed visual stereotypes (Pörksen 1997; Holly 2003a; Machin 2004). The increasingly visual nature of the media, which, parallel to writing and reading, also asks for new skills in users, has been called a modernising process of "visualisation" (Ludes 1993, 1998). However, the term is a misnomer and inappropriate for contrasting contemporary media to the "old" culture of writing, because writing itself is of course visual as well.

Perhaps more importantly, increased visuality is part of a more comprehensive process of "performing politics", which was already described some time ago (Boorstin 1961; Edelman 1964, 1971, 1988; Schwartzenberg 1980); others have conducted empirical case studies on visualisation (e.g. Holly, Kühn and Püschel 1986; Sarcinelli 1987) and, more recently, analysed a cross-section of television programs on a given day (Meyer, Ontrup, and Schicha 2000). According to the above-mentioned claim, politics have been "colonised" by the media, leaving one to question whether or not democracy has turned into "mediocracy" (Meyer 2001). The main feature of such "mediatised politics" would be the production of images:

> In a media society, politics increasingly present themselves as an ever more sophisticated sequence of visuals, camera-friendly pseudo-events, personifications and images in which gestures and symbols, episodes and takes, surroundings, scenery and props, in short visual messages of all kinds become the central structures. In parts, these are even conceived by advertising and communication experts and re-enacted by actors to generate maximum media attention. (Meyer 2001: 109–110)

Although visual performances in politics are of course not new, they have recently been discussed with renewed vigour (see e.g. Müller 1997; Hofmann 1998, 1999). Images are part of the all-encompassing "theatricality" of politics, which operates with devices used in the theatre. At its centre, we find the actions of the human body, including facial expression, gestures, proxemics (spatial communicative behaviour), props, scenery and also linguistic and paralinguistic signs (Meyer 2001: 112). The latter, however, are understood as mere parts of a performance geared towards the visual. In this context, techniques of impression management, as they have been described in social psychology (Schütz 1992; Laux and Schütz 1996), also take effect. Marketing activities such as event politics, image projections and pseudo-actions, which we know not only from election campaigns, are the concrete strategies employed in such political performances (Meyer 2001: 112).

Instead of "visualisation", the more accurate term may be one that has been used in the same context, namely "aestheticisation of the public sphere". It better captures what is occasionally implied by the term "performance"; that it remains unclear "whether or not the staged images are covered by political actions" (Meyer 2001: 111). Just like images in other aestheticised areas, like art or advertising, they are not bound by truthfulness, even though they are not necessarily "false". In addition, their features of personalisation and intimisation (Sennett 1974), emotionalisation and dramatisation, banalisation and entertainment ultimately "depoliticise" communication in the public sphere in a politically meaningful way.

The forecast is not entirely pessimistic, however. There are also positive aspects to "symbolic expressivity", which is said to potentially "focus attention, provide motives, trigger action" and as such is a "legitimate and often productive means of politics". In sum, the evaluation of theatrical strategies remains ambivalent (Meyer 2001: 117).

2.2. Language vs. images in politics

The partly skeptical, partly more optimistic claims about the development of public communication start out from particular political implications of visual and verbal communication, which we will now look at more closely. As a rule, certain prototypical characteristics of linguistic and visual signs are contrasted in a polarising manner. Schmitz (2003: 253) offers the following concise summary of such a contrast between verbal texts and, here, static images (for a more detailed review, see e.g. Burger 1990: 300–304):

> Texts are processed in a successive and linear fashion, while images are perceived simultaneously and holistically; texts provide arbitrary and symbolic representation, images are iconic and analogous; texts serve argumentative and images presentative purposes; texts are discursive, general and regulated, whereas images are "presentative" (Langer 1942: 103), unique and impossible to translate – if these usual contrasts are valid at all, that is.

So the core differences lie in the different semiotic foundations of linguistic and visual signs, but also, and related to that, in the different part-whole structures of communicating meaning, as Schmitz (2004: 114–115) elaborates:

Language operates with a grammar that organises the framework for relating a whole to its parts. Because of it, meaningless or decontextualised material from the linguistic repertoire (phonemes, morphemes, words, ...) can quickly be assembled into situationally meaningful utterances. This is why language lends itself well to symbolic signs whose form bears no similarity to their content. With images, however, the technicalities of relating a whole to is parts are much less pre-defined, although certain conventions, usages and styles do emerge. However, images are not used to formulate, but to design and present. Images thus operate iconically: They depict or present something. Texts are more about informing and thinking, images about showing and looking.

Even if one acknowledges that, on closer inspection, the differences are not as clear-cut, and therefore hesitates to embrace such polarisations, they do seem to at first glance make sense. Judging their respective political relevance takes us back to a number of tenaciously ambivalent idealisations of images and language, which seem to feed into often overly generalising and mostly culture critical evaluations (Sachs-Hombach 2003: 308–318). On the one hand, images are said to lack rationality, argumentative power, possible abstraction and detached reflection because they can only ever show the concrete and the individual and thus do not afford the discursive agreement necessary for democracy. Instead, they provide a direct, fast, holistically dense and partly intimate realisation. They are regarded as an attractive, expressive eye-catcher, as emotionally loaded (see some chapters in Knieper and Müller 2001) and, due to their analogous structure, as universally comprehensible: "An image says more than a thousand words". Images thus have an indispensable potential to motivate, explain and popularise. This includes mediating politics to a heterogeneous mass audience, albeit not always in a democratic sense, as witnessed by the visually powerful performances of totalitarian regimes. In addition, images have a suggestive power and credibility, in line with the old adage that "the camera never lies". Although now clearly obsolete, this belief still seems to take effect for photographic "representation", going back as it does to its "quasi-natural meaning-making" that does not seem to originate from any communicative action (Spangenberg 1988: 783–785) and that is therefore prone to an "essentialist fallacy" (Kepplinger 1987). The subsequent possible loss of reality is particularly dangerous for democratic politics – just think of the meticulous staging of visual symbols in political campaigns, e.g. the "mission accomplished" publicity stunt that depicted George W. Bush in military dress on an aircraft carrier, intended to make an end to the Iraq war visually plausible. In yet another sense, electronic visuality is also guilty of making it impossible, once and for all, for the visual sense – which is characterised by distance anyway (Köller 2004: 12–16) – to be in direct "touch" with the world (Robins 1996).

Language by contrast, especially spoken language, is the sign system that seems inherent to parliamentary democracy. Although, as elaborated above, the trustworthiness and efficiency of linguistic actors, politicians and journalists, seems to be waning, language, for its terminological and rhetorical potential alone, is still indispensable for mediating democratic politics. Thus, linguistic signs still play the central role in phrasing political matters, especially where such matters are conceptually comprised into formulaic slogans and supported by (ideally short) arguments; "waging semantic battles" and "occupying terms" (Liedtke, Wengeler, and Böke 1991) are therefore still very much part of the game. As far as language can combine the comprehensibility and brevity of images with its own unique capacity for abstraction, and as far as it "appropriately performs" (Meyer 2001: 206–209) the demands of thematic relevance and truthfulness of content, it is still a crucial factor in the democratic communication of politics.

At the same time, however, it should be noted that any theoretical considerations which decouple verbal and visual political communication have hardly any basis in reality anymore, since the vast majority of political communications is effected through the verbal-visual combinations found in the print media with their increased use of layout (see Kress and van Leeuwen 1998) and even more so in the audiovisual texts of television, which integrate the different qualities synergistically. This is why we should rather ask how we can best model the interrelations between the two components in audiovisual meaning complexes and how the two reinforce each other in a way similar to, or different from, the above-mentioned idealisations. Describing the relations between language and images, while still part of the current research agenda (see Holly, Hoppe, and Schmitz 2004; Stöckl 2005 for summaries), has stagnated and should be further developed for audiovisual texts (e.g. Burger 1990. 289 320, 354–362; Jäger and Stanitzek 2001; Liebrand and Schneider 2002; Holly 2004b, 2005; van Leeuwen 2005: 231–237).

Taking a broader view, the critique of "tabloidisation", as it concerns increased visuality, can be seen against the backdrop of the long-standing dispute between written and visual cultures, as it played out, for instance, in the conflict between Catholic visual piety and Protestant textual exegesis. At the same time, it is a critique voiced by sciences based on writing, whose self-stylisation demands discipline and asceticism and condemns the effortless, entertaining and varied ways of visual communication; by associating it with the "boulevard", communication not centered on written language is associated with pointless, if not harmful, activities. In this regard, "tabloidisation tendencies" can also be interpreted as a liberating step away from letter-based rationality, and as a counter-movement against the exclusive focus on a high culture that requests gestures of reverence and thereby serves no other purpose than elitist self-assurance.

2.3. Entertainment in media and politics: politainment

First of all, reference shall be made to Josef Klein's (1996, 1997, 1998a) theoretical reflections on the notion of entertainment. Generally speaking, one can contrast the two ideal types – information and entertainment – as basic communicative goals; following the tradition of ancient rhetoric (*docere* vs. *movere* and *delectare*), they long influenced the structure of media products (e.g. fiction vs. non-fiction, genres in newspapers, "hard news" vs. "soft news") as well as media institutions (departments in newspapers and broadcasting companies). Both come with different expectations, which also surface as the criteria of respective reviews. As for the categories linked to informative communication, Klein (1998a: 103) draws on Grice's conversational maxims (Grice 1975) and points out the parallels between the Gricean categories (plus one) and the terms commonly used in journalistic practice (in brackets below):

- informativity (currency/news value)
- foundation in fact (objectivity)
- truthfulness (reliability)
- relevance (newsworthiness)
- clarity (comprehensibility)

Klein then contrasts the Gricean information categories ("I-categories") with entertainment categories ("E-categories"), which correspond along a particular "mental processing dimension" (Klein 1997: 182).

Table 1. contrasts between I-categories and E-categories

mental processing dimension	I-categories	E-categories
quantitatively appropriate for processing capacity	informativity	variety
appropriate for processing goal	truth	lightness
appropriate for focus preference	relevance	interest
appropriate for structural processing capacity	clarity	intelligibility

These basic entertainment categories are then elaborated further, yielding sub-categories or extensions of the basic categories (Klein 1998a: 104).

basic category	sub-categories, extensions of basic categories
variety	speed, surprise, diversity, ...
lightness	amusement, fictitiousness, easy-going nature, ...
interest	emotional and/or erotic arousal, suspense, spectacular nature, ...
intelligibility	conventionality, simple structure, friendly and trustworthy presentation

Entertainment characteristics are thus rendered more systematic and more easily comparable to those of information. What about the features then that many authors keep listing for tabloidisation (see also the references given above)? In this context, Klein (1998a: 103) mentions the following:

- emotionalisation
- personalisation
- dramatisation
- aestheticisation up to the point of kitsch
- decreased distance (e.g. in formal attitude or respect).

According to his analysis, all these features can also be found as elements of entertainment categories, especially in the categories of interest and comprehensibility (Klein 1998a: 104). Only the elements variety and lightness need to be added to make for complete entertainment. Of course, we cannot speak of tabloidisation when explicit entertainment programming is entertaining, i.e. shows its typical features, nor will every occurrence of these features count as tabloidisation. The crucial point is: When, how and to what end are such elements employed? Our focus is on the tendency found with entertaining elements to penetrate text types and programming formats that are traditionally characterised by information categories, for instance in the case of so-called "infotainment" and, further on, the phenomenon that entertaining genres and programming formats are on the rise in general.

It is obvious that the tendency criticised as tabloidisation of the media has largely commercial reasons. Private for-profit media institutions are strictly geared towards sales and viewer levels, and the resulting competition for publicly held institutions lures these into using strategies that help them survive on the "media boulevard". All of this means that content is often not dictated by what makes journalistic sense but by what is most cost-efficient and sells best. In this regard, we should rather speak of a new wave of commercialisation.

If we look at individual programming formats or text types (e.g. news, reports, feature pages, science and higher education), we have to start from the premise that regardless of commercial orientation and entertaining design, there are still good and bad media products. However, quality should be assessed not only on the level of content but also with regard to presentation. Aestheticising and entertaining elements in information contexts have to be checked individually as to whether they only function as mere "icing" and "packaging", making them ultimately dysfunctional, or whether they can be seen as stimulating, enriching and facilitating comprehension.

It has to be noted that an orientation towards anticipated recipient expectations does not necessarily mean trivialisation or a decrease in quality. Since there is an overlap between the categories "comprehensibility" and "relevance" (as important factors in informative communication) on the one hand and the entertainment factors "intelligibility", "variety" and "interest" on the other, entertaining elements can indeed make informative communication more interesting, easier to understand and therefore better. In principle at least, an orientation towards entertainment on commercial grounds offers a chance for texts and programs to be better designed, even to better meet the goals of informative communication, e.g. through modular presentation, information charts and more pictures in the print media (see e.g. Lutz and Wodak 1987; Bucher 1998). The new commercialisation here meets a historically continuous tendency for modernisation that is commercially and communicatively motivated and has long tried to better reach audiences by means of media-specific design, various incentives, increasing recipient loyalty, aestheticisation, decompressed information, colloquial formulations etc. There can never be too much recipient orientation to make communication less elitist. Having said that, the loss of information under layers of packaging is by no means a rare phenomenon in commercially oriented media institutions and the criticism is therefore still valid.

The fact that media increasingly communicate in terms of entertainment, including in areas which were hitherto reserved for information, may have to do with their increased orientation towards commercial and viewer level goals. It is a much criticised consequence that the one area of public communication that is perhaps most important, i.e. politics, has also witnessed a further change in its communicative guidelines. This, however, is not steered by the media system alone. After all, the commercial orientation of the media meets with convergent interests on the part of political actors. In this perspective, we can reformulate the above-mentioned hypothesis that the media and the political system are interrelated with regard to their joint orientation towards entertainment categories. Andreas Dörner has done so by introducing the term "politainment" (Dörner 2000, 2001, 2002, 2003):

> Generally speaking, politainment always emerges on two levels, which, however, often appear as inextricably linked in media reality: *entertaining politics* and *political entertainment*. Entertaining politics is at stake whenever political actors resort to the instruments and stylistic devices of entertainment culture in order to realise their respective goals. (...) Thus, entertaining politics serve to acquire and stabilise political power.
> Political entertainment on the other hand starts from the opposite direction. The entertainment industry uses political tropes, topics and events strategically as material to construct its fictional world of images and to make its products interesting and attractive. (...) Such activities are not, or not primarily, geared towards political goals (...) – the main point is success in the mass media market. (Dörner 2001: 31–32; original emphasis)

Starting from the conditions in US "event culture", which is seen as paradigmatic, the author first shows how Hollywood films and numerous television series increasingly depict political processes. He also points out how entertainment in the US was, as a consequence of a more radical democratisation, never as suspicious as in Europe, but has been and still is an obvious and legitimate element of politics (Dörner 2001: 45–46) – which is also reflected in its academic treatment (e.g. Jewett and Lawrence 1977; Combs 1984, 1991). Dörner then analyses German election campaigns and talk shows as examples of entertaining politics, as well as soap operas and other series, but also feature films that incorporate elements of political entertainment (Dörner 2001: 112–234). The German examples show that US conditions have long since been exported to many European countries and other parts of the world.

This development is also reflected in relevant academic work. Ever since the 1960s, Cultural Studies in the UK and later in the US and Australia have investigated the relation between entertainment-oriented popular culture and political communication, especially with regard to recipient activities and practices (e.g. Hall 1980; Fiske 1987, 1989, 1993, 1994; for a summary see Dörner 1999, 2000: 98–145). Their proposals have also been drawn upon by German scholars (Hepp and Winter 1999; Hörning and Winter 1999; Winter 2001) and have given a significant boost to the hitherto scarce research in entertaining political communication, particularly linguistic work on talk shows and interviews (e.g. Linke 1985; Mühlen 1985; Holly, Kühn, and Püschel 1989; Holly 1990b; Burger 1991; Holly 1992, 1993, 1994; Holly and Schwitalla 1995; Gruber 1996). There are now a number of German articles and edited collections which address not only talk shows (e.g. Tenscher and Schicha 2002), but also other forms of politainment (e.g. Willems and Jurga 1998; Schicha and Ontrup 1999; Dörner and Vogt 2002; Schicha and Brosda 2002; Soeffner and Tänzler 2002; Nieland and Kamps 2004).

3. Tabloidisation and popularisation, performance and representation

In the Critical Theory tradition of the Frankfurt School, there was hardly any doubt that the mass communicative offers of the cultural industry first and foremost meant a mass deception that reduced a mostly passive and numb audience to unquestioning dependence. In contrast to that, Cultural Studies tried to show how recipients could independently construct entertaining texts for themselves, even act as a kind of subversive "semiotic guerilla" (de Certeau 1984) and adapt whatever the media had to offer in more or less creative ways. In any case, simple cause-effect models did not stand the test of reality (see also Holly, Püschel, and Bergmann 2001). As the notion of direct manipulation is disproved by studies of media effects on audiences, the elitist suspicion of all things entertaining is weakened as well: Entertaining programming can apparently become the object of intelligent reception games. The positive aspects of entertainment have subsequently been acknowledged, with theorists claiming that entertainment culture does not *a priori* exclude the general audience from the exclusive discourse of a politically reflecting cultural elite. Despite all skepticism, politainment and its "inclusive design" along the lines of entertaining communication can in this sense be seen as potentially opening up space for participation (Dörner 2003: 220–221).

Still, the simplification and bias brought about by an entertaining presentation must not be played down or, worse still, overlooked. The personalisation and emotionalisation of popularising formats may make them more lively and comprehensible, but the concomitant reduction in complexity soon exceeds the level that is permissible for rational political debate. If arguments cannot be understood anymore, because they do not even feature anymore, responsible decisions can no longer be taken. Election campaigns in particular, if they follow a pattern of entertaining politics only, become mere feel-good events. As such, they are out of place, and may even defeat their purpose if they diverge too much from the immediate reality as perceived by the voters. Frivolous or superficially emotional political performances and their in-your-face mood management can become counterproductive in the face of real problems requiring serious solutions. This was the lesson learned by both the former German chancellor Schröder after too many entertaining television appearances as well as by his adversary, Liberal Party chairman Westerwelle, whose self-displays were at one point perceived as "too much fun" and gave way to a more serious stylisation.

On the other hand, forms of political entertainment employing appropriate dramatic means can indeed be used to talk about, and raise public awareness of, serious political problems, as for instance done in a committed soap such as the German *Lindenstraße*. These forms can even counteract some effects of the "politics fatigue" claimed by groups in society who are particularly alienated and disengage themselves from public discourse.

In general, it would be an exaggeration to interpret aestheticising forms of political communication as merely biased and ultimately immoral performances that are meant to distract from what is really happening, and that can be unmasked to reveal an undisguised reality. On the one hand, performance is indispensable even under private and everyday conditions of communication, as shown in Erving Goffman's micro-sociological studies (e.g. Goffman 1959). On the other hand, the performance metaphor in politics cannot be reduced to a simple dichotomy of front stage with show effects and backstage with open decisions (Holly 1990a: 54–59; Soeffner 1998: 218). The structures and processes of communication are too complex to allow for that; rather, their inherent conflicts between roles force every politician into ambiguous and necessarily conflicting moves (Holly 1990a: 272–273).

According to Soeffner (1998: 220–226), politics needs ritual and ceremonies (Wulf and Zirfas 2004) exactly because public interests allows politicians to "get their hands dirty"; after all, political activity consciously factors in and uses immorality, deception and potential power abuse to redress the balance between the represented and their representatives. This relationship is redefined as a quasi "holy order", so that any "unavoidable" moral trespassing is immunised right from the outset:

> On closer inspection, the ritually supported representation agreement consists – not exclusively but also – of voters granting their representatives a kind of collective permission to commit moral trespasses when *public interest* seems to demand it: Those represented can stay "clean" because others get dirty on their behalf. (Soeffner 1998: 224; original emphasis)

This is why representative elements in political communication (Gauger and Stagl 1992) also mean that aesthetics help to cover what is ethically questionable "with the incense of ceremonial acts" and with an "aura" (Soeffner 1998: 220, 231), yet do not abandon moral control altogether. This opens up a difficult set of evaluations requiring constant negotiation, where it has to be decided in each case whether the line of what is tolerable "for the common good" has been crossed. What is not at stake, however, is whether political communication should relinquish general ethical principles of communication in general. On the contrary: Only if the structural danger to the political sphere is recognised and accepted can necessary counter-measures, such as the ones that modern public spheres have created by cultivating scandals (e.g. Ebbighausen and Neckel 1989; Hondrich 2002; Burkhardt and Pape 2003; Holly 2003b), be better understood and reinforced.

Both critical perspectives on tabloidisation in political communication come up with ambivalent results: Functionally, one has to continuously check whether the balance between far-reaching democratic inclusion and necessary rational adequacy has been maintained, and ethically, one has to ask whether the aestheticisation required by ritual has created an aura that is still legitimate, or whether this aura has to be tested and demystified against political and moral standards.

Notes

1 This chapter was translated from German (transl. V. Koller).

References

Assmann, Jan and Aleida Assmann
   1990   Kultur und Konflikt: Aspekte einer Theorie des unkommunikativen Handelns. In: Jan Assmann and Dietrich Harth (eds.), *Kultur und Konflikt*, 11–48. (edition suhrkamp NF 612.) Frankfurt/Main: Suhrkamp.
Bagehot, Walter
   1872   *Physics and Politics or Thoughts on the Application of the Principles of "Natural Selection" and "Inheritance" to Political Society.* London: King.

Baringhorst, Sigrid
   1998   *Politik als Kampagne: Zur medialen Erzeugung von Solidarität.* Opladen/ Wiesbaden: Westdeutscher Verlag.
Bennett, W. Lance and Robert M. Entman (eds.)
   2001   *Mediated Politics: Communication in the Future of Democracy.* Cambridge/New York: Cambridge University Press.
Boorstin, Daniel
   1961   *The Image or What happened to the American Dream.* New York: Atheneum.
Bucher, Hans-Jürgen
   1998   Vom Textdesign zum Hypertext: Gedruckte und elektronische Zeitungen als nicht-lineare Medien. In: Werner Holly and Bernd Ulrich Biere (eds.), *Medien im Wandel*, 63–102. Opladen/Wiesbaden: Westdeutscher Verlag
Burger, Harald
   1990   *Sprache der Massenmedien.* 2nd ed. Berlin/New York: de Gruyter.
Burger, Harald
   1991   *Das Gespräch in den Massenmedien.* Berlin/New York: de Gruyter.
Burkhardt, Armin and Kornelia Pape (eds.)
   2003   *Politik, Sprache und Glaubwürdigkeit: Linguistik des politischen Skandals.* Wiesbaden: Westdeutscher Verlag.
Choi, Yong-Joo
   1995   *Interpenetration von Politik und Massenmedien: Eine theoretische Arbeit zur politischen Kommunikation.* Münster/Hamburg: Lit.
Combs, James
   1984   *Polpop: Politics and Popular Culture in America.* Bowling Green, OH: Bowling Green University Popular Press.
Combs, James
   1991   *Polpop 2: Politics and Popular Culture in America Today.* Bowling Green, OH: Bowling Green University Popular Press.
Cook, Timothy E.
   1998   *Governing with the News: The News Media as a Political Institution.* Chicago: University of Chicago Press.
de Certeau, Michel
   1984   *The Practice of Everyday Life.* Berkeley: University of California Press.
Dieckmann, Walther
   1975   *Sprache in der Politik: Einführung in die Pragmatik und Semantik der politischen Sprache.* 2nd ed. Heidelberg: Winter.
Dörner, Andreas
   1999   Medienkultur und politische Öffentlichkeit: Perspektiven und Probleme der Cultural Studies aus politikwissenschaftlicher Sicht. In: Andreas Hepp and Rainer Winter (eds.), *Kultur – Medien – Macht: Cultural Studies und Medienanalyse*, 2nd ed., 319–335. Opladen/Wiesbaden: Westdeutscher Verlag.
Dörner, Andreas
   2000   *Politische Kultur und Medienunterhaltung: Zur Inszenierung politischer Identitäten in der amerikanischen Film- und Fernsehwelt.* Konstanz: Universitätsverlag Konstanz.

Dörner, Andreas
    2001   *Politainment: Politik in der medialen Erlebnisgesellschaft.* Frankfurt/Main: Suhrkamp.
Dörner, Andreas
    2002   Wahlkämpfe – eine rituelle Inszenierung des "demokratischen Mythos". In: Andreas Dörner and Ludgera Vogt (eds.), *Wahl-Kämpfe: Betrachtungen über ein demokratisches Ritual*, 16–42. Frankfurt/Main: Suhrkamp.
Dörner, Andreas
    2003   Demokratie – Macht – Ästhetik: Zur Präsentation des Politischen in der Mediengesellschaft. In: Hans Vorländer (ed.), *Zur Ästhetik der Demokratie: Formen der politischen Selbstdarstellung*, 200–223. Stuttgart: Deutsche Verlagsanstalt.
Dörner, Andreas and Ludgera Vogt (eds.)
    2002   *Wahl-Kämpfe: Betrachtungen über ein demokratisches Ritual.* Frankfurt/Main: Suhrkamp.
Donsbach, Wolfgang, Otfried Jarren, Hans Mathias Kepplinger and Barbara Pfetsch
    1993   *Beziehungsspiele – Medien und Politik in der öffentlichen Diskussion.* Gütersloh: Bertelsmann Stiftung.
Ebbighausen, Rolf and Sighard Neckel (eds.)
    1989   *Anatomie des politischen Skandals.* Frankfurt/Main: Suhrkamp.
Edelman, Murray
    1964   *The Symbolic Uses of Politics.* Urbana: University of Illinois Press.
Edelman, Murray
    1971   *Politics as Symbolic Action, Mass Arousal and Quiescence.* Chicago: Markham Publishing Corporation.
Edelman, Murray
    1988   *Constructing the Political Spectacle.* Chicago: University of Chicago Press.
Esser, Frank
    1999   "Tabloidization" of news: a comparative analysis of Anglo-American and German press journalism. *European Journal of Communication* 14: 291–324.
Fiske, John
    1987   *Television Culture.* London: Methuen.
Fiske, John
    1989   *Understanding Popular Culture.* London/Sidney/Wellington: Unwin Hyman.
Fiske, John
    1993   *Power Plays – Power Works.* London/New York: Verso.
Fiske, John
    1994   *Media Matters: Everyday Culture and Political Change.* Minneapolis/London: University of Minnesota Press.
Frevert, Ute and Wolfgang Braungart (eds.)
    2004   *Sprachen des Politischen: Medien und Medialität in der Geschichte.* Göttingen: Vandenhoeck & Ruprecht.
Gauger, Jörg-Dieter and Justin Stangl (eds.)
    1992   *Staatsrepräsentation.* Berlin: Reimer.
Goffman, Erving
    1959   *The Presentation of Self in Everyday Life.* New York: Doubleday Anchor.

Goodin, Robert E. and Hans-Dieter Klingemann
1996   Political Science: The Discipline. In: Robert E. Goodin and Hans-Dieter Klingemann (eds.), *A New Handbook of Political Science*, 3–49. Oxford/New York: Oxford University Press.

Graber, Doris A.
1997   *Mass Media and American Politics*. 5th ed. Washington, DC: Congressional Quarterly Press.

Gruber, Helmut
1996   *Streitgespräche: Zur Pragmatik einer Diskursform*. Opladen: Westdeutscher Verlag.

Grice, Herbert P.
1975   Logic and conversation. In: Peter Cole and J. L. Morgan (eds.), *Syntax and Semantics. Vol. 3: Speech Acts,* 41–58. New York/San Francisco/London: Academic Press.

Gurevitch, Michael and Jay G. Blumler
1977   Linkages between the mass media and politics: a model for the analysis of political communication systems. In: Curran, James, Michael Gurevitch and Janet Woollacort (eds.), *Mass Communication and Society,* 270–290. Beverly Hills, CA: Sage.

Habermas, Jürgen
1962   *Strukturwandel der Öffentlichkeit: Untersuchungen zu einer Kategorie der bürgerlichen Gesellschaft*. Darmstadt/Neuwied: Luchterhand.

Hall, Stuart
1980   Encoding/decoding. In: Hall, Stuart, Dorothy Hobson, Andrew Lowe and Paul Willis (eds.), *Culture, Media, Language,* 128–138. London: Routledge.

Hepp, Andreas and Rainer Winter (eds.)
1999   *Kultur – Medien – Macht: Cultural Studies und Medienanalyse,* 2nd ed. Opladen/Wiesbaden: Westdeutscher Verlag.

Heringer, Hans Jürgen
1990   *"Ich gebe Ihnen mein Ehrenwort": Politik, Sprache, Moral*. (Becksche Reihe 425.) Munich: Beck.

Hörning, Karl H. and Rainer Winter (eds.)
1999   *Widerspenstige Kulturen: Cultural Studies als Herausforderung*. Frankfurt/Main: Suhrkamp.

Hofmann, Wilhelm (ed.)
1998   *Visuelle Politik: Filmpolitik und die visuelle Konstruktion des Politischen*. Baden-Baden: Nomos.

Hofmann, Wilhelm (ed.)
1999   *Die Sichtbarkeit der Macht: Theoretische und empirische Untersuchungen zur visuellen Politik*. Baden-Baden: Nomos.

Holly, Werner
1990a   *Politikersprache: Inszenierungen und Rollenkonflikte im informellen Sprachhandeln eines Bundestagsabgeordneten*. Berlin/New York: de Gruyter.

Holly, Werner
1990b   Politik als Fernsehunterhaltung: Ein Selbstdarstellungsinterview mit Helmut Kohl. *Diskussion Deutsch* 21: 508–528.

Holly, Werner
   1992   Was kann Kohl, was Krenz nicht konnte? Deutsch-deutsche Unterschiede politischer Dialogrhetorik in zwei Fernsehinterviews. In: *Rhetorik. Ein internationales Jahrbuch* 11: 33–50.

Holly, Werner
   1993   Zur Inszenierung von Konfrontation in politischen Fernsehinterviews. In: Adi Grewenig (ed.), *Inszenierte Information: Politik und strategische Kommunikation in den Medien*, 164–197. Opladen: Westdeutscher Verlag.

Holly, Werner
   1994   Confrontainment: Politik als Schaukampf im Fernsehen. In: Louis Bosshart and Wolfgang Hoffmann-Riem (eds.), *Medienlust und Mediennutz: Unterhaltung als öffentliche Kommunikation*, 422–434. Munich: Ölschläger.

Holly, Werner
   1995   Secondary orality in the electronic media. In: Uta Quasthoff (ed.), *Aspects of Oral Communication* 340–363. (Research in Text Theory 21.) Berlin/New York: de Gruyter.

Holly, Werner
   2002   Fernsehkommunikation und Anschlusskommunikation: Fernsehbegleitendes Sprechen über Talkshows. In: Jens Tenscher and Christian Schicha (eds.), *Talk auf allen Kanälen: Angebote, Akteure und Nutzer von Fernsehgesprächssendungen*, 353–370. Wiesbaden: Westdeutscher Verlag.

Holly, Werner
   2003a   "Ich bin ein Berliner" und andere mediale Geschichts-Klischees. In: Ulrich Schmitz and Horst Wenzel (eds.), *Wissen und neue Medien: Bilder und Zeichen von 800 bis 2000*, 215–240. Berlin: Erich Schmidt.

Holly, Werner
   2003b   Die Ordnung des Skandals: Zur diskursanalytischen Beschreibung eines "Frame" am Beispiel der CDU-Spendenaffäre. In: Armin Burkhardt and Kornelia Pape (eds.), *Politik, Sprache und Glaubwürdigkeit: Linguistik des politischen Skandals*, 47–68. Wiesbaden: Westdeutscher Verlag.

Holly, Werner
   2004a   *Fernsehen*. (Grundlagen der Medienkommunikation 15.) Tübingen: Niemeyer.

Holly, Werner
   2004b   Sprechsprache und bewegte Bilder: Audiovisualität. *Mitteilungen des Deutschen Germanistenverbands* 51: 122–134.

Holly, Werner
   2005   Zum Zusammenspiel von Sprache und Bildern im audiovisuellen Verstehen. In: Busse, Dietrich, Thomas Nier and Martin Wengeler (eds.), *Brisante Semantik: Neue Konzepte und Forschungsergebnisse einer kulturwissenschaftlichen Linguistik*, 337–353. Tübingen: Niemeyer.

Holly, Werner
   2007   Audiovisuelle Hermeneutik: Am Beispiel des TV-Spots der Kampagne 'Du bist Deutschland'. In: Fritz Hermanns and Werner Holly (eds.), *Linguistische Hermeneutik*, 387–426. Tübingen: Niemeyer.

Holly, Werner and Bernd-Ulrich Biere (eds.)
   1998   *Medien im Wandel*. Opladen/Wiesbaden: Westdeutscher Verlag.

Holly, Werner, Almut Hoppe and Ulrich Schmitz (eds.)
 2004   *Sprache und Bild: Mitteilungen des Deutschen Germanistenverbands* 51 (1/2).
Holly, Werner, Peter Kühn and Ulrich Püschel
 1986   *Politische Fernsehdiskussionen: Zur medienspezifischen Inszenierung von Propaganda als Diskussion.* Tübingen: Niemeyer.
Holly, Werner, Peter Kühn and Ulrich Püschel (eds.)
 1989   *Redeshows: Fernsehdiskussionen in der Diskussion.* Tübingen: Niemeyer.
Holly, Werner, Ulrich Püschel and Jörg Bergmann (eds.)
 2001   *Der sprechende Zuschauer: Wie wir uns Fernsehen kommunikativ aneignen.* Wiesbaden: Westdeutscher Verlag.
Holly, Werner and Johannes Schwitalla
 1995   "Explosiv – Der heiße Stuhl": Zur Inszenierung von "Streitkultur" im kommerziellen Fernsehen. In: Klaus Neumann-Braun and Stephan Müller-Doohm (eds.), *Kulturinszenierung – Kultureffekte*, 59–88. Frankfurt/Main: Suhrkamp.
Hondrich, Karl Otto
 2002   *Enthüllung und Entrüstung: Eine Phänomenologie des politischen Skandals.* Frankfurt/Main: Suhrkamp.
Iyengar, Shanto and Richard Reeves (eds.)
 1997   *Do the Media Govern? Politicians, Voters, and Reporters in America.* Thousand Oaks/London/New Delhi: Sage.
Jäger, Ludwig and Georg Stanitzek (eds.)
 2001   *Transkribieren: Medien/Lektüre.* Munich: Fink.
Jarren, Otfried
 1998   Medien, Mediensystem und politische Öffentlichkeit im Wandel. In: Ulrich Sarcinelli (ed.), *Politikvermittlung und Demokratie in der Mediengesellschaft*, 74–94. (Schriftenreihe 352.) Bonn: Bundeszentrale für Politische Bildung.
Jewett, Robert and John Shelton Lawrence
 1977   *The American Monomyth.* Garden City, NY: Anchor Press, Doubleday.
Kepplinger, Hans Mathias
 1987   *Darstellungseffekte: Experimentelle Untersuchungen zur Wirkung von Pressefotos und Fernsehfilmen.* Freiburg/Munich: Alber.
Klein, Josef
 1996   Unterhaltung und Information: Kategorien und Sprechhandlungsebenen. Medienlinguistische Aspekte von TV-Akzeptanzanalysen mit dem Evaluationsrekorder. In: Hess-Lüttich, Ernest W. B., Werner Holly and Ulrich Püschel (eds.), *Textstrukturen im Medienwandel*, 107–119. Frankfurt/Main etc.: Lang.
Klein, Josef
 1997   Kategorien der Unterhaltsamkeit: Grundlagen einer Theorie der Unterhaltung mit kritischem Rückgriff auf Grice. In: Eckhard Rolf (ed.), *Pragmatik: Implikaturen und Sprechakte*, Linguistische Berichte. Sonderheft 8: 176–188.
Klein, Josef
 1998a   Boulevardisierung in TV-Kulturmagazinen. In: Werner Holly and Bernd Ulrich Biere (eds.), *Medien im Wandel*, 103–111. Opladen/Wiesbaden: Westdeutscher Verlag.

Klein, Josef
    1998b   Politische Kommunikation als Sprachstrategie. In: Jarren, Otfried, Ulrich Sarcinelli and Ulrich Saxer (eds.), *Politische Kommunikation in der demokratischen Gesellschaft: Ein Handbuch*, 376–395. Opladen/Wiesbaden: Westdeutscher Verlag.

Knieper, Thomas and Marion G. Müller (eds.)
    2001   *Kommunikation visuell. Das Bild als Forschungsgegenstand – Grundlagen und Perspektiven.* Cologne: Halem.

Köller, Wilhelm
    2004   *Perspektivität und Sprache: Zur Struktur von Objektivierungsformen in Bildern, im Denken und in der Sprache.* Berlin/New York: de Gruyter.

Kress, Gunther and Theo van Leeuwen
    1998   Front pages: (the critical) analysis of newspaper layout. In: Allen Bell and Peter Garrett (eds.), *Approaches to Media Discourse*, 186–219. Oxford: Blackwell.

Langer, Susanne
    1942   *Philosophy in a New Key.* New York: New American Library.

Laux, Lothar and Astrid Schütz
    1996   *"Wir, die wir gut sind": die Selbstdarstellung von Politikern, zwischen Glorifizierung und Glaubwürdigkeit.* Munich: Deutscher Taschenbuch Verlag.

Liebrand, Claudia and Irmela Schneider (eds.)
    2002   *Medien in Medien.* Cologne: DuMont.

Liedtke, Frank, Martin Wengeler and Karin Böke (eds.)
    1991   *Begriffe besetzen: Strategien des Sprachgebrauchs in der Politik.* Opladen: Westdeutscher Verlag.

Linke, Angelika
    1985   *Gespräche im Fernsehen: eine diskursanalytische Untersuchung.* Bern etc.: Lang.

Livingstone, Sonia and Peter Lunt
    1994   *Talk on Television: Audience Participation and Public Debate.* London/New York: Routledge.

Ludes, Peter
    1993   Visualisierung als Teilprozeß der Modernisierung der Moderne. In: Knut Hickethier (ed.), *Geschichte des Fernsehens in der Bundesrepublik Deutschland. Volume 1. Institution, Technik und Programm: Rahmenaspekte der Programmgeschichte des Fernsehens*, 353–370. Munich: Fink.

Ludes, Peter
    1998   *Einführung in die Medienwissenschaft: Entwicklungen und Theorien.* Berlin: Erich Schmidt.

Luhmann, Niklas
    1996   *Die Realität der Massenmedien.* 2nd ed. Opladen: Westdeutscher Verlag.

Lutz, Benedikt and Ruth Wodak
    1987   *Information für Informierte.* Vienna: Akademie der Wissenschaften.

Machin, David
    2004   Building the world's visual language: the increasing global importance of image banks in corporate media. *Visual Communication* 3(3): 316–336.

Meier, Christian
1983   *Die Entstehung des Politischen bei den Griechen.* Frankfurt/Main: Suhrkamp.
Meyer, Thomas
2001   *Mediokratie: Die Kolonisierung der Politik durch die Medien.* (edition suhrkamp 2004.) Frankfurt/Main: Suhrkamp.
Meyer, Thomas, Rüdiger Ontrup and Christian Schicha
2000   *Die Inszenierung des Politischen: Zur Theatralität von Mediendiskursen.* Wiesbaden: Westdeutscher Verlag.
Meyrowitz, Joshua
1985   *No Sense of Place: The Impact of Electronic Media on Social Behavior.* New York/Oxford: Oxford University Press.
Mill, John Stuart
1864   *On Liberty.* 3rd ed. London: Longman, Roberts & Green.
Mühlen, Ulrike
1985   *Talk als Show: Eine linguistische Untersuchung der Gesprächsführung in den Talkshows des deutschen Fernsehens.* Frankfurt/Bern/New York: Lang.
Müller, Marion G.
1997   *Politische Bildstrategien im amerikanischen Präsidentschaftswahlkampf 1828–1996.* Berlin: Akademie Verlag.
Münch, Richard
1991   *Dialektik der Kommunikationsgesellschaft.* Frankfurt/Main: Suhrkamp.
Nieland, Jörg-Uwe and Klaus Kamps (eds.)
2004   *Politikdarstellung und Unterhaltungskultur: Zum Wandel der politischen Kommunikation.* Cologne: Halem.
Norris, Pippa (ed.)
1997   *Politics and the Press: The News Media and their Influences.* Boulder/London: Lynne Rienner.
Ong, Walter J.
1982   *Orality and Literacy: The Technologizing of the Word.* London: Methuen.
Pörksen, Uwe
1997   *Weltmarkt der Bilder: Eine Philosophie der Visiotype.* Stuttgart: Klett-Cotta.
Proudhon, Pierre-Joseph
1843   *De la création de l'ordre dans l'humanité, ou Principes d'organisation politique.* Paris: Prévot.
Robins, Kevin
1996   *Into the Image: Culture and Politics in the Field of Vision.* London/New York: Routledge.
Sachs-Hombach, Klaus
2003   *Das Bild als kommunikatives Medium: Elemente einer allgemeinen Bildwissenschaft.* Cologne: Halem.
Sarcinelli, Ulrich
1987   *Symbolische Politik: Zur Bedeutung symbolischen Handelns in der Wahlkampfkommunikation der Bundesrepublik Deutschland.* Opladen: Westdeutscher Verlag.

Schicha, Christian and Carsten Brosda (eds.)
    2002   *Politikvermittlung in Unterhaltungsformaten.* Münster: Lit.
Schicha, Christian and Rüdiger Ontrup (eds.)
    1999   *Medieninszenierungen im Wandel: Interdisziplinäre Zugänge.* Münster: Lit.
Schildt, Axel
    1999   Massenmedien im Umbruch der fünfziger Jahre. In: Jürgen Wilke (ed.), *Mediengeschichte der Bundesrepublik Deutschland*, 633–648. Cologne/Weimar/Vienna: Böhlau.
Schmidt, Manfred G.
    2000   *Demokratietheorien: Eine Einführung.* Wiesbaden: Westdeutscher Verlag.
Schmitz, Ulrich
    2003   Text-Bild-Metamorphosen in Medien um 2000. In: Ulrich Schmitz and Horst Wenzel (eds.): *Wissen und neue Medien: Bilder und Zeichen von 800 bis 2000*, 241–263. Berlin: Erich Schmidt.
Schmitz, Ulrich
    2004   *Sprache in modernen Medien: Einführung in Tatsachen und Theorien, Themen und Thesen.* Berlin: Erich Schmidt.
Schneider, Beate
    1998   Mediensystem. In: Jarren, Otfried, Ulrich Sarcinelli and Ulrich Saxer (eds.), *Politische Kommunikation in der demokratischen Gesellschaft: Ein Handbuch*, 422–430. Opladen/Wiesbaden: Westdeutscher Verlag.
Schütz, Astrid
    1992   *Selbstdarstellung von Politikern: Analyse von Wahlkampfauftritten.* Weinheim: Deutscher Studien-Verlag.
Schwartzenberg, Roger Gérard
    1980   *Politik als Showgeschäft: Moderne Strategien im Kampf um die Macht.* Düsseldorf/Vienna: Econ.
Sennett, Richard
    1974   *The Fall of Public Man.* New York: Knopf.
Soeffner, Hans-Georg
    1998   Erzwungene Ästhetik: Repräsentation, Zeremoniell und Ritual in der Politik. In: Herbert Willems and Martin Jurga (eds.), *Inszenierungsgesellschaft: Ein einführendes Handbuch*, 215–234. Opladen/Wiesbaden: Westdeutscher Verlag.
Soeffner, Hans-Georg and Dirk Tänzler (eds.)
    2002   *Figurative Politik: Zur Performanz der Macht in der modernen Gesellschaft.* Opladen: Leske und Budrich.
Spangenberg, Peter M.
    1988   TV, Hören und Sehen. In: Hans Ulrich Gumbrecht and K. Ludwig Pfeiffer (eds.), *Materialität der Kommunikation*, 776–798. Frankfurt/Main: Suhrkamp.
Sparks, Colin
    2000   Introduction: the panic over tabloid news. In: Colin Sparks and John Tulloch (eds.), *Tabloid Tales: Global Debates over Media Standards*, 1–40. Lanham etc.: Rowman & Littlefield.

Sparks, Colin and John Tulloch (eds.)
2000   *Tabloid Tales: Global Debates over Media Standards*. Lanham etc.: Rowman & Littlefield.
Sternberger, Dolf
1966   Die Sprache in der Politik. In: *Die deutsche Sprache im 20. Jahrhundert*, 79–91. Göttingen: Vandenhoeck & Ruprecht.
Stöckl, Hartmut
2005   *Die Sprache im Bild – Das Bild in der Sprache: Zur Verknüpfung von Sprache und Bild im massenmedialen Text*. Berlin/New York: de Gruyter.
Straßner, Erich
1997   *Zeitung*. Tübingen: Niemeyer.
Strauß, Gerhard, Ulrike Haß and Gisela Harras
1989   *Brisante Wörter von Agitation bis Zeitgeist: Ein Lexikon zum öffentlichen Sprachgebrauch*. Berlin/New York: de Gruyter.
Tenscher, Jens
2002   Talkshowisierung als Element moderner Politikvermittlung. In: Jens Tenscher and Christian Schicha (eds.), *Talk auf allen Kanälen: Angebote, Akteure und Nutzer von Fernsehgesprächssendungen*, 55–71. Wiesbaden: Westdeutscher Verlag.
Tenscher, Jens and Christian Schicha (eds.)
2002   *Talk auf allen Kanälen: Angebote, Akteure und Nutzer von Fernsehgesprächssendungen*. Wiesbaden: Westdeutscher Verlag.
Turner, Graeme
1999   Tabloidization, journalism and the possibility of critique. *International Journal of Cultural Studies* 2: 59–76.
van Leeuwen, Theo
2005   *Introducing Social Semiotics*. London/New York: Routledge.
Weischenberg, Siegfried
1995   *Journalistik: Theorie und Praxis aktueller Medienkommunikation. Volume 2: Medientechnik, Medienfunktionen, Medienakteure*. Opladen: Westdeutscher Verlag.
Willems, Herbert and Martin Jurga (eds.)
1998   *Inszenierungsgesellschaft: Ein einführendes Handbuch*. Opladen/Wiesbaden: Westdeutscher Verlag.
Winter, Rainer
2001   *Die Kunst des Eigensinns: Cultural Studies als Kritik der Macht*. Weilerswist: Velbrück Wissenschaft.
Wulf, Christoph and Jörg Zirfas (eds.)
2004   *Die Kultur des Rituals: Inszenierungen. Praktiken. Symbole*. Munich: Fink.

IV. Language and communication in the media

15. News genres

Theo van Leeuwen

1. Introduction

The term "genre" refers to a *type* of text or communicative event. Genre analysis should therefore aim to bring out the characteristics of types of texts. The problem is, this can be done in many different ways. The everyday words we use to refer to genres of text characterize them in terms of their subject matters (e.g. "Westerns", "romances"), their functions ("advertisements" seek to persuade, "sermons" to teach a moral lesson), their truth claims (e.g. "fiction", "documentary", "report", "opinion piece"), their effects ("thrillers" seek to thrill, "comedies" to raise a laugh), or their forms and mediums (e.g. "musicals" incorporate song, "radio plays" use the medium of sound broadcasting). In this chapter "genre" will be used in the narrower and more specific sense which it has acquired in linguistics and discourse analysis over the past 30 years or so – as characterizing texts and communicative events in terms of the way they embody particular types of interaction that come with particular relationships between the interactants (e.g. participants in a dialogue, or writers and readers) and with particular communicative functions (e.g. persuading, teaching, entertaining).

In this conception "genre" is distinct from two other ways of characterizing texts (cf. e.g. Fairclough 2000; van Leeuwen 2005). The first is *discourse*, the subject matter of the text, together with the interpretation that is put on to it, in other words, the way the text constructs a particular kind of representation of the aspect(s) of reality of which it speaks. The second is *style*, the way in which a text expresses the identity of the speaker or writer (or the organisation or institution on whose behalf he or she speaks or writes). All texts and communicative events can be, and perhaps should be, analyzed in all three of these ways, as illustrated by this example from *Cosmopolitan* magazine (USA version, November 2004, p. 146):

> Sip a soothing beverage
> The act of slowly drinking any hot liquid calms you down, says New York City psychotherapist Anne Rosen Noran, PhD. Green tea is your best bet since it's packed with skin-beautifying antioxidants. Try Susan Ciminelli Afternoon Delight Tea, $ 15.

The text is based on a discourse of tea drinking – "*a*" discourse, because there can be several. Tea drinking can be interpreted as something you do as a "connoisseur", to seek refined pleasures, or as something you do for purposes of health or beauty, as in this case, where slowly drinking tea "calms you down" and beautifies your skin. And that does not exhaust the possibilities.

As a genre, the text is a typical "advertorial" – a mixture of providing information ("The act of slowly drinking [...] calms you down"), advice ("Green tea is your best bet") and persuasion ("Try Susan Ciminelli Afternoon Delight Tea"). The direct address ("you") and the use of imperatives is typical of the kind of relations which writers of such material try to set up with their readers.

In terms of style, the piece conveys a hybrid identity. It combines the voice of the expert (the mention of the psychotherapist's PhD, expressions like "the act of drinking" and terms like "antioxidants") with the voice of the advertiser ("Try Susan Ciminelli Afternoon Delight Tea") and with a casual, conversational style that makes the message sound more like the advice of a friend than the advice of an expert ("your best bet", "it's packed with").

2. The concept of genre

As mentioned above, the term "genre" is narrowed down here to refer to texts and communicative events as pieces of interaction that create specific kinds of relations between their interactants, and fulfil specific communicative functions, for instance bonding, entertaining, persuading, teaching, etc. Analysing texts and communicative events in terms of their "genre" is therefore (1) describing what people do to, for, or with each other by means of texts and communicative events, and (2) describing how the way in which they do this helps set up or maintain specific relationships (formal or informal, equal or unequal, and so on).

Longacre (1974) distinguished four basic types of genre: the narrative genre; the procedural genre (the "how-to-do-it" or "how-it-is-done" text); the expository genre, which describes, explains and interprets the world; and the hortatory genre, which aims to "influence conduct", to get people to feel or think or do in certain ways. He claimed that these genres are universal, and studied examples from various traditional societies (Longacre 1971), correlating their functions (entertaining, instructing, explaining, persuading, etc) to the linguistic features that typically manifest them, as shown in Table 1 below.

Narratives, Longacre (1974) said, are about people and their actions, and link these actions chronologically (which of course does not exclude flashbacks, parallel stories and so on). As they deal with events that have already happened, they must be told in "accomplished time", and in the first or third person. Changing one or other of these features creates special types of narratives: a narrative in "non-accomplished" time is the special case of "prophecy", for instance, and a narrative in the second person will either praise or accuse the addressee(s).

Table 1. Longacre's discourse genres

	− prescriptive	+ prescriptive
+ chronological	*Narrative* First or third person Actor-oriented Accomplished time (encoded as past or present) Chronological linkage	*Procedural* Non-specific person Goal oriented Projected time (encoded as past, present or future) Chronological linkage
− chronological	*Expository* Any person (usually third) Subject matter oriented Time not focal Logical linkage	*Hortatory* Second person Addressee oriented Commands, suggestions (encoded as imperatives or "soft" commands) Logical linkage

Procedural texts also deal with actions but for purposes of "how to do it" instruction. They may use imperatives ("wash the vegetables"), "we" ("first, we wash the vegetables") or "you" ("first you wash the vegetables"), but no specific people are addressed and the focus is on the sequence of actions that is being explained (which must be chronologically ordered if the instructions are to be effective).

Expository texts do not narrate specific events in chronological order but link more general statements in some form of logical structure, for instance an "argument" or an "explanation". Hortatory texts, finally, are like procedural texts in that they address the listeners or readers directly, in order to persuade them to do or think or feel something. Their structure, however, is logical, as in expository texts: reasons must be given, for instance, for why things should be done, or why they should be done in the way proposed.

Longacre stressed that the features that manifest these genres are "deep structure", semantic features. For instance, in a procedural text, time is always "projected", always oriented towards the future because the task that is being explained has not yet been performed by the listener or reader. But this need not be realized by future tense. A procedural text may also take the form of a "case story", or "best practice example". On the surface it will then have the features Longacre described as typical of narratives. But a closer look would show that all the stages of a particular process are included, so that the text can serve as instruction just as surely as a straightforward procedural text. As a whole, such texts will then combine the entertainment function of the narrative with the instructional function of the procedural text. As Walter Ong has shown (1982: 43), this was common in oral story telling traditions:

> The articulation of such things as navigation procedures (...) would have been encountered not in any abstract manual-style description but (...) embedded in a narrative presenting specific commands for human action or accounts of specific acts.

But it is common in today's media as well, for instance in celebrity profiles in women's magazines, which often provide what is, from the point of view of narrative flow, an excess of detail on the beauty and health regimes that keep them looking young and beautiful.

In addition to describing the typical features and functions of all four of these genres, Longacre also described the typical beginning-middle-end structure of narratives, as did Labov, more or less at the same time (Labov 1972). Later this approach was extended also to non-narrative genres (Hasan 1978; Martin 1985, 1992; van Leeuwen 1987; Ventola 1987; Swales 1990). The essential characteristics of the approach are as follows:

- A genre is described as a series of "stages", each of which has a specific function in moving the text or communicative event forward towards the realization of its ultimate communicative aim. In the analysis each stage is given a functional label to bring out this function, e.g. "Revealing a problem", "Appealing for help" etc. in the following example, which is taken from a magazine advice column in the Indian version of *Cosmopolitan* magazine (November 2001: 58):

I lied on my CV	*Revealing a problem (confession)*
Should I come clean with my boss?	*Appealing for help (question)*
Yes	*Providing a solution (answer)*
But be prepared for the possibility of losing your job if you have a scrupulous boss	*Issuing a caveat (warning)*
The bright side: you will gain her respect if you speak up and accept your mistake	*Predicting the result (prediction 1)*
and having got this burden off your chest will help you focus better on your work	*(prediction 2)*

- Each stage consists of one or more of the same speech acts (e.g. "question", "answer", "warning" etc. in the above example). In the example the first stage contains only one "confession", but in many other advice columns the "revealing a problem" stage might be a short narrative containing a *series* of confessions.
- The sequence of stages as a whole realizes a particular strategy for achieving an overall communicative goal, in this case the solution of a problem.
- Because each stage is homogeneous in terms of the communicative acts it contains, it will also be relatively homogeneous in terms of the linguistic features that characterize it. The "revealing a problem" stage of an advice

column, for instance, will have the features typical of confessions: first person, statements, past tense and verbs that express what is, in the context, considered to be a deviant action or state.

We can now see that genres are not as homogeneous as Longacre's characterizations might have us believe. Advice columns, for instance, can be characterized by the ways in which they *combine* narrative, explanatory, hortatory, and sometimes also procedural stages. Not all the stages in the above example would occur in every advice column. "Predicting the result" could be omitted, for example. For this reason genre analysts often indicate which stages are indispensable ("obligatory") and which "optional" (e.g. Hasan 1978). It is not possible, for instance, to have an advice column without, at the very least, a problem and a solution, in that order (an advertisement, on the other hand, *could* offer a solution before indicating the problems it might solve).

3. Stories

Journalists refer to news, not as "articles", but as "stories": "A good journalist 'gets good stories' or 'knows a good story'. A critical news editor asks: 'Is this really a story?' or 'Where's the story in this?'" (Bell 1991: 147).

But journalists' stories differ from most other stories, including such media stories as magazine feature articles. The best way to bring this out is by reference to Labov's (1972) classic account of narrative. It was originally written as an analysis of a specific kind of narrative, the boasting stories of Harlem teenagers, but turned out to apply to many other kinds of stories, and it uses the approach described in the previous section of this chapter: dividing narratives into stages, and showing the communicative function of each stage as well as the way these stages, through the particular order in which they occur, create the communicative function of the narrative as a whole – the way it entertains and enthrals an audience by telling a story, and the way it delivers something of relevance to the listeners' lives.

In describing Labov's stages I will use a feature article from *Cosmopolitan* magazine (USA version, November 2004: 92–95).

1 Abstract
The storyteller begins with a brief summary or indication of the topic of the story, to attract the listener's attention and interest:

> **Her Bridesmaids were Killed on Their Way to the Wedding.**
> What was to be the happiest day of Bree Mayer's life turned into the worst with one phone call. She shared her heartbreaking experience with *Cosmo*.

2 Orientation
The storyteller then introduces the setting – who is involved, when and where – and the "initial event", the event that kicks off the story. This provides orientation for the listener. Elements of orientation may also occur later in the story as new people, places and things are introduced.

> Joey and I met in 2000, when we were both freshmen at North Central University in Minnesota. We were in a gospel band on campus; he played the guitar and I sang. I was intrigued by Joey because he seemed kind of mysterious (...) One day, Joey invited me on a boat ride, but we ran out of gas in the middle of the lake. Since we didn't have any oars, we were stuck, so we started talking. By the time someone paddled out to rescue us I knew I wanted to spend a lot more time with this guy.

3 Complication
The story then moves into the events that make up its core: Joey and Bree decide to get married. Joey's three sisters will be bridesmaids and are due to attend the pre-wedding "bachelorette's party". They are late to arrive. Then there is a phonecall and Bree learns that all three have died in a road accident.

4 Evaluation
Throughout the development of the story there are moments of evaluation. At such moments the storyteller reasserts the relevance, importance and interest of the story. In this story this is done mostly by indicating and reinforcing the narrator's feelings about the events:

> "I was in total shock"
> "I felt completely numb"

5 Resolution
The final event, the outcome of the story, provides the listener with meaning. Stories are told to convey ideas about life. They have an issue, a life problem, to resolve. In this case the issue in need of resolution is whether, such a short time after the tragedy, the wedding should or should not go ahead. The resolution is that it should. Marriage is a celebration of love, and "love can heal".

6 Coda
This stage, which is "optional", has the storyteller signing off and making a bridge from the resolution to the "here and now" of the telling of the story, and to its continuing relevance for the storyteller and/or the listeners. Here is the coda of the *Cosmopolitan* story:

> Now we try to take it one day at a time. Some are more difficult than others, but we're settling into the routine of any couple. We miss the girls terribly. But we are helping each other deal with the loss and learning to balance grief with joy.

All these stages are realized by specific linguistic features, as indicated by the examples in this table:

Table 2. Speech acts and their realizations

Stages and their typical speech acts	Typical realizations	Examples
Abstract (speech acts of summarizing and attracting interest)	Action clauses summarizing the story; relational clauses with evaluative attribute	Her bridesmaids were killed on their way to the wedding. What was to be the happiest day of Bree Mayer's life turned into the worst.
Orientation (speech acts of description)	E.g. relational clauses describing people and places	He seemed mysterious. We were in a band.
Complication (speech acts of narration)	Action clauses	Alyssa then called the highway patrol. He looked at me and said: "They're dead. They're all dead."
Evaluation (speech acts of emotive expression)	E.g. first person relational clauses with mental process attributes	I was in shock. I felt completely numb.
Coda (general observations of the impact of the narrated events)	E.g. clauses of habitualized action or relational clauses with mental process attribute.	We are helping each other deal with the loss. Some (days) are more difficult than others.

4. News stories

The typical "hard news" story differs from the classic "complication-resolution" story described above in a number of ways. As van Dijk (1988: 176) has said, "News reports in the press are a member of a family of media types that need their own structural analysis". The account below is based on the analysis of van Dijk (1988), Bell (1991), Iedema, Feez and White (1994) and White (1998).

I use the first five paragraphs of the following *Sydney Morning Herald* story (22 October 2005: 15) as an example:

> **Hurricane's fury echoes that of Katrina official**
> Powerful winds and lashing rain pounded the Yutacan Peninsula, one of Mexico's top tourist destinations, as thousands of tourists went to ground in shelters to escape a weakening-then-strenghtening Hurricane Wilma.
> The category four hurricane is likely to strike densely populated Southern Florida late tomorrow.
> Described by forecasters as extremely dangerous, Wilma was expected to send a three-metre surge of water over Mexico's "Maya Riviera" early this morning.
> It killed 10 people in mudslides in Haiti earlier this week.
> Mexican authorities said yesterday nearly 22,000 tourists and residents had been evacuated from low-lying coastal areas. In one gymnasium shelter in Cancun, 1600 people spent Thursday night on mattresses.

The first point to make is this: the news story has a beginning, but no end. Like the classic complication-resolution story, it begins with an abstract. But it does not end with a resolution and a coda. And the abstract, or "lead" as it is called by journalists ("intro" in the US), does not serve to entice the listener or reader into the story, but instead conveys, without delay, the whole of the "central event" of the story, as concisely as possible, in maximally 40, preferably only 30-odd words. Any "orientation" is tightly wrapped into this, rather than presented separately. We do not have, for instance, "Yucatan is one of Mexico's top tourist destinations" but " pounded the Yucatan peninsula, one of Mexico's top tourist destinations". As former *Sunday Times* editor Harold Evans said (1972: 158), in a story, the writer "begins at the beginning and goes step by step to the stirring conclusion", but "for most hard news, story-telling is too slow a technique".

Secondly, while the "Hurricane Wilma" story is an "action story", a story recounting actions and events, these actions and events are not necessarily told in their chronological order. During most of the 19th century, news stories were still organized chronologically, as for instance in this example from the *Sydney Gazette* of March 5, 1803:

> On Tuesday, the 15th ultimo, fifteen labouring men fled from the Agricultural Settlement at Castle Hill, after having committed many acts of violence and atrocity. They at first forcibly entered the dwellinghouse of M.DECLAMB, which they ransacked, and stripped of many articles of plate, wearing apparel, some fire and side arms, provisions, spirituous liquors, a quantity of which they drank or wasted in the house. They next proceeded to the farm houses of Bradley and Bean, at Baulkham Hills. Mrs. Bradley's servant man they wantonly and inhumanly discharged a pistol at, the contents of which so shattered his face as to render him a ghastly spectacle, in all probability, during the remainder of his life. In Mrs. Beane's house they gave aloose to sensuality, equally brutal and unmanly. Numerous other delinquencies were perpetuated by this licentious banditti, whose ravages, however, could not escape the certain tread of justice.

But from the 1880s onward, the modern newspaper story developed, with its focus on a single central event, and its "inverted pyramid" structure. To bring this out, the following summary of the "Hurricane Wilma" story reconstructs the chronological order of events from the story's many time indications ("earlier in the week", "early this morning", "late tomorrow" etc.), and uses numbers in brackets to indicate the place of the events in the story as it was actually published:

1. Hurricane Wilma kills 10 people in Haiti (5)
2. Powerful winds and lashing rain pounds the Yucatan peninsula (1)
3. 22,000 tourists and residents are evacuated (2 and 6)
4. 1600 people spend the night on mattresses in a shelter in Cancun (7)
5. Hurricane will send a three-metre surge of water over Mexico's "Maya Riviera" (4)
6. Hurricane will strike densely populated Southern Florida (3)

The central event, the event that is happening *now*, on the day of publication, leads the story, and is thereby treated as the most important item of information, more important for instance than what happened in Haiti a few days earlier. Such a central event must have an "angle". It must be newsworthy (cf. Bell 1991: 156–160): recent, urgent, unexpected, relevant to the readers' interests (as construed by the newspaper), and, in some sense, "bad news", an event which threatens to "destabilise the social order" (Iedema, Feez and White 1994: 107). But there is a practical reason for starting with the whole of the most important event as well. It allows copy editors to fit the stories on the newspaper pages by taking as many paragraphs from the end as needed: the information in a newspaper story is presented in descending order of importance, with the least important details kept to the end of the story, according to the principle of the "inverted pyramid".

Still, although news stories focus on a single central event, they tie it in with many other events. For instance, in the "Hurricane Wilma" story, the central event is the storm in "Mexico's top tourist destination" and its effect on (Western) tourists. But, as has been pointed out by Allan Bell (1991), other events are related to it in a number of ways:

1 Background
Earlier events can serve as "background" or "context". As defined by Bell (1991: 170):

> The category of "background" covers any events prior to the current action. These are classed as "previous episodes" if they are comparatively recent. They probably figured as news stories in their own right at an earlier stage of the situation. If the background goes beyond the near past, it is classed as "history".

An example from the Hurricane Wilma story:

"It [Hurricane Wilma] killed 10 people in mudslides in Haiti earlier in the week".

2 Follow-up

Follow-up "covers any action subsequent to the main action of an event" and also includes reactions. It is therefore a "prime source for subsequent updating stories" (Bell 1991: 170), and journalists intending to keep a story alive will ensure that they include some follow-up. An example of "follow-up" from the Hurricane Wilma story:

"The category four hurricane is likely to strike densely populated southern Florida late tomorrow."

3 Commentary

Commentary "provides the journalist's or news actor's observations on the action" (Bell 1991: 170). It may be realized by explicit evaluation (e.g., in the "Hurricane Wilma" story, "described by forecasters as extremely dangerous"), or, for example, by comparisons with previous events. The latter happens extensively in the "Hurricane Wilma" story, as already indicated by the headline "Hurricane's fury echoes that of Katrina official" – the "official" in question was the only Federal Emergency Management Agency employee present in New Orleans when Katrina hit, and the writer of the piece uses the comparison to suggest that the authorities are once again badly prepared for the new emergency in Southern Florida.

4 Details

As Iedema, Feez and White (1994) have pointed out, the same event may be retold a number of times, each new re-telling adding further detail, for instance:

Thousands of tourists went to ground in shelters to escape (...)

Mexican authorities said yesterday nearly 22,000 tourists and residents had to be evacuated from low-lying coastal areas (...)

In one gymnasium shelter in Cancun, 1600 people spent Thursday night on mattresses (...)

Extending this term also to what Bell (1991) calls "background" and "follow-up", they called the central event the "nucleus" and these details "satellites": "Each satellite provides a new set of details about the 'crisis' event, including details about the past or details about the consequences" (Iedema, Feez and White 1994: 168). They represent this diagrammatically as shown in Figure 1, which models the structure of a news story about a car crash:

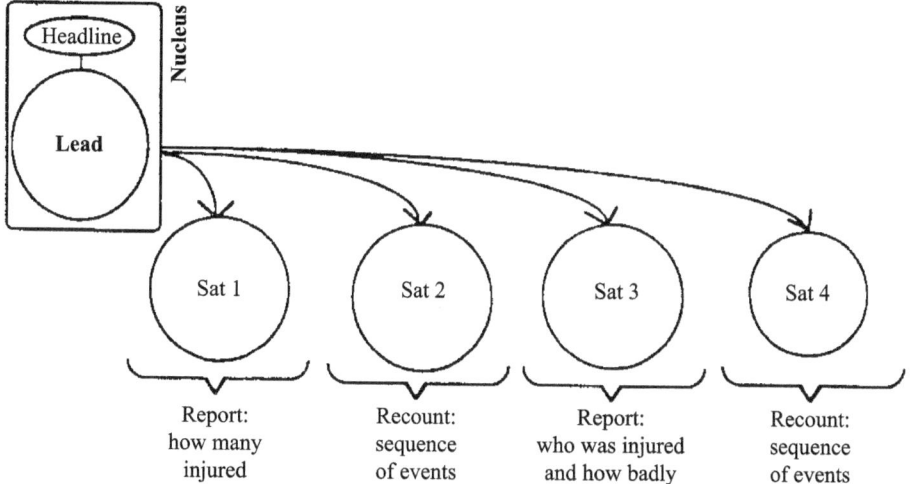

Figure 1. Nucleus-Satellite Structure (from Iedema, Feez and White 1994: 104)

In all these ways, then, news stories "knit diverse events together" (Iedema, Feez and White 1994: 168), and the "Hurricane Wilma" story, much as it may be built around a single central event, nevertheless ties this event to other events that happened, are happening, or are predicted to happen, in New Orleans, Washington, Haiti, Cancun and Florida.

We can now summarize our analysis of the "Hurricane Wilma" story (the italicized items show how orientations and evaluations are tucked into the narrative clauses in various ways, rather than featuring as separate stages):

Powerful winds and lashing rain pounded the Yucatan Peninsula, one of Mexico's top tourist destinations, as thousands of tourists went to ground in shelters to escape a weakening-then-strengthening Hurricane Wilma	*Establishing central event (1)* *Orientation* *Establishing central event (2)*
The category four hurricane is likely to strike densely populated Southern Florida late tomorrow	*Predicting follow-up event (b)* *Orientation*
Described by forecasters as extremely dangerous, Wilma was expected to send a three-metre surge of water over Mexico's "Maya Riviera" early this morning	*Evaluation (commentary)* *Predicting follow-up event (a)*

It killed ten people in mudslides in Haiti earlier this week	*Contextualizing by means of "background" event*
Mexican authorities said yesterday nearly 22,000 tourists and residents had to be evacuated from low-lying coastal areas	*Elaborating central event in more detail*
In one gymnasium shelter in Cancun, 1600 people spent Thursday night on mattresses	*Further elaborating central event*

5. Types of news stories

Many news stories (or parts of news stories) deal with opinions rather than events. Such stories often have a double structure. They are at once a narrative, a "story", a report, an expository, an "argument". This is possible because, in journalism, all opinions must be "attributed", to signify that they are the opinions of spokespeople, and not of the journalist him or herself. So from the point of view of what is conveyed by the "projecting" clauses ("he said", "Mr Bush said", etc.), the story is simply a report of what one or several spokespeople said, again presented in order of importance rather than chronologically (as shown in the left half of the example below). But from the point of view of the "projected" clauses (the reported or quoted utterances), judicious editing can turn the story into a logical argument (as shown in the right half of the example below (the example is from the *Sydney Morning Herald*, 22 October 2005: 15):

Report structure PLUS Argument structure

Event	he [Mr Bush] said	"Israel should not undertake any activity that contravenes its roadmap obligations".	*Warning*
Next event	he added that	Israel would be "held to account for any actions that hampered the peace process".	*Reason*
Next event	Mr Abbas said	Israel should stop settlement building on the West Bank	*Similar warning*
		if it wanted to foster an "atmosphere for peace".	*Condition*

Next event	he said	"Peace and security cannot be guaranteed by the construction of walls, by the erection of checkpoints and the confiscation of land, but rather by the recognition of rights".	*Reason*

So far I have discussed three media story genres: a magazine feature genre which follows the classical "complication-resolution" pattern, and the hard news "action story" and "opinion story" formats. But there are further genres of news story. The two fundamental elements of the "human interest story", for instance, as analyzed by Iedema, Feez and White (1994), are (1) the chronological narrative or *incident* which opens the story and may be preceded by an abstract and orientation and followed by details that elaborate the orientation and the incident, and (2) the *interpretation*. Their example is a story about a woman who "grew up in a close, caring and supportive family", but became a heroin addict and ended up holding up a corner shop armed with a syringe.

Abstract   After years of upheaval, Keris Hodge seemed to be finally getting her life back on track.

Orientation   She had been free of heroin for three years, her methadone was gradually being reduced and she was working at the job she liked best: nursing in an old people's home.

Incident   But then she injured her back carrying a patient and was prescribed Normison for the pain. Within days Keris was addicted. Five months later, she was holding up an all-night supermarket in Enmore, threatening the cashier with a syringe.
Keris Hodge who will be 30 tomorrow is now serving a four-year jail term, for armed robbery. The District Court judge who imposed the sentence this week, Judge Court, said that in "this era of AIDS" a syringe is as terrifying a weapon as a knife.

The "interpretation" that concludes the story has the "double structure" described above, as shown by the following short excerpt:

Event	Judge Court described it as	a crime with very serious overtones'	*Interpretation*
Next event	he said	she should get a full-time jail term	*Result*
		to reinforce the notion of deterrence (…)	*Purpose*

It follows that the "human interest" story is "not a collection of facts around a central event", like the hard news story, but a story that focuses on how particular events came about, on how someone who "grew up in a close, caring and supportive family" could end up in jail (Iedema, Feez and White 1994: 144)

Van Leeuwen (1987) focuses on a story from the Australian *Daily Mirror* (24/1/1984) interpreting it as an advice column in the form of a news story. Today, when much newsprint is devoted to "lifestyle" stories, such mixtures of news and advice are becoming an increasingly important genre. This particular example is a piece of parental advice which appeared on the first day of the new school year, and opened with a mini-narrative, in order, perhaps, to entice the reader into the story and to provide a small measure of "human interest":

> "When Mum first took me to school I started to cry because I thought I would never see her again. But after a few days I really loved school." – Mark, aged six.

It then moved into an "opinion story" in which a child psychologist explained that children might be anxious about "the first day" and that "preparation" is the answer to the problem:

		The first day at school can be a happy and a memorable one,	*Statement*
Event	Valerie said,	But the secret is to get ready and preparing now.	*Condition*
Next event	Valerie said	the main problems for new pupils were separation from families, meeting large numbers of children they didn't know and conforming to a classroom situation.	*Reason*

Finally it became "hortatory", to use Longacre's (1974) term, providing a set of "first day" do's and don'ts for parents. But the advice was still attributed to the child psychologist and therefore still read like a news story:

Event	Valerie says	it is important your child knows how to use and flush a toilet, ask for things clearly say his or her name and address.	*Suggestions*
		On the first day it is important not to rush children.	*Suggestion*

Next event   Valerie says   give them plenty of time to get   *Suggestion*
                                ready, eat breakfast and wash
                                and clean their teeth (…)

Clearly such "news" stories *do* have a beginning, a middle and an end, and do progress, step by step, towards a conclusions such as this one:

> "And finally don't worry if you or your child cries", Valerie says. "It won't last long".

Equally clearly, they mix different genres – news and advice column, narrative, exposition and procedure. Texts are rarely "pure" in terms of genre, and perhaps it is better to think of genres as resources we use to create strategies for achieving social goals of various kind, or, from the point of view of analysis, as *reference points* for analysis, rather than as schemas in which texts can be expected to fit neatly.

6. The procedural turn

Ever since the beginnings of speech act theory, the main emphasis in the study of language and text has shifted from meaning to action. The growth of genre theory has been part of this "procedural turn". Genres as defined in this tradition, and therefore also in this chapter, are conceived of as (inter)actional *formats* that can accommodate an ever widening range of discourses, and as strategies for achieving objectives, rather than, for instance, as resources for negotiation. Today this concept of genre is used, not only in text analysis, but also in text design, for instance by the designers of software (Powerpoint is a key example), the scripts used by call centre operators and other service workers (cf. Cameron 2000), and so on.

The supersedure of genre over discourse (as that term is used in this chapter) can in principle lead to a new form of social cohesion-in-diversity, a form in which it no longer matters that people believe different things, so long as they *do* more or less the same things. Universities are a good example of this principle. In universities many different and often contradictory truths can be taught. This poses no threat to the cohesion of the institution, so long as these truths are all delivered and examined in the same formats, subject to the same ritualized quality assessment procedures, and so on – so long as we all *do* the same things in increasingly homogeneous ways.

The same principle also allows us to be at once local and heterogeneous, and global and homogeneous. In a series of studies of the global magazine *Cosmopolitan*, Machin and van Leeuwen (e.g. 2003, 2004) described how different versions of the magazine used different discourses of women's work. The Dutch version, for instance, was oriented towards employees taking personal responsibility for their work, and working for the sake of job satisfaction rather than material rewards, while the Indian version was oriented towards working for status and material rewards. In the Indian version women had high status occupations, while in the Spanish and Greek versions they tended to be office workers with male bosses. The point is, all these versions were framed in the same "problem-solution" genre, as practical solutions to common problems, endorsed by psychological truths about human nature, and therefore as transcending cultural differences and legitimately "global".

This example shows that genres are not neutral containers for different discourses. The problem-solution format encountered in *Cosmopolitan,* for instance, carries a message of its own. It

> suggests a world in which there can be no solidarity with fellow human beings, no counsel from cultural and religious traditions, and no structural and political problems that can be addressed by collective political action. Instead it is all up to the individual. Each problem must be faced alone, and solved by means of the rational survival strategies sold by the global church of the corporate media in the way passports to heaven were once sold by the Catholic Church. (Machin and van Leeuwen 2004: 118)

Clearly genre is a highly important phenomenon in today's society, a prime example of Foucault's "microphysics of power" (see e.g. 1977, 1980). But it should be studied alongside discourse and style, and *critically*, with an eye for its social impact and its uses in social control, rather than only procedurally and "technically", for in that case it will inevitably contribute to an increasing homogeneity of generic practices and the increasing supersedure of procedure over meaning, whether the analyst is aware of it or not.

Note

It should be pointed out that this chapter does not deal with issues of the reception and comprehension of news. Fairclough (1995) discusses the issue of the diverse possible readings of media texts, an issue which has played an important role in the field of media studies, and van Dijk (1988) relates schematic structures such as the ones discussed in this chapter to comprehension.

References

Bell, Allan
    1991   *The Language of News Media*. Oxford: Blackwell.
Cameron, Deborah
    2000   *Good to Talk?* London: Sage.
Evans, Harold
    1972   *Editing and Design. Book One: Newsman's English*. London: Heinemann.
Fairclough, Norman
    1995   *Media Discourse*. London: Edward Arnold
Fairclough, Norman
    2000   *New Labour, New Language?* London: Routledge.
Foucault, Michel
    1977   *Language, Counter-Memory, Practice: Selected Essays and Interviews*. Ithaca, NY: Cornell University Press.
Foucault, Michel
    1980   *Power/Knowledge: Selected Interviews and Other Writings 1972–1977*. London: Pantheon.
Hasan, Ruqaiya
    1978   Text in the systemic-functional model. In Wolfgang U. Dressler (ed.), *Current Trends in Textlinguistics*, 228–246. Berlin: de Gruyter.
Iedema, Rick, Susan Feez and Peter White
    1994   *Media Literacy*. Sydney: Disadvantaged Schools Program, NSW Department of School Education.
Labov, William
    1972   *Language in the Inner City*. Philadelphia: University of Philadelphia Press.
Longacre, Robert E. (ed.)
    1971   *Philippine Discourse and Paragraph Studies in Memory of Betty McLachlin*. Canberra: Pacific Linguistics.
Longacre, Robert E.
    1974   Narrative versus other discourse genre. In Ruth Brend (ed.), *Advances in Tagmemics*, 357–376. Amsterdam: North Holland.
Machin, David and Theo van Leeuwen
    2003   Global schemas and local discourses in *Cosmopolitan*. *Journal of Sociolinguistics* 7(4): 493–512.
Machin, David and Theo van Leeuwen
    2004   Global media: generic homogeneity and discursive diversity. *Continuum: Journal of Media and Cultural Studies* 18(1): 99–120.
Martin, James R.
    1985   *Factual Writing: Exploring and Challenging Social Reality*. Geelong: Deakin University Press.
Martin, James R.
    1992   *English Text: System and Structure*. Amsterdam: Benjamins.
Ong, Walter J.
    1982   *Orality and Literacy: The Technologizing of the Word*. London: Methuen.

Swales, John
    1990   *Genre Analysis: English in Academic and Research Settings.* Cambridge: Cambridge University Press.

van Dijk, Teun A.
    1988   *News as Discourse.* Hillsdale, NJ: Lawrence Erlbaum.

van Leeuwen, Theo
    1987   Generic strategies in press journalism. *Australian Review of Applied Linguistics* 10(2): 199–221.

Van Leeuwen, Theo
    2005   *Introducing Social Semiotics.* London: Routledge.

Ventola, Eija M.
    1987   *The Structure of Social Interaction: A Systemic Approach to the Semiotics of Service Encounters.* London: Frances Pinter.

White, Peter R. R.
    1998   Telling media tales: the news story as rhetoric. Unpublished PhD thesis, Sydney University.

16. Specific genre features of new mass media

Helmut Gruber

1. Introduction

During the last fifteen years, the boost of information technology has had a far reaching cultural and social impact. Computer technology and the development of the internet play the main role in this technological revolution, but mobile telephone services have an ever increasing part in this development process. Together they represent what has been called the "new media" during the last decade.

The new information technologies offer not only the appropriate technological means for meeting the needs of the globalised information society, they also symbolise all the relevant features we associate with 21st century society: decentralisation, interactivity, multi-modality, transnationality and transculturality (Münker and Roesler 1997). Like the invention of any new technology of writing, the new media have had a tremendous effect on communicative and discursive practices and have fostered the emergence of new communicative styles and genres (Bolter 1997).

These communicative and discursive practices and their effects on the public sphere will be the main focus of this contribution, in which I will deal with the following forms of communication: hypertext, e-mail, internet relay chat (IRC), and telephone text messages.

In the first part of the remainder of this chapter, each of the four forms of communication will be characterised and their commonalities and differences will be discussed. In the following four sections I will discuss linguistic and communicative characteristics of each of the four forms of communication. For reasons of space it is impossible to present and analyse examples of each of the discussed forms of communication, therefore every section contains references to publications which present sample analyses. In the closing section, I will sum up various consequences of the communicative forms and genres in the new media and try to provide some general conclusions.

2. Forms of communication in the new media

2.1. General characteristics

Following Holly (1997), I distinguish between types of media, communicative forms, and genres. Holly suggests using the term "medium" for an array of communicative possibilities which are characterised by:

(a) Specific types of signs which they can process (e.g. spoken vs. written);
(b) The direction of communication (monological vs. dialogical);
(c) The specific possibilities of transmission and storage of data.

One specific medium may facilitate different communicative forms, which are characterised by combinations of certain features on these three dimensions (e.g. the medium "computer" may be used for the production of written, monological, stored (hyper-)texts[1] as well as for engaging in spoken, dialogical, (by default) unstored video conferences.

Forms of communication, on the other hand, are not necessarily associated with one single medium. A monological, written text may, for instance, be realised as a book, an inscription on a stone, or as an electronic text. The realisation of a form of communication in a specific medium, however, allows for media-specific variations.

Additionally, forms of communication may be realised as different genres, depending on the communicative purpose they fulfil in a certain situation type. As in the case of mediaspecific realisations of communicative forms, genres may also be realised differently in different media.

In order to characterise communicative forms in the new media, I split each of Holly's dimensions into two sub-dimensions (see table 1). The "sign type" dimension is divided into the sub-dimensions (1) "conceptual mode of communication" and (2) "communicative modality". Sub-dimension (1) draws upon a distinction which was introduced by Koch and Oesterreicher (1994), who assume that the conception of a communicative product as "spoken" or "written" is independent of its realisation in the oral or written mode. According to them, the conceptually literal pole is associated with interpersonal distance, whereas the conceptually oral pole is associated with closeness between communication partners.

Sub-dimension (2) refers to the semiotic modalities which are (in principle) available in the different forms of communication. These modalities range from oral to written, pictorial, musical etc.

Holly's second dimension is split into the sub-dimensions of (3) "monological vs. dialogical communication" and (4) "number of communication partners". Sub-dimension (3) refers to the primary communicative function a certain form of communication has.

Sub-dimension (4) specifies how many senders prototypically interact with how many addressees by the specific communicative form. It comprises three types of sender – addressee combinations: one to one (1:1), one to many (1:n), and many to many (n:n) communications.

The third dimension is split into two sub-dimensions (5) "degree of intended persistence" and (6) "synchronous vs. asynchronous communication".

Sub-dimension (5) takes up a notion of Erickson (1999), who notes that most forms of computer-mediated communication are intended to persist for a longer time period (i.e. they can be stored) and argues that this feature compensates for some of the shortcomings of computer-mediated communication (cf. below). Users may associate different degrees of intended persistence with different forms of communication (e.g. a hypertext is intended to persist for a longer time than a turn in a chat communication or a text message).

Sub-dimension (6) specifies whether communicators interact synchronously or asynchronously in a form of communication. Table 1 gives an overview of the prototypical specifications of each form of communication on the six sub-dimensions.

Table 1. Characterisation of new media as "communicative forms"

Sub-dimension	Hypertext	E-mail	Chat	Text messages
(1) conceptual mode of communication	conceptually written	conceptually written + conceptually spoken	conceptually written + conceptually spoken	conceptually written + conceptually spoken
(2) semiotic modality	multi-modal	primarily textual (hypertext possible)	textual	textual[2]
(3) primary communicative function	monological	dialogical	dialogical	dialogical
(4) no. of communication partners[3]	1:n	1:1 (personal communication) 1:n (newsgroups etc.)	n:n (1:1 possible)	1:1, (1:n possible)
(5) degree of intended persistence	high	medium	low	low
(6) synchronicity vs. asynchronicity	asynchronous	asynchronous	synchronous	asynchronous

The features of the four forms of communication on the six sub-dimensions in Table 1 show that no clear cut boundaries divide them from each other, but that they rather share different characteristics on different sub-dimensions. Hypertexts stand out as the most distinctive of the four forms. They share only the feature of asynchronicity with e-mail and text communication. On all other dimensions, hypertexts differ from the others. Hypertexts are conceptually written, multi-modal, monological,[4] one-to-many forms of communication with a high degree of intended persistence, i.e. they are produced to be accessible (yet not unchanged) at least for a certain time rather than designed as one (ephemeral) move in a multi-party communication.

E-mail, chat and texting share the same features on the first three sub-dimensions (i.e. they are conceptually written *and* spoken; their primary semiotic modality is textual; and they are dialogical), but differ in the last three. Here, e-mail and texting show the same characteristics on sub-dimensions 4 and 6 (i.e. they are used primarily for 1:1 communications and they are asynchronous forms of communication), whereas chat and texting are similar on sub-dimension 5 (i.e. their degree of intended persistence is low).

This preliminary characterisation of the four forms of communication shows that they constitute a network which we can expect to share certain discursive features, communicative practices, and genres.

2.2. Hypertext

Hypertexts are the prototypical documents on the world wide web (the graphical part of the internet). The communication situation of hypertext communication resembles that of "traditional" textual communication, i.e. it is a situation where author(s) and reader(s) are not co-present in a communication situation and the text mediates between communicative partners over distances of space and time (Ehlich 1983).

Hypertext and its communicative potentials have escaped the interest of text linguists and discourse analysts for a long period of time. Only rather recently have scholars of linguistics started to deal with this form of communication (Storrer 1999, 2002; Kress and van Leeuwen 2001; O'Halloran 2004; e.g. Jakobs and Lehnen 2005).

Hypertexts and their properties pose interesting questions for text linguistics which are not yet fully explored:

(1) Hypertexts challenge the traditional notion of "coherence". In modern text linguistics, coherence is viewed under a process perspective, i.e. as a property which is assigned to texts by producers and recipients in a communication process. Under this perspective, coherence can be viewed from a text production and a text reception perspective. The former deals with the production strategies an author employs to create a coherent text, while the latter deals with recipients' strategies to create a coherent mental representation of an actual text (Storrer 1999). In the case of linear texts, text production and reception may not coincide (e.g. if a reader skips several paragraphs or even chapters of a longer text), but both author and reader at least deal with the same document. In the case of hypertexts, however, authors provide readers with a whole array of possibilities of traversing a text. In complex hypertexts, every reader may thus

in principle take another path through the text and hence encounter a different text with a different global coherence. In Lemke's terms, users "traverse" through hypertexts and hypertext networks and this has specific semantic, generic and social consequences (Lemke 2005). This research shows that the concept of "global coherence" is not applicable for hypertexts as a whole (Storrer 1999). Only the local coherence of single text elements ("e-texts") of a hypertext is under the control of the hypertext author, but planning the global coherence of a website or of a hypertext network is impossible. The insights of coherence research, however, might be usefully applied in planning limited hypertexts and in combining multi-modal elements in a hypertext.

(2) Apart from its modules, hyperlinks are the constitutive elements of a hypertext. Links can connect pieces of information between which a variety of relations holds. To date, a theoretically informed classification of hyperlinks is still missing. It is one of the main desiderata of text linguistic hypertext research to provide a classification of hyperlinks which covers rhetorical, semantic, and functional properties (Henriquez 2000). Several partial solutions have been proposed so far (Burbules 1998; Storrer 1999, 2002) but an integrated solution is still missing.

Jakobs (2004) provides detailed sample analyses of several hypertext genres, whereas Kress (1998) discusses the historical development of multimodality in printed and electronic texts, and Baldry and O'Halloran (2008) provide a model for corpus analysis of hypertexts.

As shown in Table 1 above, hypertexts resemble "traditional" texts in their communicative functions as they are monological and persistent. It was only during the last years that two recent developments brought Ted Nelson's and Douglas Engelbart's original conception of hypertext as a collaborative endeavour (cf. Keep, McLaughlin, and Parmar 1993–2001) closer to its realisation. In 1995, Ward Cunningham developed the first "wiki", a collaborative knowledge management system. Wiki systems allow users to create parts of a hypertext (e-texts) on their own and then link them with an existing hypertext which is stored on a web server. The best known wiki system is probably wikipedia (http://en.wikipedia.org/wiki/Wikipedia:Community_Portal), an internet encyclopaedia which is compiled and maintained by its users. As Emigh and Herring (2005) show, according to differing practices of user collaboration, various genre sub-types of entries have evolved in different wiki systems.

The second recent development which allows the collaborative construction of hypertexts is provided by so called "weblogs" or "blogs". Weblogs are websites which contain series of entries like personal diaries. Weblog software makes it very easy for users to add new information to their website, and many webloggers update their website frequently, sharing their daily experiences with others. Many weblogs also offer visitors the possibility to add comments and statements to a website. Thus, similar to wiki systems, weblogs are often collaboratively maintained. Although initially mainly used as "internet diaries", weblogs have been increasingly used for "grassroot" journalism, providing local people with the possibility to report relevant local news very quickly to a broader audience (e.g. Green 2004; see also Koller, this volume).

Both wiki systems and weblogs represent new developments which help overcoming the monological nature of hypertexts and help making them a truly interactive endeavour.

2.3.   E-mail, newsgroup, and discussion list communication

As the earliest available type of computer-mediated communication, e-mail is also the most researched form of communication in the new media. Most linguistic research on e-mail communication concerns characteristics of language use in e-mails and specifics of e-mail interactions. Furthermore, gender specific aspects and interpersonal aspects of e-mail communication were also investigated. Each of these aspects will be elaborated in the following.

Like traditional letters, e-mail messages are composed of three parts: the message header (i.e. the letter head), the body of text, and the greetings and signature part. Whereas the header is automatically generated by e-mail programs, message body and signature are parts of the mail message which are produced by e-mail users. They display various linguistic features which differentiate them from traditional letters.

Firstly, the obvious "sloppiness" of many e-mails raised the interest of language scholars. In the first empirical investigation of a corpus of e-mail messages, Ferrara, Brunner, and Whittemore (1991) argued that e-mail messages display features of a "reduced register" as they frequently lack subject pronouns, copula verbs and articles and show a high frequency of abbreviations and contractions. Drawing on theoretical work on register and register variation in Systemic Functional Linguistics, they showed that their corpus of e-mail messages displayed features of spoken as well as of written language, a result which was corroborated by many other investigations. Linguistic characteristics which are associated with spoken language features include the use of first and third person pronouns, discourse particles, modal elements and hedges, and the number of prepositional phrases which are used. Written language characteristics include a high type/token ratio and high lexical density, a high proportion of subordinate clauses and a lower number of coordinated clauses (Ferrara, Brunner, and Whittemore 1991; Yates 1996; Gruber 1997a; all three references provide many sample analyses). This hybrid mode characteristic of e-mail language seems to be one of the most robust findings in computer-mediated communication research.

Another typical feature of e-mail communication is "quoting" (see Gruber 1997b, 1998; Herring 1999 for sample analyses). Quoting is a technologically facilitated mode of intertextual reference in e-mail communication through which writers of an e-mail can then directly comment on and react to the message to which they are responding. This possibility of directly referring to previous messages compensates for the limited possibilities of sequential coherence in computer-mediated communication (Gruber 1998; Herring 1999) and creates an impression of turn-adjacency which is in fact not possible in this form of communication (Herring 1999).

A last feature of e-mail communication also results from its technological characteristics. Like all forms of communication which do not require the physical co-presence of speaker and hearer, e-mail communication is characterised by reduced audio-visual cues, i.e. a lack of back channel cues. Additionally, until a few years ago, e-mail users were limited to the ASCII character set when composing messages, i.e. it was impossible to insert graphics in the message text. E-mail users overcame these shortcomings very quickly. In the late 1980s, "emoticons" (combinations of ASCII signs which create small ASCII "graphics") were invented and used to convey metacommunicative meanings (like irony) in e-mail messages. Since many modern e-mail programs allow users to produce e-mails in HTML format and thus offer rich design opportunities, nowadays emoticons are used in text messaging rather than e-mail.

Email discourse in general is characterised by the combination of spoken and written language features with technologically facilitated characteristics of language use. But e-mail communication is used in various discursive practices which shape these general features in special ways. Probably the best researched discursive practices of e-mail communication are discussions in discussion lists and newsgroup (sometimes also referred to as "discussion boards"). Discussion lists are mainly set up for scholars and used for scholarly discussions, whereas newsgroups are aimed at a broad audience and cover all possible topics of human life. Both forms of communication establish new public debate formats in the media (cf. Richardson, this volume).

"Flaming" was one of the first communicative practices which was observed and described especially in newsgroup (but also in discussion list) interaction. The term "flaming" covers all forms of communicative behaviour in computer-mediated communication through which discussants confront others in rude and hostile ways (Lea et al. 1992). For some scholars, flaming results from the "reduced cues" characteristic of computer-mediated communication (see above). Herring (1996), however, claims that flaming is a typically male behaviour on discussion lists, whereas she found women to be more supportive towards each other.

Partly in response to this latter feature of newsgroup communication, users have developed rules of conduct on the internet. Already in 1995, McLaughlin, Osborne, and Smith (1995) presented a list of norms for interaction in newsgroup discussions they identified by analysing normative postings to several newsgroups in the first half of the 1990s. These norms of conduct in internet communication soon became known as "netiquette". Today most discussion lists and newsgroups provide their subscribers with netiquette guidelines and several websites and books are devoted to this topic (e.g. Arlene 1998). As in the case of flaming behaviour, Herring (1996) argues that netiquette norms vary with gender, i.e. she found male dominated lists proclaiming antagonistic values in their netiquette guides, whereas female dominated lists propagate cooperative values.

Another interpersonal aspect of e-mail communication which found scholarly attention was its contribution to group formation and new forms of community. Baym (1995) and Reid (1995) both analyse newsgroups with members from a widespread geographical and social background for whom the newsgroup forms a relevant part of their social life. Newsgroups on recreational topics thus widen individuals' possibilities for creating social relationships. Baym's and Reid's results challenge the widespread pessimistic view of heavy computer users being socially impaired, lonesome "nerds" who spend all their leisure time in front of a machine because they do not have enough real-life social contacts.

2.4. IRC, MUDs, and MOOs

The first internet chat program ("internet relay chat", IRC) was developed in the late 1980s, and since then, internet relay chat has arguably become the most popular form of synchronous computer-mediated communication. After logging into a chat channel and choosing a nickname, the user's nickname is visible on the screens of all other logged in users and he/she can start to interact with the other "chatters". Therefore, internet relay chat is characterised as a "synchronous" form of computer-mediated communication, although Storrer (2001) rightly points out that single contributions in a chat conversation are not submitted "synchronously" but "asynchronously", i.e.; contributions are not visible for others during their production but only after the chatter hits the "enter" key on his/her keyboard. At that moment, the whole contribution is sent to the server and then transmitted to all other chatters. This transmission technique has severe consequences for the communication process in internet relay chat: (1) message order does not reflect interactional coherence (i.e. single units of adjacency pairs do not follow each other on the screen) but the speed of the respective internet connection. (2) Users who produce long contributions seem to be "quiet" for a rather long time and others may therefore "lose sight" of them.

Both factors shape linguistic features as well as interactive practices in internet relay chat. The technically organised order of contributions makes internet relay chat protocols at first sight look like documents of totally chaotic and disorderly interactions. Nonetheless, they do consist of conversational sequences (or "adjacency pairs", see Schönfeldt 2001; Storrer 2001) but lack virtually any conversational organisation above this level (Schönfeldt 2001, who provides sample analyses of this feature of internet relay chat). Users rather engage simultaneously in exchanges with many other users. Thus, chat protocols show rather complex series of simultaneous sequences rather than complex hierarchical levels of organisation. To facilitate single turn allocation to a sequence (and hence to identify the addressee of a contribution), chat users usually put the nickname of their addressee at the beginning of each turn. This phenomenon has been called "addressivity" (Werry 1996).

The reduced "visibility" of users who are not (yet) engaged in a current exchange causes some other interactional characteristics. Firstly, users who log on to a channel often engage in elaborate and lengthy greeting sequences with others (Schmidt 2000; Schönfeldt 2001). These prolonged ritual sequences have two reasons: (1) Users often frequent the same channel for a rather long time, i.e.; chatters on certain channels have known their interlocutors (or at least their nicknames) for quite a while and sometimes develop rather tight social relations with them. (2) Users have to draw attention to their presence in the channel as soon as they are logged on, as the program only sends a short line to each user (saying "***NICKNAME has joined channel #CHANNELNAME"), which is easily overlooked.

The danger of being ignored by others also causes users' tendency to compose only short messages to ensure that their contributions are distributed quickly and appear in regular intervals on the others' screens. Skilled users, who sometimes would like to compose longer messages without running the risk of being forgotten by the others, split their contribution into several single line contributions which they send as soon as they are finished. Each of these "sequel" messages is preceded by the name of the addressee and users on some channels have even developed conventions of signalling (at the end of each line of an extended message) that a sequel will follow (Storrer 2001).

Another consequence of the necessity to compose only short messages is the heavy use of acronyms and abbreviations in internet relay chat. Contracted syntactic and lexical forms are as frequently used as computer-mediated communication specific abbreviations like "IMHO" ("in my humble opinion") or "ROFL" ("rolling on the floor laughing", cf. Werry 1996). The latter forms are also used in non-English chat interactions (and also in e-mails) and have thus become part of an international computer-mediated communication register which easily combines local (dialectal) language variants with English acronyms and other foreign language elements. Special forms of acronyms which are used in IRC (and to a lesser extent in e-mails) are metacommunicative comments which are enclosed in asterisks (e.g. *g* = "grin"; or *lol* = "laughing out loud"). Like emoticons, they indicate the emotional state of the interactant and substitute missing non- and para-verbal cues in internet relay chat.

Internet relay chat shares with e-mail communication its limitation to the ASCII character set and the "reduced cues" characteristic (cf. above). Internet relay chat users, however, have developed a complex system of contextualisation cues which uses chat specific interactive resources (Schepelmann 2004). Among these are the use of emoticons (cf. section 2.3.), code switching phenomena, and the use of "action ascriptions" and "inflectives" (Schlobinski 2001; Storrer 2001; Schepelmann 2004, who provide sample analyses of these phenomena). "Action ascriptions" resemble metacommunicative acronyms (cf. above). By using a special internet relay chat command (the so called "/me" command) the user's nickname is automatically inserted into a message. Thus, when a user types "/me laughs" and then presses the enter key, all logged in chatters will see the message "NICKNAME laughs". "Inflectives" are a linguistic characteristic of German chat conversations. They resemble the linguistic features of comic strip language where metacommunicative comments (which lack an inflective morpheme and hence are ungrammatical) like *kicher* ("giggle"), *stöhn* ("moan") or *ächz* ("groan") are quite common. In German IRC conversations, these inflectives are used like other metacommunicative comments (i.e. bracketed between two asterisk signs). Schepelmann (2004) found elaborate inflectives which did not only contain an uninflected verb, but also consisted of a whole verb-final main clause (which is another "ungrammatical" feature of inflectives) written as one word.[5]

Apart from these technologically induced interactive characteristics, internet relay chat communication displays the highest amount of oral speech characteristics in computer-mediated communication, which stems from its "synchronicity". Additionally, users frequently use regional language variants which lack writing conventions and which are normally not used in writing. These features have led researchers to refer to IRC as "interactive written discourse" (Werry 1996) or as conceptually oral discourse (Storrer 2001). The latter characteristic also has a sociolinguistic explanation: Internet relay chat is mainly used in recreational contexts and has a phatic function. Additionally, many chat groups are made up of chatters from the same local area who use their local dialect as an in-group marker.

MUDs ("multi user domains" or "multi user dungeons") and MOOs ("multi user object oriented environments") are special cases of chat environments where users may acquire certain pre-defined roles and move through several virtual places where they interact with other players. Apart from their phatic function, conversations in these environments have a strong pretend play character and resemble internet based computer game interactions.

As chat interaction attracts many users and can create a high degree of social bonding (Cherny 1999, who also provides a wealth of sample analyses of several features of internet relay chat communication), it has been increasingly used by institutions during recent years. Not only do online newspapers and public and private media networks offer chats for their clients but political parties also integrate chat clients into their websites. Another institutional use of chat communication is in educational settings, where many e-learning platforms include chat options.

2.5.   Telephone text communication (texting)[6]

Texting is the "youngest" form of communication in the new media. It was originally introduced by mobile phone service providers to send service messages to their customers but has become extremely popular, especially among young people. Texting provides rather limited communication possibilities: message length is limited to 160 characters (with some new phone models allowing a message length of 420 characters) of the ASCII character set, and most phones can only store a maximum of 10 messages. Additionally, entering a text message is rather difficult as users have to use the tiny telephone keys where each key represents up to four characters.

Investigating communicative features of text communication poses many more methodological difficulties than the investigation of other forms of communication in the new media. As Table 1 above shows, texting is predominantly used in 1:1 communications and text messages are only stored for a limited time. To build up a sufficient corpus of text messages therefore requires the collaboration of several users who either type all their incoming messages verbatim into a computer data base or who regularly transmit their message from their phones to a computer via a data cable. Apart from these technical difficulties, many text messages are instances of very personal (and even intimate) communication which many users do not want to share with third parties. Empirical investigations of text communication are therefore rather sparse. An overview of the existing literature is provided in the following.

Schlobinski et al. (2001), Androutsopoulos and Schmidt (2002), Thurlow (2003), and Schmidt and Androutsopoulos (2004) are among the few researchers who have investigated linguistic and discursive features of text messages so far (and who also provide many sample analyses of various discursive features of texting in German and English). They characterise text communication as a typical in-group communication practice, which causes many of its linguistic features, like the use of in-group slang and a high number of spelling errors. Users report that they type more carefully and use different language patterns if they send messages to people whom they do not know. Text messages share many linguistic characteristics with chat communication and they are also characterised as being conceptually oral (Schlobinski et al. 2001; Androutsopoulos and Schmidt 2002). Characteristic features include the use of non-standard spelling and punctuation, emoticons, discourse particles, expressive interjections, elements of group slang and youth language, the graphematic representation of dialectal variants, and the emulation of prosodic features via spelling conventions (see also Thurlow 2003).

A further characteristic of text language is the frequent use of abbreviations and syntactic reduction (ellipsis). This feature is also reminiscent of chat communication but is probably rooted in different communicative conditions. Whereas abbreviations and syntactic reductions in chat communication result from users' aspirations to spend only little time on typing a message, in text communication these phenomena result from the typing difficulties users encounter. These difficulties (and the technical support many mobile phones offer for solving them) cause another linguistic characteristic of text messages. Androutsopoulos and Schmidt (2002) found a high amount of words in their text corpus which were obviously the wrong lexical choices in the context they were used. When they asked their informants why they had used these lexemes, informants reported that they had simply accepted the suggestions of the built-in dictionary (the so-called T9 function) of their mobile phones, which can be switched to "auto-completion" mode like many computer programs. These "wrong" (but phonetically similar) lexical choices offer users a source for language games and also foster the emergence of group language.

Like internet relay chat, texting has mainly a social and phatic function which is reflected in the typical topics of text message conversations. Schlobinski et al. (2001), Androutsopoulos and Schmidt (2002), and Krause and Schwitters (2002) found that text messages are most frequently used for making appointments between friends. The second most frequent category is "flirting, greeting, extending good wishes" and other interpersonal communication practices. The third frequent topic category is "boredom of the user", i.e. users send short messages to friends if they are bored. Thurlow (2003) reports similar results in his study on American adolescents' use of texting.

Apart from the predominantly personal use of short messages by young people, text communication is increasingly used in commercial and institutional communication. Concert organizers and railway companies offer text ticketing services, municipalities collect parking fees via text messages and many institutions offer text message newsletters.

3. Conclusions

The social consequences of communication in the new media have often been discussed in terms of various dichotomies which, although they all characterise these new forms of communication, do not provide the "whole picture" of computer-mediated communication. The first dichotomy (computer-mediated communication as a form of "reduced" language" vs. "flexible adaptation of users") concerns linguistic features in a narrow sense. The above overview of research has shown that computer-mediated communication has some technologically caused shortcomings, like reduced audio-visual cues and disrupted turn adjacency (Herring 1999). Research results also show that users flexibly and creatively adapt to these shortcomings but the shortcomings nonetheless remain and software developers and language researchers are called upon to solve these problems in order to make communication in the new media easier.

The second dichotomy concerns the social consequences of communication in the new media and can be framed as "increased separation of individuals" vs. "new possibilities for creating communities" via computer-mediated communication. As research on newsgroup and IRC interaction has shown, computer-mediated communication (and especially its "reduced cues" characteristic) opens up new possibilities for its users to create social bonds across national, geographic and social boundaries. On the other hand, internet relationships are extremely vulnerable as users may deceive others and invent a "persona" who exploits the social relationships others establish with them. Thus, relationships which are solely based on computer-mediated communication may immediately break down if people meet in real life, which may cause psychological stress and troubles (Döring 2003).

The third dichotomy relates to the former and can be formulated as "possibilities of playing with different identities" vs. "identity formation". Especially research on multi user dungeons and multi user object oriented environments has stressed that these forms of computer-mediated communication enable users to playfully realise aspects of their identity or personality they would never realise in real life and thus offers them new experiences. Miller and Shepherd (2004), on the other hand, stress that blogs offer users possibilities to develop their identities in new ways and may contribute to the development of stable personal identities.

The last dichotomy concerns the difference between "privacy" and "publicity". The internet is a medium which allows every user to become a "publisher" and to make public anything he/she wants, even very "private" things. Being an "anonymous" medium (i.e. nobody "out there" can "really" get into contact with you unless you want it), the internet even fosters the revelation of private details in order to establish social relationships (Miller and Shepherd 2004), which results in a blurring of the border between the "public" and the "private".

All in all, the new communicative practices and genres the new media make possible require users to develop new communicative skills. If they do so (and if they are aware of the vagaries of these new forms of communication), users may benefit from the new communicative possibilities they are offered. The possibility to develop this kind of "computer literacy", however, is not equally distributed across social strata and geographic regions.

As *Interrogate the Internet*, an interdisciplinary working group on the impacts and implications of cyberspace, already noted in 1996, there are several structural barriers to access to the internet (Interrogate 1996). The first barrier is the availability of the necessary infrastructure. Internet statistics show that (as of September 2002)[7] inhabitants of Europe, Canada and the USA, and of the Asian/Pacific region make up about 90 per cent of the estimated internet users of 605.6 million persons (NUA.com 2004). The rest of the world contributes the remaining 10 per cent of users (with Latin America contributing 5.5 per cent). These statistics show that inhabitants of the economically more developed countries have a much higher chance to participate in the global communication network than people from other parts of the world.

Language competence poses a second barrier for prospective internet users. As of November 2004, 35.2 per cent of the internet users came from English speaking countries (global-reach.biz 2004).[8] Although speakers of European languages (excluding English) make up 35.7 per cent and Asian language speakers make up 32.3 per cent of internet users, these latter figures have to be interpreted with caution as in this statistic, "European languages" represent a total of 23 languages and "Asian languages" comprise 10 languages (including Arabic [sic!]). Thus, English is still "the" language of the internet, and users who do not speak English, or do not speak it well enough, are excluded from a vast array of communicative possibilities (see also Gruber 2004). A last barrier is posed by technical knowledge (Interrogate 1996). For quite a long time, computer and internet use was limited to a male, white, middle-class population of college and university students and teachers. Although this bias in computer use is gradually diminishing, elderly people, less educated people and women still use computers to a lesser extent than the former group (Epodio 2003).

This short description of the "digital divide" between those who have access to and use computer technology and the new communication possibilities, and those who do not, shows that "old" sociolinguistic variables like gender, class, age and national background are still important factors. Their influence on language and communication in the new media has so far been largely ignored but would deserve more attention by language researchers.

Notes

1 Before going into further detail, a short definition of two basic terms is necessary: Although a core feature of many communicative forms in the new media is their multi-modality (i.e. the possible integration of written and spoken language, sounds, pictures, and even video clips into one communicative product) I use the term "text" to refer to a single functional communicative unit (in the sense of de Beaugrande and Dressler 1981) even if this text contains non-linguistic elements and exists only in digital form. I use the term "document" to refer to written (i.e. printed) records of digital texts and/or interactions. In this terminology, an e-mail message is a "text" and if it is printed out, this printout is the "document" of this e-mail. On the other hand, in IRC a participant's move is a single "text", but the printout of the entire chat interaction is the "document" of this interaction (which consists of a multitude of textual units).

2 In this paper, I deal only with the "classical" form of text messages in which users are confined to transmitting text messages and emoticons. Newer technologies facilitate the transmission of pictures and videos via mobile phones too (MMS), but these technologies are still in their developing phase and many mobile phones are not capable of them, nor have any investigations of the communicative and discursive consequences of these new technologies been carried out to date.
3 As regards hypertexts, the sender (author) of a hypertext is not necessarily a single person but may also be an institution or a web design team. But even in these cases different aspects of text production are performed by single specialists who cooperate to produce a hypertext which is intended to be viewed as a communicative product of one single source.
4 This characterisation needs a qualification: of course, complex websites may also contain interactive elements like e-mail or chat clients. But the interactivity these elements provide are not hypertext features but features of e-mail or chat.
5 E.g.: *NickNameletzterippevonmilkaschenk* (literal translation: 'NICKNAME last piece of chocolate give"); this construction lacks the first person singular pronoun, a preposition and the obligatory German verb inflection form and means roughly: "I give the last piece of chocolate to NICKNAME" (Schepelmann 2004).
6 Also known as short messaging service (SMS)
7 More recent statistics were not available at the end of 2004 when this article was written.
8 This statistic does not even include counts for areas outside Europe, Northern America, Australia and Asia.

References

Androutsopoulos, Jannis and Gurly Schmidt
    2002   SMS-Kommunikation: Ethnographische Gattungsanalyse am Beispiel einer Kleingruppe. *Zeitschrift für Angewandte Linguistik* 36: 49–81.
Arlene, Rinaldi
    1998   The Net: User Guidelines and Netiquette. Available online at http://www.fau.edu/netiquette/net/index.html. Accessed 11 Marche 2005.
Baldry, Anthony and Kay O'Halloran
    2008   *Multimodal Corpus-Based Approaches to Website Analysis*. London: Equinox.
Baym, Nancy
    1995   The emergence of community in computer-mediated communication. In: Stephen G. Jones (ed.), *Cybersociety: Computer Mediated Communication and Community,* 138–164. London: Sage.
Bolter, Jay David
    1997   Das Internet in der Geschichte der Technologie des Schreibens. In: Stefan Münker and Alexander Roesler (eds.), *Mythos Internet,* 37–56. Frankfurt/Main: edition suhrkamp.
Burbules, Nicholas C.
    1998   Rhetorics of the Web. In: Ilana Snyder (ed.), *Page to Screen: Taking Literacy into the Electronic Era,* 102–123. London: Routledge.

Cherny, Lynn
    1999   *Conversation and Community: Chat in a Virtual World.* Stanford: CSLI Publications.
de Beaugrande, Robert and Wolfgang U. Dressler
    1981   *Einführung in die Textlinguistik.* Tübingen: Niemeyer.
Döring, Nicola
    2003   *Sozialpsychologie des Internet: Die Bedeutung des Internet für Kommunikationsprozesse, Identitäten, soziale Beziehungen und Gruppen.* 2nd ed. Göttingen: Hogrefe.
Ehlich, Konrad
    1983   Text und sprachliches Handeln. In: Aleida, Assmann, Jan Assmann and Christof Hardmeier (eds.), *Schrift und Gedächtnis,* 24–43. Munich: Fink.
Emigh, William and Susan C. Herring
    2005   *Collaborative Authoring on the Web: A Genre Analysis of Online Encyclopedias.* Available online at http://ella.slis.indiana.edu/~herring/wiki.pdf. Accesed 23 October 2005.
Epodio, Rita Mijumbi
    2003   Bridging the Gender Gap. *UN Chronicle* 36: 41–42.
Erickson, Thomas
    1999   Persistent conversation: an introduction. *Journal of Computer Mediated Communication* 4. Available online at http:/jcomputer-me diatedcommunication.indiana.edu. Accessed 19 November 2004.
Ferrara, Kathleen, Hans Brunner and Greg Whittemore
    1991   Interactive written discourse as an emergent register. *Written Communication* 8(1): 8–35.
global-reach.biz
    2004   *Global Internet Statistics (by Language).* Available online at http://global.reach.biz/globstats/index.php3. Accessed 19 November 2004.
Green, Bob
    2004   *Bob Green's Anguilla News.* Available online at http://news.ai/daily.php3. Accessed 19 November 2004.
Gruber, Helmut
    1997a   E-mail discussion lists: a new genre of scholarly communication? *Wiener Linguistische Gazette* 60–61: 24–43.
Gruber, Helmut
    1997b   Themenentwicklung in wissenschaftlichen E-mail Diskussionslisten: Ein Vergleich zwischen einer moderierten und einer nichtmoderierten Liste. In: Rüdiger Weingarten (ed.), *Sprachwandel durch Computer,* 105–131. Opladen: Westdeutscher Verlag.
Gruber, Helmut
    1998   Computer-mediated communication and scholarly discourse: forms of topic-initiation and thematic development. *Pragmatics* 8(1): 21–47.
Gruber, Helmut
    2004   Die Globalisierung des wissenschaftlichen Diskurses: Sprachliche und nicht-sprachliche Teilnahmebarrieren in internationalen E-mail Diskussionen. *Wiener Slawistischer Almanach* 52: 91–109.

Henriquez, Jaime
2000   One-way doors, teleportations and writing without prepositions: an analysis of world wide web hypertext links. In: Lynn Pemberton and Simon Shurville (eds.), *Words on the Web: Computer Mediated Communication*, 4–13. Exeter: Intellect Books.

Herring, Susan C.
1996   Posting in a different voice: gender and ethics in computer-mediated communication. In: Charles Ess (ed.), *Philosophical Perspectives on Computer-Mediated Communication*, 115–147. New York: State University of New York Press.

Herring, Susan C.
1999   Interactional coherence in computer-mediated communication. *Journal of Computer Mediated Communication* 4(4). Available online at www.ascusc.org/jcomputer-mediated communication/vol4/issue4/herring.html. Accessed 19 November 2004.

Holly, Werner
1997   Zur Rolle von Sprache in Medien. Semiotische und kommunikationsstrukturelle Grundlagen. *Muttersprache* 107: 64–75.

Interrogate the Internet
1996   Contradictions in cyberspace: collective response. In: Rob Shields (ed.), *Cultures of Internet: Virtual Spaces, Real Histories, Living Bodies*, 125–133. London: Sage.

Jakobs, Eva-Maria
2004   Hypertextsorten. In: Angelika Storrer (ed.), *Deutsche Sprache im Internet und in den neuen Medien. Zeitschrift für Germanistische Linguistik* 31: 232–252.

Jakobs, Eva-Maria and Katrin Lehnen
2005   Hypertext: Klassifikation und Evaluation. In: Siever, Torsten, Peter Schobinski and Jens Runkehl (eds.), *Websprache.net: Sprache und Kommunikation im Internet*, 159–184. Berlin: de Gruyter.

Keep, Christopher, Tim McLaughlin and Robin Parmar
1993–2001   *The Electronic Labyrinth*. Available online at http://www.iath.virginia.edu/elab/elab.html. Accessed 28 February 2005.

Koch, Peter and Wulf Oesterreicher
1994   Schriftlichkeit und Sprache. In: Hartmut Günther and Otto Ludwig (eds.), *Schrift und Schriftlichkeit: ein interdisziplinäres Handbuch internationaler Forschung*, 587–604. Berlin: de Gruyter.

Krause, Melanie and Diana Schwitters
2002   *SMS-Kommunikation: Inhaltsanalyse eines kommunikativen Phänomens*. Available online at www.mediensprache.net/networx/networx-27.pdf. Accessed 18 October 2004.

Kress, Gunther
1998   Visual and verbal modes of representation in electronically mediated communication: the potentials of new forms of text. In: Ilana Snyder (ed.), *Page to Screen: Taking Literacy into the Electronic Era*, 53–80. London: Routledge.

Kress, Gunther and Theo van Leeuwen
2001   *Multimodal Discourse: The Modes of Media and Contemporary Communication*. London: Edward Arnold.

Lea, Mary, Tim O'Shea, Pat Fung and Russell Spears
    1992   "Flaming" in Computer Mediated Communication. In: Mary Lea (ed.), *Contexts of Computer Mediated Communication,* 89–113. Hemel Hempstead: Harvester Wheatsheaf.

Lemke, Jay L.
    2005   Multimedia genres and traversals. In: Helmut Gruber and Peter Muntigl (eds.), *Approaches to Genre (special issue of "Folia Linguistica"),* 45–57. Berlin: de Gruyter.

McLaughlin, Margaret L., Kerry K. Osborne and Christine B. Smith
    1995   Standards of conduct in Usenet. In: Stephen G. Jones (ed.), *Cybersociety. Computer-Mediated Communication and Community,* 90–112. London: Sage.

Miller, Carolyne R. and Dawn Shepherd
    2004   *Into the Blogosphere: Rhetoric, Community, and Culture of Weblogs.* Available online at http://tc.eserver.org/24397.html. Accessed 7 July 2005.

Münker, Stefan and Alexander Roesler
    1997   Vorwort. In: Stefan Münker and Alexander Roesler (eds.), *Mythos Internet,* 7–15. Frankfurt/Main: edition suhrkamp.

NUA.com
    2004   *How Many Online?* Available online at http://www.nua.ie/surveys/how_many_online/index.html. Accessed 19 November 2004.

O'Halloran, Kay (ed.)
    2004   *Multimodal Discourse Analysis.* London: Continuum.

Reid, Elizabeth
    1995   Virtual worlds: culture and imagination. In: Stephen G. Jones (ed.), *Cybersociety: Computer Mediated Communication and Community,* 164–184. London: Sage.

Schepelmann, Alexandra
    2004   *Kontextualisierungskonventionen im Internet Relay Chat.* Unpublished M. A. Thesis, Vienna University, Vienna Available online at http://www.univie.ac.at/linguistics/publikationen/diplomarbeit/schepelmann/start.htm. Accessed 19 November 2004.

Schlobinski, Peter
    2001   *knuddel – zurueckknuddel – dich ganzdollknuddel*. Inflektive und Inflektivkonstruktionen im Deutschen. *Zeitschrift für germanistische Linguistik* 29(2): 192–218.

Schlobinski, Peter, Nadine Fortmann, Olivia Groß, Florian Hogg, Frauke Horstmann and Rena Theel
    2001   *Simsen: eine Pilotstudie zu sprachlichen und kommunikativen Aspekten in der SMS Kommunikation.* Available online at http:/www.websprache.net/networx/docs/networx-22.pdf. Accessed 18 October 2004.

Schmidt, Gurly
    2000   Chat Kommunikation im Internet – eine kommunikative Gattung? In: Caja Thimm (ed.), *Soziales im Netz: Sprache, Beziehungen und Kommunikationskulturen im Internet,* 109–131. Wiesbaden: Westdeutscher Verlag.

Schmidt, Gurly and Jannis Androutsopoulos
    2004   *löbbe döch*: Beziehungskommunikation mit SMS. *Gesprächsforschung – Online Zeitschrift zur verbalen Interaktion* 5: 50–71.

Schönfeldt, Juliane
    2001   Die Gesprächsorganisation in der Chat-Kommunikation. In: Michael Beißwenger (ed.), *Chat-Kommunikation. Sprache, Interaktion, Sozialität und Identität in synchroner computervermittelter Kommunikation: Perspektiven auf ein interdisziplinäres Forschungsfeld*, 25–55. Stuttgart: ibidem Verlag.
Storrer, Angelika
    1999   Kohärenz in Text und Hypertext. In: Henning Lobin (ed.), *Text im digitalen Medium: Linguistische Aspekte von Textdesign, Texttechnologie und Hypertext Engineering*, 33–67. Wiesbaden: Westdeutscher Verlag.
Storrer, Angelika
    2001   Sprachliche Besonderheiten getippter Gespräche: Sprecherwechsel und sprachliches Zeigen in der Chat-Kommunikation. In: Michael Beißwenger (ed.), *Chat-Kommunikation. Sprache, Interaktion, Sozialität und Identität in synchroner computervermittelter Kommunikation: Perspektiven auf ein interdisziplinäres Forschungsfeld*, 3–25. Stuttgart: ibidem Verlag.
Storrer, Angelika
    2002   Coherence in text and hypertext. *Document Design: Journal of Research and Problem Solving in Organizational Communication* 3(2): 156–168.
Thurlow, Crispin
    2003   Generation Txt? The sociolinguistics of young people's text-messaging. *Discourse Analysis Online*. Available online at www.shu.ac.uk/daol. Accessed 5 April 2005.
Werry, Christopher C.
    1996   Linguistic and interactional features of internet relay chat. In: Susan C. Herring (ed.), *Computer Mediated Communication: Linguistic, Social and Cross-cultural Perspectives*, 47–65. Amsterdam: Benjamins.
Yates, Simeon J.
    1996   Oral and written linguistic aspects of computer conferencing: a corpus based study. In: Susan C. Herring (ed.), *Computer Mediated Communication: Linguistic, Social and Cross-Cultural Perspectives*, 29–47. Amsterdam: Benjamins.

17. Specific debate formats of mass media

Kay Richardson

1. Introduction

Is mediated public debate valuable to society? Mediated debate comes in a wide variety of formats, across many channels – the press, radio, television, the internet; and in many different local, national and trans-national contexts. This alone would make it impossible to formulate any generalisations about the benefit of such debate to our cultures and democracies. Value judgements about particular formats are not easy either, and prima facie interpretations of particular formats – that *Jerry Springer* is obviously bad "trash TV", making an entertainment spectacle of people's troubles, or that news interviews are obviously good, holding the powerful to account – have been challenged and interrogated (see, for example, Fairclough 1995, Lunt and Stenner 2005 on Springer, chapter 7 on radio news interviews), often exposing tensions around the underlying criteria of evaluation.

The present chapter will restrict itself to discussion of mediated debate in broadcasting, grounded not only in the scholarly literature, which now extends well beyond English language programming, but also in my experience of such debate as a media consumer experiencing television and radio in the British context. After a preliminary framing of the subject, the chapter proceeds to offer an overview of research on mediated debate. This is followed by a section which illustrates the application of discourse analysis to broadcast debate, by focusing on two examples, chosen to represent opposite ends of a spectrum from "traditional" to "modern" formats. The chapter concludes by suggesting some questions which can be posed in respect of any particular format, and some discussion of how this kind of programming functions within the contemporary public sphere.

2. Context

The idea of debate in the public sphere suggests interaction, voices responding to other voices. It suggests positions being aired and negotiated between a number of participants, with audiences witnessing the play of opinion and perhaps also joining in, where this is allowed by the structures and norms of the format. Public debate in this sense can exist independently of mass media, including some venerable formats, such as parliamentary debate, or meetings held as part of electioneering.

Mediated debate formats, by contrast, are regarded as politically significant because of the role they play in the construction of "the public": its values, tastes, beliefs and opinions, as well as the terms on which this "public" is able to participate in debate, "speak truth to power" and itself exercise discursive power – or, alternatively, in some arguments, be exploited by the powerful via their ability to exploit the formats and undermine, subvert and "devalue the public's contribution" – as suggested by Zhong (2004) in relation to the prestige programme *Dialogues*, on air on various channels in China's quasi-commercial broadcasting service since 2001, and viewed principally by "intellectuals and university students" (Zhong 2004: 822). The spaces provided by mass media for such discourse take many forms: broadcast interviews and debates, both live and recorded; newspaper letters pages; radio phone-ins and internet forums of various types (see Gruber, this volume). Those provided by broadcasting, as opposed to the print media or to the internet, continue to take centre stage, commanding the largest audiences at the national level.

Clayman (2004), in an overview of mediated interaction formats in broadcasting, is largely positive about their collective value to democracy. Seen in historical perspective the various arenas of mediated interaction on air have "reduced the social distance separating government officials and other elites from the public at large" (Clayman 2004: 47), producing journalists who are willing to hold elite agents of power to account before the public and, where they incorporate audience participation, giving ordinary people a voice in a domain which was previously monopolised by elites. Clayman tempers this positive evaluation in his recognition that for any particular arena "there must be a realistic assessment of how conditions of access and norms of conduct impose constraints on participation" (Clayman 2004: 47). However, Clayman's project, in this and other work, is in general less concerned with evaluation and more with the use of conversation analysis methods to explore the character of mediated debate as a form of institutional discourse.

Less positive commentators writing about televised debate have concentrated on particular programmes and formats, finding that power relations, marketisation/informalisation, cynicism on the part of hosts and overall control of programming by the State and by news corporations variously compromise the promise of the interactional forms. For example, Dahlgren, a media studies researcher writing about *Ikväll med Robert Aschberg (Tonight with Robert Aschberg)* – an influential programme broadcast on Swedish satellite/cable television from the 1980s until 1993, suggests that: "after the fireworks, not much light remains" (Dahlgren 1995: 65). Blum-Kulka (2001), who grounds her approach in linguistic discourse analysis, offers the view that in Israeli television's *ecel meni (With Meni),* telling personal stories has become an end in itself, although the sociability of the telling somewhat redeems a public forum potential. *With Meni* is Israel's longest running talk show, undergoing many changes of approach over its 13 year history, showing firstly on the country's monopoly public channel, and then on public television in the multiple-channel era. Fairclough (1995), as a discourse analyst with a critical purpose, demonstrates the linguistic realisations of a populist tone in radio news interviews conducted on BBC Radio 4's *Today* programme, the principal early morning radio news vehicle and a major contributor to the British public sphere because of the elite nature of its audience. Carpentier (2001) considers, from a media studies perspective, how the contribution of the "public" is managed on the north Belgian audience discussion television programme *Jan Publiek*, 'Joe Public', broadcasting on a public service network. The most negative view is that of Zhong (2004), mentioned above. Zhong is a media researcher who finds *Dialogues*, a Chinese television talk show, to be little more than State propaganda, constructed to foster a false image of interchange and participation.

Since television and radio are predominantly media of entertainment, any assessment of their contribution to the contemporary public sphere must come to terms with trends favouring various kinds of "infotainment" formula (see Holly, this volume). In the world of daytime talk shows, the "showing" may be as significant as the "talking" and the spectacle of talk performance as significant as the content and linguistic form of what is being said. Public interaction does not have to offer itself on public service terms, or concern itself with public issues. Even when it does not, it is worthy of examination as a "cultural" public sphere, just as significant in the construction of publics as the political one.

Some of the themes in the recent literature on televisual interaction, notably participation frameworks, power relations amongst participants, face, and host persona, were anticipated as long ago as 1957 in an article by Donald Horton and Anselm Strauss (Horton and Strauss 1957), for whom "audience participation" included talent shows, quiz programmes and shows of the "Candid Camera" type, the fore-runners of reality television. Horton and Strauss, for example, talk of devices which "have the effect of creating a drama out of the responses of unskilled and unpractised volunteers from the audience; of creating a situation in which the star can reveal himself as a parasocial personality, cheerful, urbane, witty and masterful but if need be sympathetic and tender" (Horton and Strauss 1957: 584) – a description which fits Oprah Winfrey just as well as it fits any of the celebrities with whom the authors would have been familiar.

3. Researching mediated debate: An overview

This section provides a general overview of research on broadcast mediated debate, with a brief mention of the role of the press. Mediated debate on the internet is the subject of a separate chapter in this volume (see Gruber).

In many countries, the importance of the daily press is not so much as the provider of debate forums, but in the way that it contributes to the overarching public sphere of that society. In Britain and elsewhere, the celebrity hosts of TV talk shows are provoked by press stories into raising particular topics with their interviewees, the on-air discussion then itself feeding back into print journalism.

Within broadcasting research, the three most significant research clusters relate to television talk shows, radio call-in programmes, and news interviews/ press conferences.[1] The work on TV talk shows is the most extensive of these clusters. Tolson's (2001b) critical overview of this research remains extremely valuable. Some further significant work has been published since this review appeared, including work which looks beyond the Anglo-American English language examples.[2] There is no such overview of work on news interviews, though the journal literature has now been enhanced by the addition of a book-length study by Clayman and Heritage (2002) on American and British forms of mediated interaction, written from a conversation analysis perspective. Hutchby (1996), also adopting a CA perspective, remains the most substantial piece of work on radio call-in shows (though for an early media studies foray into this field, see Higgins and Moss 1982).

In relation to the broadcast mass media, the term "debate" evokes the public service conception of TV and radio, where broadcasters are under an obligation to facilitate intelligent, rational, worthwhile discussion over the airwaves. There are both worthy reasons for "debate" being as popular as possible in this context (see Holly, this volume), such as the importance of accessibility across wide variations of educational level, and less worthy ones, such as the pursuit of entertainment values for economic reasons at the expense of the public service principles. An important line of research on broadcast discussion, with the Habermasian concept of the public sphere at its heart, is thus concerned with both the limitations of mediated debate conceived in these terms, and its strengths, which often requires considerable "reframing" of what it is we can and should expect from television in particular. For Livingstone and Lunt (1994), the appropriate way to think about television talk shows like *Kilroy* is via the concept of "oppositional public sphere" (pp. 24–28). A distinguishing feature of such shows is that the voice of "common" sense and lay experience is consistently privileged over that of expertise.

Tolson (2001b) observed that much of the academic discussion of TV talk shows up to that point was highly judgmental and polarised. The moralistic variant of this polarisation, exemplified by Abt and Seesholtz (1994), amongst others, addressed whether talk shows demeaned their participants and corrupted the values of audiences. The political variant asked whether talk show formats made a positive contribution to the public sphere, providing a new space for voices not usually heard on television (see Livingstone and Lunt 1994). Feminists discussed whether talk shows were progressive, because they allowed space for female voices and experience (e.g. Masciarotte 1991) or conservative, reducing social issues to personal problems (e.g. Peck 1995). The contributors to the Tolson volume, including Myers (2001), Thornborrow (2001), Wood (2001) as well as others referenced elsewhere in this chapter, sought to move some of these questions on to more analytic terrain, on the basis of contributions from conversation and discourse analysis.

Haarman's (1999a) typology of TV talk shows recognises three basic formats: the celebrity format (e.g. *The Late Show with David Letterman*, broadcasting since 1993 on weekdays late at night in the USA, its home market, with a mix of showbusiness and political/satirical content, on the mainstream national network CBS; currently available on a minor network via satellite/cable in the UK); the issue-oriented format (e.g. *Question Time*, a weekly late night panel discussion on BBC 1 in the UK with a national public service remit); and the audience discussion format (e.g. *Kilroy,* a former British audience discussion programme where all "guests" were simultaneously "audience members" and vice-versa. This long-running popular daytime programme, airing on the main public service channel BBC 1 early each weekday morning, was cancelled in 2004 after the host used the press to publicise his personal political views).

The issue-oriented format is itself further divided into three subtypes: those centred on current affairs (e.g. *Question Time*); those centred on social issues in a personal perspective (e.g. *The Oprah Winfrey Show* and its successors, nationally syndicated in its home market, the USA, since 1986 and also available at times in various international markets, including the UK, with variable scheduling though generally daytime or early evening); and those centred on social and personal problems as spectacle – otherwise identified as the "trash talk" brand (exemplified by *Jerry Springer,* on air in the USA nationwide since 1991, brought to the UK in the late 1990s, initially on cable/satellite then transferring to the terrestrial commercial Channel 4. This show is no longer in production).

Variations on this typology are exemplified by *The Mrs Merton Show* (Montgomery 1999) where the host adopts a fictional persona, subverts the rules of the format and routinely threatens the face of the guest for comic effect. *The Mrs Merton Show* was essentially a BBC 1 after-the-watershed comedy programme of the mid-1990s, closer in format to the celebrity type of media debate than to any of the others in Haarman's typology, though parodic of this format. "The watershed" occurs at 9.00 p.m. – after which more adult content is permissible on mainstream British television. There is also an American brand of talk show which hybridises the celebrity chat show and the current affairs subtype of issue show, exemplified by *Politically Incorrect with Bill Maher* (Jones 2005).

The next most extensive body of work focuses on news interviews and press conferences (see Clayman and Heritage 2002; Clayman 2004). The news interview does not refer to a particular type of *programme*. Instead, it refers to a particular form of institutional talk on television or radio which can be inserted into different programme formats, specifically those with a journalistic focus on news and current affairs. Some interviews are dyadic: a single interviewer and a single interviewee. Others involve a panel of guests (Greatbatch 1992; Clayman 2002, 2004).

4. Forms of discourse in broadcast debate

The two programmes to be discussed below – *Any Questions?* and *Sally* – are different in many ways, as the accounts below will show. Nevertheless, both of them coexist as part of the contemporary public sphere, since both were, in principle, accessible to the British audience during the winter months of 2004/05 when this chapter was written. Unlike Lunt and Stenner 2004 (see below) I do not regard either of these shows as a "public sphere" in its own right. For me, the "public sphere" is ultimately realised not in any particular format, standing alone, but in the mix which is available within any given country as well as trans-nationally, and in the interaction between available formats. Assessment of the quality of this public sphere is not a question that textual analysis alone can answer, for it also depends on the material and cultural conditions favouring different formats in different socio-political contexts. This must include the conditions by which the citizenries of the world encounter the various formats and the sense which they make of them. For the purposes of this chapter, the two chosen formats represent, respectively, tradition and modernity.

4.1. Maintaining tradition on talk radio

BBC Radio Four's *Any Questions?* is a broadcast debate format which has stood the test of time, celebrating its 50th anniversary in October 1998. It goes out, from early September until mid-July the following year, at 8.00 p.m. on Friday evenings and is repeated on Saturdays at 1.00 p.m. on BBC Radio 4 – the BBC's major "speech" network on radio.[3] The most recent presenter, out of a total of 4, is Jonathan Dimbleby, who has chaired *Any Questions?* since 1987. *Any Questions?* has a sister programme, *Any Answers,* where the listening public responds to what it has heard. This is broadcast live at 2.00 p.m. on Saturdays, immediately following the repeat of *Any Questions?* Although radio in 2005 is less prominent than television in terms of audience numbers, Radio 4's contribution to the elite sector of the public sphere in Britain is indisputable, and this programme is an important element in that contribution. The *Any Questions/Any Answers* enterprise has, over the years, made some accommodations to changing times. In the 1970s *Any Answers* was reconstructed as a phone-in programme rather than one based on readers' letters. By the end of the 1990s it allowed email as well as phone contributions. Most recently, it has made itself electronically available beyond its broadcasting slots via the internet, and also providing online transcripts (http://www.bbc.co.uk/radio4/news/anyquestions.shtml), although it does not have its own message board.

Any Questions? most closely approximates the panel interview: "a panel of participating interviewees offering a variety of perspectives on some newsworthy topic" (Clayman and Heritage 2002: 299). Like American TV panel interviews, this programme features "legislators, certified experts of various stripes, and representatives of advocacy groups" and the discussion consists of "expert analysis and commentary on current events" (Clayman and Heritage 2002: 299). Unlike American TV panels, *Any Questions?* usually includes some "movers and shakers" – senior politicians with input into policymaking. The effect on the content is interesting: Some but not all topics result in more pressure on the most senior panellist. On 25 February 2005, half of all the chairman's follow-up questions were addressed to the only Minister of State on the panel, whilst one of the "certified experts" was asked no such follow-up questions.

Any Questions? adopts the alternating form of panel interview: "each successive question is asked of a different interviewee on the panel" (Clayman and Heritage 2002: 304), in contrast to the serial form, "wherein each member of the panel is questioned separately, with the interviewer interrogating first one interviewee at length before turning to the next" (Clayman and Heritage 2002: 303). It adopts the least conflictual alternating approach, the chairman merely inviting each panellist to present his or her views on the same topic, in response to a question from the floor. On some topics this results in four successive short speeches, one from each panellist. Before each speech the chairman takes a turn, and uses it preferentially to select the next panellist, by simply naming him or her. Each panellist, especially panellist 1, must orient to the wording and/or the agenda of the original question. However, panellists 2, 3 and 4 may also optionally orient to the monologue of the previous panellist. This sequence is then repeated as many times as there are new questions (generally between 5 and 7), varying the order in which the panellists speak. Only the chairman speaks to questioners, and does not challenge them, though he may try to establish if there is a lifeworld basis for their questions by politely questioning them about their background.

28 January 2005
Q: (Robert Buckley) It has been suggested this week that history should be a compulsory element in the school curriculum. As the timetable pot is now full, what should be poured out to make room?
DIMBLEBY: You sound, I may be completely wrong, I have no clue, I can see you're a man of the cloth but are you also a teacher?
Q: (Robert Buckley) Former head teacher and a governor of three schools.

This "serial monologue" approach is a template which is frequently modified on the chairman's initiative. He can, for example, add something purposeful when nominating a panellist, like mentioning something relevant from the panellist's past. Here, the subject is educational reform, Tomlinson is the author of a report on that subject, and Dimbleby is nominating Miliband:

11 February 2005
DIMBLEBY: There was – there was a bright young Labour thinker called David Miliband who in 1991 co-authored a report which looked at the virtues enthusiastically of the British Baccalaureate, which has many things in common with Tomlinson. Was that the same David Miliband as the present minister?[4]

Alternatively, he can use any one of his turns for a follow-up question:

11 February 2005
DIMBLEBY: We will allow him to answer those questions in due course but I'm going next to Ben Page.
PAGE: [takes a turn]
DIMBLEBY: Given that you are a walking encyclopaedia of what in some cases even the minutiae of public opinion research, do you think they get a good grade out of this – because we're being asked too not just what the public thinks, important though that is, but whether or not the diploma is a way of resolving a perceived crisis in education where 50 per cent, I think it is, of the kids are alleged to fail by only getting – by not getting their five GCSEs A–C?
PAGE: [takes another turn].

Follow-up turns are at no point required as a preferred next turn, and some topics feature none at all. But such turns are obligatory at the level of the programme: no episode will be performed without any such turns.

Although *Any Questions?* involves "audience participation", the role of the studio audience is highly constrained. There are the usual collective acts of approval and disapproval, such as clapping, laughing and booing in descending order of frequency. In addition, some members contribute individually by asking, through the chair, their pre-scripted and vetted questions related to the current news agenda. The preferred wording is succinct, presuming considerable familiarity on the part of the audience with current affairs: "Should the Attorney General's advice on the legality of the Iraq war be made public?" It is also often mildly witty: "If there was an A level in educational reform, what grade would the government get?" (A major report on educational reform was not wholly acceptable to the Government.)

Any Questions? conforms to the protocols, described by Clayman and Heritage (2004), that ensure the interviewer's footing is neutralistic and non-partisan. The interviewer requires three devices, for his part, to bring off this footing: he must confine himself to asking questions, withhold news receipts and attribute challenging propositions to other sources rather than originating them. The interviewee must refrain from interpreting the presuppositions in loaded questions as elements in the host's own political belief system:

11 February 2005
DIMBLEBY: Minister, one of the members of the Commons Intelligence and Security Committee (...) he was on the radio and some listeners will have heard it – saying there were two or three occasions in the past when law officers' advice to the government has been published. Well if there's no security problem now, as George Osborne says there isn't, why not now publish so that the public, some of whom may be dubious, can be reassured?
MILIBAND: Well I'd like to see that. All of my information is that this has not been the case, that legal advice has not been published. (...)

It is provocative to suggest that there are precedents for the disclosure of legal advice to the Government, because Miliband has previously denied this. But it is not Dimbleby himself making the suggestion. He is the animator for the un-named committee member. Miliband's resistance to the suggestion involves the words "I'd like to see that" rather than "I don't believe you", thus accepting the Chairman's disinterested footing. The provocation also illustrates the chairman's task of instigating/intensifying disagreement. As a broadcast programme, *Any Questions?* is required to produce entertainment as well as elucidation, and the clash of voices is one way to achieve this. *Any Questions?* panellists are chosen in the expectation they will have divergent, conflicting opinions and that this divergence of views will be hearable even in their initial responses to questions. But "disagreement" can also involve engagement *between* the panellists. When panellists do want to take issue with one another, the default option is to be indirect, to speak *to* the chairman *about* the other panellist, rather than addressing criticisms and objections directly to that panellist:[5]

11 February 2005
MILIBAND: (...) Now the second thing that's important is that George raised intercept evidence and he said intercept evidence should be used as the way to get out of this hole. Let me just read you something. Decisions to authorise the detention of terrorist suspects are often made on the basis of sensitive information, if such information were revealed it might well give rise to a serious risk to persons assisting the police or lead to the loss of valuable intelligence. That is the reason why we do not disclose intercept evidence in court.

Miliband addresses himself to Dimbleby, in order to disagree with George Osborne's suggestion that the State should use intercept evidence (phone-tapping) in deciding whether to prosecute suspected terrorists. Miliband refers to Osborne in the third person, and only when the chairman allots him a turn. Escalation of conflict is apparent in departures from this default form – when speakers address one another rather than the chair, and when they do not wait for their proper turns. Such escalation need not involve audible passion in terms of raised voices or other vocal qualities:

MILIBAND: (…) Bea is right that fourteen-to-nineteen education has been a very, very difficult area traditionally for English education, of course the Scottish system is different.
BEA CAMPBELL: Better.
MILIBAND: Well actually the evidence on that is shifting. But the Tomlinson report made some important recommendations I think about the importance of basic skills, about the strengthening of vocational education (…)

Restrained as this is as an example of "conflict", it is nevertheless noteworthy that Miliband does not wait for Dimbleby to ask him to resume the floor, but neither does he ignore the interruption: he orients to it, and disagrees with it – he is in effect talking *to* Campbell at this point, though only briefly, quickly reverting to a more acceptable footing.

4.2. A new kind of public sphere

If *Any Questions?* stands for Public Service and the Citizen, then daytime TV talk shows such as *Sally*[6] stand for Entertainment and the Consumer. Livingstone and Lunt (1994) and Tolson (2001a) offer two major landmarks in the study of televised discussion. In 1994, Livingstone and Lunt proposed an account of television audience discussion programming in terms of an "oppositional public sphere" (pp. 24–28), on the basis of the privilege given to the voice of experience in such programmes, at the expense of the voice of expertise. By 2001, Tolson was talking about "the melodramatic performance of talk" (Tolson 2001b: 27). In the intervening period, the landscape of televised talk had changed. The number of TV talk shows had expanded enormously, and the "daytime" talk show, formerly represented by *Oprah Winfrey* and *Donahue*, had undergone further modification with the introduction of the "trash talk" subgenre exemplified by *The Jerry Springer Show*. In 2005, the landscape has changed again. The American daytime talk show is no longer significant in the British broadcasting schedules, and even in the USA the famous hosts are retiring and not being replaced. *Sally* is one programme that still survives as the tide of daytime talk shows ebbs.

It is in the world of these shows that the production of conflict for the purposes of entertainment has been taken the furthest. Lunt and Stenner (2005), writing about *Jerry Springer*, recognise it as the mirror image of the world of *Any Questions?* and its analogues. If in "proper" debate programmes, any emotional involvement can only be disruptive of rational goals, in Springer, according to Lunt and Stenner, the reverse is the case (Lunt and Stenner 2005: 65). Nevertheless, this does not disqualify it as a putative public sphere. Rather, it constitutes it as an *emotional* public sphere – as distinct from a bourgeois, rational one – where an ideal conflict situation in which the force of the spectacular, not the force of argument, prevails. "Conduct that would usually lead to exclusion from the media (vernacular language, swearing, threatening) is accepted as part of the difficulty of bringing emotional issues out in public" (Lunt and Stenner 2005: 70). Furthermore, although entertainment "potentially gets in the way of discussion (…) it smoothes the path of emotional expression and conflict" (Lunt and Stenner 2005: 75).

The production of conflict in Jerry Springer should not be viewed as exploitative. It too, performs a kind of public service. Lunt and Stenner (2005) work through aspects of the show in relation to Habermasian principles of discourse ethics. The host tests the meaning and sincerity of claims made by speakers, and the right of speakers to say what they do, while other participants challenge the truthfulness of claims. All this is consistent with Habermasian validity claims in respect of free and open dialogue aimed at mutual understanding. In private life, communication is distorted. So says Habermas (1984, 1987), and so says *The Jerry Springer Show* in respect of its participants. Communicative action is meaningful when it engages with high moral themes. So says Habermas and so says *The Jerry Springer Show*, by invoking moral norms to assess the behaviour of individuals. If there is a problem with the Lunt and Stenner argument, it is in downplaying the extent of self-conscious, melodramatic, public display on the part of the participants, which may be quite distinct from the emotional problems they are ostensibly trying to resolve.

Where the excesses of *Jerry Springer* mark it as an extreme case, at the limits of what the dominant culture can allow, *Sally* has become an unremarkable example of its genre. Episodes of *Sally*, in Britain, are broadcast daily, (at 9.30 a.m. and at 5.00 p.m. at the time of writing) but they go out several years after their original transmission in the USA, currently on a minor channel. Their contribution to the British public sphere, via viewers who are available to watch at such times of day, is their promotion of personal/ethical agendas rather than ones which are directly news-related. As with all the daytime TV talk shows, the remit of *Sally* is to produce dramatic entertainment. The production of conflict (en route to resolution of conflict) between participants is certainly one of its goals, though not the only one. In an episode originally transmitted in the USA prior to 2003 but broadcast in Britain on 23 January 2005, with the title *Did you kill someone I love*? each segment is devoted to a different cluster of guests, brought together, on the one hand, as a bereaved family and on the other, as someone they blame for the death. The framing of the episode anticipates confrontation. Narrated "case histories" precede the on-screen encounters between participants. This develops tension: the "accused" is kept off-set until the history is established. When he or she appears, the audience is ready for the accusations which are made and denied as well as the questions which are asked and responded to. The audience joins in, sometimes as audible witnesses, with cheers and boos, and sometimes as individual questioners. The camerawork participates in the confrontation too, especially when it deploys the "split-screen" technique to show the faces of accuser and accused in simultaneous close-up, enhancing the sense of proximity between them.

The structural management of conflict is exactly as for *Any Questions*: interviewees begin by talking with the moderator, about their fellow-interviewees and others: "escalation" is effected by exchanging that footing for direct interaction. This is exactly what happens when Alan, the supposed killer of Sandra, takes the floor. Jim is the father of Sandra and Jenny is Jim's girlfriend: Jim's intervention is directed (through bodily orientation) at the studio audience and the host, but Jenny's gaze and her verbal address singles out Alan as the addressee and ensure that his next comment is directed at her not Sally.

ALAN: (to Sally Jessy Raphael) (...) I called the police, state police, and asked if she could leave. I never said that I'm going to kill this woman, never, never.
JIM: It's in the court record.
JENNY: You *did* kill her.
(Alan turns away from looking at SJR, and looks to his left side where Jenny and Jim are sitting).
ALAN: I did not kill her, Jenny.
JENNY: You murdered her.

The visual semiotics of daytime talk shows are as important as the language, structurally via what Grindstaff (2002) refers to as "the money shot":

> Ordinary people are expected not just to discuss personal matters but to do so in a particular way. They're expected to deliver what I call, borrowing from film pornography, the "money shot" of the talk-show text: joy, sorrow, rage or remorse expressed in visible, bodily terms. It is the moment when tears well up in a woman's eyes and her voice catches in sadness and pain as she describes having lost her child to a preventable disease; when a man tells his girlfriend that he's been sleeping with another woman and her jaw drops in rage and disbelief, when members of the studio audience lose their composure as they listen to a victim recount the lurid details of a crime. These moments have become the hallmark of the genre, central to its claim to authenticity as well as to its negative reputation (Grindstaff 2002: 20–21).

These shows require meaning to be embodied. A key trope of talk show discourse, particularly the "trash talk" brand, is "talking to the hand":

> (...) no guest on the show has ever been told, 'Put your hand in the other guest's face and look away', which is a common motion now among the talk shows. It's called 'talk to the hand' which is short for 'talk to the hand because the face doesn't understand'. It didn't start on talk shows, it started somewhere on the street, somewhere in urban life" (David Roth, a talk show producer, quoted in Gamson 1998: 64).

Although Roth's point is that the gesture and the expression did not originate on talk shows but on the street, its appropriacy for the format could not be better, since its references to body parts, "hand" and "face", rather than mental faculties as the locus of hearing/understanding is entirely congruent with the overall focus on embodied expression.

The "money shot" in *Did you kill someone I love?* comes when Jim, after some time spent in exchanges with Alan, loses patience with Alan's continuing resistance to accusations, and loudly declaims:

ALAN: You are in denial, denial, denial that you took my daughter's life. You are in denial.

As he says this, he leans forward and across Jenny so as better to lock gaze with Alan, who takes up a reciprocal pose. Cue substantial audience applause.

"Money shots" in this episode are mild compared with what we have come to expect from Jerry Springer. In this sequence, for example, although Jim and Jenny show passion in their behaviour (through body language, rhetoric and voice qualities) Alan, the accused, is more restrained. He defends himself robustly as the argument unfolds, and he makes eye contact with Jenny, Jim, Sally and audience members as required, but his demeanour is defensive rather than angry, and his voice is held at a consistent, even volume.

5.   Discussion: Mediated debate and the public sphere

The mediated debate formats discussed in this paper were chosen because they represent such strong contrasts in the contemporary context. The comparison of *Sally* with *Any Questions?* shows up a contrast between formats in commercially-driven, entertainment-led broadcasting and formats dominated by traditional public service principles, though other differences are also involved (radio versus television; British versus American; news-dominated agenda versus personal agendas, and so on).

The contrast is not absolute. The formality of the *Any Questions?* approach does not make confrontation impossible, and its occurrence livens up the proceedings in ways that are acceptable to its particular target audience. Conversely, the entertainment orientation of the daytime talk shows does not necessarily make their contribution to the public sphere negative or irrelevant. As Lunt and Stenner (2005) have argued in relation to *Jerry Springer*, it may be these very melodramatic excesses which make it possible for such programmes to bring painful personal issues into the public domain and address them safely and cogently. But they are sufficiently different to underline Clayman's (2004) point that each debate format must be assessed individually in respect of its contribution to democracy. I suggest that in doing so the following questions should be addressed:

- Is the public a participant in the debate, and if so, on what terms?
- Is the focus of debate on public issues (including issues of morality) or on private concerns?
- Do the most powerful members of society make themselves available for interrogation, and if so, on what terms?
- Do participants orient to shared norms of interaction for the purposes of the encounter?
- Is there an obligation to provide entertainment as well as/by means of, the exploration of issues, and what are the effects of this on the discourse?

Each of these questions can be answered differently in respect of the interactive forms examined above. For *Any Questions?* public participation is tightly controlled, though it has a large audience based at home providing passive participation, and this audience is likely to include an elite component. Daytime TV talk structures the participation of its audiences quite differently. Its fortunes in the ratings have fluctuated, though it reaches a much more working-class demographic, and the American shows also have an international audience.

Mediated debate certainly has the potential to be valuable to society. The question is whether that potential is realised in practice. Where the public service ethos dominates, programming may be judged virtuous in intention but too high-minded to reach a popular audience. Where broadcasting is more directly in the service of the State, the appearance of open discussion may be a cloak disguising more authoritarian positions. Where consumer/entertainment values dominate, even the *display* of civic virtue may be irrelevant. "Best practice" should not be sought only in particular programmes, but in the range of formats available, including the terms of their availability such as "niche" marketing or free-to-air distribution. This need not preclude criticism and praise for particular formats, based on sensitive and thorough textual analysis, and oriented to explicit articulations of how the public might best be served.

Notes

1 There are national differences regarding the relative prominence of any of these forms in practice. News interviews can appear on either television or radio in Britain, but perhaps only on TV in the United States; similarly, mediated press conferences are more salient in the US than in the UK.
2 Published work on non-English examples of mediated debate includes studies of such debate in Israel (Blum-Kulka 2001), Belgium (Carpentier 2001), Sweden (Dahlgren 1995; Ekström 2001), China (Zhong 2004), Italy (Haarman 1999b), France (Haarman 1999b) and Norway (Ytreberg 2004).
3 Since 2006 *Any Questions/Answers* are both broadcast all year round.
4 All transcriptions are idealised, so as to show only the relevant details. All words are reproduced but non-verbal vocalisations are omitted and no attempt has been made to capture aspects of vocal delivery.
5 Compare the convention in the House of Commons, where MPs address the Speaker rather than each other.
6 *Sally (*formerly *Sally Jessy Raphael)* is an American show but widely distributed in other markets. No fresh episodes were produced after May 2003, but old ones are still being recycled. See Brunavatne and Tolson (2001) for more discussion of this programme.

References

Abt, Vicky and Mel Seesholtz
   1994   The shameless world of Phil, Sally and Oprah: Television talk shows and the deconstructing of society. *Journal of Popular Culture* 28(1): 171–191.
Blum-Kulka, Shoshana
   2001   The many faces of With Meni: The history and stories of one Israeli talk show. In: Andrew Tolson (ed.), *Television Talk Shows: Discourse, Performance, Spectacle*, 89–116. London: Lawrence Erlbaum.
Brunavatne, Raina and Andrew Tolson
   2001   "It makes it okay to cry": two types of "therapy talk" in TV talk shows. In: Andrew Tolson (ed.), *Television Talk Shows: Discourse, Performance, Spectacle*, 139–154. Mahwah, NJ: Lawrence Erlbaum.
Carpentier, Nico
   2001   Managing audience participation: the construction of participation in an audience discussion programme. *European Journal of Communication* 16(2): 209–232.
Clayman, Steven
   2002   Disagreements and third parties: dilemmas of neutralism in panel news interviews. *Journal of Pragmatics* 34: 1427–1446.
Clayman, Steven
   2004   Arenas of interaction in the mediated public sphere. *Poetics* 32: 29–49.
Clayman, Steven and John Heritage
   2002   *The News Interview: Journalists and Public Figures on the Air.* Cambridge: Cambridge University Press.

Dahlgren, Peter
   1995   *Television and the Public Sphere: Citizenship, Democracy and the Media*. London: Sage.
Ekström, Mats
   2001   Politicians interviewed on TV news. *Discourse & Society* 12(5): 563–584.
Fairclough, Norman
   1995   *Media Discourse*. London: Arnold.
Gamson, Joshua
   1998   *Freaks Talk Back: Tabloid Talk*. Chicago: University of Chicago Press.
Greatbatch, David
   1992   The management of disagreement between news interviewees. In: Peter Drew and John Heritage (eds.), *Talk at Work*, 268–301. Cambridge: Cambridge University Press.
Grindstaff, Laura
   2002   *The Money Shot: Trash, Class, and the Making of TV Talk Shows*. Chicago: University of Chicago Press.
Haarman, Louann
   1999a   Performing Talk. In: Louann Haarman (ed.), *Talk about Shows: La Parola e lo Spettacolo*, 1–51. Bologna: CLUEB.
Haarman, Louann (ed.)
   1999b   *Talk about Shows: La Parola e lo Spettacolo*. Bologna: CLUEB.
Habermas, Jürgen
   1984, 1987   *The Theory of Communicative Action*, Vols. 1 and 2. Cambridge: Polity Press.
Higgins, Christine and Peter Moss
   1982   *Sounds Real: Radio in Everyday Life*. St. Lucia/London/New York: University of Queensland Press.
Horton, Donald and Anselm Strauss
   1957   Interaction in audience participation shows. *The American Journal of Sociology* 62(6): 579–587
Hutchby, Ian
   1996   *Confrontation Talk: Arguments, Asymmetry and Power on Talk Radio*. Mahwah, NJ: Lawrence Erlbaum.
Jones, Jeffrey
   2005   *Entertaining Politics: New Political Television and Civic Culture*. Oxford: Rowman and Littlefield.
Livingstone, Sonia and Peter Lunt
   1994   *Talk on Television: Audience Participation and Public Debate*. London: Routledge.
Lunt, Peter and Paul Stenner
   2005   The Jerry Springer Show as an emotional public sphere. *Media Culture and Society* 27(1): 59–81.
Masciarotte, Gloria-Jean
   1991   "C'mon girl: Oprah Winfrey and the discourse of feminine talk." *Genders* 11: 81–110.
Montgomery, Martin
   1999   Talk as entertainment: the case of the Mrs Merton Show. In: Louann Haarman (ed.), *Talk About Shows: La Parola e lo Spettacolo*, 101–150. Bologna: CLUEB.

Myers, Greg
   2001   "I'm out of it; you guys argue": Making an issue of it on The Jerry Springer Show. In: Andrew Tolson (ed.), *Television Talk Shows: Discourse, Performance, Spectacle*, 173–192. London: Lawrence Erlbaum.

Peck, Janice
   1995   TV talk shows as therapeutic discourse: the ideological labour of the televised talking cure. *Communication Theory* 5(1): 58–81.

Thornborrow, Joanna
   2001   "Has it ever happened to you?": Talk show stories as mediated performance. In: Andrew Tolson (ed.), *Television Talk Shows: Discourse, Performance, Spectacle*, 117–138. London: Lawrence Erlbaum

Tolson, Andrew (ed.)
   2001a   *Television Talk Shows: Discourse, Performance, Spectacle*. London: Lawrence Erlbaum.

Tolson, Andrew
   2001b   Talking about talk: the academic debates: In: Andrew Tolson (ed.), *Television Talk Shows: Discourse, Performance, Spectacle*, 7–30. London: Lawrence Erlbaum.

Ytreberg, Espen
   2004   Formatting participation within broadcast media production. *Media, Culture and Society* 26(5): 677–692.

Wood, Helen
   2001   No, YOU rioted! The pursuit of conflict in the management of "lay" and "expert" discourses on Kilroy. In: Andrew Tolson (ed.), *Television Talk Shows: Discourse, Performance, Spectacle*, 65–89. Mahwah, NJ: Lawrence Erlbaum.

Zhong, Yong
   2004   CCTV 'dialogue' = speaking + listening: a case analysis of a prestigious CCTV talk show series Dialogue. *Media, Culture and Society* 26(6): 821–840.

18. The sounds of silence in the media: Censorship and self-censorship

Christine Anthonissen

1. Introduction

This chapter will refer to the nature of censorship in the media. Such censorship is viewed as an action of silencing that occurs in at least two ways: (i) an authoritative body imposes censorship in order to obscure information it believes to be harmful either to itself or to others, and (ii) an individual or a group exercises self-censorship by withholding information believed to be harmful to themselves or to others. Between the two extremes of imposing silence by killing the speaker and achieving silence by self-censorship of a speaker, there are a range of ways and means of dictating what can be said and what cannot.

Media censorship functions as an instrument for dealing with tabooed news; it prohibits publication and it inhibits those who would otherwise speak out. News media, I would argue, are more than texts used in "sites of engagement" (cf. Scollon 1998: 11–13, 123–125, 143–144); they are themselves sites of engagement where individuals or institutions compete for public attention, and attempt to foreground certain kinds of information while obscuring others. As such, news media are often also sites seeking disengagement, they may become sites of silencing that disallow public engagement of opposing perspectives.

Thiesmeyer's (2003: 11) claim that "silencing results from an act of language where language is used in order to enable some kinds of expression and to disable others" provides a useful point of departure. This paper will consider overt and covert forms of censorship that range from ignoring the voices of minority groups or digressing opinions, through forbidding publication, to burning newspapers and even murdering writers of provocative texts. It will specifically consider the structure and use of two kinds of censorship prevalent in media discourses, namely censorship of the powerful who may forcibly silence others or authoritatively withhold information, and censorship of the vulnerable who are forcibly silenced or withhold information in fear, in shame, in uncertainty or sometimes in resistance.

Illustratively, reference will be made to South African legislation used in censoring the media during the 1980s, and to political, historical and social circumstances which gave rise to the publication (or not) of censored media texts. The focus will be on silencing the media in 1986 when severe state censorship attempted to subdue and stamp out the growing protest of disenfranchised citizens. A majority, who had for decades been silenced in many more ways than being denied access to the media, had engaged in more and less active forms of protest. Material will be drawn from a case, popularly referred to as the "Guguletu Seven", where much of the complexity of silences operative at the time, only became clear ten years later, through the work of the Truth and Reconciliation Commission (TRC).

The chapter is organised as follows: first, the notion of silence in language will be considered; second, the relation between censorship and free speech will be discussed; third, legal and other means of assuring silence in the media will be introduced; finally, to illustrate various forms of silencing in the media, the media coverage of the "Guguletu Seven" will be investigated.

2. On silence and silencing in language

A number of scholars have, from various perspectives, considered the way in which silence functions in language. For example, in conversation analysis, the occurrence and significance of pauses have been recorded and analysed,[1] in ethnographic studies research has focussed on the comfort or discomfort particular groups have with long silences in conversation,[2] and in studies on cross-cultural communication the role of silence in miscommunication between different groups has been noted.[3] Here I shall briefly consider the possible meanings of intentional and unintentional silences[4] in spoken discourse, and how such silences are made manifest in written discourse. For example, one needs to consider how the silence of non-disclosed police violence is variously articulated in writing by either perpetrator or victim. As silence is opposed to speech, white space on a printed page becomes a visual equivalent of silence; such conspicuous silence makes manifest the intention to communicate by keeping quiet, by deliberately holding one's tongue.[5] But there is more to silence than stillness or white space. This chapter will highlight ways in which words in the media rather than empty spaces, articulate silence, and will consider how "written silences" carry meaning.

Thiesmeyer (2003) puts forward the perspective that silencing is an action which entails more than merely turning off the sound or leaving something unsaid; silencing is an act that takes place where discourse of one kind disables or replaces another. It is "a way of using language to limit, remove or undermine the legitimacy of another use of language" (Thiesmeyer 2003: 2). This chapter will follow the theoretical position taken by various critical discourse analysts who work with language as "an irreducible part of social life" (Fairclough 2003: 2), who see discourse as a form of social practice (Fairclough and Wodak 1997; Reisigl and Wodak 2001), and who view media discourse as a form of social interaction (Scollon 1998). An important focus in this analytic framework is on the relation between language and power (cf. Kress and Hodge 1979; Fairclough 1989, 1995b; Wodak 1996; Reisigl and Wodak 2001; Dedaić and Nelson 2003). Much scholarly attention has been devoted to the use of language in establishing, maintaining and challenging power relations; where silence is a critical part of discourse, acts of silencing oneself or others will necessarily also be a substantial part of the discourse. Then the meaning and use of silence has to be made explicit.

The kinds of silence considered in Thiesmeyer (2003) include the silence of the powerless who cannot speak (e.g. abused women or prison inmates – cf. O'Connor 2003: 139–169; Towns, Adams and Gavey 2003: 43–77), the silence of those who will not speak (e.g. a presidential candidate who gives no reference to embarrassing, perhaps even shameful events in his past – cf. Wodak 1991; Mitten 1992; Wodak et al. 1994; Wodak 2003: 185–187 on the "Waldheim affair"), the silence of those who speak in new turns of phrase, (e.g. people who relexicalise and rephrase tabooed references – cf. Wodak 2003: 179–209 on anti-Semitic discourse), and the silence of subjects denied the right to speak in powerful institutions (e.g. in the courtroom, by legislation or by policing – cf. Fridland 2003: 119–138; Galasiński 2003: 211–232; Lambertus 2003: 233–272).

Jaworski (1993), considering the functions of silence as a significant part of any communicative system, finds that speech and silence complement each other, that "silence is not a mere background to speech, and that it is not a negative category devoid of communicative properties" (1993: 48). He notes that silence manifests in speech in different forms, that it can have both positive and negative value. He also notes "that silence and speech do not stand in total opposition to each other, but form a continuum of forms ranging from the most prototypical instances of silence to the most prototypical instances of speech" (1993: 34). The assumption that an essentially ambiguous phenomenon such as silence can be finally categorised and given a fixed set of possible functions, as has been attempted by Dauenhauer (1980), is criticised.

Silence can be considered as absence of sound, and also as absence of speech. Kurzon (1997: 21) supports the idea of regarding silence and speech as "phenomena on a continuum". In remaining silent a speaker can indicate that she has nothing to say, or that she has chosen to remain silent on a matter where she could have spoken. Silence is covert when a person speaks about one thing in order to conceal another, is overt when a person refuses a designated turn explicitly, and is insignificant when a person chooses to speak directly and explicitly. Jaworski (1993: 71–73) discusses these distinctions by referring to different verbs in Polish that denote the different absences of sound (*cisza*) and of speech (*milczec*).[6] In discussing the latter, he highlights the simultaneous use of speech and silence when talking or writing while withholding information. Such silence of withholding would occur (e.g.) in circumstances where a government disallows public scrutiny of important, topical information, such as the causes of death of those who died in a police shoot-out. Similarly, there are "speaking silences" that need to be investigated where newspapers promote certain discourses, such as those of the elite protesting against high crime levels, and neglect others, such as those of social security organisations that highlight the correlation between poverty, neglect, abuse and crime.

In the media those in power speak more loudly than those in subordinate positions, in-groups get coverage that is denied out-groups, criticism that re-enforces popular perceptions is favoured above criticism that is aimed at correcting popular commonplaces. In such a way the voices of the subordinate, the disempowered, of out-groups and minority groups, of less popular, socially critical groups, may be silenced. Less covertly, the power of the media can be controlled, by means of official censorship. Even in well established democracies, powerful institutions such as the government, big business corporations, owners of the media, professional communities, and the likes, have recourse to censorship. Such institutions are in a position to silence facts themselves, and at the same time to silence those who know (or suspect) facts potentially embarrassing to the institution, and would otherwise publish them.

Silencing achieved by means of censorship legislation that also provides for punitive measures usually has the additional effect of self-censorship. This is made manifest when police, plaintiffs or defendants at an inquest or other legal process, withhold self-incriminating information. The kind of silence that withholds information can and often does occur, where a person would, perhaps even should, speak but cannot. A similar kind of silence follows trauma, when a person who has experienced pain will withdraw as he finds himself unable to relate what is intolerable, even in memory.[7] In the media this would be effected by means of omission (as when details are left out, when critical aspects of a story are simply not told) or more visibly through leaving blank spaces, or deleting offensive words and phrases – but also by relexicalising, by retelling in terms that are perhaps ambiguous, perhaps obscure. As an alternative to not saying anything at all, indirect speech acts give clues and messages are given "between the lines" (cf. Anthonissen 2003: 91–111).

In censorship silence becomes a tool of sociopolitical oppression. Jaworski (1993: 98, 99) refers to the "silences" in politicians' public speaking when they deliberately avoid reference to sensitive issues, or use "irrelevant words", i.e. empty words that merely beat about the bush. This kind of censorship is disguised in that a conventionalised routine is used, which will habitualise perception[8] and blunt the audience's ability to recognize deceptive and discordant messages. Jaworski also refers to "strategic silence" used to create "mystery, uncertainty, passivity and relinquishment". Such silence, not only withholds information, but is also used to bluff, to establish the impression that the politician (e.g.) is knowledgable and reliable.

Silence is imposed by censorship; conversely, silence can oppose censorship. White, open spaces and black lines across print have been used to protest censorship (cf. Anthonissen 2002, 2003). When censorship silences by having untraceable information obviously and deliberately withheld, there is an obscuring effect that protects the publisher; however, when traceable information such as a name is withheld, but it is evident who is implied, the silence becomes telling, and the publisher is still protected. Also, there can be words that silence by replacing others, and there can be words that challenge and defy the imposed silence. Such articulations of censorship in the media will be illustrated in section 5 below, in the discussion of the reporting on the Guguletu Seven.

3. On censorship

The practice of censorship has been variously defined as an action of berating, denouncing, rebuking, reproaching, strongly criticising or disapproving of something. Related to, but distinguished from this, is the practice of censorship which refers to the official examination and approval or prohibition of plays, books, news, correspondence, and so on, in order to suppress what is regarded as immoral, seditious or inopportune.[9] Censorship of printed matter is effected in various ways, including prohibition of publishing certain references, ordering excisions of offensive sections of text, banning of an entire publication, legislating restrictions even before any text is produced, demanding clearance from an appointed official prior to publication, or seizure of disapproved literature. Incidentally, as the discussion of legislation below will make clear, all such measures were in place at some stage in the strained years before the 1994 elections that brought representative democratic rule to South Africa.

There are social practices beyond media uses of language, whereby a community disallows certain acts, including speech acts of various kinds, because they are in some way offensive to views and beliefs widely held and respected in that community. Censure is often related to social taboos[10] such as child abuse, paedophilia, incest, verbal abuse, sheep stealing, gossip, and so on. Censure can be effected by direct rebuke, social isolation or formal community intervention, as when a church committee or a group of tribal elders rely on consensually afforded authority[11] in discussing and taking decisions on such matters. Often legal recourse is also available as a form of censure.

Censure of certain taboos becomes institutionalised in that those who violate recognised behavioural codes become legally liable. A person who is found guilty of (e.g.) theft, assault, public indecency, etc. will be censured by means of legal action that provides retribution, discipline, repair of damage, and to limit possible repetition of such criminal acts. Forms of censorship related to publishing tabooed information, ideas or views, are mostly constitutionally or legally defined. Offensive uses of language such as libel, *crimen injuria*, and the like, are prohibited. When there is a reasonable threat that hurtful information will be published, of which the damaging effect cannot be reversed after publication, an interdict may prohibit such publication *prior* to the act; alternatively, if tabooed information has been published the offender may be censured *after* the act, by means of a fine, banning of the publication, an obligatory public apology, or an explicit withdrawal of any harmful implications. "Censorship" in this context, in contrast to 'censure' that bars or repudiates, typically refers to restricting what may be published,[12] by inhibiting speakers through threats of rejection, scandal or more seriously, being put out of work or being incarcerated.

Censorship can be introduced by means of laws or proclamations that limit representation and discussion of certain topics, or by regulations *ex post facto* to remove the whole or certain sections from texts already published and prepared for public circulation. Such legally defined censorship determines that certain things may not be said, certain information may not be published, and certain topics may not be publicly discussed, weighed, developed or put forward for wider consideration. Such publicly sanctioned ways of restricting what may be said or printed, are widely institutionalised. Discussion of censorship in modern states such as Holland (cf. Buelens et al. 2000) or the German Federal Republic (cf. Kienzle and Mende 1980) as well as under repressive regimes such as National Socialism, Fascism or Stalinist Russia, often refers to similar conditions and considerations of state censorship and corresponding self-censorship.[13] Although the South African context is invoked illustratively in this chapter, generic aspects of the phenomenon should not be missed.

3.1. The right to free speech

Censorship is often regarded as a negative action that removes an established and well recognised human right, namely the right to free speech. This is a right that in constitutional democracies is not simply honoured as one of a variety of fundamental liberties, but is mostly explicitly and specifically protected.[14] The protection of such a right is legally and philosophically justified on one or more of three grounds (cf. Barendt 1987: 8–23). First, there is John Stuart Mill's argument from truth, which emphasises the importance of open discussion for discovering true facts and arriving at accurate judgements. Second, there is reference to free speech as an aspect of self-fulfilment to which each individual has a right in her/his intellectual and spiritual development. Third, there is the argument from citizen participation in a democracy, which recognises not only the right of all citizens to understand political issues in order to participate effectively in the working of democracy, but also asserts the crucial role of freedom of expression in the formulation of public opinion on political questions.

Due consideration of the right to free speech implies that people cannot be prosecuted simply for speaking their minds. The right to freedom of speech underlies another well-established democratic right, namely "freedom of the press". Due consideration of this right ensures that political views opposing those of the government in power may be published, discussed, circulated and developed without fear of retribution. Particularly notable is that freedom of speech is distinguished from other personal liberties such as those of privacy, housing, education or family life in that it is primarily a liberty against the state (Barendt 1987: 15). Although a number of separate principles are suggested as possible bases for safeguarding freedom of expression, Schauer (1982) finds that the various principles are unified in a deeper notion residing in an argument from government incompetence. Freedom of speech, then, is based on the assumption that political leaders are fallible, on distrust of governmental determinations of truth and falsity and on a somewhat deeper distrust of governmental power in a more general sense.

Censorship, thus, is a state initiative that infringes on the basic liberty of being able to publish, through whichever mode, facts, ideas and opinions without restraint or fear of prosecution. Provisions that secure free speech are typically assembled against the government: constitutions give a more significant degree of protection against state intrusion than against interference by individuals. The limits of freedom of speech are often discussed. The question is what kinds of conditions justify an encroachment on such freedom that is patently designed to protect the right to criticise the government, to safeguard minorities and to keep alive the possibilities of political change. Considering the above-mentioned argument from democracy, political speech expressing opinions and communicating facts from whichever perspective is taken to be crucial for the maintenance of a confident democracy. Unrestricted use of such political speech is covered in virtually all circumstances by articles protecting freedom of expression in constitutions. Other categories of speech, such as commercial speech, moral discourse, literature and other forms of art or pornography appear generally to enjoy less protection.

During the 1980s in South Africa, censorship was clearly aimed against open discussion of forms of government and political ideas – a form of speech generally afforded maximum and barely disputable protection. Illustratively I refer to some of the legislation that instituted such censorship, and on the effects of such legislation on the media, in section 4. Since 1994, the governmental dispensation has changed considerably. Although much of the restrictive legislation remains in place, there are considerably fewer court cases that refer to censorship laws and certainly, much of what was formerly prohibited is now allowed. Even so, censorship prevails in new forms and in relation to different topics. Media language use is restricted in contextually sensitive ways, as will be illustrated in the considerations that follow. Consideration of former as well as more recent applications of censorship will assist in defining the kinds of circumstance in which the regulation or suppression of speech in the media may typically occur.

3.2. Limiting the right to free speech

In spite of a long-established and highly valued tradition of protecting free expression, censorship is still a regular practice in democratic societies. In fact, censorship in one form or another is considered to be acceptable on the grounds that freedom of speech is not an unqualified freedom. If, in speaking his or her mind, one person mischievously damages the good name of another, this freedom has been abused. The other's right to privacy, to protection of integrity and human dignity may have been violated. Also, if a person freely expresses his/ her views in such a way as to incite violence or seriously threaten public security, this is regarded as an infringement of the rights of others to safety from bodily harm. Then sanctions of some kind are in order. Such sanctions may be provided in the form of legally mandated censorship.

In one view, the freedom of expression principle[15] that secures public discussion of political matters may at times be best preserved by temporary suppression of certain kinds of speech (Barendt 1987: 21). Here considerations of public welfare are generally raised; for instance, during times of extreme emergency, speech that may result in public violence is regarded as being best prohibited. Also raised in this context are considerations of national security. When audience response to a particular kind of speech may be rioting, disruption of crucial services such as provision of electricity, destruction of vital resources such as crude oil reserves, disintegration of proper order in the armed forces, and the like, the state assumes the authority to prohibit such speech.

Censorship is regarded as an extreme measure justified only in extreme circumstances. Where a state presents itself as a democracy, a clear case would have to be made for resorting to censorship rather than to other democratically more acceptable means of dealing with a purported emergency. Crucial questions here are (i) whether the threats to public welfare, public order and national security are real, perceived or fabricated and (ii) whether the government itself, through its policies and practices, is in part responsible for the emergency it is seeking to ward off.

Legislators and legal practitioners have to decide under which circumstances censorship is justified, and under which circumstances censorship defeats justified causes. From various historic situations it is clear that censorship has often been used as a repressive tool and not as one that protects recognised human or societal rights that are under serious threat.

Jaworski and Galasiński (2000: 185–200) report on and analyse the *Black Book of Polish Censorship* – a document which records instructions, principles and practices of censorship in Poland during the 1970s. This gives insight into the topics that were scrutinised for possibly unacceptable renderings of virtually every aspect of community life in the country, as well as into specific ways in which materials were questioned, cut, reformulated or completely banned. The process illustrates how censorship was accomplished in what is described as a totalitarian regime. However, even in modern democracies censorship of more or less overt kinds have been used to make sure that only preferred constructions of particular conflicts get media coverage, such as in the United States during the Vietnam War (Arnett 1995) and the Gulf War (Traber and Lee 1991), and in the UK during the Falklands War (Glasgow Media Group 1995) and the IRA protests in Northern Ireland (Miller 1995).

It is not only through legislation and other overt forms of prohibition that censorship is achieved. There are more covert forms of silencing minority groups, marginalised groups or critical voices in the media. If a publication is conceptualised as a site of engagement where a variety of perspectives may be presented, debated, motivated and recognised for their validity, then control of the space will decide which voices are heard and which are muted. For example, if government and publishers are in opposition, the media become contested spaces. The media can silence voices of government and amplify critical voices. Government can respond by employing its power to censor, to assure that they gain greater control of the public space embodied in the media.

In another, similarly political domain, the media have been tardy in yielding space to gay and lesbian discourses, by which the positions, contributions and civil rights of members of such groups would be recognised. Not only have the media denied these discourses the opportunity to engage, often the lack of engagement is due to self-censorship. On the one hand groups that challenge received positions in mainstream culture are silenced and so made to be invisible; on the other hand their invisibility is often intentional as some prefer not to make the private public or political.[16] Then the silence is self-imposed and the opportunity to topicalise, eventually even normalise, human conditions that have been placed on the periphery, is forfeited.

Self-censorship is also illustrated in what has lately been termed "embedded journalism". This practice of attaching reporters to military units was initiated during the Persian Gulf War of 1991. During the United States invasion of Iraq in 2003 this practice particularly came under scrutiny.[17] In more and less deliberate ways, journalists aligned to US and British forces obscured much of the horrifying reality of the war. Some, through being close to and confined to working with US soldiers, could not gain access to alternative experiences such as those of Iraqi civilians (cf. David Zucchino of the *Los Angeles Times*). Then silence on the experiences of those not mentioned was to some extent "accidental". Others, through an apparent choice to sanitise their own group's military action, and with the bravado and romanticism often encountered among those disengaged from the real horrors of war, avoided reference to, for example, civilian deaths or casualties resulting from "friendly fire" (cf. Ron Harris of the *St.Louis Post-Dispatch*).[18] Then the silence on e.g. the killing of civilians at checkpoints, or the use of depleted uranium, is self-imposed deliberately.

Silencing may also be achieved by pre-empting censorship. In anticipating the advantages of limiting free speech or the penalties that may indirectly arise from speaking freely, publishers may advise, even enforce, self-censorship. Jasper Becker, former bureau chief for a Hong Kong based newspaper, refers to the pressure of working under constant surveillance and the risk of a journalist compromising his contacts. He refers to the dismissal of the paper's cartoonist, a satirical writer, and a British editor, before his own dismissal that followed his protest. In this case, he reports, there was no legislation that insisted on the newspaper towing the line; the publishers and the editor apparently urged collaboration, "writing to allow readers to read between the lines", ahead of any government demands (Becker 2002).[19]

In Zimbabwe media censorship was recently exercised in the form of intimidation of journalists or editors who criticise the President, the governing party or their actions. During the 2005 election campaign, even foreign correspondents that had in some way annoyed the governing party were detained. Earlier, in 2000, an editor of one of the more liberal newspapers was imprisoned and only released after substantial public protest. Editors critical of government controlled newspapers were retrenched,[20] and a South African journalist at the scene of a bomb blast was arrested and accused of complicity. Within six months after the introduction of the USA Patriot Act, three newspaper editors had lost their jobs for criticising American policy (Free Expression Network 26 April 2002). Harassing and firing the editor expressly for his/her criticism is more overt than doing the same under false pretences or without giving reasons.

Public debate in South Africa ten years after the introduction of democracy indicates that a degree of tension between government and the media is virtually inevitable, even when the government is democratically elected and the press is free. Members of Parliament sensitive to scrutiny by journalists suggested that in the process of transformation in the country the media should refrain from probing and criticising new structures of government. Others more sensitive to fallibility of any government pointed out that the new constitution and a Bill of Rights protecting liberal freedoms provide checks and balances that serve transformation better.

Even if censorship is seen as an acceptable remedy in justifiable circumstances, it remains a remedy that has to be carefully monitored. Coetzee (1996: 9) argues strongly against any form of censorship. He holds that whichever evils censorship may intend to deter, "the cure is always worse than the disease".[21] Often there is silence on the real intentions of censoring regulations: enabling public safety may be put forward to justify surveillance and investigation that goes against established democratic rights. The USA Patriot Act passed in October 2001[22] in response to the 11 September attacks was motivated by arguments for public security. However, consideration of the effects of this law did not endorse such justification. According to the Free Expression Network

(2002) the law "created a climate chilling to speech, debate, and dissent in the very places intended to foster discussion and dialogue – schools, colleges and universities, and newspapers". Knowing how easily personal communication by telephone, e-mail, internet, library subscription, and the likes could be monitored certainly had an inhibiting effect. This is reminiscent of the Emergency Regulations in South Africa during the 1980s when a taboo on discussion of topics, such as who and how many political detainees were being held, was presented as being in the interest of national security, while in fact the true intention was to disable discourses of social justice potentially embarrassing to the legislator.

4. Obliging silence by legislating censorship

From general considerations of the functions of silence in communication, the right to free expression and censorship that limits such a right, we now move to more specific conditions of censorship in South Africa from 1985 to 1990. The printed media of the late 1980s often referred to the governmental procedures that imposed restrictions, and to the issues on which the media were expected to remain silent[23] (cf. Tomaselli and Louw 1991). Even government supporters acknowledged and justified the media regulations.[24]

A revealing feature of state censorship, according to Coetzee (1996: 35) is that "it is not proud of itself, never parades itself". State attempts to control the media clandestinely were already introduced in the 1970s. The media history that preceded the censorship associated with state of emergency legislation of the 1980s is documented from various perspectives in works by (*inter alia*) de Villiers (1980), Rees and Day (1980), Rhoodie (1983), Hachten and Giffard (1984).

Related to ancient practices of taboo, where certain acts and expressions were prohibited for cultural and religious reasons, the custom of controlling the written word in a similar way to earlier practices of controlling the spoken word has almost universally become a regular part of governmental rule. Galasiński (2003) elaborates on 1981 legislation in Poland that regulated official control of performances and publications. Such legislation, introduced more or less simultaneously as the South Africa media restrictions, was justified by a similar argument, namely the state's obligation to safeguard its subjects, purportedly protecting freedom of speech (Galasiński 2003: 216–217). Governments' authority in presiding over the right to publish is rarely contested. Nevertheless, there is much controversy over the limits of such authority. For example, where censorship on the publishing of pornography is expected and accepted, there is still debate on what kinds of publication can rightly be categorised as such, and on whether the state should indeed be a guardian of moral values of this kind.

Concerning the publication of politically sensitive material, the state's claim to control is much less tolerated than its claim to oversee matters of public decency.

To measure the potential harm that can be done by publishing controversial matter, many communities rely on religious instructions and customary law. Additionally, there is governmental legislation that regulates the printing and distribution of specifically defined issues and concerns.

The South African laws and proclamations of the 1980s that determined what content news media were allowed to publish as well as the style, modes and attitudes these media were allowed to adopt clearly threatened an established democratic right to freedom of expression. Such laws to a large extent determined the context in which news could (or could not) be published. Media responses varied between open challenges, subtle references to the gagging orders, and self-censorship aimed at avoiding controversy or repudiation.

4.1. General media regulations in South Africa

At the beginning of 1986 when the first state of emergency (announced in June 1985) prevailed, there were more than 100 laws circumscribing what journalists in South Africa may write about (Standbridge 1986). These laws were of course not all directly related to the state of emergency (which was continually renewed until 1990). For example, there were measures that proscribed reporting on socially sensitive issues such as details of divorce proceedings or publishing pictures of people in mental institutions. Nevertheless, many of the laws already in place by 1985 became particularly pertinent during the state of emergency.

To illustrate, the Publications Act (42 of 1974) authorised the Publications Advisory Board (PAB) to control publications it found to be undesirable on various grounds,[25] such as indecency and obscenity, blasphemy, ridiculing sections of the population, impairing relations between any sections of the population, or disclosing offensive or harmful material with reference to any judicial proceedings. This controversial law constructed the "reasonable person" in the community as immature, of very average intelligence and incapable of making good moral judgements. Under emergency conditions this act provided for censorship of publications carrying a threat to "state security, general welfare or peace and good order". Thus a text originally motivated by concern for moral principles in a multicultural community obscured and was extensively used for additional aims of silencing criticism against government.

A large number of laws that intended to secure public order and to regulate the role of the media in socially sensitive domains contained regulative measures. Included in the collection of laws that in some way limited what newspapers could publish and in what form are the Defence Act (44 of 1957), the Police Act (7 of 1958), the Post Office Act (44 of 1958), the Internal Security Act (74 of 1982), and the Protection of Information Act (84 of 1982). Effectively, these acts tabooed media discussion of or comment on specified military and police activities, national intelligence activities, access to secret documents, and so on. They also silenced the dissemination of information on unlawful organisations, resistance campaigns and other protest activities.

During the 1970s enormous amounts of public funds were channelled into secret accounts used to gain control of internal and foreign media in attempts to present South African policies and experiences in a more favourable light. On the argument that the irregularity and aggressiveness of the propaganda against the country justified using unconventional and irregular methods, vigorous governmental media control proceeded. Not surprisingly, but most ironically, silence on the enormous misappropriation of funds, misrepresentations and accompanying malpractices aimed at using the media to strengthen the state was broken in the news. Indeed, it was the *Rand Daily Mail*,[26] a publication which had for a long time been a thorn in the flesh for the government, to whom the first disenchanted collaborator turned to leak the story.

The introduction of stricter media control during the 1980s has to be understood against the history of the media conflict of the preceding years. During 1985 to 1990 a set of specific media restrictions was added to the existing ones. Government was acutely aware not only of the way in which the media gave access to news that could shape public perceptions and opinions, but also of the fact that the oppositional press was strong and highly articulate. The partial independence of the press necessitated, from the government's perspective, aggressive intervention. There was no apparent appreciation of the potential value a free press may have in developing political ideas or just practices in society.

5. The Guguletu Seven

At an early stage in the 5-year period when a state of emergency gave security forces special powers in the repression of political protest, an event occurred in Cape Town that eventually became a leading case in claiming restitution for unsolicited repressive state violence. The event, referred to as the case of the "Guguletu Seven", happened early on a Monday morning, 3 March 1986. I shall refer to the silencing, and later the disclosure, of how and why seven youngsters were killed in a police shoot-out. In tracing what was given and what obscured, three sources assisted: (i) newspaper reports published in the aftermath of the event, (ii) transcripts of the Guguletu Seven TRC hearing ten years later, where this particular event was investigated anew, and (iii) a documentary film[27] that used police videotapes, films made in investigating the submissions of a number of the victims' relatives and video recordings of the TRC hearing. These sources illustrate generally how censorship measures intended to silence may succeed in some aspects, but may be challenged and defeated in others.

Briefly, what happened was that a group of seven young unemployed men living in Guguletu, a township outside Cape Town, were recruited to join an underground resistance group allegedly aligned to the African National Congress (ANC), a banned organisation at the time. The men were promised financial support for participating in dissident activities, the details of which were not made clear to them. On the very first day of taking up their relatively uncertain commitment, they ran into a police ambush which ended in the death of all seven youngsters. The immediate official media release on the event differed considerably from the recount of journalists who were barred from the scene of the event, but had independently obtained eyewitness reports. The police version suggested that their unit had responded to a tip off, ran into an ambush apparently set by terrorists, and survived due to their effective self-defence. Reports from the community suggested another version, but emergency regulations precluded a proper investigation.

Ten years later, when the TRC was established to investigate gross human rights violations, the full picture emerged. The anguish and objections of the mothers and of others who had known the men proved to be justified: their children had not been involved in political activity until they were recruited by an undercover military agent who posed as a leader in the resistance movement. They were deceitfully recruited for the sole purpose of taking part in a staged ambush set up by a secret military unit, to support state propaganda on the severity of internal terrorist threats and to justify intensified police "intervention" in the townships. The youngsters had been lured into the ambush and intentionally, brutally shot down. Attempts to silence the reports alternative to those officially released continued for the next ten years. Questions of eye witnesses and of people close to the deceased, were left unanswered; tributes of their home community at the funerals were banned; military and police collaborators were protected from thorough interrogation, at a number of occasions. The breaking of the silence in the TRC hearings offers unique insight into the nature and structure of media silences.

Analysis of media coverage discloses how censorship silences on at least two levels. First, there is the silence of the powerful, the censors. The legal documents that prohibit publication include discourse that obscures, or at least attempts to obscure, the full intent of the prohibition. In responding to media enquiry, police officers give limited information, false information or refuse to give any – thus silencing one text by offering another. Government officials responsible for the prohibiting legislation and for the actions of security force members also took part in muzzling community voices, eye witnesses and the media. Second, there is the silence of the vulnerable, the censored. Youngsters were silenced by being killed rather than being arrested. Community members and relatives who had witnessed parts of the event were silenced in their access to public media, as well as in the course of police investigation and inquests that followed. Reporters were silenced by any number of restrictive measures including summonses to disclose the names of witnesses and to answer for having passed restricted material on to foreign journalists.

5.1.   Acts of language that enable media censorship – the silencers

The announcement of a State of Emergency in various regions of the country in 1985 immediately put a considerable degree of censorship in place. However, the regulations proved to be inadequate to stop the flow of information about the extent of protest as well as about the manner and intensity of preventive and retributive measures taken by the police and the military. On a daily basis media reports voiced and fuelled indignation and outrage at government actions in the areas affected by the emergency regulations. The government responded by imposing more measures of media control. I shall refer here specifically to the censorship measures that applied in March 1986 when the shooting of the Guguletu Seven took place.

5.1.1. Legal documents: Media restrictions during the State of Emergency, 1985–1986

Before the 1985 State of Emergency it was illegal to publish information on matters such as defence, external military actions, liberation wars in southern Africa, nuclear activities and fuel supplies without official permission. Publication without due clearance ran the risk of high penalties (Breytenbach 1997). In September 1985 a Bureau of Information was established under the aegis of the Office of the State President. The Bureau was assigned to improve the South African government's image abroad, and simultaneously to keep an eye on how the internal media represented the state, state policies and state initiatives. It was not openly established as a censoring institution, but was given such responsibilities (Tomaselli and Louw 1991).

Emergency regulations published in the *Government Gazette* of November 1985 had a silencing effect by determining that the police would decide who to allow as journalists in the magisterial districts under emergency regulations, and how those chosen ones were to go about their professional duties. Taking or publishing photographs, sound recordings and even drawings of unrest-related material were prohibited, except with the permission of a police officer. Journalists entering the restricted areas had to display their accreditation at all times, and had to report to the officer in charge. The Minister of Police, Louis Le Grange, rephrased such covert censorship as a regulation introduced so that the police could "render the necessary assistance".[28]

The only reason given overtly for such control of the professional practices of journalists, was the government's concern that "the presence of television and other camera crews in unrest situations (...) proved to be a catalyst to further violence" (Le Grange, cited in *Sunday Tribune,* 10 November 1985).

State proscriptions silenced by obscuring the intention of the particular regulations, which apparently was to keep security force brutality from public scrutiny. Justification of the media restrictions stated that they would repair and maintain internal stability.

5.1.2. *Police statements to the media*

On 5 March, two days after the shooting in Guguletu, the *Cape Times* adhered to emergency regulations, telexing allegations made by the families of deceased youngsters to Police Headquarters in Pretoria and asking permission to publish them. Censorship of these allegations began by delaying the answers so that they were not in time for the newspaper going to press. Suggestions of eye witnesses that contradicted police claims and resultant probing questions in the media were constructed as malicious and aimed at undermining state security. Police responses then took the form of overt refusals to give further comment. Thus the discourse between publishers and censoring authorities on conflicting versions of the event was replaced by a discourse of stubborn refusal to either ratify or deny information obtained in independent news gathering. Such refusals then became the printed news, as in:

> "The Commissioner of Police has already made a statement. I have nothing further to add." (Police liaison officer cited in *Cape Times*, 15 March 1986: 2)
>
> According to the Commanding officer of the Public Relations Division of the South African Police (SAP) in Pretoria "police had already made statements on the issue and were not prepared to comment any further". (*Cape Times*, 15 March 1986: 2)

Another form of silencing by police authorities occurred when reporters indicated that between 6,000 and 15,000 people (some reported even more) had attended the funeral of the seven.[29] The police version, however, assured that in monitoring the crowd, they had counted no more than 3,000 mourners.

5.1.3. *Statements by Government officials*

The Economist[30] commented that none of the media regulations seemed to have much to do with averting a guerrilla onslaught – a justification often used by politicians. Rather, the regulations would frustrate those who had opted for the only alternative to violence open to the disenfranchised. Civic protest in the form of speeches, demonstrations, strikes and boycotts became outlawed. The media regulations of 1985 and 1986 thus silenced verbal as well as non-verbal forms of communication. The justification of extreme emergency was used, although no objective support was given for such a claim, and public scrutiny or ratification was foreclosed.

In parliament, members of the opposition asked questions related to the Guguletu Seven incident. On 19 March, more than two weeks after the shooting, Louis le Grange, Minister of Law and Order, contradicted eye witness accounts. According to the *Cape Times* the opposition spokesman for Law and Order, Tian van der Merwe, pertinently asked whether one victim had in fact attempted to surrender as was alleged by an eye witness. The Minister reportedly answered with a blunt "no". He also refused to disclose and so remained silent on: the causes of death; the nature of the victims' wounds; the name and rank of the officers in charge of the police operation; details of who had stolen the vehicle used by the youngsters; whether the men had been known to the police through e.g. former arrests, detentions, or charges in terms of security laws.

Readers were left to guess the reasons for such self-censorship of the minister. At the time it was possible to imply that he did not have the requested information. However, in 1996 it emerged that this was highly unlikely; the Truth and Reconciliation Commission investigations revealed that the youngsters had in fact been recruited by an "askari", a person co-opted as informer and collaborator, working for a clandestine government agency, the Civil Co-operation Bureau (CCB). The existence of this particular Bureau, later referred to as the government's "dirty tricks" section, was shrouded in silence. This institution was licenced to remove state opposition by means outside and above the law.

This was a clear government cover-up, though at first there was little evidence of the full extent of the gross abuse of state power. The government's silence and silencing was most likely motivated by their desire to keep their considered use of criminal methods undisclosed. By replacing the discourse on facts of the event with a discourse on the untrustworthiness of certain media, they intended to deceive a supposedly naïve polity.

5.2.   Acts of language that disable full disclosure in the media – the silenced

Legal restrictions on journalists were not unambiguous in distinguishing between standard criminal activity (on which reporting was allowed) and political protest constructed as criminal activity (on which reporting was disallowed). Journalists were able to gather information, but would have to screen what they published carefully to avoid the penalties attached to censorship.

5.2.1.   Silencing by "permanently removing" those who could speak

All seven youngsters, referred to as "terrorists" (*Die Burger* 4–3–1986: 2) or "guerillas" (*Cape Times* 4–3–1986: 1; 5–3–1986: 2) in the first reports on the shoot-out were killed. Thus their own testimony was silenced. Even so, there were attempts to censor information on who they were, and what kind of standing they had in their home communities. The *Cape Times* of 7 March 1986 reports on a set of questions their reporters had asked the police and which the police had not answered. One such unanswered question had requested the names of those who had been killed. Nevertheless, a journalist got in touch with relatives of the men, and some of the critical media broke the silence about names and identities. Two media techniques challenged the official discourse, i.e. the use of quotation marks in printing pejorative terms such as "terrorist" and "guerilla", and giving alternative renderings of the referents' identities.

Die Burger of 5 and 6 March 1986 referred to the seven as "terroriste" and "vermeende terroriste" ("terrorists, alleged terrorists") without using quotation marks. In contrast the *Cape Times* of 5 March reported under the heading "Mothers of 'guerillas' speak" – quotation marks used – how the families to whom they had spoken denied that their children had been active, or even interested, in the political activities alleged by the police:

> "Jabulani was just a sweet boy who knew nothing about politics. He was the only son I had (...) they have shot the wrong people." (Eunice Miya, cited in *Cape Times*, 5 March 1986: 2)

5.2.2. *Silencing eye-witnesses and relatives*

The immediate responses of police spokesmen made it clear that they had an interest in silencing eye-witness reports. A *Cape Times* journalist assigned specifically as a crime reporter had arrived at the scene of the shoot-out in the regular course of his day's work. When police on site refused to give any information and referred him to "Pretoria", he proceeded to a nearby hostel where he collected the critical eye-witness reports. The police urgently and insistently demanded that the *Cape Times* give them the names of the witnesses by having a subpoena delivered by a senior officer, the commander of the Murder and Robbery Squad. They also denied the truth of the eye-witness allegations. In doing so they signalled their dissatisfaction with an alternative version. The discourse between competing daily newspapers, *Die Burger* and *Cape Times*, highlighted inconsistencies between the eye-witness accounts and the police accounts. *Die Burger* alluded to the civilians' version as

> 'n poging om die indruk te wek dat die mense wat doodgeskiet is onskuldige werksoekers was (alhoewel hulle swaar bewapen was).
> [an attempt to create the impression that the people who were shot and killed were innocent jobseekers (although they were heavily armed)] (*Die Burger*, 15 March 1986: 2)

Again, silencing took the form of withholding the names of the eye-witnesses. The *Cape Times,* as a standard measure of source protection, did not publish their names. Even so, the witnesses soon came forward themselves to have their accounts officially recorded. These accounts were available ten years later at the Truth and Reconciliation Commission enquiry. Then, in 1997, the *Cape Times* journalist who had "broken" the news gave their names explicitly, indicating that the taboo on naming had been removed; Bowers Mzonke, Cecil Mthuthu and General Sibaca were at last publicly heard and recognised as respectable, honest witnesses.

In raising doubt as to the credibility of eye-witness reports and relatives' characterisations, the official discourses displaced those of the people closest to the seven youngsters. So, discourses portraying one as a worker in a bakery who supported his mother, another as a sensitive son who walked his mother to the station as she was leaving for work, and a third as a friend who liked to make music, were replaced. Official discourse portrayed the Guguletu Seven as delinquents who had joined the underground and had misled their families. The more complex detail of vulnerable, naive young men desperate for an income and thus easily lured into an offer that promised reasonable remuneration was not heard until ten years after the event. The Truth and Reconciliation Commission gave the first opportunity for the local community's version of the story to be afforded status similar to that of the official versions circulated in 1986. The 1986 version has now largely been replaced by the 1996 version.

5.2.3. *Silencing the media: The stories as well as the narrators*

The narrators, the journalists, sub-editors and editors had virtually stumbled upon the Guguletu Seven event. Chris Bateman of the *Cape Times* related to the Truth and Reconciliation Commission how he had arrived at police headquarters at 9 am, found no-one in, and gathered that "something major had happened". Silencing of media voices started by police denying reporters access to the scene, and it continued in miscellaneous ways. Headlines on the front page of the *Cape Times* of 4 and 5 March read:

Man with hands in air shot – witness
7 die in battle with police
Jeers as police wash away blood

In text under such headings as the above, the censorship was challenged by means of implications regarding the nature of the event, as in:

"In what appeared to be a *carefully planned police operation*, detectives confronted the suspects" [my italics]
"Certain *allegations made by the families* have been withheld pending the police reply which had not been received at the time of going to press." [my italics]

The police immediately drew on the emergency regulations, attempting to silence by legal action against two journalists of the *Cape Times*. Newspapers' persistent questions were referred to the Bureau of Information in Pretoria, where requests for permission to run the stories that they had uncovered were either left unanswered or given brusque, uninformative responses.

Information on the extraordinary circumstances of the event had been silenced. There were nagging questions concerning who had been responsible for the security force action, who had been in command, how the police managed such a prompt and extensive presence at that particular time and place, why there was no attempt to arrest the youngsters, why in circumstances alleged to be excessively threatening, police injuries had been virtually negligible, and so on. Such discourse was censored and replaced by another that topicalised the reluctance of officials in responding to questions and by the punitive measures against journalists, who insisted on their right to publish an alternative, more likely representation of the event.

The media became sites of engagement between the publishers and the state, as well as between two local morning papers, *Die Burger* and *Cape Times*. In the discursive web of questions, implications, scant details and lies, the tug of war between powerful institutions such as state and media was patent. Within days the *Cape Times* reporter responsible for the alternative version of the chain of events was subpoenaed to supply the names of the witnesses. Also, a colleague was charged for passing the story on to a foreign news agency, the BBC. After the event Bateman was barred from attending the regular crime report meetings at police headquarters. That he had embarrassed and annoyed the police went unmentioned. His exclusion was justified by the sham claim that he did not have the required police accreditation. In fact, many journalists worked without such accreditation: a number of newspapers had deliberately decided not to apply for it as they regarded the instruction to be a form of censorship and had chosen to resist such state surveillance.

Die Burger, traditionally aligned to the ruling National Party, published a front page report on the Guguletu event on 4 March. Their representation challenged the *Cape Times* version by giving open support for the police account, with headlines such as

> **ANC-lokval gefnuik** (*ANC trap foiled*)
> **Bloedbad was hul doel** (*Bloodbath was their aim*)
> **Al hoe meer terroriste loop hul vas** (*More and more terrorists confounded*)

The Afrikaans paper reported more on the summons brought against the *Cape Times* reporters than did the *Cape Times* itself. In referring to the journalist's eye-witness account of police shooting a man who was giving himself up, and another who was lying on the ground already wounded, *Die Burger* cited a Captain Calitz, who said the police would never shoot to kill a suspected terrorist.

polisiemanne – uitgesoekte spesialiste – weet watter waarde 'n gevange terroris vir die polisie inhou ... (maar as) 'n AK47 op jou skiet is daar geen tyd om te redekawel nie
[policemen – elected specialists – know what value a captured terrorist has for the police ... (but if) an AK47 is firing at you there is no time for dispute] (*Die Burger,* 4 March 1986: 1)

In referring to the slight injuries of police officers in comparison to the excessive wounds of the deceased, *Die Burger* cited the police response that their men had had "noue ontkomings" ("narrow escapes").

Also, *Die Burger* (4–3–1986: 8) commented protractedly on an escalating "rewolusionêre patroon" ("revolutionary pattern") and "aaklige geweldspolitiek van die ANC en sy terroriste-bendes" ("ghastly violence politics of the ANC and its terrorist gangs").

Much of the information tabooed in 1986 was silenced through censorship regulations. However, a fair amount was not published because journalists at the time could not even collect the information. Instead of a story on the deception and a staged ambush on susceptible youngsters, the story of March 1986 was replaced by one of seven terrorists caught in the act of a bungled ambush they had planned and poorly executed. The discourse given prominence in 1986 focussed on whether the intensity of the police violence had been justified, and whether the threat they allegedly experienced had been real. The silence on who had planned and commanded the operation and what they had set out to achieve on the morning of 3 March was resounding. Censorship of these particulars was achieved not through media regulations, but in fact through a decision of senior security force members to enable a fabricated story of terrorists frustrated in an attempt to ambush a police vehicle, and to disable a story of security force members covertly luring the unsuspecting men into naive political protest that would cost them their lives.

A detailed analysis of censorship under a repressive political system highlights a number of very obvious instances of silencing in the media. There are examples from across the range: silencing by murdering witnesses, silencing by legal prohibition, silencing by telling lies, by replacing one story with another, by foregrounding one story and discrediting another; offenders remain silent on their own motives and actions, reporters remain silent to protect witnesses, relatives remain silent in horror and vulnerability. It is clear that between destroying documents and killing witnesses on the one hand, and the self-censorship of those who cannot or will not speak on the other, there is a continuum of more and less forceful tabooing. To marginalise discourses that publish minority perspectives, or to secure biased reviews by employing the journalist illustrate more covert forms of silencing. Covert silencing may seem relatively innocent but may be as damaging as many more overt forms. Reflection on the variety of ways in which discourse spaces are occupied and organised should serve to raise awareness of the power of language and the power of silence in the media. Such reflection also assists in recognising, interpreting and challenging deceptive or hegemonic discourses.

Notes

1. cf. discussion in Levinson (1983: 299, 300).
2. As discussed in Tannen and Saville-Troike (1985).
3. cf. Wardhaugh (1986: 234–237); also Scollon (1985) and Scollon and Scollon (1996).
4. cf. Kurzon (1997: 12, 20) on notions of intentional and unintentional silence.
5. cf. reference to such "gagging made graphic" in Anthonissen (2003: 305, 306)
6. A similar distinction is to be found in nouns of Dutch and Afrikaans, where *stilte* can denote absence of sound or of speech, but *"swye"* denotes specifically absence of speech. Cf. the German cognates *Stille* vs. *Schweigen*.
7. Cf. a theatre review of *Primo*, a play by Anthony Sher based on Primo Levi's Auschwitz memoir, titled "From horror comes stillness".
8. Cf. Fowler (1996) on "defamiliarization" as a means of challenging "habitualization", where he refers to general laws of perception that tend to repress sensitivity to stable, regular forms and patterns.
9. Cf. *The New Collins Thesaurus* (1985). London: Guild Publishing; *Oxford Dictionary* Oxford: Oxford University Press.
10. Obviously different communities have different conventions relating to the acceptability or not of various kinds of behaviour. Therefore, what has to be censored, what kind of behaviour is dubious but tolerable in given circumstances, and what kind is entirely acceptable and respectable are not universal or generic. Various forms of censure and censorship are often culture and group specific.
11. Such authority often enjoys legal protection such as is recognised in customary law or the statutes of local authorities, constitutions of community organisations, and so on.
12. The term "publish" in this context is used for any means of making public a text, i.e. a spoken announcement, written text or visual image such as a photograph or a film.
13. Coetzee (1996) refers extensively to censorship measures in the USSR, although his interest is in state control of literature rather than of the media. He refers not only to state prescription and proscription, but also to how censorship was resisted (e.g.) as when Isaac Babel elected for a "genre of silence" (1996: 147), for rather not writing at all than writing according to objectionable rules. Coetzee refers also to censorship in related regimes such as Hungary and Cuba.
14. Such protection is guaranteed, for example, in the First Amendment to the United States Constitution, in Article 5 of the German *Grundgesetz* and in Article 10 of the European Convention. In Britain the freedom exists residually in that, where statute or common law rules do not restrict it, it is naturally established.
15. Many legal systems protect not only the right to speak freely, but also the right to remain silent. The right to remain silent is mostly one that allows silence as an alternative to giving self-incriminating evidence (cf. Kurzon 1997: 51–71).

16 Cf. reference to the phrase "the personal is political", coined by Carol Hanish in the feminist protest against the Miss America Contest in 1968, in Sebek (2002). On (self-)censorship of gay and lesbian discourses in mainstream media, see also Henriques (1978); Dickey (1987); Higgins (1995).
17 Media coverage of the gulf wars and a definition of the notion of embedded journalism are elaborated in the web-based encyclopedia Wikipedia. See also web-reports by Turnley (2002) and Silver (2002) on televising the Gulf War; comments published by Goodman (n.d.) and Newshour (2003) regarding embedded journalism.
18 Cf. reference to Harris and Zucchino in Rockwell (2005).
19 On censorship and self-censorship in Hong Kong, see also Lee and Lin (2006: 331–358), where the discourse on censorship in two local newspapers is analysed.
20 Cf. *The Cape Times*, 1 September 2000, p. 4.
21 See also Butler (1997) for an elaborate investigation of hate speech, and a strong position against recourse to state control and censorship as a means of challenging this.
22 For specific details and comment on the provisions of the USA Patriot Act see also American Civil Liberties Union (2001), Electronic Frontier Foundation (2001) and Feingold (2001).
23 Cf. *Weekly Mail, Cape Times*.
24 For example, *Die Kerkbode* (17 December 1986) surveyed editors of a number of publications of Afrikaans churches and was convinced that *"verantwoordelike kerkpers nie geraak (word) deur media-beheer(nie)"* ("responsible church publications are not affected by media control"). A front page article went on to mention that it was a pity that restrictions had become necessary because we were living in "revolutionary times".
25 For specific details cf. Stuart (1990: 86–89).
26 Due to economic pressure not unrelated to the political strife in the country, this publication was discontinued in 1985. However, it re-emerged as an independent weekly newspaper, *The Weekly Mail*, currently published as the *Mail and Guardian*.
27 "The Guguletu Seven" produced and directed by Lindi Wilson.
28 Cf. Gavin Stewart's "The Walls of Jericho", article published in the *Sunday Tribune*, 10 November 1985.
29 In fact, at the funeral on 15 March only six of the seven were buried; the seventh person's family had opted for a less public ceremony.
30 *The Economist*, 20 December 1986, p. 17–20.

References

American Civil Liberties Union
   2001   How the anti-terrorism bill allows for detention of people engaging in innocent associational activity. Available online at http://www.aclu.org/natsec/emergpowers/12482log20011023.html. Accessed 8 September 2007.
Anthonissen, Christine
   2002   Interaction between visual and verbal communication: Changing patterns in the printed media. In: Gilbert Weiss and Ruth Wodak (eds.) *Critical Discourse Analysis: Theory and Interdisciplinarity*, 297–313. Basingstoke: Palgrave.

Anthonissen, Christine
    2003   Challenging media censoring: In: Jim Martin and Ruth Wodak (eds.) *Re/reading the Past: Critical and Functional Perspectives on Time and Value*, 91–111. Amsterdam: Benjamins.

Arnett, Peter
    1995   *Live From the Battlefields: From Vietnam to Baghdad: 35 Years in the World's War Zones*. London: Corgi.

Barendt, Eric
    1987   *Freedom of Speech*. Oxford: Clarendon Press.

Becker, Jasper
    2002   On Hong Kong's self-censorship. Taipei Times (22 May). Available online at http://taipeitimes.com/News/editorial/archives/2002/05/21/story/0000136986. Accessed 4 July 2006.

Breytenbach, Marlene M.
    1997   The Manipulation of Public Opinion by State Censorship of the Media in South Africa (1974–1994). PhD dissertation, University of Stellenbosch.

Buelens, Geert, Bert Bultinck, Pieter de Buysser and Dirk Mertens (eds.)
    2000   *De Militanten van de Limiet: Over Censuur en Vrije Meningsuiting*. Antwerpen: Van Halewyck.

Butler, Judith
    1997   *Excitable Speech: a Politics of the Performative*. New York: Routledge.

Coetzee, John M.
    1996   *Giving Offense: Essays on Censorship*. Chicago: University of Chicago Press.

Dauenhauer, Bernard P.
    1980   *Silence: The Phenomenon and its Ontological Significance*. Bloomington: Indiana University Press.

De Villiers, Les
    1980   *Secret Information*. Cape Town: Tafelberg Publishers.

Dedaić, Mirjana N. and Daniel N. Nelson (eds.)
    2003   *At War With Words*. Berlin: Mouton de Gruyter.

Dickey, Julienne
    1987   Heterosexism and the lesbian image in the press. In: in Kath Davies, Julienne Dickey and Teresa Stratford (eds.) *Out of Focus: Writings on Women and the Media*, 81–89. London: The Women's Press.

Electronic Frontier Foundation
    2001   Analysis of the provisions of the USA Patriot Act that relate to online activities. Available online at http://www.eff.org/Privacy/Surveillance/Terrorism/20011031_eff_usa_patriot_analysis.php. Accessed 30 November 2007.

Fairclough, Norman
    1989   *Language and Power*. London: Longman.

Fairclough, Norman
    1995   *Media Discourse*. London/New York/Sydney: Edward Arnold.

Fairclough, Norman
    2003   *Analysing Discourse: Textual Analysis for Social Research*. London: Routledge.

Fairclough, Norman and Ruth Wodak
   1997   Critical discourse analysis. In: Teun A. van Dijk (ed.) *Discourse as Social Interaction*, 258–283. London: Sage.
Feingold, Russ
   2001   Statement of U.S. Senator Russ Feingold on the anti-terrorism bill. Available online at http://www.epic.org/privacy/terrorism/usapatriot/feingold.html. Accessed 8 September 2007.
Fowler, Roger
   1996   *Linguistic Criticism*. Oxford: Oxford University Press.
Free Expression Network (FEN)
   2002   The USA Patriot Act six months later. Available online at http://www.freeexpression.org/patriotstmt.htm. Accessed 4 July 2006.
Fridland, Valérie
   2003   Quiet in the court: Attorneys' silencing strategies during courtroom cross-examination. In: Lynn Thiesmeyer (ed.) *Discourse and Silencing*, 119–138. Amsterdam: Benjamins.
Galasiński, Dariusz
   2003   Silencing by law: The 1981 Polish Performances and Publications Control Act. In: Lynn Thiesmeyer (ed.) *Discourse and Silencing*, 211–232. Amsterdam: Benjamins.
Glasgow Media Group
   1995 [1985]   The Falklands War: Making good news. In: Greg Philo (ed.) *Glasgow Media Group Reader*, 76–101. London: Routledge.
Goodman, Amy
   n.d.   Independent media in a time of war. Available online at http://www.democracynow.org/static/IMIATOW.shtml. Accessed 8 September 2007.
Hachten, William A. and C. Anthony Giffard
   1984   *Total Onslaught: The South African Press under Attack*. Johannesburg: Macmillan, SA.
Henriques, Nikki
   1978   Why gays in media?. *Sappho* 6: 11, 15–16, 21.
Higgins, Ross
   1995   Murder will out: Gay identity and media discourse in Montreal. In: William Leap (ed.) *Beyond the Lavender Lexicon: Authenticity, Imagination and Appropriation in Lesbian and Gay Languages*, 107–132. New York: Gordon and Breach Press.
Jaworski, Adam
   1993   *The Power of Silence: Social and Pragmatic Perspectives*. London/New Delhi: Sage.
Jaworski, Adam and Dariusz Galasiński
   2000   Strategies of silence: Omission and ambiguity in *The Black Book of Polish Censorship*. *Semiotica* 131(1/2): 185–200.
Kienzle, Michael and Dirk Mende (eds.)
   1980   *Zensur in der Bundesrepublik*. Munich: Wilhelm Heyne Verlag.
Kress, Gunther and Hodge, Robert
   1979   *Language as Ideology*. London: Routledge.

Kurzon, Dennis
    1997   *Discourse of Silence*. Amsterdam: Benjamins.
Lambertus, Sandra
    2003   News discourse of Aboriginal resistance in Canada. In: Lynn Thiesmeyer (ed) *Discourse and Silencing*, 233–274. Amsterdam: Benjmains.
Lee, Francis and Angel My Lin
    2006   Newspaper editorial discourse and the politics of self-censorship in Hong Kong. *Discourse & Society* 17(3): 331–358.
Levinson, Stephen
    1983   *Pragmatics*. Cambridge: Cambridge University Press.
Miller, David
    1995   The media and Northern Ireland: Censorship, information management and the broadcasting ban. In: Greg Philo (ed.) *Glasgow Media Group Reader*, 45–75. London: Routledge.
Mitten, Richard
    1992   *The Politics of Anti-Semitic Prejudice: The Waldheim Phenomenon in Austria*. Boulder: Westview Press.
Newshour
    2003   Pros and cons of embedded journalism. Available online at http://www.pbs.org/newshour/extra/features/jan-june03/embed_327.html. Accessed 8 September 2007.
O'Connor, Patricia E.
    2003   Telling bits: Silencing and the narratives behind prison walls. In: Lynn Thiesmeyer (ed.) *Discourse and Silencing*, 139–169. Amsterdam: Benjamins.
Rees, Mervin and Chris Day
    1980   *Muldergate*. Johannesburg: Macmillan.
Reisigl, Martin and Ruth Wodak
    2001   *Discourse and Discrimination: Rhetorics of Racism and Antisemitism*. London/New York: Routledge.
Rhoodie, Eschel
    1983   *The Real Information Scandal*. Pretoria: Orbis.
Rockwell, Paul
    2005   Embedded journalism at its worst: The Ron Harris smear campaign against marine sgt. Jimmy Massey. Available online at http://www.inmotionmagazine.com/opin/pr_rh.html. Accessed 4 July 2006.
Saville-Troike, Muriel
    1985   The place of silence in an integrated theory of communication. In: Deborah Tannen and Muriel Saville-Troike (eds.) *Perspectives on Silence*, 3–18. New York: Ablex.
Schauer, Frederick F.
    1982   *Free Speech: A Philosophical Enquiry*. Cambridge: Cambridge University Press.
Scollon, Ron
    1985   The machine stops: Silence in the metaphor of malfunction. In: Deborah Tannen and Muriel Saville-Troike (eds) *Perspectives on Silence*, 21–30. New York: Ablex.
Scollon, Ron
    1998   *Mediated Discourse as Social Interaction*. London/New York: Longman.

Scollon, Ron and Suzanne Scollon
    1995   *Intercultural Communication: A Discourse Approach.* Oxford: Blackwell.
Sebek, Anezka
    2002   Lesbian media activism. (Unpublished MA thesis proposal). Available online at http://beard.dialnsa.edu/~treis/pdf/Lesbian%20Media%20Activism.pdf. Accessed on 4 July 2006.
Silver, Rosalind
    2002   Gulf War: the more we watched, the less we knew. Available online at http://www.medialit.org/reading_room/article595.html. Accessed 8 September 2007.
Standbridge, R.
    1986   A SA newspaper stands its ground. In *New African* (February): 40.
Stuart, Kelsey
    1990   *Kelsey Stuart's The Newspaperman's Guide to the Law.* Durban: Butterworths.
Tannen, Deborah and Muriel Saville-Troike
    1985   *Perspectives on Silence.* New York: Ablex.
Thiesmeyer, Lynn (ed.)
    2003   *Discourse and Silencing.* Amsterdam: Benjamins.
Tomaselli, Keyan and P. Eric Louw (eds)
    1991   *The Alternative Press in South Africa.* Bellville, SA: Anthropos.
Towns, Alison, Peter Adams and Nicola Gavey
    2003   Silencing talk of men's violence towards women. In: Lynn Thiesmeyer (ed.) *Discourse and Silencing*, 43–78. Amsterdam: Benjamins.
Traber, Michael and Philip Lee (eds)
    1991   Reporting the Gulf War. Special issue of *Media Development* (October).
Turnley, Peter
    2002   The unseen Gulf War. Available online at http://digitaljournalist.org/issue0212/pt_intro.html. Accessed 8 September 2007.
Wardhaugh, Ronald
    1986   *An Introduction to Sociolinguistics.* Oxford: Basil Blackwell.
Wodak, Ruth
    1991   The Waldheim Affair and anti-semitic prejudice in Austrian public discourse. *Patterns of Prejudice* 24(2–4): 18–33.
Wodak, Ruth
    1996   *Disorders of Discourse.* London: Longman.
Wodak, Ruth
    2003   Anti-Semitic discourse in post-war Austria. In: Lynn Thiesmeyer (ed.) *Discourse and Silencing*, 179–209. Amsterdam: Benjamins.
Wodak, Ruth, Florian, Menz, Richard Mitten and Frank Stern
    1994   *Die Sprachen der Vergangenheiten: Öffentliches Gedenken in österreichischen und deutschen Medien.* Frankfurt/Main: Suhrkamp.

Websites (see also references):

http://en.wikipedia.org/wiki/Embedded_journalist Accessed 4 July 2006.
http://en.wikipedia.org/wiki/Gulf_War#Media Accessed 4 July 2006.
http://en.wikipedia.org/wiki/USA_PATRIOT_Act Accessed 8 September 2007.
http://en.wikipedia.org/wiki/Usa_patriot_act Accessed 4 July 2006.

South African Legislation

Defence Act 44/1957
Police Act 7/1958
Post Office Act 44/1958
Publications Act 42/1974
Internal Security Act 74/1982
Protection of Information Act 84/1982
Government Gazette, November 1985

Newspapers

Cape Times: 4 March 1986, 5 March 1986, 7 March 1986, 15 March 1986, 20 March 1986, 11 February 1999, 1 September 2001.
Die Burger: 4 March 1986, 5 March 1986, 6 March 1986, 15 March 1986.
Die Kerkbode: 17 December 1986.
Sunday Tribune: 10 November 1985.
The Economist: 20 December 1986.
Weekly Mail: 20–26 June 1986, 4–10 July 1986, 22 August 1986, 12–18 December 1986, 13–19 March 1987.

19. Technology, democracy and participation in space

Rodney H. Jones

1. Participation and space

Much has been written about the new possibilities for participation in civil and political life in cyberspace. New information technologies have made possible new ways for people to construct social identities, form social networks and take social action. Attention has been paid to the use of the internet in political movements and political processes, the ways flows of information affect relationships of power, and the development of on-line communities, particularly among the marginalised.

We construct cyberspace by the way we study it. Technologies, as Hine (2000) points out, are both tools for communication and artifacts that we create through the symbolic meanings we invest in them. Studies in computer mediated communication and politics always define computer mediated participation based on a particular definition of the space in which that participation is seen to occur, a particular metaphor by which cyberspace is understood (Stefik 1996), whether it is seen as a "communication conduit", "a digital library", "an electronic marketplace", "a collection of virtual worlds" or an "information superhighway", to name just a few possibilities. What cyberspace is is determined by the theoretical frames and terminological screens we bring to it.

This paper compares and contrasts the approaches of various scholars in applied linguistics and communication studies regarding political participation and the internet, analysing them in terms of the ways they construct participation by constructing the space in which it occurs. It reviews approaches which see cyberspace as a kind of virtual public square, and define participation in terms of access to this virtual property, those which focus more on the generic or textual spaces constructed in cyberspace and see participation as mastery of particular sets of discursive conventions, and finally, those which view participation in terms of concrete, everyday social actions within overlapping layers of activity spaces, both physical and virtual. These studies constitute a range of interests, methodologies and theoretical frameworks from mass communication studies to genre analysis to mediated discourse analysis.

In order to fully understand the potential for the internet to alter modes of political participation, I will argue, all of these ways of perceiving space need to be accounted for. Most importantly, however, analysts must recognise that participation with computer technologies is always participation in spaces which are shaped by users themselves through the kinds of metaphors and communicative expectations they bring to them.

2. Participation and the electronic commons

Most contributions to the debate about the internet and democracy from the field of communication studies have conceptualised cyberspace as a kind of "electronic commons" in which users can deliberate, debate, organise and otherwise exchange information. In this approach the key criteria by which participation is defined are access, visibility, community, and the free flow of information, and the key questions involve the extent to which the internet alters citizens' ability to affect public policy or exercise collective political power in the public sphere. Central to this construction of a "virtual public sphere" are liberal values of transparency, participation, openness, collaboration and egalitarianism.

Many scholars taking this approach focus on the internet's potential to bring about "a revitalized democracy characterized by a more active informed citizenry" (Corrado 1996: 29). They credit it with widening political debate by providing the resources for disseminating information to a greater number of people, providing a forum for debating policy, and providing a means of holding those in power more accountable. Characteristic of this perspective is the work of Dahlgren (2000, 2001), who sees the internet as changing what Habermas (1989) calls "the public sphere". The internet, he argues, more than any other medium, has created a communal public space which, due to its near universal accessibility, its social decontextualisation, its lack of usage conventions, and the difficulty of enforcing censorship in it, satisfies Habermas's conditions for increased democratic discourse.

Whereas in the past sources of information tended to be concentrated among a few major commercial and governmental outlets, the internet allows those with limited resources to publish information, and for users all over the world to bypass traditional gatekeepers of information and avail themselves of primary sources and of a wide range of perspectives on these sources. This feature has proved particularly important in nations in which traditional media (newspapers, television) are tightly controlled by governmental or commercial interests (Zheng and Wu 2005).

Not only has information itself become decentralised, so has the power to decide what kinds of information are important and what kinds are not – the process of "agenda setting" (Harper 2003). In the past, large media corporations and governments perpetuated a top-down model of political discourse in which those at the top of the information business held control over the public discussion. Now, even web pages or weblogs run by individuals can have an enormous impact on the shape of the political debate (Drezner and Farrell 2004) (see, for example, the role the Drudgereport had in the Monica Lewinsky scandal). Individuals can also effect policy change by rallying support through mainstream channels or through more subversive forms of online political activism or "hacktivism" (Taylor 2005).

The extent to which these new flows of information and new processes of agenda setting can actually cultivate the kind of "informed public" seen as necessary for democracy, however, is uncertain. Just because a public has more information available to it does not necessarily mean it is "more informed". First, much of the information that circulates on the web can be inaccurate or biased, bypassing as it does traditional systems of responsibility, regulation, and accountability. As Bazerman (2004: para. 34) writes "while the increased opportunities for participation and affiliation seem to foster the ideals of democracy, there are also fewer filters on the partisanship, controversialism, and unreliability of reports that can become widely visible and seem to have some spillover effect into more traditional media." Second, this information often comes at a rate at which it is difficult to process: the fundamental changes in the political economy of information have been accompanied by an enormous speeding up of the rate at which texts are produced and consumed, and this increased speed of information can have negative effects on the political decision making processes of both leaders and citizens, forcing them, in many cases, to make hastier decisions in response to the furious flow of information (Hartley 2003).

Another oft-cited advantage of the internet is that is provides spaces for the development and the strengthening of communities, increasing citizens' ability to engage in lobbying or identity politics (Graham and Khosravi 2002). Rheingold (1993), the most famous early proponent of electronic communities, insisted as far back as the early nineties that cyberspace provides individuals with the freedom to form their own communities free of physical and political limitations. This aspect of the medium has been especially important for people in socially or politically marginalised groups who are able to network with one another for the purposes of social support or political organisation and to construct a kind of visibility in the virtual public sphere that may not be possible in the physical one. By calling on the rhetoric of inclusion associated with the electronic commons, excluded groups can argue for their rights as part of an active public. Examples of this can be seen in the creation of digital "queer spaces" by gays and lesbians (Woodland 2000). Marginalised communities can also work in less visible ways, using electronic communication more quietly to undermine powerful discourses, as with democracy activist in places like China and Burma (Zheng and Wu 2005).

At the heart of the ability of the internet to foster free speech and political activism is the fact that new technologies of communication fundamentally change how people are able to manage their identities in various kinds of "publics". The Internet has altered what Saco (2002: xi) calls "the politics of visibility": On one hand, it has increased the visibility of previously invisible groups and perspectives, but on the other hand, much of this visibility depends upon the invisibility of individual participants that the web affords. What chiefly facilitates free speech on the internet is the fact that it gives people ways to conceal or alter their identities and thus simultaneously advance their agendas and disassociate themselves from them.

Many of those who see the internet as an inclusive public sphere rest as much of their claim on the invisibility it affords as on the visibility. Anonymity, it is argued, breeds egalitarianism. As Heim (1992: 72) puts it, "we are more equal because we can either ignore or create the body that appears in cyberspace". Perhaps the most extreme version of this argument comes from some corners of the "cyberfeminism" movement, best characterised by the writings of Donna Haraway (1991) and her theory of the "cyborg". In this perspective the internet is seen as freeing women (and men) from the limits of biology, lessening hierarchy and providing new opportunities for nurturing.

At the same time, many have questioned this view of equality based on disembodiment and anonymity. First, while the anonymity that is possible on the internet can facilitate free speech and democratic deliberation by creating conditions under which people feel more comfortable expressing themselves, it can also inhibit free speech and serious deliberation by creating the conditions under which people do not have to take responsibility for what they say. Thus, while the Internet is a bastion of free expression for the socially and politically marginalised, it is also a major forum for those who seek to further marginalise them – purveyors of racist, sexist and extreme nationalist ideas and other forms of "hate speech" (Irvine 2006).

Second, as Travers (2000) points out, anonymity does not necessarily foster inclusively, as the norms that prevail when people's particularity is bracketed tend to be based on existing hegemonies. Even if the internet allows us to "dispose of physical spaces and bodies" (Saco 2002: xxv), this does not necessarily result in more egalitarian public spaces since ignoring the body does not have the effect of legitimating difference, but of erasing it. As Stone (1992: 103) writes, "forgetting about the body is an old Cartesian trick, one that has unpleasant consequences for those bodies whose speech is silenced by the act of forgetting (…) usually women and minorities."

The key problem here is the assumption that technologically mediated spaces are politically neutral when, in fact, racism, sexism and other forms of discrimination are not left behind with our bodies. Nakamura (2002), in her study of race and the internet, claims that the kinds of racism that exist in physical space are often mirrored, or even accentuated in cyberspace. Similarly, Herring (1993), in her studies of gender and online language use, has found that attempts by females to participate on an equal basis in on-line discussions are often ignored or delegitimised by male users.

Others critical of the potential for the net to foster political participation within the "virtual public sphere" model point to the fact that the identities most internet websites make available for their users are not empowering political identities, but rather consumer identities. Despite the use of cyberspace for political activism, ninety percent of all web pages are commercial in nature. Finally, any discussion of participation and the internet would not be complete without mentioning the "digital divide", the fact that many people in the world do not have access to the material resources or the skills to even enter the "virtual commons".

3. Textual performance: Participation as identity

One limitation of approaches that see the internet as a discrete "public space" into which people bring ready made identities is that they are based on a view of identity as separate from participation. Others, working from a different theoretical paradigm, see identity not as separate from cyberspace itself, but as constituted in the discursive practices that cyberspace makes possible. In this perspective, space is not just constructed by technologies but by the discourse through which the "polity continuingly speaks and inscribes itself into existence and by which individuals talk and write themselves" (Bazerman 2002: 37). For scholars like this, the key point of the information age is not so much the information, but the generic patterns through which it is transmitted and the social roles and relationships these genres make possible. We develop and form identities, they insist, through participation in systems of discourse; "identities and forms of life get built within the evolving social spaces identified by recognizable communicative acts" (Bazerman 2002: 17).

The internet has introduced an entirely new generic architecture into our lives with new ways of amplifying (and limiting) possibilities for participation in social and political life. The weblog, the instant messaging session and the newsgroup are just a few of the emergent genres that are taking advantage of the multimodal affordances of new media; integrating older conventions of the printed text with newer dynamic image-and-sound technologies, along with the special capability of hypertext to let users form multiple pathways through an area of interest (Lemke 2002, 2003).

One of the chief questions in this approach is whether or not the new discourse practices that have evolved in cyberspace are actually conducive to the egalitarianism and rational deliberation seen as hallmarks of democratic life. A number of studies from applied linguistics and communication studies have suggested they are not (Fung 1998; Weger and Aakhus 2003). Weblogs and other forms of political participation, it is argued, rather than giving rise to rational deliberation, can sometimes limit users' access to opposing points of view by engaging them in discourse practices in which like minded perspectives are hyperlinked in tight ideological networks. It has also been suggested that the patterns of interaction fostered by the internet give rise to discourses full of "flaming" (Dery 1994), exclusions, persuasions and misunderstandings: an attack oriented and polemic form of interaction which turns participants into partisans. "Fooled by the cool surface of electronic text," writes Dibbell (1994: 261), people "lob messages cast in aggressively forensic impersonality into the midst of this combustively personal medium."

Bazerman (2002), in his genre analysis of American political discourse on the web, found that, while the internet opens opportunities for non-politicians and non-journalists "to perform political and journalistic activities, elevating their local talk into a public performance" (Bazerman 2002: 28), rather than deliberation, exchanges of opinion often become a kind of identity play (Billig 1988), in which users exchange tokens of allegiance to a particular group. Bazerman (2004) concludes that "[t]he internet, while changing the dynamics and opportunities of communication, nonetheless, continues a complex system of political communication forged in previous media and still contains means to degrade or elevate our politics" (Bazerman 2004: para. 2).

Wodak and Wright (2006), on the other hand, similarly focusing on how the structure of internet genres helps to shape the content and conduct of political debates, present a slightly more optimistic picture. In their analysis of a the European Union's "Futurum" discussion forum, they find not only that the expression of diverse views (in diverse languages) is facilitated, but also that users' contributions follow conventions of relevance and politeness. What makes Wodak and Wright's approach particularly illuminating is, first, that it combines the quantitative analysis of identity makers and surface linguistic forms with a close critical discourse analysis of selected interactions, and second, that their conceptualisation of the communicative space of the internet does not isolate it from other spaces, seeing it instead as part of a "vast and complex system of communicative multilingual practices" (p. 256) within which ideas, ideologies and identities are reconfigured and recontextualized (Iedema 1999) as they move from one communicative space to another.

Central to the construction of participation in this more discourse analytical perspective is the notion of "literacy", in terms of both the basic language and IT skills needed to participate in electronic life, and the mastery of particular genres and discourses (Gee 1996) which, when used, mark participants as being particular kinds of people. In computer-mediated communication, language use itself cannot be studied as a neutral linguistic phenomenon, but needs to be seen in terms of access, power and identity (Murray 2000). Travers (2000: 14) writes that "access to computer-based public spheres needs to be understood partially in terms of socially determined competence and partly in terms of the sense of entitlement that inspires certain groups to make public their written statements".

For many in literacy studies, the central political fact about new media is that it has given rise to "new literacies". Lankshear and Knobel (2002) enumerate some of these, from the more pedestrian, like sorting and evaluating information and participating discursively in on-line marketplaces like eBay (http://www.ebay.com/), to the more subversive, like "culture jamming" (see http://www.adbusters.org/home/). Lanham (1993) posits that the most important new literacies will revolve around our ability to manage attention, both our own and others'. Traditional school and work based ways of organising knowledge, he suggests, have become obsolete, and real political power belongs to those who are able to develop and control the "attention structures" through which the mass of disparate information that characterises post-modern societies can be navigated.

According to Lemke (2001, 2002, 2003), the internet has already fundamentally altered the politics of reading though hypertext, which frees readers from the argumentative grasp of authors, allowing them to "explore alternative pathways [and] create their own traversals" through texts, and to make meanings that are not intended by the author. Hypertext reading invites a "more complex dialogical (...) chaining of offers and demands, choices and constraints between users and designers/sites" (Lemke 2002: 322). The multimodality of the internet, he argues, further contributes to this proliferation of meanings and viewpoints by presenting subjects and objects in more "multidimensional ways" in which matters of "degree and possibility rather than category and constraint" are communicated (Lemke 2002: 322).

But Lemke (2002) does not stop there. He goes even further to suggest that the internet is changing the meaning of "genre" altogether, creating opportunities for linkages of meaning making that cross standardised genre boundaries. Meanings and the identities that grow from communication are no longer constructed primarily through fixed genres (with their fixed social and discourse roles) but rather as we travel between and among genres along what Lemke calls "traversals." The "political" result of this is that when "people cross institutional and genre boundaries they not only hybridize formerly insulated genres," but also "make new (and potentially subversive) meanings along the new traversals they map out across traditional genres" (Lemke 2003: 1), creating new possibilities for participation and changing the dynamics of power between individuals and institutions.

4. Participation and power in everyday life

Lemke's focus on traversals, the sense of traveling from space to space in cyberspace, brings us to a third approach, one which focuses less on understanding the influence of the internet on the macro-political context and more on understanding how technologies have altered the micro-politics of everyday life. This perspective seeks to understand the ways the political changes brought about by the internet manifest in the subtle tactics of resistance woven into the fabric of the mundane, day to day practices of individuals (de Certeau 1984).

One limitation of the metaphors upon which the approaches discussed above are based is that they take an essentially bifurcated view of space; cyberspace, whether technologically or discursively constituted, is seen as separate from the "real" spaces in which people use their computers and live their "flesh and blood" lives. Even Lemke's formulation of "traversals" which link different on-line and off-line spaces is still predicated on a conceptual separation of the virtual and the physical. Perhaps the greatest impact that new communication technologies have had on politics, however, has to do with the way they have erased (and continue to erase) these boundaries, how the "virtual" has fundamentally altered the patterns of participation and power that we construct with others on a moment to moment basis in our everyday physical lives, in offices, in schools and in our homes.

One branch of sociolinguistics particularly concerned with this aspect of cyberspace is mediated discourse analysis (Scollon 2001; Norris and Jones 2005). Scollon and Scollon (2004) argue that, while the role of the internet in disseminating political information and facilitating organised political deliberation and action is certainly important, a much more important impact of the medium has been the way it makes possible new linkages of social practices in the physical world, and, through these, new identities. The internet, they say, has altered the participation frameworks (Goffman 1981) and power relations associated with face to face communication: People once separated by more stable social boundaries of age, power and geographical location are communicating more, identities are becoming more fluid and contingent, and the distinctions between conversational topics and activities (at work and at play) are becoming blurred. What discourse analysts should focus on when studying the internet, they insist, is not just the discourse that they find on it, but the kinds of everyday social actions it makes possible for users.

Mediated discourse analysis does not limit its metaphor of cyberspace to the spaces visible on users' screens, but considers cyberspace a collection of multiple overlapping spaces, virtual, geographical and physical, which accommodate multiple "forms of life" and communicative possibilities (Jones 2005c; Leander 2005). This conceptualization of space is reminiscent of Goffman's (1971) use of the word *umwelt* ("surroundings"), which he borrows from the study of animal behaviour, and defines as "the region around an individual from which signs of alarm can come" (Goffman 1971: 252). More broadly, it is the space within which communicative signals can be sent to and received from others – an individual's environment of communicative potential (Jones 2004).

Unmediated, the individual's *umwelt* is limited by his or her physical capacities for perception and production of communicative signals. When mediated by technologies like telephones and computers, however, the *umwelt* expands – with other spaces being layered upon the physical space users occupy. Simply having the telephone or computer next to one already expands one's *umwelt*, as it makes available to one the "calls" of people situated a great distance away.

At the same time, technologies have also increased our control over if and how we are perceived within the *umwelt* of others. Animals in the wild protect themselves not just through extending their range of perception and their ability to warn their companions, but also through *camouflage*, modulating their "presence", being able to make themselves available to the perception of friends and shield themselves from the perception of predators. Computer mediated communication provides ways of constructing not just public, but also private spaces through the increased control the medium affords over the communicative environment, its ability to maximise choices with regard to whom one is "available" and how one is available to them. The effect of new communiucation technologies on power is not a matter of their ability to create virtual spaces in exchange for our physical ones. With computers we are able to inhabit multiple spaces at once, and to layer and separate those spaces in multiple ways. This ability to strategically operate within several spaces at once is a source of considerable interactional power, for it facilitates opportunities for "audience segregation" (Goffman 1959), allowing users to play many roles and occupy many communicative positions at the same time.

In his famous exploration of power and discourse in modern societies, Foucault (1979) insists that relations of power are organised around the visibility of the body and technologies of partitioning space which affect that visibility. His model for this is the image of the *panopticon*, a spatial arrangement in which individuals are under constant surveillance from a central authority yet cannot see each other. In many ways, computer mediated communication creates a kind of reverse *panopticon* in which users are afforded myriad ways of concealing their activities from authorities while colluding in various ways on various levels with others. The internet has confounded spatial patterns of surveillance by confounding notions of what space itself is, how it is shaped and the actions we are able to perform within it.

5. Two teenagers

Based on this view of cyberspace, mediated discourse analysis asks how the different possibilities of perception and of presence afforded by new media technologies affect participation in our social worlds, particularly when it comes to issues of power, domination and resistance. This question is the starting point for a number of studies focusing on how "less powerful" or marginalised individuals such as gay men (Jones 2005c), the physically disabled (Al Zidjaly 2004) and teenagers (Lam and Kramsch 2003; Jones 2004, 2005a,b; Leander 2005) use computers to alter power relations in the physical spaces they inhabit. In this section I will illustrate this potential by describing briefly the computer use of two teenagers in Hong Kong.

The strategic layering of spaces that computers facilitate seems especially important in Hong Kong, where the "privacy" of physical space is not usually available to teenagers. As Scollon and his colleagues (1999: 35) put it, Hong Kong teenagers are:

> virtually never alone. Whether at home or at (school) – for many of them even in transit – they do what they do together with others (...) There are virtually no private spaces available. Students find that the only way they experience something like individual privacy is to stay up very late until all of the other members of the family have gone to sleep. (Scollon et al. 1999: 35)

It is often only through their computers, and the ways they use them to construct borders between public and private activity frames, that these young people are able to attain a certain level of control over how and by whom their involvements can be monitored.

Ka Ho, for example, is a sixteen-year-old Chinese gay boy for whom the computer is an essential tool for managing social identity. In the evenings he often visits gay chat rooms and web pages to meet friends and explore his developing sexual and social interests. Like most Hong Kong teenagers, his computer is in the living room of his home, but he has become very good at using game screens and word documents to cover up his chat room activities whenever any of his family members come within eyeshot of the computer. For Ka Ho, the computer is an important "boundary object" in the physical space of his home. It allows him to establish an alternate space in which a whole range of alternate social actions are possible without having to leave the watchful gaze of his parents.

The communicative surround created by Ka Ho's computer not only allows him to participate in interactions with others in ways he could not or would not in face-to-face contexts, but also to participate in particular social identities and communities of practice that would not be so immediately available to him without his computer. Like many other gay youth in Hong Kong and elsewhere, the internet has expanded Ka Ho's access to resources with which to construct his own emerging gay identity, and, more importantly, a means through which to "try on" different ways of participating in this community of practice from the relative safety of his home (Jones 2005d). Other routes to such experimentation (gay bars, public toilets) are either restricted to him because of his age or dangerous. As he himself observes:

the internet has brought me to my real world – gay life, it has let me start my first time of different aspects: have fun, have sex, meeting gay guys, falling in love, meeting friends to play badminton (…) Also, it trained me to be more mature as I can share and listen to others' experiences.

At the same time, just as the computer helps him to construct barriers between the space of his living room and gaze of his parents and the space of the gay world he is exploring, it also functions as a boundary object within this virtual space itself, allowing him to restrict the access "unwanted" online others have to him. Text-based communication allows him to evaluate the character and intention of his interlocutors and disclose his own identity and intentions in an incremental way based on those evaluations. One example of this is the way he decides whether or not to share his pictures with others. He says:

If he asks for my photo only after a few words, I always try to put a test on him before giving my picture. Most people who are asking for a picture are either looking for fun or giving it to others. This is what I am afraid of it. If he asks me for a photo after a really short conversation, I will never give my picture out. And if we have been chatting for a few days and I think that we can really talk to each other and make friends with each other, I will give him my photo if he asks for it and is willing to give his picture to me first.

The involvement screens of computer mediated communication also allow him to master the "orders of indexicality" (Blommart 2005) of this community, to learn about the different kinds of social positions created by different kinds of self-descriptions and the social value commanded by different kinds of identities. "Sometimes I change my nickname ten times in a night," he says, "and every time I change it, different people click on me." This ability to deploy different sorts of "virtual bodies" is also a strategy for testing how far he will allow his interactions to develop. "Before I met my boyfriend," he says, "I often mentioned I was ugly. However, he still wanted to see me as he felt I was very nice. He never cared about my face. Well, it demonstrated that he was not for fun as he still wanted to meet an ugly guy. Actually it was a test, if someone still wants to meet after I tell him I am very ugly, he is probably not for fun. That guy passed the test!"

Finally, the internet allows Ka Ho "legitimate peripheral participation" (Lave and Wenger 1991) within a community of gay men, participation that enables him to hover safely on the periphery without having to commit to the physical actions of full membership. The chat room affords him the opportunity to present himself as simultaneously available and not available, making it possible for him to practice sexual negotiation without necessarily having to practice sex. Ka Ho himself has very clear ideas about his physical boundaries. He says:

> A large number of guys in the chat room often asked me whether I was for fun or liked fucking, sucking, kissing (…) it doesn't mean I don't like these things. I am quite sure that most of guys, including me, like fucking, sucking, kissing so much. However, I will only consider to do these things with my [boyfriend] as I don't want to get any disease, especially AIDS. I think it is safer to have a stable partner.

Ka Ho's situation is not unique. In fact, the internet has become an important avenue for many young people, gay and straight, to experiment with different sex roles, personas and modes of participation (Cooper, McLoughlin and Campbell 2000). This phenomenon is the source of considerable consternation in media constructions of the internet which portray it as place where teenagers are susceptible to manipulation by older sexual predators, and much of this concern is justified. At the same time, what is often missing from these constructions is an understanding of the skills these young people have developed to manage these interactions, and the self-protection strategies they are able to make use of, strategies that teenagers, more familiar with the possibilities of the virtual communicative surround, are often more adept at than adults.

It should be clear from the above example that one of the most important things about the internet for young people is that it not just enables them to participate in different kinds of social interactions and social relationships, but that it allows them to participate as different kinds of people. Danny is the kind of student whose internet use has become a concern for his parents and teachers, the kind of student that is often the subject of alarmist media reports of internet addiction (see for example Chan 1999).

At school, Danny has figured out how to disable the teacher monitoring system at his workstation in the multimedia learning center. Now, when his class is taken there for English lessons to do on-line grammar exercises, he can play Counter Strike, a popular on-line game, while the teacher is not looking. Before his English lessons end, he usually logs onto the English learning website and quickly fills in the blanks in the grammar exercises that have been assigned, and sometimes he even gets a few right. In the physical space of the classroom, Danny is just a mediocre student. In the world of Counter Strike, he is a man to respect.

What is not considered in media, parental and school based discourses about students like Danny, which see the time he spends on Counter Strike as interfering with his studies and isolating him from "real" social relationships with his peers and family members, is an understanding of the kind of social participation on-line gaming does make available to him.

Like the gay chat room, the social environment around Counter Strike is, for Danny, a "figured world" (Holland et al. 1998) with its own sets of social roles and its own "orders of indexicality" which open up possibilities for participation that are not available in Danny's home and school. In particular, what it gives Danny, and many like him, is an opportunity to enact "identities of expertise." Although the interaction order of Counter Strike is intensely hierarchical, this hierarchy is based solely on one's skill in playing the game. A fifteen-year-old can be far more worthy of attention than a fifty year old. "It's all about respect," says Danny, "and it's all about teamwork. You learn how to build up social networks. You learn how to interact with others. Rules about how to act. You get to learn all that stuff."

Danny's participation in Counter Strike involves not just playing the game, but also maintaining a website and a personal server for his friends and team members. All of this requires considerable technical skill, which Danny has mastered without the benefit of school-based instruction. What is different about the learning that takes place within the "figured-world" of Counter Strike and the learning that takes place in Danny's school is that the tasks he masters around Counter Strike are immediately consequential to his standing in his social world and his ability to build positions of power and identities of expertise in ways that performing on-line exercises about the past perfect tense are not. "I've learned a lot about myself as a person," he says, "how to fit into society. What I want to become in the future. It's a reflection of myself."

What these examples illustrate is that understanding the political consequences of computer technology for many individuals involves understanding how, as Leander puts it, "practice travels" across multiple spaces. They show how youth "use digital literacies in distinct ways to alter, extend, transform, and manipulate the space-times of their lives, including the space-times of schooling" (Leander 2005: 3). This layering of multiple contexts, which allow users to strategically enact multiple ways of being socially present, has fundamentally altered power relations in the physical spaces of their everyday lives. The kinds of political action taken by the young people in these studies is not usually targeted towards governments or public policy, but it nevertheless has a considerable impact on the way power is distributed in the immediate social environments of their homes and schools. The nightly virtual gatherings they engage in via message boards, blogs, on-line games and instant messaging programs are important sites where social relationships and social hierarchies formed off-line are rehearsed and ratified, or challenged and contested.

A large part of these teenagers' ability to use the computer to alter power relations is, of course, their special historical position as members of a generation that has grown up with a technology unavailable to their parents when they were young. In many ways, a fifteen-year-old has access to modes of participation that his or her parents will never have access to. The important point, however, is not just that their parents and others of their generation do not have the technical tools available to enact the kinds of participation teenagers do, but that these modes of participation themselves are foreign to them, for what underpins these new modes of participation is not just the technology, but totally different orientations towards time and space (Jones 2005a).

5. Conclusion

The lesson from this comparison of different metaphors for cyberspace from different academic perspectives is not just that our definitions of participation alter with the kinds of conceptual spaces that we make available for that participation, but also that we as citizens or social interactants participate in cyberspace contingent on the metaphors we ourselves bring to it, metaphors that are grounded in the views of time and space that are dominant in our social worlds.

The internet has introduced new "ways of operating" (de Certeau 1984) within the discourses and institutions that police our social lives, and that cycle through them on multiple levels – on the level of public policy, and on the level of private interaction. It has created new spaces, new traversals across spaces, and new ways of "layering" space, through which we can navigate our relationships with others, and as we do, give meaning to these spaces, populating them with our goals, our struggles, our deceptions and our intrigues.

References

Al Zidjaly, Najma
    2004   Nexus analysis and agency: How a quadriplegic Omani man claims power through discourse. A paper presented at the Annual Conference of the American Association of Applied Linguistics, 1–4 May, Portland, OR.

Bazerman, Charles
    2002   Genre and identity: Citizenship in the age of the internet and the age of global capitalism. In: Richard Coe, Lorelei Lingard and Tatiana Teslenko (eds.) *The Rhetoric and Ideology of Genre: Strategies for Stability and Change*, 13–37. Cresskill, NJ: Hampton Press.

Bazerman, Charles
    2004   Hot politics: the changing places of political participation in the age of the internet. Available online at http://www.education.ucsb.edu/~bazerman/chapters/44.politicswired.doc. Accessed 18 September 2004.

Billig, Michael
    1988   *Ideological Dilemmas: A Social Psychology of Everyday Thinking*. London: Sage.

Blommart, Jan
    2005   *Discourse: A Critical Introduction*. Cambridge: Cambridge University Press.

Chan, Quinton
    1999   Internet users suffer withdrawal symptoms: Survey Web habit is hard to kick. *South China Morning Post* (7 November): 2.

Cooper, Al, Irene McLoughlin and Kevin Campbell
    2000   Sexuality in cyberspace. *Cyberpsychology and Behavior* 3 (4): 521–536.

Corrado, Anthony
1996 Elections in cyberspace: prospects and problems. In: Anthony Corrado and Charles M. Firestone (eds.) *Elections in Cyberspace*, 1–31. Aspen, CO: Aspen Institute.
Dahlgren, Peter
2000 The internet and the democratization of civic culture. *Political Communication* 17(4): 335–340.
Dahlgren, Peter
2001 The public sphere and the net: Structure, space and communication. In: W. Lance Bennett and Robert. M Entman (eds.) *Mediated Politics: Communication in the Future of* Democracy, 33–54. Cambridge: Cambridge University Press.
de Certeau, Michel
1984 *The Practice of Everyday Life* (Transl. S. Rendell). Berkeley: University of California Press.
Dery, Mark
1994 Flame wars. In: Mark Dery (ed.) *Flame Wars: The Discourse of Cyberculture*, 1–10. Durham, NC: Duke University Press.
Dibbell, Julian
1994 A rape in Cyberspace. In: Mark Dery (ed.) *Flame Wars: The Discourse of Cyberculture*, 237–262. Durham, NC: Duke University Press.
Drezner, Daniel W. and Henry Farrell
(2004) The web of influences. *Foreign Policy* 145: 32–40.
Foucault, Michel
1979 *Discipline and Punish: The Birth of the Prison.* (Transl. A. Sheridan). New York: Vintage Books.
Fung, Anthony
1998 Representative publics, politics and Chinese discourses in a degenerated public sphere on Internet. *Perspectives*. City University of Hong Kong. Available online at http://sunzi1.lib.hku.hk/hkjo/view/10/1000150.pdf. Accessed 4 February 2008.
Gee, James P.
1996 *Social Linguistics and Literacies.* 2nd ed. London: Taylor and Francis.
Goffman, Erving
1959 *The Presentation of Self in Everyday Life.* New York: Anchor.
Goffman, Erving
1971 *Relations in Public.* New York: Harper and Row.
Goffman, Erving
1981 *Forms of Talk.* Philadelphia: University of Pennsylvania Press.
Graham, Mark and Shahram Khosravi
2002 Reordering public and private in Iranian cyberspace: identity politics and mobilization. *Identities* 9(2): 219–247.
Habermas, Jürgen
1989/1996 *The Structural Transformation of the Public Sphere.* Cambridge: Polity Press.
Haraway, Donna
1991 A cyborg manifesto: Science, technology, and socialist-feminism in the late twentieth century. In: *Simians, cyborgs and women: The reinvention of nature*, 149–181. New York: Routledge.

Harper, Christopher
   2003   Journalism in a digital age. In: Henry Jenkins and David Thorburn (eds.) *Democracy and New Media*, 271–280. Cambridge, MA.: MIT Press.
Hartley, John
   2003   The frequencies of public writing: tomb, tome, and time as technologies of the public. In: Henry Jenkins and David Thorburn (eds.) *Democracy and New Media*, 247–269. Cambridge, MA: MIT Press.
Heim, Michael
   1992   The erotic ontology of cyberspace. In: Michael Benedikt (ed.) *Cyberspace: First Steps*, 59–80. Cambridge MA: MIT Press.
Herring, Susan
   1993   Gender and democracy in computer-mediated-communication. *Electronic Journal of Communication* 3(2). Available online at http://www.cios.org/www/ejc/v3n293.htm. Accessed 4 February 2008.
Hine, Christine
   2000   *Virtual Ethnography*. London: Sage.
Holland, Doroth, William Lachicotte Jr., Debra Skinner and Carole Cain
   1998   *Identity and Agency in Cultural Worlds*. Cambridge, MA: Harvard University Press.
Iedema, Rick
   1999   Formalizing organizational meaning. *Discourse & Society* 10(1): 49–66.
Irvine, Janice M.
   2006   Anti-gay politics on the web. *Gay and Lesbian Review Worldwide* 13(1): 15–19.
Jones, Rodney
   2004   The problem of context in computer mediated communication. In: Philip LeVine and Ron Scollon (eds.) *Discourse and Technology: Multimodal Discourse Analysis*, 20–33. Washington DC: Georgetown University Press.
Jones, Rodney
   2005a   Navigating the emic and etic in participatory research on on-line literacies. Paper presented at the 14th World Congress on Applied Linguistics, 24–29 July, Madison, USA.
Jones, Rodney
   2005b   Attention structures and computer mediated communication among Hong Kong secondary school students. Paper presented at the Annual Meeting of the American Educational Research Association (AERA), 11–15 April, Montreal, Canada.
Jones, R.
   2005c   Sites of engagement as sites of attention: Time, space and culture in electronic discourse. In: Sigrid Norris and Rodney Jones (eds.) *Discourse in Action: Introducing Mediated Discourse Analysis*, 141–154. London: Routledge.
Jones, Rodney
   2005d   The Internet and gay men. In: James T. Sears (ed.) *Youth, Education and Sexualities*, 433–437. Westport, CT: Greenwood/Oryx Press.

Lam, Wan Shun and Claire Kramsch
   2003   The ecology of an SLA community in a computer-mediated environment. In: Jonathan Leather and Jet van Dam (eds) *Ecology of Language Acquisition*, 141–158. Dordrecht, Netherlands: Kluwer Academic.

Lanham, Richard A.
   1993   *The Electronic World: Democracy, Technology and the Arts.* Chicago: University of Chicago Press.

Lankshear, Colin and Michele Knobel
   2002   Do we have your attention? New literacies, digital technologies and the education of adolescents. In: Donna E. Alverman (ed.) *Adolescents and Literacies in a Digital World*, 19–39. New York: Peter Lang.

Lave, Jean and Etienne Wenger
   1991   *Situated Learning: Legitimate Peripheral Participation.* Cambridge: Cambridge University Press.

Leander, Kevin
   2005   Home/schooling, everywhere: digital literacies as practices of space-time. Paper presented at the Annual Meeting of the American Educational Research Association (AERA), 11–15 April, Montreal, Canada.

Lemke, Jay
   2001   Texts and discourses in technologies of social organization. In: Gilbert Weiss and Ruth Wodak (eds.) *Critical Discourse Analysis: Theory and Interdisciplinary*, 130–149. Basingstoke: Palgrave.

Lemke, Jay
   2002   Travels in hypermodality. *Visual Communication* 1(3): 299–325.

Lemke, Jay.
   2003   Multimedia genres and traversals. Paper presented at the Conference of the International Pragmatics Association, 13–18. July, Toronto, Ontario, Canada.

Murray, Denise E.
   2000   Protean communication: the language of computer mediated communication. *TESOL Quarterly* 34(3): 397–421.

Nakamura, Lisa
   2002   *Cybertypes: Race and Ethnicity in Cyberspace.* London: Routledge.

Norris, Sigrid and Rodney Jones (eds.)
   2005   *Discourse in Action: Introducing Mediated Discourse Analysis.* London: Routledge.

Rheingold, Howard
   1993   *Virtual Communities: Homesteading on the Electronic Frontier.* Boston: Addison-Wesley.

Saco, Diana
   2002   *Cybering Democracy: Public Space and the Internet.* London: University of Minnesota Press.

Scollon, Ron
   2001   *Mediated Discourse: The Nexus of Practice.* London: Routledge.

Scollon, Ron and Suzanne W. Scollon
   2004   *Nexus Analysis: Discourse and the Emerging Internet.* London: Routledge.

Scollon, Ron, Vijay Bhatia, David Li and Vicki Yung
   1999   Blurred genres and fuzzy identities in Hong Kong public discourse: foundational ethnographic issues in the study of reading: *Applied Linguistics* 20(1): 22–43.

Stefik, Mark
   1996   *Internet Dreams: Archetypes, Myths and Metaphors*. Cambridge, MA: MIT Press.

Stone, Allucquére R.
   1992   Will the real body please stand up?: Boundary stories about virtual cultures. In: Michael Benedikt (ed.) *Cyberspace: First steps*, 81–118. Cambridge, MA: MIT University Press.

Taylor, Paul A.
   2005   From hackers to hacktivists: Speed bumps on the global superhighway? *New Media and Society* 7(5): 625–646.

Travers, Ann
   2000   *Writing the Public in Cyberspace: Redefining Inclusion on the Net*. New York: Garland Publishing.

Weger, Harry Jr. and Mark Aakhus
   2003   Arguing in internet chat rooms: argumentative adaptations to chat room design and some consequences for public deliberation at a distance. *Argumentation and Advocacy* 40: 23–38.

Wodak, Ruth and Scott Wright
   2006   The European Union in cyberspace: multilingual democratic participation in a virtual public sphere. *Journal of Language and Politics* 5(2): 253–277.

Woodland, Randal
   2000   Queer spaces, modem boys and pagan statues: gay/lesbian identity and the construction of cyberspace. In: David Bell and Barbara M. Kennedy (eds). *The Cybercultures Reader*, 416–431. London: Routledge.

Zheng, Yongnian N. and Guaguano Wu
   2005   Information technology, public space and collective action in China. *Comparative Political Studies* 38(5): 507–536.

Biographical notes

Christine Anthonissen is an Associate Professor and Chairperson of the Department of General Linguistics at Stellenbosch University (South Africa). Her recent research has been in critical discourse analysis, looking specifically at mediation and consultation related on the one hand to discourses originating in the South African Truth and Reconciliation Committee processes, and on the other hand to discourses in an HIV/AIDS day clinic. Other than that, multilingualism in South Africa has been a research focus, with attention to aspects of language choice, language shift and language identity of speakers from a historically Afrikaans speaking community in the Western Cape. Recent publications include *Discourse and Human Rights Violations* (co-edited with Jan Blommaert; Benjamins, 2007). Email: ca5@sun.ac.za

Paul Chilton is a cognitive linguist and discourse analyst working in an interdisciplinary and inter-cultural context. He obtained his first degree and doctorate at Oxford University and has held posts at Nottingham, Warwick, Aston and the University of East Anglia. Currently, he is a Professor of Linguistics in the Department of Linguistics and English Language at Lancaster University. In the field of cognitive linguistics he has published books and articles on metaphor and spatial conceptualization and has developed a formal model of discourse on geometrical principles. In discourse analysis he has investigated numerous aspects of political discourse and critically examined the methods of CDA. He is also principal coordinator of the Leverhulme-funded project New Discourses in Contemporary China. Email: p.chilton@lancaster.ac.uk

Guy Cook is Professor of Language and Education at the Open University. He has published extensively on discourse analysis, literary stylistics, English-language teaching, and applied linguistics. Recent research has been on the discourse of food politics (see http://creet.open.ac.uk/projects/language-of-food-politics/projects.cfm). His books are *Genetically Modified Language* (2004), *Applied Linguistics* (2003), *The Discourse of Advertising* (2001), *Language Play, Language Learning* (2000), *Discourse and Literature* (1994) and *Discourse* (1989). He is co-editor of the journal *Applied Linguistics*. Email: G.Cook@open.ac.uk

Nick Couldry is Professor of Media and Communications at Goldsmiths College, University of London. He is the author or editor of seven books, including most recently *Listening Beyond the Echoes: Media, Ethics and Agency in an Uncertain World* (Paradigm Books, 2006) and (with Sonia Livingstone and Tim Markham) *Media Consumption and Public Engagement: Beyond the Presumption of Attention* (Palgrave Macmillan, 2007). Email: cos02nc@gold.ac.uk

Lidia De Michelis is Professor of English Literature and British Cultural Studies at the State University of Milan. She is the author of *La poesia di Thom Gunn* (1978), *'More Worlds in Trade to Conquer': la cosmografia mercantile di Daniel Defoe* (1995), *L'Isola e il Mondo. Intersezioni culturali nella Gran Bretagna d'oggi* (2008), and of several essays on eighteenth-century literature, especially Defoe and writings by women (Haywood, Manley, Lennox). Among her publications are also translations and articles on Anita Brookner, Ian McEwan and the Sixties. Her current interests include the discursive strategies and cultural politics of New Labour, analysed through a cultural studies and discourse analytical approach, with a particular emphasis on issues of nationhood and identity. Email: lidia.demichelis@unimi.it

Phil Graham is Professor of Communication and Culture and Director of the Institute for Creative Industries and Innovation at Queensland University of Technology. He is co-editor of *Critical Discourse Studies* and author of *Hypercapitalism* (2005). He has published numerous works on critical social analysis, political economy of communication, and media studies. Before moving into academia, Phil had a long career as a professional musician working in the fields of advertising, television, film, and publishing industries. Email: p.graham@qut.edu.au

Helmut Gruber is Associate Professor of Applied Linguistics at the University of Vienna. He studied psychology, applied linguistics and education at Vienna University and finished his PhD in 1987 and his *Habilitation* (post-doctoral thesis) in 1995. He has published in various fields of applied linguistics such as critical discourse analysis, media studies, political discourse analysis, Gricean pragmatics, conflict communication, computer mediated communication, and students' academic writing. He is co-editor of *Pragmatics*, the quarterly journal of the International Pragmatics Association (IPrA), and member of IPrA's consultational board. Email: Helmut.K.Gruber@univie.ac.at

Werner Holly studied German language and literature, politics and sociology in Heidelberg, Munich and Freiburg. After teaching at the universities of Trier, Sao Paulo, Rostock and Saarbrücken, he was appointed Professor for German Linguistics at the Technical University of Chemnitz in 1993. His work focuses on pragmatics, text linguistics and conversation analysis, the language of politics, language and the media, and audio-visuality. Major recent publications include *Der sprechende Zuschauer* [The Talking Viewer] (Wiesbaden 2001, co-edited with Ulrich Püschel and Jörg Bergmann), *Einführung in die Pragmalinguistik* [Introduction to Pragmalinguistics] (Berlin 2001), *Fernsehen* [Television] (Tübingen 2004, co-authored with Stephan Habscheid, Frank Kleemann, Ingo Matuschek and G. Günter Voß), *Linguistische Hermeneutik* [Linguistic Hermeneutics] (Tübingen 2007). Email: werner.holly@phil.tu-chemnitz.de

Rodney Jones is an Associate Professor of English and Communication at City University of Hong Kong. His research interests include mediated discourse analysis, multimodal discourse analysis, health communication and language and sexuality. Email: enrodney@cityu.edu.hk

Veronika Koller is Lecturer in English Language at the Department of Linguistics and English Language at Lancaster University. Her research interests include critical discourse analysis, cognitive semantics and social cognition as well as language, gender and sexual identity. She is the author of *Metaphor and Gender in Business and Media Discourse* (2004) and *Lesbian Discourses: Images of a Community* (2008). Veronica is currently working on corporate discourse in the public sphere, with a special focus on the communication of corporate brands. Email: v.koller@lancaster.ac.uk

Michelle M. Lazar is Associate Professor in the Department of English Language and Literature at the National University of Singapore. Her research interests are in critical discourse analysis, gender and feminism, multimodality, media and political discourse. She is editor of *Feminist Critical Discourse Analysis: Gender, Power and Ideology in Discourse* (Palgrave, 2005), and has published in a range of journals including *Discourse & Society, Feminist Media Studies, Nations & Nationalism, Social Semiotics,* and *Critical Discourse Studies*. She is on the editorial/advisory boards of six journals, and is series editor of *Routledge Critical Studies in Discourse*. Email: ellmml@nus.edu.sg

Gerlinde Mautner is Professor of English Business Communication at *Wirtschaftsuniversität Wien* (Vienna University of Economics and Business Administration). A graduate from the University of Vienna, she has spent a year each at the linguistic departments of the universities of Birmingham (UK), Lancaster, and, most recently, Cardiff. Combining critical discourse analysis with corpus linguistic methodology, her research focuses on corporate and marketing communications, as well as on the discourse of the public and nonprofit sectors. E-mail: gerlinde.mautner@wu-wien.ac.at

Florian Oberhuber (M.A., PhD) is a Research Associate at the Research Center "Discourse, Politics, Identity" (Vienna). He studied sociology, political science, philosophy and history at the Universities of Salzburg, Bowling Green (Ohio, USA) and Vienna. Florian has been a Jean Monnet Fellow at the European University Institute, Florence, and a collaborator for the Dictionary of Political Language in Austria. He teaches political theory and qualitative methodology at the Universities of Salzburg and Vienna. His main research fields are European studies, political sociology and political theory. He is a member of the editorial board of the cultural studies journal *sinn-haft* (Vienna) and board member of the "International Voegelin-Society for Politics, Culture and Religion" (Munich). Email: florian.oberhuber@univie.ac.at

Martin Reisigl teaches Applied Linguistics at the University of Vienna and works on his post-doctoral thesis (*Habilitation*), which is supported by research fellowships of the German Alexander von Humboldt Foundation and the Austrian Academy of Sciences (APART). His research interests include discourse analysis, text linguistics, sociolinguistics, rhetoric, argumentation theory and semiotics. Among his books are: *The Discursive Construction of National Identity*. Edinburgh: EUP (1999, with Ruth Wodak, Rudolf De Cillia, Karin Liebhart); *Discourse and Discrimination. Rhetorics of Racism and Antisemitism*. London et al.: Routledge (2001, with Ruth Wodak); *Nationale Rhetorik in Fest- und Gedenkreden. Eine diskursanalytische Studie zum "österreichischen Millennium" in den Jahren 1946 und 1996*. Tübingen: Stauffenburg (2007).
Email: Martin.Reisigl@univie.ac.at

Kay Richardson is a Reader in Communication Studies in the School of Politics and Communication Studies at the University of Liverpool. Her publication record includes joint and single authored books on a variety of media related topics, health discourse on the internet, the history of World in Action (a TV current affairs series), European satellite broadcasting, language and poverty, audiovisual discourse on nuclear power, and the politics and ethics of language research, as well as a range of scholarly articles on aspects of language and media. She is currently working on a book about television drama dialogue to be published by Oxford University Press in 2009.
Email: kay100@liverpool.ac.uk

Aud Solbjørg Skulstad holds a Personal Chair in English Language and Didactics (*Didaktik*) in the Department of Foreign Languages at the University of Bergen, Norway. She has been engaged in preservice training of teachers of English at that university since 1996. Her authorship includes *Established and Emerging Business Genres* (Norwegian Academic Press, 2002) and a number of research articles within the fields of genre analysis, English for specific purposes, and the teaching of English as a foreign language.
E-mail: aud.skulstad@if.uib.no

Theo van Leeuwen is Dean of the Faculty of Humanities and Social Sciences at the University of Technology, Sydney. He has published widely in the areas of critical discourse analysis, multimodality and visual semiotics. His books include *Reading Images – The Grammar of Visual Design* (with Gunther Kress); *Speech, Music, Sound*; *Multimodal Discourse – The Modes and Media of Contemporary Communication* (with Gunther Kress); *Handbook of Visual Analysis*

(with Carey Jewitt) and *Introducing Social Semiotics*. His new book *Global Media Discourse* (with David Machin) was published in 2007. He is a founding editor of the journal *Visual Communication.*
Email: Theo.VanLeeuwen@uts.edu.au

Ruth Wodak is Distinguished Professor of Discourse Studies at Lancaster University. Besides various other prizes, she was awarded the Wittgenstein Prize for Elite Researchers in 1996. Her research interests focus on discourse studies, gender studies, language and/in politics, prejudice and discrimination, and on ethnographic methods of linguistic field work. She is member of the editorial board of a range of linguistic journals and co-editor of the journals *Discourse and Society, Critical Discourse Studies*, and *Language and Politics,* and co-editor of the book series *Discourse Approaches to Politics, Society and Culture* (DAPSAC). She has held visiting professorships in Uppsala, Stanford University, University Minnesota, University of East Anglia and Georgetown University. In 2008, she was awarded the Kerstin Hesselgren Chair of the Swedish Parliament (at University Örebrö). Recent book publications include *Qualitative Discourse Analysis in the Social Sciences* (with M. Krzyżanowski, 2008), *Migration, Identity and Belonging* (with G. Delanty, P. Jones, 2008) and *The Discursive Construction of History* (with H. Heer, W. Manoschek, A. Pollak, 2008). Email: r.wodak@lancs.ac.uk

Scott Wright is Lecturer in Media and Society in the School of Political, Social and International Studies at the University of East Anglia. He previously held research fellowships at De Montfort University and at the University of East Anglia, where he also completed his PhD. He has published widely in the fields of e-participation and e-deliberation, including articles in: *The British Journal of Politics and International Relations, Journal of European Public Policy, New Media and Society, Parliamentary Affairs, Information Polity*, and the *Journal of Language and Politics*. Email: scott.wright@uea.ac.uk

Index

Names of groups, as well as titles of newspapers, magazines, radio and television programmes, are set in italics. References to persons do not include bibliographical references.

A

advertising *see also* discourse, advertising 10–11, 55, 104, 113–124, 131, 157–159, 168, 172 n.4, 182, 215, 246–247, 252–253, 258, 273, 284 n.9, 323–324
advertorial 117, 346
aestheticisation 13, 323, 324, 328, 329, 332
affordances 137, 433
Afrikaans 420, 422 n.6
androcentrism *see also* sexism 98, 101
annual report 11, 136, 137, 138, 158, 186, 187, 189
anti-Semitism *see also* discourse, anti-Semitic; ethnicism; racism; xenophobia 295
– syncretic 308 n.6
Any Answers (radio programme) 388
Any Questions? (radio programme) 14, 388–397
applied linguistics v–xix, 10, 15, 114, 117, 132, 139, 208, 262, 429, 433
argument, argumentation 2, 3, 30, 50, 195, 196, 245, 253, 254, 263 n.4, 276, 293, 295, 296, 302, 304, 305, 308 n.13, 326, 331, 347, 356, 393
argumentation theory 262, 273, 308 n.13
Aristotle 45–46, 182, 225, 244, 263 n.3
assistive technologies 144
audience 5–6, 14, 31, 52–53, 55, 57, 68–75, 77–78, 117, 124, 131, 143, 157, 158, 162–163, 165, 166, 189, 191, 196, 243, 252, 255–259, 263, 319–320, 325, 329–330, 349, 368, 369, 383–388, 390, 392, 394–396, 404, 408, 437
Austria 5, 84, 247, 255, 263 n.5, 295, 300, 301, 303–308, 321

B

Belgium 397 n.2
Big Brother (TV programme) 78, 83
Big Brother *see also* Orwell, George 319
Birmingham Centre for Contemporary Cultural Research 69
blogs 53, 155, 163–164, 166–170, 367–368, 375, 430, 433, 441
boundaries vi–vii, 6, 7, 15, 68, 134, 208, 229, 365, 375, 435–436, 439
Bourdieu, Pierre 6, 28, 51, 60, 67, 75, 79, 82, 85 n.4, 134, 146, 183, 205, 247, 296, 298
bourgeoisie 2, 29, 318
branding 114, 115, 116, 135, 141–142, 145, 146, 158, 167, 204–210, 214, 216–218, 218 n.2
– brand image 7, 135–140
– brand positioning 135
– brand values 8, 10, 135
– re-branding 203, 205–206, 208, 211, 216
Britain 2, 84, 123, 144, 145, 182, 191, 203, 205, 210–219, 230, 279, 303, 330, 386–388, 393, 397 n.1, 409, 422 n.14
Britishness 11, 203, 213–216
broadcasting *see also* radio; television (TV) 5, 14, 55, 322, 327, 345, 383–387, 389, 392, 395, 396
business studies 122

C

call centres 122, 136
camerawork 394
capitalism 10, 57, 120, 156, 164, 205, 206, 211, 212
celebrities 81, 117, 385
censorship *see also* freedom of speech; silence 7, 14, 29, 54, 163, 401–402, 404–412, 414–417, 419–423, 430

454 Index

- covert 401, 403, 404, 409, 415, 421
- laws 406, 407, 412, 422 n.15
- overt 401, 403, 409, 410, 416
- self-censorship 14, 401, 404, 406, 409, 410, 412, 417, 421, 423 n.19
chat *see* internet relay chat (IRC)
China, People's Republic of 54, 384, 397 n.2, 431
civic, civil *see also* citizen, citizenship 4, 5, 32, 97, 134, 146, 278, 318, 396, 409, 416, 417, 429
citizen, citizenship *see also* civic, civil 1–6, 31, 32, 34, 36 n.9, 45, 47–49, 89, 144, 158, 203, 208, 225, 228, 245, 294, 296, 318, 388, 392, 401, 406, 430–431, 442
cognitive linguistics 159
cognitive semantics 15, 228
coherence 137, 162, 184, 366–367, 369, 370
Cold War 53, 206, 237
communication vii, xiv, 3–15, 21–36, 47–61, 69, 75, 89–107, 113–118, 120–125, 131–149, 155–159, 165, 166, 167, 169, 173 n.7, 194, 203, 206, 207, 212, 213, 229, 232, 233, 235, 254, 257–258, 259, 272, 273, 279, 282, 283 n.3, 298, 317–332, 363–366, 368–376, 393, 411, 429–431, 433–436, 439
- asynchronous 14, 364–366, 370
- communicative forms 11, 363–365, 376 n.1
- communicative style 99, 363
- computer-mediated *see also* discourse, electronic; internet, communication; new media 6, 15, 50, 364, 365, 368–372, 374–375, 429, 434, 437, 439
- cross-cultural 402
- miscommunication 28, 402
- synchronous 14, 364–366, 370
- transmission model of 6, 24–25, 27, 68, 250, 257, 364, 370
concepts viii, 3, 8, 12, 33, 52, 92, 132, 155, 159, 162, 165, 208, 209, 225, 226, 227–232, 234, 235, 236, 238, 239, 244, 259, 262, 271–283, 293, 295, 296, 297–298, 305
- contested 227–229, 232

- disseminated 8, 12, 271–276, 278–279, 281–282, 283 n.6
- implemented 8, 12, 271–273, 275–282, 283 n.7
consumer 6,7, 29, 31, 55, 91, 119, 120, 131, 158, 159, 163, 164, 170, 173 n.4, 192, 204, 205, 210, 383, 396, 433
- consumption communities 119, 120
containment 237–238
conversation analysis (CA) 68, 84, 156, 158, 273, 384, 386, 402
corporate communication *see also* discourse, corporate 6, 28, 131, 133, 138, 139, 142, 157–158
- integrated 10, 131, 138
corporate cultures 28, 139, 163, 205
corporate design 137, 149 n.11
corporate discourse *see* discourse, corporate
corporate image 11, 169, 181–182, 186, 187, 189, 196
Cosmopolitan (magazine) 300, 345, 348, 349, 350, 359, 360
critical discourse analysis (CDA) *see* discourse analysis, critical
critical linguistics 13, 225, 273, 291, 297
Cuba 422 n.13
cultivation analysis 69–70
culture *see also* multiculturalism 5, 25, 27, 48, 50, 52, 56–57, 60, 103, 185, 204, 208–209, 210, 213, 293, 298
- collectivistic 23
- corporate *see* corporate cultures
- cultural competence 293
- cultural values 57–59, 61
- culture jamming 435
- enterprise *see* enterprise culture
- event *see* event culture
- political *see* politics, political culture
cultural studies 27, 74, 208, 330
culturalisation 205
customer service 136, 142, 168

D
debate 1, 2, 4, 5, 7, 8, 9, 14, 28, 29, 30–32, 34–35, 36 n.11, 54, 58, 59, 245, 246,

Index   455

249, 251–253, 255–256, 272, 280, 284 n.9, 296, 300, 318, 322, 331, 369, 383–388, 393, 395–396, 397 n.2, 410, 411, 430, 431, 434
deliberation 4, 8, 32–36, 56, 244–245, 251, 254–255, 257–259, 318, 321, 430, 432–434, 436
democracy 32–34, 48–52, 55, 57, 124, 163, 225–229, 231–235, 254, 259, 263, 317–321, 323, 325, 384, 396, 406–410, 429–433
democratisation 13, 14, 34, 317, 329
dialogue *see also* monologue 1–4, 14, 30, 35, 89, 93, 99, 102, 116, 122, 124, 166, 171, 217, 260, 262, 318, 345, 364–366, 393, 411, 435
– rational 2, 4
Dialogues (TV programme) 384–385
dichotomy 6, 31, 89, 90, 93, 105–107, 125 n.1, 331, 374–375
digital divide *see also* communication, computer-mediated; internet, communication; new media 7, 14, 26, 137, 148 n.6, 376, 433
disenfranchisement 401, 416
discourse *see also* interdiscursivity 2, 3, 5, 6–15, 21, 30, 31, 33, 35, 46, 50–51, 54, 55, 57, 59, 61, 67–69, 71, 73–75, 78–84, 90–95, 101–103, 105, 116, 120–121, 123, 125 n.17, 130, 131–134, 136, 140, 143, 145, 155–162, 169–170, 182–188, 191, 195, 196, 203–206, 208–211, 214, 216, 226–227, 229, 233, 235–236, 239, 247–249, 263 n.4, 272–284, 291, 295–297, 299–302, 304–306, 331, 345, 347, 359–360, 366, 368, 369, 372, 373, 384, 388, 393, 395, 396, 401–404, 407, 409, 411, 414, 416–423, 430–431, 433
– anti-Semitic 308 n.6, 403
– business 31, 156
– chains 196
– corporate *see also* corporate communication; discourse, institutional; discourse, organisational 11, 155–162, 169–170, 218
– democratic 35, 430
– discriminatory 295

– electronic, electronically mediated *see also* communication, computer-mediated; internet, communication 50
– emancipatory 90, 107
– environmental 182, 279
– discourse ethics 30, 393
– external 155, 276
– gay/lesbian 409, 423 n.16
– global, globalisation, globalising 51, 204, 276
– hegemonic 12, 46, 279, 280, 422
– institutional, institutionalisation, institutionalised *see also* discourse, corporate; discourse, organisational 33, 120, 195, 196, 279–280, 384
– internal 155
– literary 121
– managerial 11, 146
– marketised 134
– media *see also* media 9, 14, 67–83, 401
– metadiscourse 187
– neo-fascist 292–293
– New Labour 11, 203, 216
– organisational *see also* discourse, corporate; discourse, institutional 155–156, 169, 172
– political 5, 11, 13, 235, 247, 249, 293, 430, 434
– practice *see* discursive practices
– private 6, 130, 205, 226, 229
– processing, deep 233
– processing, shallow 233–235, 237–238
– professionalisation of 7
– public 6–9, 21, 50, 51, 94, 130, 157, 158, 159, 203, 205, 233, 235, 294, 295, 299–301, 331
– racist *see also* racism 293, 294
– religious 121
– spoken 156, 402
– technologisation of 134
– written 196, 372, 402
discourse analysis, discourse studies 8, 67, 71, 125 n.16, 156, 157, 169, 172 n.2, 173 n.5, 182, 185, 226, 244, 383, 384, 387, 429
– critical (CDA) 3, 12, 13, 15, 33, 67, 71, 74, 75, 79, 84, 107 n.1, 119, 155, 170,

203, 225, 262, 274–275, 291, 299, 385, 434
 – approaches in 208, 284 n.10, 300–301
 – feminist 9, 89–107, 107 n.1
 – mediated *see also* media 429, 436
discourse community 7, 183–184, 186–188
discourse semantics 272, 273, 281
discrimination see also discourse, discriminatory 9, 13, 89, 98, 144, 145, 291–297, 299–302, 304–307, 432
discursive practices 13, 15, 133–134, 146, 247, 260, 275, 278, 302, 363, 369, 433–434
discussion list 100, 368–370
Donahue (TV programme) 392
Durkheim, Emile 67, 79–81
Dutch 360, 422 n.6

E
email 54, 389
emancipation *see also* feminism, feminists 9, 50, 89–90, 92–93, 97, 100, 103, 107
English 54, 93–94, 101, 103, 120–121, 157, 251, 292, 376
enlightenment 2, 3, 47–48, 59, 217
enterprise culture 135
entertainment 5, 13, 57, 60, 61, 317, 322–324, 327–331, 347, 383, 385–386, 391–393, 395–396
environmental reports 6, 11, 158, 181–182, 186–187, 192, 196–197, 201
ethical, ethics *see also* morals 30, 32, 46, 118, 147, 157, 159, 236, 261, 262, 263, 332, 393
 – business ethics 188–189
ethnicism *see also* anti-Semitism; racism; xenophobia 291
euphemism 121, 226, 251, 255, 259
evaluation 10, 57, 121, 158, 262, 276, 306, 321–322, 325, 350–351, 354–355, 383–384, 439
event culture 329
exclusion *see also* inclusion 4, 6, 7–8, 12–15, 73, 100–101, 148 n.5, 170, 226, 251, 275, 291, 295, 299, 301–302, 304, 307, 393, 420, 434

F
fascism *see also* national socialism; regime, totalitarian 123, 292–293, 406
 – feminism, feminists *see also* emancipation; discourse analysis, critical, feminist 1, 9, 89–95, 98, 100–101, 103, 105, 106, 423 n.16, 432
flaming 369–370, 434
Focus (magazine) 322
footing 390–392, 394
Foucault, Michel 12, 91, 183, 225, 263 n.4, 277, 360, 437
frames, framing 83, 85 n.3, 231–233, 302
 – frame semantics 238–239
France 2, 292, 298, 303, 397 n.2
freedom of speech *see also* censorship 54, 406–408, 411
Freedom Party 226–227
Frege, Gottlob 226
functional linguistics 185, 368

G
Gallie, W.B. 227–229, 235, 239
gender 9, 89–93, 98–100, 102–107, 121, 148 n.6, 156–157, 273, 368, 370, 376, 432
genealogy 275, 278, 281
genre 5–7, 11–14, 114–117, 136–137, 156–158, 162–163, 169–170, 181–189, 196, 212, 243–249, 251, 257–258, 261–262, 276, 282, 296, 298–299, 345–349, 357–360, 363–367, 375
 – chains 211, 276–277
 – emerging 7, 11, 163, 181, 182, 187, 196, 363, 433–435
 – established 124, 181, 186, 187
 – genre analysis 11, 15, 156–158, 162, 182–183
 – genre membership 182, 183, 184, 186, 251
 – genre name 187
German 1, 250, 251, 272, 292, 321, 372, 377 n.5, 422 n.6
German Democratic Republic 225, 272
German Federal Republic 273, 406
Germany *see also* German Democratic Republic; German Federal Republic 252, 255, 263 n.5, 272, 273

Glasgow Media Group 67, 71, 73–75, 77, 79, 84, 409
globalisation *see also* glocalisation 5, 6, 9, 13, 135, 145, 204, 205, 207–208
glocalisation *see also* globalisation 8, 138
grassroots movement 6, 33
Greece, ancient 45
greenwashing *see* image, green
Guguletu Seven 402, 405, 413–420

H
Habermas, Jürgen 1–4, 8, 21, 28–35, 47–48, 52, 318, 393, 430
habitus 28, 75, 79, 296
harassment 91, 95
hegemony *see* discourse, hegemonic
heterosexuality 96, 97
history 272–273, 300, 353
Holland *see* Netherlands, The
Hong Kong *see also* China, People's Republic of 8, 15, 410, 438
Hungary 422 n.13
hybridity 6, 57, 158, 209, 212, 346, 368, 387, 435
hyperlink 367, 434
hypertext 144, 363, 365–368, 377 n.3, 433, 435

I
identity 11, 75, 114, 119–120, 155–180, 204–205, 345–346, 375, 433–434
– corporate (CI) 10, 132, 157
– feminine 96, 97
– gay 438–439
– national *see* national identity
identity politics 251, 431
ideology 4, 11, 69, 90–91, 106, 107, 159, 184, 203, 206, 211, 233, 239, 296–300, 434
image 133, 143–146, 155–180, 155, 162, 163, 164, 169, 204, 205, 207, 213, 217, 258, 261, 300, 323–326, 329, 415
– brand *see* branding, brand image
– corporate *see* corporate image
– externally addressed 181, 189–192, 196–197
– externally constructed 181, 189, 192–195, 196–197
– green 7, 181–201
– internal 181, 189
image schema 236–237
imagined community 15, 208, 216, 253
implicature 304
in-group/out-group *see also* other, othering 13, 51, 246, 254, 294–295, 302, 372, 373, 404
inclusion *see also* exclusion 6, 7, 14, 251, 295, 301–302, 431
information (and communication) technology *see also* communication, computer-mediated; internet, communication; new media 49, 51, 52, 144, 170, 363, 429
institutions *see also* organisations 1, 4, 9, 48, 57, 67, 79, 82–83, 92, 95, 98, 122, 141, 213, 272, 274–278, 281–282, 291, 293, 296, 298, 299, 306, 320, 327–329, 401, 403–404, 442
institutionalisation *see also* discourse, institutional 33, 95, 183, 276, 278–282, 405–406
intensification 60, 302
interaction, interactivity 23, 24, 52–53, 78, 98–100, 131, 155, 158–164, 169, 247, 254–255, 276, 278, 282, 318, 346, 363, 368–372, 375, 383–386, 396, 402, 434, 439–442
interdiscursivity 162, 169, 208, 211, 212, 218, 249, 257–258, 260, 275, 281
internet *see also* new media 5, 8, 21, 26, 28, 34–35, 50, 54, 56–57, 99, 114, 131, 136, 137, 144–145, 211, 243, 252, 256, 259, 363, 366–376, 383–385, 389, 429–442
– communication *see also* communication, computer-mediated; discourse, electronic 57, 370
internet relay chat (IRC) 8, 10, 14, 53, 363, 365–366, 370–377, 438–440
intimidation 410
Israel 356, 384, 397 n.2
Italy 397 n.2

J

jargon 121, 145, 209
Jerry Springer Show (TV programme) 14, 35, 383, 387, 392–393, 395–396
Joe Public (TV programme) 385
journalism 356, 368, 386
– embedded 319, 409, 423 n.17

K

Kennan, George 237
Kilroy (TV programme) 386, 387

L

Lakoff, George 232–233, 236, 278
language history 12, 272, 273
langue *see also* parole; Saussure 231
Late Show with David Letterman, The (TV programme) 387
Leonard, Mark 205, 218 n.5
lexical density *see* type-token ratio
lexicon *see also* relexification 227, 228, 235
liberalism 89–90, 97, 235–237
– neo-liberalism 58, 203, 206
lifestyle 14, 358
Lindenstraße (TV programme) 331
literacy 48, 49, 89, 103, 107, 375, 434, 435
– practices 103, 163
logo 114, 125 n.3, 137, 142, 149 n.11, 214

M

manager-academics 141
market research 55
marketing 10, 11, 52, 53, 55–56, 102, 114–115, 116–117, 131, 136, 138, 139, 141–143, 148 n.7, 149 n.11, 157–159, 169, 181, 192, 203–212, 214, 217, 324, 396
– higher education 141
media *see also* censorship; discourse, mediated; new media; newspapers; radio; television (TV) 1–2, 5, 6–9, 13, 28, 31, 47, 67–85, 250, 256–258, 273, 282, 291–293, 317–330
– comprehension of 72, 328
– influence 12, 72–79, 84, 85 n.2, 252, 259–262
– producer 5
– mass media 12, 13, 14, 49, 117, 259–261, 276, 280, 299–300, 383–399
– multimodal 12, 243, 319
– recipient 257, 328–330, 366
– studies 15, 67, 71, 300, 360, 384, 385, 386
mediascape 55, 57, 319
mediatisation 217, 320, 323
melodrama 392, 393, 396
memory 74, 75, 209, 214, 216, 232, 243, 260
metadiscourse *see* discourse, metadiscourse
metaphor 11, 12, 116, 118, 134, 142, 167, 203, 207, 211, 212–213, 217, 233, 235–238, 252, 278, 279, 281, 282, 283 n.6, 302, 429, 430, 436, 442
– visual 119
migrants *see also* refugees 291–295, 306, 308 n.7
mission statements 10, 121, 155, 157–159, 162–170
mitigation 95–96, 295, 302, 306
mobile phone *see also* texting 363, 373, 374, 377
modality 136–137, 142, 146, 159, 165, 211, 365–366
monologue *see also* dialogue 14, 35, 243, 254, 318, 364–368, 389, 390
morals *see also* ethical, ethics 14, 30, 47–48, 305, 332, 386, 393, 396, 407, 411–412
move-step analysis 187
Mrs Merton Show, The (TV programme) 387
Mulgan, Geoff 218 n.5
multiculturalism *see also* culture 291, 293, 412
multimodal analysis 10, 15
multimodality 13, 96, 116, 123, 125 n.16, 144, 158, 367, 376 n.1, 433, 435
multi user domain, multi user dungeon (MUD) 372, 375
multi user object oriented environment (MOO) 372, 375

N

narration *see* story
national identity 11, 75, 203–222, 247, 248, 253
 – transnationalisation *see also* communication 33
 – transnationality 363
national socialism *see also* fascism; regime, totalitarian 123, 225, 255, 260, 272, 283 n.4, 292, 406
nationalism 84, 206, 208, 209, 212, 251, 272, 292–293, 432
Nationwide (TV programme) 69
naturalisation 45, 67–84, 89, 93, 96, 305
negation 192–193
Netherlands, The 406
netiquette 370
newsgroup 13, 365, 368–370, 375, 433
new media *see also* internet; texting 4, 14, 48, 51, 55–57, 60, 256, 319, 363–381, 433, 435, 437
 – communicative practices in *see also* communication, computer-mediated; discourse, electronic; internet, communication 369, 375
newspapers *see also* media 5, 7, 13, 47, 53, 96, 301, 318, 323, 327, 353, 372, 384, 401, 404, 410–413, 416, 418, 420, 428, 430
non-profit sector 135, 140
Norway 397 n.2

O

oppression *see also* regime, totalitarian 89, 95, 404
Oprah Winfrey Show, The (TV programme) 385, 387, 392
organisations *see also* institutions 115, 184, 204
Orwell, George 225
other, othering *see also* in-group/out-group 13, 96–97, 166, 212, 258, 292–295, 301–302, 304–305

P

panel discussion 387
parody 387
parole *see* also langue; Saussure 231

performance 57, 92, 256, 261, 323–325, 330–331, 382, 392, 433–434
 – environmental 181, 187–195
persona 47, 147, 375, 385, 387, 440
persuasive language 10, 11, 115, 123, 158, 196, 226, 254, 258, 261, 347
poetry 119, 121, 123, 133
Poland 295, 408, 411
policy 51–52, 54, 55, 117, 122, 182, 188, 189, 191, 235–238, 244, 246, 252, 278–280, 430–431, 441, 442
 – analysis 276, 279
Polish 403
politainment *see also* entertainment 327–330, 331
political correctness 147, 295
political discourse *see* discourse, political
political practice *see* practice, political
Politically Incorrect with Bill Maher (TV programme) 387
politics 6, 8, 11–14, 34–35, 46, 49–50, 52, 90, 107, 117, 206, 217, 226, 229, 237, 244, 246, 251, 253, 259, 261, 272, 279, 291–296, 299–300, 317–320, 322, 323–326, 327, 329–331, 429, 431, 434–436
 – political culture 7–8, 11, 232, 235, 236, 246, 252, 263, 322
 – symbolic 13, 317
polity 12, 33, 228, 229, 230, 244, 246, 253, 254, 417, 433
politolinguistics 244, 261–263, 272
pornography 394, 407, 411
postmodernism 1, 3–4, 170, 214
power relations 15, 28, 54, 91 93, 96, 277, 298, 384, 385, 403, 436, 438, 441
pragmatics 8, 15, 118, 119, 226, 234, 239, 254, 296, 304
predication 302
privacy 93, 319, 375, 407, 438
 – right to 408
private sphere 1, 6–8, 10, 13, 29, 31, 89–91, 93, 96, 102, 104–105, 133, 319
 – intimate 89, 93, 96
projection 10, 196, 216, 324
propaganda 49, 115, 116, 123–124, 207, 262, 319, 385, 413, 414
prototypes 115

public diplomacy 204, 206–210, 212, 213, 217–218
public relations (PR) 9, 10, 11, 12, 113–125, 131–132, 139, 157–158, 170, 186, 189, 259, 319–320, 416
public sector 45, 134, 135, 139
public space *see* public sphere
public sphere 1–16, 6, 8–9, 21–35, 28, 45–61, 89–105, 134, 146, 155, 157–159, 161–162, 164, 167, 169–170, 181–196, 203, 206, 208, 211, 217–218, 244, 252–254, 257–258, 262, 282, 294–295, 296, 299, 300, 304, 306, 317–332, 363, 383, 385, 386, 388, 392–393, 395–396, 409, 430–434
Putnam, Hilary 230–231, 235, 239

Q
Question Time (TV programme) 31, 387
quotations 116, 190, 210, 212

R
race 215, 291–295, 432
racialisation 293, 294–295
racism *see also* anti-Semitism; discourse, racist; ethnicism; xenophobia 147, 291–296, 299–300, 305–306, 308 n.5, 432
– anti-racism 293
– cultural 291, 292
– syncretic 293
– xeno-racism 293
radio *see also* broadcasting; media 14, 28, 47, 49, 55, 68, 250, 252, 259, 318, 322, 383–386, 388–389, 395, 397 n.1
– talk radio 388
reader 5–6, 27, 70, 74, 163, 165, 166, 193–195, 196, 212, 276, 322, 345–347, 352–353, 358, 366, 410, 435
Real World, The (TV programme) 81
recontextualisation 95, 155, 167, 204, 207, 209–210, 212, 215, 247, 259, 275–276, 281, 296, 301, 304
reflexivity 92, 94, 100, 101, 107, 157, 213
refugees *see also* migrants 292, 294

regime 136, 275, 277, 279, 280, 348, 406, 422 n.13
– totalitarian *see also* fascism; national socialism 225, 320, 325, 409
relevance theory 119, 234
relexification *see also* lexicon 403, 404
religion 52, 58, 60, 81, 83, 120–121, 213, 261, 294, 295, 304, 360, 411
representation 3, 4, 6, 78, 82, 85 n.4, 93–97, 101, 104–105, 159, 162, 163, 168, 173 n.7, 203, 208, 209, 214, 231, 234, 236, 257, 259, 299, 302, 324, 330–332, 345, 366, 373, 420
rhetoric, rhetorical 11–13, 15, 94, 123, 158, 182–189, 196, 203, 210, 216, 226, 243–263, 273, 276, 296, 305, 318, 326–327, 367, 395, 431
– genre 184, 243–244, 251, 258
– movement 187
– organisation 186
– rightwing populist 301
– strategies 94, 187–189, 196, 215
rhyme 113, 130
rhythm 35, 113–114, 121, 123
ritual 56–57, 79, 80, 82, 83, 121, 209, 252, 331, 332, 371
Rorty, Richard 235–239
Russia *see* Soviet Union

S
Sally (TV programme) 388, 392–395, 397 n.6
satire 245, 387, 410
Saussure, Ferdinand de *see* also langue; parole 27, 231
semantics 12, 225, 226, 228, 231, 282
– cognitive *see* cognitive semantics
– discourse *see* discourse semantics
– frame *see* frame, frame semantics
– historical *see* language history
semiotics 4, 21, 23, 25, 26, 27, 70, 118–119, 137, 139, 144, 156, 157, 182, 185, 247, 259, 276, 283 n.3, 300, 321, 324, 364, 365, 366, 394
sexism *see also* androcentrism 9, 89, 91, 93–95, 432
– sexist language 93, 95

Index   461

sexuality *see* heterosexuality; discourse, gay/lesbian; identity, gay
silence 100, 401–422, 432
– self-incrimination 14, 404, 422
– strategic *see* censorship, self-censorship
Singapore 8, 94, 96, 102, 104, 107 n.2
situatedness 184–185
slogan 113, 123, 125 n.20, 137, 292, 296, 304, 326
social cognition 74, 161, 173 n.5
social network 4, 15, 429, 441
social organisation 61, 84, 276
social practice 9, 67, 71, 89, 90, 91–92, 146, 107, 263 n.4, 274, 275, 277, 278, 282, 292, 297, 299, 402, 405, 436
social structures 2, 61, 107, 184, 274, 299
South Africa 7, 8, 14, 401, 405–407, 410–413, 415–416, 428
Soviet Union 237, 294, 406, 422 n.13
spectacle 383, 385, 387
speech community 230–231, 234, 278, 284 n.8
speeches 12, 157, 217, 296, 389, 416
– commercial 157
– criticism 261–262
– political 12, 210, 243–263, 292
– production 260–261
stereotypes 13, 96, 102, 103, 106, 209, 215, 291–302, 322, 323
story 57, 67, 73, 76, 78, 168, 211, 214–216, 253, 302, 347, 349–358, 404, 413, 419–421
– storylines 70, 280–282
– storytelling 73, 76, 78, 347, 349, 350, 352
– types of 356–359
struggle 9, 91, 101, 209, 213, 272, 275, 296, 298, 299, 319
style 49, 98, 99, 137, 141, 143, 147, 149 n.11, 183, 208, 215, 279, 321, 322, 325, 345–346, 348, 360
styling 122
sustainability 8, 135, 278
swearing 393
Sweden 384, 397 n.2
synthetic personalisation 120, 158

T
tabloidisation 6, 7, 13, 317–332
taboo 120, 401, 403, 405–406, 411, 413, 419, 421
talk 21, 50, 68, 82, 83, 84, 91, 92, 100, 122, 136, 142, 146, 156, 279, 282, 318, 388, 392, 434
– radio *see* radio, talk radio
– talkshows *see also* television (TV) 14, 68, 82, 318, 330, 384–387, 392–396
– trash talk *see also* television (TV), trash 387, 392, 395
teenagers 8, 349, 437–441
television (TV) *see also* broadcasting; media 5, 14, 28, 31, 47, 53, 55, 68–70, 72, 78–79, 81, 83, 102, 113, 119, 120, 250–253, 300, 303, 318–319, 322, 323, 326, 329, 331, 383–389, 392, 395, 416, 430
– daytime 385, 387, 392–394, 396
– programming format 328, 384, 388, 395
– reality 78, 82–83, 385
– satellite 5, 55, 384, 387
– terrestrial 387
– trash *see also* talk, trash talk 383
terrorism 53, 234, 237–239
texting, text messaging *see also* mobile phone; new media 14, 363, 365–366, 369, 373–374, 377 n.6
think tanks 11, 203, 205, 211, 217
Today (radio programme) 385
Tonight with Robert Aschberg (TV programme) 384
topoi, topos 276, 296, 301–302, 304, 305, 308 n.13
– of authority 304
– of definition 304
– of responsibility 304–305
trauma 301, 404
Truth and Reconciliation Commission (TRC) 402, 413–414, 417, 419
type-token ratio 368

U
Union of Soviet Socialist Republics (USSR) *see* Soviet Union
United Kingdom (UK) *see* Britain

United States (US, USA) 51, 53–55, 58, 60, 69, 84, 105, 141, 144, 149 n.14, 163, 182, 191, 233, 252, 261, 303, 329–330, 376, 387, 392, 393, 397 n.1, 409–410
universities 94, 117, 139, 140, 141–143, 146, 359, 411
us/them construction *see* in-group/out-group; other, othering

V
vagueness 116, 123, 166, 322
violence 91, 95, 192, 238–239, 402, 408, 413, 421
– symbolic 298, 317
visuality 323, 325–326
visuals *see also* metaphor, visual 11, 194, 196, 323

W
web accessibility *see also* internet 131, 140, 144–145, 149 ns. 15 and 17, 430
With Meni (TV programme) 384
wiki 367–368
workplace 98–99, 105, 156
world wide web *see* internet
women's magazines 348

X
xenophobia *see also* anti-Semitism; ethnicism; racism 293, 303

Z
Zimbabwe 410

www.ingramcontent.com/pod-product-compliance
Lightning Source LLC
Chambersburg PA
CBHW050301010526
44108CB00040B/1910